NOBEL LECTURES LITERATURE

NOBEL LECTURES

INCLUDING PRESENTATION SPEECHES
AND LAUREATES' BIOGRAPHIES

PHYSICS

CHEMISTRY

PHYSIOLOGY OR MEDICINE

LITERATURE

PEACE

PUBLISHED FOR THE NOBEL FOUNDATION
BY
ELSEVIER PUBLISHING COMPANY
AMSTERDAM–LONDON–NEW YORK

NOBEL LECTURES

INCLUDING PRESENTATION SPEECHES AND LAUREATES' BIOGRAPHIES

LITERATURE

1901–1967

Edited by

HORST FRENZ

Professor of English and Comparative Literature,
Indiana University, Bloomington, Indiana, U.S.A.

PUBLISHED FOR THE NOBEL FOUNDATION
IN 1969 BY
ELSEVIER PUBLISHING COMPANY
AMSTERDAM–LONDON–NEW YORK

ELSEVIER PUBLISHING COMPANY
335 JAN VAN GALENSTRAAT
P.O. BOX 211, AMSTERDAM, THE NETHERLANDS

ELSEVIER PUBLISHING CO. LTD.
BARKING, ESSEX, ENGLAND

AMERICAN ELSEVIER PUBLISHING COMPANY, INC.
52 VANDERBILT AVENUE
NEW YORK, N.Y. 10017

LIBRARY OF CONGRESS CARD NUMBER 68–20649
STANDARD BOOK NUMBER 444–40685–9

PRINTED IN THE NETHERLANDS BY
KONINKLIJKE DRUKKERIJ G.J. THIEME N.V., NIJMEGEN
BOOK DESIGN: HELMUT SALDEN

Foreword

In his foreword to the Nobel Lectures in Physics, Chemistry and Physiology or Medicine the then President of the Nobel Foundation, Professor Arne Tiselius, wrote:

«The Nobel Foundation has, by agreement, granted the Elsevier Publishing Company of Amsterdam the right to publish in English language the Nobel Lectures for 1901–1962. The lectures in the five Nobel Prize domains: Physics, Chemistry, Physiology or Medicine, Literature, and Peace will appear separately, according to the subject. The scientific lectures will each cover three volumes and those in literature and peace one volume each. Short biographical notes and the presentation speeches will also be included.

The Nobel Foundation has since 1901 each year published *Les Prix Nobel* which contains all Nobel Lectures of that year, always in the language in which they were given, as well as short biographies of the laureates. In addition an account is given of the prize-award ceremonies in Stockholm and in Oslo, including presentation addresses and after-dinner speeches, etc., thus covering the whole field of Nobel Prize events of one particular year.

In the Elsevier series the Nobel Lectures, presentation addresses, and biographies will now be more readily accessible to those who wish to follow the development in only certain of the Nobel subjects, as reflected in the prize awards during the years passed. For practical reasons English has been chosen as common language for this series.

It is the hope of the Nobel Foundation that the volumes to be published by Elsevier Publishing Company will supplement *Les Prix Nobel* and that together they will serve to spread knowledge of those landmarks on the road of human progress that have been honoured by Nobel Prizes.»

The publication of the Nobel Lectures in Literature and in Peace brings the beginning of this series to completion. It is hoped that the new volumes shall succeed in conveying to readers in all parts of the world the spiritual message laid down in these Lectures and meet with an equally favourable response as the previously published Nobel Lectures in the Sciences.

Ulf von Euler, President, Nobel Foundation

Introduction

Sponsored by the Nobel Foundation and the Swedish Academy and based largely on the annual *Les Prix Nobel*, this volume presents for the first time in a complete English version all of the presentation and acceptance speeches which have been given during the sixty-seven-year history of the granting of the Nobel Prize in Literature. Since the French author Sully Prudhomme received the initial award in 1901, poets, novelists, dramatists, and occasionally a philosopher or a historian – sixty-three men and women from twenty-two countries – have been honoured for literary achievements which had gained international recognition. This collection brings together important historical documents connected with the official awarding of the Nobel Prize in Literature. The statements reflect the shifting of tastes and values in world literature during the twentieth century and, at the same time, indicate that the Nobel Prize has actually contributed to the shaping of literary taste and has directed world attention to some authors, particularly those from smaller countries writing in languages not widely known.

The donor of this award, Alfred Nobel, stipulated in his will that the literary Prize should honour «the person who shall have produced in the field of literature the most outstanding work of an idealistic tendency». A consecutive reading of the presentations reveals the interesting fact that, in choosing the candidates for the award, the members of the Swedish Academy at first interpreted the phrase «of an idealistic tendency» in a highly restricted sense but throughout the decades changed their point of view. In more recent times an interpretation of the phrase as humanitarian concern has led to «unorthodox» choices, to consideration of «revolutionary» writers or those who actually defied the idealism of old.

Another statement in Nobel's will, that the Prize should be given to a person who «during the preceding year, shall have conferred the greatest benefit on mankind», was clarified in the statutes of the Nobel Foundation and taken to mean that awards should be made «for the most recent achievements in the field of culture» and that older works should be considered only in cases where their importance «has not become apparent until recently».

Furthermore, it was stated that literature comprises not only belles-lettres but also other writings which «possess literary value». This interpretation explains the inclusion of two historians and three philosophers among the Nobel Prize recipients.

Most of the material included for each author consists of 1. a title page with the official commendation; 2. a presentation; 3. an acceptance; 4. banquet remarks; and 5. a biography. The presentation speech, usually given by the President of the Nobel Committee of the Swedish Academy, reflects the critical opinion which guided the Academy in its selection of the particular laureate. In a few instances, this speech is replaced by an announcement (as in the cases of Pasternak and Sartre) or by a critical essay (as during the years of both world wars when no celebrations were held). Most of the presentation speeches have never before been translated into English. The acceptances by the laureates, who are expected to comment on their work or to discuss some aspects of their vocation, take the form either of a special lecture, or of a short address at the banquet. Generally the writers, at the height of their success, evaluate the role of the artist in the changing times which their works mirrored and shaped. The acceptance speeches thus offer an eloquent survey of the relations between art and society in the last six decades.

At the banquet, it is customary that a distinguished member of one of the Swedish Prize awarding institutions offers his congratulations on the achievements of each Nobel Prize winner. The comments concerning the recipients of the award in literature are printed here for the general record as well as for their testimony to the writers' standing in the literary world community. The biographies, using data and information given in Les Prix Nobel, have been revised considerably either to eliminate material already covered in the presentation or to add important publications and biographical items for the period following the award of the Nobel Prize. Occasionally, the laureates have provided autobiographies (in the first or third person). In these instances, no changes have been made in the text but, wherever necessary, biographical sketches have been added to bring the information up to date. It should be pointed out that the brief bio-bibliographical essays are predominantly factual and that no attempt has been made to give full critical evaluations.

The original speeches delivered at the annual celebration of the Nobel Prize award are in a variety of languages. In this volume all speeches, addresses, and comments not in English have been translated into contemporary idiomatic English. The greater liberties have been taken with the early presentation addresses, which followed the involved style of formal nineteenth-century

Swedish. In these as in all the other translations, the goal has been to achieve clarity and accuracy while retaining the original flavour and spirit. Brief deletions in a few of the early presentation addresses are indicated by ellipses within the text (as, for instance, in the material on Carducci, where a number of poems quoted in Italian have been deleted); the great majority of speeches, however, are given in their complete form, except that salutations and proposals for toasts have consistently been left out.

In all but the speeches by Americans, spelling has been normalized according to British standards. However, when there was a choice between two spellings, the one also current in American usage has been adopted. In the American and British speeches, the editing has been kept to a minimum; only factual and mechanical errors have been corrected. The accuracy of dates and titles has been thoroughly checked. Titles of the laureates' works are first given in the original language, followed by the year of initial publication in parentheses; then translations of titles into English (except for proper names and cognates) are added in brackets, italicized if the works have been published in English translations. Book titles are fully cited only the first time they are mentioned in the text, and again in the biographies.

I am grateful to numerous colleagues and students for answering my questions concerning the various authors and their works and for translating sections of the material or some difficult passages. However, a few of them deserve special mention for having assisted me in the translating, editing and indexing of the whole manuscript; Larry Clark, Dr.Dolores Gros Louis, Monique Hyde, Marie Jochim, Dr.Martin Mueller, Ardis Sanders, and Dr. Hans-Joachim Schulz.

Bloomington, Indiana   Horst Frenz
January 1969

Contents

CONTENTS

Literature 1901

SULLY PRUDHOMME

(pen name of René François Armand Prudhomme)

«in special recognition of his poetic composition, which gives evidence of lofty idealism, artistic perfection, and a rare combination of the qualities of both heart and intellect»

Presentation

by C. D. af Wirsén, Permanent Secretary of the Swedish Academy

When Alfred Nobel decided to make the great donation which has justly received much attention, his entire life's work led him to favour the study of nature and to reward discoveries in some of the sciences concerned with it. Likewise, his cosmopolitan aspirations made him an advocate of peace and of the brotherhood of nations. In his will he also included literature, although he placed it after the sciences, to which he felt most drawn.

Literature is grateful to him that its practitioners have also been the object of his solicitude; one could argue that it comes last in the group of Swedish prizes for the very sound reason that the supreme flower of civilization, perhaps most beautiful yet also most delicate, will now bloom on the firm ground of reality.

In any event, the laureates receive in these floral tributes of modern times a recompense surpassing in material value the golden violets of a past era.

The award of the Nobel Prize in Literature poses its own problems. «Literature» is a very inclusive term and the statutes of the Nobel Foundation rightly specify that the competition must include not only belles-lettres but also works which, by their form as well as by their exposition, have literary value. But thereby the field is expanded and the difficulties are compounded. If it is difficult to decide–supposing that the merits of the proposed authors otherwise are approximately equal–whether the Prize should be granted to a lyric, an epic, or a dramatic poet, the task is complicated even more if it becomes a matter of choosing among an eminent historian, a great philosopher. and a poet of genius. The dimensions become, as the mathematicians say, incommensurable. But one may be consoled with the thought that, since the Prize is an annual one, more than one writer of merit who has to yield his place to another equally great, may be able to receive some other year the award he deserves.

Numerous and excellent recommendations for the literary Prize have reached the Swedish Academy. It has submitted them to the most scrupulous examination and in its choice among different names of universal reputation and almost equal literary importance, it has decided on one which it believed should have priority this time from several points of view. It has awarded the first Nobel Prize in Literature to the poet and philosopher Sully Prudhomme of the French Academy.

Sully Prudhomme was born March 16, 1839, and in 1865 emerged as an accomplished poet in his *Stances et Poèmes* [Stanzas and Poems]. This volume was followed by several others of verse, philosophy, and aesthetics. If the imagination of other poets is primarily turned outward and reflects the life and the world surrounding us, Sully Prudhomme has an introvert nature as sensitive as it is delicate. His poetry is rarely concerned with images and exterior situations as such, but principally with the extent to which they can serve as a mirror of poetic contemplation. The love of the spiritual, his doubts, his sorrows, which nothing earthly can dissipate, are the usual subjects of his work which, in its finished form and sculptural beauty, suffers no useless word. His poetry appears in exuberant colours and only rarely takes on the character of melodious music; but it is all the more plastic in the creation of forms suited to expressing feelings and ideas. Noble, profoundly pensive, and turned toward sadness, his soul reveals itself in this poetry, tender yet not sentimental – a sorrowful analysis which inspires a melancholy sympathy in the reader.

Through the charm of his exquisite diction and through his consummate art, Sully Prudhomme is one of the major poets of our time, and some of his poems are pearls of imperishable value. The Swedish Academy has been less attracted by his didactic or abstract poems than by his smaller lyric compositions, which are full of feeling and contemplation, and which charm by their nobility and dignity and by the extremely rare union of delicate reflection and rich sentiment.

In conclusion, it is necessary to emphasize one characteristic. Sully Prudhomme's work reveals an inquiring and observing mind which finds no rest in what passes and which, as it seems impossible to him to know more, finds evidence of man's supernatural destiny in the moral realm, in the voice of conscience, and in the lofty and undeniable prescriptions of duty. From this point of view, Sully Prudhomme represents better than most writers what the testator called «an idealistic tendency» in literature. Thus the Academy believed it was acting in the spirit of Nobel's will when, for the first time it awarded the Prize, it gave its approval, among so many illustrious men of letters, to Sully Prudhomme.

As the laureate has agreed to accept this distinction but is unfortunately prevented by illness from being in our midst today, I have the honour to ask the Minister of France to receive the Prize and to present it to him in the name of the Swedish Academy.

At the banquet, C. D. af Wirsén addressed himself to the Minister of France and asked him to convey the homage intended for the French poet who has combined, to such a notable degree, the best qualities of the heart and the mind. Also, he asked the Minister to present to the French Academy greetings from her younger Swedish sister, who was proud to be able to send from the country of Tegnér and Geijer testimony of esteem to the country which had witnessed the births of Racine, Corneille, and Victor Hugo. The Minister of France, Mr. Marchand, answered in a lively and spirited speech.

Biography

René François Armand Prudhomme (1839–1907) was the son of a French shopkeeper. He wanted to become an engineer, but an eye disease terminated his training at a polytechnic institute. He studied literature, and after a brief and unsuccessful interlude in industry, he took up law, though without much conviction, and worked in a solicitor's office. Sully Prudhomme was a member of the «Conférence La Bruyère», a distinguished student society, and the favourable reception that his fellow members gave to his juvenilia encouraged him to go on writing poetry. His first volume, *Stances et Poèmes* (1865) [Stanzas and Poems], was well reviewed by Sainte-Beuve and established his reputation. Sully Prudhomme combined a Parnassian regard for formal perfection and elegance with philosophic and scientific interests, which are revealed, for instance, in his translation of the first book of Lucretius' *De Rerum Natura* (1878–79). Some of his other poetic works are: *Croquis Italiens* (1866–68) [Italian Notebook]; *Solitudes* (1869); *Impressions de la guerre* (1870) [Impressions of War]; *Les Destins* (1872) [Destinies]; *La Révolte des fleurs* (1872) [Revolt of the Flowers]; *La France* (1874); *Les Vaines Tendresses* (1875) [Vain Endearments]; *La Justice* (1878); and *Le Bonheur* (1888) [Happiness]. *Les Epaves* (1908) [Flotsam], published posthumously, was a collection of miscellaneous poems. A collected edition of his writings in five volumes appeared in 1900–01. He also wrote essays and a book on Pascal, *La Vraie Religion selon Pascal* (1905) [Pascal on True Religion]. Sully Prudhomme was a member of the French Academy from 1881 until his death in 1907.

Literature 1902

CHRISTIAN MATTHIAS THEODOR MOMMSEN

«the greatest living master of the art of historical writing, with special reference to his monumental work, History of Rome*»*

Presentation

by C. D. af Wirsén, Permanent Secretary of the Swedish Academy

The second paragraph of the Nobel statutes states that «Literature» should include not only belles-lettres, «but also other writings that in form or content show literary value». This definition sanctions the award of the Nobel Prize in Literature to philosophers, writers on religious subjects, scientists, and historians, provided that their work is distinguished by artistic excellence of presentation as well as by the high value of its content.

The Swedish Academy this year had to make its choice among many brilliant names that have been suggested. In giving the Prize to the historian Theodor Mommsen, whose name had been proposed by eighteen members of the Royal Prussian Academy of Sciences, it has selected one of the most celebrated among them.

A bibliography of Mommsen's published writings, compiled by Zangemeister on the occasion of his seventieth birthday, contains nine hundred and twenty items. One of Mommsen's most important projects was editing the *Corpus Inscriptionum Latinarum* (1867–1959), a Herculean task despite the assistance of many learned collaborators, for not only did Mommsen contribute to each of the fifteen volumes but the organization of the total work is his lasting achievement. A veritable hero in the field of scholarship, Mommsen has done original and seminal research in Roman law, epigraphy, numismatics, the chronology of Roman history, and general Roman history. Even an otherwise prejudiced critic admitted that he can speak with equal authority on an Iapygian inscription, a fragment of Appius Caecus, and agriculture in Carthage. The educated public knows him chiefly through his *Römische Geschichte* (1854–55, 1885) [*History of Rome*], and it is this monumental work in particular that induced the Swedish Academy to award the Nobel Prize to him.

The work began to appear in 1854; Volume IV has not yet been published, but in 1885 he brought out Volume V, a masterly description of the state of the provinces under the Empire, a period so close to our own that the descriptions could be made to apply to more recent fields of activity which are mentioned in the Nobel statutes and which one can use as a starting point in assessing the total work of the writer. Mommsen's *Römische Geschichte*, which has been translated into many languages, is distinguished by its thorough and comprehensive scholarship as well as its vigorous and lively style. Mommsen combines his command of the vast material with acute judgment, strict method, a youthful vigour, and that artistic presentation which alone can give life and concreteness to a description. He knows how to separate the wheat from the chaff, and it is difficult to decide whether one should give higher praise and have more admiration for his vast knowledge and the organizing power of his mind or for his intuitive imagination and his ability to turn carefully investigated facts into a living picture. His intuition and his creative power bridge the gap between the historian and the poet. Mommsen felt this relationship when in the fifth volume of his Roman history he said that imagination is the mother not only of poetry but also of history. Indeed, the similarities are great. Ranke's detached objectivity is reminiscent of Goethe's calm greatness, and England did right in burying Macaulay in the poets' corner of Westminster Abbey.

In a few bold strokes Mommsen has drawn the character of the Roman people and shown how the Roman's obedience to the state was linked to the obedience of son to father. With extraordinary skill he has unrolled the huge canvas of Rome's development from slight beginnings to world rule. He has shown how with the growth of the Empire new tasks outgrew the old and stubbornly preserved constitution; how the sovereignty of the comitia gradually became a fiction, only incidentally realized by demagogues for their own purposes; how the Senate took care of public affairs in an honourable manner, but how the old aristocratic oligarchy that had once served its purpose failed to meet new demands; how a frequently unpatriotic capitalism abused its powers in political speculations; and how the disappearance of the free peasant led to disastrous consequences for the commonwealth. Mommsen also has demonstrated how the frequent change of consuls hampered the unified and consistent conduct of wars, which led to the prolongation of military commands; how at the same time the generals became increasingly independent and how Caesarism became a necessity for many reasons but especially because of the lack of institutions commensurate with the needs of the actual Empire; and how absolutism in many cases would have caused less hardship than the oligarchic rule. False grandeur vanishes before the uncompromising eye of the historian, the wheat is separated from the chaff and, like his admired Caesar, Mommsen has a clear eye for practical needs and that freedom from illusions which he praised in the conquerors of Gaul.

Various critics have objected that Mommsen is sometimes carried away by his genius for subjective passionate judgments, especially in his frequently unfavourable remarks concerning the last partisans of dying freedom and the opponents of Caesar, and concerning those who wavered between the parties during those hard times. Objections, perhaps not always totally unjustified, have been raised to Mommsen's admiration of the power of genius even where it breaks the law, as well as to his statement that in history, which has no trials for high treason, a revolutionary can be a farsighted and praiseworthy statesman. On the other hand, it must be emphasized that Mommsen never glorifies brute power, but extols that power which serves the high goals of the state; and one has to record his firmly stated conviction that «praise that is corrupted by the genius of evil sins against the sacred spirit of history.» It has also been remarked that Mommsen occasionally applies to ancient conditions modern terms that cannot fully correspond to them (*Junkertum*, the Roman Coblenz, *Camarilla, Lanzknechte, Marschälle, Sbirren*, etc.). But this method of stressing the similarities between historical phenomena of different ages is not a product of Mommsen's imagination but of his learning, which has at its disposal many analogues from various periods of history. If it adds too much colour to the narrative, it also adds freshness. Mommsen, by the way, is not a historical materialist. He admires Polybius, but he blames him for overlooking the ethical powers of man, and for having a too mechanical *Weltanschauung*. Concerning C. Gracchus, the inspired revolutionary whose measures he sometimes praises and sometimes blames, he says that every state is built on sand unless the ruler and the governed are tied together by a common morality. A healthy family life is to him the core of the nation. He severely condemns the curse of the Roman system of slavery. He has seen how a people that still has energy can be morally strengthened by disaster, and there is a pedagogical truth in his words that just as Athens' freedom was born out of the flames with which the Persians ravaged the Acropolis, so today the unity of Italy resulted from the conflagration that the Gauls caused in Rome.

Learned, lively, sarcastic, and versatile, Mommsen has shed light on the domestic and foreign affairs of Rome, her religion, literature, law, finances, and customs. His descriptions are magnificent; no reader can forget his accounts of the battles of Lake Trasimene, Cannae, Aleria, and Pharsalus. His character sketches are equally lively. In sharp and clear outlines we see the profiles of the «political incendiary» C. Gracchus; of Marius in his last period «when insanity became a power and one plunged into abysses to avoid giddiness»; of Sulla, in particular, an incomparable portrait that has become an anthology piece; of the great Julius Caesar, Mommsen's Roman ideal; of Hannibal, Scipio Africanus, the victor of Zama–not to mention the lesser figures whose features have been drawn clearly by the master's hand.

With regard to these portraits the historian Treitschke has said that *Römische Geschichte* is the finest historical work of the nineteenth century and that Mommsen's Caesar and Hannibal must cause enthusiasm in every young man, every young soldier.

One finds in Mommsen a curious combination of qualities. He is profoundly learned, a sober analyst of sources; yet he can be passionate in his judgments. He describes in great detail and with profound knowledge the inner workings of government and the complexities of economics; but at the same time his battle scenes and character sketches are brilliant. He is perhaps above all an artist, and his *Römische Geschichte* is a gigantic work of art. Belles-lettres, that noble flower of civilization, receives the last mention in Nobel's will; Mommsen will always be counted among its prime representatives. When he delivered the first volume of his *Römische Geschichte* to the publisher, he wrote, «the labour has been immense», and on the fiftieth anniversary of his doctorate he spoke fervently of the boundless ocean of scholarship. But in his completed work the labour, however great it may have been, has been obliterated as in any true work of art which receives its own form from nature. The reader treads on safe ground, unmolested by the surf. The great work stands before our eyes as if cast in metal. In his inaugural address in Cambridge, Lord Acton justly called Mommsen one of the greatest writers of the present, and from this point of view especially Mommsen deserves a great *literary* prize. The most recent German edition of *Römische Geschichte* has just appeared. There are no changes. The work has retained its freshness; it is a monument which, though it may not possess the soft beauty of marble, is as perennial as bronze. The scholar's hand is visible everywhere, but so is the poet's. And, indeed, Mommsen did write poetry in his youth. The *Liederbuch dreier Freunde* [*Songbook of Three Friends*] of 1843 is witness that he might have become a servant of the Muses if, in his own words, circumstances had not brought it about that «what with folios and with prose/not every bud turned out a rose». Mommsen the historian was a friend of Theodor Storm and an admirer of Mörike; even in advanced years he translated works by the Italian poets Carducci and Giacosa.

Arts and Sciences have often shown the capacity to keep their practitioners young in spirit. Mommsen is both a scholar and an artist, and at eighty-five he is young in his works. Even in old age, as late as 1895, he made valuable contributions to the Proceedings of the Prussian Academy of Sciences.

The medal of the Nobel Prize in Literature depicts a young man listening to the inspirations of the Muses. Mommsen is an old man, but he possesses the fire of youth, and one rarely realizes as clearly as when reading Mommsen's *Römische Geschichte* that Clio was one of the Muses. That example of pure history aroused our enthusiasm when we were young; it has kept its power over our minds, as we learn when we reread it now in our older days. Such is the power of historical scholarship if it is combined with great art.

For the above reasons we are sending today a homage from the country of Erik Gustaf Geijer to Theodor Mommsen.

At the banquet, C. D. af Wirsén delivered a speech in German in which he praised «the master of the art of historical exposition» and, in the name of the Swedish Academy, invited those present to empty their glasses in honour of the «great master of German historical research». The Minister of Germany Count von Leyden, replied for Theodor Mommsen, who was absent.

Biography

Theodor Mommsen (1817–1903), the greatest classical historian of the nineteenth century, was born in Garding, Schleswig, the son of a Protestant minister. He read law and classics at Kiel from 1838–43, and after a few years in France and Italy and a short career in journalism, he became a professor of law at the University of Leipzig. His involvement in the revolution of 1848–49 led to his dismissal in 1850. After holding academic positions at the universities of Zürich and Breslau he was appointed to the chair of Ancient History at the University of Berlin in 1858. He was permanent secretary of the Prussian Academy of Arts and Sciences. In the seventies he was an active and prominent member of the Prussian Parliament, first as a National Liberal and later as a Liberal.

Mommsen's many writings–a bibliography up to 1887 lists over 900 items–revolutionized the study of Roman history. He was the general editor of, and chief contributor to, the *Corpus Inscriptionum Latinarum*, the gigantic collection of Roman inscriptions published by the Berlin Academy (1867–1959). This work laid the foundations for a systematic study of Roman government, administration, economics, and finance. Mommsen's books on Roman coinage and on Roman constitutional and criminal law are still classics in their fields. But he was more than a brilliant scholar with a tremendous grasp of detail and a powerful talent of organization. He was a vivid and powerful writer. His passionate involvement in the revolution of 1848–49 deeply affected the point of view of his main work, the incomplete *Römische Geschichte* (1854–55, 1885) [*History of Rome*]. His contempt for the senatorial oligarchy and the «weakling» Cicero, as well as his boundless admiration for the energy and statesmanship of Julius Caesar, for a long time dominated the standard view of the history of that era. The work covers the history of the Roman Republic; a history of the Empire was planned but never written, except for a volume on provincial administration under the Empire.

Literature 1903

BJØRNSTJERNE MARTINUS BJØRNSON

« as a tribute to his noble, magnificent, and versatile work as a poet, which has always been distinguished by both the freshness of its inspiration and the rare purity of its spirit»

Presentation

by C. D. af Wirsén, Permanent Secretary of the Swedish Academy

Again this year the names of several candidates for the Nobel Prize in Literature have been submitted to the Swedish Academy for its approval; some of them are authors of European reputation. The Academy thinks that this year it should give priority to the poet Bjørnstjerne Bjørnson. Although we have the pleasure of seeing the illustrious laureate at this ceremony, custom requires that I speak of him in the third person as I give an account of the Academy's decision. But I reserve the right to address a few personal remarks to him at the end.

Bjørnstjerne Bjørnson is so generally known and his works are so familiar to educated Swedes that it is unnecessary to give a comprehensive appreciation of his universally and gladly acknowledged merits. Therefore I shall limit myself on this solemn occasion to the following remarks.

The poet to whom with true satisfaction the Swedish Academy has awarded the Nobel Prize in Literature was born at Kvikne, Norway, where his father was a minister and where as a child he could listen to the waters of the Orkla boiling at the bottom of a gorge. The last years of his childhood were, however, spent at Naesset in the beautiful valley of Romsdal where his father had been transferred. The vicarage of Naesset is situated between the two inlets of Langfjord, Eidsvaag and Eirisfjord. In that picturesque countryside of Norway, between these two fjords, the young boy often looked at the splendour of the sun setting behind the mountain or in the sea. There he learned to do farmwork. His love of the rustic nature of his country and his intimate knowledge of the life of the people date from that time. At the age of eleven he was sent to school at Molde. He did not do brilliantly, but the development of a great poet is not always measured by such standards. During his studies he came across one author who was to have a profound influence on his life: he began to read Sturleson. At this period, too, he became acquainted with the stories of Asbjørnson and the works of Oehlenschläger and Walter Scott. At the age of seventeen he went to Christiania (Oslo) to prepare for his baccalaureate, which he passed in 1852. Bjørnson has said that he knew of his poetic vocation after he took part in the First

Student Assembly in Uppsala in 1856. In unforgettable words he has given us his impressions of the church of Riddarholm lit up by the rays of the setting sun, and of Stockholm in the splendour of the summer. Then he wrote *Mellem slagene* (1857) [Between the Battles] in a fortnight, to be followed by other works, among them the story *Synnøve Solbakken* (1857) [*Sunny Hill*]. Henceforth the reputation of Bjørnson was solidly established and an uninterrupted series of new works spread his name all over the world.

Bjørnson is a great epic and dramatic writer, but he is also a great lyric poet. *Synnøve Solbakken, Arne* (1858), and *En glad gut* (1860) [*A Happy Boy*] put him in the first rank of painters of contemporary life. In these sombre accounts he reveals himself as a man of the country and of the old saga; indeed it has been said, not without reason, that he describes the life of the peasant in the light of saga. But it should be added that the peasants whom he knew so well since his Romsdal days have–in the judgments of competent persons–preserved the laconic and reserved manner of talking which the poet has reproduced with such felicity. Although this reproduction is idealized and profoundly poetic, it is nonetheless faithful and true to nature.

As a dramatist Bjørnson has treated historical subjects, e.g. *Kong Sverre* (1861), *Sigurd Jorsalafar* (1872) [Sigurd the Crusader], the masterly *Sigurd Slembe* (1862) [Sigurd the Bad], in which the love of Audhild brings some light into a sombre situation and where the figure of Finnepigen stands in the splendour of an aurora borealis, the passionate drama *Maria Stuart i Shotland* (1864), and other creations of genius. But he has been equally successful in his choice of contemporary subjects, as in *Redaktøren* (1874) [*The Editor*], *En fallit* (1874) [*The Bankrupt*], etc. Even as an old man he has created a disinterested portrait of love in *Paul Lange og Tora Parsberg* (1898); in *Laboremus* (1901) he has extolled the right of the moral life against the natural forces of unrestrained passion. Finally, in *På Storhove* (1902) [At Storhove] he has paid dramatic homage to the guardian forces of the home as represented by Margareta, the faithful and constant support of her family. It should in fact be observed that Bjørnson's characters are of a rare purity, that his genius is always positive and in no way negative. His works are never adulterated; on the contrary they are pure metal, and whatever modifications the years and experience have imposed upon his point of view and that of others, he has never ceased to combat the claim of the senses to dominate man.

It is sometimes said that the Nobel Prize in Literature, designed for the best literary work, should preferably be awarded to young writers. That may be true, but even so the Academy believes it has met all reasonable demands.

The creative power of this man of seventy-one is so great that he published *På Storhove* in 1902, and the works published afterward bear witness to the youthful spirit that he has been able to preserve.

As a lyric poet Bjørnson is exemplary by his fresh simplicity and his profound sentiments. His poems are an inspirational source of inexhaustible wealth, and the melodious character of his verse has tempted many a composer to set it to music... No country has a more beautiful anthem than «Ja, vi elsker dette Landet» [Yes, we love this country] by Bjørnson, and when one reads the sublime song of «Arnljot Gelline», in which the rhythms are like the majestic movements of waves, one likes to think that in future times the waves of memory will murmur «i store maaneskinsklare Naetter» [in clear moon-lit nights] as they play the name of the great national poet on the coasts of Norway.

Mr. Bjørnstjerne Bjørnson – Your genius has served the purest and most elevated ideas; it has put the highest demands on human life, in certain cases (*En hanske*, 1883 [*A Gauntlet*]) even thought too high by many. But in their noble severity they are infinitely preferable to the laxness that is all too prevalent in the literature of our day. Your inspired and universally acknowledged poetic achievement, rooted in nature and in the life of the people as well as in strong personal convictions, combines morality and a healthy poetic freshness. Hence the Swedish Academy has seen fit to render homage to your illustrious genius by awarding you the Nobel Prize for this year, and it respectfully asks His Majesty the King to deign to give you this proof of its admiration.

Acceptance

I believe that the Prize I have received today will be regarded by the public as a gift from one nation to another. After the long struggle in which I have taken part to gain for Norway an equal place within the Union, a struggle which was often bitterly resented in Sweden, may I say that the decision is a credit to her name.

I am glad of this opportunity to express very briefly my views on the role of literature.

Let me, in the interest of brevity, evoke a picture I have had in my mind since my early youth, whenever I think of human progress. I see it as an endless procession in which men and women move steadily along. The line they follow is not invariably straight but it does take them forward. They are urged on by an irresistible force, purely instinctive at first but eventually more and more conscious. Not that human progress is ever entirely a matter of conscious effort, and no man has ever been able to make it so. It is in this no man's land between conscious progress and subconscious forging ahead that imagination is at work. In some of us, the gift of prescience is so great that it enables us to see far ahead to the new paths along which human progress will travel.

Nothing has ever moulded our conscience so strongly as our knowledge of what is good and what is evil. Therefore, our sense of good and evil is so much a part of our conscience that, to this day, no one can disregard it and feel at ease with himself. That is why I have always been so puzzled by the idea that we writers should lay down our sense of good and evil before we take up our pens. The effect of this reasoning would be to turn our minds into cameras indifferent to good and evil, to beauty and ugliness alike!

I do not want to dwell here on the extent to which modern man – always assuming he is a sane individual – can shake off a conscience that is the heritage of millions of years, and by which all the generations of mankind have been guided to the present day. I shall merely ask why those who subscribe to this theory choose certain images instead of others? Is their choice a purely mechanical one? Why are the pictures that present themselves to their imagination almost invariably shocking? Are they sure that it is not they, in fact, who have chosen them?

I do not think we need to wait for the answer. They can no more shake off the ideas that have come down to them through centuries of inherited morality than we can. The only difference between them and ourselves is that, whereas we serve these ideas, they try to rebel against them. I should quickly add here that not all is immoral that appears to be so. Many of to-day's guiding ideas were revolutionary ones in the past. What I do say is that the writers who reject tendentiousness and purpose in their work are the very ones who display it in every word they write. I could draw count-less examples from the history of literature to show that the more a writer clamours for spiritual freedom, the more tendentious his work is liable to be. The great poets of Greece were equally at home with mortals and im-mortals. Shakespeare's plays were a great Teutonic Valhalla with brilliant sunshine at times and violent tempests at others. The world to him was a battlefield, but his sense of poetic justice, his sublime faith in life and its in-finite resources guided the battles.

We may invoke from their graves, as often as we wish, the characters of Molière and Holberg, to see nothing but a procession of figures in frilly costumes and wigs who, with affected and grotesque gestures, fulfill their mission. They are as tendentious as they are verbose.

I spoke just now of our Teutonic Valhalla. Did not Goethe and Schiller bring something of the Elysian fields into it? The sky was loftier and warmer with them, life and art happier and more beautiful. We may perhaps say that those who have basked in this warmth, in this sunshine–young Tegnér, young Oehlenschläger, and young Wergeland, not forgetting Byron and Shelley–have all had something of the Greek gods in them.

This time and this trend are gone now but I should like to mention two great men who belong to it. First, I think of my old friend in Norway who is now ill. He has lit many a beacon along our Norwegian coast to guide the mariner, to warn him of the danger that lies ahead. I think, too, of a grand old man in a neighbouring country to the east, whose light shines forth and gives happiness to many. Their spirit, their many years of work, were lit by a purpose that was ever brighter, like a flame in the evening wind.

I have said nothing here of the effect of tendentiousness on art, which it can make or mar. «Ich rieche die Absicht und werde verstimmt.»

If tendentiousness and art appear in the same proportion, all is well. Of the two great writers I have mentioned, it may well be that the former's warnings are so severe as to be frightening. And the latter may lure us with the charms of an ideal that passes human understanding and therefore frightens, too. But what is necessary is that our courage to live is strengthened, not weakened. Fear should not turn us back from the paths which open before us. The procession must go on. We must be confident that life is fundamentally good, that even after frightening disasters and the most tragic events, the earth is bathed in a flood of strength whose sources are eternal. Our belief in it is its proof.

In more recent times, Victor Hugo has been my hero. At the bottom of his brilliant imagination lies the conviction that life is good and it is that which makes his work so colourful. There are those who talk of his shortcomings, of his theatrical mannerisms. Let them. For me, all his deficiencies are compensated by his *joie de vivre*. Our instinct of self-preservation insists on this, for if life did not have more good than evil to offer us, it would have come to an end long ago. Any picture of life that does not allow for this fact is a distorted picture. It is wrong to imagine, as some do, that it is the dark aspects of life which are bad for us. That is not true.

Weaklings and egotists cannot abide harsh facts but the rest of us can. If those who choose to make us tremble or blush were also able to hold out a promise that, for all that may befall us, life has happiness to offer us, we might say to ourselves: all right, we are faced in this plot and in these words with a mystery that is part of life, and we should be roused to fear or amusement according to the author's will. The trouble is that writers seldom achieve more than a sensation, and often not even that! We feel doubly dissatisfied, because the author's attitude to life is so negative and because he is not capable of leading us. Incompetence is always galling.

The greater the burden a man takes upon his shoulders, the stronger he must be to carry it. No words are unmentionable, no action or horror beyond powers of description, if one is equal to them.

A meaningful life—this is what we look for in art, in its smallest dewdrops as in its unleashing of the tempest. We are at peace when we have found it and uneasy when we have not.

The old ideas of right and wrong, so firmly established in our consciousness, have played their part in every field of our life; they are part of our search for knowledge and our thirst for life itself. It is the purpose of all art to disseminate these ideas and, for that, millions of copies would not be one too many.

This is the ideal I have tried to defend, as a respectful servant and enthusiast. I am not one of those who believe that an artist, a writer, is exempt from responsibility. On the contrary, his responsibility is greater than that of other men because he who is at the head of the procession must lead the way for those who follow.

I am deeply grateful to the Swedish Academy for recognizing my efforts in this direction and I now wish to raise my glass to the success of its work in promoting all that is sound and noble in literature.

Biography

Bjørnstjerne Bjørnson (1832–1910) was the son of a Norwegian pastor. At school in Christiania (Oslo) Ibsen was one of his fellow students. Bjørnson participated early in the movement for a national Norwegian theatre and wrote some poetic plays which he did not publish. While a student, he became a literary critic for the *Morgenbladet* in 1854 and contributed criticism as well as stories to various other newspapers. In 1857 he succeeded in starting a literary career when he wrote the historical play *Mellem slagene* [Between the Battles] and became stage director at the Norwegian Theatre in Bergen. During the following years he took part in national politics (as he did all his life) and divided his creative activities between historical tragedies and country tales such as *Arne* (1858) and *En glad gut* (1860) [*A Happy Boy*], both of which were meant to show a kinship between the contemporary peasant and the saga heroes of old in their taciturnity and love of adventure. The years 1860–1863 he spent abroad, mostly in Italy, where he was deeply affected by Michelangelo and Greek sculpture.

The seventies were marked by a second visit to Italy (1873–1875) and a turn toward realism and social problems which produced the plays *En fallit* [*The Bankrupt*] and *Redaktøren* [*The Editor*], both in 1875. In *Kongen* (1877) [*The King*] he dealt with the loss of Christian ideals in today's secular society, a concern which led him into a religious crisis and to a rejection of the church dogma. In 1882 he left Norway and spent five years abroad where *En hanske* (1883) [*A Gauntlet*] was written, a play in which he attacked hypocrisy concerning sexual matters as well as the liberal attitude of the Bohemians. During the following years he wrote educational novels such as *Det flager i byen og på havnen* (1884) [*The Heritage of the Kurts*] and *På Guds veie* (1889) [*In God's Way*], with its main theme of religious tolerance, as well as the educational play *Over oevne, annet stykke* (1895) [*Beyond Human Power*].

His last important plays were *Paul Lange og Tora Parsberg* (1899), which treats the theme of political tolerance, and finally *Nar den ny vin blomstrer* (1909) [*When the New Wine Blooms*]. Bjørnson's collected works were published in nine volumes in 1919.

Literature 1904

FRÉDÉRIC MISTRAL

«in recognition of the fresh originality and true inspiration of his poetic production, which faithfully reflects the natural scenery and native spirit of his people, and, in addition, his significant work as a Provençal philologist»

JOSÉ DE ECHEGARAY Y EIZAGUIRRE

«in recognition of the numerous and brilliant compositions which, in an individual and original manner, have revived the great traditions of the Spanish drama»

Presentation

by C. D. af Wirsén, Permanent Secretary of the Swedish Academy

One sometimes hears it said that the Nobel Prizes should be awarded to authors still in the prime of life and consequently at the height of their development, in order to shelter them from material difficulties and assure them a wholly independent situation.

The institutions charged with awarding these Prizes should like to bear such striking witness to the value of a young genius; but the statutes of the Nobel Foundation stipulate that the works eligible for such a reward must be of exceptional importance and confirmed by experience. Thus there cannot be any hesitation in choosing between a talent in process of formation and a proven genius at the end of his development. The jury does not have the right to ignore a still active author of European fame, merely because he is old. The works of an old writer are often proof of a unique and youthful energy. The Swedish Academy therefore was right to render homage to Mommsen and Bjørnson in awarding them Nobel Prizes even at a time when both were past their prime. In making its choice among the candidates proposed this year for the Nobel Prize, the Academy has again given its attention to several literary veterans of recognized fame, and it has wished to renew its pledge to genius held in high esteem in the literary world.

The Academy has thought particularly of two authors who would both have been worthy of the whole Nobel Prize. Both have attained the final limits not only of the poetic art, but even of human life; one is seventy-four years old, the other two years younger. Therefore the Academy believes it should not wait longer to confer on them a distinction they both equally merit, although from different points of view, and it has awarded half the annual Prize to each. If the material value of the award is thus diminished for each of the laureates, the Academy nonetheless wishes to state publicly that, in this particular case, it considers each of these two Prizes as the equivalent of the whole Prize.

I

The Academy has given one of the awards to the poet Frédéric Mistral. In the freshness of his poetic inspiration this venerable old man is younger than most of the poets of our time. One of his principal works, *Lou pouèmo dóu rose* [*The Song of the Rhone*], was published not long ago, in 1897, and when the Provençal poets celebrated their fiftieth anniversary on May 31, 1904, Mistral tuned his lyre for a poetry that in verve and vigour does not yield to any of his previous works.

Mistral was born on September 8, 1830, in the village of Maiano (in French, Maillane), which is situated midway between Avignon and Arles in the Rhone Valley. He grew up in this magnificent natural setting among the countryfolk and soon became familiar with their work. His father, François Mistral, was a well-to-do farmer, devoted to the customs of his faith and of his ancestors. His mother nursed the soul of the child with the songs and traditions of his birthplace.

During his studies at the College of Avignon, the young boy learned the works of Homer and Virgil, which made a profound impression on him, and one of his professors, the poet Roumanille, inspired in him a deep love for his maternal language, Provençal.

According to the wish of his father, Frédéric Mistral took a law degree at Aix-en-Provence; after that he was left free to choose his career as he pleased. His choice was soon made. He devoted himself to poetry and painted the beauties of Provence in the idiom of the country, an idiom which he was the first to raise to the rank of a literary language.

His first attempt was a long poem about rustic life; then he published poems in a collection entitled *Li Prouvençalo* (1852). After that he spent seven consecutive years on the work that established his universal fame, *Mirèio* (1859).

The action of this poem is very simple. A good and attractive peasant girl cannot marry a poor young man whom she loves because her father refuses his consent. In despair she flees from the paternal home and goes to seek succour at the church on the site of the pilgrimage of the Three Saint Marys on the island of Camargue in the Rhone delta. The author recounts in charming fashion the youthful love of the young people and retraces with masterly hand how Mirèio rushes across the rocky plains of the Crau. Smitten by a sunstroke in the torrid Camargue, the unfortunate young girl crawls to the chapel of the pilgrimage site to die. There, in a vision, the three Marys appear to her at the very instant in which she breathes her last.

The value of this work is not in the subject nor in the imagination displayed in it, no matter how interesting the figure of Mirèio may be. It lies in the art of linking together the episodes of the story and of unreeling before our eyes all Provence with its scenery, its memories, its ancient customs, and the daily life of its inhabitants. Mistral says that he sings only for the shepherds and the country people; he does so with Homeric simplicity. He is, indeed, by his own admission, a student of the great Homer. But far from imitating him slavishly, he gives proof of a very personal originality in his descriptive technique. A breath of the Golden Age animates a number of his descriptions. How can one forget his paintings of the white horses of the Camargue? Galloping, with manes flying in the wind, they seem to have been touched by Neptune's trident and set free from the sea god's chariot. If you remove them from their beloved pastures at the edge of the sea, they always escape in the end. Even after long years of absence, they return to the well-known plains which they salute with their joyous neighing as they hear again the breaking of the waves on the shore.

The rhythm of this poem has beauty and harmony, and its artistic composition succeeds on all counts. The source from which Mistral has drawn is not psychology; it is nature. Man himself is treated purely as a child of nature. Let other poets sound the depths of the human soul! Mirèio is a half-opened rose, still all shining from the rosy light of dawn. This is the spontaneous work of an original spirit and not the fruit of purely reflective labour.

The poem was greeted with enthusiasm from its first appearance. Lamartine, worn out with personal cares but always smitten by beautiful poetic works, wrote «A great poet is born!» He compared Mistral's poem to one of the islands of an archipelago, to a floating Delos which must have detached itself from its group in order to join, in silence, the fragrant Provence. He applied to Mistral these words of Virgil: «Tu Marcellus eris!»

Seven years after the publication of Mirèio, Mistral published a second work of equal dimensions, Calendau (1867). It has been said that the action of this poem is too fantastic and improbable. But it matches its predecessor in the charm of its descriptions. How could one question the grandeur of its ideas about the ennoblement of man through trial? While Mirèio celebrates peasant life, Calendau presents a gripping picture of the sea and the forests. It is like a brilliant glistening of water in several remarkably precise scenes about the life of the fisherman.

Mistral is not only an epic poet; he is also a great lyricist. His collection, Lis Isclo d'or (1876) [Islands of Gold], contains some poems of an immortal beauty. Suffice it to recall the stanzas on the drum of Arcole, on the dying mower, on the chateau of Roumanin with its memories of the times of the troubadours that seem to evoke the splendour of the sunsets, or, again, the beautiful mystic chant that should be spoken in the veiled twilight of the evening, «la coumunioun di sant».

In other lyric poems Mistral insists with fervour on the rights of neo-Provençal to an independent existence and seeks to protect it against all attempts to neglect or discredit it.

The poem in the form of a short story, «Nerto» (1884), offers many beautiful pages for the reader's admiration. But the epic narrative, *Lou pouèmo dóu Rose*, is more profound. Composed by a poet of sixty-seven years, it is still full of life, and its numerous vignettes of the regions washed by the Rhone are most engaging. What a superb type is that proud and devout captain of the ship *Aprau*, who thinks that one must be a sailor to know how to pray! Another ravishing little scene shows us the pilot's daughter, Anglora, whose imagination has been fed on old legends. One night she imagines that she has seen Lou Dra, the god of the river, in the moonlit waves of the Rhone and that she has been touched by him. The very verses here seem to stream and sparkle in the moonlight.

In short, Mistral's works are all lofty monuments to the glory of his beloved Provence.

This year is a year of celebration for him. Fifty years ago on St. Estelle's day he founded, together with six literary friends, the Association of Provençal Poets, whose goal was to purify and give a definitive form to the Provençal language. The language which is spoken from St. Remy to Arles and, without significant differences, in all the Rhone Valley from Orange to Martigues, served as a basis for a new literary language, as earlier the Florentine dialect had served to form Italian. Experts such as Gaston Paris and Koschwitz tell us that this movement was not at all retrograde. It did not seek to restore to life the old Provençal, but on the basis of dialects in use among the people, it attempted to create a national language understood by all. The efforts of the Provençal poets have not been slow to be crowned with success. In his great neo-Provençal dictionary, *Tresor dóu Félibrige* (1879–1886), a giant work on which he has worked for more than twenty years, Mistral has recorded the wealth of the Provençal dialects and built an imperishable monument to the *lengo d'O*.

It goes without saying that a man like Mistral has received all kinds of honours. The French Academy has awarded him a prize four times. The

Institute of France gave him the Reynaud prize of 10,000 francs for his dictionary. The universities of Halle and Bonn have conferred honorary doctorates on him. Several of his poems have been translated into various foreign languages. *Mirèio* has been set to music by Gounod, and *Calendau* by the composer Maréchal.

One knows the motto given by Mistral to the Association of Provençal Poets: «Lou soulèu me fai canta» («The sun makes me sing»). His poems have, in effect, spread the light of the Provençal sun in many countries, even in Northern regions where they have made many hearts rejoice.

Alfred Nobel demanded idealism from an author to be judged worthy of the Prize he established. Is it not amply found in a poet whose work, like that of Mistral, is distinguished by a healthy and flourishing artistic idealism; in a man who has devoted his entire life to an ideal, the restoration and development of the spiritual interests of his native country, its language and its literature?

II

After the splendour of the Greek theatre, it is principally among the English and the Spanish that a national dramatic art has developed. To understand modern Spanish drama, it is necessary to know what conditions in the life of past periods lie behind it. For a long time Spanish drama has displayed sharp contrasts. On the one hand, there is the most luxurious flowering of fantasy; on the other, an extremely subtle and at times conventional casuistry. In one place, there is brilliant colouring, and in another, a great affection for rhetorical antithesis. Emphatic language is coupled with tangled intrigue. Striking effects are violent, the lyric order intense. Disharmonies are sharp, and conflicts almost always have a tragic resolution. Dialectic is vigorous. However, interior life is very rich, and the severe, inflexibly applied dictates of honour do not exclude the luxury of sudden expressions of fantasy. In Spanish drama the artificial has managed to become fused with a genuine originality.

The heir and continuator of these glorious and characteristic traditions is the writer who has been awarded half of the Nobel Prize this year. A son of the modern age and perfectly independent in his judgments, he has not the same conception of the world Calderón had. Loving liberty and having fought often for tolerance, he is no friend of despotism or of hierarchy, but still there is in him the same exotic ardour and the same dignity which from oldest times have been the distinctive marks of Spanish dramatists. This writer is José de Echegaray. Like his forebears, he knows how to present conflict, is extremely moving and vitally interested in different temperaments and ideals, and like them he enjoys studying the most complicated cases of conscience. He is complete master of the art of producing in the audience pity and fear, the well-known fundamental effects of tragedy. Just as in the masters of the old Spanish drama, there is in him a striking union of the most lively imagination and the most refined artistic sense. For this it can be said of him–as a critic otherwise unsympathetic to him declared–«that he is of pure Spanish breed». However, his conception of the world is vast. His sense of duty has been purified, his fundamental conceptions are benevolent, and his moral heroism, while retaining a peculiar national character, has the features of a universal humanity.

José de Echegaray was born in Madrid in 1833 but spent his childhood years in Murcia, where his father held the chair of Greek Studies at the Institute. Receiving his bachelor's degree at fourteen, he soon entered the School of Civil Engineering, where he distinguished himself by his zealous application and his penetrating skill. Five years later, in 1853, he completed his engineering career after having compiled a most brilliant record. Mathematics and mechanics had been his favourite studies, and his singular understanding of these branches of learning enabled him, after one year, to be appointed a professor in the very school which he had so recently attended as a student. It appears that for some years his struggle for existence was quite hard, and he had to give private lessons in order to sustain the most modest way of life. In spite of everything, he soon became an eminent professor, distinguishing himself both in pure and applied mathematics, and became an outstanding engineer. At the same time he energetically studied political economy, embracing the ideas of free trade. Soon, that great talent, that vivacious engineer, was called to the highest and greatest tasks. Three times he has been a minister of his country's government. According to those who know him, whether they were adversaries or friends, he has always shown a singular skill in the administration of public finance and public works.

We can easily understand the general astonishment when this scholar, who had published treatises on analytic geometry, physics, and electricity, dedicated his indefatigable energy to writing for the theatre. It has been said that his creations for the stage had the form of equations and problems. If the new manifestation of his genius was enthusiastically acclaimed by numerous admirers, it also found severe critics. Nevertheless, no one could deny that his works were distinguished by a deep moral sense. In a way, the critics were not mistaken who maintained that in his dramas, following the example of some surgeons, he rarely used any other method than that of «urere et secare»; still, however, there is something to admire in this Muse of romantic exaltation and austere severity which condemns any compromise with duty.

Despising the transient approval of fashion and listening only to the inspirations of his genius, Echegaray pursued his triumphal career, demonstrating a dramatic fecundity which makes us think of Lope de Vega and Calderón.

Even in his youth, when he was attending the School of Civil Engineering, he was enthusiastic about drama and used his savings to obtain theatre tickets. In 1865 he wrote a play entitled *La hija natural* [The Illegitimate Daughter], which was followed by *El libro talonario* [Book of Accounts] in 1874. The playbill carried a pseudonym instead of the author's name, but it did not take the public long to guess that the acclaimed dramatist was Echegaray, then Spain's Minister of Finance. Some months later *La última noche* [The Last Night] was staged, and since then his fertile imagination has not stopped engendering ever-new creations. He works with such speed that in one year he has published three or four works. Since lack of time prohibits a complete review here of all of his productions, suffice it to make brief mention of some which have won general attention. Echegaray scored his first triumph in November, 1874, with the drama *La esposa del vengador* [The Avenger's Wife], in which his true genius was revealed and in which, side by side with certain exaggerations, the greatest beauties can be admired. The public could imagine that it had been taken back to the Golden Age of Spanish drama, and it saluted Echegaray as the regenerator of the most brilliant era of the nation's dramatic poetry. *En el puño de la espada* [The Sword's Handle], presented the following year, was received with the same applause. The sublime power that is manifest in this noble conception so moved the many spectators that the applause did not stop with the performance, and, after the last act, Echegaray had to appear on stage seven times to receive the acclaim of the audience. But great controversies arose in 1878 when, in *En el pilar y en la cruz* [The Stake and the Cross], the poet showed himself the defender of free thought against intolerance, of humanity against fanaticism. Typical of Echegaray, as he himself has observed, is his *Conflicto entre dos deberes* [Conflict of Duties], which was presented in 1882. A conflict of duties is found in almost all of his dramas, but rarely has the conflict been pushed to such an extreme as in this piece. Two other dramas have made his name famous. These two inspired, excellent plays are *O locura ó santidad* [*Madman or Saint*] and *El gran Galeoto* [*Great Galeoto*], the former presented in January, 1877, and the latter in March, 1881. In *O locura ó santidad* there is a great wealth of ideas and profound genius. It shows a man who, moved by his righteousness to sacrifice his prosperity and worldly goods, is considered crazy and treated as such by his friends and by the world at large. Lorenzo de Avendano renounces a name and a fortune when he learns unexpectedly but undeniably that they do not legally belong to him, and he persists in his resolution when the one indisputable proof of his illegitimacy has disappeared. Such idealism is judged madness by his family, and Lorenzo is looked upon by everybody as a Don Quixote, stubborn and simple-minded. The structure of the drama is firm and solid, demonstrating that it is the work of an engineer who calculates precisely all the elements that have gone into it, but it shows us to a still greater degree the poet of mature creative genius. More than an external collision, it treats the internal conflict of an extremely sad figure. It consists of a struggle between duty and opportunism, and Lorenzo in following the dictate of his conscience reaches martyrdom. Experience has always shown that very frequently he who faithfully obeys his conscience must be prepared to bear the fate of a martyr.

El gran Galeoto made an even greater impression. In the first month after it opened, it went through no fewer than five editions and inspired a national subscription to honour its author. Because of the masterful portrayal of the psychology of the characters the play has a lasting value. It shows the power of slander. The most innocent trait is disfigured and scandalously deformed by the gossip of people. Ernesto and Teodora have nothing for which to reproach themselves, but the world believes them guilty, and at last, abandoned by everyone, they end by throwing themselves into one another's arms. Subtlety of psychological analysis is revealed with such masterly detail of observation that those two noble spirits, in no way desirous of stealing the right of their neighbour, become mutually enamoured without suspecting it. They discover the fact of their love only by means of the persecution to which they see themselves exposed. Romanticism triumphs in this drama whose poetic beauty is clearly perceptible, whose lyric details possess a dazzling colouring, and whose structure is without a flaw.

Echegaray goes on working as a dramatist. This year (1904) he has published a new play, *La desequilibrada* [The Disturbed Woman], whose first act is a genuine masterpiece of exposition and individualization, and which in its entirety reveals no weakening of poetic inspiration. In this play, we are shown Don Mauricio de Vargas, a clear type of that chivalry so dear to Echegaray, that chivalry which does not want to buy even its own happiness at the cost of compromising duty.

Thus it is just that the Nobel Prize be awarded to this great poet, whose production is distinguished by its virile energy and whose mode of seeing is impregnated with such high ideals that with abundant reason an eminent German critic has been able to say of him: «Er verlangt Recht und Pflichterfüllung unter allen Umständen.»

Echegaray has put in the mouth of one of the characters of *El gran Galeoto* the most pessimistic words about the world, which «never recognizes the subtleties of the genius until three centuries after his death».

No doubt this can happen. But against the general application of the above thesis we can offer the justified admiration which the work of Echegaray has aroused. To those tributes of appreciation the Swedish Academy has agreed to add still one more, awarding the Nobel Prize in homage to the celebrated poet, the honour and glory of the Spanish Academy, José de Echegaray.

At the banquet, C. D. af Wirsén pointed out that sharing in the Prize did not diminish in any way the value of the laureates. He recalled to mind the works–pure, limpid, and fresh–of Frédéric Mistral, naming the principal ones and asking the Minister of France, Mr. Marchand, to convey to the famous Provençal poet the homage which the Swedish Academy and all those assembled took pleasure in rendering him. The speaker then reviewed the imposing work of Echegaray and expressed regrets for his state of health and explained that the Minister of Spain had been prevented from attending this banquet and from receiving the congratulations for his famous countryman.

The Minister of France, Mr. Marchand, replied to the Secretary of the Swedish Academy and recalled that in the preceding year he had thanked them for the Prize awarded to Mr. and Mrs. Curie; this time he spoke for the great poet of whom Provence is justly proud. He told of a most touching event. Forty-five years ago the French Academy, which did not have at its disposal resources as great as those with which the great Nobel had endowed the Swedish Academy, decided, at the suggestion of Lamartine, who was enthusiastic about *Mirèio*, to award the prize of 3000 francs to Mistral. When they asked the author, who had been leading a simple life in the country, what he would do with the Prize, he answered, «It is a prize for poetry; it is not to be touched!» The modest poet shared his «overabundance» with others.

Mr. Marchand also acted as spokesman for his colleague, the Minister of Spain, to express Mr. Echegaray's gratitude.

Biography

Frédéric Mistral (1830–1914) came from an old and well-to-do family of landowners that had settled in Provence in the sixteenth century. He was deeply influenced by his early years in the leisurely and patriarchal manor of his father. Mistral read law, but after taking his degree devoted himself entirely to writing poetry in Provençal, the passion for which had been aroused during his school days by one of his masters, the Provençal poet Joseph Roumanille. Mistral's aim was to make neo-Provençal a literary language conforming to fixed standards of purity. For this purpose he spent many years on the compilation of the *Trésor dóu Félibrige*, a dictionary of Provençal published by the «Félibrige», a literary society that Mistral had founded.

Mistral was both an epic and a lyrical poet. His work is determined by Provence, not only in language, but in content and feeling. Provence is the true hero of all his poems. His first great success was *Mirèio* (1859), a story of two star-crossed lovers. It was followed by *Calendau* (1867), a fantastic narrative poem about a Provençal fisherman. Other works include *Lis Isclo d'or* (1876) [*Islands of Gold*], a collection of poems; «Nerto» (1884), a narrative poem based on a chronicle of the Avignon Popes; *La Rèino Jano* (1890); and *Lou pouèmo dóu rose* (1897) [*The Song of the Rhone*]. A five-volume edition of his works appeared between 1887 and 1910; three volumes of unpublished works appeared posthumously (1926–30). Mistral wrote an autobiography *Moun espelido: Memori è raconte* (1906) [Memoirs of Mistral]. His efforts to revive Provençal were at various times supported by the Académie Française and the Institut de France.

Biography

José de Echegaray (1833–1916), son of a professor of Greek, was born in Madrid. He went to an engineering school, studied economics, and had a distinguished career in the Spanish Government. He was successively Minister of Public Works and Finance Minister. At the height of his career he turned to the stage, a passion that dated back to his youth. A mathematician, engineer, and administrator, he built his plays with the same regard for exactitude and duty that inspired his public life. Conflicts involving duty are at the heart of most of his plays, and he upheld the idea with uncompromising severity. His exalted romanticism appears in his choice of subjects. Like his great predecessors of the Spanish Golden Age, Echegaray was a prolific playwright. His most famous plays were: *La esposa del vengador* (1874) [The Avenger's Wife]; *En el puño de la espada* (1875) [The Sword's Handle]; *En el pilar y en la cruz* (1878) [The Stake and the Cross], a play defending the freedom of thought, which aroused much controversy; *Conflicto entre dos deberes* (1882) [Conflict of Duties], the title of which is programmatic for Echegaray's entire work; *O locura ó santidad* (1877) [*Madman or Saint*]; and *El gran Galeoto* (1881) [*Great Galeoto*].

Literature 1905

HENRYK SIENKIEWICZ

«because of his outstanding merits as an epic writer»

Presentation

by C. D. af Wirsén, Permanent Secretary of the Swedish Academy

Wherever the literature of a people is rich and inexhaustible, the existence of that people is assured, for the flower of civilization cannot grow on barren soil. But in every nation there are some rare geniuses who concentrate in themselves the spirit of the nation; they represent the national character to the world. Although they cherish the memories of the past of that people, they do so only to strengthen its hope for the future. Their inspiration is deeply rooted in the past, like the oaktree of Baublis in the desert of Lithuania, but the branches are swayed by the winds of the day. Such a representative of the literature and intellectual culture of a whole people is the man to whom the Swedish Academy has this year awarded the Nobel Prize. He is here and his name is Henryk Sienkiewicz.

He was born in 1846. His youthful work *Szkice weglem* (1877) [Charcoal Sketches] breathes deep and tender sympathy for the oppressed and disinherited of society. Of his other early works one remembers especially the moving story of *Janko muzykant* (1879) [*Janko the Musician*] and the brilliant portrait of the *Lighthouse Keeper* (*Latarnik*, 1882). The novella *Niewola tatarska* (1880) [Tartar Prison] gave a foretaste of Henryk Sienkiewicz's future performance in the historical novel, in which he did not show his full ability until the appearance of his famous trilogy. Of the three volumes *Ogniem i mieczem* [*With Fire and Sword*] appeared in 1884, *Potop* [*The Deluge*] in 1886–87, and finally *Pan Wolodyjowski* [*Pan Michael*] in 1888–89. The first volume describes the revolt of the Cossacks supported by the Tartars in 1648–49; the second deals with the Polish war against Charles Gustave; and the third with the war against the Turks, during which the fortress of Kamieniec was taken after a heroic defence. The climax of *Ogniem i mieczem* is the description of the siege of Sbaraz and of the internal struggle of the inflexible Jeremi Wisniowiecki, debating within himself whether his being indubitably the most resourceful general gives him the right to usurp supreme command. The struggle of conscience ends in the hero's victory over his ambition. Let us mention in passing that in his trilogy the author has described three sieges, that of Sbaraz, that of Czestochowa, and finally that of Kamieniec, without ever repeating himself in his treatment of the theme. *Potop* contains many excellent tableaux that remain in the reader's memory. There is Kamicia, at the beginning of the novel hardly more than an outlaw induced to fight against his king, who under the influence of his love for a noble woman regains the esteem that he had lost and accomplishes a series of brilliant exploits in the service of the legal order. Olenka, one of Sienkiewicz' many beautiful female characters, is ravishing in her religious faith, her incorruptible rigour, and her devout patriotism. Even the villains in this story are interesting. There is the sombre and masterly portrait of Prince Janusz Radziwill, who took up arms against his country, and the description of the banquet at which he tried to inveigle his officers into betraying Poland. Even the traitor has his beauty, and an English critic has drawn attention to the psychological refinement with which Henryk Sienkiewicz shows us the prince debating with his conscience and wilfully deluding himself into believing that his rebellion would serve the cause of Poland. Incapable of persisting for long in this voluntary blindness, the prince dies of remorse vainly repressed. Even in the unreliable and libertine Prince Boguslaw there are certain attractive traits of personal courage, of courtly grace and cheerful insouciance. Henryk Sienkiewicz knows people too well to present them uniformly white or black. Another distinctive trait is Sienkiewicz' habit of never shutting his eyes to the faults of his compatriots; rather he exposes them mercilessly, while he renders justice to the abilities and courage of the enemies of Poland. Like the old prophets of Israel he often tells his people strong truths. Thus in his historical tableaux he blames the excessive Polish desire for individual liberty, which frequently led to a dissipation of energy and made impossible the sacrifice of private interests to the public good. He upbraids the lords for their quarrels and their unwillingness to adapt themselves to the justifiable needs of the state. But Sienkiewicz is always a patriot who certainly puts the brave chivalry of the Polish people in its proper light and who emphasizes the great role effectively played by Poland, formerly the bulwark of Christendom against the Turks and the Tartars. This high objectivity is above all proof of the wisdom of Sienkiewicz' mind and his conception of history. As a good Pole he must disapprove the attack of Charles Gustave against Poland, but nonetheless he gives brilliant portraits of the personal courage of the king and of the excellent discipline and cohesion of the Swedish troops.

It has often been said that *Pan Wolodyjowski* is the weakest part of the trilogy. We find it hard to subscribe to that opinion. One need only remember the moving account of how the wife of Wolodyjowski escapes from the wily Tartar Azya who combines the qualities of serpent and lion, or the admirable portrait of Basia herself, that beautiful and dauntless soldier wife who combines sweetness with gaiety and courage. The last part of the trilogy is especially rich in gentle and purely human features, as in the beautiful and sublime scene of farewell between Basia and Wolodyjowski, who is about to let himself be blown up with his fort. While the victorious Turks surround the fortress of Kamieniec, when all means of rescue have been exhausted and disaster is imminent, husband and wife are united during an August night in a sort of niche formed by a walled-up gate. He comforts her and reminds her how much happiness they had been granted together and that death is merely a transition. The first to begin the journey to the beyond would only prepare for the coming of the other. The episode is marvellous and enchanting. Although it is not sentimental, it contains such a wealth of pure and true feeling that it is difficult to read it without emotion. The description of Wolodyjowski's burial is equally grandiose, though in a different manner. At the foot of the coffin Basia, stretched out on the tiles of the church, is overcome by grief. The chaplain beats the tambourine as if he were giving a signal of alarm and exhorts the dead hero to rise from the catafalque and combat the enemy as before. Then, mastering this outburst of grief, he praises the manly courage and virtues of the dead and prays to God that in this time of extreme danger for the country He may give rise to a liberator. At this moment Sobieski enters the church. All eyes turn toward him. Seized by prophetic enthusiasm, the priest exclaims «Salvator» and Sobieski falls to his knees at the side of Wolodyjowski's bier.

All of these descriptions are distinguished by great historical truthfulness. Because of Sienkiewicz' extensive researches and his sense of history, his characters speak and act in the style of the period. It is significant that among the many persons who suggested Henryk Sienkiewicz for the Nobel Prize there were eminent historians.

The trilogy abounds in descriptions of nature admirable in their freshness. Where would one find the equivalent of the very short but unforgettable description in *Ogniem i mieczem* of the steppe as it awakens in the spring, when flowers rise from the soil, insects buzz, wild geese pass over, birds sing, and wild horses with floating manes and dilated nostrils rush away like a whirlwind at the sight of a troop of soldiers?

Another remarkable trait of this grandiose trilogy is its humour. The little knight Wolodyjowski is certainly admirably drawn, but the portrait of the jovial nobleman Zagloba imprints itself perhaps even more firmly in our memory. His vainglory, his girth, and his taste for wine recall Falstaff, but these are their only common traits. Whereas Falstaff is of a dissipated and questionable character, Zagloba has a heart of gold; he is faithful to his friends in times of danger. Zagloba himself pretends to be a sober man, made to be a good priest, but in truth he is much addicted to the pleasures of the table. He loves wine and declares that only traitors renounce it because they are afraid to give away their secrets when drunk; what makes him especially abhor the Turks is the fact that they do not drink wine. Zagloba is a terrible gossip—a quality that he considers necessary in winter because otherwise the tongue might freeze and become numb. He flaunts military decorations and boasts of military exploits in which he never took part. In reality his courage—for he has courage—is of another kind. He trembles before every encounter like a coward, but once the battle has begun he is seized by rage against the enemy who will not let him live in peace and he becomes capable of true feats of courage, as when he defeats the terrible Cossack Burlaj. Moreover, he is wily and resourceful like Odysseus and often finds a way out when the others have come to the end of their tether. He is basically a debonair and emotional man, who sheds tears when some great mishap befalls his friends. He is a good patriot and unlike so many others he does not desert his king. It has been said that the character of Zagloba lacks consistency because in the last volume of the trilogy the grotesque gossip becomes more serious and acquires more social consideration. This opinion is inconsiderate. Sienkiewicz wanted to show us precisely how Zagloba develops and becomes somewhat ennobled while at the same time retaining his old faults. Such a relative improvement is all the more natural as Zagloba despite all his bizarre faults is basically as good as a child. Such as he is, Zagloba belongs forever to the gallery of immortal comic characters of world literature, and he is thoroughly original.

The diversity of Henryk Sienkiewicz' talent became apparent when in 1890 he passed from the warrior portraits of his trilogy to a modern psychological novel and published *Bez dogmatu* [*Without Dogma*], which is considered by many critics his main work. The novel is in the form of a journal, but unlike so many other journals, it is never tiresome. With an art hardly surpassed elsewhere it presents to us the type of a wordly man, a religious and moral sceptic, who becomes unproductive because of his morbid need for self-analysis. Through his perpetual indecision, he prevents his own happiness, sacrifices that of others, and finally succumbs. Ploszowski is a highly gifted man, but he lacks moral bones, so to speak: he is without dogma. He is hyper-aesthetic and extremely sophisticated, but the sophistication cannot replace his lack of faith and spontaneity. There is the figure of Anielka, delightful in her sad melancholy, who watches the best hopes of her life pass away through the egotism of Ploszowski, yet until the end remains faithful to the laws of duty. The author shows us with insight how in a soul that has once been Christian, like that of Ploszowski, the cult of beauty is insufficient to fill the void left by the loss of religious sentiment. Sienkiewicz has portrayed a type which exists in all countries, a brilliant figure marred by intellectual neurasthenia. *Bez dogmatu* is a profoundly serious book that invites reflection, but at the same time it is an exquisite work of art, delicately chiselled. The inspired account vibrates with controlled melancholy, and if the book appears at times cold, it is the cold of a work of sculpture inherent in many beautiful and noble works of art. We find this frequently, for instance, in the works of Goethe.

Bez dogmatu was followed in 1894 by *Rodzina Polanieckich* [*Children of the Soil*], a work less inspired than *Bez dogmatu* but characterized by great depth in its description of the contrast of a useful country life and hollow cosmopolitanism. Here again we find the figure of a superb woman, the candid, devoted, and tender Marynia. Critics have raised objections to a detail; that is, the sin of passion which Polanieckich commits. Far from defending him, the author has illustrated how a man whose life is neither abnormal nor excessive, let alone perverted, is nonetheless capable of committing a fault, but soon comes to his senses and repents it without soft complacency. The ties between Polanieckich and his wife are re-established even more firmly at the end of the book, and the novel is really a glorification of domestic virtues and of sane and salutary social activity. There is much charm in the delicately drawn portrait of the sick child Litka, who sacrifices her child's love for Polanieckich in order to reconcile him with Marynia. The episode is sublime and rich in purity and moving poetry.

The same critics who blamed his trilogy for being too long have cavilled at the rapid pace of the short tale *Pojdzmy za nim* (1892) [*Let Us Follow Him*], a simple sketch that paints with great poetic beauty how the countess Antéa, ill and suffering from painful and dangerous hallucinations, is cured by the dying and resurrected Saviour. In each case the criticism is irrelevant, for the different subjects demand a different treatment. *Pojdzmy za nim* is admittedly a sketch, but it is a story of deep and moving sensibility. Thus a master's casual chalk sketch because of its intimate characters is often almost equal in value to his more elaborate works. *Pojdzmy za nim* is written with noble piety; it is a modest flower growing at the foot of the cross and enclosing in its blossom a drop of the blood of the Saviour.

Religious subjects soon led Sienkiewicz to a vast work that has become universally famous. In 1895–96 he wrote *Quo Vadis*. This history of the persecutions under Nero had an extraordinary success. The English translation sold 800,000 copies in England and America in one year. Professor Brückner, the historian of Polish literature in Berlin, estimated in 1901 that about two million copies had been sold in these two countries alone.

Quo Vadis has been translated into more than thirty languages. Although one should not overestimate the importance of such a success–bad books also spread easily provided they are seductive–it still points clearly to the value of a work that never addresses itself to the lower instincts of man but treats an elevated subject in an elevated manner. *Quo Vadis* excellently describes the contrast between the sophisticated but gangrened paganism with its pride, and humble and confident Christianity, between egotism and love, between the insolent luxury of the imperial palace and the silent concentration of the catacombs. The descriptions of the fire at Rome and the bloody scenes in the amphitheatre are without equal. Henryk Sienkiewicz discreetly avoids making Nero a major character, but in a few strokes he has portrayed to us the dilettante crowned with all his vanity and the folly of his grandeur, all his false exaltation, all his cult of superficial art void of moral sense, and all his capricious cruelty. The portrait of Petronius, drawn in greater detail, is even better. The author was able to rely on the inspired sketch in the two short chapters of the sixteenth book of Tacitus' *Annals*. Starting from these very brief hints Sienkiewicz has constructed a psychological picture that gives a strong appearance of truthfulness and is extremely penetrating. Petronius, the man of sophisticated culture, *arbiter elegantiae*, is a bundle of contradictions. Epicurean and above all sceptic, he considers life a deceptive mirage. Pleasures have made him effeminate, but he still has the courage of a man. While free of prejudices, he is at times superstitious. His sense of good and evil is not strongly developed, but his sense of the beautiful is all the more marked. He is a man of the world and in delicate situations he is capable of acquitting himself with skill and sang-froid without compromising his dignity. The sceptic Pyrrhon and the poet of pleasure Anacreon please him more than the uncouth moralists of the Stoa. He despises the Christians, whom he knows little. It seems to him pointless and unworthy of a man to render good for bad according to Christian doctrine. To hope for a life after death, as the Christians do, seems to him as strange as if one were to announce that a new day begins at night. Ruined by the favourite Tigellinus, Petronius dies with the serenity of a death that he had sought himself. The entire description is perfect in its genre. But *Quo Vadis* contains many other admirable things. Especially beautiful is the episode, lit by the setting sun, in which the apostle Paul goes to his martyrdom repeating to himself the words that he had once written: «I have fought a good fight, I have finished my course, I have kept the faith» (2 Tim., 4:7).

After this major work Henryk Sienkiewicz returned to the national Polish novel and in 1901 wrote *Krzyzacy* [*The Knights of the Cross*]. The task was this time less easy than in the case of the trilogy because there were fewer sources. But Sienkiewicz overcame the difficulties and gave to his version a strong medieval colour. The subject of the novel is the fight of the Polish and Lithuanian nations against the Teutonic Knights who, having long ago finished their original mission, had become an oppressive institution more occupied with power and terrestrial gains than with the cross whose insignia the members of the order bore on their coats. It was the Archduke Jagiello, later King of Poland under the name of Wladislaw II, who broke the dominance of the order. He plays a role in the novel, although he is only sketchily drawn according to Sienkiewicz' custom of not giving too much prominence to historical characters. The many characters which are entirely the product of the author's rich fancy attract our attention more strongly and furnish excellent examples of medieval civilization. It was a superstitious epoch and, although the country had been Christianized for a long time, people still put food out at night for vampires and revenants. Each saint had his particular function. Apollonia was invoked for toothaches, Liberius for stones. It is true that God the Father rules the universe, but this very fact proves that he has no time to look after human affairs of minor importance; consequently he has delegated certain functions to saints. That epoch was indeed superstitious, but it was also full of energy. Huge and solid, the castle of the order stands at Marienburg. The Polish and Lithuanian opponents of the monastic knights do not lack force, either. There is Macko, crude, greedy, bent on the interests of his family, but brave. There is the noble Zbyszko, his mind full of chivalrous adventures. Surpassing all the others, colossal, as if cut in granite, there is the redoubtable Jurand, cruel in his hatred of the Teutonic Order and finally the victim of its terrible revenge. In the hour of his humiliation he is more sublime than ever because of his self-victory and the power of his forgiveness. He is one of the most grandiose of Sienkiewicz' warrior characters. Tableaux of gentleness alternate with those of force. Queen Jadwiga is gentle, but her appearance is elusive. The description of the funeral for the poor, sorely tested Danusia is delicately beautiful like a softly chanted passion service. On the other hand, the fresh and springlike picture of Jagienka is radiant with exuberant health and liveliness. All these creations have their individual life. Among the outstanding minor characters are the irascible and bellicose Abbé, unable to brook any contradiction, and Sanders, the seller of indulgences, who sells a hoof of the donkey on which the flight to Egypt took place, a piece of the ladder of Jacob, the tears of the Egyptian Mary, and a little rust from the keys of St. Peter. The closing episode, the battle of Tannenberg in 1410 in which the squadrons of the Teutonic Order were crushed after a heroic battle, is like the finale of a splendid musical drama.

Henryk Sienkiewicz is certainly the first to recognize his debt to old Polish literature. That literature is indeed rich. Adam Mickiewicz is its true Adam, its ancestor by virtue of the full nature of the poetry that distinguishes his great epic. Brilliant as the stars in the sky of Polish literature are the names of Slowacki, a man of fertile imagination, and of the philosopher Krasinski. The epic art has been successfully practised by men like Korzeniowski, Kraszewski, and Rzewuski. But with Henryk Sienkiewicz that art has reached its full bloom and presents itself in its highest degree of objectivity.

If one surveys Sienkiewicz' achievement it appears gigantic and vast, and at every point noble and controlled. As for his epic style, it is of absolute artistic perfection. That epic style with its powerful over-all effect and the relative independence of episodes is distinguished by naive and striking metaphors. In this respect, as Geijer has remarked, Homer is the master because he perceives grandeur in simplicity as, for example, when he compares the warriors to flies that swarm around a pail of milk, or when Patroklos, who all in tears asks Achilles to let him fight against the enemies, is compared to a little girl who weeping clings to the dress of her mother and wants to be taken in her arms. A Swedish critic has noticed in Sienkiewicz some similes that have the clarity of Homeric images. Thus the retreat of an army is compared to a retreating wave that leaves mussels and shells on the beach, or the beginning of gunfire is compared to the barking of a village dog who is soon joined in chorus by all the other dogs. The examples could be multiplied. The attack on the front and rear of an army surrounded and subject to fire from both sides is compared to a field that is reaped by two groups of mowers who begin their work at opposite sides of the field with the purpose of meeting in the middle. In *Krzyżacy* the Samogites rising from furrows attack the German knights like a swarm of wasps whose nest has been damaged by a careless wanderer. In *Pan Wolodyjowski* we also find admirable images; in order to judge them we should remember that, as often in Homer, the two terms of the comparison converge only in one point, while the rest remains vague. Wolodyjowski with his unique sword kills human lives around him as rapidly as a choir boy after the mass snuffs the candles on the altar one after the other with his long extinguisher. Hussein Pasha, the commander of the Turkish army who vainly tries to leave by the gate that leads to Jassy, returns to the camp to try another exit, just as a poacher who has been tracked in a park tries to escape now on one side and now on the other. The Christian martyrs of *Quo Vadis* who are prepared for death are already as removed from earthly places as mariners who have pushed off and left the quay. Many more situations equally Homeric and yet equally natural and spontaneous could be cited; thus in *Krzyżacy* Jagienka at the unexpected sight of Zbyszko, who resembles a young prince, stops short at the gate and nearly drops the jug of wine.

The literary production of Henryk Sienkiewicz is far from over. At the moment he is in the process of publishing a new trilogy entitled *Na polu chwaly* (1906) [*On the Field of Glory*] that deals with the time of Sobieski.

His own poetic career has indeed unfolded on the field of glory. He has received valuable tokens of the devotion of his people, all the more precious since, despite his ardent patriotism, he has never flattered his country. On the occasion of his twenty-fifth anniversary as an author a grand national subscription provided the means to buy the castle that had been the original seat of his family and to offer it to him as a present. He was saluted by delegations, congratulatory messages were sent, and the Warsaw theatre staged a gala performance in his honour.

An homage from the North has now been added to these proofs of admiration, for the Swedish Academy has decided to award the Nobel Prize in Literature of 1905 to Henryk Sienkiewicz.

Acceptance

Nations are represented by their poets and their writers in the open competition for the Nobel Prize. Consequently the award of the Prize by the Academy glorifies not only the author but the people whose son he is, and it bears witness that that nation has a share in the universal achievement, that its efforts are fruitful, and that it has the right to live for the profit of mankind. If this honour is precious to all, it is infinitely more so to Poland. It has been said that Poland is dead, exhausted, enslaved, but here is the proof of her life and triumph. Like Galileo, one is forced to think «E pur si muove» when before the eyes of the world homage has been rendered to the importance of Poland's achievement and her genius.

This homage has been rendered not to me – for the Polish soil is fertile and does not lack better writers than me – but to the Polish achievement, the Polish genius. For this I should like to express my most ardent and most sincere gratitude as a Pole to you gentlemen, the members of the Swedish Academy, and I conclude by borrowing the words of Horace: «Principibus placuisse non ultima laus est».

Biography

Henryk Sienkiewicz (1846–1916), the most outstanding and prolific Polish writer of the second half of the nineteenth century, was born in Wola Okrzejska, in the Russian part of Poland. His father's family was actively engaged in the revolutionary struggles for Polish independence, which accounts for the strong patriotic element in Sienkiewicz' work. Historical scholarship on the other hand ran in his mother's family.

Sienkiewicz studied in Warsaw, but without any visible results. His talent as a writer was soon discovered. His early works are satirical sketches, betraying a strong social conscience. He made a trip to America in 1876 and travelled as far as California. His impressions were published in Polish newspapers and received very favourably. His travels provided him with material for several works, among them the brilliant short story *Latarnik* (1882) [*The Lighthouse Keeper*].

After his return to Poland, Sienkiewicz devoted himself to historical studies, the result of which was his great trilogy about Poland in the mid-seventeenth century. *Ogniem i mieczem* [*With Fire and Sword*], *Potop* [*The Deluge*] and *Pan Wolodyjowski* [*Pan Michael*] were published in 1884, 1886, and 1888 respectively. The historical novels were followed by works on contemporary subjects: *Bez dogmatu* (1891) [*Without Dogma*], a psychological study of a sophisticated decadent man, and *Rodzina Polanieckich* (1894) [*Children of the Soil*], a peasant novel. In 1895 Sienkiewicz published his greatest success, *Quo Vadis*, a novel of Christian persecutions at the time of Nero.

In his later novels he returned again to historical subjects. *Krzyzacy* (1900) deals with a period of medieval history, the victory of the Poles over the Teutonic Knights; *Na polu chwaly* (1906) [*On the Field of Glory*] is a sequel to his seventeenth-century trilogy. His last works *Wiry* (1910) [*Whirlpools*] and *W pustyni i w puszczy* (1912) [*In Desert and Wilderness*] again deal with contemporary subjects.

Sienkiewicz was immensely popular. In 1900, a national subscription raised enough funds to buy for him the castle in which his ancestors had lived. The complete edition of his works, published 1948–55, runs to sixty volumes.

Literature 1906

GIOSUÈ CARDUCCI

«*not only in consideration of his deep learning and critical research, but above all as a tribute to the creative energy, freshness of style, and lyrical force which characterize his poetic masterpieces*»

Presentation

by C. D. af Wirsén, Permanent Secretary of the Swedish Academy

From the unusually large number of poets and authors proposed for the Nobel Prize this year, the Swedish Academy has chosen a great Italian poet who for a long time has attracted the attention both of the Academy and of the entire civilized world.

Since antiquity, Northern men have been drawn to Italy by her history and her artistic treasures as well as by her sweet and gentle climate. The Northerner does not stop until he has arrived in the eternal city of Rome, just as the war for Italian unity could not stop before Rome was conquered. But before arriving in Rome the visitor is fascinated by the beauty of so many other places. Among these, in the Appenines, is the Etruscan city of Bologna, which is known to us through the *Songs of Enzo* by Carl August Nicander.

Since the Middle Ages, when a famous university gave it the title of learned, Bologna has been of great importance in the cultural history of Italy. Although in ancient times it was renowned as an authority on jurisprudence, it has now become especially famous for its poetic marvels. Thus, it is today still worthy of the expression «Bononia docet» (Bologna teaches). For its greatest poetic attainments of the present, it is indebted to the man to whom the Nobel Prize has been awarded this year–Giosuè Carducci.

Carducci was born on July 27, 1835, in Val di Castello. He himself has given an interesting account of his impressions from his childhood and youth, and he has been the subject of several good biographies.

In order to judge properly the development of his mind and his talents, it is important to know that his father, Dr. Michele Carducci, was a member of the Carboneria (a secret political society working for Italian unity) and was active in the political movements for Italian liberty, and that his mother was an intelligent and liberal woman.

Michele obtained a position as a doctor in Castagneto. The young poet thus spent his earliest years in the Tuscan Maremma. He learned Latin from his father, and Latin literature was to become very familiar to him. Although Carducci later opposed Manzoni's ideas with great fervour, he was also strongly influenced for a long time by his father's admiration for the poet. At this time he also studied the *Iliad* and the *Aeneid*, Tasso's *Gerusalemme*, Rollin's Roman history, and Thier's work on the French Revolution.

It was a time of great political tension, and one can well believe that in those days of discord and oppression the young poet's fiery imagination absorbed everything which had to do with ancient liberty and the impending unification.

The boy soon turned into a little revolutionary. As he himself recounts, in his games with his brothers and friends he organized little republics which were governed by archons or consuls or tribunes. Vigorous brawls frequently broke out. Revolution was considered a normal state of affairs; civil war was always the order of the day. The young Carducci stoned a make-believe Caesar who was about to cross the Rubicon. Caesar had to flee and the republic was saved. But the next day the little patriotic hero got a sound trouncing from the conquering Caesar.

Not too much stress need be laid on these games, since they are frequent among young boys. But Carducci did, in fact, embrace strong republican sympathies in later life.

In 1849 the family moved to Florence, where Carducci was enrolled in a new school. Here, in addition to his required studies, he first read the poetry of Leopardi, Schiller, and Byron. And soon he started writing poetry–satiric sonnets. He later studied at the Scuola Normale Superiore in Pisa, where he seems to have shown a great deal of energy in his work. After finishing his studies he became a teacher of rhetoric in San Miniato. Because of his expressions of radical ideas, the grand-ducal government annulled his later election to a post at the Arezzo elementary school. Afterward, however, he taught Greek at the lyceum in Pistoia. Finally he obtained a chair at the University of Bologna, where he has had a long and highly successful career.

These in brief are the general lines of his external life. There has been no lack of struggle in his career. He was, for example, even suspended for some time from teaching in Bologna, and on several occasions he was involved in lively polemics with several Italian authors. He suffered great personal tragedies, of which his brother Dante's suicide was undoubtedly the most painful. But his family life and his love for his wife and children have offered him great consolation.

The fight for Italian liberty was extremely important to the development of his sensibility. Carducci was a passionate patriot; he followed the war with all the fire of his soul. And no matter how much he may have been embittered by the defeats at Aspromonte and Mentana, and no matter how much he was disillusioned by the new parliamentary government, which was not being organized in accordance with his desires, he was, nevertheless, overjoyed at the triumph of his sacred patriotic cause.

His ardent nature was tormented by anything which in his opinion interfered with the fulfillment of the work for Italian unity. He was not one to wait patiently; he continuously demanded immediate results and felt a strong aversion to diplomatic delays and the diplomatic *festina lente*.

In the meantime his poetry blossomed abundantly. Although he is also the author of excellent historical and literary criticism, we should be concerned above all with his poetry, for it is through his poetry that he has won his greatest fame.

The volume *Juvenilia* (1863) contains, as the title indicates, his youthful work of the 1850's. Two qualities characterize this collection: on the one hand, its classical cast and intonation, sometimes carried to the point where Carducci salutes Phoebus Apollo and Diana Trivia; and on the other, its profoundly patriotic tone, accompanied by a violent hatred of the Catholic Church and of the Pope's power, the strongest obstacles to Italian unity.

In strong opposition to ultramontanism, Carducci in his songs evokes the memories of ancient Rome, the images of the great French Revolution, and the figures of Garibaldi and Mazzini. At times, when be believes Italy's state hopeless and fears that all of its ancient virtues and valiant deeds have been vitiated, he plunges into the profoundest despair.

This bitterness helps to explain Carducci's numerous attacks on various authors and on other people; Carducci was generally violent in his polemics. But in *Juvenilia* there are also poems with a more positive content, like the song to Victor Emanuel, written in 1859 at the moment when it became obvious that a war with Austria would soon break out. In this song he jubilantly celebrates the monarch who bore the banner of Italian unity.

True patriotism is expressed in the sonnet «Magenta» and in the poem «Il Plebiscito», in which he renews his enthusiastic praise of Victor Emanuel... The most beautiful of the poems in *Juvenilia* is probably the poem to the Savoy cross...

The later collection called *Levia Gravia* (1868) [*Light and Heavy*] contains the poems of the sixties. A certain sadness can be heard in many of these poems. The long delay of the conquest of Rome contributed much to Carducci's bitter feelings, but there were a great many other things which Carducci passionately regretted in the prevailing politics of the day. Carducci had expected more from the new political conditions than they could offer. Yet we encounter some very beautiful poems in this collection. Carducci was familiar with fourteenth-century poetry, and a great many echoes of this epoch are heard, for instance, in «Poeti di Parte Bianca» [«Poets of the White Party»] and in his poem on the proclamation of the Italian kingdom.

Only in the *Rime nuove* (1877) [New Rhymes] and in the three collections of the *Odi barbare* (1877–89) [*The Barbarian Odes*] do Carducci's full lyrical maturity and accomplished stylistic beauty appear. Here we no longer find the same disdainful poet who fought with sword and fire under the pseudonym of Enotrio Romano. Instead, the character of the poet seems wholly transformed; sweeter, softer melodies are to be heard. The introductory poem «Alla Rima» [«To Rhyme»] is extremely musical, a true hymn to the beauty of rhyme. Its ending excellently characterizes Carducci himself... Evidently Carducci understood his own temperament, which he compares with the Tyrrhenian Sea. But his uneasiness is not continuous, and notes of real joy resound in the enchanting poem «Idillio di Maggio» [«A May Eclogue»]. «Mattinata» [«Morning»], which clearly recalls Hugo, is also lovely, as are the songs entitled «Primavere Elleniche» [«Hellenic Springtimes»]...

«Ca Ira» [«The Rebellion»], a section of the *Rime nuove*, is composed of a series of sonnets. Although it is not of great poetic value, it does represent Carducci's more or less unreserved apotheosis of the French Revolution.

The poet's greatness is more fully revealed in his *Odi barbare*, the first collection of which came out in 1877, the second in 1882, and the third in 1889. There is some justification, however, for criticism of the work's form.

Although Carducci adopted ancient meters, he transformed them so entirely that an ear accustomed to ancient poetry will not hear the classical rhythms. Many of these poems attain the pinnacle of perfection in their poetic content. Carducci's genius has never reached greater heights than in some of his *Odi barbare*. One need only name the fascinating «Miramar» and the melodious and melancholy poem «Alla Stazione in una Mattinata d'Autunno» [«To the Station On an Autumn Morning»], products of the most noble inspiration. The song «Miramar» is about the unfortunate emperor Maximilian and his brief Mexican adventure. It excels as much in its moving tragic tone as it does in its vivid nature imagery. The Adriatic shore is depicted with perfect mastery. This song exhales a certain feeling of compassion which is rare in Carducci's treatment of Austrian subject matter, but which he expressed yet another time in the beautiful song on the Empress Elizabeth's sad fate in *Rime e Ritmi* (1898) [Rhymes and Rythms]...

Many contrasts clearly are to be found in a violent and rich poetic nature like Carducci's. Disapproval from many sides has thus been mixed with the just admiration for this poet. Yet Carducci is without doubt one of the most powerful geniuses of world literature, and such disapproval, voiced also by his compatriots, has not been spared even the greatest poets. No one is without defect.

The blame is not, however, directed at his sometimes passionate republican tendencies. Let his opinions remain his own possession. No one will contest his independent political position. In any case, his hostility toward the monarchy has subsided with the years. He has come more and more to consider the Italian dynasty as the protector of Italian independence. In fact, Carducci has even dedicated poems to the queen mother of Italy, Margherita. A venerable woman revered by almost all factions, her poetic soul has been celebrated by Carducci's grandiose art. He has paid her beautiful and affectionate homage in the magnificent song «Alla Regina d'Italia» [«To the Queen of Italy»] and in the immortal poem «Il Liuto e la Lira» [«Lute and Lyre»], in which, through the Provençal *sirventes* and the pastoral, he expresses his admiration of the noble princess... The petty, obstinate republicans, because of these and other tributes, have looked upon Carducci as a deserter of their cause. He justly responded, however, that a song of admiration dedicated to a magnanimous and good woman has nothing whatever to do with politics, and that he reserved the right to think and write whatever he pleased about the reigning Italian family and its members.

The reasons for the antagonism of his friends and political partisans toward him are of a completely different origin. This antagonism is occasioned less by his ferocious assaults on persons of differing political opinions than by his overenthusiastic paganism, which often assumes a biting tone toward Christianity itself. His anti-Christian sentiments have above all produced his much discussed hymn to Satan.

There is a good deal of justice in many of the attacks on Carducci's anti-Christianity. Although one cannot perfectly approve of the way in which he has tried to defend himself in *Confessioni e battaglie* [Confessions and Battles] and in other writings, a knowledge of the attendant circumstances helps to explain, if not to justify, Carducci's attitudes.

Carducci's paganism is understandable to a Protestant, at least. As an ardent patriot who saw the Catholic Church as in many ways a misguided and corrupt force opposed to the freedom of his adored Italy, Carducci was quite likely to confuse Catholicism with Christianity, extending to Christianity the severe judgments with which he sometimes attacked the Church.

Still we must not forget the genuine religious sentiments expressed in some of his poems. It is helpful to remember the end of «La Chiesa di Polenta» [«The Church of Polenta»], which stands in healthy contrast to «In una Chiesa Gotica» [«In a Gothic Church»].

And as to the impetuous *Inno a Satana* (1865) [*Hymn to Satan*], it would be a great wrong to Carducci to identify him, for example, with Baudelaire and to accuse Carducci of poisonous and unhealthy «Satanism». In fact, Carducci's Satan has an ill-chosen name. The poet clearly means to imply a Lucifer in the literal sense of the word–the carrier of light, the herald of free thought and culture, and the enemy of that ascetic discipline which rejects or disparages natural rights. Yet it seems strange to hear Savanarola praised in a poem in which asceticism is condemned. The whole of the hymn abounds with such contradictions. Carducci himself in recent times has rejected the entire poem and has called it a «vulgar sing-song». Thus, there is no reason to dwell any longer on a poem which the poet himself has disavowed.

Carducci is a learned literary historian who has been nurtured by ancient literature and by Dante and Petrarch. But he cannot be easily classified. He is not devoted to romanticism, but rather to the classical ideal and Petrarchan humanism. Regardless of the criticism which can justly be launched against him, the irrefutable truth remains that a poet who is always moved by patriotism and a love of liberty, who never sacrifices his opinions to gain favour, and who never indulges in base sensualism, is a soul inspired by the highest ideals.

And insofar as his poetry in the aesthetic sense attains a rare force, Carducci can be considered worthy in the highest degree of the Nobel Prize in Literature.

The Swedish Academy thus pays respect to a poet who already enjoys a world-wide reputation, and adds its homage of admiration to the many praises already given him by his country. Italy has elected Carducci senator and repaid the honour he has brought her by assigning him a life-long pension amounting to a considerable sum.

At the banquet, C. D. af Wirsén spoke in Italian about the poet whom illness had prevented from coming to Stockholm. Subsequently he addressed himself to the Italian chargé d'affaires, Count Caprara, and recalled that through the Nobel Prize Sweden had wanted to honour his country and one of her greatest sons at the same time. Mr. Caprara expressed his gratitude in French and, after a speech addressed to the country of Alfred Nobel, promised to convey the homage to the poet.

Biography

Giosuè Carducci (1835–1907) was born in Val di Castello, a small town near Pisa. He was early attracted to the Greek and Roman authors; in addition, he conscientiously studied the Italian classics: Dante, Tasso, and Alfieri. At the age of twenty he graduated with a degree in philosophy and letters from the University of Pisa. After several difficult years in which he taught in various high schools, he was appointed to the chair of Italian Literature at the University of Bologna, a post that he held until his retirement in 1904.

Inspired both by his own time as well as by his study of the classical and Italian poets, Carducci began writing poetry when he was a child. The first two collections of his poetry were *Rime* (1857) [*Rhymes*] and *Levia Gravia* (1868) [*Light and Heavy*]. Both reveal his enthusiasm for and imitation of the ancients as well as a strong revolutionary tendency. *Inno a Satana* (1865) [*Hymn to Satan*], for which Carducci was considered to be a «notorious praiser of Satan», is the full expression of his free thought and of modern ideas, inventions, and revolutions. *Giambi ed epodi* (1882) [*Iambics and Epodes*], a collection of satiric poems of a political nature, expresses Carducci's indignation with his compatriots. In the *Nuove poesie* (1873) [*New Poems*] and the three collections of *Odi barbare* (1877, 1882, and 1889) [*The Barbarian Odes*], his poetic forms reach perfection.

Carducci was also an excellent translator, and the lyrics of Goethe and Heine greatly influenced the development of his own poetry.

In addition to his fame as a poet he was a noted literary historian and an eminent orator. He conducted research in every phase of literature and eloquently expressed his findings in *Studi letterati* (1874) [*Literary Studies*], *Bozzetti critici e discorsi letterari* (1876) [Critical Sketches and Literary Discussions], and many other works.

Carducci, moreover, led an active political life. After having been named an honorary citizen of Bologna, he was elected to the Senate in 1890; he served as deputy in the House of Representatives for a short time. Carducci's poetry inspired his compatriots in the war for Italian independence, and he enjoyed an immense popularity both at home and abroad. Having manifested a scholarly and dynamic personality in all his endeavours, he stands as the greatest Italian literary figure in the latter part of the nineteenth century.

Literature 1907

RUDYARD KIPLING

« in consideration of the power of observation, originality of imagination, virility of ideas, and remarkable talent for narration which characterize the creations of this world-famous author»

Presentation

by C. D. af Wirsén, Permanent Secretary of the Swedish Academy

The suggestions for names of suitable recipients of this year's Nobel Prize in Literature have been numerous, and there has been no dearth of exceedingly well-qualified candidates for this honourable and coveted distinction.

From these candidates, the Swedish Academy has selected for this occasion a writer who belongs to Great Britain. For centuries past the literature of England has flourished and blossomed with marvellous luxuriance. When Tennyson's immortal lyre was silenced forever, the cry which is so customary at the passing of literary giants was raised. With him the glorious reign of poetry is over; there is none to take up the mantle. Similar despairing notes were struck in this country on the demise of Tegnér, but it is not so with the fair goddess Poetry. She does not perish, is not deposed from her high estate; she but arrays herself in a fresh garb to suit the altered tastes of a new age.

In the works of Tennyson idealism is so pervasive that it meets the eye in a very palpable and direct form. Traits of idealism, however, may be traced in the conceptions and gifts of writers who differ widely from him, such writers who seem primarily concerned with mere externals and who have won renown especially for their vivid word-picturings of the various phases of the strenuous, pulsating life of our own times, that life which is often chequered and fretted by the painful struggle for existence and by all its concomitant worries and embarrassments. This description applies to Rudyard Kipling, to whom the Swedish Academy has awarded the Nobel Prize in Literature this year. Of him a French author, who has devoted much time and study to English literature, wrote more than six years ago: «He, Kipling, is undoubtedly the most noteworthy figure that has appeared within recent years in the domain of English literature.»

Kipling was born in Bombay on December 30, 1865. At the age of six he was placed in the care of some relatives in England, but he returned to India on reaching the age of seventeen. He obtained a position on the staff of *The Civil and Military Gazette*, published at Lahore, and in his early twenties edited *The Pioneer* at Allahabad. In his capacity as a journalist, and for his own purposes, he travelled extensively throughout India. On those journeys he acquired a thorough insight into Hindu conceptions and sentiments and became intimately acquainted with the different Hindu groups, with their varying customs and institutions, and with the special features of English military life in India. This firm grasp of the true inwardness of all things Indian is abundantly reflected in Kipling's writings, so much so that it has even been said that they have brought India nearer home to the English nation than has the construction of the Suez Canal. Of his early works the satirical *Departmental Ditties* (1886) attracted notice by the audacity of the allusions it contained, and by the originality of its tone. Also among the early productions are *Plain Tales from the Hills* (1888) and *Soldiers Three* (1888), collections of stories famous among other things for the three lovingly drawn soldier types: Mulvaney, Ortheris, and Learoyd. Other works in the same category are, for instance, *The Story of the Gadsbys* (1888), *In Black and White* (1888), and *Under the Deodars* (1889), all of which are concerned with society life in Simla. The series entitled *Life's Handicap*, embracing some stories of serious import, appeared in 1891. The same year saw the publication of *The Light that Failed*, a novel somewhat harsh in style but containing some strongly coloured descriptive passages of excellent effect.

As a poet Kipling was already full-fledged at the appearance of *Barrack-Room Ballads* (1892), magnificent soldier-songs brimming over with virile humour and depicting realistically Tommy Atkins in all his phases, valiantly marching onward to encounter dangers and misery wherever it pleases «the Widow of Windsor», or her successor on the throne, to dispatch him. In Kipling the British Army has found a minstrel to interpret in a new, original, and tragicomical manner the toils and deprivations through which it has to pass, and to depict its life and work with abundant acknowledgment of the great qualities it displays, but without the least trace of meretricious embellishment. In his verses descriptive of soldiers and sailors he so happily expresses their own thoughts, often in the very language they themselves employ, that they appreciate him deeply and, as we are told, sing his song whenever they have a pause in the day's occupations. Surely, there is hardly any greater mark of honour that can be given to a poet than to be beloved by the lower orders.

In the cycle entitled *The Seven Seas* (1896) Kipling reveals himself as an imperialist, a citizen of a world-wide empire. He has undoubtedly done more than any other writer of pure literature to draw tighter the bonds of union between England and her colonies.

In Sweden, as elsewhere, «the jungle books» by Kipling, the first of which appeared in 1894, are much admired and beloved. A primordial type of imaginative power inspired the creator of these mythlike tales of the animals in whose midst Mowgli waxed in strength: Bagheera the Black Panther, Baloo the Bear, Kaa the cunning and mighty Rock-Python, Nag the White Cobra, and the chattering, foolish Monkeys. Some of the scenes are simply sublime; for instance, the one where Mowgli is resting in the «living arm-chair» Kaa, while the latter, who has witnessed so many generations of trees and animals, dreams of bygone ages; or again when Mowgli causes Hathi the Elephant to «let in the jungle» to take over the fields of men. These descriptions display an instinctive feeling for a poetry of nature which is quite phenomenal, and Kipling is far more in his true element in the primeval grandeur of these jungle stories than, for instance, in «The Ship that Found Herself» (in *The Day's Work*, 1898), an interesting though eccentric personi-fication of mechanical inventions. The *Jungle Book* tales have made Kipling a favourite author among children in many countries. Adults share the de-light experienced by the young and relive their childhood while perusing these marvellously delightful, wonderfully imaginative fables of animals.

Among the large number of Kipling's creations, *Kim* (1901) deserves special notice, for in the delineation of the Buddhist priest, who goes on a pilgrimage along the banks of the stream that purifies from sin, there is an elevated diction as well as a tenderness and charm which are otherwise un-usual traits in this dashing writer's style. There is, too, in the figure of the little rascal Kim, the priest's chela, a thorough type of good-humoured ro-guishness.

The accusation has occasionally been made against Kipling that his lan-guage is at times somewhat coarse and that his use of soldier's slang in some of the broadest of his songs and ballads verges on the vulgar. Though there may be some truth in such remarks, their importance is offset by the invig-orating directness and ethical stimulus of Kipling's style. He has won im-mense popularity, not only in the Anglo-Indian world, which possesses in him a great literary master, but also far beyond the limits of the vast British Empire. During his serious illness in America in 1899, the American news-papers issued daily bulletins regarding his condition, and the German Em-peror dispatched a telegram to his wife to express his earnest sympathy.

What is then the cause of this world-wide popularity that Kipling enjoys? Or, rather: In what way has Kipling shown himself to deserve it? How is it, too, that he has been deemed worthy of the Nobel Prize in Literature, for which a writer must especially show an idealism in his conceptions and in his art? The answer follows:

Kipling may not be eminent essentially for the profundity of his thought or for the surpassing wisdom of his meditations. Yet even the most cursory observer sees immediately his absolutely unique power of observation, capable of reproducing with astounding accuracy the minutest detail from real life. However, the gift of observation alone, be it ever so closely true to nature, would not suffice as a qualification in this instance. There is something else by which his poetical gifts are revealed. His marvellous power of imagination enables him to give us not only copies from nature but also visions out of his own inner consciousness. His landscapes appear to the inner vision as sudden apparitions do to the eye. In sketching a personality he makes clear, almost in his first words, the peculiar traits of that person's character and temper. Creativeness which does not rest content with merely photographing the temporary phases of things but desires to penetrate to their inmost kernel and soul, is the basis of his literary activity, as Kipling himself says: «He draws the thing as he sees it for the God of things as they are.» In these weighty words lies a real appreciation of the poet's responsibility in the exercise of his calling.

Rudyard Kipling's manly, at times brusque, energy does not preclude tenderness and delicacy of touch, though these qualities never clamour affectedly for recognition in his works. The simple «Story of Muhammad Din» is imbued with the poetry of genuine heartfelt emotion, and who can ever forget the little drummer boys in «The Taking of Lungtumpen» (in *Plain Tales*)?

In the innermost being of this indefatigable observer of life and human nature vibrate strings attuned to a lofty note. His poem «To the True Romance» reveals that yearning for a patiently sought, never to be attained ideal that resides in living form in the breast of every true poet, from where the scenes and impressions of the sensuous world can never dislodge it:

> *Enough for me in dreams to see*
> *And touch thy garment's hem:*
> *Thy feet have trod so near to God*
> *I may not follow them!*

This writer's philosophy of life is diffused with a piety characteristic of the Old Testament, or rather perhaps of Puritan times, wholly devoid of pretentiousness or wordiness, based upon a conviction that «the fear of the Lord is the beginning of wisdom» and that there exists a

> *God of our fathers, known of old,*
> *Beneath whose awful Hand we hold*
> *Dominion...*

If Kipling is an idealist from an aesthetic point of view by reason of poetical intuition, he is so, too, from an ethical-religious standpoint by virtue of his sense of duty, which has its inspiration in a faith firmly rooted in conviction. He is acutely conscious of the truth that even the mightiest states would perish unless they rested upon the sure foundation in the citizens' hearts of a loyal observance of the law and a reasoned self-restraint. For Kipling, God is first and foremost Almighty Providence, termed in *Life's Handicap* a «Great Overseer». The English as a nation can well appreciate these conceptions, and Kipling has become the nation's poet, owing not only to his numerous highly prized soldier-songs, but perhaps quite as much to the brief lines of the hymn («Recessional») which he composed on the occasion of Queen Victoria's Diamond Jubilee in 1897. Especially striking are these words expressing genuine and humble religious feelings:

> *The tumult and the shouting dies;*
> *The Captains and the Kings depart:*
> *Still stands Thine ancient sacrifice,*
> *An humble and a contrite heart.*

The recessional hymn voices the spirit of national pride, yet it also conveys a warning against the dangers of presumptuous pride...

Quite naturally, during the Boer War Kipling sided with his own nation, the English. He has, however, done full justice to the heroic courage of the Boers, for his imperialism is not of the uncompromising type that pays no regard to the sentiments of others.

Many and varied are the movements that have had their vogue in English literature, a literature unparalleled for wealth of output and adorned to surpass all others by the immortal figure of Shakespeare. In Kipling may be traced perhaps more of Swift and Defoe than of Spenser, Keats, Shelley, or Tennyson. Clearly, however, imagination is as strong in him as empirical observation. Though he does not possess the refined and sensuously beautiful style of Swinburne, yet he escapes, on the other hand, all tendency toward a pagan worship of pleasure for pleasure's sake. He avoids all morbid sentimentality in matter and Alexandrian superflorescence in form.

Kipling favours concreteness and concentration; empty abstractions and circumlocutionary descriptions are wholly absent from his works. He has a knack for finding the telling phrase, the characteristic epithet, with swift accuracy and certainty. He has been compared now to Bret Harte, now to Pierre Loti, now to Dickens; he is, however, always original, and it would seem that his powers of invention are inexhaustible. Nevertheless, the apostle of the imagination is likewise, as stated above, the standard-bearer of law-abidingness and discipline. The Laws of the Jungle are the Laws of the Universe; if we ask what their chief purport is, we shall receive the brief answer: «Struggle, Duty, Obedience». Kipling thus advocates courage, self-sacrifice, and loyalty; unmanliness and lack of self-discipline are abominations to him, and in the world order he perceives a nemesis before which presumption is constrained to surrender.

If Kipling is quite independent as a writer, it does not follow that he has learned nothing from others; even the greatest masters have done so. With Bret Harte, Kipling shares his appreciation of the picturesqueness of vagabond life, and with Defoe his accuracy in depicting every detail and his sense of the values of exactness in the use of terms and phrases. Like Dickens he feels a keen sympathy with those of low degree in the community, and like him he can perceive the humour in trifling traits and acts. But his style is distinctively original and personal. It accomplishes its ends by suggestion rather than by description. It is not quite uniformly brilliant but it is always eminently expressive and picturesque. The series *From Sea to Sea* (1899) is a veritable model of graphic description, whether the scene is laid in the Elephant City governed by the Grand Divinity of Laziness, in Palm Island, or in Singapore, or whether the story deals with manners and customs of Japan. Kipling has at his command a large fund of irony–sometimes highly pungent–but he has abundant resources of sympathy, too, sympathy for the most part extended to those soldiers and sailors who have upheld the honour of England in far-distant lands. He has every right and reason to tell them: «I have eaten your bread and your salt, I have drunk your water and wine, I have lived your life, I have watched o'er your beds of death.»

He attained fame and success as a very young man, but he has continued to develop ever since. One of his biographers has stated that there are three «notes» to be traced in his authorship. The satirical note is found in *De-*

partmental Ditties, Plain Tales from the Hills, The Story of the Gadsbys, with its amusing commendation of single blessedness, and in the much-debated novel, *The Light that Failed*. The second, the note of sympathy and human kindness, is most clearly marked in «The Story of Muhammad Din» and in «Without Benefit of Clergy» (in *Life's Handicap*), a gem of heartfelt emotion. The third, the ethical note, is clearly traceable in *Life's Handicap*. Whether there be much value or not in this classification which, as is usually the case in such matters, cannot be consistently applied to the whole of his production, one thing is certain: Kipling has written and sung of faithful labour, fulfilment of duty, and love of one's country. Love of one's country with Kipling does not mean solely devotion to the island kingdom of England, but rather an enthusiastic affection for the British Empire. The closer uniting of that Empire's separate members is a long and fervently cherished aspiration of the poet's. That is surely clear from his exclamation: «What should they know of England who only England know?»

Kipling has given us descriptions in vivid colours of many different countries. But the picturesque surface of things has not been the principal matter with him; he has always, in all places, had a manly ideal before him: ever to be «ready, ay ready at the call of duty» and then, when the appointed time comes, to «go to God like a soldier».

The Swedish Academy, in awarding the Nobel Prize in Literature this year to Rudyard Kipling, desires to pay a tribute of homage to the literature of England, so rich in manifold glories, and to the greatest genius in the realm of narrative that that country has produced in our times.

There was no banquet because of the death of King Oscar II of Sweden on December 8, 1907.

Biography

Rudyard Kipling (1865–1936) was born in Bombay, but educated in England at the United Services College, Westward Ho, Bedford. In 1892 he returned to India, where he worked for Anglo-Indian newspapers. His literary career began with *Departmental Ditties* (1886), but subsequently he became chiefly known as a writer of short stories. A prolific writer, he achieved fame quickly. Kipling was the poet of the British Empire and its yeoman, the common soldier, whom he glorified in many of his works, in particular *Plain Tales from the Hills* (1888) and *Soldiers Three* (1888), collections of short stories with roughly and affectionately drawn soldier portraits. His *Barrack Room Ballads* (1892) were written for, as much as about, the common soldier. In 1894 appeared his *Jungle Book*, which became a children's classic all over the world. *Kim* (1901), the story of Kimball O'Hara and his adventures in the Himalayas, is perhaps his most felicitous work. Other works include *The Second Jungle Book* (1895), *The Seven Seas* (1896), *Captains Courageous* (1897), *The Day's Work* (1898), *Stalky and Co.* (1899), *Just So Stories* (1902), *Trafficks and Discoveries* (1904), *Puck of Pook's Hill* (1906), *Actions and Reactions* (1909), *Debits and Credits* (1926), *Thy Servant a Dog* (1930), and *Limits and Renewals* (1932). During the First World War Kipling wrote some propaganda books. His collected poems appeared in 1933.

Kipling was the recipient of many honorary degrees and other awards. In 1926 he received the Gold Medal of the Royal Society of Literature, which only Scott, Meredith, and Hardy had been awarded before him.

Literature 1908

RUDOLF CHRISTOPH EUCKEN

«in recognition of his earnest search for truth, his penetrating power of thought, his wide range of vision, and the warmth and strength of presentation with which in his numerous works he has vindicated and developed an idealistic phi-losophy of life»

Presentation

by Harald Hjärne, Director of the Swedish Academy

Alfred Nobel was a man of action who, during his successful business career in the competing markets of many countries and in the international trade centres, had developed an awareness of the inner contradictions and dangers of modern developments. Mankind still seemed to him to need help, and therefore he thought that the best investment for his own fortune would be to use its interest to support those of whom the future would reveal that–in the words of his will–«mankind profited most from them».

The ambiguity of all human work and its tools or weapons challenged him to a personal deed in behalf of human progress. He knew the enormous usefulness of his own technical inventions for military purposes; therefore, he wanted to support any promising efforts toward international peace. How could his worldly mind have overlooked that all our civilization is full of strife, that it invites abuse as well as proper use, and that it can be turned toward evil as well as good?

His chief interest, however, was the intellectual sphere, despite its inherent contradictions. It appeared to him, the cosmopolitan familiar with the languages and civilizations of France and England, as a complex of arts and sciences, of exact natural science and humanistic belles-lettres. The former he sought to stimulate by supporting discoveries and inventions for the benefit of mankind. Turning to literature with the same philanthropic concern, he established a prize for what he called «excellence in works of an idealistic tendency».

Alfred Nobel was deeply influenced by the outlook of Victor Rydberg's poetry and philosophy. He knew what ideals mean to the human mind, to the will that creates and maintains civilization, cultivates and reaps its fruits, and through the struggle and darkness of life breaks a path toward a new dawn of light and peace. Wherever such ideals are manifested in their infinite variety and strengthen the willingness of men to serve each other–whether in the poet's inspiration, the philosopher's attempt to solve the riddle of life, the historian's biographies, or the work of any scholar or writer that looks toward those ideals as models in his freedom and independence–

there one finds the literature that Alfred Nobel had in mind. This literature makes use of whatever art and science can offer, and from it mankind «profits the most» precisely because it mirrors the ideal truth without any regard for the useful. The creations and forms of this literature are as manifold as the ideals, and they are forever new and free.

The Swedish Academy has therefore felt that it acted with the sanction of Alfred Nobel when it decided this year to award the literary prize founded by Nobel to one of the most prominent thinkers of our age, Professor Rudolf Eucken, «in recognition of his earnest search for truth, his penetrating power of thought, his wide range of vision, and the warmth and strength of presentation with which in his numerous works he has vindicated and developed an idealistic philosophy of life».

For over thirty years Professor Eucken has been publishing profound contributions in several areas of philosophy. His activity as a writer has yielded increasingly many and important books as his basic philosophy has become both more coherent and more comprehensive. Particularly in recent years he has published the works that afford us the most thorough introduction to his thought; moreover, the wider public has received from him uncommonly lucid and powerful expositions of his attempts to resolve the most urgent problems of contemporary civilization. Thus he is in the midst of giving the final shape to his mature thought, and everywhere one can see new ideas which we hope he will be able to develop fully in the near future.

I cannot here give a detailed account of Eucken's long and versatile career as a philosopher, because time is short and the subject difficult for one with little knowledge of most of his special fields. I can only make some generalizations and dwell in particular on the historical foundations of his *Weltanschauung* and his views on the meaning of historical processes. Professor Eucken considers history a decisive influence on his philosophy, and it was philological and historical studies that led him toward philosophy. Ever since his early days the actual life of man and society has meant much more to him than the abstractions of mere thought analysis. Unfortunately we shall have to omit many interesting ramifications of his thought in order to get a clear picture at least of its main results.

The confident and rising idealism today in the intellectual life not only of Germany but everywhere on the higher and freer levels of civilized life is very different from those proud constructions which bore that name and which went bankrupt half a century ago with Hegel's magnificent system.

It was an attempt to derive the inexhaustible wealth of life and the world from abstract categories and concepts by means of a daring dialectic, and to force all human research, all civilization, under the yoke of a complete system of thought. But closer analysis revealed this attempt to be beyond the competence of the philosophical search for truth, and in fact it accelerated the change to an equally dogmatic materialism.

We Swedes know that even at the zenith of dialectic absolutism Boström directed his logical criticisms toward its basic attitudes. By going back to earlier views both here and abroad, he developed a different outlook which has had its adherents in this country up to the present. There is an indisputable resemblance between his views and those developed by Professor Eucken in his writings. This is not surprising, for they both represent a basic type that since the earliest days of civilization—notwithstanding temporary eclipses—has preserved its vitality in the face of pantheistic abstractions as well as materialistic fear of thought. But this characteristic agreement in their basic views does not exclude independent and personal development; on the contrary it rather promotes it, and no branch of philosophy has produced so many marked profiles as realistic idealism. Socrates and Plato were led by this idealism to hold that philosophy is a search for truth rather than a fixed dogma, and this tireless search, by whatever means, has characterized philosophy throughout the ages. Thus Eucken and Boström reached their common goal by quite different means.

Since his youth Eucken has carefully observed the busy and steady philosophical attempts to reassess external and inner experience and to gain firm ground again after the collapse of the bold philosophical systems. Philosophy turned in different directions with varying expectations and success. Sometimes the motto was «Back to Kant», and the great metaphysical iconoclast served as a model for thorough studies of the limits of human knowledge, or else one listened hesitantly to his declaration of an eternal realm of reason based on unassailable moral postulates. Again there were attempts to give philosophy a safe position by tying it to the victorious advances of modern science or, more successfully, by independently questioning its presuppositions and methods. There were attempts to discover the secrets of the human soul in its manifestations, whether by observation or experiment, and there was hope that such research would lead toward the discovery of the proper relation of physical and psychological existence.

Eucken has been familiar with all these schools, but his main field has been historical and critical research on the emergence and development of main streams of thought in connection with the evolution and change of general culture. Like so many pioneers in his field, he has always been convinced that there can be no true progress without a proper regard for tradition and that there is more to the annals of philosophy than a kaleidoscope of systems rising and falling with equal suddenness. As Eucken has often emphasized, there can be no continuity in philosophy unless it grows like the other sciences and continually treats and develops the same problems, lest every mind should believe that he could start all over from the beginning only to be replaced by someone else in the same manner.

Apart from collections of monographs and essays in this field, Eucken as early as 1878 published the first comprehensive results of his method. In *Grundbegriffe der Gegenwart* [Basic Concepts of Modern Thought] he discusses the origin, formulation, and development of common modern concepts since the days of ancient philosophy and scholasticism. Such terms are «subjective and objective», «experience and evolution», «monism and dualism», «mechanistic and organic», «law and individuality», «personality and character», «theoretical and practical», «immanence and transcendence». But he is not interested merely in a definition of terms; he wants to describe the leading goals and attitudes of a period by elucidating, in his own words, «concepts as a mirror of their time». With each dissection the object becomes more clearly delineated. In the fourth edition, which appeared this year, the scope of the book has widened; it has become a thorough critique of the conflicts in modern civilization; accordingly, the title of the book has been changed to *Geistige Strömungen der Gegenwart* (1908) [*Main Currents of Modern Thought*]. Indeed, the author has developed his own basic ideas in it, and it is a rewarding labour to study them in their wealth and complexity.

A thinker who considers the perennial questions of human civilization from this point of view will soon learn that he cannot solve them either by ignoring their close interrelation or by limiting himself to epistemological questions. Undoubtedly these problems constantly impinge upon each other; they cover the whole of human existence, influence individuals that are particularly susceptible to their importance, and thereby exercise a reforming power over entire communities and ages. The attempt to trace them in their vital and seminal role amounts to giving a comprehensive survey of human intellectual history. At the same time such a project is more conducive to arousing and widening philosophical interest than a mere analysis of conflicting dogmas, schools, and sects. Eucken undertook such a task in *Die Lebensanschauungen der grossen Denker: Eine Entwicklungsgeschichte des Lebens-*

problems der Menschheit von Plato bis zur Gegenwart (1890) [*The Problem of Human Life as Viewed by the Great Thinkers from Plato to the Present Time*]. This work, revised and expanded through seven editions, bears witness not only to the depth and scope of Eucken's research but to his mastery of marshalling his thoughts and to the maturity of his style.

Eucken has developed his own philosophy in several works such as *Der Kampf um einen geistigen Lebensinhalt: Neue Grundlegung einer Weltanschauung* (1896) [The Struggle for a Spiritual Content of Life: New Principles of a Philosophy] and *Grundlinien einer neuen Lebensanschauung* (1907) [*Life's Basis and Life's Ideal: The Fundamentals of a New Philosophy of Life*] as well as the more popular *Der Sinn und Wert des Lebens* (1908) [*The Meaning and Value of Life*] and *Einführung in eine Philosophie des Geisteslebens* (1908) [Introduction to a Philosophy of the Mind]. The last mentioned work in particular is a masterly and lucid exposition of his views.

In recent years Eucken has also turned his attention to religious questions, in *Der Wahrheitsgehalt der Religion* (1901) [*The Truth of Religion*] and *Hauptprobleme der Religionsphilosophie der Gegenwart* (1907) [Main Problems of Contemporary Philosophy of Religion], the latter based on three lectures delivered during a theological summer institute at the University of Jena. This year he has developed his ideas about the philosophy of history at some length in a treatise that forms part of the great encyclopaedic work *Die Kultur der Gegenwart* [Contemporary Civilization]. According to hints in recent works he is now planning a thorough re-examination of ethical problems.

His deep insights into history and his significant attempts to relate his own thoughts on the forces of life to the evidence of history place Eucken far above the superficial attitudes that exaggerate and misinterpret the inner meaning of history. These attitudes, at the cost of an unprejudiced love of truth, have become all too common in this century of history.

Furthermore, Eucken sees a threat to civilization in the caricature of historicism, which partly intends to drag all firm goals and higher aims into the whirlpool of a misunderstood relativity and partly supports the frequent attempts to limit and paralyze the human will by fitting all human developments and achievements into a supposed naturalistic and fatalistic causal nexus. But in contrast to Nietzsche, for instance, he does not believe in the right or ability of the overweening individual to maintain his own will to power in the face of the obligations to the eternal majesty of moral laws. It is not the individual or the superman in his separate existence, but the strong character formed in the consciousness of free harmony with the intellectual forces of the cosmos, and therefore profoundly independent, that in Eucken's view is called upon to liberate us from the superficial compulsion of nature and the never completely inescapable pressure of the historical chain of cause and effect.

In history as well as in his personal existence man has life of a higher nature, a life originating not in nature but existing in itself and through itself, a life of the mind, which is in reality beyond time but which is revealed to us only in temporal manifestations. All true development presupposes some basis of existence. To the extent to which man comes to participate in the intellectual life, he acquires a power that is eternal and above the vicissitudes of time. This eternal life is a realm of truth, for truths with a limited existence are unthinkable. At the same time it is an infinite whole of living power, far above the world as it appears to us but exercising its influence in the world for us and through us. It is not an abstract castle in the air to which we can escape on the wings of a mystical and supposedly logical imagination, but as a wholly living power it confronts our entire personality with an either–or, a choice of the will that makes the evolution of man and mankind a ceaseless struggle between the higher and the lower life.

History is the mirror of mankind's victories and defeats in this struggle, the vicissitudes of which have been due to the self-determination of the free personality. Hence no philosophy of history can predict the future of this struggle. Even the civilization handed to us as a heritage does not survive by itself but demands our persistent and personal struggle for the true and genuine life of the mind. Nothing else can justify and support our endeavours for morality and art and our political and social work.

«Utilitarianism,» Eucken says, «whichever form it assumes, is irreconcilably opposed to true intellectual culture. Any intellectual activity degenerates unless it is treated for its own sake.» Although a great admirer and lover of art, Eucken has turned with equal severity against the aestheticism which is preached so loudly in our days and which «infects only reflective and pleasure-loving hedonists». «No art that values itself and its task can afford to condemn morality. A creative artist of the highest order has hardly ever been a follower of an aesthetic view of life.» Our Runeberg is a poet after his heart, for such an outlook «with its indifference to moral values and its arrogant exclusiveness is quite foreign to him». And only those nations, whether great or small, that have created and maintained a civilization full of genuine intellectual life have a contribution to make to mankind. A contribution may be made only by those nations whose future consists not in a vain endeavour to use material force and weapons to «transform quantity into quality», but in the ever growing revelation of eternal life within the limits of temporal existence.

Eucken does not reject a metaphysics that tries to express conceptually those things that are accessible to us in the infinite realm of truth and life. But he has not constructed an everlasting system, nor did he want to do so. His philosophy, which he himself calls a philosophy of action, operates primarily with the forces of human evolution and is therefore more dynamic than static. We may regard him as a *Kulturphilosoph* who fully meets the standards and needs of our age.

Professor Eucken – The lofty and scholarly idealism of your *Weltanschauung*, which has found such vigorous expression in your many and widely read works, has justified the Swedish Academy in awarding to you the Nobel Prize in Literature for this year.

The Academy greets you with sincere and respectful admiration and hopes that your future works, too, will bear ample fruit for the benefit of culture and humanity.

At the banquet, Harald Hjärne addressed, in German, his personal congratulations to Professor Eucken. He recalled Thuringia and, in particular, the University of Jena, the heart of German humanism, and the relations of that university with the history of the Swedish Reformation. In his reply, Mr. Eucken spoke enthusiastically about the idealism for which he had struggled and expressed his gratitude toward Sweden and the Swedish Academy.

Naturalism or Idealism?

Nobel Lecture, March 27, 1909

The history of mankind knows of certain questions that are at once very old and always new: they are very old because any way of life contains an answer to them, and always new because the conditions on which those ways of life depend are constantly shifting and may at critical stages change so much that truths safely accepted for generations may become open problems causing conflict and bewilderment.

Such a question is the contrast between naturalism and idealism with which we are dealing today. The meaning of these words has been blunted by usage; they cause many a misunderstanding, and only through laziness do we put up with such catchwords. But their inadequacy cannot conceal the great contrast which lies behind them and which sharply divides men. This contrast concerns our attitude to the whole of reality and the resulting task that dominates our life; it concerns the question whether man is entirely determined by nature or whether he can somehow–or indeed essentially–rise above it. We are all agreed on the very close ties between man and nature which he should not abandon. But it has been argued and is still being argued vehemently whether his whole being, his actions and sufferings, are determined by these ties or whether he possesses life of another kind which introduces a new stage of reality. The one attitude characterizes naturalism, the other idealism, and these two creeds differ fundamentally both in their goals and in their pursuits of them. For if the additional life of man exists only in his imagination, we should eradicate all traces of it from human opinions and institutions. Instead, we should aim at the closest ties with nature and develop to a pure state the natural character of human life; for thus life would restore the ties with its true origins which it severed unjustly and to its lasting damage. But if one recognizes in man a new element beyond nature, the task will consist in giving it the strongest possible support and contrasting it clearly with nature. In this case life will take up its main position in the new element and look at nature from that point of view. This contrast in attitudes emerges nowhere as clearly as in the place of the soul in the two systems. Nature, of course, has its share in the life of the soul and in numerous manifestations deeply influences human life. But this natural life of the soul is peripheral, mere appendix to the material phenomena of nature. Its only purpose is the preservation of physical life, for man's higher psychological development, his cleverness and resourcefulness, compensate for the brute strength, swiftness of movement, or sharpness of the senses in which animals excel. But even in its extreme form this life has neither purpose nor content in itself; it remains a conglomeration of disparate points. It does not coalesce in an inner community of life, nor does it constitute an inner world peculiar to itself. Thus action is never directed toward an inner purpose but toward the utilitarian purpose of preserving life. Naturalism, if it remains true to its purpose, reduces human life to that norm. Idealism, on the other hand, maintains the emancipation of inwardness; according to it the disparate phenomena of life coalesce in an all-embracing inner world. At the same time, idealism demands that human life should be governed by its peculiar values and goals, the true, the good, and the beautiful. In its view the sub-ordination of all human aspiration to the goal of usefulness appears an in-tolerable humiliation and a complete betrayal of the greatness and dignity of man. Such divergent and even contradictory attitudes seem to be irrec-oncilable: we have to choose between harsh alternatives.

With regard to this choice the present time is undeniably divided against itself, particularly since profound changes in the setup of life have brought new aspects of the problem to light. Centuries of tradition had accustomed us to striving primarily for an invisible world and to valuing the visible world only to the degree of its relation to the invisible world. To the medieval mind man's home is a transcendental world; in this world we are merely travellers abroad. We cannot penetrate it, nor does it give us any scope for achievements or hold us by any roots. In such a conception nature easily appears as a lower sphere which one approaches at one's own peril. When Petrarch had climbed Mount Ventoux and was enraptured by the splendour of the Alps, he had serious doubts whether such delight at the creation was not an injustice to the Creator and did not deprive Him of the worship due to Him alone. Thus he took refuge with St. Augustine to regain the security of a religious mood.

These things have changed. We set greater store by the world of im-mediate experience and many things have helped to make it completely our home. Science has been the leader in this movement, for it has brought about a closer relationship with nature, resulting in many new impulses that have not only enriched parts of our life but have deeply affected its totality. The speculative and subjective thought of former ages was unable to analyze sensual perceptions and did not penetrate to the essence of things. Moreover, its recognition of certain regularities in nature lagged far behind the discovery of mathematical laws of nature first formulated by the genius of Kepler. And not only did it fail to penetrate nature, it failed equally to turn its powers to the use of man and to the advancement of his welfare. Occasional technical inventions were the result of chance rather than superior insight; on the whole, man remained defenceless against nature. Only a century ago men were still awkward and powerless in this regard. In that age of great poets and thinkers, how much time was wasted with overcoming natural obstacles, how inconvenient was travelling, and how cumbersome postal services. In all these respects our age has seen changes never dreamed of by history before. The accumulation of scientific knowledge since the seventeenth century was brought to a triumphant conclusion in the nineteenth. By unravelling the separate strands of natural processes and tracing them back to their ultimate elements, by formulating the effects of these elements in simple formulas, and finally by using the idea of evolution to combine what had been separated, scientific research has given us a closer and more direct experience of nature in all its aspects. At the same time the theory of evolution has shown man's dependence on nature: understanding himself in nature, his own essence appeared to become clearer to him.

The change of concepts was accompanied by a change of the realities of life. Technology seized upon the results of science and caused a revolution in man's relationship with his environment. Former ages had held that his position in the world was essentially determined and not subject to change; man had to suffer whatever dark fate or the will of God had decreed. Even if he could–and was expected to–alleviate suffering in individual instances, he was no match for the totality of suffering and there was no hope of either tearing up evil by the root or making life richer and more joyous. In our age, however, we are translating into action the conviction that by common effort mankind can raise the level of life, that a rule of reason can gradually replace the tyranny of irrational forces. Man may again feel victorious and creative. Even if his powers are limited at any given moment, that moment is only one in a long chain. The impossibilities of a former age have been realized in ours. We have witnessed surprising breakthroughs in our own age and can see no limit to this progressive movement. Man's existence has been immeasurably enriched; it has become an attraction and a challenge for him.

Technological progress becomes even more exciting when it enters into the service of the social idea which demands that not only a small élite but humanity at large should profit by it. This demand creates an entirely new challenge, requiring tremendous energy but also giving rise to new complications and harsh contrasts which, in turn, intensify the passion of man's work in this world and enrich its meaning. The transformation of environment has become the purpose of human life; life seems real only insofar as it deals with things. Man no longer needs the escape to an invisible world in order to find and realize exalted goals.

These facts are indisputable. Our material environment and our relation to it have assumed tremendous importance. Any philosophy and any course of action based on it must reckon with this fact. But naturalism goes beyond this fact, for it maintains that man is completely defined by his relationship with the world, that he is only a piece of the natural process. That is a different contention which requires careful examination. For history has taught us that our judgment is easily confused and exaggerated when revolutionary changes upset the old balance of things. Facts and opinions are confused by man, who is helpless against error and passion. At such a time, it becomes an urgent task to separate the facts from the interpretations given to them. Naturalism, too, is subject to such a scrutiny when it turns a fact into a principle, sees the totality of human life determined by man's closer relation to nature, and adjusts all values accordingly.

The chief argument against such a limitation of human life is the result not of subjective reflection but of an analysis of the modern movement itself. The emergence and the progress of that movement reveal an intellectual capacity which, whether it manifests itself as intellectual and technical mastery of nature or as practical social work, proves the existence of a way of life that cannot be accounted for, if man is understood as a mere natural being. For in coming closer to nature man shows himself superior to it. As a mere part of nature, man's existence would be a series of isolated phenomena. All life would proceed from and depend on contact with the outside world. There would be no way of transcending the limitation of the senses. There would be no place at all for any activity governed by a totality or superior unity, nor for any inner coherence of life. All values and goals would disappear and reality would be reduced to mere actuality. But the experience of human work shows a very different picture.

Modern science has not been the result of a gradual accumulation of sensual perceptions but a deliberate break with the entire stock of traditional knowledge. Such a break was deemed necessary because the old concepts had been too anthropomorphic, whereas a scientific understanding of nature presupposed an acknowledgment of its complete independence from man. But our concepts could not have formulated the independence of nature unless thought had emancipated itself from sensual impressions, and through analysis and new synthesis created a new view of nature. This re-creation was caused by the search for truth and the desire to identify with things as they are and thus to bring about an inner expansion of life. But how could nature be conceived in such a manner without the element of chance and distortion, inherent in the perspective of the individual, unless thought could operate independently of sensual perception? Logical thought, striving for a unified conception of the universe, transformed the immediate sensual perception; it provided the sensual existence with the foundation of a world of thought. Man's tremendous intellectual achievement of a conception of nature in its totality proves his superiority over the natural world and the existence of another level of reality. Thus we may say that naturalism with its emphasis on nature is refuted nowhere with more cogency than in modern science as it transformed nature into an intellectual conception. The more we recognize the intellectual achievement and inner structure of modern science, the clearer becomes the distance from naturalism.

The superiority of man to mere nature is also proved by modern technology, for it demands and proves imaginative anticipation and planning, the tracing of new possibilities, exact calculations, and bold ventures. How could a mere natural being be capable of such achievements?

The social movement, too, reveals man as not entirely limited by a given order, but as a being that perceives and judges a given situation and is confident that it can change it essentially by its own efforts. We have come to set greater store by material things, but we value them not because of their sensual characteristics but because they serve us to enhance life and to dominate the world completely. We do not aim at an increase in sensual pleasures but at a situation in which any man and all men together can develop their full strength. The mere mention of a social idea implies common interests beyond the egotism of the individual, and this idea would never have reached the power it has had it not been conceived of both as a duty and as a privilege. The ethical element inherent in it gave it the power to win over minds, to attract enthusiastic disciples, and to prevail even over reluctance. But there is no place at all for such an ethical element in the realm of mere nature; thus the mere existence of a social movement refutes naturalism.

These considerations lead to the conclusion that naturalism is by no means an adequate expression of the modern way of life. On the contrary, that way of life has outgrown its origins and has revealed far greater spiritual independence than naturalism could acknowledge. Life itself has contradicted that interpretation of life. The fact that environment means more to us does not mean that we are a mere part of it. Naturalism makes the mistake of ascribing to nature itself the changes the mind effected in it. The mistake resulted from concentrating on the effects and ignoring the power which alone could produce them.

Still the fact remains that mind needs environment as an object to work on, and to that extent it is dependent on it. But does not such a situation confront life with an intolerable conflict? The transformation of the environment has released vast intellectual energies which fortify the claim of life for happiness and satisfaction. Will life not feel intolerably confined if man must deal only with the outside world, if he may never return to himself and use the results of his stupendous labours for his own welfare? The achievement itself is limited narrowly if its object is invariably outside ourselves and can never be taken into our own life. Scientific research in an external object can never lead to true, complete, and inner knowledge. As long as we regard man simply as a being next to us, there can be no inner community of mutual love. Energy that is not dominated by, and does not return to, a centre, will never constitute the content of life; it leaves us empty in the midst of bustling excitement. This is a common and painful modern experience. But is not such a sensation of emptiness itself proof that there are more profound depths within us which demand satisfaction? Thus we are faced with the question whether life does not somehow go beyond the position reached so far, whether it could not return from an occupation with outside objects to an occupation with itself and to the experience and shaping of itself. Only life's own movement can give such an answer; let us see whether it is in the affirmative.

I think we can say confidently that it is. We need only regard clear and indisputable individual phenomena as a whole and appreciate that whole in its full significance in order to recognize that there is indeed a great movement within us which generates an essentially new way of life. Hitherto our discussion had seen life as something between subject and object, between man and world, between energy and thing. However, the thing was touched only from the outside; it remained inwardly foreign to us. But now intellectual activity takes a turn to the effect that the object is taken into the process of life, is incorporated into the soul and excites and moves us as part of our own life. The artist's creative activity, for instance in Goethe, is an example of this. We call such creativity objective, but that is not to say that the outside world is pictured in its sensual being without any addition of the soul; rather, the external object becomes part of the soul. There is a fruitful relation of energy and object; they combine, enhance one another, and create a new complete living entity. In such life a soul is breathed into the object, or the soul that is in it is made to sound, and in effecting the object, energy loses its initial indeterminate character and assumes full definition. The poet appears as a magician who gives to things a language in which they proclaim their own being, but they come alive only in the soul of the poet, only in an inner world. Something similar to this artistic process occurs in practical life, in the relationship of men as it finds its expression in law and morality. The other man who at first seems a complete outsider is taken into the circle of our own life when we become capable of identifying ourselves with him. Nowhere is the process of making the seemingly strange your own as marked as in love, the highest relationship of two individuals. For here the gap between oneself and the other is completely bridged; what was strange becomes an integral part of one's own life. Nor can we love our people, our country, or the whole of mankind unless we find in them our own life and being. In another direction the search for truth leads to a broadening of our inner life. For how could we desire so powerfully to recognize the object unless it did not somehow exist within our own life, unless the toil spent on it did not contribute to the perfection of our own being?

Thus the beautiful, the good, and the true agree in that the object becomes part of the inner process of life, but this cannot possibly happen without deep changes in the structure and meaning of that process. For now life is dealing primarily with itself; energy and object meet in it and demand a balance. However, there can be no balance unless both are comprehended in one whole, which finds its life and perfection in them. Thus life enters into a relationship with itself, it is structured in itself in different degrees and begets within itself a new depth, a comprehensive and persistent energy. If this happens, the whole can be present and effective in each detail. It is only in this way that convictions and attitudes are possible, and character and personality can manifest themselves in their manifold activities. The integration into the process of life gives to the object a new and higher form, and so life is not merely the representation or appropriation of a given reality; it enhances and creates; it does not find a world, but must make a world for itself.

Thus life faces not only the outside world, but itself. It creates its own realm of the mind. By combining with each other, the different movements produce an inner world, and this inner world, through a complete reversal of the initial situation, becomes the point of departure for all intellectual activity. This world is not a private world; the good, true, and beautiful are not peculiar to each individual. We live in a common world and the individual achievement is valid for all and becomes their possession. In this consists the greatness of that new world. The new life in the individual has a universal character, and in the quest for this life the individual more and more finds his true self and abandons his limited point of departure. Mere self-preservation becomes increasingly less satisfying.

If we look more closely at this development of life and consider its energies and forms, the complete reversal it caused and the new tasks it created, we cannot really doubt any more that it is not a mere figment of man's imagination designed for his pleasure and comfort. It is obviously a new level of reality which creates new tasks for man. The movement toward the new goals, the development of a more intimate basic relationship with reality, and the grafting of an infinite life onto human existence cannot possibly be mere human creations. Man could not even imagine such things. There must be an impulse of life from the universe that embraces and carries us and gives us the strength to fight for the new reality, to introduce it into the world of natural reality, and to participate in the movement of the universe. Without being rooted in the actuality of the universe, our aspirations could never gain a firm foothold and direction. Life on our level could not exist within itself and enhance itself unless the totality of reality exists within itself and is in an inward motion.

The importance of man and the tension of his life increase immeasurably in this process of change. Belonging at first to the level of nature, he rises to a new level of reality in which he is active with the energy of the whole, and so he does not remain a mere part of a given order but becomes a stage on which worlds meet and search for their further development. And he is more than a stage. For although that movement of the world cannot arise out of him, it cannot be activated on this stage without his decision and action. He cooperates in the totality of worlds so that limitation and freedom, finiteness and infinity, meet in him. The world ceases to be foreign to him, and with the whole of its life it becomes his own and inmost essence.

It is this development of life to its full self-realization which idealism seizes upon and on which it models its goals and concentrates its efforts, even though the level of nature remains and man's intellectual life can develop only in constant intercourse with it. But this does not dispose of the fundamental contrast that idealism, unlike naturalism, understands not mind by nature but nature by mind.

The ever-renewed conflict between the two convictions is due to the fact that the new world, however much it must be effective from the bottom of our souls, can be gained only in a constant struggle that always creates new complications. It is not only the individual who has to make this world his own; mankind at large has to fight for its more definite form, which is not given to us but has to be discovered and realized by ourselves. History knows of many approaches to this goal, but none has proved perfect in the end. We experience the world of the mind at first only separately and vaguely; it is our task to achieve a comprehensive form to give it a fully definite character and make it a complete and safe possession. Now at high points of history, humanity has made the attempt at such a synthesis of life that would embrace and give form to the whole of being. Success may seem to attend such an effort in its first surge, but soon obstacles arise, and as they grow it becomes clear that life does not in its entirety fit the measure prescribed for it. Individual movements free themselves from the projected structure, and the period of positive creation and coalescence of the elements is followed by a period of criticism and disintegration, so that the search for the unity of life leads to a new synthesis. Thus, epochs of concentration and expansion follow upon each other, and both serve man's aspiration for a spiritual content of life. Past achievements will always appear too small, and the need for spiritual preservation of life will always lead to a new effort. In such tenacity of purpose, such continuous progress, and such struggle with infinity the tremendous greatness of mankind is realized.

The experience of European civilization since the Greek era has revealed this process with particular forcefulness. Greek life has its lasting importance in the cheerful energy with which it engaged upon an original synthesis of the entire range of our existence. It did so by means of art, in particular fine arts, and this synthesis served as a point of departure for the manifold ramifications of civilization. Science tried to determine the permanent artifice of the cosmos behind the chaos of shifting phenomena. Action was to turn the human commonwealth into a strictly measured and well-constructed work of art, and the individual was to combine in perfect harmony all the manifold energies and desires of his soul. These endeavours resulted in a thorough patterning of life. Activity was aroused everywhere, a balance of conflicting sides was achieved together with stability and an inner cheerfulness. All these achievements have become a permanent gain. But mankind could not stop at this. The experience of life created greater tasks, greater contrasts and conflicts than could be solved by it. It became apparent that an end had been set abruptly and prematurely, and that the soul had depths not fully sounded by it. The whole had rested on the assumption of the immediate presence and irresistible power of the intellect in human life, and a weaker age came to doubt this presence. A period of disintegration followed. The manifold elements separated, but despite all its negative aspects, this period prepared for a new synthesis. Such a synthesis appeared in original Christianity, where the whole of reality was subordinated to the moral idea, and the variety of life was made subject to the moral obligation. But considering man's moral frailty and the lack of reason in the human world, the strength for the solution of such a task had to be derived from a superhuman order. Thus, the moral synthesis had at the same time a religious character and together with it affected the entire range of life. This concentration led to an enormous deepening of life; it created a pure inner world and first established the absolute supremacy of mind over nature.

But though this life remains valid in our world, its original form has encountered increasingly strong opposition ever since the beginning of the modern period. A new humanity full of high spirits found in it too little for the development of its power. At the same time, a desire for a universal culture that would embrace all branches of life with equal love, felt confined by that moral-religious synthesis. Hence a new synthesis arose, in which the basic idea is the unlimited development of all energies and in which the enhancement of life has become its purpose. This urge has set in motion whatever appeared to be at rest. Constant progress has affected not only nature, but man himself. Nothing seems to be more characteristic of man than his ability to rise toward the infinite by the powers of his mind despite his natural limitations. This life is still flooding about us from all sides and is penetrating ever more deeply into the ramifications of being. However, at the bottom of our souls and at the height of intellectual effort, new doubts are beginning to arise about this solution. First we have begun to doubt

whether the entire range of being can really be turned into an upward movement, and whether this movement itself does not create new problems and
complications that it could not cope with; whether the release of all energies
has not conjured up contrasts and passions that are threatening the sanity
of our existence. And even if we could suppress these doubts, other and
greater ones arise from the question whether the transformation into incessant activity really exhausts life and satisfies the soul. For if motion does
not find its balance in a state of rest superior to it from which it can be comprehended, the possibility of life's existence within itself disappears. We can
no longer assign any content to life; it is a constant and impatient longing
for the remote which never returns to itself and forms itself. Nor can we
defend ourselves against a boundless relativism, if the truth of today is super-
seded tomorrow. The restlessness and haste of such progressive activity cannot prevent a growing emptiness and the consciousness of it. Despite the
greatness of technical achievements in particular fields, man in the entirety
of his existence is doomed to decline: the powerful and individual personality
will gradually disappear.

But as soon as we realize the limitations and defects of this modern synthesis of life, we cease to believe in it. The old order will disintegrate and
the contrasts will again emerge in full power. Self-assured activity once more
will give way to brooding reflection; we shall once more enter from a
positive into a critical period.

If life thus lacks a dominating unity and a centre, while at the same time
the transformation of the outside world achieves splendid triumphs, it is understandable if the balance of life is lost, and external successes gradually
come to dominate the picture. The achievement makes us forget the power
that produced it. Education works from the outside to the inside, and in the
end man appears completely a product of his environment because the central
energy could no longer cope with the affluence of the outside world. In such
an atmosphere naturalism wields power over souls, and we fully understand
how it gains ground as the expression of a peculiar situation. But it is precisely
through our understanding of it that we are more firmly convinced that it
is not the whole truth of human experience.

Its attempt to reduce man entirely to the level of nature can succeed only
so long as human existence does not bring forth new energies and goals.
But since we have recognized that man represents a new degree of reality
which makes intellectual activity possible, we can no longer simply return
to nature. The new reality may temporarily be lost in the consciousness of

man, but the results of history are embedded in his soul, in the midst of all struggles, doubts, and errors. Even in the midst of negation they have put him far above the level of mere nature, and naturalism appears to be sufficient only because it borrows widely and unscrupulously from idealism. If these borrowings disappear and naturalism has to rely on its own resources, its inadequacies become glaring. There will be a decisive rebellion against an intolerably shallow view of life, accompanied by a strong movement toward idealism and the search for a new synthesis of life.

For certainly the new and strong desire for life's existence within itself and for a rich inner world cannot be satisfied by a return to an earlier stage. There may be imperishable truths in the older syntheses of life, but how can we explain the tremendous shocks and the feeling of uncertainty about the whole of life if those truths, as they have been historically transmitted, contained the final truth? We have considered the deep changes that the modern age has brought about, and we have recognized the closer concatenation of man with his environment and the greater importance of that environment. At the same time, we have seen the harsh obstacles met by the striving for a complete intellectualization of existence, we feel the deep gap between the immediate being of man and the demands of intellectual life, and we realize that we must revise our image of man in order to reach the point of intellectual creativity. We can no longer hope to set the whole of existence in motion at one stroke. First of all we must try to form a nucleus of life and to fortify that position; then we shall have to cope with environment and gradually encroach upon it. The new insights and tasks of the modern age will be fully utilized in this endeavour, especially the tremendous progress made in human welfare which we owe to science. Only we must not assimilate these new elements in their immediate sensual form. We shall have to extract the nucleus of truth, and this can be done only in the context of our entire historical experience. Any conviction that is to carry mankind needs an open mind for the movements of the time, but such open-mindedness should not lead to helpless drifting in their wake.

A revival of idealism may well face many difficulties and obstacles, but the task is imperative and we cannot shirk it. Once mankind has attained an existence of life within itself it cannot resign it again; it has to use all its power and ingenuity to carry out that imperative demand. Once man has escaped from the fetters of natural life, he cannot possibly agree to them again; once risen to independent activity, he cannot again be the plaything of inscrutable powers; having penetrated to the universe and its infinity, he cannot again return to the limitations of a natural being; once the desire for an inner relationship to the world has stirred within him, external relationships will no longer satisfy him. Thus, there is an urge beyond naturalism in all directions.

The peculiar experiences and needs of our own time most strongly demand the revival of the movement toward idealism. The steady increase of work and the rush of the struggle for existence have obscured the meaning of life and deprived our life of a dominating goal. Can we hope to regain such a goal without a powerful concentration and elevation in the soul of man? There are senile features in the colorful picture of modern life, and there is a great urge for rejuvenation, for a production of pure and original beginnings. Would not such an urge be folly if man were wholly determined by the necessity of a natural process? The creativity of the mind has at all times been surrounded and often covered by petty interests, but it makes a considerable difference whether we can check such obscurantism or not. If we can, we need a goal that unites and elevates men; otherwise we are at the mercy of human pettiness, and there is far too much of it in our world today. In the confusion of everyday life little distinction is made between what is high and low, true or seeming, genuine or spurious. There is no sense of the substantial, no acknowledgement of the great either–or pervading human life. We shall have to separate the wheat from the chaff and in an act of concentration gather whatever the time contains in good and important things, the wealth of good will and readiness to sacrifice, so that these things will unite for a common effort and give to life a content worth living for. But how can we carry out such a separation and such a collection unless there is an inner synthesis of life that lifts mankind above the insecurity of individual reflection?

The contrast expressed in the struggle of naturalism and idealism is not confined to the general outline of life; it is found in any particular realm which represents a totality of conviction. It makes a tremendous difference whether man submits to a given existence and tries to improve it only in spots or whether, inspired by the belief in an ascending movement of the universe, he is able to contribute independently to that movement, to discover new goals, and to release new energies. Literature is a case in point, as I shall indicate in a few words. Naturalism cannot give to literature an inner independence or allow it an initiative of its own; for if literature is only a hand of life on the dial of time, it can only imitate and register events as they happen. By means of impressive descriptions it may help the time to understand its own desires better; but since creative power is denied to it, it cannot contribute to the inner liberation and elevation of man. At the same time it necessarily lacks dramatic power, which cannot exist without the possibility of an inner change and elevation. But the perspective and the task change completely if literature acknowledges the possibility of a decisive turn in human life, of the ascension to another level, and if it feels called upon to help bring about that ascension. In that case it can help to shape life and to lead the time, by representing and simultaneously guiding what is rising in man's soul. Literature can clarify and confirm by drawing certain simple outlines in the bewildering chaos of the time and by confronting us with the chief problems of our intellectual existence and persuading us of their importance. It can raise our life to greatness above the hubbub of everyday life by the representation of eternal truths, and in the midst of our dark situation it can strengthen our belief in the reason of life. It can act in the way envisaged by Alfred Nobel when he gave to literature a place of honour in his foundation.

Thus there are strong reasons for our continued belief in idealism and for our attempt to give it a form that corresponds to the sum of our historical experiences. But such an attempt will never truly succeed unless it is considered a personal necessity and is carried out as a matter of intellectual self-preservation. Exhilaration, courage, and firm belief can arise only from such an acknowledgement of a binding necessity, not from a hankering after remote and alien goals but from a belief in life as it is active within us and makes us participate inwardly in the large context of reality. Only such faith can enable us to cope with the enormous obstacles and fill us with the confidence of success.

> *Du musst glauben, du musst wagen*
> *Denn die Götter leihn kein Pfand;*
> *Nur ein Wunder kann dich tragen*
> *In das schöne Wunderland.*

Biography

Rudolf Eucken (1846–1926) was born in Aurich, Germany. He studied philosophy, philology, and history at the universities of Göttingen and Berlin and wrote his dissertation on the language of Aristotle. He became a professor of philosophy at Basle in 1871 and from 1874 on held the chair of philosophy at Jena. Eucken was an idealist philosopher who developed his flexible system in many works. He revised his books and brought them up to date over a period of several decades, so that some of his works ran into more than a dozen editions. His main works were *Geistige Strömungen der Gegenwart* (1908) [*Main Currents of Modern Thought*], *Die Lebensanschauungen der grossen Denker* (1890) [*The Problem of Human Life as Viewed by the Great Thinkers from Plato to the Present Time*], *Der Kampf um einen geistigen Lebensinhalt* (1896) [The Struggle for a Spiritual Content of Life], *Der Wahrheitsgehalt der Religion* (1901) [*The Truth of Religion*], *Grundlinien einer neuen Lebensanschauung* (1907) [*Life's Basis and Life's Ideal: The Fundamentals of a New Philosophy of Life*], *Present Day Ethics in their Relation to the Spiritual Life* (the Deem Lectures given at New York University in 1913), and *Der Sinn und Wert des Lebens* (1908) [*The Meaning and Value of Life*]. Eucken developed his philosophy of history in an essay entitled «Philosophie der Geschichte» (1907), which appeared in the series *Die Kultur der Gegenwart* [Contemporary Civilization].

Literature 1909

SELMA OTTILIANA LOVISA
LAGERLÖF

«*in appreciation of the lofty idealism, vivid imagination, and spiritual perception that characterize her writings*»

Presentation

by Claes Annerstedt, President of the Swedish Academy

History tells us that there was a time when Sweden fought for a world prize on the field of martial honour. The time of arms has passed, but in the international competition for peaceful prizes our people have for a long time held a position of esteem, and now the hour has finally come when Sweden can enter into literary competition with the great nations. The realm of the mind is determined by living powers that are not measured by population or golden millions but by the idealistic and ethical demands which they satisfy.

Geijer, Tegnér, or Runeberg, to mention only them, could justly have laid claim to the Nobel Prize, and the development which these great men have started has grown to fuller bloom. But among the writers of the younger generation who have contributed so much to our literature, there is one name that enjoys the special splendour of a star of the first magnitude. In the works of Selma Lagerlöf we seem to recognize the purest and best features of our Great Swedish Mother. Five years ago the Swedish Academy recognized the importance and strength of her achievement for Swedish poetry by awarding her the Gold Medal «because of the imaginative wealth, idealism, and narrative talent that are evidenced in her works, which are beloved inside and outside the borders of Sweden». This homage was strongly appreciated by all classes in our nation. Surely the same nation will be proud to hear today that the Swedish Academy has found Selma Lagerlöf's literary achievement so important that her works should be counted among those considered the property of all mankind and that they are full of the idealism which Nobel required for the award of the Nobel Prize. It should not be thought that this decision was inspired by excessive national self-esteem, especially since many important foreign opinions have supported her candidacy. Nor would anybody consider it a lack of modesty if the Nobel Prize, which is now being awarded for the ninth time, remains in the country of its founder; on the contrary, such modesty could be interpreted as a lack of national self-confidence.

Few first novels have attracted so much attention as *Gösta Berlings Saga*

(1891). The work was significant not only because it broke decisively with the unhealthy and false realism of the times, but also because of its own original character. Yet the work was not unanimously praised; if most people admired it greatly, some criticized it severely. There could be no better proof of its extraordinary character. One could not help admiring an imagination that had not had its peer since Almqvist's days. However peculiar the characters and situations created by this imagination might be, they were covered by the marvellous bloom of artistic genius, and the presentation at times exhibited rapturous beauty. The reader was particularly moved by the profound feeling that in this work he was encountering a forgotten piece of what had once been Swedish country life; his heart was captured, just as the curious, radiant surface of the picture enchanted his senses. This first novel did have its weaknesses; how could it be otherwise! Where is gold found pure; when does a genius enter the world completely mature? But one thing was abundantly clear: a new genius of genuine Swedish nature was trying its wings.

Soon she was to enter the realm of her true heritage, the mystical world of fairy tales and legends. Only a soul that had fed on legends since the days of childhood, and that added love to a rich imagination, could dare to interpret the secrets of the invisible world that the visionary always sees beside or rather beneath the visible world. The visionary quality that is so characteristic in Lagerlöf's writings has been stronger in her than in anyone since the days of St. Birgitta. Just as refractions in the hot air of the desert create a vivid fata morgana for the wanderer, so her warm and colourful imagination possesses a wonderful power of giving to her visions the force of living reality, which is instinctively recalled by whoever listens to her poetry. This is particularly true of her description of nature. For her, everything, even what is called inanimate nature, has its own, invisible, but real life; and therefore her artist's hand is not content with representing the outward beauty of nature. Her loving eye follows the inner life whose silent language has been caught by her fine ear. That is why she has succeeded in eliciting beautiful secrets from fairy tales, living folk legends, and saints' stories; secrets that had been hidden from the wordly-wise but which true simplicity perceives because, as the poet has the old grandmother say, it «has eyes to see the secrets of God».

As a painter of peasant life she is completely original and can compete with the best of other countries. *Tösen från Stormyrtorpet* (1908) [*The Girl from the Marsh Croft*] is inimitable in its realistic and faithful descriptions, and it contains a new and deeper beauty in the irresistible power of unselfish love which underlies the whole work. And there are many other pieces of equal beauty. But Selma Lagerlöf's talent comes out most clearly in the proud achievement that bears the name *Jerusalem* (1901–02) [*The Holy City*]. The deep spiritual movements that have from time to time aroused the peasant population of our country have rarely been traced so clearly as in this description of the pilgrimage of the people of Dalekarlia to the Holy Land. The reader sees things as clearly as if he himself were experiencing how this strong breed with its serious and introspective character goes its way, brooding heavily over the riddles of life. And it is not surprising if these people, torn between belief and superstition, in the painful struggle between their love of the inherited soil and their fear that they may not walk with God, finally abandon home, since they believe that the bells on high admonish them to march toward the holy city. But it is no less natural if these children of voluntary exile, in the midst of their delight at having seen the earth that had been touched by the foot of the Saviour, are deep in their hearts consumed by the desire for the simple green soil far north in old Dalarna. The sound of rivers and forests is always in their ears. With loving perception the poet has sounded the secret depth of their souls and a bloom of purest poetry transforms the realistic and faithful description of their touching and simple lives. The introduction to *Jerusalem*, entitled «Ingemarssönerna» [Ingemar's Sons], movingly intimates that the lives and deeds of the fathers work like a force of destiny on later generations.

Selma Lagerlöf's style deserves our full appreciation. Like a loyal daughter, she has administered the rich heritage of her mother tongue; from this source come the purity of diction, the clarity of expression, and the musical beauty that are characteristic of all her works.

Purity and simplicity of diction, beauty of style, and power of imagination, however, are accompanied by ethical strength and deep religious feeling. And indeed it could not be otherwise in someone to whom the life of man is a «thread on God's great loom». In poetry of such elevation the air is always pure; more than one of her beautiful legends reflect the simplicity and loftiness of Scripture. But what makes Selma Lagerlöf's writings so lovable is that we always seem to hear in them an echo of the most peculiar, the strongest, and the best things that have ever moved the soul of the Swedish people. Few have comprehended the innermost nature of this people with a comparable love. It is her own heart that speaks when in *Tösen från Stormyrtorpet* the strict judge, whose severe features have increasingly brightened at the sight of the sacrificial love of the young girl, finally says with deep emotion to himself: «That is my people. I shall not be angry with them since there is so much love and fear of God in one of their humblest creatures.» Such an intimate and profound view is possible only for one whose soul is deeply rooted in the Swedish earth and who has sucked nourishment from its myths, history, folklore, and nature. It is easy to understand why the mystical, nostalgic, and miraculous dusk that is peculiar to the Nordic nature is reflected in all her works. The greatness of her art consists precisely in her ability to use her heart as well as her genius to give to the original peculiar character and attitudes of the people a shape in which we recognize ourselves.

We are acting according to the will of the founder if we honour those who have had such success in appealing to the best sides of the human heart, and whose name and achievement have penetrated far beyond the borders of Sweden. Nor should anyone who bears a famous literary name, whether inside or outside the country, be envious if the Swedish Academy today pronounces that it has awarded this year's Nobel Prize in Literature to Sweden's distinguished daughter, Selma Lagerlöf.

Acceptance

A few days ago I was sitting in the train, bound for Stockholm. It was early evening; there was little light in my compartment and none at all outside. My fellow passengers were dozing in their respective corners, and I was very quiet, listening to the rattling of the train.

And then I began to think of all the other times I had come up to Stockholm. It had usually been to do something difficult–to pass examinations or to find a publisher for my manuscript. And now I was coming to receive the Prize in Literature. That, too, I thought would be difficult.

All through this autumn I had lived at my old home in Värmland in complete solitude, and now I should have to step forward in the presence of so many people. I had become shy of life's bustle in my solitary retreat and was apprehensive at the thought of facing the world.

Deep within me, however, was a wondrous joy at receiving this Prize, and I tried to dispel my anxiety by thinking of those who would rejoice at my good fortune. There were my good friends, my brothers and sisters and, first and foremost, my old mother who, sitting back home, was happy to have lived to see this day.

But then I thought of my father and felt a deep sorrow that he should no longer be alive, and that I could not go to him and tell him that I had been awarded the Nobel Prize. I knew that no one would have been happier than he to hear this. Never have I met anyone with his love and respect for the written word and its creators, and I wished that he could have known that the Swedish Academy had bestowed on me this great Prize. Yes, it was a deep sorrow to me that I could not tell him.

Anyone who has ever sat in a train as it rushes through a dark night will know that sometimes there are long minutes when the coaches slide smoothly along without so much as a shudder. All rustle and bustle cease and the sound of the wheels becomes a soothing, peaceful melody. The coaches no longer seem to run on rails and sleepers but glide into space. Well, that is how it was as I sat there and thought how much I should like to see my old father again. So light and soundless was the movement of the train that I could hardly imagine I was on this earth. And so I began to daydream: «Just think, if I were going to meet Father in Paradise! I seem to have heard of such things happening to other people – why, then, not to myself?» The train went gliding on but it had a long way to go yet, and my thoughts raced ahead of it. Father will certainly be sitting in a rocking chair on a veranda, with a garden full of sunshine and flowers and birds in front of him. He will be reading Fritjof's *Saga*, of course, but when he sees me he will put down his book, push his spectacles high up on his forehead, and get up and walk toward me. He will say, «Good day, my daughter, I am very glad to see you», or «Why, you are here, and how are you, my child», just as he always used to do.

He will settle again in his rocking chair and only then begin to wonder why I have come to see him. «You are sure there is nothing amiss?» he will ask suddenly. «No, Father, all is well», I will reply. But then, just as I am about to break my news to him, I will decide to keep it back just a while longer and try the indirect approach. «I have come to ask you for advice, Father,» I will say, «for I am very heavily in debt.»

«I am afraid you will not get much help from me in this matter», Father will reply. «One may well say of this place that, like the old estates in our Värmland, it has everything except money.»

«Ah, but it is not money that I owe, Father.» «But that's even worse», Father will say. «Begin right at the beginning, daughter.»

«It is not too much to ask that you should help, Father, for it was all your fault right from the beginning. Do you remember how you used to play the piano and sing Bellman's songs to us children and how, at least twice every winter, you would let us read Tegnér and Runeberg and Andersen? It was then that I first fell into debt. Father, how shall I ever repay them for teaching me to love fairy tales and sagas of heroes, the land we live in and all of our human life, in all its wretchedness and glory?»

Father will straighten up in his rocking chair and a wonderful look will come into his eyes. «I am glad that I got you into this debt», he will say.

«Yes, you may be right, Father, but then remember that that is not all of it. Think how many creditors I have. Think of those poor, homeless vagabonds who used to travel up and down Värmland in your youth, playing the fool and singing all those songs. What do I not owe to them, to their mischief and mad pranks! And the old men and women sitting in their small grey cottages as one came out of the forest, telling me wonderful stories of water-sprites and trolls and enchanted maidens lured into the mountains.

It was they who taught me that there is poetry in hard rocks and black forests. And think, Father, of all those pale, hollow-cheeked monks and nuns in their dark cloisters, the visions they saw and the voices they heard. I have borrowed from their treasure of legends. And our own peasants who went to Jerusalem – do I owe them nothing for giving me such glorious deeds to write about? And I am in debt not only to people; there is the whole of nature as well. The animals that walk the earth, the birds in the skies, the trees and flowers, they have all told me some of their secrets.»

Father will smile and nod his head and look not at all worried. «But don't you understand, Father, that I carry a great burden of debt?» I will say, and look more and more serious. «No one on earth knows how I can repay it, but I thought that you, in Heaven, would know.» «We do», Father will say and be as carefree and relaxed as he used to be. «Never fear, child, there is a remedy for your trouble.»

«Yes, Father, but that's not all. I am also heavily in debt to those who have formed and moulded our language into the good instrument that it is, and taught me to use it. And, then, am I not in debt to those who have written in prose and in verse before my time, who have turned writing into art, the torchbearers, the pathfinders? The great Norwegians, the great Russians who wrote when I was a child, do I not owe them a thousand debts? Has it not been given to me to live in an age in which my own country's literature has reached its highest peak, to behold the marble emperors of Rydberg, the world of Snoilsky's poetry, Strindberg's cliffs, Geijerstam's countryfolk, the modern men of Anne-Charlotte Edgren and Ernst Ahlgren, Heidenstam's Orient? Sophie Elkan, who has brought history to life, Fröding and his tales of Värmland's plains, Levertin's legends, Hallström's *Thanatos*, and Karlfeldt's Dalekarlian sketches, and much else that was young and new, all that nourished my fantasy, drove me on to compete, and made the dreams bear fruit–do I not owe them anything?»

«Yes, yes», Father will say. «You are right, yours is a heavy debt but, never fear, we will find a way.»

«I don't think, Father, that you really understand how hard it is for me. You don't realize that I am also in debt to my readers. I owe them so much –from the old King and his youngest son, who sent me on my apprentice's wanderings through the South, to the small schoolchildren who scribbled a letter of thanks for *Nils Holgersson*. What would have become of me if no one had wanted to read my books? And don't forget all those who have written of me. Remember the famous Danish critic who, with a few words, won me friends all over Denmark! And he who could mix gall and ambrosia in a more masterly fashion than anyone in Sweden had ever done before his time. Now he is dead. Think of all those in foreign lands who have worked for me. I owe them gratitude, Father, both for their praise and for their censure.»

«Yes, yes», Father will say, and I shall see him look a little less calm. Surely, he will begin to understand that it will not be easy to help me.

«Remember all who have helped me, Father!» I shall say. «Think of my faithful friend, Esselde, who tried to open doors for me when no one dared to believe in me. Think of others who have cared for and protected my work! Think of my good friend and travelling companion, who not only took me south and showed me all the glories of art but made life itself happier and lighter for me. All the love that has come to me, the honours, the distinctions! Do you not understand now that I had to come to you to ask how such debts can be paid?»

Father has lowered his head and does not look so hopeful any more.

«I agree, Daughter, it is not going to be easy to find help for you but, surely, there is nothing more you owe anyone?»

«Yes, Father, I have found it difficult enough to bear all that I owed before, but my biggest debt has not yet come. That is why I had to come to you for advice.» «I cannot understand how you could owe still more», Father will say. «Oh, yes», I will reply, and then I will tell him all about *this*.

«I just cannot believe the Academy...», Father will say but, looking at me and seeing my face, he will know it is all true. And, then, every wrinkle in his face will tremble and tears will come into his eyes.

«What am I to say to those who put my name up for the Prize and to those who have made the decision – think, Father, it is not only honour and money they are bestowing on me. They have shown that they have trust enough in me to single me out before the whole world. How shall I repay this debt?»

Father will sit and still no words will come as he thinks. Then, drying tears of joy from his eyes, he will bang down his fist on the arm of the rocking chair and say, «I will not rack my brains about problems that no one in Heaven or on earth can solve. I am too happy that you have been given the Nobel Prize to worry about anything!»

Your Majesties, Your Royal Highnesses, Ladies and Gentlemen – having received no better answer than this to all my questions, it only remains to me to ask you to join me in the toast which I have the honour to propose to the Swedish Academy.

Biography

Selma Lagerlöf (1858–1940) was born in Östra Emterwik, Värmland, Sweden. She was brought up on Mårbacka, the family estate, which she did not leave until 1881, when she went to a teachers' college at Stockholm. In 1885 she became a teacher at the girls' secondary school in Landskrona. She had been writing poetry ever since she was a child, but she did not publish anything until 1890, when a Swedish weekly gave her the first prize in a literary competition and published excerpts from the book which was to be her first, best, and most popular work. *Gösta Berlings Saga* was published in 1891, but went unnoticed until its Danish translation received wide critical acclaim and paved the way for the book's lasting success in Sweden and elsewhere. In 1895 financial support from the royal family and the Swedish Academy encouraged her to abandon teaching altogether. She travelled in Italy and wrote *Antikris mirakler* (1897) [*The Miracles of Antichrist*], a novel set in Sicily. After several minor works she published *Jerusalem* (1901–1902) [*The Holy City*], a novel about Swedish peasants who emigrated to the Holy Land and whom she had visited in 1900. This work was her first immediate success. A book intended as a primer for elementary schools became one of the most charming children's book in any language: *Nils Holgerssons underbara resa genom Sverige* (1906) [*The Wonderful Adventures of Nils*].

None of her later works matched the power or success of *Gösta Berlings Saga*. In the mid-twenties she published the historical trilogy: *Löwensköldska Ringen* (1925), *Charlotte Löwensköld* (1927), and *Anna Svärd* (1928) [*The Ring of the Löwenskölds*, 3 vols.]. She also published several volumes of reminiscences under the title *Mårbacka* (1922–32).

Literature 1910

PAUL JOHANN LUDWIG HEYSE

«as a tribute to the consummate artistry, permeated with idealism, which he has demonstrated during his long productive career as a lyric poet, dramatist, novelist, and writer of world-renowned short stories»

Presentation

by C. D. af Wirsén, Permanent Secretary of the Swedish Academy

Many famous writers from several countries have been proposed for this year's Nobel Prize in Literature. The Swedish Academy has awarded it to a writer whose nomination has been supported by more than sixty German experts on art, literature, and philosophy. His name is Paul Heyse. The name revives the memory of our youth and manhood; we still remember the literary pleasure that his novellas, in particular, gave to us. Now an old but still active man, he is a figure that the jury could not pass over if it was to express its admiration by awarding the high distinction to the most significant literary work. Nor was the jury to be swayed by considerations of age or, indeed, anything other than true merit.

Paul Heyse was born in Berlin in 1830. His father was the philologist Karl Wilhelm Heyse, a gentle but determined scholar. From his Jewish mother, Julie Saaling, Heyse perhaps inherited his warm and lively temperament. Heyse, who was nature's favourite in so many ways, had the good fortune of growing up in a carefree home. His school years passed quickly. He was an easy learner. For a while he was a student in Berlin and later he studied Romance philology under Friedrich Diez at Bonn University. In 1852 he received his doctorate in Berlin *multa cum laude*. Subsequently Heyse was awarded a scholarship that enabled him to travel in Italy, with whose art and literature he was to become so familiar. He soon became engaged to Margarete Kugler, the daughter of the art historian to whose house he had been introduced by his patron, the poet Emanuel Geibel. Not sure where to look for a position, he was freed from all material worries by Geibel, who once more helped him. At Geibel's recommendation Maximilian II offered him a titular professorship at Munich. His only duty consisted in taking part in the literary soirées of the King. On May 15, 1854, he was married to Margarete and the happy young couple settled in Munich, where Heyse has lived ever since, with the exception of occasional sojourns in his beloved Italy. Soon he became the central figure of a thriving cultural life. Since this is not the place for a detailed biography of Heyse, suffice it to say that several years after the death of Margarete he married again, this time the charming Anna Schubart.

Between 1855 and 1862 Heyse wrote the first four volumes of his prose novellas, a genre in which he became a master. Among Heyse's many novellas we may mention here *L'Arrabbiata* (1853); *Andrea Delfin* (1859), rich in Venetian colours; the deeply felt *Nerina* (1875), an episode from Leopardi's life; the profoundly moral *Bild der Mutter* (1859) [Portrait of a Mother]; and the marvellous troubadour novella *Marion* (1855). In his novellas Heyse observes strict rules of composition without doing violence to the charm and freedom of the story. He developed his own theory of the novella. «A novella of literary value», he wrote, «should represent an important human destiny. It must not be an everyday occurrence but should reveal to us a new side of human nature. The narrow scope of the tale calls for strict concentration.»

It has rightly been said that Heyse is the creator of the modern psychological novella. He is rarely tendentious in his novellas, and that is probably the reason we prefer their Goethean objectivity to his longer narratives *Kinder der Welt* (1872) [*The Children of the World*] and *Im Paradiese* (1875) [*In Paradise*], which deal with moral problems, the former with the independence of morality from narrow dogmas, the latter with a defence of art against an austere puritanism. Both works unmistakably show the humanism of their creator. In *Im Paradiese* there is in addition a vivid description of the artists' world in Munich. In *Gegen den Strom* (1904) [Against the Stream] Heyse courageously challenged engrained prejudices by turning against the practice of duelling. A curiously youthful power is evident in the book *Geburt der Venus* (1909) [Birth of Venus], which appeared last year and in which he consistently and emphatically develops his lifelong aesthetic convictions both by defending the freedom of art from a one-sided asceticism and by polemizing against the naturalistic technique of copying the low, the common, and the simple-minded.

Heyse, however, is not only a writer of novels and novellas; he is the most important lyrical poet of contemporary Germany. He has written delightful novellas in verse, of which the admirable *Salamander* (1879) in terza rima is especially memorable. Although drama was not his natural medium, he has nonetheless written excellent plays, among them—to select two from a total of over fifty—the patriotic play *Kolberg* (1865) and the interesting drama *Hadrian* (1865), in which the wisdom and sadness of Hadrian are combined and represented in a most moving manner.

Heyse's taste is very independent. While he had great admiration for *The Pretenders* and *Vikings at Helgeland* by his friend Ibsen, he liked neither *Ghosts* nor the following symbolic plays. He is deeply musical, but not so much moved by Wagner as by Beethoven, Mozart, Schubert, Chopin, and Brahms.

In all critical situations of life Heyse has maintained the same independence. When his friend Geibel lost his salary as a poet at the Bavarian court because of a poem to King William in which he expressed his hope for a united Germany under Prussia, Heyse, too, in a respectful letter offered to resign his position, since he agreed with Geibel on every point and therefore wished to share his fate as well.

Heyse is almost as popular in Italy as in Germany. His numerous brilliant translations have made Italian literature known in Germany. It is due to him that Leopardi, Manzoni, Foseolo, Monti, Parini, and Giusti are now widely read and admired there.

But it would be wrong to assume that the brilliant Heyse, so often called the laurel-crowned favourite of fortune, was always free from cares or was always acknowledged in the leading circles of his country. As a father he was deeply afflicted by the loss of several of his beloved children. He expressed his grief in deeply poetic songs which despite their gloom radiate an unending beauty...

As for literary opinion, it is true that the Apollonian and charming poet enjoyed early popularity, but it is equally true that there was a time when the situation changed. Naturalism, which burst forth in the eighties and dominated the scene for the next decade, directed its iconoclastic attack especially against Heyse, its most powerful opponent. He was too harmonious, too fond of beauty, too Hellenic and lofty for those who, slandering him at any price, demanded sensation, effect, bizarre licentiousness, and crass reproductions of ugly realities. Heyse did not yield. His sense of form was offended by their uncouth behaviour; he demanded that literature should see life in an ideal light that would transfigure reality. In his detailed and sensitive story *Merlin* (1892) he expressed his sense of injury in a manly way. Now the tide has turned again, and Heyse would probably have been proposed earlier by his country for the world prize had it not been for the partisan dislike of the naturalists. Now a miracle seems to have changed everything. The honourable veteran has been the object of admiration everywhere; he is an honorary citizen of Munich where a street has been named after him; he has been flooded with honours. To the manifold distinctions, the Swedish Academy, acting at the recommendation of many critics, has now added its token of admiration by presenting to the old poet the rare homage of the Nobel Prize.

Heyse has gone his own ways. Aesthetically he has been faithful to truth, but in such a manner that he mirrored inner in external reality. Schiller's wellknown words, «Life is serious, art serene», properly understood, express a profound truth which can be found in the life and work of Heyse. Beauty should liberate and recreate: it should neither imitate reality slavishly nor drag it into the dust. It should have a noble simplicity. Heyse reveals beauty in this aspect. He does not teach morals, which would deprive beauty of its immediacy, but there is much wisdom and nobility in his works. He does not teach religion, but one would look in vain for anything that would seriously hurt religious feelings. Although he puts greater emphasis on the ethical than on the dogmatic side of religion, he has expressed his deep respect for every serious opinion. He is tolerant but not indifferent. He has praised love, but it was its heavenly and not its earthly aspect that he glorified. He likes men who are faithful to their nature, but the individuals to whom Heyse is most sympathetic adhere to their higher rather than their lower nature.

On this festive occasion, which Heyse has not been able to attend because of illness, we thank him for the joy that his works have given to thousands, and we send our regards to the house in the Louisenstrasse in Munich, which has been for so many years the home of the Muses: «Glaubt mir, es ist kein Märchen, die Quelle der Jugend sie rinnet/wirklich und immer. Ihr fraget, wo? ‹In der dichtenden Kunst.› »

At the banquet, Professor Oscar Montelius made the following comments: «I regret that we do not have the pleasure to see among us the great poet to whom this year's Nobel Prize in Literature has been awarded. But he is being worthily represented by the German Minister, Count von Pückler— and I ask you, Count, to assure him that, when toasts were proposed to the laureates, we did not forget him. »

The Minister, Count von Pückler, speaking in behalf of Paul Heyse, recalled that two years ago the Nobel Prize in Literature had been given to a German philosopher, this time to a popular poet. He attested to the lively exchange between Swedish and German literature, which had increased ever since the Swedish Academy became the Areopagus in charge of following closely the literary production of the entire world and of distributing the Nobel Prizes among the great masters of letters. He ended by paying his respect to the first of the international Areopaguses, the Swedish Academy.

Autobiography

I was born in Berlin on March 15, 1830, the second son of the royal university professor K. W. L. Heyse and his wife Julie, née Saaling, who came from a Jewish family. After attending the Gymnasium between my eighth and seventeenth years, I studied classical philology at Berlin University for two years under Boeckh and Lachmann, and with the friendly support of Emanuel Geibel and Franz Kugler I dabbled in all sorts of poetry. In Bonn, where I studied for a year, I changed from classical to Romance philology, taught there by its great founder, F. Diez, and at the beginning of 1852 I received the doctorate for a dissertation on the refrain in Provençal poetry. In the autumn of the same year I went to Rome on a grant by the Prussian Ministry of Culture. For a year I stayed at various Southern places, continuing my Romance studies at Italian libraries. The findings were published by W. Hertz in 1856 under the title *Romanische Inedita*.

The year 1853 yielded even greater results in creative writing. In the spring of 1854 some of my publications persuaded King Maximilian II of Bavaria to offer me, at the suggestion of Emanuel Geibel, a position in Munich with an annual salary of 1000 guilders, to take part in his so-called symposia, weekly soirées at which scholars and poets were gathered. Before I moved I was married to Kugler's daughter Margarete, whom death took away from me in the autumn of 1862 after she had borne me four children. Five years later I married a young woman from Munich, Anna Schubart, with whom for forty-four years I have lived happily, except for the premature deaths of two children and a son from my first marriage.

I have given a detailed account of the first four decades of my life until the death of my dear royal patron in my *Jugenderinnerungen und Bekenntnisse* (Berlin, 1900) [Memories of my Youth and Confessions]. From that time on outward events receded; my life has passed without particular events or adventures and has been devoted entirely to writing. Here is a list of books published by the Cotta Publishing House:

Gesammelte Werke (1871–1910) [Collected Works], 36 vols.; *Dramatische Dichtungen* (1864–1905) [Dramatic Works], 36 vols.; *Romane, Novellen, ly-*

rische und epische Gedichte (1902–1912) [Novels, Novellas, Lyrical and Epic Poems], series I, 12 vols.; series II, 40 vols.; *Italienische Dichter seit der Mitte des 18ten Jahrhunderts: Übersetzungen und Studien* (1889–1905) [Italian Poets since the Middle of the 18th Century: Translations and Studies], 5 vols.

Published by other publishers: *Deutscher Novellenschatz* (1871–76) [Treasury of German Novellas], 24 vols.; *Novellenschatz des Auslands* (1872–76) [Treasury of Foreign Novellas], 14 vols.; *Neuer Deutscher Novellenschatz* (1884–88) [New Treasury of German Novellas], 24 vols. Also, a translation of José Caveda y Nava's history of Spanish architecture, *Geschichte der Spanischen Baukunst* (1858).

Biographical note on Paul Heyse

Paul Heyse (1830–1914) was made a nobleman by the King of Bavaria in 1910. His complete works were published in fifteen volumes in 1924, ten years after his death.

Literature 1911

Count MAURICE POLYDORE

MARIE BERNHARD MAETERLINCK

«in appreciation of his many-sided literary activities and especially of his dramatic works, which are distinguished by a wealth of imagination and by a poetic fancy which reveal, sometimes in the guise of a fairy tale, a deep inspiration, while in a mysterious way they appeal to the readers' own feelings and stimulate their imaginations»

Presentation

by C. D. af Wirsén, Permanent Secretary of the Swedish Academy

This year highly competent persons have proposed several men of letters as candidates for the Nobel Prize in Literature. Several among them presented such great and unusual qualities that it has been very difficult to weigh their respective merits. In giving this year's award to Maurice Maeterlinck, who has been proposed and seriously considered several times before, the Swedish Academy has been determined first by the profound originality and singularity of his talent as a writer, so different from the usual forms of literature. The idealistic character of this talent is elevated to a rare spirituality and mysteriously causes delicate and secret strings to vibrate in us. He is certainly not of a shallow nature, this unusual man, who has not yet reached the age of fifty and who, as an author, follows his own quite personal voice and possesses the marvellous faculty of being at once mystical, profound, and popular through the charm of his expression. While reading him one sometimes recalls the words of Sophocles, «Man is only a trivial shadow», or the words of Calderon that life is a dream; and yet Maeterlinck knows how to render the fine nuances of our moral life with the force of a visionary. What in ordinary circumstances dwells in us latently and belongs to the secret depths of our being, he calls up with the tap of a wand, and we acknowledge that he has evoked features of our most intimate being, which ordinarily remains hidden in a mysterious twilight. He does it without affectation and mannerisms and mostly with an unfailing sureness and classical refinement, although action and scenery are often vague–like a Chinese shadow show –and in keeping with the great subtlety of his poetry. Legendary and fantastic as the narration may be, the dialogue is pointed. With the sounds of muted music, the poet introduces us to unsuspected regions of our inner being, and we feel with Goethe that «Alles Vergängliche/ Ist nur ein Gleichnis». We have the foreboding that our true home is far away, well beyond the limits of our earthly experiences. We hardly ever pass beyond this foreboding with Maeterlinck, although his poetry opens for us glimpses of inaccessible distances.

Maurice Maeterlinck was born in 1862 at Ghent. His family appears to have been well-to-do. He was educated at the Jesuit college of Saint-Barbe. He did not like it, but this conventional school probably influenced his intellectual development very strongly by orienting him toward mysticism. After finishing school and passing the baccalaureate, Maeterlinck followed the wishes of his parents, read law, and established himself in Ghent as a lawyer. But he succeeded, according to his biographer Gerard Harry, only in demonstrating brilliantly his ineptitude for the legal career, having the «happy defects» that render a man absolutely unfit for the pettifogging quarrels and public counsel's speeches in the law court. He was attracted by literature, and this attraction increased during a stay in Paris where he became acquainted with a number of writers, one of whom, Villiers de l'Isle Adam, apparently had a great influence on him. Paris fascinated Maurice Maeterlinck so much that he established himself there in 1896. Nonetheless, the great metropolis did not really suit this solitary contemplative mind as a permanent place to live. He goes there, from time to time, to deal with his editors, but in the summer he likes to live at Saint-Wandrille, an old Norman abbey which he bought and saved from imminent vandalism. In the winter he seeks refuge in the mild climate of the town of Grasse, known for its flowers.

The first work published by Maurice Maeterlinck was a slim collection of verses entitled *Serres chaudes* (1889) [Ardent Talons]. These poems appear more tormented than one would have expected from his calmly meditative disposition. The same year (1889) he published a dramatic fantasy, *La Princesse Maleine*. It is sombre, terrifying, and deliberately monotonous due to numerous repetitions intended to give an impression of duration; but a delightful fairy-tale charm reigns in this little drama, which is written with a vigour one would not have suspected in the author of the *Serres chaudes*. It is in any case an important work of art. *La Princesse Maleine* was enthusiastically praised by Octave Mirbeau in *Le Figaro*, and from that day on Maurice Maeterlinck was no longer unknown. Later on, Maeterlinck wrote a whole series of dramatic compositions. Most unfold in eras that we could not determine and in places not to be found on any map. The scene is usually a fairy castle with underground passages, a park with lovely shady places, or a lighthouse with the sea in the distance. In these melancholy regions figures often move veiled like the idea itself. In several of his most perfect scenic works, Maurice Maeterlinck is a symbolist and an agnostic; but one should not conclude that he is a materialist. With the instinct and imagination of the poet he feels that man does not belong solely to the tangible world, and he expressly says that poetry does not satisfy if it does not make us perceive a reflection of the more profound and secret reality that is the source of phenomena. Sometimes this background appears to him in an obscure and misty fashion like an ensemble of occult powers of which men are easily the victims, and he then attributes to the occult force a fatal omnipotence that destroys our freedom. But in several dramatic works he has mitigated this conception; he has given more room to hope and to mixed mystic influences, less to reality. The main idea which always dominates, especially in his best works, is that the spiritual, real, intimate, and profound life of man, which is manifested precisely in his most spontaneous acts, must be sought in the realms beyond thought and discursive reason. It is these acts which Maeterlinck excels in representing with the almost somnambulant imaginative power and dreaming spirit of a visionary but with the precision of a perfect artist. At the same time the expression is stylized; the simplification of the technique is pushed as far as possible without harming the understanding of the drama.

A more pronounced deism would have had a beneficial influence on his dramas because it would have made them less similar to shadow plays; but one should not disparage the creations of his genius. Like Spinoza and Hegel, who were great thinkers though not deists, Maeterlinck is a very great poet although his conception of things and of life is not that of a deist. He does not deny anything: he simply finds the principle of existence hidden in the shadows. Besides, is not agnosticism in some degree excusable, since no human reason could ever formulate an exact notion of the origin of existence which in many aspects is accessible only to intuition and to faith? And if Maurice Maeterlinck's characters are sometimes creatures of dreams, they are still very human, for Shakespeare was not wrong in stating:

> *We are such stuff*
> *As dreams are made on, and our little life*
> *Is rounded with a sleep.*

Besides, Maeterlinck is in no way a polemist; in almost all his works there breathes a sweet, sometimes melancholy soul, so that in poetic beauty he excels many writers whose conception of the world rests perhaps more on the concept of personality. Maurice Maeterlinck is evidently a man who has felt and thought profoundly. Homage must be rendered to his sincere thirst for truth, and it must be remembered that there exist for him a law and an inner right which invariably command and direct man in the midst of a world where so many things seem to encourage injustice. If Maurice Maeterlinck, who has passed through so many stages of inner development, sometimes speaks of «gravitation» as the power that rules the world, and apparently wants to substitute it for religion, one would hardly be wrong (considering his symbolism) in taking the word «gravitation» as a symbolic expression of that law of religio-ethical gravity to which, if I may say so, all are obedient.

There is no time to list all of Maeterlinck's works; however, it seems right to me on this solemn occasion to recall very briefly the most characteristic ones.

The pitiless, mysterious power of death has rarely been rendered in more poignant fashion than in Maeterlinck's little piece, *L'Intruse* (1890) [*The Intruder*]. Among all those who surround the sick mother and who hope for her recovery, only the old blind grandfather notices furtive and sliding steps in the garden where the cyprus trees are beginning to rustle and where the nightingale is hushed; he feels a cold breeze pass, he hears a scythe being whetted, he reckons that someone invisible to the others has entered to sit in their circle. On the stroke of midnight there is a noise as if someone had suddenly stood up and gone away; at the same instant the sick one dies. The guest no one can escape has passed there. The portent is described with great force and subtlety. The short play *Les Aveugles* (1890) [*The Blind*], which shows the same foreboding of disaster, is perhaps even more melancholy. The sightless have followed their guide, an old sick priest; and there in the middle of the forest they believe they have lost him. In reality he is in the middle of them but he is dead. Little by little they realize his death. How will they now find their refuge?

In *Pelléas et Mélisande* (1892) and *Alladine et Palomides* (1894) we find in different variants the fatal power of love which Maeterlinck describes with a fantastic imagination – that love which, fettered by other bonds or by external circumstances, neither could nor should attain a happy ending, but which is crushed by a fatality against which human strength breaks.

The most inspired of Maeterlinck's dramas is unquestionably his *Aglavaine et Sélysette* (1896), one of the purest jewels in world literature. This play is deeply melancholic but contains poetic treasures. Méléandre, who has married the sweet, timid Sélysette, begins to love the noble Aglavaine, a love Aglavaine returns. Theirs is a pure love which raises them above the common lot. But Sélysette suffers from not possessing Méléandre's heart alone. The tender creature, full of abnegation, resolves to sacrifice herself for the happiness of her husband and Aglavaine. She leans so far out of the embrasures of an old turret that a crumbling part of the wall collapses and Sélysette falls, not into the sea as she had thought, but onto the sand of the beach. Wounded, she is carried to the house, and even on the verge of death she is unselfish; wishing to spare them remorse, she tries to pretend to Méléandre and Aglavaine that her fall from the tower was accidental. In this drama in which delicately shaded states of soul abound, all the characters are noble and generous. Both Aglavaine and Méléandre feel that a happiness that is purchased at the price of another's suffering is fugitive and vain and, if they do not feel less irresistibly drawn to one another, they do not by any means yield to low desires but to a powerful, spiritualized attraction. They struggle against fate, a struggle all the more painful as they well suspect that fraternal love will ultimately be impossible and that everything will lead them to the complete union which they flee as a sin. These words of Aglavaine are beautiful: «If somebody must suffer, it should be us. There are a thousand duties, but I think one is rarely mistaken in the attempt to relieve a weaker creature by taking its suffering upon oneself.» This play has a charm which ranks it among the most beautiful poetic creations of the century.

   Aglavaine et Sélysette, Maeterlinck's masterpiece, appeared in 1896. In 1902 the author published the drama of *Monna Vanna*, known and played even here in Sweden. The action takes place against the historical background of the Renaissance in Italy; its composition is very clear-cut and entirely free from that kind of twilight which generally characterizes Maeterlink's art. The dramatic idea of duty which sustains the action has often been disputed, with very diverse opinions. The play is certainly bold and of great psychological interest, but Maeterlinck is perhaps more himself in the short, delicately symbolic plays in which the great, flooding light of day does not hold sway but which open up marvellous perspectives for the most intimate presentiments of the human heart.

   Maurice Maeterlinck, a many-sided writer, has written works of a philosophical nature, if not purely philosophical works. Such, for example, is *Le Trésor des humbles* (1896) [*The Treasure of the Humble*] which, among other interesting studies, contains inspired pages about the mystic Ruysbrock and about the spiritual life. Maeterlinck's idealism finds a happy expression here in his words on the most exalted poetry, which, he says, aims at keeping open the principal paths which lead from the visible to the invisible world. In many places in this book appears the thought mentioned earlier that there is behind our visible self another self which is our true being. This idea may appear mystical to the empiricists; at bottom it is quite as plausible as Kant's doctrine of intelligibility which, after all, is the source of the empirical character. In *Le Temple enseveli* (1902) [*The Buried Temple*] is found the idea of an invisible personality, the basis of the visible and earthly personality. If, however, Maeterlinck is accused of fatalism, one should remember the glowing optimism of his book *La Sagesse et la destinée* (1893) [*Wisdom and Destiny*], in which man's fate is said to reside in himself and to depend on the way in which he exercises his will. The downfall of great historical personages is represented here as caused by their own faults or originating from the fact that they lost their old confidence in themselves through errors, and indeed through evil actions, and thereby lost the strength to combat perils victoriously.

In 1900 *La Vie des abeilles* [*The Life of the Bee*] appeared. This book had strong repercussions. Although Maurice Maeterlinck is an enthusiastic bee-keeper and thoroughly familiar with the life of the bees, he did not intend to write a scientific treatise. His book is not an abstract of natural history but an exuberantly poetic work abounding in reflections, the sum total of which is almost a declaration of incompetence. It is useless, the author seems to say, to inquire if the strange cooperation among the bees, their apportionment of work, and their social life are the product of a reasoning mind. It matters little whether the term «instinct» or the term «intelligence» is used, for they are but ways of revealing our ignorance in the matter. What we call instinct among the bees is perhaps of a cosmic nature, the emanation of a universal soul. One immediately thinks of Virgil's immortal description of the bees in which he says that a thinker attributes to them a share of *divina mens*, the divine thought, the divine spirit.

L'Intelligence des fleurs (1907) [The Intelligence of Flowers], another of Maeterlinck's works, is interesting for its bold representation of plants as having wisdom and self-interest. Here one finds the same richness of poetic imagination and, occasionally, profound reflections.

With his creative force, which never runs dry, Maeterlinck composed in 1903 the fascinating dramatic phantasy *Joyzelle*, which shows, through difficult trials and sombre episodes, the triumph of love faithful to its own nature. *Marie Magdeleine* (1909) represents the change in the soul of the repentant sinner and her victory over a temptation that was all the stronger as it touched precisely the noblest side of her nature and urged her to save the Messiah at the sacrifice of herself and of the new moral life which he himself had created in her; that is to say, at the sacrifice of the vital work of the Messiah. Finally, we admire the spectacle *L'Oiseau bleu* (1909) [*The Blue Bird*], a profound fairy tale which sparkles with the poetry of childhood, even if it seems to include too much reflection to have quite enough naive spontaneity. Alas! the blue bird of happiness exists only beyond the limits of this perishable world, but those who have pure hearts will never seek it in vain, for their emotional lives and their imaginations will enrich them and purify them in their journey across the countries of the land of dreams.

And so we return to the place we started from, the land of dreams. Perhaps we would not be wrong in saying that for Maurice Maeterlinck, all reality in time and space, even when it is not a product of the imagination, always carries a veil woven of dreams. Under this veil is hidden the real truth of existence, and when the veil is lifted someday, the essence of things will be discovered.

I have tried to give an account of Maeterlinck's conception of life, using his works as a guide. One cannot doubt the beauty and nobility of this conception; moreover, it is presented in the original form of a poetry that is strange and sometimes bizarre but always inspired.

Maurice Maeterlinck belongs to the chosen ones in the field of poetry. Tastes may change, but the charm of *Aglavaine et Sélysette* will remain. Today Sweden, the land of sagas and folk songs, offers her world prize to the poet who has made us perceive the tender vibrations of the melody that is hidden in the hearts of men.

Acceptance

by Mr. Charles C. M. A. Wauters, Minister of Belgium

The absence of my illustrious countryman, Mr. Maurice Maeterlinck, whom a serious illness retains at home, has—as Count Mörner has already said—caused great disappointment to all those who admire his remarkable literary work and who were eager to meet him in person.

I know that his own disappointment is no less than yours. He was quite eager himself to come and to receive the laurels which have been bestowed upon him and to see this country which fascinates him.

Although Mr. Maeterlinck's absence has given me the honour to receive from the hands of His Majesty the King the Prize awarded to him and to speak to you in his name, nobody regrets his absence more than I do. I would have been happy to meet again a countryman, a fellow citizen from Ghent, and a fellow student from college days; and I know how difficult it is to try to replace him by evoking his image.

Tall, robust, of athletic appearance, with a full face and a dull complexion, easily excited, always bareheaded, he hardly gives the impression of a dreamer, poet, or philosopher. For those who know him well, he is a thinker and a shy man who reveals himself only to his friends. One recognizes here the author of his works; endowed with an extreme sensibility, he rises above the abyss of rationalistic scepticism to a height where morality and logic, with a touch of paradox and antithesis, almost assume the sense of a religion without dogma.

Although Flemish and from Flanders, Maeterlinck wrote French in a most flexible, subtle, and harmonious manner. Still, he is the genius of his race, the incarnation of the Flemish soil.

Those who have travelled through Belgium only by train or car cannot appreciate the intimate and fascinating charm which characterizes the Flemish plains—strewn with monuments in stone whose façades recall the lacework that Flemish peasant women do on their lace pillows, sitting on the threshholds of their houses. Often one hears, in the calm of the countryside, strong, deep voices singing slow and dreamy chants. And in the old towns of Flanders with their winding and picturesque streets, the silence of night is interrupted at regular intervals by the clear sound of bells which, silvery and poetic, impart a sense of medieval times, of centuries of glory, heroism, and prosperity.

Into this milieu Maeterlinck was born, here he grew up, and here lie the sources of his talent and his genius. It is here that I have known him, that I have seen, in the back of a flower garden, the row of hives whose inhabitants he studied and described.

Maeterlinck's success justly adds to the glory of French literature, but also to the glory of his country. The Swedish Academy, in awarding the literary Prize to him, has paid tribute to the French form of a Flemish idea.

I thank the members of the Nobel Institute and ask them to accept the expression of profound gratitude of my absent countryman, whose glory reflects on the country whose representative I have the honour to be.

Prior to the acceptance, K. A. H. Mörner, Director of the Royal Institute of Medicine and Surgery, expressed his disappointment that Maurice Maeterlinck, «a writer universally known and esteemed, whose poetic creations have filled us with enthusiasm», was unable to be present because of illness, and he asked the Minister of Belgium, Mr. Wauters, to convey to him the regrets of those present and their respect.

Biography

Maurice Maeterlinck (1862–1949), born in Ghent, Belgium, came from a well-to-do family. He was educated at a Jesuit college and read law, but a short practice as a lawyer in his home town convinced him that he was unfit for the profession. He was drawn toward literature during a stay in Paris, where he associated with a number of men of letters, in particular Villiers de l'Isle Adam, who greatly influenced him. Maeterlinck established himself in Paris in 1896 but later lived at Saint-Wandrille, an old Norman abbey that he had restored. He was predominantly a writer of lyrical dramas, but his first work was a collection of poems entitled *Serres chaudes* [Ardent Talons]. It appeared in 1889, the same year in which his first play, *La Princesse Maleine*, received enthusiastic praise from Octave Mirbeau, the literary critic of *Le Figaro*, and made him famous overnight. Lack of action, fatalism, mysticism, and the constant presence of death characterize the works of Maeterlinck's early period, such as *L'Intruse* (1890) [*The Intruder*], *Les Aveugles* (1890) [*The Blind*], and the love dramas *Pelléas et Mélisande* (1892), *Alladine et Palomides* (1894), and *Aglavaine et Sélysette* (1896). The shadow of death looms even larger in his later plays, *Joyzelle* (1903) and *Marie Magdeleine* (1909), Maeterlinck's version of a Paul Heyse play, while *L'Oiseau bleu* (1909) [*The Blue Bird*] is marked by a fairy-tale optimism. *Le Bourgmestre de Stilemonde* (1919) [*The Burgomaster of Stilemonde*] was written under the impact of the First World War.

Maeterlinck developed his strongly mystical ideas in a number of prose works, among them *Le Trésor des humbles* (1896) [*The Treasure of the Humble*], *La Sagesse et la destinée* (1898) [*Wisdom and Destiny*], and *Le Temple enseveli* (1902) [*The Buried Temple*]. His most popular work was perhaps *La Vie des abeilles* (1900) [*The Life of the Bee*], which was followed by studies of the «intelligence of flowers» (1907), of termites (1927), and of ants (1930). In later life, Maeterlinck became known chiefly for his philosophical essays. In 1932 he was given the title of Count of Belgium.

Literature 1912

GERHART JOHANN ROBERT HAUPTMANN

«primarily in recognition of his fruitful, varied, and outstanding production in the realm of dramatic art»

Presentation

by Hans Hildebrand, Acting Secretary of the Swedish Academy

There is an old saying that times change and men change with them. If we look back on past ages we discover its truth. We, who are no longer young, have had the opportunity in our bustling lives to experience the truth of the saying, and every day confirms it anew. As far back as history extends we find that new things emerged, but were not at first recognized although they were to be important in the future. A seed came alive and grew to magnificent size. Certain names in contemporary science illustrate the discrepancy between modest beginnings and later developments.

The same is true of dramatic poetry. This is not the place to trace its development through twenty-five centuries. There is a tremendous difference, however, between the satyr choruses of the Dionysiac festivals, called tragedies because of the goat skins worn by the chorus, and the demands the modern age makes on dramatic poetry, and this difference indicates considerable progress.

In our time Gerhart Hauptmann has been a great name in the field of drama. He turned fifty recently; he is thus in his prime of life and can look back on an exceptionally rich career as an artist. He submitted his first work to the stage at the age of twenty-seven. At the age of thirty he proved himself a mature artist with his play *Die Weber* (1892) [*The Weavers*]. This work was followed by others which confirmed his reputation. In most of his plays he deals with conditions of the low-class life which he had numerous occasions to study, especially in his native Silesia. His descriptions are based on keen observations of man and his milieu. Each of his characters is a fully developed personality–there is not a trace of types or clichés. Nobody even for a moment could doubt the truthfulness of his observations; they have established Hauptmann as a great realist. But he nowhere praises the life of these so-called low characters. On the contrary, when one has seen or read these plays and identified himself deeply with the conditions they represent, he feels the need for fresh air and asks how such misery can be abolished in the future. The realism in Hauptmann's plays leads necessarily to brighter dreams of new and better conditions and to the wish for their fulfilment.

Hauptmann has also written dramas of a totally different nature: he calls them «Märchendramen». Among them is the delightful *Hanneles Himmel-fahrt* (1893) [*The Assumption of Hannele*], in which the misery of life and the bliss of heaven emerge with such striking contrast. Among these plays is also *Die versunkene Glocke* (1897) [*The Sunken Bell*], the most popular of his plays in his own country. The copy used by the Nobel Committee of the Swedish Academy bore the stamp of the sixtieth impression.

Hauptmann has also distinguished himself in the genres of historical drama and comedy. He has not published a collection of his lyrical poems, but incidental poems in his plays bear witness to his talent in this field.

In his early years he had published a few short stories, but in 1910 he brought out his novel *Der Narr in Christo Emanuel Quint* [*The Fool in Christ: Emanuel Quint*], the result of many years of work. The story «Der Apostel» of 1892 is a sketch of the final work in which we learn about the inner life of a poor man who, without any education other than that acquired from the Bible and without any critical judgment of what he has read, finally reaches the conclusion that he is the reincarnation of Christ. It is not easy to give a correct account of the development of a human soul that can be considered normal, in view of all the forces and circumstances that affect its development. But it is even more difficult to attain the truth if one describes the inner development of a soul that is in certain respects abnormal. The attempt is bold; its execution took decades of creative work. Judgment of the work has differed widely. I am happy to join the many who consider *Emanuel Quint* a masterly solution of a difficult problem.

Hauptmann's particular virtue is his penetrating and critical insight into the human soul. It is this gift that enabled him in his plays and in his novels to create truly living individuals rather than types representing some particular outlook or opinion. All the characters we meet, even the minor ones, have a full life. In his novels one admires the descriptions of the setting, as well as the sketches of the people that come in more or less close contact with the protagonist of the story. The plays reveal his great art by their powerful concentration which holds the reader or spectator from beginning to end. Whatever subject he treats, even when he deals with life's seamy side, his is always a noble personality. That nobility and his refined art give his works their wonderful power.

The preceding remarks were intended to sketch the reasons why the Swedish Academy has awarded this year's Nobel Prize to Gerhart Hauptmann.

Dr. Hauptmann–In your significant and controversial book *Der Narr in*

Christo Emanuel Quint you say: «It is impossible to uncover the necessary course of a human life in all its stages, if only because every human being is something unique from beginning to end and because the observer can comprehend his object only within the limits of his own nature.»

That is indeed true. But there are many kinds of observers. The everyday man in the midst of his bustling life has neither the opportunity nor the will to study his fellow men in greater depth. We see the outside but do not care to see beneath it unless we happen to have a special interest in learning another's motives. Even those who are not drawn into the turmoil of present life, who limit their intercourse with the outside world and are on intimate terms with their immediate surroundings, do not generally go very far in their study of the human soul. We are attracted or repelled; we love or hate, if we are not indifferent. We praise or blame.

The poet, however, is not an everyday man. He is able to extend the scope of his imagination much further. For he has the divine gift of intuition. And you, Dr. Hauptmann, possess this wonderful gift to the highest degree. In your many works you have created innumerable characters. But they do not exist merely as so many types of such and such a nature. To the reader and spectator of your plays, each of your characters is a fully developed individual, living and acting together with others, but different from all of them. That is the reason for much of the magic of your work.

It has been said that at least in some of your works you have been a marked realist. You have had rich opportunities to use your gift of observation and become acquainted with the misery of whole classes of people, and you have described it faithfully. If after seeing or reading such a play one is deeply moved by it, he cannot help thinking, «These conditions must be improved.» One cannot deny the existence of the seamy side of life, and it must have its place in literature in order to teach wisdom to the living.

Your manifold activities as a writer have given us other marvellous works. I shall mention only two here, *Hanneles Himmelfahrt* and *Die versunkene Glocke*. The latter seems to enjoy great popularity in your country.

Through the mouth of the ambitious and unfortunate Michael Kramer you say:

If someone has the effrontery to paint the man with the crown of thorns—it will take him a lifetime to do it. No pleasures for him: lonely hours, lonely days, lonely years. He must be alone with himself and with his God. He must consecrate himself daily. Nothing common must be about him or in him. And then when he struggles and toils in his solitude the Holy Ghost comes. Then he can sometimes catch a glimpse. It swells, he can feel it. Then he rests in the eternal and he has it before him in quiet and beauty. He has it without wanting it. He sees the Saviour. He feels him.

Although in your work you have not represented the Saviour with the crown of thorns, you have represented a poor man ultimately driven to the delusion that he is the second Christ. But Kramer's words reflect your own attitude. Your novel *Der Narr in Christo Emanuel Quint* appeared in 1910, but the story «Der Apostel» of 1892 shows that the plan for writing the novel had occurred to you twenty years earlier.

True art does not consist in writing down and handing to the public the thoughts of the moment, but rather in subjecting potentially useful ideas to close scrutiny, to the conflict of different opinions and the apprehensive consideration of their eventual effect. This process will gradually lead the true artist to the precious conviction, «I have finally reached the truth.» You have attained the highest rank of art by painstaking but never pedantic preparatory research, by the consistency of your feelings, thoughts, and actions, and by the strict form of your plays.

The Swedish Academy has found the great artist Gerhart Hauptmann worthy of receiving this year's Nobel Prize, which his Majesty the King will now present to him.

Acceptance

As the recipient of this year's Nobel Prize in Literature, I thank you for the kind and cordial words which have been addressed to me. You may rest assured that I and my nation understand and deeply appreciate the honour conferred upon me. The Nobel Prize has become a cultural concern of the entire globe, and its magnificent donor has for all times given his name a place in the cultural life of nations. Distinguished people the world over will utter the name of Nobel with the same emotions as people of former ages uttered that of a patron saint whose power of protection is beyond doubt, and the medal will be passed on from generation to generation and honoured by families of all peoples.

Today I cannot but pay my share of the ever-renewed tribute of respect to this great donor, and after him to the Swedish nation that has brought him forth and is so faithfully administering the heritage of his humanitarianism. Let me also recall the memory of those men whose self-denying and lyncean task on this earth consists in attending to the cultivation of the mind's soil, so that the weeds may be rooted out and the good shoots be nurtured. Let me thank you and express the wish that you may never tire in the most blessed of all activities and that you may never lack truly rich harvests.

And now let me drink to the eventual realization of the ideal that underlies this foundation, I mean the ideal of world peace, which comprehends the final ideals of art and science. For art and science that serve war are neither pure nor ultimate; they are so only when created by, and in turn creating, peace. And let me drink to that great, ultimate, and purely ideal Nobel Prize which humanity will bestow upon itself when brute violence is banished from the intercourse of nations, as it has been banished from that of individuals in civilized societies.

Prior to Mr. Hauptmann's acceptance, the President of the Royal Academy of Sciences, H. G. Söderbaum, addressed the laureate: «This is the twelfth time that the Swedish Academy has awarded the Nobel Prize in Literature; and it is the fourth time that this award goes to a German writer. This only proves the great esteem literature enjoys among a people with whom we share a common origin. At the same time it shows our desire to justly appreciate this literature. I do not know whether you have been in Sweden before; but I do know that for many years your masterpieces have found their way to our stages. Be assured that among us there are none but admirers of your great talent.»

Autobiography

I was born on November 15, 1862. The place of my birth is Bad Obersalz-
brunn, a spa famous for its medicinal springs. The house of my birth is the
inn «Zur Preussischen Krone». My father was Robert Hauptmann, my
mother Marie Hauptmann, née Straehler. I am the youngest of four children.
I remember growing up in an educated and lively middle-class house.

I attended the village school, learned some Latin from a tutor, and had
violin lessons. Later I went to Breslau, the capital of our province, where I
lived in boardinghouses and attended a Gymnasium. Fortunately, my Breslau
school period did not crush me, but it left scars from which I only slowly
recovered.

I should have perished if there had not been a way out. I went to the
country and began to study agriculture. The tortures of school, begun in
1874, ended in 1878. But agriculture remained an episode. Once in solitude
I learned to stand on my own feet and have my own thoughts. I grew
conscious of myself, my value, and my rights. In this way I gained independence, firmness, and a freedom of intellect that I still enjoy today.

Hungry for culture, I returned to Breslau where I spent a second, happier
period. I attended the art academy, did sculpturing, learned what youth,
hope, and beauty are, the value of friends, masters, and teachers.

I drew, sculptured, drank, wrote poems, made plans, and built castles in
Spain. In this mood I exchanged the art academy of Breslau for the University
of Jena in Thuringia. In this mood I exchanged Jena for Rome, and later
Rome for Berlin.

Although I still worked as a sculptor in Rome, it was here that I finally
decided upon literature. A play *Vor Sonnenaufgang* [*Before Dawn*] made me
publicly known in 1889.

My later works I wrote partly in Berlin, partly in Schreiberhau in the
Riesengebirge, partly in Agnetendorf, partly in Italy: they are the condensation of outward and inward fortunes.

Biographical note on Gerhart Hauptmann

Gerhart Hauptmann (1862–1946) gained fame as one of the founders of German Naturalism. After *Vor Sonnenaufgang*, which created a scandal and, at the same time, was hailed as the beginning of naturalistic drama in Germany, he wrote his most successful play, *Die Weber* (1892) [*The Weavers*], the comedy *Der Biberpelz* (1893) [*The Beaver Coat*], the historical drama *Florian Geyer* (1896), *Fuhrmann Henschel* (1898) [*Drayman Henschel*], *Rose Bernd* (1903), and *Die Ratten* (1911) [*The Rats*]. But he also wrote symbolic works like *Haneles Himmelfahrt* (1893) [*The Assumption of Hannele*] and *Die versunkene Glocke* (1896) [*The Sunken Bell*]. Hauptmann's later works are often literary in inspiration to the point of being – in the widest sense – revisions of European classics. *Der arme Heinrich* (1902) [*Henry of Auë*] is modelled on a German medieval romance; *Hamlet in Wittenberg* (1935) challenged Shakespeare and *Der grosse Traum* (1942–43) [The Great Dream] Dante. Greece influenced him deeply, but in his image of Greece archaic and chthonic features predominated: *Griechischer Frühling* (1908) [Greek Spring], *Der Bogen des Odysseus* (1914) [The Bow of Odysseus], and above all the *Atridentetralogie*, of which the last two parts, *Agamemnons Tod* [Agamemnon's Death] and *Elektra*, were published posthumously in 1948.

Other works include the erotic novel *Der Ketzer von Soana* (1918) [*The Heretic of Soana*], *Buch der Leidenschaft* (1930) [Book of Passion], a thinly veiled account of his divorce and remarriage in 1904, and the two autobiographical volumes *Abenteuer meiner Jugend* (1937 and 1949) [*Adventure of My Youth*]. His collected works in seventeen volumes were published in 1942.

Literature 1913

RABINDRANATH TAGORE

«because of his profoundly sensitive, fresh, and beautiful verse, by which, with consummate skill, he has made his poetic thought, expressed in his own English words, a part of the literature of the West»

Presentation

by Harald Hjärne, Chairman of the Nobel Committee of the Swedish Academy

In awarding the Nobel Prize in Literature to the Anglo-Indian poet, Rabindranath Tagore, the Academy has found itself in the happy position of being able to accord this recognition to an author who, in conformity with the express wording of Alfred Nobel's last will and testament, had «during the current year» written the finest poems «of an idealistic tendency.» Moreover, after exhaustive and conscientious deliberation, having concluded that these poems of his most nearly approach the prescribed standard, the Academy thought that there was no reason to hesitate because the poet's name was still comparatively unknown in Europe, due to the distant location of his home. There was even less reason since the founder of the Prize laid it down in set terms as his «express wish and desire that, in the awarding of the Prize, no consideration should be paid to the nationality to which any proposed candidate might belong.»

Tagore's *Gitanjali: Song Offerings* (1912), a collection of religious poems, was the one of his works that especially arrested the attention of the selecting critics. Since last year the book, in a real and full sense, has belonged to English literature, for the author himself, who by education and practice is a poet in his native Indian tongue, has bestowed upon the poems a new dress, alike perfect in form and personally original in inspiration. This has made them accessible to all in England, America, and the entire Western world for whom noble literature is of interest and moment. Quite independently of any knowledge of his Bengali poetry, irrespective, too, of differences of religious faiths, literary schools, or party aims, Tagore has been hailed from various quarters as a new and admirable master of that poetic art which has been a never-failing concomitant of the expansion of British civilization ever since the days of Queen Elizabeth. The features of this poetry that won immediate and enthusiastic admiration are the perfection with which the poet's own ideas and those he has borrowed have been harmonized into a complete whole; his rhythmically balanced style, that, to quote an English critic's opinion, «combines at once the feminine grace of poetry with the virile power of prose»; his austere, by some termed classic, taste in the choice of words and his use of the other elements of expression in a borrowed tongue–those features, in short, that stamp an original work as such, but which at the same time render more difficult its reproduction in another language.

The same estimate is true of the second cycle of poems that came before us, *The Gardener, Lyrics of Love and Life* (1913). In this work, however, as the author himself points out, he has recast rather than interpreted his earlier inspirations. Here we see another phase of his personality, now subject to the alternately blissful and torturing experiences of youthful love, now prey to the feelings of longing and joy that the vicissitudes of life give rise to, the whole interspersed nevertheless with glimpses of a higher world.

English translations of Tagore's prose stories have been published under the title *Glimpses of Bengal Life* (1913). Though the form of these tales does not bear his own stamp–the rendering being by another hand–their content gives evidence of his versatility and wide range of observation, of his heartfelt sympathy with the fates and experiences of differing types of men, and of his talent for plot construction and development.

Tagore has since published both a collection of poems, poetic pictures of childhood and home life, symbolically entitled *The Crescent Moon* (1913), and a number of lectures given before American and English university audiences, which in book form he calls *Sādhanā: The Realisation of Life* (1913). They embody his views of the ways in which man can arrive at a faith in the light of which it may be possible to live. This very seeking of his to discover the true relation between faith and thought makes Tagore stand out as a poet of rich endowment, characterized by his great profundity of thought, but most of all by his warmth of feeling and by the moving power of his figurative language. Seldom indeed in the realm of imaginative literature are attained so great a range and diversity of note and of colour, capable of expressing with equal harmony and grace the emotions of every mood from the longing of the soul after eternity to the joyous merriment prompted by the innocent child at play.

Concerning our understanding of this poetry, by no means exotic but truly universally human in character, the future will probably add to what we know now. We do know, however, that the poet's motivation extends to the effort of reconciling two spheres of civilization widely separated, which above all is the characteristic mark of our present epoch and constitutes its most important task and problem. The true inwardness of this work is most clearly and purely revealed in the efforts exerted in the Christian mission-field throughout the world. In times to come, historical inquirers will know better how to appraise its importance and influence, even in what is at present hidden from our gaze and where no or only grudging recognition is accorded. They will undoubtedly form a higher estimate of it than the one now deemed fitting in many quarters. Thanks to this movement, fresh, bubbling springs of living water have been tapped, from which poetry in particular may draw inspiration, even though those springs are perhaps intermingled with alien streams, and whether or not they be traced to their right source or their origin be attributed to the depths of the dreamworld. More especially, the preaching of the Christian religion has provided in many places the first definite impulse toward a revival and regeneration of the vernacular language, i.e., its liberation from the bondage of an artificial tradition, and consequently also toward a development of its capacity for nurturing and sustaining a vein of living and natural poetry.

The Christian mission has exercised its influence as a rejuvenating force in India, too, where in conjunction with religious revivals many of the vernaculars were early put to literary use, thereby acquiring status and stability. However, with only too regular frequency, they fossilized again under pressure from the new tradition that gradually established itself. But the influence of the Christian mission has extended far beyond the range of the actually registered proselytizing work. The struggle that the last century witnessed between the living vernaculars and the sacred language of ancient times for control over the new literatures springing into life would have had a very different course and outcome, had not the former found able support in the fostering care bestowed upon them by the self-sacrificing missionaries.

It was in Bengal, the oldest Anglo-Indian province and the scene many years before of the indefatigable labours of that missionary pioneer, Carey, to promote the Christian religion and to improve the vernacular language, that Rabindranath Tagore was born in 1861. He was a scion of a respected family that had already given evidence of intellectual ability in many areas. The surroundings in which the boy and young man grew up were in no sense primitive or calculated to hem in his conceptions of the world and of life. On the contrary, in his home there prevailed, along with a highly cultivated appreciation of art, a profound reverence for the inquiring spirit and wisdom of the forefathers of the race, whose texts were used for family devotional worship. Around him, too, there was then coming into being a new literary spirit that consciously sought to reach forth to the people and to make itself acquainted with their life needs. This new spirit gained in force as reforms were firmly effected by the Government, after the quelling of the widespread, confused Indian Mutiny.

Rabindranath's father was one of the leading and most zealous members of a religious community to which his son still belongs. That body, known by the name of «Brahmo Samaj», did not arise as a sect of the ancient Hindu type, with the purpose of spreading the worship of some particular godhead as superior to all others. Rather, it was founded in the early part of the nineteenth century by an enlightened and influential man who had been much impressed by the doctrines of Christianity, which he had studied also in England. He endeavoured to give to the native Hindu traditions, handed down from the past, an interpretation in agreement with what he conceived to be the spirit and import of the Christian faith. Doctrinal controversy has since been rife regarding the interpretation of truth that he and his successors were thus led to give, whereby the community has been subdivided into a number of independent sects. The character, too, of the community, appealing essentially to highly trained intellectual minds, has from its inception always precluded any large growth of the numbers of its avowed adherents. Nevertheless, the indirect influence exercised by the body, even upon the development of popular education and literature, is held to be very considerable indeed. Among those community members who have grown up in recent years, Rabindranath Tagore has laboured to a pre-eminent degree. To them he has stood as a revered master and prophet. That intimate interplay of teacher and pupil so earnestly sought after has attained a deep, hearty, and simple manifestation, both in religious life and in literary training.

To carry out his life's work Tagore equipped himself with a many-sided culture, European as well as Indian, extended and matured by travels abroad and by advanced study in London. In his youth he travelled widely in his own land, accompanying his father as far as the Himalayas. He was still quite young when he began to write in Bengali, and he has tried his hand in prose and poetry, lyrics and dramas. In addition to his descriptions of the life of the common people of his own country, he has dealt in separate works with questions in literary criticism, philosophy, and sociology. At one period, some time ago, there occurred a break in the busy round of his activities, for he then felt obliged, in accord with immemorial practice among his race, to pursue for a time a contemplative hermit life in a boat floating on the waters of a tributary of the sacred Ganges River. After he returned to ordinary life, his reputation among his own people as a man of refined wisdom and chastened piety grew greater from day to day. The open-air school which he established in western Bengal, beneath the sheltering branches of the mango tree, has brought up numbers of youths who as devoted disciples have spread his teaching throughout the land. To this place he has now retired, after spending nearly a year as an honoured guest in the literary circles of England and America and attending the Religious History Congress held in Paris last summer (1913).

Wherever Tagore has encountered minds open to receive his high teaching, the reception accorded him has been that suited to a bearer of good tidings which are delivered, in language intelligible to all, from that treasure house of the East whose existence had long been conjectured. His own attitude, moreover, is that he is but the intermediary, giving freely of that to which by birth he has access. He is not at all anxious to shine before men as a genius or as an inventor of some new thing. In contrast to the cult of work, which is the product of life in the fenced-in cities of the Western world, with its fostering of a restless, contentious spirit; in contrast to its struggle to conquer nature for the love of gain and profit, «as if we are living», Tagore says, «in a hostile world where we have to wrest everything we want from an unwilling and alien arrangement of things» (*Sādhanā*, p. 5); in contrast to all that enervating hurry and scurry, he places before us the culture that in the vast, peaceful, and enshrining forests of India attains its perfection, a culture that seeks primarily the quiet peace of the soul in ever-increasing harmony with the life of nature herself. It is a poetical, not a historical, picture that Tagore here reveals to us to confirm his promise that a peace awaits us, too. By virtue of the right associated with the gift of prophecy, he freely depicts the scenes that have loomed before his creative vision at a period contemporary with the beginning of time.

He is, however, as far removed as anyone in our midst from all that we are accustomed to hear dispensed and purveyed in the market places as Oriental philosophy, from painful dreams about the transmigration of souls and the impersonal *karma*, from the pantheistic, and in reality abstract, belief that is usually regarded as peculiarly characteristic of the higher civilization in India. Tagore himself is not even prepared to admit that a belief of that description can claim any authority from the profoundest utterances of the wise men of the past. He peruses his Vedic hymns, his *Upanishads*, and indeed the theses of Buddha himself, in such a manner that he discovers in them what is for him an irrefutable truth. If he seeks the divinity in nature, he finds there a living personality with the features of omnipotence, the all-embracing lord of nature, whose preternatural spiritual power nevertheless likewise reveals its presence in all temporal life, small as well as great, but especially in the soul of man predestined for eternity. Praise, prayer, and fervent devotion pervade the song offerings that he lays at the feet of this nameless divinity of his. Ascetic and even ethic austerity would appear to be alien to his type of divinity worship, which may be characterized as a species of aesthetic theism. Piety of that description is in full concord with the whole of his poetry, and it has bestowed peace upon him. He proclaims the coming of that peace for weary and careworn souls even within the bounds of Christendom.

This is mysticism, if we like to call it so, but not a mysticism that, relinquishing personality, seeks to become absorbed in an All that approaches a Nothingness, but one that, with all the talents and faculties of the soul trained to their highest pitch, eagerly sets forth to meet the living Father of the whole creation. This more strenuous type of mysticism was not wholly unknown even in India before the days of Tagore, hardly indeed among the ascetics and philosophers of ancient times but rather in the many forms of *bhakti*, a piety whose very essence is the profound love of and reliance upon God. Ever since the Middle Ages, influenced in some measure by the Christian and other foreign religions, *bhakti* has sought the ideals of its faith in the different phases of Hinduism, varied in character but each to all intents monotheistic in conception. All those higher forms of faith have disappeared or have been depraved past recognition, choked by the superabundant growth of that mixture of cults that has attracted to its banner all those Indian peoples who lacked an adequate power of resistance to its blandishments. Even though Tagore may have borrowed one or another note from the orchestral symphonies of his native predecessors, yet he treads upon firmer ground in this age that draws the peoples of the earth closer together along paths of peace, and of strife too, to joint and collective responsibilities, and that spends its own energies in dispatching greetings and good wishes far over land and sea. Tagore, though, in thought-impelling pictures, has shown us how all things temporal are swallowed up in the eternal:

Time is endless in thy hands, my lord. There is none to count thy minutes.
Days and nights pass and ages bloom and fade like flowers. Thou knowest how to wait.
Thy centuries follow each other perfecting a small wild flower.
We have no time to lose, and having no time, we must scramble for our chances. We are too poor to be late.

And thus it is that time goes by, while I give it to every querulous man who claims it, and thine altar is empty of all offerings to the last.

At the end of the day I hasten in fear lest thy gate be shut; but I find that yet there is time.   (*Gitanjali*, 82.)

Acceptance

Telegram from Rabindranath Tagore, read by
Mr. Clive, British Chargé d'Affaires

I beg to convey to the Swedish Academy my grateful appreciation of the breadth of understanding which has brought the distant near, and has made a stranger a brother.

Biography

Rabindranath Tagore (1861–1941) was the youngest son of Debendranath Tagore, a leader of the Brahmo Samaj, which was a new religious sect in nineteenth-century Bengal and which attempted a revival of the ultimate monistic basis of Hinduism as laid down in the *Upanishads*. He was educated at home; and although at seventeen he was sent to England for formal schooling, he did not finish his studies there. In his mature years, in addition to his many-sided literary activities, he managed the family estates, a project which brought him into close touch with common humanity and increased his interest in social reforms. He also started an experimental school at Shantiniketan where he tried his Upanishadic ideals of education. From time to time he participated in the Indian nationalist movement, though in his own non-sentimental and visionary way; and Gandhi, the political father of modern India, was his devoted friend. Tagore was knighted by the ruling British Government in 1915, but within a few years he resigned the honour as a protest against British policies in India.

Tagore had early success as a writer in his native Bengal. With his translations of some of his poems he became rapidly known in the West. In fact his fame attained a luminous height, taking him across continents on lecture tours and tours of friendship. For the world he became the voice of India's spiritual heritage; and for India, especially for Bengal, he became a great living institution.

Although Tagore wrote successfully in all literary genres, he was first of all a poet. Among his fifty and odd volumes of poetry are *Manasi* (1890) [The Ideal One], *Sonar Tari* (1894) [The Golden Boat], *Gitanjali* (1910) [Song Offerings], *Gitimalya* (1914) [Wreath of Songs], and *Balaka* (1916) [The Flight of Cranes]. The English renderings of his poetry, which include *The Gardener* (1913), *Fruit-Gathering* (1916), and *The Fugitive* (1921), do not generally correspond to particular volumes in the original Bengali; and in spite of its title, *Gitanjali: Song Offerings* (1912), the most acclaimed of them, contains poems from other works besides its namesake. Tagore's major plays are *Raja* (1910) [*The King of the Dark Chamber*], *Dakghar* (1912) [*The Post*

Office], *Achalayatan* (1912) [The Immovable], *Muktadhara* (1922) [The Waterfall], and *Raktakaravi* (1926) [*Red Oleanders*]. He is the author of several volumes of short stories and a number of novels, among them *Gora* (1910), *Ghare-Baire* (1916) [*The Home and the World*], and *Yogayog* (1929) [Crosscurrents]. Besides these, he wrote musical dramas, dance dramas, essays of all types, travel diaries, and two autobiographies, one in his middle years and the other shortly before his death in 1941. Tagore also left numerous drawings and paintings, and songs for which he wrote the music himself.

Literature 1914

Prize not awarded

Literature 1915

(Prize awarded in 1916)

ROMAIN ROLLAND

«as a tribute to the lofty idealism of his literary production and to the sympathy and love of truth with which he has described different types of human beings»

Biographical - Critical Essay

by Sven Söderman, Swedish Critic

Romain Rolland was born on January 29, 1866, in the district of Nièvre. He studied literature, music, and philosophy, and in 1895 he published two doctoral theses: *Les Origines du théâtre lyrique moderne*, an erudite and penetrating work which was awarded a prize by the French Academy, and a Latin thesis, *Cur ars picturae apud Italos XVI saeculi deciderit*, a study of the decline of Italian painting in the sixteenth century. After several tiresome years as a schoolmaster, he was appointed to the École Normale as *maître de conférences* and thereafter (1903) to the Sorbonne, where until 1910 he gave a remarkable course on the history of music. In addition to his duties at the university, he devoted himself to music criticism during these years and acquired a wide reputation not only in France but all over Europe when he published his articles and reviews in book form under the titles *Musiciens d'autrefois* (1908) [*Some Musicians of Former Days*] and *Musiciens d'aujourd'hui* (1908) [*Musicians of Today*]. They reveal him as a critic of great judgment, both fair and bold, without prejudices or allegiance to any one party, and as one always striving to reach through music the very sources of life. His biographies of Beethoven (1903) and Händel (1910), inspired as well as learned, are proof of his understanding of music. Besides these, he has written equally remarkable biographies of François Millet (1902), Michelangelo (1905–06), and Tolstoi (1911), in which he has stressed the heroic character of the lives and talents of these artists.

Rolland made his debut in pure literature in 1897 with a play in five acts, *Saint-Louis*, which he published together with *Aërt* (1898) and *Le Triomphe de la raison* (1899), under the common title *Les Tragédies de la foi* (1909) [Tragedies of Faith]. In these plays he sought to set forth, under the mask of historial events, the miseries that souls faithful to their ideals meet in their struggle with the world. He also wrote *Théâtre de la révolution* (1909), which includes *Le 14 Juillet* (1902), *Danton* (1900), *Les Loups* (1898) [*The Wolves*], and a pacifist drama about the war in the Transvaal, *Le Temps viendra* (1903) [*The Time Will Come*]. The plays about the Revolution were conceived during a period when Rolland dreamed of a dramatic reform. He wanted to create a new theatre, to free the art from the domination of a selfish clique, and to entrust it to the people. He had previously outlined his ideas in an essay called *Le Théâtre du peuple* (1900–03) [*The People's Theatre*]. He tried to make his own contribution to this new popular drama by describing the principal episodes of the French Revolution and by representing in a dramatic cycle the Iliad of the French nation. These dramas, which seek moral truth at the sacrifice of anecdotal color, reveal historical intuition, and their characters are fully alive. They are very interesting to read and deserve to be staged.

From 1904 to 1912 Rolland published his great novel *Jean-Christophe*, which is composed of a series of independent narratives: *L'Aube, Le Matin, L'Adolescent, La Révolte, La Foire sur la place, Antoinette, Dans la maison, Les Amies, Le Buisson ardent,* and *La Nouvelle Journée* [*Dawn, Morning, Youth, Revolt, The Market Place, Antoinette, The House, Love and Friendship, The Burning Bush, The New Dawn*]. In 1910 he resigned from his duties at the University; since then he has devoted himself entirely to writing, living most of the time in Rome and Switzerland. During the war, he wrote a series of articles in Swiss newspapers; these were subsequently published in a volume called *Au-dessus de la mêlée* (1915) [*Above the Battle*]. In this, he maintains that the future of mankind is superior to the interests of nations. War for him is barbarous violence, and over the bloody struggles of nations which seek power he turns our eyes toward the cause of humanity. Rolland's recent works are a novel, *Colas Breugnon* (1918), a dramatic fantasy, *Liluli* (1919), and a study of Empedocles (1917).

Romain Rolland's masterpiece, for which he has received the Nobel Prize in Literature in 1915, is *Jean-Christophe*. This powerful work describes the development of a character in whom we can recognize ourselves. It shows how an artistic temperament, by raising itself step by step, emerges like a genius above the level of humanity; how a powerful nature which has the noblest and most urgent desire for truth, moral health, and artistic purity, with an exuberant love of life, is forced to overcome obstacles that rise up ceaselessly before it; how it attains victory and independence; and how this character and this intelligence are significant enough to concentrate in themselves a complete image of the world. This book does not aim solely at describing the life of the principal hero and his environment. It seeks also to describe the causes of the tragedy of a whole generation; it gives a sweeping picture of the secret labour that goes on in the hidden depths and by which nations, little by little, are enlightened; it covers all the domains of life and art; it contains everything essential that has been discussed or attempted in the intellectual world during the last decades; it achieves a new musical aesthetic; it contains sociological, political and ethnological, biological, literary, and artistic discussions and judgments, often of the highest interest. The artistic personality which is revealed in *Jean-Christophe* is one of rare resoluteness and strong moral structure. In this work Rolland has not simply followed a literary impulse; he does not write to please or to delight. He has been compelled to write by his thirst for truth, his need for morality, and his love of humanity. For him the purpose of the aesthetic life consists not merely in the creation of beauty; it is an act of humanism. *Jean-Christophe* is a profession of faith and an example; it is a combination of thought and poetry, of reality and symbol, of life and dream, which attracts us, excites us, reveals us to ourselves, and possesses a liberating power because it is the expression of a great moral force.

In addition to the Romain Rolland who is concerned about truth and altruism there is also the artist. He is a poet of great scope. Although he has assigned the novel only to second place in his work, his mastery of the genre is superb. The character study of Jean-Christophe is an inspired creation, astonishing in spontaneity, with individuality in every trait, every movement, every thought.

Around this central, monumental figure, we find a whole series of characters of great human interest. Rolland's observation is precise and profound. He penetrates to the depths of the beings whom he describes; he studies their characters and paints their souls with incomparable psychological art. His portraits of women, especially, are masterpieces. His characters come from all walks of life and are astonishingly true to type—the bourgeois, the politician, the artist. Sometimes the descriptions are brief but powerful sketches full of drama and pathos; sometimes they are extended to form immense tableaux of manners that are striking because of their keenness of vision and their singular penetration. His innate sincerity prevents Rolland from using rhetorical devices. He says in an exact and natural manner what he has to say—and nothing more. But when his thought is inflamed, when his heart is filled with emotion—love, anger, enthusiasm, scorn, joy, or sadness—then a wind swells the sentence and gives to the text a beauty that, before Rolland, only the greatest masters of French prose have attained.

The author of *Jean-Christophe* is one of the most imposing literary figures of the contemporary era; he is a mighty spirit and an original poet. His masterpiece has taken its place in world literature among the most original, the boldest, and the healthiest works of our century.

Biographical note on Romain Rolland

The works of Romain Rolland (1866–1945) written after the First World War continued to reflect all his earlier interests. During the twenties he began another «roman fleuve», *L'Ame enchantée* (7 vols., 1922–33) [*The Soul Enchanted*]. Music and the problem of the artist are the subject of his *Beethoven: Les grandes époques créatrices* (1928) [*Beethoven the Creator*]. Rolland persisted in his quest for peace and was attracted by the non-violence movement of Ghandi, about whom he wrote a book (1924). His fascination with India and Buddhism led to the study *Essai sur la mystique et l'action de L'Inde vivante* (1929–30) [*Prophets of the New India*]. His political ideas were increasingly influenced by socialism, as is evident from his many essays. Other works of his later period are *Les Précurseurs* (1919) [*The Forerunners*], *Clerambault: histoire d'une conscience libre pendant la guerre* (1920) [*Clerambault*], *Le Jeu de l'amour et de la mort* (1925) [*The Game of Love and Death*], and *Péguy* (1944), the study of his boyhood friend.

CARL GUSTAF VERNER
VON HEIDENSTAM

«in recognition of his significance as the leading representative of a new era in our literature»

Biographical – Critical Essay

by Sven Söderman, Swedish Critic

In the constellation of original artists who regenerated Swedish poetry at the end of the last century, Verner von Heidenstam was the most brilliant star. He was the leader of the generation of poets of 1890; he was the first to set forth in theory and also to realize in his works the ideal of new Swedish generations. Even in his first poems he opened new paths for imagination and form; and his later collections are in large part pure masterpieces of the lyric art. Not less significant – but more impressive because of its great dimensions – is his work in prose. Inspired by national subjects from the very beginning, it succeeds in capturing the most genuine characteristics of national life; it depicts the destinies of the Swedish people in epic poems, which by the richness of their imagination, the sharpness of their contours, and their composition, are works of the highest order in Scandinavian literature. No competent and impartial judge has ever questioned the rare originality of his genius, and Heidenstam has long been ranked among the masters of Swedish national literature.

Born in 1859 into an old family of the Swedish nobility, he first wanted to be a painter, but he abandoned the study of painting to devote himself to his vocation as a poet. His first collection of poems, *Vallfart och vandringsår* (1888) [*Pilgrimage: The Wander Years*], which contains predominantly Oriental themes, marked an epoch in the modern literature of Sweden. In truth it gave the final blow to the realistic school, enemy of all imagination, which was then dominant in Sweden and which since 1880 had darkened literature with its sadness and its gloom. This was the first manifestation of a new poetry in which free individuals, led only by the logic of their imagination, worshipped beauty for its own sake. This «renaissance», which a small polemical work (*Renässans*, 1889) announced a little later, was already completely realized in these poems, rich in colours and bold in form. They reaffirmed the right of man to the naive pleasure of living and surprised with their new rhythms and their poetic accents.

The Oriental poems which played so charmingly with colours and forms had inaugurated a new era and had made the renewal of Swedish poetry apparent to the eyes and to the imagination. In the great prose-poem intermixed with verse, *Hans Alienus* (1892), the tragic Odyssey of an uprooted worshipper of beauty, and especially in his *Dikter* (1895) [Poems] Heidenstam opens perspectives to an inner life. The time of hymns to voluptuousness is past; gravity and sadness are now persistent moods. Sentiment and duty are appreciated at their just value and what is firmly rooted in the depths of the human personality finds itself intuitively explained. What is characteristic in this conception of life, born of noble and unhappy experiences, is a proud and tolerant virility which constitutes the very essence of the suffering, the hope, and the intoxication of the poet, and a newly acquired capacity to reach the spiritual world by renunciation. An ample and profound imagination, genial sentiment, and pure humanity fill these poems – which are also admirable in the sense of form – and make Heidenstam a manly poet and a master of the lyric genre.

A new aspect of Heidenstam's development appeared in his patriotic poetry. He had discovered early that love for the ancestral hearth and for the home of one's birth is what most strongly links man to life. To this love he gave an intense expression even in the poems of his youth; this love henceforth linked him more closely to his country and to his people and oriented his poetic genius toward the historic tales and memories of Sweden. Compelled by such love, he summarized, in a cycle of poems, *Ett folk* (1902) [One People], all that is Swedish into a unity with the same rights and obligations for those who enter therein; and his love finally suggested a patriotic dream of grandeur and called forth this passionate demand: «No people may be greater than you; that is the goal, no matter what the cost.» A whole series of great prose-poems bears witness to his patriotism. In *Karolinerna* (1897–98) [*The Charles Men*] he describes, in the form of separate narratives, the inevitable ruin of Swedish greatness through the act of Charles XII; with a few quick strokes he sketches the tragic character of this national hero and shows that in the end he was only the echo of an ancient saga. In *Heliga Birgittas pilgrimsfärd* (1901) [Saint Bridget's Pilgrimage] he gives a penetrating explanation of this remarkable woman, suggesting that she quite consciously sought sainthood but that she attained it unconsciously when of her own will she divested herself of her pride. Truly monumental are the two volumes of *Folkunga Trädet* (1905–07) [*The Tree of the Folkungs*], *Folke Filbyter* and *Bjälboarvet* [*The Bjälbo Inheritance*], which constitute the trunk and lower branches of «the genealogical tree of the Folkungs», a great historical prose epic in which he retraces the character of a clan of chieftains and the destinies of the Swedes during a period of the Middle Ages. Here the historical imagination of the author, sustained by an inspiration forever fresh, follows all threads in weaving the fates of his characters. His imagination, with its symbolic visions, glistens before the eye.

While Heidenstam was working on this epic about the life and character of the Swedes, his cult for man was taking shape, and one finds traces of it in the work. This cult often includes the necessity to renew life through sacrifice and to aspire to a more elevated earthly existence, an idea which is opposed to love and the cult of woman and results logically in the exaltations of stories *Sankt Göran och draken* (1900) [St. George and the Dragon] and *Skogen susar* (1904) [The Forest Whispers]. This collection contains, in particular, the great prose-poem «Herakles».

Beside these works, Heidenstam has published, among other things, stories and memories of a trip, *Från Col di Tenda till Blocksberg* (1888) [From Col di Tenda to Blocksberg]; the novel *Endymion* (1889), Oriental to the core; the book of historical lectures *Svenskarna och deras hövdingar* (1908–10) [*The Swedes and Their Chieftains*]; and the collections *Tankar och teckningar* (1899) [Thoughts and Notes] and *Dagar och händelser* (1909) [Days and Occurrences]. In this last book he has notably treated subjects of aesthetics and general culture.

The final aspect of Heidenstam's concept of life is offered us through his *Nya dikter* (1915) [New Poems], a collection mainly of philosophical poems of an elevated humanity, of a mellow wisdom, of a beauty of images strangely serene. In loneliness men come to understand themselves; love is the bond which should unite them, and creative humility is the great force which builds the world and which raises statues of the gods.

«O Man, you will become wise only when you reach the summit of the evening-cool heights where all the earth is beheld.»

Biographical note on Verner von Heidenstam

The literary career of Verner von Heidenstam (1859–1940) practically came to an end with the publication of his *Nya dikter*. His only work of importance after this date was his idealized autobiography *När kastanjerna blommade* [When the Chestnuts Bloomed], which was published posthumously in 1941. His collected works in 23 volumes were published between 1943 and 1945.

Literature 1917

KARL ADOLPH GJELLERUP

«for his varied and rich poetry, which is inspired by lofty ideals»

HENRIK PONTOPPIDAN

«for his authentic descriptions of present-day life in Denmark»

Biographical – Critical Essay

by Sven Söderman, Swedish Critic

Karl Gjellerup was born in 1857 and died on October 13, 1919. Like Henrik
Pontoppidan, he came from a family of ministers. He chose a career in the
clergy although he felt no special calling for it; rather his inclinations drew
him strongly toward literature, and alongside his «bread and butter studies»
he devoted himself to reading the Greek, English, and especially the German
classics. In the course of his theological studies, he came gradually to take
a purely negative attitude toward theology and became attracted by the
literary radicalism led by Georg Brandes. In 1878 he made his literary début
under the pseudonym of «Epigonos» with a short novel entitled *En idealist*
[An Idealist]. He published next, in quick succession, a series of tales and
poems in which he posed as a fanatic enemy of all theology and as a sworn
partisan of Darwin and the doctrine of evolution.

   After this first period of anti-theological battles, not marked by a profound
originality, Gjellerup undertook a trip abroad during which he collected
his thoughts and found his intellectual equilibrium. At the same time his
literary talent took on more distinct outlines: the description of an era, «*Romulus*» (1883); the beautiful short story «*G-Dur*» (1883) [G-Major], a portrait of intimacy; and especially the great drama *Brynhild* (1884), which marks
the peak of his talent during this period. The theme of this drama is the
episode of the Volsunga Saga in which Sigurd and Brunhilde, finding themselves on the same mountain, are separated by their destiny but dream of
and desire one another. This waiting, full of torment, this quiet desire, imbues
with sentiment the tragedy which is presented with strength and with great
poetic and pictorial richness. The verse, especially in the choruses composed
in the ancient fashion, attains great lyric beauty. The scope of the work is
due to its depth and form; through its idealism and moral elevation it contrasts absolutely with the other productions of the naturalistic period during
which it was written. In spite of his freedom of thought, Gjellerup had at
bottom only a few common bonds with the naturalistic school. He had, on
the contrary, many more affinities with German classicism, with the literature
of antiquity, and with the wealth of sentiments of Wagner, and when he

realized this fact, he broke sharply and publicly with the school of Brandes in his travel book, *Vandreaaret* (1885) [Wander Year]. His literary production (plays, lyric poems, stories) was henceforth oriented toward idealism, but at the beginning it only barely succeeded from the artistic point of view, even though the richness of his poetic gifts was always visible in it. The best of the books he published during the last years of this period was the charming novel *Minna* (1889), a truly beautiful love story and a delicate study of feminine psychology which must be classed in the highest rank of Scandinavian novels. Let us cite also that novel with the broadest foundations and a solid construction, *Møllen* (1896) [*The Mill*], a curious analysis of the state of mind of a murderer who becomes remorseful and denounces himself; it is a work of tragic grandeur. Less remarkable as works of art, but expressive of Gjellerup's high moral ideas about marriage and the relationship between the sexes, are his modern bourgeois dramas *Herman Vandel* (1891), *Wuthhorn* (1893), and *Hans Excellence* (1895). These dramas are not a plea for marriage. Indeed, the author puts the idea of marriage above banal conventions, and precisely because he puts it so high, he does not find it realized in ordinary marriages. He proposes as a purer model the free union, even though it would not have the consecration of church or state, provided that this union is the only one in a human life.

These dramas, whose tendency is religious despite their individualistic revolts, form a transition between the first ideas of the author and those which characterize the last and most significant period of his literary life. It was without doubt the enthusiasm for the musical drama of Wagner, to which he devoted a masterly work, which led him to the study of Buddhist wisdom with its annihilation of the personality in the universal world of Nirvana. Among the works written by Gjellerup in the twentieth century, the best ones are inspired precisely by these speculations on India and place on stage Hindu subjects which he has treated so poetically and idealistically that they have aroused general admiration. This period of his work began with a musical play, *Offerildene* (1903) [The Sacrificial Fires], the legend of a young disciple of Brahma who in the simplicity of his pious soul discovers wisdom beneath the literal sense of the law, and who wishes to preserve in the world the three sacrificial fires: the fire of the soul, the flame of love, and the fire of the funeral pyre which consumes the body. Philosophical thought is here allied freely and harmoniously with the creative imagination of a poet. In the great mythic novel, *Pilgrimen Kamanita* (1906), which contains a history of Buddha's era, Gjellerup has elucidated the essential characteristics of the

Buddhist conception of the world, its doctrine of renunciation, its effort toward perfection, and its dreams of paradise, of Nirvana, and of universal destruction. Kamanita is the man in search of earthly satisfactions who, after seeing the fragility of all things, desires instead eternal treasures. We follow him not only during his earthly life but also during the different transformations he undergoes in the «Western Paradise», in which the tropical sumptuousness of India is rediscovered. Those who have destroyed themselves awaken here and leave their lotus buds to participate in the dance of the blessed and to undergo new incarnations, following which their souls begin a new existence in the empire of the Buddha of the hundred thousand cycles. In spite of its uninterrupted speculations on Hindu philosophy, this poem exercises a singular fascination. Quite intuitively the poet seems to have penetrated into the spiritual life of a far-off people and to have expressed their dreams of it with the visionary's gift. In certain passages of this poem one finds the spirit of the Arabian Nights, and certain parts of the Western Paradise present a penetrating picture of the sumptuous magnificence of the life of the blessed. In the same way the drama *Den fuldendtes hustru* (1907) [The Wife of the Perfect One], which deals with the purifications that Buddha's wife must undergo to attain perfection, is a masterpiece. The author has succeeded in permitting his own nature and genius to shine through these dogmatic and philosophical revelations of a millennial philosophy. Gjellerup's last great work, *Verdens vandrerne* (1910) [World Wanderers], with its half-Oriental, half-Western moral, does not attain the same artistic beauty, but it contains beautiful details and holds our interest through a mysticism full of imagination as much as through the development of the action.

Karl Gjellerup was that strange combination, a scholar as well as a poet. His inventive imagination and his gifts of visionary poetry were often difficult to harmonize with his specific knowledge and his lively intelligence. His earlier works are characterized by very broad but sometimes clumsy descriptions, philosophical rather than spontaneous. They occasionally neglect artistic form, but they are always rich in ideas and full of promises of originality. Among them are such remarkable works as *Brynhild* and *Minna*. A poet who gathers all the flowers; a spirit that seeks tirelessly until it reaches its true domain in the world of Hindu mysticism, in which his profound thought and his ideal effort to clarify the enigmas of truth and life are combined with his artistic instinct: such is the Gjellerup of the second period. Thought charged with emotion, a great knowledge of the soul, a great desire for beauty, and a poetic art have given birth to works of enduring value. The author of *Pilgrimen Kamanita* and *Den fuldendtes hustru* has justifiably been called the «classic poet of Buddhism».

Autobiography

I was born on June 2, 1857, in the Roholte vicarage at Praestö. My father was Pastor Carl Adolph Gjellerup, my mother, Anna Fibiger. After my father's death in 1860, in Landet vicarage on Lolland (from which I still have a number of memories), I went in November of the same year to the home of my mother's cousin, Pastor Johannes Fibiger, parish minister of the garrison church in Copenhagen, and author of *Johannes den Døber* (1857) [John the Baptist], *Nogle sagn* (1865) [Some Stories], *Kors og kaerlighed* (1858) [Cross and Love], *Den evige strid* (1878) [The Eternal Strife], and *Mit liv og levned* (1898) [My Life]. I was graduated summa cum laude from Haerslevs Grammar School in 1874. Before this I had made several attempts at writing; immediately after graduation I wrote a tragedy, *Scipio Africanus*, and a drama, *Arminius*, both of which were shown to my uncle, Professor Edvard Holm, who encouraged me and showed the latter to Christian Molbech. Nevertheless, I studied theology and lived much in the country (in Vallensved on South Sjaelland, where Fibiger was the minister, and after 1881 in Ønslev on Falster), a country life which made an indelible impression on my mind and has left its mark in all of my novels. I earned my B.D. (summa cum laude) in June of 1878. I immediately began writing *En idealist* (1878) [An Idealist], which was published in November on the same day as *Den evige strid*, both under a pseudonym. Because both books created something of a sensation, I then came into contact with Høffding, Drachmann, Schandorph, Borchsenius, the brothers Brandes, J. P. Jacobsen, and many artists. Ceaseless production followed, temporarily taking a scientific direction in *Arvelighed og moral* (1881) [Heredity and Morals], a book with an evolutionary viewpoint, which was awarded the University Gold Medal. The novel *Germanernes laerling* (1882) [The Apprentice of the Teutons] (in its very title a program for existence), a collection of poems entitled *Rødtjørn* (1881) [Hawthorne], and *Aander og tider* (1882) [Spirits and Times], a requiem on Darwin, are the most noteworthy works from this time. A small inheritance made it possible for me to undertake a longer trip abroad in 1883. During a three-month stay in Rome, I pursued studies in water colour with Kronberg; later I studied pastel and oil painting. My return trip went through Switzerland, Greece, and Russia, and via Stockholm I arrived home at Christmastime. In the meantime two short stories, «Romulus» (1883) and «G-Dur» (1883) [G-Major], had come out. The travel impressions, *En klassisk maaned* (1884) [A Classical Month] and *Vandreaaret* (1885) [Wander Year], followed. In the latter of these two I broke off from the followers of Georg Brandes. Then appeared the first work of mine which was received with excitement, the lyrical tragedy *Brynhild* (1884), which had already been sketched during my student years, and which was dedicated to Eugenia. From the summer of 1885 to the fall of 1887 I lived in Dresden, where I wrote the scenes from the revolution, *Saint Just* (1885) (reworked for the stage in German in 1913 and still not published), and the dramatic-lyrical poem «Thamyris» (1887). The latter along with *Brynhild* was responsible for my receiving a state pension for life. In October of 1887 I married Eugenia Bendix, née Heusinger, and settled in Hellerup. The lyrical tragedy *Hagbard og Signe* (1888) [Hagbard and Signe], the novel *Minna* (1889), the poetry collection *Min kaerligheds bog* (1889) [The Book of my Love], and the plays *Herman Vandel* (1891) and *Wuthhorn* (1893) (performed at the Dagmar Theatre over 100 times) were written in Hellerup. I also wrote an essay about Wagner's Nibelungenring and translated the songs of the gods in the *Edda*.

In March of 1892 I settled in Dresden. The tragedy *Kong Hjarne* (1893) [King Hjarne] and the verse comedy *Gift og modgift* (1898) [Toxin and Antitoxin] were performed at the Dagmar Theatre. After *Fabler* [Fables], *Fra vaar til høst* [From Spring to Autumn], and *To fragmenter* [Two Fragments] I bade farewell to Danish poetry. The novels *Møllen* (1896) [The Mill], *Ved graensen* (1897) [At the Border], *Tankelaeserinden* (1901) [The Soothsayer], and *Rudolf Stens Landpraxis* or *Reif für das Leben* (1913) [Ripe for Life] were written in German, and this language, in which I had made my debut with *Pastor Mors* (1894), now became my true artistic medium. The dramas *Die Opferfeuer* (1903) [The Sacrificial Fires] (produced at the court theatres in Dresden and Dessau) and *Das Weib des Vollendeten* (1907) [The Wife of the Perfect One] (produced at the court theatre in Stuttgart) and the poetic novels *Der Pilger Kamanita* (1906) [*The Pilgrim Kamanita*], *Die Weltwanderer* (1910) [The World Travellers], *Der goldene Zweig* (1917) [The Golden Bough], and *Die Gottesfreunde* (1916) [The Friends of God] belong chiefly to German literature and – like *Reif für das Leben* – have found their true understanding and appreciation almost exclusively in Germany. When my first book appeared forty years earlier, it had been influenced by German idealism. Just three years later (in the thesis awarded the gold medal) I was a follower of English naturalism, after which I returned to a position under those elevated signs of the zodiac which constitute my rightful habitat, only this time the guiding star was not Hegel as in *En idealist*, but Kant and Schopenhauer.

Karl Gjellerup died in Klotzsche, near Dresden, in 1919.

Biographical - Critical Essay

by Sven Söderman, Swedish Critic

Henrik Pontoppidan belongs to the generation of writers who followed closely the «modern renaissance» of Danish literature after 1870, which had as its principal representatives Georg Brandes, Holger Drachmann, and J. P. Jacobsen. As a writer, his particular province is the novella. As an observer of human nature, as historian of the moral life of his time, he assuredly ranks first among contemporary Danish novelists. Born in Jutland in 1857, he was the son of a Protestant minister whose ideas were tinged with the doctrine of Grundtvig. He was educated at a polytechnical college. Later he taught school, but soon he gave up all professions to follow only his vocation as a writer. His first book, *Staekkede vinger* [Clipped Wings], appeared in 1881; since then he has published a great number of books, among them works of great and lasting value. During his youth he had bitter experiences of the Danish character and life which must have been a determining influence on his career as a writer. All his work is a struggle against what seemed to him deceptive and perfidious illusions, false authority, romanticism, superstitious belief in beautiful phrases, and the intoxication of lofty words, exalted sentiments, and moral fear. In a word, it is «the process of lyric putrefaction» by which the society of the Old World, in his judgment, is heading toward its ruin.

Thus in *Sandinge menighed* (1883) [The Parish of Sandinge], he finds fault with the falsities in the higher educational system; in *Skyer* (1890) [Clouds], he criticizes the leftist Danish politician of sonorous but empty phrases under the provisory laws of Estrup; in *Den gamle Adam* (1894) [The Old Adam] and *Højsang* (1896) [Song of Songs], he exposes the ravings of the amorous imagination and lofty sentiments; and in *Natur* (1890), he exercises his irony on the exaltation of nature. *Mimoser* (1886) [Mimosas] supports a theory completely opposed to the idea which had been dominant since Björnson defended it in *En hanske* [A Gauntlet], the idea which demanded man's purity and fidelity in sexual relations. *Det ideale hjem* (1900) [The Ideal Home] is a defence of matriarchy against marriage. *Nattevagt* (1894) [Night Watch] and the play *Asgaardsrejen* (1906) [The Wild Chase] contain attacks against modern art and lyric poetry which are only objects of luxury. To anaemic culture, the enemy of life, Pontoppidan opposes nature as it is developed in freedom. He shows an ardent sympathy especially for the social and revolutionary struggle and for the ideas of rational positivism. However, he never speaks in his own name; the characters whom he puts on stage speak for themselves, but the spirit of his books is revolutionary. What is curious, however, is that he himself was nourished on the «stale milk of romanticism» and that he is a lyricist in spite of his realistic spirit–a deep-seated contradiction which has permitted him to clothe reality in romantic veils and at the same time to undermine romanticism by means of irony.

Pontoppidan's masterpieces are the three-volume novel *Det forjaettede land* (1891–95) [The Promised Land] and the novel *Lykke-Per* [Lucky Peter), originally published in eight volumes (1898–1904) but later condensed (1905)–two monumental works which give a tableau of the spiritual life of Denmark after 1860. The first of these novels, a vast picture of rustic life, portrays the opposition between the peasants and the inhabitants of the cities. It shows that even the most enthusiastic attempts to restore these classes to unity are doomed to certain failure. The principal character, an idealistic priest from Copenhagen, motivated by a strong feeling of duty, wishes to live with the peasants in order to lift them out of their condition; but he finds himself deceived in his faith in the people, as well as in his mission as a priest and the possibility of adapting it to everyday life and actions. He ends as an unbalanced visionary. Lykke-Per, on the contrary, is a young provincial, an engineer, who has firmly decided to achieve happiness in the capital. Contrary to the priest of *Det forjaettede land*, he is a man who is interested only in positive reality; he dislikes everything religious, metaphysical, or aesthetic. He behaves like a man of energy whom nothing can stop in the realization of his bold plans. But he also lacks that strength of domination over himself which is the necessary condition for a free soul, and he falls victim to that Christian romanticism which he has in his blood and which is precisely what he scorned. What is remarkable in this book is the masterly exposition of the essential differences between Jewish and Germanic ideas. A third cycle of novels, *De dødes rige* (1912–1916) [*The Kingdom of the Dead*], whose last parts were completed during the World War, also gives a whole series of images of Denmark at the end of the nineteenth and beginning of the twentieth century. Its subject is the unfortunate attempt of a radical politician to awaken a «people who are sleeping». It contains interesting social descriptions and vivid portraits (based on living models), but on the whole this work cannot be compared with the key works of the preceding period.

Henrik Pontoppidan has been called the classicist of the new Danish realism. He writes in a nervous and supple prose which has the peaceful, regular rhythm of healthy breathing. He narrates simply and easily without vain search for artistic words, but he has the rare gift of expressing reality clearly and in a lively manner. One finds the whole of Denmark in his writings: Jutland, the islands, and the capital; the commercial city and the country with its manors, its parsonages, its schools, and its taverns. One feels that the author has lived what he writes about. Moreover, the countryside is not described for itself but for the men who live there; it has value only because it conditions men. The essential object of Pontoppidan is man and his destiny, and in the objective description of human destiny he reveals himself as an incomparable artist. He has knowledge of the different classes of Danish people; he really knows their language, their manners, their habits, and their disposition. He is skilled in making out of his characters portraits in prominent relief, but he knows also how to endow them with an intense interior life which expresses their personalities. When one has read his work, one remembers a great number of distinctly individualized characters and the conditions of their existence. It is a broad avenue traced across Danish life during several decades. In the two central works, especially, there are admirable descriptions and characters whose emotional lives are portrayed in changing psychological situations and in scenes of great beauty. All the details appear, but the different parts of each novel and its details are put together effortlessly to give a generally unified work. Henrik Pontoppidan is an epic author of great range who, in an imposing endeavour, seeks to realize a work of monumental dimensions.

Autobiography

My father, Dines Pontoppidan, belonged to an old family of clergymen and was himself a minister. My mother, whose maiden name was Oxenbøl, was the daughter of a government official. They had sixteen children. One of the middle ones in the flock, I was born on July 24, 1857, in the small Jutland town of Fredericia. In 1863, my father was transferred to Randers, another Jutland town, where a year later, at the age of six, I experienced the invasion of the allied Prussian and Austrian armies. When I was seventeen I went to Copenhagen, where I was accepted at the Polytechnical College. After a summer trip to Switzerland, which was rich in experiences, I started writing. In the beginning I aimed at descriptions of nature and folk life until, as the years passed, the description of man became my chief interest.

My first book was published in 1881. I began with a few volumes of smaller tales, among which was *Fra hytterne* (1887) [From the Cottages]. But the subjects which especially attracted me demanded a more spacious form and a broader style. I turned to the novel, an artistic form which had in former days been neglected and had thus acquired a bad reputation, but which during the nineteenth century had developed and elevated itself to the ranks occupied by drama and the ancient epic. In a trilogy, *Det forjaettede land* (1891–95) [The Promised Land], *Lykke-Per* (1898–1904) [Lucky Peter], and *De dødes rige* (1912–16) [The Kingdom of the Dead], I have attempted to give a continuous picture of the Denmark of today through descriptions of human minds and human fates which reflect the social, religious, and political struggles of the time. Aside from this, over the years I have produced a number of minor and more personal works, wherein imagination has been allowed to play more freely. I mention *Ung elskov* (1885) [Young Love], *Minder* (1893) [Memoirs], *Den gamle Adam* (1894) [The Old Adam], *Højsang* (1896) [Song of Songs], *Borgmester Hoeck og hustru* (1905) [Mayor Hoeck and Wife], *Den kongelige gaest* (1908) [The Royal Guest], and *Hans Kvast og Melusine* (1907) [Hans Kvast and Melusine]. My collected works comprise approximately forty volumes.

Biographical note on Henrik Pontoppidan

Henrik Pontoppidan (1857–1943) wrote his last novel, *Mands himmerig* [Man's Heaven], in 1927. The most significant work of his later years consisted of five volumes of memoirs, published between 1933 and 1943.

Literature 1918

Prize not awarded

Literature 1919

(Prize awarded in 1920)

CARL FRIEDRICH GEORG SPITTELER

«*in special appreciation of his epic,* Olympischer Frühling»

Presentation

by Harald Hjärne, Chairman of the Nobel Committee of the Swedish Academy

The Swedish Academy, in accordance with the statutes of the Nobel Foundation, has awarded the Nobel Prize in Literature for 1919, which was not
awarded last year, to the Swiss poet Carl Spitteler for his epic, *Olympischer
Frühling* (1906) [Olympian Spring].

Of this work it can be truly said that its «significance has become apparent
only in recent years», and that all doubts that prevented a full appreciation
had to be carefully considered until its merits, not immediately obvious,
could be fully recognized, not only as ornaments of the poetic form but
above all as the artistic and harmonious expressions of a superior genius of
rare independence and idealism.

This is not to say that we in any way subscribe to the opinion that this
poem represents the fruit of a persistent struggle with the darkness of thought
rather than of a lucid liberal inspiration. The original gap between the poet's
art and its appreciation by critics and readers does not in this case point to
a shortcoming on either side, but rather proves the deep and rich meaning
of the work, which needs careful critical judgment to be revealed in its entirety.

Spitteler's *Olympischer Frühling* achieved popularity in Switzerland and
Germany only in the revised final version of 1909. But with every year and
especially since the end of the war, interest in it has grown and its circle
of readers has widened; this year's impression is expected to run into several
thousand copies. That is a considerable number for something as out of step
with the times as a verse epic of 600 pages about the gods of Olympus, which
because of its genre must be read as a whole and which demands the leisure
and concentration of the reader. The writer, who has for decades devoted
all his energies to such an enterprise, has indeed deliberately and ruthlessly
isolated himself from hectic contemporary life and has given little thought
to the modern demand for adequate material compensation.

He has done nothing to soften these contrasts. On the contrary, he has
intentionally chosen a subject and an approach which were bound to bewilder and even repel many readers of different dispositions and inclinations

or of different backgrounds of taste and education, as they tried to understan
the poetic world that he opened before their eyes. From the beginning h
was bold enough to appeal to their patience and endurance to follow hin
to the end of his curious paths, illuminated only by the clear and uninter
rupted thread of the action and the soliloquies and dialogues of the heroes
which are highly dramatic despite the epic framework. The connoisseur rec
ognizes Homeric traits, but to his surprise he is led on toward an unknow
and never anticipated goal.

But for the rest, what a harsh and striking contrast between Homer'
Olympus and Spitteler's idiosyncratic mythology! Nothing could be mor
unjust than the reproach that he likes to attract philologists and other disciple
of scholarship by means of recondite allusions and profound symbols bor
rowed from their disciplines. His Olympians and heroes, his myths an
oracles only rarely remind one of the style or tone of the older Greek poet
philosophers. They can neither be derived from the latest findings of classica
scholarship nor cited as evidence of the poet's dependence on any kind o
allegorical interpretation. Equally misguided are those who have spoken o
a third part of *Faust*. Spitteler does not imitate anyone, not even the aging
Goethe in his attempt to reconcile Romantic passion and classical balanc
in the masks of Faust and Helen. Spitteler's mythology is a purely persona
form of expression which grew naturally out of his education and whicl
gives shape to the living turmoil of struggling characters that he evokes ir
order to represent on the level of ideal imagination, human sufferings, hopes
and disillusions, the vicissitudes of different human fortunes in the struggle o
the free will against imposed necessity. Why should he care that the curren
aesthetic enlightenment finds it difficult to accept this seemingly fantasti
mixture of dream and reality with its wilful abuse of mythological names

Even if I attempted to give a careful and comprehensive summary of th
action of *Olympischer Frühling*, I could not give a clear picture of the wealtl
of its content, of the radiant vividness and moving power of the changing
episodes, nor of their firm interrelation in an effective whole. Suffice it tc
say that the brilliant life of Olympus and the cosmos, manifesting itself ir
pleasure and trials of strength, ends in impotent despair in the face of humar
ingratitude, licence, crime, and misery. Herakles, the mortal son of Zeus,
equipped with all perfections by his father, his relatives, and friends, but a
the same time burdened with the curse and hatred of Hera, the queen of
the gods, must leave Olympus to accomplish ungrateful tasks of pity and
courage on earth.

The Olympians, with their deeds and adventures, their victorious fights and their quarrels among themselves are in reality supermen whom the poet values only inasmuch as they are able to curb their whims and desires.

«Der Weise zügelt, der Tor lässt Willkür walten.» Above them all there is an inexorable universal law that assumes shape in gloomy powers of fate. Below them and closer to us are the mechanizing, soulless powers of nature which gods and men should put into their service for the benefit of themselves and of others, but which, abused by malice and pride, drive them into folly and ruin. The epic is full of airships and other curious inventions and its gorgeous buildings with cupolas and stately porches leave Homeric simplicity far behind. But the plot of the impudent flatfoot people to deprive Apollo of his universal rule by means of an artificial sun and their overweening attempt to attack him in the air by means of a treacherously constructed vehicle and poison gas testify to the decay that threatens mankind when it pushes too far a self-confidence based on material power.

Spitteler describes such pranks and the strange quests and enterprises of his heroes with a playful humour reminiscent of Ariosto. His style has a great variety of tones and colors ranging from solemn pathos to the careful brush strokes of the similes and the lively descriptions of nature, which reflect his native Alps rather than the regions of Greece. The iambic hexameters with their alternating masculine and feminine rhymes carry the flow of his masterly language, which is always powerful and splendid, never without vitality, and often unmistakably Swiss.

The Academy takes pleasure in expressing its admiration for the independent culture of Spitteler's poetry by awarding him this Prize. Since Mr. Spitteler has been prevented by illness from attending this ceremony, the Prize will be forwarded to him through the Swiss Embassy.

At the banquet, Professor Oscar Montelius addressed the Swiss Minister of Foreign Affairs, Count Wrangel, who received the Prize for Carl Spitteler, and asked him to inform the poet of the Academy's concern for his health and of the hope that he would soon be able to write other works as remarkable as *Olympischer Frühling*.

Autobiography

I was born on April 24, 1845, in the little town of Liestal in the Canton of Baselland. When I was four we moved to Bern, where my father had been appointed treasurer of the newly established Swiss Confederacy. In the winter of 1856–57 I returned home with my parents. I attended the Gymnasium at Basle and lived with an aunt; later I lived in Liestal and went by train to Basle daily to attend the Obergymnasium called the «Pädagogium». Wilhelm Wackernagel and Jacob Burckhardt were my teachers there. At my father's request I took up the study of law at the University of Zürich in 1863. Later, 1865–70, I studied theology in Zürich, Heidelberg, and Basle. After taking my theological examination at Basle I went to Petersburg at the invitation of General Standertskjöld to be the tutor of his younger children. I left for Petersburg in August, 1871 and stayed there until 1879. During this period, spent partly in Russia and partly in Finland, I worked on *Prometheus und Epimetheus*, which, after my return to Switzerland, I published in 1881 at my own expense under the pseudonym Carl Felix Tandem. The book was completely neglected; because it was not even reviewed I abandoned all hope of making poetry my living and was compelled instead to teach school (Neuveville, Canton Bern, 1881–1885) and work for newspapers (*Grenzpost*, Basle, 1885–86; *Neue Zürcher Zeitung*, 1890–92). In July, 1892, fate suddenly granted me financial independence. I moved to Lucerne, where I have lived happily with my family ever since. The following works of mine appeared after *Prometheus und Epimetheus*: *Extramundana* (1883), a book which I consider mediocre; *Schmetterlinge* (1889) [Butterflies]; *Friedli der Kolderi* (1891); *Gustav* (1892); *Litterarische Gleichnisse* (1892) [Literary Parables]; *Balladen* (1896); *Der Gotthard* (1897); *Conrad der Leutnant* (1898); *Lachende Wahrheiten* (1898) [Laughing Truths]. Between 1900 and 1906 the four volumes of my epic *Olympischer Frühling* [Olympian Spring] were published: I. *Die Auffahrt* [Overture]; II. *Hera die Braut* [Hera the Bride]; III. *Die Hohe Zeit* [High Tide]; IV. *Ende und Wende* [End and Change].

The first two parts remained as unnoticed as all my other books. But between the publication of the second and third volumes, a musician, the famous Felix Weingartner, suddenly announced *Olympischer Frühling* (together with *Prometheus*) to the German public in a special pamphlet called *Carl Spitteler, ein künstlerisches Erlebnis* (München, 1904). That was the breakthrough. Felix Weingartner had discovered me for the world. To the Swiss public I had long before been recommended by J. V. Widmann.

In 1909 a revised edition of my epic in five volumes was published; by the end of 1920 it had run into several editions. After *Olympischer Frühling* I published *Glockenlieder* (1906) [Bell Songs]; *Imago* (1908); *Gerold und Hansli, die Mädchenfeinde* (1907) [*Two Little Misogynists*], translated into several languages; and *Meine frühesten Erlebnisse* (1914) [My Earliest Experiences]...

Biographical note on Carl Spitteler

Carl Spitteler (1845–1924) revised his early Prometheus epic and published it under the title *Prometheus der Dulder* (1924) [*Prometheus the Sufferer*]. His collected works have been published in nine volumes (Zürich, 1945–50).

Literature 1920

KNUT PEDERSEN HAMSUN

«for his monumental work, Growth of the Soil*»*

Presentation

by Harald Hjärne, Chairman of the Nobel Committee of the Swedish Academy

In accordance with the statutes of the Nobel Foundation, the Swedish Academy has awarded the literary Prize for 1920 to the Norwegian novelist Knut Hamsun for his work, *Markens Grøde* (1917) [*Growth of the Soil*].

It would be superfluous to give a detailed account of a book that in a short time has spread everywhere in its original form or in translation. Through the originality of its plot and style, it has aroused the liveliest interest in many countries and has found favourable reception with the most diverse groups of readers. Only recently a leading and distinctly conservative English reviewer wrote that this book, which had appeared in England only this year, was universally acclaimed as a masterpiece. The reasons for this incontestable success will no doubt hold the attention of literary critics for a long time, but even now, under the impact of first impressions, they deserve to be pointed out at least in their broad features.

In spite of current opinions of our time, those who want to find in literature above all a faithful reproduction of reality, will recognize in *Markens Grøde* the representation of a life that forms the basis of existence and of the development of societies wherever men live and build. These descriptions are not distorted by any memories of a long, highly civilized past; their immediate effect is due to the evocation of the harsh struggle all active men must in the beginning endure (in varying external conditions, of course) against an indomitable and rebellious nature. It would be difficult to conceive of a more striking contrast with works usually called «classic».

Nonetheless, this work may rightly be called classic, but in a deeper and more profound sense than usual if this epithet is to express something other and more than vague praise. The classic, in the culture we have inherited from antiquity, is less the perfect which calls for imitation than the significant which is taken directly from life and which is rendered in a form of enduring value even for future ages. The insignificant, that which in itself is of no consequence, cannot be comprehended in this notion any more than that which is formally provisional or defective. But apart from that, whatever is precious in human life, although it may appear common, can be placed in the same category as the extraordinary and the brilliant, with a significance and a form of equal value, once it is presented for the first time in its proper light. In this sense it is no exaggeration to maintain that in *Markens Grøde* Hamsun has given to our times a classic that can be measured against the best we already have. Antiquity does not possess in this respect a monopoly inaccessible to future generations; for life is always new and inexhaustible and as such can always be presented in new forms created by new geniuses.

Hamsun's work is an epic of labour to which the author has given monumental lines. It is not a question of disparate labour which divides men within and among themselves; it is a question of the concentrated toil which in its purest form shapes men entirely, which mollifies and brings together divided spirits, which protects and increases their fruits with a regular and uninterrupted progress. The labour of the pioneer and the first farmer with all its difficulties, under the poet's pen, thus takes on the character of a heroic struggle that yields nothing to the grandeur of the manly sacrifice for one's country and companions in arms. Just as the peasant poet Hesiod described the labours of the field, so Hamsun has put in the foreground of his work the ideal labourer who dedicates his whole life and all his powers to clearing the land and to triumphing over the obstacles with which men and the forces of nature confront him. If Hamsun has cast behind him all the weighty memories of civilization, he has by his own work contributed to a precise understanding of the new culture that our era expects to arise from the progress of physical labour as a continuation of ancient civilization.

Hamsun does not present so-called types on his stage. His heroes and heroines are all very much alive, all in quite modest circumstances. Certain among them, and the best, are unimaginative in their goals and thoughts, the principal example being the tireless and silent farmer himself. Others are drifting, troubled, and often even bewildered by egoistic aspirations and follies. They all carry the mark of their Norwegian origin; they are all conditioned in some manner by «the fruits of the earth». It is one of the characteristics of our sister languages that often the same words express very different nuances of meaning by the images they evoke. When we Swedes speak of «the fruits of the earth», we think immediately of something fertile, abundant, succulent, preferably in an agricultural region that has been cultivated for a long time. The thought of Hamsun's book is not oriented in this direction. «The earth» here is the rugged and forbidding fallow soil. Its fruits do not fall from a cornucopia of abundance; they comprise all that can germinate and grow in this ungrateful soil, the good and the bad, the beautiful and the ugly, among men and animals as well as in the forest and the fields. Such are the kinds of fruits Hamsun's work offers for our harvest.

However, we Swedes, or at least many Swedes, do not feel strange in the regions and circumstances described to us here. We rediscover the atmosphere of the North with all that is a part of its natural and social milieu, and with many parallels on both sides of the frontier. Moreover, Hamsun also presents Swedish characters who are drawn to the newly cultivated land, most of them no doubt attracted by the mirage of brilliant economic success, as the cities on the Norwegian coasts appear on the horizon like snares of the great worldly life enticing defenceless hearts from the heavy toil of the land.

These and other quite human projections, far from weakening, reinforce the impression produced by the classic content of the story. They dissipate the apprehension one could feel in seeing the light of the ideal at the expense of truth; they guarantee the sincerity of the design, the truth of the images and the characters. Their common humanity escapes no one. The proof is in the welcome this work has found among peoples of different mentalities, languages, and customs. Furthermore, through the light touch of smiling humour with which the author treats even the saddest things he relates, he has proved his own compassion for human destiny and human nature. But in the story, he never departs from the most complete artistic serenity. The style, stripped of vain ornaments, renders the reality of things with certainty and clarity, and one rediscovers in it, under a personal and powerful form, all the richness of nuance of the writer's mother tongue.

Mr. Knut Hamsun – In facing the rigours of the season as well as the fatigues of a long trip particularly arduous at this time in order to come to receive the Prize awarded you, you have given great joy to the Swedish Academy, which will certainly be shared by all the persons present at this ceremony. In the name of the Academy, I have tried as well as possible in the short time accorded me to express at least some of the major reasons for which we appreciate so highly your work which has just been crowned. Thus, in addressing myself now to you personally, I do not wish to repeat what I have said. It remains for me only to congratulate you in the name of the Academy and to express the hope that the memories you will keep of your visit with us will be ties that will link you to us also in the future.

Acceptance

What am I to do in the presence of such gracious, such overwhelming generosity? I no longer have my feet planted on the ground, I am walking on air, my head is spinning. It is not easy to be myself right now. I have had honours and riches heaped on me this day. I myself am what I am, but I have been swept off my feet by the tribute that has been paid to my country, by the strains of her national anthem which resounded in this hall a minute ago.

It is as well perhaps that this is not the first time I have been swept off my feet. In the days of my blessed youth there were such occasions; in what young person's life do they not occur? No, the only young people to whom this feeling is strange are those young conservatives who were born old, who do not know the meaning of being carried away. No worse fate can befall a young man or woman than becoming prematurely entrenched in prudence and negation. Heaven knows that there are plenty of opportunities in later life, too, for being carried away. What of it? We remain what we are and, no doubt, it is all very good for us!

However, I must not indulge in homespun wisdom here before so distinguished an assembly, especially as I am to be followed by a representative of science. I will soon sit down again, but this is my great day. I have been singled out by your benevolence, chosen amongst thousands of others, and crowned with laurels! On behalf of my country I thank the Swedish Academy and all Sweden for the honour they have bestowed on me. Personally, I bow my head under the weight of such great distinctions, but I am also proud that your Academy should have judged my shoulders strong enough to bear them.

A distinguished speaker said earlier tonight that I have my own way of writing, and this much I may perhaps claim and no more. I have, however, learned something from everyone and what man is there who has not learned a little from all? I have had much to learn from Sweden's poetry and, more especially, from her lyrics of the last generation. Were I more conversant with literature and its great names, I could go on quoting them *ad infinitum* nd acknowledge my debt for the merit you have been generous enough o find in my work. However, coming from a person like me, this would ›e mere name-dropping, shallow sound effects without a single bass note o support them. I am no longer young enough for this; I have not the trength.

No, what I should really like to do right now, in the full blaze of lights, ›efore this illustrious assembly, is to shower every one of you with gifts, vith flowers, with offerings of poetry–to be young once more, to ride on he crest of the wave. That is what I should wish to do on this great occasion, his last opportunity for me. I dare not do it, for I would not be able to escape idicule. Today riches and honours have been lavished on me, but one gift ıas been lacking, the most important one of all, the only one that matters– he gift of youth. None of us is too old to remember it. It is proper that we vho have grown old should take a step back and do so with dignity and ;race.

I know not what I should do–I know not what is the right thing to do, ›ut I raise my glass to the youth of Sweden, to young people everywhere, o all that is young in life.

›rior to the acceptance, Professor Oscar Montelius addressed Mr. Hamsun: I know that you prefer to be talked about as little as possible; but I cannot efrain from assuring you that all of us who admire your *Growth of the Soil* ejoice in having made your personal acquaintance.»

Biography

Knut Hamsun (1860–1952) was born in Lom, Norway, and grew up in poverty on the Lofoten Islands. At the age of seventeen he became an apprentice to a ropemaker, and at about the same time he began to write. He spent some years in America, travelling and working at odd jobs, and published his impressions, chiefly unfavourable, under the title *Fra det moderne Amerikas Aandsliv* (1889) [The Intellectual Life of Modern America]. The novel *Sult* (1890) [Hunger] and even more so *Pan* (1894) established him as one of the foremost Norwegian writers.

Hamsun's work is determined by a deep aversion to civilization and the belief that man's only fulfilment lies with the soil. This primitivism (and its concomitant distrust of all things modern) found its fullest expression in Hamsun's masterpiece *Markens Grøde* (1917) [*Growth of the Soil*]. His early works usually centre on an outcast, a vagabond figure, aggressively opposed to civilization. In his middle period, Hamsun's aggressiveness gives way to melancholy resignation about the loss of youth. The decay of age is the theme of such plays as *Livets Spil* (1896) [Game of Life] and *Aftenrøde* (1898) [Sunset], as well as of the novels *Under Høststjernen* (1906) [*Under the Autumn Star*], *Benoni* (1908), and *En Vandrer Spiller med Sordin* (1909) [*A Wanderer Plays on Muted Strings*]. In 1904 Hamsun also published a volume of poems, *Det vilde Kor* [The Wild Chorus].

Hamsun's later works focused less on individual characters and more on broad attacks on civilization. Apart from *Marken's Grøde* one should mention *Børn av Tiden* (1913) [*Children of the Age*], *Segelfoss By* (1915) [*Segelfoss Town*], *Landstrykere* (1927) [*Vagabonds*], *August* (1930), *Men Livet lever* (1933) [*The Road leads on*], and *Ringen sluttet* (1936) [*The Ring is Closed*].

Hamsun's admiration for Germany, which was of long standing, made him sympathetic toward the Nazi invasion of Norway in 1940. After the war he was sentenced to the loss of his property, temporarily put under psychiatric observation, and spent his last years in poverty. A fifteen-volume edition of his complete works was published in 1954, two years after his death.

Literature 1921

ANATOLE FRANCE

(pen name of Jacques Anatole Thibault)

in recognition of his brilliant literary achievements, which are characterized
y nobility of style, magnanimous human sympathy, charm, and a true French
temper»

Presentation

by E. A. Karlfeldt, Permanent Secretary of the Swedish Academy

Anatole France was no longer a young man when, in 1881, he captured the attention of the literary public in France and subsequently in the civilized world with his curious novel, *Le Crime de Sylvestre Bonnard*. He had behind him a long stretch of years during which his development had been carried on without attracting wide attention. But if, during this period of slow growth, his literary efforts had been infrequent and not very energetic, the work to which he had subjected his intellect, his thought, and his taste had been proportionately wider and more vigorous. No immoderate desire for fame moved him. Ambition seems to have played a small role in his life. Indeed, he tells the story that at the age of seven he wanted to be famous. Excited by the legends of saints told to him by his good, pious mother, he wanted to settle in the desert and as a hermit match the glory of St. Anthony and St. Jerome. His desert was the *Jardin des Plantes* where the huge beasts lived in houses and cages, and where God the Father seemed to him to raise his arms to heaven blessing the antelope, the gazelle, and the dove. His mother was frightened by such vanity but her husband soothed her: «My dear, you will see that at twenty he will be disgusted with fame.» «My father was not mistaken», France says. «Like the King of Yvetot, I lived quite well without fame and no longer had the least desire to engrave my name on the memory of men. As for the dream of becoming a hermit, I refashioned it every time I believed I felt life was thoroughly bad; in other words, I refashioned it every day. But every day nature took me by the ear and led me to the amusements in which our humble lives pass away.» At the age of fifteen the young Anatole France dedicated his first essay, «La Légende de Sainte Radegonde, Reine de France», to his father and his beloved mother. This work is now lost, but even much later, when his faith in saints had vanished, he was still able to write legends with a pen dipped in the gold of haloes.

The poet's star seems to have been illuminated first in that bright constellation bearing the name Anatole France. In the old library of his worthy father, he soon felt a thirst for knowledge, amidst the noble dust of old books. Into this shop, whose proud sign «Aux Armes de France» inspired father and son to take up the literary name, came collectors and bibliophiles to examine the recently acquired treasures and to discuss authors and editions. Thus the young Anatole, always a good listener, was initiated into the mysteries of erudition, a pursuit he considered the highest pleasure of a peaceful life. We need only look at the Abbé Coignard, all beaming as he leaves the grill room of the «Reine Pédauque» where he pays for the material pleasures of this world by giving some lessons to a young spit-turner and by dispensing the treasures of an eloquence full of wisdom, irony, and Christian faith; we see him turn toward the library to feast his spirit free of charge on the latest books arrived from Holland, the country of classical editions. And, bored with domestic tedium, here is Mr. Bergeret, who comes to pass the finest hours of his day in conversation with friends gathered around the library's display shelves. Anatole France is the poet of libraries and bookworms. His imagination revels in the visions of bibliophiles, as when he praises that marvellous *Astaracienne*, a giant collection of books and manuscripts in which a noble cabalist sought proofs to bolster his superstition. «More fervently than ever», says Coignard toward the end of his adventurous career, «I want to sit down behind a table, in some venerable gallery, where many choice books would be assembled in silence. I prefer their conversation to that of men. I have found diverse ways of life and I judge that the best way is to devote oneself to study, to support calmly one's part in the vicissitudes of life, and to prolong, by the spectacle of centuries and of empires, the brevity of our days.» Love of intellectual work is a fundamental characteristic of Anatole France's personal religion and just like his Abbé, he prefers, from the height of the ivory tower of knowledge and thought, to turn his gaze toward far-off times and countries. His irony lives in the present, his devotion in the past.

Yet though our existence is fragile, beauty lives everywhere, and for the writer it materializes in form and style. Anatole France's vast studies and great meditation have bestowed a rare solidity on his work, but no less serious is the labour he has devoted to the perfecting of his style. The language which he had to shape is one of the noblest; French is the most richly endowed daughter of the mother tongue Latin. It has served the greatest masters. Now grave, now merry, it possesses serenity and charm, strength and melody. In many places France calls it the most beautiful language on earth and lavishes the most tender epithets on it as to a beloved woman. But as a true son of the ancients, he wishes it *simplex munditiis*. He is an artist, certainly one of the greatest, but his art aspires to keep his language, through severe purification, as simple and, at the same time, as expressive as possible. In contemporary Europe, where flourishes a superficial dilettantism, dangerous for the purity of languages, his work is a richly instructive example of what art can do with true resources. His language is the classical French, the French of Fénélon and Voltaire, and rather than contribute new ornaments to it, he gives it a slightly archaic stamp which admirably suits his subjects, often taken from antiquity. His French is so transparent that one would like to apply to it what he said of Leila, daughter of Lilith, one of the luminous and fragile beings sprung from his imagination: «If crystal could speak, it would speak in this fashion.»

Let us recall now, for our own pleasure, some of the works which have secured for the name of Anatole France the world-wide renown which he has so little desired but which nevertheless he cannot avoid. By so doing we will often encounter France himself, for he is less inclined than most writers to hide behind his characters and words.

He is recognized as a master of the tale, which he has made a wholly personal genre, in which erudition, imagination, serene charm of style, and depth of irony and passion combine to produce marvellous effects. Who can ever forget his Balthazar? The Negro King of Ethiopia comes to pay a visit to Balkis, the beautiful Queen of Sheba, and soon wins her love. But shortly the fickle queen forgets him to give herself to another. Wounded to death physically and emotionally, Balthazar returns to his country to devote himself to the highest wisdom of the seers, astrology. Suddenly an astonishing and sublime light spreads over the intense gloom of his passion. Balthazar discovers a new star and, high in the heavenly concourse, the star speaks to him, and in the light it sheds he joins with two neighbouring kings. No longer can Balkis hold him. His soul is detached from voluptuousness and he undertakes the pursuit of the star. The star which spoke was no other than the star which led the Three Wise Men to the manger at Jerusalem.

Another time France opens before our eyes a mother-of-pearl casket filled with priceless jewels, chased by the hand of a master of antiquity. We find in it the legend, slightly ironic but most seductive, of Célestin and d'Amyers, of the old hermit and the young faun singing together the Easter Alleluia, the one exalting in the return of Christ and the other in the return of the sun, worshippers communing in a single innocent piety, reunited at last– under the alarmed eye of the historian–in a single sacred tomb. This story shows us France in a realm in which he delights, the realm between paganism

nd Christianity, where twilight and dawn are mingled, where satyrs meet
vith apostles, where sacred and profane animals wander, where ample ma-
erials are found to exercise his fantasy, his contemplation, and his spiritual
rony in all its nuances. One often does not know whether to call it fiction
r reality.

Romantic chastity is celebrated in the legends of the saints Oliverie and
Liberette, Euphrosine and Scolastica. These are pages taken from the chron-
cles of saints, literary pastiches perhaps, executed with talent and a sense
or the miraculous.

Still another time France takes us to the pits outside of Sienna where, in
he spring twilight, a sweet barefooted Carmelite narrates the story of St.
Francis of Assisi and St. Claire, the daughter of his soul, and that of the
holy satyr who served masters as different as Jupiter, Saturn, and the Gali-
ean, a profound if hardly edifying legend, but recounted by France in the
most exquisite style.

In his famous novel *Thaïs* (1890) he enthusiastically penetrates the Alexandrine world at the time when the scourging thorns of Christianity were
ravaging among the last effeminate survivors of Hellenic civilization. Ascet-
cism and voluptuousness are at their heights here, mysteries and aesthetic
orgies flower side by side, angels and demons incarnate press around the
Fathers of the Church and the neo-Hellenic philosophers, disputing over
human souls. The story is steeped in the moral nihilism of that era, but it
includes beautiful passages such as the magnificent descriptions of the desert
solitude in which the anchorites preach from atop their columns or are
ubject to nightmares in the mummies' tombs.

However, one must put *La Rôtisserie de la Reine Pédauque* (1893) [*At the
Sign of the Reine Pédauque*] in the first rank of Anatole France's novels. There
he has sketched a group of true-to-life characters, legitimate or natural offspring of his mind in their own colourful world. The Abbé Coignard is so
alive that one can study him as a real character who reveals all his complexity
only when one has penetrated his privacy. Perhaps others have had the same
experience I had. At first I had but little sympathy for this clumsy, loquacious
priest and doctor of theology, who has so little concern for his dignity that
sometimes he even steals or commits other equally heinous crimes, which
he nevertheless defends with shameless casuistry. But he improves on better
acquaintance, and I have learned to love him. He is not only a brilliant
sophist, but an infinitely amusing character who exercises his irony not only
no others but also on himself. There is profound humour in the contrast

between his lofty views and his shabby life, and one must regard him with the smiling tolerance of his creator. Coignard is one of the most remarkable figures in contemporary literature. He is a new and vigorous plant in the Rabelaisian vineyard.

A type at once grotesque and lovable is the cabalist of Astarac. The crude mystic evidently must be included in a novel dealing with eighteenth-century manners. But the beings this magician evokes are of a singularly ethereal species; freed of earthly bonds, he enjoys the sweet and useful society of salamanders and sylphs. As proof of the talents of these beings, d'Astarac tells how once a sylph obliged a French scholar by arranging delivery of a message to Descartes, who was then living in Stockholm where he was teaching philosophy to Queen Christine. Sworn enemy of superstition that he may be, Anatole France should be grateful to that superstition for all the happy suggestions it has given him for his work.

Admirably rendered is the accent of pious simplicity with which the Abbé's student, the young spit-turner, recounts all these turbulent events. When his master, revered despite everything, after having suffered to his last moments the assault of the powers of darkness, finally dies a holy death in a Church he had never ceased to recognize openly, the student traces in Latin an ingenuous epithet praising the Abbé's wisdom and virtues. The author himself, in a later work, delivers an obituary eulogy for his principal hero. Presenting him as a blend of an Epicurean with a St. Francis, one who scorned men tenderly, France speaks of his benevolent irony and his merciful scepticism. Aside from the religious aspect, this characterization applies equally well to Anatole France himself.

Let us accompany him then without fear in his philosophical strolls in the garden of Epicurus. He will teach us humility. He will say to us: the world is infinitely large and man is infinitely small. What do you imagine? Our ideals are luminous shades but it is in following them that we find our only true happiness. He will say that human mediocrity is widespread, but he will not exclude himself from it. We may reproach him for the sensuality that occupies too large a place in some of his works and for the hedonistic sentiments, for example, which he describes under the sign of the red lily of Florence, and which are not made for serious minds. He will reply, according to the maxims of his spiritual father, that the pleasures of the mind surpass by far those of the flesh, and the serene calm of the soul is the port into which the wise man steers his boat in order to escape the tempests of sensual life. We shall hear him express the wish that time, which deprives us of so many things, may allow us compassion for our fellow man, so that in our old age we do not find ourselves shut up as in a tomb.

Following this inclination Anatole France left his aesthetic seclusion, his «ivory tower», to throw himself into the social fray of his time, to clamour like Voltaire for the restoration of the rights of persons unjustly condemned as well as of his own wounded patriotism; and he has gone into the workers' quarters to look for means of reconciling classes and nations. His old age has not become a walled tomb. The end has been good for him. After having been accorded many sunny years at the court of the Graces, he still throws the glint of gay learning into the idealistic struggle that, at an advanced age, he wages against the decadence of societies and against materialism and the power of money. His activity in this regard does not interest us directly, but we obtain from it the inestimable advantage of being able to fix his literary image against the background of a lofty nobility of sentiments. There is nothing of the careerist about him. His much discussed work on Joan of Arc, which has cost him enormous toil and which was intended to tear the veil of mysticism from the inspired heroine of France and to restore her to nature, to real life, was a thankless enterprise in an era prepared to canonize her.

«The Gods are Athirst!» The great drama of the Revolution unfolds and, as with the battle of ideas, the trivial destinies of men are reflected in blood. Do not believe, however, that France would wish to present this squaring of accounts as being definitive. A century is far too short a period of time to permit delineating distinctly the march of men toward more tolerance and humanity. How have events fulfilled his predictions! Several years after the appearance of this book the great catastrophe occurred. What beautiful arenas have been prepared now for the games of salamanders! The smoke of battles still hangs over the earth. And out of the fog surge gnomes, sinister spirits of the earth. Are these the dead who return? Sombre prophets announce a new revelation. A wave of superstition threatens to flood the ruins of civilization. Anatole France wields the subtle and corrosive weapon which puts to flight the ghosts and the false saints. For our times, faith is infinitely necessary–but a faith purified by healthy doubts, by the spirit of clarity, a new humanism, a new Renaissance, a new Reformation.

Sweden cannot forget the debt which, like the rest of the civilized world, she owes to French civilization. Formerly we received in abundance the gifts of French Classicism like the ripe and delicate fruits of antiquity. Without them, where would we be? This is what we must ask ourselves today. In our time Anatole France has been the most authoritative representative of that civilization; he is the last of the great classicists. He has even been called the last European. And indeed, in an era in which chauvinism, the most criminal and stupid of ideologies, wants to use the ruins of the great destruction for the building of new walls to prevent free intellectual exchange between peoples, his clear and beautiful voice is raised higher than that of others, exhorting people to understand that they need one another. Witty, brilliant, generous, this knight without fear is the best champion in the sublime and incessant war which civilization has declared against barbarism. He is a marshal of the France of the glorious era in which Corneille and Racine created their heroes.

Today, as we in our old Germanic country award the world prize of the poets to this Gallic master, the faithful servant of truth and beauty, the heir of humanism, of the lineage of Rabelais, Montaigne, Voltaire, Renan, we think of the words he once spoke at the foot of Renan's statue–his profession of faith is complete in them: «Slowly but surely humanity realizes wise men's dreams.»

Mr. Anatole France – You have inherited that admirable tool, the French language, the language of a noble and classical nation, which is reverently guarded by the famous academy you adorn and is maintained by it in an enviable condition of purity. You have that brilliant tool of piercing sharpness, and in your hand it acquires a scintillating beauty. You have used it masterfully to cut out *chefs-d'oeuvre* very French in their style and refinement. But it is not your art alone that charms us: we revere your creative genius as well, and we have been enticed by the generous, compassionate heart which so many exalted pages of your works reveal.

Acceptance

I have cherished the prospect of visiting in the evening of my life your beautiful country which has brought forth brave men and beautiful women. With gratitude I receive the prize that crowns my literary career. I consider it an incomparable honour to have received this Prize established by a man of noble sentiment and awarded to me by judges so just and competent. Invited by you as a member of the French Academy to give advice on the Nobel Prize in Literature, I have several times had the pleasure of directing your choice. It happened in the case of Maeterlinck, who combines a brilliant style with thought of great independence; it also happened in the case of Romain Rolland, in whom you have acknowledged a lover of justice and peace and who has been able to defy unpopularity in order to remain a good man.

Perhaps I am overstepping the limits of my competence, if I now talk about the peace Prize of the Norwegian Storting. If I do it, nonetheless, it is to praise the choice that the Storting has made. I may perhaps be permitted to say that in my view you have honoured in Branting a statesman impassioned for justice. Would that the destinies of peoples could be guided by such men! The most horrible of wars has been followed by a peace treaty that is not a treaty of peace but a continuation of war. Unless common sense finally finds its place in the council chambers of ministers, Europe will perish. If one cannot with good reason hope for the triumph of union and harmony among the countries of Europe, I wish at least to believe, gentlemen, that under the influence of brave, just, and loyal men like you the good will sometimes prevail.

In the official record, the following event is reported: After Anatole France had received his Prize from the hands of the King, there occurred an incident which left a strong impression on all present. When the venerable writer had gone up to the rostrum again, he turned to Professor Walther

Nernst, Prize winner in Chemistry, and exchanged a long and cordial hand-shake with him. The Frenchman, the «last classic», and the German, the great scientist and representative of intellectual sobriety, the citizens of two countries which had for a long time been enemies, were united in a handshake –a profoundly symbolic gesture. The audience applauded, feeling that the two nations, which for years had fought against one another, had just met in reconciliation.

Biography

Anatole France, pseudonym for Jacques Anatole Thibault (1844–1924), was the son of a Paris book dealer. He received a thorough classical education at the Collège Stanislas, a boys' school in Paris, and for a while he studied at the École des Chartes. For about twenty years he held diverse positions, but he always had enough time for his own writings, especially during his period as assistant librarian at the Senate from 1876 to 1890. His literary output is vast, and though he is chiefly known as a novelist and storyteller, there is hardly a literary genre that he did not touch upon at one time or another. France is a writer in the mainstream of French classicism. His style, modelled on Voltaire and Fénélon, as well as his urbane scepticism and enlightened hedonism, continue the tradition of the French eighteenth century. This outlook on life, which appears in all his works, is explicitly expressed in a collection of aphorisms, *Le Jardin d'Épicure* (1895) [*The Garden of Epicurus*].

France had written several stories and novels before he achieved his first great success with *Le Crime de Sylvestre Bonnard* (1881). The novel received a prize from the Académie Française, of which France became a member in 1896.

In 1885 he published *Le Livre de mon ami* [*My Friend's Book*], a kind of autobiographical novel, which he continued with *Pierre Nozière* (1899), *Le Petit Pierre* (1918), and *La Vie au fleur* (1922) [*The Bloom of Life*]. From 1888 to 1892 France was the literary critic of the newspaper *Le Temps*. His reviews, inspired by the scepticism of Renan, but highly subjective, were collected in four volumes under the title *La Vie littéraire* (1888–92) [*On Life and Letters*]. About this time France turned sharply against the naturalism of Zola. His own work of this period consists of historical fiction that evokes past civilizations with great charm and deep insight. The period of transition from paganism to Christianity was one of his favourites. In 1889 appeared *Balthazar*, a fanciful version of the story of one of the Magi, and in 1890 *Thaïs*, the story of the conversion of an Alexandrian courtesan during the Christian era. *L'Étui de nacre* (1892) [*Mother of Pearl*] is the story of a hermit and a faun, an ironic conjunction typical of France's art.

In 1893 France published his most celebrated novel, *La Rôtisserie de la Reine Pédauque* [*At the Sign of the Reine Pédauque*], a vast tableau of life in eighteenth-century France. The central figure of the novel, the Abbé Coignard, a complex, ironical, and lovable character, reappears in *Les Opinions de Jérôme Coignard* (1893) and the collection of stories *Le Puits de Sainte Claire* (1895) [*The Well of Saint Claire*]. With the tragic love story, *Le Lys rouge* (1894) [*The Red Lily*], France returned to a contemporary subject and in the following years wrote *Histoire contemporaine* (1896–1901), a group of prose works, not really novels, that have their unity in the character of Professor Bergeret, one of France's most famous creations.

In his later years France became increasingly interested in social questions. He protested the verdict in the Dreyfus case and developed some sympathies for socialism. Among his last important works were a biography of Joan of Arc (1908), *Les Dieux ont soif* (1912) [*The Gods are Athirst*], and *La Révolte des anges* (1914) [*The Revolt of the Angels*]. The collected works of Anatole France were published in twenty-five volumes between 1925 and 1935.

Literature 1922

JACINTO BENAVENTE

«for the happy manner in which he has continued the illustrious traditions of the Spanish drama»

Presentation

by Per Hallström, Chairman of the Nobel Committee of the Swedish Academy

Jacinto Benavente has devoted his imaginative gifts mainly to the theatre, and it seems as if he has systematically guided the course of his development in this direction through many varieties of experience. But with this imaginative artist, system seems to be a free and direct expression of his whole being. It appears that no one could have reached his goal with less effort and brooding in comparison with the value of the achievement.

The feeling which has carried him on has also been of an unusually complete and harmonious nature: it is not only the dramatic art and the atmosphere of the theatre that he has loved; he has cherished an equally warm affection for life outside, for the world of realities which it was his task to bring to the stage. It is not a matter of mere uncritical and superficial worship of life. He has observed his world with extremely clear and keen eyes, and what he has seen he has measured and weighed with an alert and flexible intelligence. He has not allowed himself to be duped either by men or by ideas, not even by his own ideas or his own pathos. Nevertheless, he does not strike one as being in the least bitter, or even blasé.

His writing has thus obtained its most distinctive quality–grace. This is such a rare value, especially in our own times, that there is little demand for it on the market and it is not recognized by most people. Grace, however, is as precious as it is uncommon. It is the token of the balance of powers, of the self-discipline and assurance of art, especially when it is not an end in itself and a mere frivolity, but when, without apparent effort, it stamps its mark on the entire form-giving process. It does not, then, merely play on the surface, affecting the style; it also determines each proportion in the treatment of the subject and every line in its depiction.

This is precisely the case with Benavente. The effect he attains may vary greatly in strength, but it is based on unfailing tact and strict loyalty to the subject. He gives what the subject is able to give without effort and without bombast. The fare he provides may be more or less rich and interesting, but it is always unadulterated. This is a classic feature in Benavente.

Nevertheless, his bent is above all realistic, if we eliminate from that label

ll the customary flavour of social tendency, commonplace philosophy, or
ross striving for effect. To reproduce the wealth and mobility of life, the
lay of characters, and the struggle between wills, in a way that comes as
ear truth as possible – that is his chief aim. When he aims at something
eyond this – to stimulate thought, to solve problems, to demolish pre-
udices, to enlarge human sympathy–he does so with the most scrupulous
are not to tamper with the objective accuracy of the literary description.
He exercizes this unusual discipline even when he is faced with the strongest
emptation for a dramatist – dramatic and scenic effect. However easily a
cene could be made more telling by increasing the tension of the conflict
nd plot, by putting on more flaring colours, by flogging up the emotions
o their highest pitch, Benavente never does this at the expense of truth:
e permits no blurring of the tone. He is a rare example of a born dramatist,
ne whose imagination, by itself, creates in accordance with the laws of the
tage, but yet avoids anything theatrical as fully as all other false conventions.

His activity lies especially in comedy, but that term in Spanish is more
nclusive than with us; it comprises what we may in general call middle-
lass plays without tragic conclusions. If there is such a conclusion, the pieces
re called dramas, and Benavente has also written such plays, including the
emarkable and moving play, *La Malquerida* (1913) [The Wrongly Loved].
He has also composed many romantic and fantastic pieces, among which
re exquisite achievements of poetic art, especially on a small scale.

But his central significance lies in his comedies, which, as we have seen,
nay well be as serious as they are gay; and in the short forms of comedy,
which in Spanish literature have been developed into special species with
ld and glorious traditions. In the latter Benavente is an enchanting master
ecause of his unlaboured wit and comic verve, his radiant good nature,
nd his grace, which combines all these qualities. I have time for only a few
ames: *De pequeñas causas* (1908) [For Small Reasons]; *El amor asusta* (1907)
Love Frightens]; *No fumadores* (1904) [Smoking Prohibited]. But there are
nany others, an entire treasury of merry jest, where the battle is waged so
ightly and so elegantly that it is always good-tempered, however sharp the
weapon itself may be.

In the larger works we encounter an amazing range of spheres of life and
ubject matter. They are taken from peasant life, from all circles of society
n the town, from the artist's world down to the travelling circus people
whom the poet embraces with a strong human sympathy and whom he
values more highly than many other classes.

But it is mainly the life of the upper classes that he has treated in its two characteristic centres, Madrid and Moraleda, the latter a place not found on the map, but which in its sunny and alluring variety comprises the typical features of a provincial town in Castile. In *La farándula* (1897) [The Company of Comedians] the ambitious politician goes to this town in order to rally and to gain the support of the uncorrupted energies of the people for a somewhat vaguely defined ideal; in the play *La Gobernadora* (1901) [The Governor's Wife], conceived ambition dreams of a larger stage for its greater talents. Moraleda is really a planetary world, which is attracted and illuminated by Madrid and does not reveal the full force of its comedy except in comparison with Madrid.

The capital and its spiritual content are made understandable much more fully through personal vicissitudes of fortune which are determined, as are its fashions and its culture, by the strata of its society. We see a distinct development in the art of Benavente. He begins by stressing the description of environment, with an abundant wealth of colour and life and features that reveal character. The dramatic element proper—unsought, like all the rest of the apparatus—exists for the most part merely to keep the action going. Its function is to arrange the whirl of life in a picture, composed in groups, with strong individual scenes. He has taken pains to create a faithful and artistic mirror of reality, which is then left to speak for itself.

Later his composition becomes more rigid. Although it is arranged firmly around a stronger, deeper, and more spiritual dramatic conflict, it is, nevertheless, almost as simple as when Benavente was merely writing episodes describing society. There is nothing artificial, nothing abstract and isolated in the human fates which are represented. As before, they are still connected with the world around them, but the light is strictly limited, revealing only what is central from a dramatic point of view. The sharp characterization is carried just far enough to make the action clear; the psychology is merely a means, not an end. Nothing is laboriously prepared beforehand, nothing strikes one really as being prepared at all: every feature in the action comes, as it were, with the improvisation of life and may take one by surprise until one has reflected for a moment, just as happens in life itself. The technique, too, is purely realistic and has not searched for models in ancient tragedy. Summing up the past is not the main function of this kind of drama, nor is the dialogue a kind of cross-examination to discover the past. The required discoveries are made by life itself by means of the unforced course of the action.

Broadly speaking, Benavente does not seek to harrow the spectator; his
bject is a solution of conflicts that is harmonious even in melancholy and
orrow. This harmony is usually gained by resignation, not weary or aloof
r pathetic, and without great gestures. The characters suffer, tear at their
onds, are attracted by fortune (the way to which is to pass over others'
ortune), wrestle in conflicts, measure their world and themselves, and gain
clearer and wider vision through their constraint. That which has the last
vord is not passion, in fact not the ego at all, but the spiritual value that
roves so great that, were it lost, the ego would be poor and fortune empty.
he decision is made without capitulation, merely through the fact that the
ersonality is face to face with the consequences of its choice of fate and
hooses freely, on the basis of instinctive feeling rather than in accordance
vith theories.

I have time for only one or two titles of his strange, simple, and quiet
dramas: *Alma triumfante* (1902) [Conquering Soul], *La propria estimacion*
1915) [Self-respect], and *Campo de armiño* (1916) [The White Scutcheon].
There are many others of equal value which are more or less like these. The
distinctive mark of them all is a peculiarly pure humanity, which at first
glance is surprising in the keen and flashing satirist, while the moderation
nd the freedom from all sentimentality in the mode of expression are in
complete accordance with his schooling. As a matter of fact his qualities go
vell together: as his grace of form is a classic feature, so are his feeling and
is insight classic, strictly schooled, well balanced, farsighted, and clear. His
implicity of expression and hushed tone come from the same source.

Nevertheless, Teutonic readers are often reminded, even when it comes
to an art as good as this, that it has sprung from a national temperament other
than ours and from other poetic traditions. The kind of lyric we desire, at
least in the atmosphere of the world of drama, is on the whole probably unknown to the Romance nations. Half-light, both in nature and in the human
soul, is lacking in them: all that human beings contain is expressed, or it
seems that it *can* be expressed. Their thoughts may have brilliance, rapidity,
and, of course, clarity; but they strike us as lacking in power, as belonging
to a somewhat more vacant atmosphere, and as having less life in their inner
being. What southerners say of our art may reveal equally great defects;
but we must mutually accustom ourselves to admire what we understand
and to leave outside our aesthetic judgments things which, for the reasons
mentioned, fail to satisfy us.

In the works in which the Spaniard Benavente has abandoned his comedy descriptive of society and individuals, and instead has ranged over large complexes of ideas and has sought to interpret all the unrest and yearning of our times, we cannot follow him with the admiration that has been bestowed upon him by his countrymen. This is true of *El collar de estrellas* (1915) [The Belt of Stars] and several other pieces.

I have not dwelt on the limitations of his art, but sought to indicate the central qualities of his craftsmanship in his country and in his time. I believe that scarcely any other contemporary dramatist has anywhere captured the life about him in such a many-sided and faithful manner and given it a form so immediate and, through its simple and noble art, so durable. The traditions of Spanish poetry comprise a strong, bold, and sound realism, a prolific power of growth, and an inimitable charm in the comic spirit which is merry and built on realities, not on conversational wit. Benavente has shown that he belongs to this school and, in a form peculiar to himself, has worked out a modern comedy of character containing much of the classic spirit. He has proved himself to be a worthy adherent of an ancient and elevated style of poetry; and that is to say a great deal.

Acceptance

by Count de Torata, Spanish Ambassador

t is difficult to express the deep satisfaction I feel today. It would take Bena-vente's talent to come up to the level of my task and that of my audience. Also, I doubly regret the absence of the great author, for my sake as well as yours. The honour you have so rightfully bestowed on Jacinto Benavente you have also bestowed on Spain and all those countries in which our lan-guage is spoken, some of whose representatives I am happy to see among us. I hope that this Prize will contribute to a strengthening of the ties which unite us, to a mutual understanding between our countries, to reinforcing the cordiality of our friendship. Finally, permit me to express all the admira-tion and affection I feel for your country.

Prior to the acceptance, Professor H. G. Söderbaum made the following remarks: «The art of poetry has this year donned the gleaming attire of drama and greets us from the far-reaching lands where the noble speech of Castile, the mother tongue of Lope de Vega and Calderon, forms the means of communicating thought for a considerable part of the population of our globe.

It has been said that ‹the business of the dramatist is to keep himself out of sight and to let nothing appear but his characters›. We regret that circum-stances have compelled the Prize winner in Literature to follow this rule so literally that on this occasion also he has kept out of sight; but we hope that the near future will give us the opportunity of forming a closer acquaintance with him and also with his work.»

Biography

Jacinto Benavente (1866–1954), the son of a well-known pediatrician, was born in Madrid. He studied law, but when his father died and left him with a comfortable income, he abandoned his studies and travelled widely in France, England, and Russia. On his return to Spain he edited, and contributed to, several newspapers and journals. He published a collection of poems (1893) and achieved some fame with *Cartas de mujeres* (1892–93) [Women's Letters], a series of women's letters, which was followed by another series in 1902. These letters gave Benavente a reputation as a brilliant stylist. His career as a dramatist began in 1892 with a collection of plays under the title «The Fantastic Theatre», but his first successes were *El nido ajeno* (1894) [Another's Nest] and *Gente conocida* (1896) [High Society], a satire of Madrid society. Benavente's plays deal with all strata of life; they are both serious and comic, realistic and fantastic, but it is chiefly as a writer of comedies of manners and of one-act farces that he made his name. His comedies usually take place in Madrid or in Moraleda, an imaginary provincial town in Castile. Whereas in his earlier plays Benavente had been chiefly interested in giving a faithful portrait of society, his later works show an increasing concern for a tight dramatic structure.

Benavente is best known for such plays as *La Gobernadora* (1901) [The Governor's Wife], *Rosas de otoño* (1905) [Autumnal Roses], and particularly *Señora ama* (1908) [The Lady of the House] and *La Malquerida* (1913) [The Wrongly Loved], two psychological dramas which take place in a rural atmosphere. *Los intereses creados* (1907) [*The Bonds of Interest*] has repeatedly been called Benavente's masterpiece, and it is certainly, of all his plays, the one that has most often been seen on the stage. A note of ironic resignation marks the delicate allegory of this play, the thesis of which affirms the necessity of evil. Mention should also be made of the play *Hijos, padres de sus padres* [*Sons, Fathers of Their Parents*], which appeared in the year of Benavente's death. His collected plays were published in ten volumes between the years 1941 and 1955.

Literature 1923

WILLIAM BUTLER YEATS

*for his always inspired poetry, which in a highly artistic form gives expression
to the spirit of a whole nation»*

Presentation

by Per Hallström, Chairman of the Nobel Committee of the Swedish Academy

Very early, in the first bloom of youth, William Butler Yeats emerged as a poet with an indisputable right to the name; his autobiography shows that the inner promptings of the poet determined his relations to the world even when he was a mere boy. He has developed organically in the direction indicated by his emotional and intellectual life from the very beginning.

He was born in an artistic home–in Dublin–thus beauty naturally became a vital necessity for him. He showed artistic powers, and his education was devoted to the satisfying of this tendency; little effort was made to secure traditional schooling. He was educated for the most part in England, his second fatherland; nonetheless his decisive development was linked to Ireland, chiefly to the comparatively unspoiled Celtic district of Connaught where his family had their summer home. There he inhaled the imaginative mysticism of popular belief and popular stories which is the most distinctive feature of his people, and amidst a primitive nature of mountain and sea he became absorbed in a passionate endeavour to capture its very soul.

The soul of nature was to him no empty phrase, for Celtic pantheism, the belief in the existence of living, personal powers behind the world of phenomena, which most of the people had retained, seized hold of Yeats' imagination and fed his innate and strong religious needs. When he came nearest to the scientific spirit of his time, in zealous observations of the life of nature, he characteristically concentrated on the sequence of various bird notes at daybreak and the flight of moths as the stars of twilight were kindled. The boy got so far in his intimacy with the rhythm of the solar day that he could determine the time quite exactly by such natural signs. From this intimate communion with the sounds of morning and nighttime, his poetry later received many of its most captivating traits.

He abandoned his training in the fine arts soon after he had grown up in order to devote himself to poetry, for which his inclination was strongest. But this training is evident throughout his whole career, both in the intensity with which he worships form and personal style and, still more, in the paradoxically audacious solution of problems in which his acute but fragmen-

:ary philosophical speculation sought its way to what he needed for his own peculiar nature.

The literary world he entered, when he settled down in London at the end of the eighties, did not offer him much positively, but it at least offered him fellowship in opposition, which to pugnacious youth seems particularly dear. It was filled with weariness and rebellion toward the spirit of the times which had prevailed just before, namely that of dogmatic natural science and naturalistic art. There were few whose hostility was so deeply grounded as that of Yeats, altogether intuitive, visionary, and indomitably spiritualistic as he was.

He was disturbed not only by the cocksureness of natural science and the narrowness of reality-aping art; even more, he was horrified by the dissolution of personality and the frigidity which issued from scepticism, by the desiccation of imagination and emotional life in a world which at best had faith only in a collective and automatic progression to the sacred land of Cockaigne. Events proved him to be terribly right: the «paradise» which could be reached by humanity with such schooling, we have now the dubious advantage of enjoying.

Even more beautiful kinds of social utopianism, represented by the greatly admired poet William Morris, did not captivate such an individualist as young Yeats. Later he found his way to the people, and then not as an abstract conception, but as the Irish people, to whom he had been close as a child. What he sought in that people was not the masses stirred by present-day demands, but an historically developed soul which he wished to arouse to more conscious life.

In the intellectual unrest of London, things nationally Irish remained dear to Yeats's heart; this feeling was nurtured by summer visits to his homeland and by comprehensive studies of its folklore and customs. His earlier lyrics are almost exclusively built on his impressions from these. His early poems immediately won high esteem in England because the new material, with its strong appeal to the imagination, received a form which, despite its special characteristics, was nevertheless linked closely with several of the noblest traditions of English poetry. The blending together of Celtic and English, which had never been successfully effected in the political sphere, became a reality here in the world of poetic imagination—a symptom of no small spiritual significance.

However much Yeats had read of English masters, his verse has a new character. The cadence and the colours have changed, as if they had been moved to another air – that of the Celtic twilight by the sea. There is a greater element of song than is usual in modern English poetry. The music is more melancholy, and, under the gentle rhythm, which for all its freedom moves as securely as a sleepwalker, we have a hint of yet another rhythm with the slow breathing of the wind and the eternal pulse of the powers of nature. When this art reaches its highest level it is absolutely magical, but it is seldom easy to grasp. It is indeed often so obscure that an effort is needed to understand it. This obscurity lies partly in the mysticism of the actual subject, but perhaps just as much in the Celtic temperament, which seems to be more distinguished by fire, delicacy, and penetration than by clearness. But no small part may have been played by the tendencies of the time: symbolism and *l'art pour l'art*, chiefly absorbed by the task of finding the boldly appropriate word.

Yeats's association with the life of a people saved him from the barrenness which attended so much of the effort for beauty that marked his age. Around him as the central point and leader arose, within a group of his countrymen in the literary world of London, that mighty movement which has been named the Celtic Revival and which created a new national literature, an Anglo-Irish literature.

The foremost and most versatile poet of this group was Yeats. His rousing and rallying personality caused the movement to grow and flower very quickly, by giving a common aim to hitherto scattered forces or by encouraging new forces previously unconscious of their existence.

Then, too, the Irish Theatre came into existence. Yeats's active propaganda created both a stage and a public, and the first performance was given with his drama *The Countess Cathleen* (1892). This work, extraordinarily rich in poetry, was followed by a series of poetic dramas, all on Irish subjects drawn mainly from the old heroic sagas. The most beautiful among these are *Deirdre* (1907), the fateful tragedy of the Irish Helen; *The Green Helmet* (1910), a merrily heroic myth of a peculiarly primitive wildness; and above all *The King's Threshold* (1904), where the simple material has been permeated by thought of a rare grandeur and depth. The quarrel about the place and rank of the bard at the king's court here gives rise to the ever-burning question as to how much spiritual things are to hold good in our world, and whether they are to be received with true or false faith. With the claims on which the hero stakes his life, he defends in the supremacy of poetry all that makes the life of man beautiful and worthy. It would not become all poets to put forward such claims, but Yeats could do so: his idealism has never been

dulled, nor has the severity of his art. In these dramatic pieces his verse attains a rare beauty and sureness of style.

Most enchanting, however, is his art in *The Land of Heart's Desire* (1894),
which has all the magic of fairy poetry and all the freshness of spring, in
its clear but as it were dreamy melody. Dramatically, also, this work is one
of his finest; and it might be called the flower of his poetry, had he not also
written the little prose drama *Cathleen ni Hoolihan* (1902), which is at once
his simplest folk play and his most classically perfect work.

Here more powerfully than anywhere else he touches the patriotic string.
The subject is Ireland's struggle for liberty throughout the ages, and the chief
personage is Ireland herself, impersonated by a wandering beggar woman.
But we hear no simple tone of hatred, and the profound pathos of the piece
is more restrained than in any other comparable poem. We hear only the
purest and highest part of the nation's feeling; the words are few and the
action the simplest possible. The whole thing is greatness without a touch
of affectation. The subject, having come to Yeats in a dream, has retained
its visionary stamp of being a gift from above—a conception not foreign to
Yeats's aesthetic philosophy.

Much more might be said of Yeats's work, but it must suffice to mention
the ways followed by his dramas of recent years. They have often been romantic by virtue of their strange and uncommon material, but they have
generally striven after classic simplicity of form. This classicism has been
gradually developed into bold archaism; the poet has sought to attain the
primitive plasticity found in the beginning of all dramatic art. He has devoted much intensive, acute thought to the task of emancipating himself
from the modern stage, with its scenery that disturbs the picture called up
by the imagination, with its plays whose features are necessarily exaggerated
by the footlights, with its audience's demand for realistic illusion. Yeats
wishes to bring out the poem as it was born in the poet's vision; he has given
form to this vision following Greek and Japanese models. Thus he has revived
the use of masks and has found a great place for the actors' gestures to the
accompaniment of simple music.

In the pieces thus simplified and brought to a strict stylistic unity, whose
subjects are still taken by preference from the hero legends of Ireland, he has
sometimes attained a fascinating effect, even for the mere reader, both in
the highly compressed dialogue and in the choruses with their deep lyrical
tone. All this, however, is in its period of growth, and it is not yet possible
to decide whether the sacrifices made are fully compensated for by what

has been gained. These pieces, though in themselves highly noteworthy, will probably find greater difficulty in becoming popular than the earlier ones.

In these plays as well as in his clearest and most beautiful lyrics, Yeats has achieved what few poets have been able to do: he has succeeded in preserving contact with his people while upholding the most aristocratic artistry. His poetical work has arisen in an exclusively artistic milieu which has had many perils; but without abjuring the articles of his aesthetic faith, his burning and questing personality, ever aiming at the ideal, has contrived to keep itself free from aesthetic emptiness. He has been able to follow the spirit that early appointed him the interpreter of his country, a country that had long waited for someone to bestow on it a voice. It is not too much to call such a life's work great.

Acceptance

have been all my working life indebted to the Scandinavian nation. When
was a very young man, I spent several years writing in collaboration with
friend the first interpretation of the philosophy of the English poet Blake.
Blake was first a disciple of your great Swedenborg and then in violent revolt
nd then half in revolt, half in discipleship. My friend and I were constantly
driven to Swedenborg for an interpretation of some obscure passage, for
Blake is always in his mystical writings extravagant, paradoxical, obscure.
Yet he has had upon the last forty years of English imaginative thought the
influence which Coleridge had upon the preceding forty; and he is always
in his poetry, often in his theories of painting, the interpreter or the antagonist
of Swedenborg. Of recent years I have gone to Swedenborg for his own
sake, and when I received your invitation to Stockholm, it was to his biography that I went for information. Nor do I think that our Irish theatre
could have ever come into existence but for the theatre of Ibsen and Bjørnson.
And now you have conferred upon me this great honour. Thirty years ago
a number of Irish writers met together in societies and began a remorseless
criticism of the literature of their country. It was their dream that by freeing
it from provincialism they might win for it European recognition. I owe
much to those men, still more to those who joined our movement a few
years later, and when I return to Ireland these men and women, now growing old like myself, will see in this great honour a fulfilment of that dream.
in my heart know how little I might have deserved it if they had never
existed.

Prior to Mr. Yeats's acceptance, Einar Lönnberg, President of the Academy
of Sciences, addressed the Irish writer: «Mr. Yeats – A worthier tongue than
mine has already given us a review of your literary work. What more, then,
can I do on this occasion than express our admiration and thank you for
the beautiful visions you have revealed to us from the Emerald Isle? We

have delighted in listening to the tales of the fairies and elves, with which
you have made us acquainted. We have been especially charmed by your
poem about the little ‹silver trout›. In another of your poems you have said
‹Time drops in decay / Like a candle burnt out›. It is true, but we should
be happy if this day would remain long in your memory, as it certainly will
in ours.»

The Irish Dramatic Movement

Nobel Lecture*, December 15, 1923

I have chosen as my theme the Irish Dramatic Movement because when I remember the great honour that you have conferred upon me, I cannot forget many known and unknown persons. Perhaps the English committees would never have sent you my name if I had written no plays, no dramatic criticism, if my lyric poetry had not a quality of speech practised upon the stage, perhaps even – though this could be no portion of their deliberate thought – if it were not in some degree the symbol of a movement. I wish to tell the Royal Academy of Sweden of the labours, triumphs, and troubles of my fellow workers.

The modern literature of Ireland, and indeed all that stir of thought which prepared for the Anglo-Irish War, began when Parnell fell from power in 1891. A disillusioned and embittered Ireland turned away from parliamentary politics; an event was conceived and the race began, as I think, to be troubled by that event's long gestation. Dr. Hyde founded the Gaelic League, which was for many years to substitute for political argument a Gaelic grammar, and for political meetings village gatherings, where songs were sung and stories told in the Gaelic language. Meanwhile I had begun a movement in English, in the language in which modern Ireland thinks and does its business; founded certain societies where clerks, working men, men of all classes, could study those Irish poets, novelists, and historians who had written in English, and as much of Gaelic literature as had been translated into English. But the great mass of our people, accustomed to interminable political speeches, read little, and so from the very start we felt that we must have a theatre of our own. The theatres of Dublin had nothing about them that we could call our own. They were empty buildings hired by the English travelling companies and we wanted Irish plays and Irish players. When we thought of these plays we thought of everything that was romantic and poetical, for the nationalism we had called up – like that every generation had called up

* Yeats maintained that his lecture was written down from memory. It seems therefore appropriate to incorporate here certain improvements he made in a version published in *The Bounty of Sweden* (The Cuala Press, Dublin, 1925).

in moments of discouragement–was romantic and poetical. It was not, however, until I met in 1896 Lady Gregory, a member of an old Galway family, who had spent her life between two Galway houses, the house where she was born and the house into which she was married, that such a theatre became possible. All about her lived a peasantry who told stories in a form of English which has much of its syntax from Gaelic, much of its vocabulary from Tudor English, but it was very slowly that we discovered in that speech of theirs our most powerful dramatic instrument, not indeed until she began to write. Though my plays were written without dialect and in English blank verse, I think she was attracted to our movement because their subject matter differed but little from the subject matter of the country stories. Her own house has been protected by her presence, but the house where she was born was burned down by incendiaries some few months ago; and there has been like disorder over the greater part of Ireland. A trumpery dispute about an acre of land can rouse our people to monstrous savagery, and if in their war with the English auxiliary police they were shown no mercy they showed none: murder answered murder. Yet ignorance and violence can remember the noblest beauty. I have in Galway a little old tower, and when I climb to the top of it I can see at no great distance a green field where stood once the thatched cottage of a famous country beauty, the mistress of a small local landed proprietor. I have spoken to old men and women who remembered her, though all are dead now, and they spoke of her as the old men upon the wall of Troy spoke of Helen; nor did man and woman differ in their praise. One old woman, of whose youth the neighbors cherished a scandalous tale, said of her, «I tremble all over when I think of her»; and there was another old woman on the neighbouring mountain who said, «The sun and the moon never shone on anybody so handsome, and her skin was so white that it looked blue, and she had two little blushes on her cheeks.» And there were men that told of the crowds that gathered to look at her upon a fair day, and of a man «who got his death swimming a river», that he might look at her. It was a song written by the Gaelic poet Raftery that brought her such great fame and the cottagers still sing it, though there are not so many to sing it as when I was young:

> O star of light and O sun in harvest,
> O amber hair, O my share of the world,
> It is Mary Hynes, the calm and easy woman,
> Has beauty in her body and in her mind.

It seemed as if the ancient world lay all about us with its freedom of imagination, its delight in good stories, in man's force and woman's beauty, and that all we had to do was to make the town think as the country felt; yet we soon discovered that the town could only think town thought.

In the country you are alone with your own violence, your own heaviness, and with the common tragedy of life, and if you have any artistic capacity you desire beautiful emotion; and, certain that the seasons will be the same always, care not how fantastic its expression.[1] In the town, where everybody crowds upon you, it is your neighbour not yourself that you hate and, if you are not to embitter his life and your own life, perhaps even if you are not to murder him in some kind of revolutionary frenzy, somebody must teach reality and justice. You will hate that teacher for a while, calling his books and plays ugly, misdirected, morbid or something of that kind, but you must agree with him in the end. We were to find ourselves in a quarrel with public opinion that compelled us against our own will and the will of our players to become always more realistic, substituting dialect for verse, common speech for dialect.

I had told Lady Gregory that I saw no likelihood of getting money for a theatre and so must put away that hope, and she promised to find the money among her friends. Her neighbour, Mr. Edward Martyn, paid for our first performances; and our first players came from England; but presently we began our real work with a little company of Irish amateurs.[2] Somebody had asked me at a lecture, «Where will you get your actors?» and I said, «I will go into some crowded room and put the name of everybody in it on a piece of paper and put all those pieces of paper into a hat and draw the first twelve.» I have often wondered at that prophecy, for though it was spoken probably to confound and confuse a questioner, it was very nearly fulfilled. Our two best men actors were not indeed chosen by chance, for one was a stage-struck solicitor's clerk and the other a working man who had toured Ireland in a theatrical company managed by a negro. I doubt if he had learned much in it, for its methods were rough and noisy, the negro whitening his face when he played a white man, and, so strong is stage convention, blackening it when he played a black man. If a player had to open a letter on the stage I have no doubt that he struck it with the flat of his hand, as I have seen players do in my youth, a gesture that lost its meaning generations ago when blotting paper was substituted for sand. We got our women, however, from a little political society which described its object as educating the children of the poor, which meant, according to its enemies, teaching them a catechism that began with this question, «What is the origin of evil?», and the answer, «England».

And they came to us for patriotic reasons and acted from precisely the same impulse that had made them teach, and yet two of them proved players of genius: Miss Allgood and Miss «Maire O'Neill». They were sisters, one all simplicity, her mind shaped by folk song and folk stories; the other sophisticated, lyrical, and subtle. I do not know what their thoughts were as that strange new power awoke within them, but I think they must have suffered from a bad conscience, a feeling that the old patriotic impulse had gone, that they had given themselves up to vanity or ambition. Yet I think it was that first misunderstanding of themselves that made their peculiar genius possible, for had they come to us with theatrical ambitions they would have imitated some well known English player and sighed for well known English plays. Nor would they have found their genius if we had not remained for a long time obscure like the bird within its shell, playing in little halls, generally in some shabby, out-of-the-way street. We could experiment and wait, with nothing to fear but political misunderstanding. We had little money and at first needed little, twenty-five pounds given by Lady Gregory and twenty pounds by myself and a few pounds picked up here and there. And our theatrical organization was preposterous, players and authors all sat together and settled by vote what play should be performed and who should play it. It took a series of disturbances, weeks of argument, during which no performance could be given, before Lady Gregory and John Synge and I were put in control. And our relations with the public were even more disturbed. One play was violently attacked by the patriotic press because it described a married peasant woman who had a lover, and when we published the old Aran folk tale upon which it was founded, the press said the story had been copied from some decadent author of Pagan Rome. Presently Lady Gregory wrote her first comedy. My verse plays were not long enough to fill an evening and so she wrote a little play on a country love story in the dialect of her neighbourhood. A countryman returns from America with a hundred pounds and discovers his old sweetheart married to a bankrupt farmer. He plays cards with the farmer and, by cheating against himself, gives him the hundred pounds. The company refused to perform that play because they said to admit an emigrant's return with a hundred pounds would encourage emigration. We produced evidence of returned emigrants with much larger sums but were told that only made the matter worse. Then after this interminable argument had worn us all out, Lady Gregory agreed to reduce the sum to twenty and the actors gave way. That little play was sentimental and conventional, but her next discovered her genius. She, too, had desired to serve, and that genius must have seemed miraculous to herself. She was in middle life and had written nothing but a volume of political memoirs and had no interest in the theatre.

Nobody reading today her *Seven Short Plays* can understand why one of them, now an Irish classic, *The Rising of the Moon*, could not be performed for two years because of political hostility. A policeman discovers an escaped Fenian prisoner and lets him free, because the prisoner has aroused with some old songs the half forgotten patriotism of his youth. The players would not perform it because they said it was an unpatriotic act to admit that a policeman was capable of patriotism. One well known leader of the mob wrote to me, «How can the Dublin mob be expected to fight the police if it looks upon them as capable of patriotism?» When performed at last the play was received with enthusiasm, but only to get us into new trouble. The chief Unionist Dublin newspaper denounced it for slandering his Majesty's forces, and Dublin Castle, the centre of English Government in Ireland, denied to us a privilege, which we had shared with the other Dublin theatres, of buying for stage purposes the cast off clothes of the police. Castle and Press alike knew that the police had frequently let off political prisoners but «that only made the matter worse». Every political party had the same desire to substitute for life, which never does the same thing twice, a bundle of reliable principles and assertions.[3] Nor did religious orthodoxy like us any better than political; my *Countess Cathleen* was denounced by Cardinal Logue as an heretical play, and when I wrote that we would like to perform «foreign masterpieces», a Nationalist newspaper declared that «a foreign masterpiece is a very dangerous thing». The little halls where we performed could hold a couple of hundred people at the utmost and our audience was often not more than twenty or thirty, and we performed but two or three times a month and during our periods of quarrelling not even that. But there was no lack of leading articles, we were from the first a recognised public danger. Two events brought us victory, a friend gave us a theatre, and we found a strange man of genius, John Synge. After a particularly angry leading article I had come in front of the curtain and appealed to the hundred people of the audience for their support. When I came down from the stage an old friend, Miss Horniman, from whom I had been expecting a contribution of twenty pounds, said, «I will find you a theatre.» She found and altered for our purpose what is now the Abbey Theatre, Dublin, and gave us a small subsidy for a few years.

I had met John Synge in Paris in 1896. Somebody had said, «There is an Irishman living on the top floor of your hotel; I will introduce you.» I was very poor, but he was much poorer. He belonged to a very old Irish family and though a simple, courteous man, remembered it and was haughty and lonely. With just enough to keep him from starvation, and not always from half starvation, he had wandered about Europe travelling third class or upon foot, playing his fiddle to poor men on the road or in their cottages. He was the man that we needed because he was the only man I have ever known incapable of a political thought or of a humanitarian purpose. He could walk the roadside all day with some poor man without any desire to do him good, or for any reason except that he liked him. He was to do for Ireland, though more by his influence on other dramatists than by his direct influence, what Robert Burns did for Scotland. When Scotland thought herself gloomy and religious, Providence restored her imaginative spontaneity by raising up Robert Burns to commend drink and the devil. I did not, however, see what was to come when I advised John Synge to go to a wild island off the Galway coast and study its life because that life «had never been expressed in literature». He had learned Gaelic at College, and I told him that, as I would have told it to any young man who had learned Gaelic and wanted to write. When he found that wild island he became happy for the first time, escaping as he said «from the nullity of the rich and the squalor of the poor». He had bad health, he could not stand the island hardship long, but he would go to and fro between there and Dublin.

Burns himself could not have more shocked a gathering of Scotch clergy than did he our players. Some of the women got about him and begged him to write a play about the rebellion of '98, and pointed out very truthfully that a play on such a patriotic theme would be a great success. He returned at the end of a fortnight with a scenario upon which he had toiled in his laborious way. Two women take refuge in a cave, a Protestant woman and a Catholic, and carry on an interminable argument about the merits of their respective religions. The Catholic woman denounces Henry VIII and Queen Elizabeth, and the Protestant woman the Inquisition and the Pope. They argue in low voices because one is afraid of being ravished by the rebels and the other by the loyal soldiers. But at last either the Protestant or the Catholic says that she prefers any fate to remaining any longer in such wicked company and climbs out. The play was neither written nor per-

ormed, and neither then nor at any later time could I discover whether
ynge understood the shock that he was giving. He certainly did not foresee
1 any way the trouble that his greatest play brought on us all.

When I had landed from a fishing yawl on the middle of the island of Aran,
few months before my first meeting with Synge, a little group of islanders,
who had gathered to watch a stranger's arrival, brought me to «the oldest
man upon the island». He spoke but two sentences, speaking them very
lowly, «If any gentleman has done a crime we'll hide him. There was a
gentleman that killed his father and I had him in my house three months
ill he got away to America.» It was a play founded on that old man's story
ynge brought back with him. A young man arrives at a little public house
nd tells the publican's daughter that he has murdered his father. He so tells
: that he has all her sympathy, and every time he retells it, with new exaggerations and additions, he wins the sympathy of somebody or other, for
: is the countryman's habit to be against the law. The countryman thinks
he more terrible the crime the greater must the provocation have been.
'he young man himself under the excitement of his own story becomes gay,
nergetic, and lucky. He prospers in love and comes in first at the local races
nd bankrupts the roulette table afterwards. Then the father arrives with his
ead bandaged but very lively, and the people turn upon the impostor. To
vin back their esteem he takes up a spade to kill his father in earnest, but
orrified at the threat of what had sounded so well in the story, they bind
im to hand over to the police. The father releases him and father and son
valk off together, the son, still buoyed up by his imagination, announcing
1at he will be master henceforth. Picturesque, poetical, fantastical, a master-
iece of style and of music, the supreme work of our dialect theatre, it roused
1e populace to fury. We played it under police protection, seventy police
1 the theatre the last night, and five hundred, some newspaper said, keeping
rder in the streets outside. It is never played before any Irish audience for
1e first time without something or other being flung at the players. In New
'ork a currant cake and a watch were flung, the owner of the watch claiming
. at the stage door afterwards. The Dublin audience has, however, long
nce accepted the play. It has noticed, I think, that everyone upon the stage
: somehow lovable and companionable, and that Synge described, through
n exaggerated symbolism, a reality which he loved precisely because he
oved all reality. So far from being, as they had thought, a politician working
1 the interests of England, he was so little a politician that the world merely
mused him and touched his pity. Yet when Synge died in 1910 opinion had

hardly changed, we were playing to an almost empty theatre and were continually denounced in the Press. Our victory was won by those who had learned from him courage and sincerity but belonged to a different school. Synge's work, the work of Lady Gregory, my own *Cathleen ni Houlihan* and my *Hour glass* in its prose form, are characteristic of our first ambition. They bring the imagination and speech of the country, all that poetical tradition descended from the middle ages, to the people of the town. Those who learned from Synge had often little knowledge of the country and always little interest in its dialect. Their plays are frequently attacks upon obvious abuses, the bribery at the appointment of a dispensary Doctor, the attempt of some local politician to remain friends with all parties. Indeed the young Ministers and party politicians of the Free State have had, I think, some of their education from our plays. Then, too, there are many comedies which are not political satires, though they are concerned with the life of the politic ridden people of the town. Of these Mr. Lennox Robinson's are the best known; his *Whiteheaded Boy* has been played in England and America. Of late it has seemed as if this school were coming to an end, for the old plots are repeated with slight variations and the characterization grows mechanical. It is too soon yet to say what will come to us from the melodrama and tragedy of the last four years, but if we can pay our players and keep our theatre open, something will come.⁴ We are burdened with debt, for we have come through war and civil war and audiences grow thin when there is firing in the streets. We have, however, survived so much that I believe in our luck, and think that I have a right to say I end my lecture in the middle or even perhaps at the beginning of the story. But certainly I have said enough to make you understand why, when I received from the hands of your King the great honour your Academy has conferred upon me I felt that a young man's ghost should have stood upon one side of me and at the other a living woman in her vigorous old age. I have seen little in this last week that would not have been memorable and exciting to Synge and to Lady Gregory, for Sweden has achieved more than we have hoped for our own country. I think most of all perhaps of that splendid spectacle of your court, a family beloved and able that has gathered about it not the rank only but the intellect of its country. No like spectacle will in Ireland show its work of discipline and of taste, though it might satisfy a need of the race no institution created by English or American democracy can satisfy.

Notes

1 I was in my Galway house during the first months of civil war, the railway bridges blown up and the roads blocked with stones and trees. For the first week there were no newspapers, no reliable news, we did not know who had won nor who had lost, and even after newspapers came, one never knew what was happening on the other side of the hill or of the line of trees. Ford cars passed the house from time to time with coffins, standing upon end between the seats, and sometimes at night we heard an explosion, and once by day saw the smoke made by the burning of a great neighbouring house. Men must have lived so through many tumultuous centuries. One felt an overmastering desire not to grow unhappy or embittered, not to lose all sense of the beauty of nature. A stare (our West of Ireland name for a starling) had built in a hole beside my window and I made these verses out of the feeling of the moment:

> The bees build in the crevices
> Of loosening masonry, and there
> The mother birds bring grubs and flies.
> My wall is loosening, honey bees
> Come build in the empty house of the stare.

> We are closed in, and the key turned
> On our uncertainty; somewhere
> A man is killed, or a house is burned,
> Yet no clear fact to be discerned:
> Come build in the empty house of the stare.

That is only the beginning but it runs on in the same mood. Presently a strange thing happened; I began to smell honey in places where honey could not be, at the end of a stone passage or at some windy turn of the road and it came always with certain thoughts. When I got back to Dublin I was with angry people, who argued over everything or were eager to know the exact facts. They were in the mood that makes realistic drama.

2 Our first performances were paid for by Mr. Edward Martyn, a Galway landowner with a house, part fourteenth century, part that pretentious modern Gothic once dear to Irish Catholic families. He had a great hall adorned

with repeating patterns by that dreary decorator Crace, where he played Palestrina upon an organ, and a study with pictures of the poets in poor stained glass, where he read Ibsen and the Fathers of the Church and nothing else. A sensible friendly man with intelligence, strength of purpose, and a charming manner, he shrank from women like a medieval monk and between him and all experience came one overwhelming terror–«If I do such and such a thing or read such and such a book I may lose my soul.» My *Countess Cathleen* and a play of his own were our first performances. My play's heroine, having sold her soul to the devil, gets it back again because «God only sees the motive not the deed» and her motive is to save starving people from selling their souls for their bodies' sake. When all our announcements had been made Martyn withdrew his support because a priest told him that the play was heretical. I got two priests to say that it was not and he was satisfied, for we have democratic ideals. He withdrew permanently, however, after a few months, foreseeing further peril to his soul. He died a couple of months ago and with him died a family founded in the twelfth century. An unhappy, childless, laborious, unfinished man, typical of an Ireland that is passing away.

3 Josef Strzygowski in his *Origin of Christian Church Art* (a translation of a series of lectures, delivered in Upsala in 1919) says that art «flourishes less at courts than anywhere else in the world. For at the seat of power everything is subordinated to politics; the forces willing to accept this fact are always welcome; those which are not willing must either emigrate or remain aloof». The danger to art and literature comes today from the tyranny and persuasions of revolutionary societies and forms of political and religious propaganda. The persuasion has corrupted much modern English literature; and during the twenty years that led up to our national revolution the tyranny wasted the greater part of the energy of Irish dramatists and poets. They had to remain perpetually on the watch to defend their creation; and the more natural the creation the more difficult the defence.

4 Since I gave my lecture we have produced *Juno and the Paycock* by Mr. O'Casey, the greatest success we have had for years. In this play, which draws its characters and scenes from the Dublin slums, a mind, not unlike that of Dostoevsky, looks upon the violence and tragedy of civil war. There is assassination, sudden poverty, and the humour of drunkards and the philosophy of wastrels, and there is little but the out-worn theme of seduction,

and perhaps a phrase or two of mechanical humour, to show that its author has not finished his artistic education. He is a working bricklayer who was taken out to be shot by English soldiers in mistake for somebody else, but escaped in a moment of confusion. He knows thoroughly the life which he describes.

Biography

William Butler Yeats (1865–1939) was born in Dublin. His father was a lawyer and a well-known portrait painter. Yeats was educated in London and in Dublin, but he spent his summers in the west of Ireland in the family's summer house at Connaught. The young Yeats was very much part of the *fin de siècle* in London; at the same time he was active in societies that attempted an Irish literary revival. His first volume of verse appeared in 1887, but in his earlier period his dramatic production outweighed his poetry both in bulk and in import. Together with Lady Gregory he founded the Irish Theatre, which was to become the Abbey Theatre, and served as its chief playwright until the movement was joined by John Synge. His plays usually treat Irish legends; they also reflect his fascination with mysticism and spiritualism. *The Countess Cathleen* (1892), *The Land of Heart's Desire* (1894), *Cathleen ni Houlihan* (1902), *The King's Threshold* (1904), and *Deirdre* (1907) are among the best known.

After 1910, Yeats's dramatic art took a sharp turn toward a highly poetical, static, and esoteric style. His later plays were written for small audiences; they experiment with masks, dance, and music, and were profoundly influenced by the Japanese Noh plays. Although a convinced patriot, Yeats deplored the hatred and the bigotry of the Nationalist movement, and his poetry is full of moving protests against it. He was appointed to the Irish Senate in 1922. Yeats is one of the few writers whose greatest works were written after the award of the Nobel Prize. Whereas he received the Prize chiefly for his dramatic works, his significance today rests on his lyric achievement. His poetry, especially the volumes *The Wild Swans at Coole* (1919), *Michael Robartes and the Dancer* (1921), *The Tower* (1928), *The Winding Stair and Other Poems* (1933), and *Last Poems and Plays* (1940), made him one of the outstanding and most influential twentieth-century poets writing in English. His recurrent themes are the contrast of art and life, masks, cyclical theories of life (the symbol of the winding stairs), and the ideal of beauty and ceremony contrasting with the hubbub of modern life.

Literature 1924

WLADYSLAW STANISLAW REYMONT

(pen name of Reyment)

«for his great national epic, The Peasants*»*

Critical Essay[*]

by Per Hallström, Chairman of the Nobel Committee of the Swedish Academy

This Polish work of imagination has its starting point in the naturalistic novel, especially in the form which that genre received from Zola in France. Reymont has acknowledged that the idea of his book was evoked by *La Terre*, not through his admiration of it, but through the indignation and opposition it provoked. He found in it a conventionalized, distorted, and coarse characterization of the class of society in which he had grown up and which he loved with all the warmth that had been cherished by his childhood memories. He knew this class of society from abundant experience, from within, and with full understanding – not, like Zola, merely through hasty journalistic studies made in accordance with a program mapped out beforehand with preconceived results; and he wished to describe it in its reality, without any distortion through theories. But Zola had a decisive influence on the work in a quite different and more positive fashion. *Chlopi* (1904–09) [*The Peasants*], in the final form in which we have it, would hardly be conceivable without the lessons that Reymont learned from Zola's work as a whole – its searching description of the environment, its orchestral mass effects, its uncompromising verism, and the harmonious working together of external nature and human life. Nevertheless *Chlopi*, rather than turning out to be a naturalistic novel, has taken on epic proportions – certainly naturalistic in method but epic in scope.

For us moderns that which most profoundly marks a narrative poem as an epic, is a certain completeness and harmony, a general impression of rest, however the various episodes may be charged with suffering and struggle. It is not easy to express this effect in a conceptual form, for it is our feelings that perceive it. It achieves its results mainly from the fact that all the elements of strife and unrest are gradually smoothed out before us, like waves that wrestle with one another; the circles never reach as far as the tranquil horizon that bounds the poem; the unrest puts no question and sends no lament beyond that limit. The world that we have before our eyes is a

* Since no official ceremony took place, the critical essay was prepared by Per Hallström in lieu of a presentation speech.

definite one and is unshakable in its foundations; but it is not a world of compulsion and imprisonment. It is wide enough for human beings to express themselves in action according to the measure of their powers. Hence the harmony of the poem. Whatever happiness is recorded, the most irremediable suffering–the disparity between given reality and ideal requirements–is not to be found there, or at least it does not reach consciousness. The most permanently bitter tragedy, that which from within shatters a being to fragments, has not yet been created; the figures we see are entire and simple and move in *one* piece. Whether the figures be large or small, whether their features be fair or foul, they assume a kind of plastic beauty and monumentality.

It is this that the Polish writer has attained in *Chlopi*; and that he achieved it, in spite of a quite modern training which scarcely promised to lead to such a goal, is surely due to the fact that his chosen subject moved of itself toward this happy form. He probably did not seek the form himself–that is evidenced by the rest of his very different production; but when it offered itself to him in the course of his work, he understood it and followed its laws. This is surely merit enough and worthy of great honour.

His Polish peasants possess in their primitive conditions, and perhaps only in consequence thereof, the simple nature, the archaism in their contours, demanded by epic art – a great aesthetic value, which, however, has been obtained at the expense of being defective in other ways. This throng of figures has extremely little of what ordinarily is called character. Among the men only few have even the raw material of character in mental energy and firmness; and their working up of this material inspires but little respect. The manliness which consists in self-discipline, a sense of responsibility, and a personal grasp of the idea of right, has barely attained any development beyond collective and vague mass feeling. What we see of the life of conscience is the common ground of the village, not the guarded estate of the individual. Consequently one must not expect more from the women: hence it is much that in one figure, the sorely tried Hanus, the pliant forces of her nature become welded together into a stubborn sense of duty.

There is really hardly any moral backbone to be found in this low-lying tract round the sluggishly flowing river. Passion bounces in men's wills like a storm in the reeds, and they bend before every breath of wind, and a spark sets everything ablaze. The sense of honesty is uncertain, perhaps chiefly because it has not had free air to grow in. From time immemorial this people has had to protect itself against oppression by those who owned the soil–

all they had to subsist on. And when the soil at last became theirs, the gift came from foreign masters, who grudged them a soul of their own. The passivity, fatalism, and naive good humour, which under similar circumstances were developed in their Slavonic brethren to the east, held no power in the Polish temperament. Here we meet instead a peculiar nervousness which is not elsewhere a characteristic of the peasant, and which readily expresses itself in anger and violent deeds. All their ill-treatment has not sufficed to crush their pride, but that pride is abundantly mixed with vanity; it is touchy, lacking in balance, and gives no trustworthy support to human dignity. Their virtues have as little root as those of children. They consist in directness, in easily stirred susceptibility, in inflexible and lively spirits: they point to a superfluity of unexhausted gifts; and over the whole there extends a never-failing charm, a certain glamour of nobility. But above all, these people appeal to us through their strong imaginative life. In their poverty and frailty they have windows opened to the world of dreams; and all that is tender and good and beautiful in them flourishes there.

The Church has preserved for them this city of refuge, and to her they are attached with a deep love, piety, and reverence; through her, they expect some day atonement and transfiguration; and in a poetical sense they are already partaking of these good things. By constantly returning to this feature Reymont has contrived to keep the air of beauty over his epic.

Without effort, he has found the gleam of heroism which an epic needs, although his subject matter did not provide him with heroic figures. Heroism was to be found only in their primitively strong, deep attachment to the soil, which gives and takes their lives and lends to their struggle and their love something of the greatness of the forces of nature. Epic breadth and greatness have been attained, too, through the simple touch of genius in the composition of the work, which has been cast in the form of a cycle of the seasons. Autumn, winter, spring, and summer, in symphonically balanced parts, give their contrasts and their harmony in a mighty hymn to life; and when the year has swung full circle in the vicissitudes of human fate, it continues in our imagination in constant novelty and constant recurrence. The episodes in the richly developed action do not occur once only: they have a typical validity. Whether they are idyllic or passionate, tragically wild or merrily diverting, they have all been turned to a rhythm of «Works and Days» in a kind of Hesiodic peasant-world: they have in them a dash of the eternal youth of the earth.

The monotony tending to threaten the peasant novel through its diffuseness of detail, has here generally been avoided by the range and the mobility of the material. Unity of style has been combined with an uncommon power and delight in colour in the painting of the several parts; and the characterization of the figures, in their dramatic working, has received due attention within the given frame. Everything gives the impression of a reality faithfully described – possibly with one exception, the chief female character Jagna, who is quite as much a symbol as a type. But the symbol is poetically justified. In fact, it is the poetry of the Polish soil and the Polish peasant woman, all the natural magic, the blind working of natural impulses, the pliancy and imaginativeness, the hunger for beauty, and the absence of responsibility, which flourish and intoxicate and are smirched and trampled in times of trouble and guilt. She is the embodiment of all the flaws that Reymont has revealed in his people, despite his love for them; yet she also represents all those qualities which are rich and splendid in human nature. He has made her the tragic heroine of his work; and if, there as elsewhere (and perhaps in consequence of a weakness he shares with the circles he describes), he has passed no clear judgment, he has not allowed any lessening of the tragic tension.

To sum up, this epic novel is characterized by an art so grand, so sure, so powerful, that we may predict a lasting value and rank for it, not only within Polish literature but also within the whole of that branch of imaginative writing which has here been given a distinctive and monumental shape.

Autobiography

I was born on May 6th, 1868, in the village of Kobielo Wielkie in that part of Poland which was under Russian rule.

My father was the church organist; the village curate was my mother's brother, a former monk from the order of Pijar, a very well educated and ascetic man who loved nothing but solitude. The most ardent Catholicism ruled in our house. We led a hard life, almost like peasants. My family had taken a very active part in the insurrections of 1863 against Russia; some of its members had been killed; one of my uncles had been condemned to forced labour in Siberia. My mother had done her share of collaborating by serving as a messenger between various armed detachments. During my childhood I had a long, dangerous spell of illness, and my health has always been delicate. I was hardly a year old when my uncle was transferred to a small locality called Tuszyn, very close to the great manufacturing town of Lodź. There my father acquired a few acres of land without abandoning his post as organist. The management of our property was left to my mother who was helped by some servants and her oldest children.

When I was six and already able to read and write Polish, my uncle the curate taught me Latin. Since he had no suitable textbook, he simply used the breviary. The lessons were tedious; the long stem of the curate's pipe assisted him daily in his instruction. At that time I discovered very interesting books in the parish library. I plunged into the history and classics of the country. Reading became a passion with me. I carried books hidden under my clothes and read wherever I could. The study of Latin was maintained throughout the winter, but the spring turned me into a shepherd; as before I was to tend my father's sheep, and I plunged only more eagerly into the Crusades and Walter Scott. That reading led to painful misunderstanding by its very contrast to my ordinary existence.

I was slowly preparing to enter the college attended by my elder brother. But unfortunately my uncle the curate died, and my father, deprived of sufficient resources to give me a higher education, decided to make an organist of me. He put me behind a piano and thus began my study of sacred music, so vigorously and so often punctuated by the cane that I quickly learned to abhor it.

Apart from my musical studies I had to help my father at the church and keep the parish register of baptisms, marriages, births, and deaths, assist daily at Mass, help the priest with the dying, etc.

I loved these diverse occupations since nobody checked my spare time, which I was able to devote entirely to reading. By the age of nine I had a thorough knowledge of contemporary Polish literature as well as of foreign literature in Polish translation, and I began to write poems in honour of a lady of thirty years. Naturally, she knew nothing about them.

During this period my brother, who had left college, tried systematically to make me pursue a regular program of studies. He took infinite pains, but did not succeed in tearing poetry out of my heart. I was at that time intoxicated by the romantic poetry of our great writers. I arranged the world according to my private use, looking at it through the poems I had devoured.

Within myself I felt vague enchantments, dull restlessness, and uncertain desires. I had hallucinations when I was awake. What wings carried me to unknown worlds!

Already I felt sick and confined at home; daily life was a burden. I dreamed of great actions, of voyages–rovings across the oceans of a free and independent life.

For entire weeks I would keep away from the house and try to live in the woods like a savage. I formed monstrous shapes in potter's clay, or cut them in trees; I filled my notebooks and the margins of my books with rough sketches, and I spent more than one night crying without reason.

Such was my life until the age of twelve. I shall skip the following years until the age of twenty.

I lived in Warsaw and – being twenty years old – I naturally had a wild imagination and a tender heart. Misery was my inseparable companion; I was a socialist and the punishment was inevitable. The Russian authorities expelled me from Warsaw after suspecting me of having taken part in the strike that had then broken out in Lodź for the first time. Considering me an irresponsible minor, they entrusted me to the custody of my father and the surveillance of the local police. At that time my parents had a watermill and land of some importance in the vicinity of Piotrków, close to the railway from Warsaw to Vienna. I could tolerate neither the tyranny of my father nor the extreme conservatism and Catholicism of my family. After a few weeks I ran away with a small troupe of actors and travelled with them across the country. After a year I had enough of the wandering artist's life with its miseries and lack of a future; besides, my talent for acting was non-existent.

I was able to find a job in the technical service of the railway. I lived in the province in a peasant's house between two stations. My income was pitiable, my life hard and tedious, my surroundings primitive. I had hit rock bottom. I was lucky to make the acquaintance of a German professor, a convinced and practising spiritualist. He dazzled and conquered me. A world of fantastic dreams and possibilities opened before my eyes. I left my job and went to join the professor, who lived at Czestochowa. He had constant and close contact with spiritualist circles in Germany and England, corresponded regularly with Madame Blavatsky and Olcot, wrote in spiritualist journals, and was always giving *ad hoc* séances. For him, spiritualism was both a science and a religion–a mystical atmosphere prevailed in his entire house. He was kind, childishly naive, and at every séance cheated by his medium. It was not difficult for me to see that very soon, and once my faith in his miracles was lost I abandoned them immediately. Once more I was free, penniless, and without a tomorrow. For a while I worked for a land-surveyor; I was a clerk in a shop that sold devotional articles, then a sales-man for a lumberyard. Finally I returned to the theatre. For several months I toured small places with a travelling company and did a great deal of acting, but when the company was dissolved I was left on the road. I tried to give recitations, for I knew entire poems by heart. I offered my services as producer in amateur theatres and I wrote for provincial journals. But I soon learned to loathe these occupations and returned willy-nilly to the railway. As before I was employed in the technical service; I was to live in a village lost between two distant stations. There was no office building for the agents of the company; I had to content myself with a peasant cottage very close to the railway.

For a while I had a roof over my head, literally a piece of dry bread, and quiet. I was surrounded by impenetrable forests in which the Czar of all Russians hunted every year. I had installed myself at the end of autumn. I did not have much to do and I had free time for writing and being foolish. I lived on tea, bread, and dreams. I was twenty-two years old. I was healthy, had only one suit, and boots with holes in them. I had faith in the world and a thousand bold projects in my mind. I wrote feverishly: dramas in ten acts, novels without end, stories in several volumes, poems. Then I tore up everything mercilessly and burned it. I lived in solitude; I had no friends;

e authorities as well as my fellow-workers were unfavourably disposed
ward me; I did my duties badly. I could adapt myself neither to the
entality of those around me nor to the conditions of my existence. All
is was painful and hard for me to endure. Misery did not release me; it
ndermined me, and then the cold... I had to spend whole days in the open
rveying the workers; the nights I spent in a room so cold that I wrote
rapped in a fur, keeping the inkwell under the lamp lest the ink should
eeze.

I suffered these torments for two years, but as a result I had finished six
ort stories that seemed to have possibilities. I sent them to a critic in Warsaw,
t it took over six months until I received a favourable reply. He even
ndescended to recommend me to a publisher. After new efforts my stories
ere printed. My whole being was filled with unspeakable happiness: at
st I had found my way. But this good fortune was not without results for
y bureaucratic career. The management dismissed me; they needed work-
s, not men of letters.

I gathered my belongings, consisting chiefly of manuscripts, and with the
enerous amount of three rubles and fifty kopecks I went to Warsaw to
nquer the world. I began a new Odyssey of misery, roving and struggling
ith destiny.

No help from anywhere! I broke completely with my family. They did
t understand me and lamented my fate. For the first six months I did not
now the taste of the most ordinary dinner. I went out only in moonlight.
y rags were too shabby for any occasion. I lived with people as miserable
I was. I wrote in the cathedral that was opposite my refuge; it was warm,
lemn, and silent. I fed my soul on organ music and the sight of religious
remonies. It was there, too, that I read Augustine, the Bible, and the Church
athers, for days on end. I contemplated suicide more and more seriously.
he earth was already opening under my feet. An irresistible fascination
ith terrifying death killed me ahead of time.

The more profound my faith became, the more violent my fascination
ith annihilation, and then incessant hunger pushed me toward the abyss.

At the beginning of spring, in April, I saw pilgrims going to Czestochowa,
e bright mountain that had the picture of the Madonna famous for its
iracles. I broke my chains and joined them. I do not remember which
urnal gave me an advance of twenty-five rubles for the description of that
lgrimage.

For eleven days I walked in marvellous spring weather, under the sun and in the green. The account of that pilgrimage (*Pielgrzymka do Jasney Góry* 1895 [Pilgrimage to the Mountain of Light]) appeared in a Warsaw illustrated daily and attracted the attention of the critics. Some months later I wrote *Komedjantka* (1896) [*The Comedian*]. During this period I made the acquaintance of a group of spiritualists who included the famous Dr. Ochorowiecz. I went to London to pursue spiritualist problems at the Theosophical Society. On my return I wrote *Fermenty* (1897) [Ferments], the sequel to *Komedjantka*. I then went to Lodź to study conditions in heavy industry and after beginning *Ziemia obiecana* (1899) [The Promised Land] I left for Paris. I spent long months in a French village near Tours. I wrote *Lili* and some short stories. I travelled through Italy in a more systematic fashion and stayed especially at Sorrente. In 1902 I was wounded in a train accident near Warsaw, and I have never regained my health completely.

In 1903–04 I published the first verion of *Chlopi*; at first it was only one volume. I burned it and rewrote it. This time it was divided into four volumes (1904–09). Next I wrote *Wampir* (1911) [*The Vampire*]–the reflection of my spiritualist exercises–two volumes of novellas, and I began historical studies concerning the decline of Poland toward the end of the seventeenth century. I wrote a trilogy called *Rok 1794* (1913–18) [*The Year 1794*]. The last volume of that work, *Insurekcja* [Insurrection], was written in Warsaw during the German occupation after the explosion of the Great War. I also published another volume of novellas. In April 1919 I left for the United States in order to visit my compatriots in that country.

I returned in 1920. In 1922–23 I wrote *Bunt* [Defiance], and I began to have heart trouble. I still have many things to say and desire greatly to make them public, but will death let me?

Biographical note on Wladyslaw Stanislaw Reymont

W. S. Reymont (1868–1925) died the year after he received the Nobel Prize. His complete works were published in thirty-six volumes (Warsaw 1930–32), his selected works in twelve volumes (Cracow, 1957).

Literature 1925

(Prize awarded in 1926)

GEORGE BERNARD SHAW

for his work which is marked by both idealism and humanity, its stimulating satire often being infused with a singular poetic beauty»

Presentation

by Per Hallström, Chairman of the Nobel Committee of the Swedish Academy

George Bernard Shaw showed in the novels of his youth the same conception of the world and the same attitude to social problems that he has maintained ever since. This provides a better defence for him than anything else against the repeated accusations of lack of honesty and of acting as a professional buffoon at the court of democracy. From the very beginning his convictions have been so firm that it seems as if the general process of development, without having any substantial influence on himself, has carried him along to the tribune from which he now speaks. His ideas were those of a somewhat abstract logical radicalism; hence they were far from new, but they received from him a new definiteness and brilliance. In him these ideas combined with a ready wit, a complete absence of respect for any kind of convention, and the merriest humour – all gathered together in an extravagance which has scarcely ever before appeared in literature.

What puzzled people most was his rollicking gaiety: they were ready to believe that the whole thing was a game and a desire to startle. This was so far from being true that Shaw himself has been able to declare with a greater justice that his careless attitude was a mere stratagem: he had to fool people into laughing so they should not hit upon the idea of hanging him. But we know very well that he would hardly have been frightened out of his outspokenness by anything that might have happened, and that he chose his weapons just as much because they suited him as because they were the most effective. He wielded them with the certitude of genius, which rested on an absolutely quiet conscience and on a faithful conviction.

Early he became a prophet of revolutionary doctrines, quite varied in their value, in the spheres of aesthetics and sociology, and he soon won for himself a notable position as a debater, a popular speaker, and a journalist. He set his mark on the English theatre as a champion of Ibsen and as an opponent of superficial tradition, both English and Parisian. His own dramatic production began quite late, at the age of thirty-six, in order to help satisfy the demands that he had aroused. He wrote his plays with instinctive sureness based on the certainty that he had a great deal to say.

In this casual manner he came to create what is to some extent a new kind
of dramatic art, which must be judged according to its own special principles.
Its novelty does not lie so much in structure and form; from his wide-awake
and trained knowledge of the theatre, he promptly and quite simply obtains
any scenic effect he feels necessary for his ends. But the directness with which
he puts his ideas into practice is entirely his own; and so too are the bellicosity,
the mobility, and the multiplicity of his ideas.

In France he has been called the Molière of the twentieth century; and there
is some truth in the parallel, for Shaw himself believes that he was following
classical tendencies in dramatic art. By classicism he means the rigorously
rational and dialectical bent of mind and the opposition to everything that
could be called romanticism.

He began with what he calls *Plays Unpleasant* (1898), so named because
they brought the spectator face to face with unpleasant facts and cheated
him of the thoughtless entertainment or sentimental edification that he expected from the stage. These plays dwell on serious abuses – the exploitation
and prostitution of poor people, while those who perpetrate these abuses
manage to retain their respectability.

It is characteristic of Shaw that his orthodox socialistic severity toward
the community is combined with a great freedom from prejudice and a genuine psychological insight when he deals with the individual sinner. Even in
these early pieces one of his finest qualities, his humanity, is fully and clearly
marked.

Plays Pleasant (1898), with which he varied his program, have on the whole
the same purport but are lighter in tone. With one of these he gained his
first great success. This was *Arms and the Man*, an attempt to demonstrate
the flimsiness of military and heroic romance, in contrast to the sober and
prosaic work of peace. Its pacifist tendency won from the audience a more
ready approbation than the author had generally received. In *Candida*, a kind
of *Doll's House* with a happy ending, he created the work which for a long
time was his most poetical one. This was due chiefly to the fact that in this
play the strong superior woman which for him – for reasons unknown to
us – has become the normal type, has here been given a richer, warmer, and
more gentle soul than elsewhere.

In *Man and Superman* (1903) he took his revenge by proclaiming that
woman, because of her resolute and undisguisedly practical nature, is destined
to be the superman whose coming has been so long prophesied with such
earnest yearning. The jest is amusing, but its creator seems to regard it more

or less seriously, even if one takes into account his spirit of opposition to the earlier English worship of the gentle female saint.

His next great drama of ideas, *Major Barbara* (1905), has a deeper significance. It discusses the problem of whether evil ought to be conquered by the inner way, the spirit of joyful and religious sacrifice; or by the outer way, the eradication of poverty, the real foundation of all social defects. Shaw's heroine, one of his most remarkable female characters, ends in a compromise between the power of money and that of the Salvation Army. The process of thought is here carried out with great force, and naturally with a great deal of paradox. The drama is not entirely consistent, but it reveals a surprisingly fresh and clear conception of the joy and poetry of the life of practical faith. Shaw the rationalist here shows himself more liberal and more chivalrous than is customary with the type.

Time does not permit us to hint at the course of his further campaign even in his more outstanding works: suffice it to say that without a trace of opportunism he turns his weapons against everything that he conceives as prejudice in whatever camp it may be found. His boldest assault would seem to be in *Heartbreak House* (1919), where he sought to embody – always in the light of the comic spirit – every kind of perversity, artificiality, and morbidity that flourishes in a state of advanced civilization, playing with vital values, the hardening of the conscience, and the ossification of the heart under a frivolous preoccupation with art and science, politics, money-hunting, and erotic philandering. But, whether owing to the excessive wealth of the material or to the difficulty of treating it gaily, the piece has sunk into a mere museum of eccentricities with the ghost-like appearance of a shadowy symbolism.

In *Back to Methuselah* (1921) he achieved an introductory essay that was even more brilliant than usual, but his dramatic presentation of the thesis, that man must have his natural age doubled many times over in order to acquire enough sense to manage his world, furnished but little hope and little joy. It looked as if the writer of the play had hypertrophied his wealth of ideas to the great injury of his power of organic creation.

But then came *Saint Joan* (1923), which showed this man of surprises at the height of his power as a poet. This it did especially on the stage, where all that was most valuable and central in the play was thrown into due relief and revealed its real weight, even against the parts that might evoke opposition. Shaw had not been happy in his previous essays in historical drama and this was natural enough, as he happened to combine with his abundant and quick intelligence a decided lack of historical imagination and sense of historical reality. His world lacked one dimension, that of time, which according to the newest theories is not without significance for space. This led to an unfortunate lack of respect for all that had once been and to a tendency to represent everything as diametrically opposite to what ordinary mortals had previously believed or said.

In *Saint Joan* his good head still cherishes the same opinion on the whole, but his good heart has found in his heroine a fixed point in the realm of the unsubstantial, from which it has been able to give flesh and blood to the visions of the imagination. With doubtful correctness he has simplified her image, but he has also made uncommonly fresh and living the lines that remain, and he has endowed *Saint Joan* with the power of directly holding the multitude. This imaginative work stands more or less alone as a revelation of heroism in an age hardly favourable to genuine heroism. The mere fact that it did not fail makes it highly remarkable; and the fact that it was able to make a triumphal progress all around the world is in this case evidence of considerable artistic worth.

If from this point we look back on Shaw's best works, we find it easier in many places, beneath all his sportiveness and defiance, to discern something of the same idealism that has found expression in the heroic figure of Saint Joan. His criticism of society and his perspective of its course of development may have appeared too nakedly logical, too hastily thought out, too unorganically simplified; but his struggle against traditional conceptions that rest on no solid basis and against traditional feelings that are either spurious or only half genuine, have borne witness to the loftiness of his aims. Still more striking is his humanity; and the virtues to which he has paid homage in his unemotional way – spiritual freedom, honesty, courage, and clearness of thought–have had so very few stout champions in our times.

What I have said has given a mere glimpse of Shaw's life-work, and scarcely anything has been said about his famous prefaces – or rather treatises –accompanying most of the plays. Great parts of them are insurpassable in their clarity, their quickness, and their brilliance. The plays themselves have given him the position of one of the most fascinating dramatic authors of our day, while his prefaces have given him the rank of the Voltaire of our time – if we think only of the best of Voltaire. From the point of view of a pure and simple style they would seem to provide a supreme, and in its way classic, expression of the thought and polemics of an age highly journalistic in tone, and, even more important, they strengthen Shaw's distinguished position in English literature.

At the banquet, Mr. Shaw's thanks were presented by the British Ambassador, Sir Arthur Grant Duff, who expressed particular appreciation of the fact that the Prize given to Mr. Shaw would be used to strengthen the cultural relations between Sweden and Great Britain.

Biography

George Bernard Shaw (1856–1950) was born in Dublin, the son of a civil servant. His education was irregular, due to his dislike of any organized training. After working in an estate agent's office for a while he moved to London as a young man (1876), where he established himself as a leading music and theatre critic in the eighties and nineties and became a prominent member of the Fabian Society, for which he composed many pamphlets. He began his literary career as a novelist; as a fervent advocate of the new theatre of Ibsen (*The Quintessence of Ibsenism*, 1891) he decided to write plays in order to illustrate his criticism of the English stage. His earliest dramas were called appropriately *Plays Pleasant and Unpleasant* (1898). Among these, *Widower's Houses* and *Mrs. Warren's Profession* savagely attack social hypocrisy, while in plays such as *Arms and the Man* and *The Man of Destiny* the criticism is less fierce. Shaw's radical rationalism, his utter disregard of conventions, his keen dialectic interest and verbal wit often turn the stage into a forum of ideas, and nowhere more openly than in the famous discourses on the Life Force, «Don Juan in Hell», the third act of the dramatization of woman's love chase of man, *Man and Superman* (1903).

In the plays of his later period discussion sometimes drowns the drama, as in *Back to Methuselah* (1921), although in the same period he worked on his masterpiece *Saint Joan* (1923), in which he rewrites the well-known story of the French maiden and extends it from the Middle Ages to the present.

Other important plays by Shaw are *Caesar and Cleopatra* (1901), a historical play filled with allusions to modern times, and *Androcles and the Lion* (1912), in which he exercised a kind of retrospective history and from modern movements drew deductions for the Christian era. In *Major Barbara* (1905), one of Shaw's most successful «discussion» plays, the audience's attention is held by the power of the witty argumentation that man can achieve aesthetic salvation only through political activity, not as an individual. *The Doctor's Dilemma* (1906), facetiously classified as a tragedy by Shaw, is really a comedy the humour of which is directed at the medical profession. *Candida* (1898), with social attitudes toward sex relations as objects of his satire, and

Pygmalion (1912), a witty study of phonetics as well as a clever treatment of middle-class morality and class distinction, proved some of Shaw's greatest successes on the stage. It is a combination of the dramatic, the comic, and the social corrective that gives Shaw's comedies their special flavour.

Shaw's complete works appeared in thirty-six volumes between 1930 and 1950, the year of his death.

Literature 1926

(Prize awarded in 1927)

GRAZIA DELEDDA

(pen name of Grazia Madesani, *née* Deledda)

«for her idealistically inspired writings which with plastic clarity picture the life on her native island and with depth and sympathy deal with human problems in general»

Presentation

by Henrik Schück, President of the Nobel Foundation

The Swedish Academy has awarded the Nobel Prize of 1926 to the Italian author Grazia Deledda.

Grazia Deledda was born in Nuoro, a small town in Sardinia. There she spent her childhood and her youth, and from the natural surroundings and the life of the people she drew the impressions which later became the inspiration and the soul of her literary work.

From the window of her house she could see the nearby mountains of Orthobene with their dark forests and jagged gray peaks. Farther off was a chain of limestone mountains which sometimes appeared violet, sometimes lemon-coloured, sometimes dark blue, depending on the variations of the light. And in the distance, the snowy peaks of Gennargentù emerged.

Nuoro was isolated from the rest of the world. The few visitors to the town usually arrived on horseback, with the women mounted behind the men. The monotony of daily life was interrupted only by traditional religious or popular holidays and by the songs and dances in the main street at carnival time.

In this environment, Grazia Deledda's view of life developed into something uniquely ingenuous and primitive. In Nuoro it was not considered shameful to be a bandit. «Do you think», says an old peasant woman in one of Deledda's novels, «that bandits are bad people? Well, you're wrong. They are only men who need to display their skill, that's all. In the old days men went to war. Now there aren't any more wars, but men still need to fight. And so they commit their holdups, their thefts, and their cattle stealing, not to do evil but only to display somehow their ability and their strength.» Thus the bandit rather enjoys the sympathy of the people. If he is caught and put in prison, the peasants have an expressive phrase which means that he has «run into trouble». And when he is freed no stigma is attached to him. In fact, when he returns to his home town, he is greeted with the words, «More such trouble a hundred years from now!»

The vendetta is still the custom in Sardinia, and a person is respected if he takes blood revenge on the killer of a kinsman. Indeed, it is considered

crime to betray the avenger. One author writes, «Even if the reward on
his head were three times its size, not a single man in the whole district of
Nuoro could be found to betray him. Only one law reigns there: respect
for a man's strength and scorn of society's justice.»

In this town, so little influenced by the Italian mainland, Grazia Deledda
grew up surrounded by a savagely beautiful natural setting and by people
who possessed a certain primitive grandeur, in a house that had a sort of
biblical simplicity about it. «We girls», Grazia Deledda writes, «were never
allowed to go out except to go to Mass or to take an occasional walk in the
countryside.» She had no chance to get an advanced education, and like the
other middle-class children in the area, she went only to the local school.
Later she took a few private lessons in French and Italian because her family
spoke only the Sardinian dialect at home. Her education, then, was not extensive. However, she was thoroughly acquainted with and delighted in the
folk songs of her town with its hymns to the saints, its ballads, and its lullabies.
She was also familiar with the legends and traditions of Nuoro. Furthermore,
she had an opportunity at home to read a few works of Italian literature
and a few novels in translation, since by Sardinian standards her family was
relatively well-to-do. But this was all. Yet the young girl took a great liking
to her studies, and at only thirteen she wrote a whimsical but tragic short
story, «Sangue Sardo» (1888) [Sardinian Blood], which she succeeded in
publishing in a Roman newspaper. The people at Nuoro did not at all like
this display of audacity, since women were not supposed to concern themselves with anything but domestic duties. But Grazia Deledda did not conform; instead she devoted herself to writing novels: first, *Fior di Sardegna*
[Flower of Sardinia], published in 1892; then *La via del male* (1896) [The
Evil Way], *Il vecchio della montagna* (1900) [The Old Man of the Mountain],
Elias Portolú (1903), and others with which she made a name for herself.
She came to be recognized as one of the best young female writers in Italy.

She had, in fact, made a great discovery – she had discovered Sardinia. In
the middle of the eighteenth century a new movement had arisen in European
literature. Writers at that time were tired of the models constantly drawn
from Greek and Roman literature. They wanted something new. Their
movement quickly joined forces with another which had begun in the same
epoch with Rousseau's adoration of man in his natural state, untouched by
civilization. The new school formed from these two movements advanced
and gained force, particularly in the great days of Romanticism. The school's
most recent trophies have been won by the work of Grazia Deledda. It is

true that in descriptions of local colour and peasant life she had predecessor
even in her own country. The so-called «regionalist» school in Italian literature had had such notable representatives as Verga, in his descriptions o
Sicily, and Fogazzaro, in his descriptions of the Lombardo-Veneto region
But the discovery of Sardinia decidedly belongs to Grazia Deledda. She knew
intimately every corner of her native land. She stayed in Nuoro until sh
was twenty-five; only then did she find the courage to go to Cagliari, th
capital of Sardinia. Here she met Madesani, the man whom she married i
1900. After her marriage she and her husband moved to Rome, where sh
divided her time between her work as a writer and her family duties. I
the novels written after she moved to Rome, she continued to deal wit
Sardinian subjects as in the work entitled *L'Edera* (1908) [The Ivy]. But i
the novels written after *L'Edera*, the action frequently takes place in a le:
localized atmosphere, as, for example, in her most recent novel *La Fuga i
Egitto* (1925) [The Flight into Egypt], which the Academy has examine
and appreciated. However, her conception of man and nature is, as alway:
fundamentally Sardinian in character. Although she is now artistically mor
mature, she remains the same serious, eloquent, but unpretentious write
who wrote *La via del male* and *Elias Portolú*.

It is rather difficult for a foreigner to judge the artistic merit of her styl
I shall therefore quote one of the most famous Italian critics on this matte
«Her style», he writes, «is that of the great masters of the narrative; it ha
the characteristic marks of all great novelists. No one in Italy today write
novels which have the vigour of style, the power of craftsmanship, the struc
ture, or the social relevance which is found in some, even the latest, work
of Grazia Deledda such as *La Madre* (1920) [*The Mother*] and *Il Segreto dell'uo
mo solitario* (1921) [The Secret of the Solitary Man].» One might note onl
that her composition does not have the strong consistency which might b
desired; unexpected passages often give the impression of hasty transition:
But this defect is more than generously compensated for by her many virtue:
As a painter of nature she has few equals in European literature. She doe
not uselessly waste her vivid colours; but even then, the nature which sh
describes has the simple, broad lines of ancient landscapes, as it has their chast
purity and majesty. It is a marvellously lively nature in perfect harmony wit
the psychological life of her characters. Like a truly great artist, she succeed
in incorporating her representation of people's sentiments and customs int
her descriptions of nature. Indeed, one need only recall the classic descriptio
of the pilgrim's sojourn on Mount Lula in *Elias Portolú*. They depart on

lay morning. Family after family ascends toward the ancient votive church, me on horseback, some in old wagons. They carry along enough provisions to last a week. The wealthier families lodge in the great shelter standing xt to the church. These families are descended from the church's founders, d each has a spike in the wall and a hearth to indicate the area which be-ngs to it. No one else can set foot in this area. Each evening the families ther in their respective areas for as long as the feast lasts. They cook their od over the fireplace and tell legends, play music, and sing during the long mmer night. In the novel *La via del male*, Grazia Deledda describes equally vidly the strange Sardinian marriage and funeral customs. When a funeral to take place, all of the doors are shut, all of the shutters are closed, every re is put out, no one is permitted to prepare food, and hired mourners wail eir improvised dirges. The descriptions of such primitive customs are so elike and so simple and natural that we are almost moved to call them omeric. In Grazia Deledda's novels more than in most other novels, man d nature form a single unity. One might almost say that the men are plants hich germinate in the Sardinian soil itself. The majority of them are simple asants with primitive sensibilities and modes of thought, but with some-ing in them of the grandeur of the Sardinian natural setting. Some of them most attain the stature of the monumental figures of the Old Testament. nd no matter how different they may seem from the men we know, they ve us the impression of being incontestably real, of belonging to real life. hey in no way resemble theatrical puppets. Grazia Deledda is a master of e art of fusing realism with idealism.

She does not belong to that band of writers who work on a thesis and scuss problems. She has always kept herself far removed from the battles the day. When Ellen Key once tried to interest her in such discussions, e answered, «I belong to the past.» Perhaps this confession of attitude is t completely just. Certainly Grazia Deledda feels tied by strong bonds to e past, to the history of her people. But she also knows how to live in d respond to her own times. Although she lacks interest in theories, she as a great deal of interest in every aspect of human life. She writes in a tter, «Our great anguish is life's slow death. This is why we must try to ow life down, to intensify it, thus giving it the richest possible meaning. ne must try to live above one's life, as a cloud above the sea.» Precisely cause life seems so rich and admirable to her, she has never taken sides in e political, social, or literary controversies of the day. She has loved man ore than theories and has lived her own quiet life far from the world's uproar. «Destiny», she writes in another letter, «caused me to be born i the heart of lonely Sardinia. But even if I had been born in Rome or Stock holm, I should not have been different. I should have always been what am–a soul which becomes impassioned about life's problems and whic lucidly perceives men as they are, while still believing that they could b better and that no one else but themselves prevents them from achievin God's reign on earth. Everything is hatred, blood, and pain; but, perhap everything will be conquered one day by means of love and good will.»

These last words express her vision of life, a serious and profound visio with a religious cast. It is frequently sad, but never pessimistic. She believ that the forces of good ultimately will triumph in the life struggle. Th principle which dominates all her work as a writer is represented clearly an concisely at the end of her novel *Cenere* (1904) [*Ashes*]. Anania's mother i ruined. In order not to be an obstacle to her son's happiness, she has take her own life and now lies dead before him. When he was only a baby, sh had given him an amulet. He opens it and finds that it contains only ashe «Yes, all was ashes: life, death, man; the very destiny which produced he And still in the last hour, as he stood before the body of the most miserabl of human creatures, who after doing and suffering evil in all of its manifesta tions had died for someone else's good, he remembered that among the ashe there often lurks the spark of a luminous and purifying flame. And he hoped And he still loved life.»

Alfred Nobel wanted the Prize in Literature to be given to someone who in his writings, had given humanity that nectar which infuses the health an the energy of a moral life. In conformity with his wishes, the Swedis Academy has awarded the Prize to Grazia Deledda, «for her idealisticall inspired writings which with plastic clarity picture the life on her nativ island and with depth and sympathy deal with human problems in general»

At the banquet, Archbishop Nathan Söderblom, Member of the Swedis Academy, addressed the laureate: «Dear Madame–The proverb says, ‹Al roads lead to Rome.› In your literary work, all roads lead to the human heart You never tire of listening affectionately to its legends, its mysteries, con flicts, anxieties, and eternal longings. Customs as well as civil and social in stitutions vary according to the times, the national character and history faith and tradition, and should be respected religiously. To do otherwise an

duce everything to a uniformity would be a crime against art and truth.
ut the human heart and its problems are everywhere the same. The author
ho knows how to describe human nature and its vicissitudes in the most
vid colours and, more important, who knows how to investigate and unveil
e world of the heart–such an author is universal, even in his local confine-
ent.

You, Madame, do not limit yourself to man; you reveal, first of all, the
ruggle between man's bestiality and the high destiny of his soul. For you
e road is extended. You have seen the road sign which many travellers pass
y without noticing. For you the road leads to God. For this reason you
elieve in rebirth in spite of the degradation and frailty of man. You know
at it is possible to reclaim the swamp so that it becomes firm and fertile
nd. Therefore, a bright ray gleams in your books. Through darkness and
uman misery you let shine the solace of eternal light.»

Autobiography

I was born in the little town of Nuoro in Sardinia in 1875. My father w
a fairly well-to-do landowner who farmed his own land. He was also
hospitable man and had friends in all of the towns surrounding Nuoro. Wh
these friends and their families had to come to Nuoro on business or f
religious holidays, they usually stayed at our house. Thus I began to kno
the various characters of my novels. I went only to elementary school
Nuoro. After this, I took private lessons in Italian from an elementary scho
teacher. He gave me themes to write about, and some of them turned o
so well that he told me to publish them in a newspaper. I was thirteen ar
I didn't know to whom I should go to have my stories published. But
came across a fashion magazine. I took the address and sent off a short stor
It was immediately published. Then I wrote my first novel, *Fior di Sardeg*
(1892) [Flower of Sardinia], which I sent to an editor in Rome. He publishe
it, and it was quite successful. But my first real success was *Elias Portolú* (1903
which was first translated by the *Revue des deux mondes*, and then into a
of the European languages. I have written a great deal:

Novels: *Anime oneste, romanzo famigliare* (1895) [Honest Souls], with pr
face by Ruggero Bonghi; *Il vecchio della montagna* (1900) [The Old Man of th
Mountain] followed by a dramatic sketch *Odio vince* (1904) [Hate Wins]; *Eli*
Portolú (1903); *Cenere* (1904) [Ashes]; *Nostalgie* (1905); *La via del male* (189
[The Evil Way]; *Naufraghi in porto* [originally *Dopo il divorzio*, 1902] (192
[*After the Divorce*]; *L'edera* (1908) [The Ivy]; *Il nostro padrone* (1910) [O
Master]; *Sino al confine* (1910) [Up to the Limit]; *Nel deserto* (1911) [In th
Desert]; *Colombi e sparvieri* (1912) [Doves and Falcons]; *Canne al vento* (191
[Canes in the Wind]; *Le colpe altrui* (1914) [The Others' Faults]; *Mariann*
Sirca (1915); *L'incendio nell'oliveto* (1918) [The Fire in the Olive Grove]; *L*
Madre (1920) [*The Mother*]; *Il segreto dell'uomo solitario* (1921) [The Secr
of the Solitary Man]; *Il Dio dei viventi* (1922) [The God of the Living]; *La danz*
della collana (1924) [The Dance of the Necklace], followed by the dramat
sketch *A sinistra* (1924) [To the Left]; *La fuga in Egitto* (1925) [The Fligl
into Egypt]; *Annalena Bilsini* (1927).

Short Stories: «Il giuochi della vita» (1905) [The Gambles in Life]; «Chia-roscuro» (1912) [Light and Dark]; «Il fanciullo nascosto» (1915) [The Hidden Boy]; «Il ritorno del figlio» (1919) [The Son's Return]; «La bambina rubata» (1919) [The Stolen Child]; «Cattive compagnie» (1921) [Evil Company]; «Il flauto nel bosco» (1923) [The Flute in the Wood]; «Il sigillo d'a-more» (1926) [The Seal of Love].

L'edera (1912) [The Ivy], a play in three acts, with the collaboration of Camillo Antona-Traversi.

In 1900 I took my first trip. It was to Cagliari, the beautiful Sardinian capital. There I met my husband. We later moved to Rome, where I am presently living. I have also written some poems which have not been collected in a volume.

Biographical note on Grazia Deledda

Grazia Deledda (1875–1936) continued to write extensively after she received the Nobel Prize. *La casa del poeta* (1930) [The Poet's House] and *Sole d'estate* (1933) [Summer Sun], both collections of short stories, reflect her optimistic vision of life even during the most painful years of her incurable illness. Life remains beautiful and serene, unaltered by personal suffering; man and nature are reconciled in order to overcome physical and spiritual hardship.

In many of her later works, Grazia Deledda combined the imaginary and the autobiographical; this blend is readily apparent in her novel, *Il paese del vento* (1931) [Land of the Wind]. In another novel, *L'argine* (1934) [*The Barrier*], the renunciation of worldly things, including love, mirrors the life of the author who, accepting self-sacrifice as a higher manner of living, is reconciled with God. The common trait of all her later writings is a constant faith in mankind and in God.

Two of Grazia Deledda's novels were published posthumously: *Cosima* (1937) and *Il cedro di Libano* (1939) [*The Cedar of Lebanon*].

Literature 1927

(Prize awarded in 1928)

HENRI BERGSON

«in recognition of his rich and vitalizing ideas and the brilliant skill with which they have been presented»

Presentation

by Per Hallström, President of the Nobel Committee of the Swedish Academy

In his *L'Évolution créatrice* (1907) [*Creative Evolution*], Henri Bergson has declared that the most lasting and most fruitful of all philosophical systems are those which originate in intuition. If one believes these words, it appears immediately with regard to Bergson's system how he has made fruitful the intuitive discovery that opens the gate to the world of his thought. This discovery is set forth in his doctoral thesis, *Essai sur les données immédiates de la conscience* (1889) [*Time and Free Will*], in which time is conceived not as something abstract or formal but as a reality, indissolubly connected with life and the human self. He gives it the name «duration», a concept that can be interpreted as «living time», by analogy with the life force. It is a dynamic stream, exposed to constant qualitative variations and perpetually increasing. It eludes reflection. It cannot be linked with any fixed point, for it would thereby be limited and no longer exist. It can be perceived and felt only by an introspective and concentrated consciousness that turns inward toward its origin.

What we usually call time, the time which is measured by the movement of a clock or the revolutions of the sun, is something quite different. It is only a form created by and for the mind and action. At the end of a most subtle analysis, Bergson concludes that it is nothing but an application of the form of space. Mathematical precision, certitude, and limitation prevail in its domain; cause is distinguished from effect and hence rises that edifice, a creation of the mind, whose intelligence has encircled the world, raising a wall around the most intimate aspirations of our minds toward freedom. These aspirations find satisfaction in «living time»: cause and effect here are fused; nothing can be foreseen with certainty, for certainty resides in the act, simple in itself, and can be established only by this act. Living time is the realm of free choice and new creations, the realm in which something is produced only once and is never repeated in quite the same manner. The history of the personality originates in it. It is the realm where the mind, the soul, whatever one may call it, by casting off the forms and habits of intelligence becomes capable of perceiving in an inner vision the truth abou its own essence and about the universal life which is a part of our self.

In his purely scientific account, the philosopher tells us nothing of the origin of this intuition, born perhaps of a personal experience skillfully seized upon and probed, or perhaps of a liberating crisis of the soul. One can only guess that this crisis was provoked by the heavy atmosphere of rationalistic biology that ruled toward the end of the last century. Bergson had been brought up and educated under the influence of this science, and when he decided to take up arms against it, he had a rare mastery of its own weapons and full knowledge of the necessity and grandeur it had in its own realm, the conceptual construction of the material world. Only when rationalism seeks to imprison life itself in its net does Bergson seek to prove that the dynamic and fluid nature of life passes without hindrance across its meshes.

Even if I were competent, it would still be impossible to give an account of the subtlety and scope of Bergson's thought in the few minutes at my disposal. The task is even more impossible for one who possesses only a very limited sense of philosophy and has never studied it.

At his starting point, the intuition of a living time, Bergson borrows in his analysis, in the development of his concepts, and in the sequence of his proofs, something of the dynamic, flowing, and almost irresistible essence of this intuition. One has to follow every movement; every moment introduces a new element. One has to follow the current, trying to breathe as best one can. There is scarcely time for reflection, for the moment one becomes static oneself, one loses all contact with the chain of reasoning.

In a singularly penetrating refutation of determinism our philosopher demonstrates that a universal intellect, which he calls Pierre, could not predict the life of another person, Paul, except in so far as he can follow Paul's experiences, sensations, and voluntary acts in all their manifestations, to the extent of becoming identical with him as completely as two equal triangles coincide. A reader who wants to understand Bergson completely must to a certain extent identify himself with the author and fulfil enormous requirements of power and flexibility of mind.

This is by no means to say that there is no point in following the author in his course, for good or ill. Imagination and intuition are sometimes capable of flights where intelligence lags behind. It is not always possible to decide whether the imagination is seduced or whether the intuition recognizes itself and lets itself be convinced. In any event, reading Bergson is always highly rewarding.

In the account, so far definitive, of his doctrine, *L'Évolution créatrice*, the master has created a poem of striking grandeur, a cosmogony of great scope and unflagging power, without sacrificing a strictly scientific terminology. It may be difficult at times to profit from its penetrating analysis or from the profundity of its thought; but one always derives from it, without any difficulty, a strong aesthetic impression.

The poem, if one looks at it in that way, presents a sort of drama. The world has been created by two conflicting tendencies. One of them represents matter which, in its own consciousness, tends downwards; the second is life with its innate sentiment of freedom and its perpetually creative force, which tends increasingly toward the light of knowledge and limitless horizons. These two elements are mingled, prisoners of each other, and the product of this union is ramified on different levels.

The first radical difference is found between the vegetable and the animal world, between immobile and mobile organic activity. With the help of the sun, the vegetable world stores up the energy it extracts from inert matter; the animal is exempt from this fundamental task because it can draw energy already stored up in the vegetables from which it frees the explosive force simultaneously and proportionately to its needs. At a higher level in the chain, the animal world lives at the expense of the animal world, being able, due to this concentration of energy, to accentuate its development. The evolutionary paths thus become more and more diverse and their choice is in no way blind: instinct is born at the same time as the organs that it utilizes. Intellect is also existent in an embryonic stage, but still mind is inferior to instinct.

At the top of the chain of being, in man, intelligence becomes predominant and instinct subsides, without however disappearing entirely; it remains latent in the consciousness that unites all life in the current of «living time»; it comes into play in the intuitive vision. The beginnings of intelligence are modest and manifestly timid. Intelligence is expressed only by the tendency and the ability to replace organic instruments instinctively by instruments sprung from inert matter, and to make use of them by a free act. Instinct was more conscious of its goal, but this goal was, on the other hand, greatly limited; intelligence engaged itself, on the contrary, in greater risks, but tended also toward infinitely vaster goals, toward goals realized by the material and social culture of the human race. Inevitably a risk existed, however: intelligence, created to act in the spatial world, might distort the image of the world by the modality thus acquired from its concept of life and might remain deaf to its innermost dynamic essence and to the freedom that presides

over its eternal variation. Hence the mechanistic and deterministic conception of an external world created by the conquests of intelligence in the
natural sciences.

We will find ourselves, then, irremediably cornered in an impasse, without any consciousness of freedom of mind and cut off from the sources of
life we carry within us, unless we also possess the gift of intuition when we
trace ourselves back to our origin. Perhaps one can apply to this intuition
the central point of the Bergsonian doctrine, the brilliant expression that he
uses about intelligence and instinct: the perilous way toward vaster possibilities. Within the limits of its knowledge, intelligence possesses logical
certainty, but intuition, dynamic like everything that belongs to living time
must without doubt content itself with the intensity of its certainty.

This is the drama: creative evolution is disclosed, and man finds himself
thrust on stage by the *élan vital* of universal life which pushes him irresistibly
to act, once he has come to the knowledge of his own freedom, capable of
divining and glimpsing the endless route that has been travelled with the
perspective of a boundless field opening onto other paths. Which of these
paths is man going to follow?

In reality we are only at the beginning of the drama, and it can scarcely
be otherwise, especially if one considers Bergson's concept that the future is
born only at the moment in which it is lived. However, something is lacking
in this beginning itself. The author tells us nothing of the will inherent in the
free personality, of the will that determines action and that has the power to
trace straight lines across the unforeseeable curves of this personality. Furthermore, he tells us nothing about the problem of life dominated by will power
about the existence or non-existence of absolute values.

What is the essence of the irresistible *élan vital*, that onslaught of life against
the inertia of matter, which, according to Bergson's audacious and magnificent expression, will one day triumph perhaps over death itself? What will
it make of us when it places at our feet all earthly power?

However complicated they may be, one cannot escape these questions. Is
the philosopher perhaps at this very moment on his way to the solution
certainly as tentative and audacious as his previous work has been and richer
still in possibilities?

There still remain some points to clarify. Does he perhaps seek to put an
end to the dualism of the image he gives of the world in seeking out a kind
of *élan vital* that applies to matter? We know nothing in this regard, but
Bergson has himself presented his system as constituting, on many points

nly an outline that must be completed in its details by the collaboration f other thinkers.

We are indebted to him, nevertheless, for one achievement of impor- ance: by a passage he has forced through the gates of rationalism, he has cleased a creative impulse of inestimable value, opening a large access to the vaters of living time, to that atmosphere in which the human mind will be ble to rediscover its freedom and thus be born anew.

If the outlines of his thought prove sound enough to serve as guides to he human spirit, Bergson can be assured, in the future, of an influence even reater than the influence he is already enjoying. As stylist and as poet, he ields place to none of his contemporaries; in their strictly objective search or truth, all his aspirations are animated by a spirit of freedom which, reaking the servitude that matter imposes, makes room for idealism.

Acceptance

I wish I had been able to express my feelings in person. Permit me to d
so through the French Minister, Mr. Armand Bernard, who has kindly con
sented to convey my message. I thank the Swedish Academy from the botto
of my heart. It has bestowed upon me an honour to which I should nc
have dared aspire. I recognize its value even more, and I am even more move
by it, when I consider that this distinction, given to a French writer, ma
be regarded as a sign of sympathy given to France.

The prestige of the Nobel Prize is due to many causes, but in particula
to its twofold idealistic and international character: idealistic in that it ha
been designed for works of lofty inspiration; international in that it is awarde
after the production of different countries has been minutely studied and th
intellectual balance sheet of the whole world has been drawn up. Free fror
all other considerations and ignoring any but intellectual values, the judge
have deliberately taken their place in what the philosophers have called
community of the mind. Thus they conform to the founder's explicit inten
tion. Alfred Bernhard Nobel declared in his will that he wanted to serv
the causes of idealism and the brotherhood of nations. By establishing
peace Prize alongside the high awards in arts and sciences, he marked h
goal with precision. It was a great idea. Its originator was an inventive geniu
and yet he apparently did not share an illusion widespread in his century
If the nineteenth century made tremendous progress in mechanical inven
tions, it too often assumed that these inventions, by the sheer accumulatio
of their material effects, would raise the moral level of mankind. Increasin
experience has proved, on the contrary, that the technological developmer
of a society does not automatically result in the moral perfection of the me
living in it, and that an increase in the material means at the disposal c
humanity may even present dangers unless it is accompanied by a cor
responding spiritual effort. The machines we build, being artificial organ
that are added to our natural organs, extend their scope, and thus enlarg
the body of humanity. If that body is to be kept entire and its movemen
regulated, the soul must expand in turn; otherwise its equilibrium will b

threatened and grave difficulties will arise, social as well as political, which will reflect on another level the disproportion between the soul of mankind, hardly changed from its original state, and its enormously enlarged body. To take only the most striking example: one might have expected that the use of steam and electricity, by diminishing distances, would by itself bring about a moral *rapprochement* between peoples. Today we know that this was not the case and that antagonisms, far from disappearing, will risk being aggravated if a spiritual progress, a greater effort toward brotherhood, is not accomplished. To move toward such a *rapprochement* of souls is the natural tendency of a foundation with an international character and an idealistic outlook which implies that the entire civilized world is envisaged from a purely intellectual point of view as constituting one single and identical republic of minds. Such is the Nobel Foundation.

It is not surprising that this idea was conceived and realized in a country as highly intellectual as Sweden, among a people who have given so much attention to moral questions and have recognized that all others follow from them, and who, to cite only one example, have been the first to grasp that the political problem par excellence is the problem of education.

Thus the scope of the Nobel Foundation seems to widen as its significance is more deeply realized, and to have benefited from it becomes an honour all the more deeply appreciated. No one is more fully aware of this than I am. I wished to say so before this illustrious audience, and I conclude, as I began, with the expression of my profound gratitude.

Prior to the acceptance, Professor Gösta Forssell made the following brief comment: «Henri Bergson has given us a philosophical system which could have served Nobel's idea as a basis and support, the idea of acknowledging with his Prizes not human deeds but new ideas revealed through select personalities. Bergson's high-minded works strive to regain for man's consciousness the divine gift of intuition and to put reason in its proper place: serving and controlling ideas.»

Biography

Henri Bergson (1859–1941), the son of a Jewish musician and an English woman, was educated at the Lycée Condorcet and the École Normale Supérieure, where he studied philosophy. After a teaching career as a schoolmaster in various secondary schools, Bergson was appointed to the École Normale Supérieure in 1898 and, from 1900 to 1921, held the chair of philosophy at the Collège de France. In 1914 he was elected to the Académie Française; from 1921 to 1926 he was president of the Commission for Intellectual Cooperation of the League of Nations. Shortly before his death in 1941, Bergson expressed in several ways his opposition to the Vichy regime.

Bergson's English background explains the deep influence that Spencer, Mill, and Darwin had on him during his youth, but his own philosophy is largely a reaction against their rationalist systems.

Bergson developed his philosophy in a number of books that have become famous not only for their fresh interpretation of life but also for a powerful employment of metaphor, image, and analogy. In his *Essai sur les données immédiates de la conscience* (1889) [*Time and Free Will*], Bergson offered an interpretation of consciousness as existing on two levels, the first to be reached by deep introspection, the second an external projection of the first. The deeper self is the seat of creative becoming and of free will. The method of intuitive introspection, first employed in this work, is developed further in his *Introduction à la métaphysique* (1903) [*An Introduction to Metaphysics*]. In *Matière et mémoire* (1896) [*Matter and Memory*], Bergson once again took up the study of consciousness, turning his attention to the relation of mind to body. He argued that this distinction is one of degree, not of kind. The limiting concept of matter is interpreted as a momentary mind, completely deprived of a memory that helps make possible freedom of choice. In *L'Évolution créatice* (1907) [*Creative Evolution*], Bergson developed the theory of time introduced in his other works and applied it to the study of living things, while in *Les Deux Sources de la morale et de la religion* (1932) [*The Two Sources of Morality and Religion*], he explored the moral implications of his theory of freedom. In *Le Rire* (1900) [*Laughter*], of greatest interest to the literary

ritic, Bergson provided a theory of comedy and established its place in a
urvey of aesthetics and the philosophy of art. Many of Bergson's essays and
eviews have been collected in *L'Énergie spirituelle* (1919) [*Mind-Energy*] and
.a *Pensée et le mouvant* (1934) [*Thought and Motion*]. Bergson's works were
ublished in seven volumes in 1945–46.

Literature 1928

SIGRID UNDSET

«principally for her powerful descriptions of Northern life during the Middle Ages»

Presentation

by Per Hallström, Chairman of the Nobel Committee of the Swedish Academy

In her first novels or novellas, all of them remarkable works, Sigrid Undset painted the present-day world of young women in the environs of Christiania. It was a restless generation, prompt to make the gravest decisions as soon as its aspirations for happiness were at stake, ready to take the ultimate logical and sentimental consequences of its impulsive nature, and impassioned for truth. This generation had to pay dearly for the sense of reality it acquired. It had to pass through many trials before regaining its inner unity, and some of its representatives succumbed in the struggle. The women of this generation were strangely isolated in this disconcerting world. Far from finding support in a firmly established social rule, they had, in full consciousness, renounced the heritage of the past. Hostile to all established social order, which they considered a useless yoke, they counted only on themselves to create a new society, consistent with a conviction, doubtless sincere at bottom, but easily misled.

With a lively imagination, Sigrid Undset lived the life of these women; she portrayed them sympathetically but with merciless truthfulness. She traced the tragedy of their lives without embellishing or amplifying it; and she conveyed the evolution of their destinies with the most implacable logic, which implied the condemnation of her heroines and of the world in which they were living. The picture is gripping, as far as the scope of the personages permits; it is attractive only in its marvellously fresh and brilliant descriptions of nature. Remaining forever in the reader's memory are the excursions on skis in the Norwegian solitude, the effects of the capricious play of the winter light, the exhilaration of the icy wind during the run, the mad dance of the blood in the veins, the spirit of adventure, the joy, the feeling of life and strength which makes the heart pound. And Sigrid Undset describes with the same mastery the splendours of spring, saturated with light and full of promises. In this domain her art attained greatness quite early.

This greatness began to extend to her entire work as soon as she abandoned the disunified and uprooted beings of the present time who had attracted her attention, in order to dedicate herself to the life of a distant past. She was destined by birth to do pioneer work in this area. Her father was a gifted historian, and from childhood she had lived in an atmosphere of historic legend and folklore. Moreover, she acquired a solid historical knowledge, guided, it would seem, by this premonition of the task her genius had set for her.

There she found the material which truly suited her nature, and her imagination was confronted with a task adequate to its scope. The characters she was going to make appear out of the past would offer a more complete unity and would be of a firmer cast than the contemporary characters. Far from being confined in a sterile isolation, they would participate in the great solidarity of past generations. These great masses would come alive in her work in a more vivid, firmer shape than the amorphous society of our era. Here was a great challenge to a writer who felt capable of carrying a heavy burden.

In their fashion, the generations of the Middle Ages also enjoyed a more varied inner life than the present generation, which Sigrid Undset found obsessed with the pursuit of sexual happiness, a quest which also determined their concepts of truth. These ancestors were strongly determined by the sentiment of honour and by faith. Here was the rich field for a psychology adequate to them. Moreover, the author's imagination was bound to be attracted by the difficult task of conjuring out of the darkness of a little-known past the external life of former generations in all its diversity. Sigrid Undset has done so to an extent that has aroused general admiration.

In so far as the inner life is concerned, her work can hardly be criticized. Intimately combined with the consciousness of the nation, in her depiction honour retains all the rigour and all the weight that it had for the chevalier and great landowners of the fourteenth century. The demands of honour are clearly stated, and the conflicts it creates are worked out regardless of their brutal consequences. Religious life is described with startling truth. Under Sigrid Undset's pen it does not become a continuous holiday of the mind, penetrating and dominating human nature; it remains, as in our day, insecure and rebellious, and is often even harsher. Profoundly conscious of the hold of faith on these inexperienced and unpolished souls, the author has given it, in the grave hours of existence, an overwhelming power.

The erotic life, the problem common to the two sexes, which constitutes the centre of Sigrid Undset's psychological interest, is found again, almost without modifications, in her historical novels. In this respect, objections naturally come to mind. In medieval documents, the feminist question is not known; one never finds hints of the inner personal life which later was to raise this question. The historian, demanding proofs, has the right to note this discrepancy. But the historian's claim is not absolute; the poet has at least an equal right to express himself when he relies on a solid and intuitive knowledge of the human soul. The archaeologist must admit that there existed in the past instruments of a nature other than those which have come down to us, not to mention the often fortuitous ways in which the memories of the past have reached us. The poet has the right to suppose that human nature has hardly varied in the course of ages, even if the annals of the past are silent in certain regards.

In spite of the laws imposed by necessity, the common life of man and woman could scarcely have been peaceful and simple. It was no doubt less noisy than in our day, but it was exempt from neither conflicts nor bloody disturbances. To these conflicts and disturbances Sigrid Undset gave a voice, although it sometimes seems that the voice had accents far too modern and that the sentiments were too subtle for an era in which the influence of poetry had not yet manifested itself. The heavier and harsher environment seems also to have been of a nature which hardened the characters more firmly. But it is to this dissemblance, if indeed one can speak of dissemblance, that her poetic work owes its poignant and evocative life. In the inevitable compromise between the present and the past, from which the historical novel cannot escape, Sigrid Undset has chosen a richly rewarding way.

Her narrative is vigorous, sweeping, and at times heavy. It rolls on like a river, ceaselessly receiving new tributaries whose course the author also describes, at the risk of overtaxing the reader's memory. This stems in part from the very nature of the subject. In the series of generations, conflicts and destinies assume a very concentrated form; these are whole masses of clouds which collide when the lightning flashes. However, this heaviness is also a result of the author's ardent and instant imagination, forming a scene and a dialogue of each incident in the narrative without taking the necessary backward look at the general perspective. And the vast river, whose course is difficult to embrace comprehensively, rolls its powerful waves which carry along the reader, plunged into a sort of torpor. But the roaring of its waters has the eternal freshness of nature. In the rapids and in the falls, the reader finds the enchantment which emanates from the power of the elements, as in the vast mirror of the lakes he notices a reflection of immensity, with the vision there of all possible greatness in human nature. Then, when the river reaches the sea, when Kristin Lavransdatter has fought to the end the battle of her life, no one complains of the length of the course which accumulated so overwhelming a depth and profundity in her destiny. In the poetry of all times, there are few scenes of comparable excellence.

Sigrid Undset's last novel, the two-volume story of *Olav Audunssøn* (1925-27), is generally on a level with the preceding novel, although it does not soar to its tragic finale. It attains, however, almost the same height in the scene in which Olav kills the Icelander. This scene constitutes a magnificent tableau, a masterly expression of the inner life, with a loftiness, a justice, an almost superhuman breadth of view rising above all the atrocities. One rediscovers here the same ripening of power as in *Kristin Lavransdatter* (1920-22). As far as the character studies are concerned, it seems impossible to reach higher than the portrayal of Eirik, the principal personage of the last part of the novel. Here is the complete evolution of a human being, from the first manifestations of childhood which are recorded not only with a vigorous strictness but also with a surprising superimposition of new traits, proportionate to the increasing clarity in the character delineation. One sees a human soul freely develop under one's eyes, a true creation of a truly superior art.

Sigrid Undset has received the Nobel Prize in Literature while still in her prime, an homage rendered to a poetic genius whose roots must be in a great and well-ordered spirit.

Acceptance

The preceding speakers have far better expressed our gratitude for the Prizes awarded to us than I could have done, and I subscribe to their words. I write more readily than I speak and I am especially reluctant to talk about myself. Instead, I wish to offer a salute to Sweden. Before I left for Sweden, a party was given for me – that is to say, not strictly speaking for me but because I was going to leave for Sweden – and everybody, the President of the Council of Ministers of Norway as well as my personal friends, asked me to give regards to Sweden. After all, the people of our peninsula form a distinct part of the world. Our forests and our mountains run into each other and our rivers carry their waters from one country to the other. Our houses in Norway resemble those in Sweden. God be praised! We have always lived in great number of small, private dwellings spread all over our countries. Modern technology has not yet completely intruded on the humanity of the North.

But what I wished to say here is that I have been asked to give regards to Sweden, the country we think of with joy, and to Stockholm, which we Norwegians consider the most beautiful city in the world.

Prior to the acceptance, Professor Gösta Forssell addressed these remarks to the laureate: «In her extensive work, an *Iliad* of the North, Sigrid Undset has resurrected in a new and visionary light the ideals which once guided our forefathers who built that community from which our Germanic culture derived. To an age in which it may be easier to acknowledge that the right to the greatest happiness is the duty of renunciation – to this age Sigrid Undset has shown the ideals of our forefathers: duty and faithfulness.»

Autobiography

My father's family came from Østerdalen. The first ancestor of ours of whom anything at all was known was one Peder Halvorsen who, in 1730, lived in Grytdalen in the Sollien valley of the river Atna where some men from Østerdalen had been allowed to settle and farm the land. My father's folk remained there until my grandfather, Halvor Halvorsen, came to Trondhjem as a non-commissioned officer and became warden of a workhouse. He took the name of Undset from a hamlet in which my grandmother had lived when she became a widow.

My father, Ingvald Martin Undset, obtained his doctorate in 1881 with a thesis on *The Beginnings of the Iron Age in Northern Europe*. In the same year he married my mother, Charlotte Gyth of Kallundborg, whose family had, for some obscure reason, settled in Denmark toward the end of the eighteenth century. Since most of my father's life consisted of travelling to almost every part of Europe, he set up a temporary home at Kallundborg. It was there that, in 1882, I first saw the light of day–the eldest of three sisters. In 1884 my father moved to Norway to take up a post at the Museum of Antiquities which was attached to the University of Christiania. I was sent to a school run by Mrs. Ragna Nielsen because my father was already aware that his days were numbered, and he was anxious for me to acquire a good education and follow in his footsteps. Mrs. Nielsen's school was co-educational and heavily committed to progressive educational ideas. It played an important role in shaping my character, inspiring me with an indelible distrust of enthusiasm for such beliefs! It was not that I disliked Mrs. Nielsen or suspected her of not being so noble-minded or attached to her principles as she appeared to be. No, it was those very principles which filled me with boundless scepticism; I knew not why either then or for a long time afterwards. Many years later I was to find some kind of an answer in the words uttered by St. Augustine concerning the leader of the Donatists: «securus judicat orbis terrarum». At the time, however, my only reaction was to roll myself up into a tight ball of resistance and it was thus, hedgehog-wise, that I went through my school years.

My father died in 1893 and Mrs. Nielsen offered my mother free education for all of us three children. Then when I was about fourteen, a memorable thing happened. Mrs. Nielsen called me into an empty classroom and told me that though she would keep her promise to my mother, «You, dear Sigrid, show so little interest in the school and there are so many children who would dearly love to be in your place and enjoy a free education, that I am asking you now: are you sure you want to take your entrance examinations?» «No, thank you», was my reply. Mrs. Nielsen looked somewhat startled but all she said was, «Very well then, you must now decide about your future like a grown-up person.» I am afraid that my behaviour that day was more akin to that of a small animal! Mrs. Nielsen was as good as her word where my sisters were concerned, but this was one of the few decisions in my life I have never regretted.

My mother had no choice but to send me to a commercial school in Christiania. I did not like it there but it had one great advantage over my old school; no one there expected me to like anything!

Later on, I went to work in an office and learned among other lessons to do things I did not care for, and to do them well. I remained there for ten years – from the age of 17 until I was 27. Before I left this office, two of my books had already been published – *Fru Marte Oulie* in 1907, and *Den lykkelige alder* (The Happy Age) in 1908. After leaving the office job, I went to Germany and Italy on a scholarship.

I have published a number of books since, my last two novels being set in the Middle Ages. They are *Kristin Lavransdatter*, which appeared in three volumes (1920–1922): *Kransen (The Garland)*, *Husfrue (The Mistress of Husaby)*, *Korset (The Cross)*; and *Olav Audunssøn i Hestviken* (1925) [*The Master of Hestviken*] and its sequel *Olav Audunssøn og hans børn* (1927) [*Olav Audunssøn and his Children*].

In 1912, I was married in Belgium to the Norwegian painter A. C. Svarstad. I was received into the Roman Catholic Church in 1924, and my marriage was then dissolved, since my husband had earlier been married to a woman who is still living. We have three children.

Since 1919, I have lived in Lillehammer.

Biographical note on Sigrid Undset

Sigrid Undset (1882–1949) was forced by the Second World War and th
Nazi invasion to leave her native Norway. She went to the United State
but continued to support the resistance movement. After the war she returne
to her country and received the Grand Cross of St. Olav for her writin
and her patriotic endeavours. Her later works are determined by the ex
perience of her religious conversion and are chiefly apologetic in character
Gymnadenia (1929) [*The Wild Orchid*], *Den brændende busk* (1930) [*Th
Burning Bush*], *Ida Elisabeth* (1932), and *Den trofaste hustru* (1936) [*The Faith
ful Wife*] deal with contemporary subjects. *Madame Dorothea* (1939) is
historical novel. Her biography of Catherine of Siena was published post
humously in 1951. Sigrid Undset is the author of the autobiographical vol
umes, *Etapper* (1929 and 1933) [*Stages on the Road*] and *Elleve aar* (1934) [*Th
Longest Years*].

Literature 1929

THOMAS MANN

principally for his great novel, Buddenbrooks, *which has won steadily increased recognition as one of the classic works of contemporary literature»*

Presentation

by Fredrik Böök, Member of the Nobel Committee for Literature

If one asks which innovation the nineteenth century made in the field of literature, which new form it created in addition to the old forms of epic, drama, and lyric, whose roots are in Greece, the answer must be: the realistic novel. By setting forth the innermost, secret experiences of the human soul against the background of contemporary social conditions, and by stressing the interdependence of the general and the particular, it has been able to portray reality with a faithful accuracy and a completeness that have no parallels in older literature.

The realistic novel–one could call it a modern prose epic influenced by historicism and science–has by and large been the creation of the English, the French, and the Russians; it is associated with the names of Dickens and Thackeray, Balzac and Flaubert, Gogol and Tolstoy. There was no comparable contribution from Germany for a long time; poetic creativity there chose other outlets. The nineteenth century had come to its end when a young writer, the twenty-seven-year-old son of a merchant from the old Hanse city of Lübeck, published his novel *Buddenbrooks* (1901). Twenty-seven years have passed since then, and it has become clear to all that *Buddenbrooks* is the masterpiece that fills the gap. Here is the first and as yet unsurpassed German realistic novel in the grand style which takes its undisputed and equal place in the European concert.

Buddenbrooks is a bourgeois novel, for the century it portrays was above all a bourgeois era. It depicts a society neither so great as to bewilder the observer, nor so small and narrow as to stifle him. This middle level favours an intelligent, thoughtful, and subtle analysis, and the creative power itself, the pleasure of epic narration, is shaped by calm, mature, and sophisticated reflection. We see a bourgeois civilization in all its nuances, we see the historical horizons, the changes of time, the changes of generations, the gradual transition from self-contained, powerful, and un-self-conscious characters to reflective types of a refined and weak sensibility. The presentation is lucid yet penetrates beneath the surface to hidden processes of life; it is powerful but never brutal, and touches lightly on delicate things; it is sad and serious but never depressing because it is permeated by a quiet, deep sense of humour that is iridescently reflected in the prism of ironic intelligence.

As a portrayal of a society, a concrete and objective representation of reality, *Buddenbrooks* hardly has its equal in German literature. Beyond the limits of its genre, however, the novel betrays its common features with the German mind, with metaphysical and musical transcendentalism. The young writer who had mastered the techniques of literary realism so perfectly was at heart a convert to Schopenhauer's pessimism and Nietzsche's criticism of civilization, and the main characters of the novel reveal their ultimate secrets in music.

Basically *Buddenbrooks* is a philosophical novel. The decline of a family is portrayed from the point of view that a profound insight into the essence and conditions of life is irreconcilable with naive *joie de vivre* and active energy. Reflection, self-observation, psychological refinement, philosophical profundity, and aesthetic sensibility appear to the young Thomas Mann destructive and disintegrating forces; in one of his most exquisite stories, *Tonio Kröger* (1903), he has found moving words for his love of human life in all its simplicity. Because he stood outside the bourgeois world that he portrayed, his vision was free, but he had a nostalgic feeling for the loss of naiveté, a feeling which gives him understanding, sympathy, and respect.

The painful experience of Mann's youth that gave its profound tone to *Buddenbrooks* includes a problem that he has treated and tried to solve in different ways throughout his career as a writer. Within himself he has felt the tension between the aesthetic-philosophical and the pragmatic-bourgeois outlooks, and he has tried to resolve it in harmony on a higher level. In the short stories *Tonio Kröger* and *Tristan* (1903) the exiles from life, the devotees of art, knowledge, and death, confess their desire for a simple and healthy existence, for «life in its seductive banality». It is Mann's own paradoxical love for simple and happy natures that speaks through them.

In the novel *Königliche Hoheit* (1909) [*Royal Highness*], whose realistic form disguises a symbolic story, he reconciled the life of the artist with that of the man of action, and he gave a motto to that human ideal: «highness and love–an austere happiness». But the synthesis is neither as convincing nor as deeply felt as the antithesis in *Buddenbrooks* and the short stories. In the drama *Fiorenza* (1906), in which the moralist Savonarola and the aestheticist Lorenzo di Medici appear as irreconcilable enemies, the gap is opened anew. In *Der Tod in Venedig* (1913) [*Death in Venice*] it reaches tragic significance. It was during this period, in the years that preceded the First World War,

that he became interested in the personality of Frederick the Great. He fel
that that ruler presented a historically valid solution of the problem, fo
Frederick's genius had, with unbroken vitality, combined action, contempla
tion, and a penetrating clarity free from illusions. In the ingenious essa
Friedrich und die grosse Koalition (1915) [*Frederick the Great and the Gran
Coalition*] he showed the possibility and reality of the solution, but th
problematic writer of *Buddenbrooks* did not succeed in representing this idea
in the plastic and vital form of literature.

The First World War and its consequences forced Mann to leave the worl
of contemplation, of ingenious analysis and subtle visions of beauty, for th
world of practical action. He followed his own advice, implied in his nove
Königliche Hoheit, to beware of the easy and the comfortable, and dedicate
himself to an agonizing reappraisal of the questions that his country face
in its time of affliction. His later works, especially the novel *Der Zauberber*
(1924) [*The Magic Mountain*], testify to the struggle of the ideas which hi
dialectical nature fought to the end and which preceded the statement o
his opinions.

Dr. Thomas Mann – As a German writer and thinker you have, reflect
ing realities, wrestled with ideas and created painful beauty even though yo
were convinced that art is questionable. You have reconciled the loftiness o
poetry and the intellect with a yearning love for the human and for the simpl
life. Accept from the hands of our King the Prize that the Swedish Academ
with its congratulations has awarded to you.

Acceptance

Now my turn to thank you has come, and I need not tell you how much I have looked forward to it. But alas, at this moment of truth I am afraid that words will fail my feelings, as is so often the case with born non-orators.

All writers belong to the class of non-orators. The writer and the orator are not only different, but they stand in opposition, for their work and the achievement of their effects proceed in different ways. In particular the convinced writer is instinctively repelled, from a literary standpoint, by the improvised and noncomittal character of all talk, as well as by that principle of economy which leaves many and indeed decisive gaps which must be filled by the effects of the speaker's personality. But my case is complicated by temporary difficulties that have virtually foredoomed my makeshift oratory. I am referring, of course, to the circumstances into which I have been placed by you, gentlemen of the Swedish Academy, circumstances of marvellous confusion and exuberance. Truly, I had no idea of the thunderous honours that are yours to bestow! I have an epic, not a dramatic nature. My disposition and my desires call for peace to spin my thread, for a steady rhythm in life and art. No wonder, if the dramatic firework that has crashed from the North into this steady rhythm has reduced my rhetorical abilities even beneath their usual limitations. Ever since the Swedish Academy made public its decision, I have lived in festive intoxication, an enchanting topsy-turvy, and I cannot illustrate its consequences on my mind and soul better than by pointing to a pretty and curious love poem by Goethe. It is addressed to Cupid himself and the line that I have in mind goes: «Du hast mir mein Gerät verstellt und verschoben.» Thus the Nobel Prize has wrought dramatic confusion among the things in my epic household, and surely I am not being impertinent if I compare the effects of the Nobel Prize on me to those that passion works in a well-ordered human life.

And yet, how difficult it is for an artist to accept without misgivings such honours as are now showered upon me! Is there a decent and self-critical artist who would not have an uneasy conscience about them? Only a supra-personal, supra-individual point of view will help in such a dilemma. It is always best to get rid of the individual, particularly in such a case. Goethe once said proudly, «Only knaves are modest.» That is very much the word of a grand seigneur who wanted to disassociate himself from the morality of subalterns and hypocrites. But, ladies and gentlemen, it is hardly the whole truth. There is wisdom and intelligence in modesty, and he would be a silly fool indeed who would find a source of conceit and arrogance in honours such as have been bestowed upon me. I do well to put this international prize that through some chance was given to me, at the feet of my country and my people, that country and that people to which writers like myself feel closer today than they did at the zenith of its strident empire.

After many years the Stockholm international prize has once more been awarded to the German mind, and to German prose in particular, and you may find it difficult to appreciate the sensitivity with which such signs of world sympathy are received in my wounded and often misunderstood country.

May I presume to interpret the meaning of this sympathy more closely? German intellectual and artistic achievements during the last fifteen years have not been made under conditions favourable to body and soul. No work had the chance to grow and mature in comfortable security, but art and intellect have had to exist in conditions intensely and generally problematic, in conditions of misery, turmoil, and suffering, an almost Eastern and Russian chaos of passions, in which the German mind has preserved the Western and European principle of the dignity of form. For to the European, form is a point of honour, is it not? I am not a Catholic, ladies and gentlemen; my tradition is like that of all of you; I support the Protestant immediateness to God. Nevertheless, I have a favourite saint. I will tell you his name. It is Saint Sebastian, that youth at the stake, who, pierced by swords and arrows from all sides, smiles amidst his agony. Grace in suffering: that is the heroism symbolized by St. Sebastian. The image may be bold, but I am tempted to claim this heroism for the German mind and for German art, and to suppose that the international honour fallen to Germany's literary achievement was given with this sublime heroism in mind. Through her poetry Germany has exhibited grace in suffering. She has preserved her honour, politically by not yielding to the anarchy of sorrow, yet keeping her unity; spiritually by uniting the Eastern principle of suffering with the Western principle of form–by creating beauty out of suffering.

Allow me at the end to become personal. I have told even the first delegates who came to me after the decision how moved and how pleased I was to

eceive such an honour from the North, from that Scandinavian sphere to
vhich as a son of Lübeck I have from childhood been tied by so many
imilarities in our ways of life, and as a writer by so much literary sympathy
nd admiration for Northern thought and atmosphere. When I was young,
wrote a story that young people still like: *Tonio Kröger*. It is about the South
nd the North and their mixture in one person, a problematic and productive
nixture. The South in that story is the essence of sensual, intellectual adven-
ure, of the cold passion of art. The North, on the other hand, stands for
he heart, the bourgeois home, the deeply rooted emotion and intimate hu-
nanity. Now this home of the heart, the North, welcomes and embraces
ne in a splendid celebration. It is a beautiful and meaningful day in my life,
. true holiday of life, a «högtidsdag», as the Swedish language calls any day
f rejoicing. Let me tie my final request to this word so clumsily borrowed
:om Swedish: Let us unite, ladies and gentlemen, in gratitude and con-
;ratulations to the Foundation, so beneficial and important the world over,
o which we owe this magnificent evening. According to good Swedish
ustom, join me in a fourfold hurrah to the Nobel Foundation!

?rior to the acceptance, Professor J. E. Johansson made the following com-
nents: «Thomas Mann has described the phenomena which are accessible
o us without the help of models of electrons and atoms. His investigations
:oncern human nature as we have learned to know it in the light of con-
cience. Thus his field is many centuries old; but Thomas Mann has shown
hat it offers no fewer new problems of great interest today. I take it that
ie does not feel a stranger in a group where everybody considers, as Alfred
Nobel did, the human endeavour of the study of the relations among phe-
iomena as the basis of all civilization, and I am quite sure that he will not
:eel an alien in a country so close to his own.»

Autobiography

I was born in Lübeck on June 6, 1875, the second son of a merchant and senator of the Free City, Johann Heinrich Mann, and his wife Julia da Silva-Bruhns. My father was the grandson and great-grandson of Lübeck citizens, but my mother first saw the light of day in Rio de Janeiro as the daughter of a German plantation owner and a Portugese-Creole Brazilian. She was taken to Germany at the age of seven.

I was designated to take over my father's grain firm, which commemorated its centenary during my boyhood, and I attended the science division of the «Katharineum» at Lübeck. I loathed school and up to the very end failed to meet its requirements, owing to an innate and paralyzing resistance to any external demands, which I later learned to correct only with great difficulty. Whatever education I possess I acquired in a free and autodidactic manner. Official instruction failed to instill in me any but the most rudimentary knowledge.

When I was fifteen, my father died, a comparatively young man. The firm was liquidated. A little later my mother left the town with the younger children in order to settle in the south of Germany, in Munich.

After finishing school rather ingloriously, I followed her and for the time being became a clerk in the office of a Munich insurance company whose director had been a friend of my father's. Later, by way of preparing for a career in journalism, I attended lectures in history, economics, art history, and literature at the university and the polytechnic. In between I spent a year in Italy with my brother Heinrich, my elder by four years. During this time my first collection of short stories, *Der kleine Herr Friedemann* (1898) [*Little Herr Friedemann*], was published. In Rome, I also began to write the novel *Buddenbrooks*, which appeared in 1901 and which since then has been such a favourite with the German public that today over a million copies of it are in circulation.

There followed shorter stories, collected in the volume *Tristan* (1903), of which the North-South artist's novella *Tonio Kröger* is usually considered the most characteristic, and also the Renaissance dialogues *Fiorenza* (1906), a closet drama which, however, has occasionally been staged.

In 1905 I married the daughter of Alfred Pringsheim, who had the chair of mathematics at the University of Munich. On her mother's side my wife is the granddaughter of Ernst and Hedwig Dohm, the well-known Berlin journalist and his wife, who played a leading role in the German movement for women's emancipation. From our marriage have come six children: three girls, of whom the eldest has gone into the theatre, and three boys, of whom the eldest has also devoted himself to literature.

The first literary fruit of my new status was the novel *Königliche Hoheit* (1909) [*Royal Highness*], a court story that provides the frame for a psychology of the formal-representative life and for moral questions such as the reconciliation of an aristocratic, melancholic consciousness with the demands of the community. Another novelistic project followed, the *Bekenntnisse des Hochstaplers Felix Krull* (1922) [*Confessions of Felix Krull, Confidence Man*]. It is based on an idea of parody, that of taking an element of venerable tradition, of the Goethean, self-stylizing, autobiographic, and aristocratic confession, and translating it into the sphere of the humorous and the criminal. The novel has remained a fragment, but there are connoisseurs who consider its published sections my best and most felicitous achievement. Perhaps it is the most personal thing I have written, for it represents my attitude toward tradition, which is simultaneously loving and destructive and has dominated me as a writer.

In 1913 the novella *Tod in Venedig* [*Death in Venice*] was published, which beside *Tonio Kröger* is considered my most valid achievement in that genre. While I was writing its final sections I conceived the idea of the «Bildungsroman» *Der Zauberberg* (1924) [*The Magic Mountain*], but work on it was interrupted in the very beginning by the war.

Although the war did not make any immediate demands on me physically, while it lasted it put a complete stop to my artistic activity because it forced me into an agonizing reappraisal of my fundamental assumptions, a human and intellectual self-inquiry that found its condensation in *Betrachtungen eines Unpolitischen* [*Reflections of an Unpolitical Man*], published in 1918. Its subject is the personally accented problem of being German, *the* political problem, treated in the spirit of a polemical conservatism that underwent many revisions as life went on. An account of the development of my socio-moral ideas is found in the volumes of essays *Rede und Antwort* (1922) [*Question and Answer*], *Bemühungen* (1925) [*Efforts*], and *Die Forderung des Tages* (1930) [*Order of the Day*].

Lecture tours abroad began immediately after the borders of countries

neutral or hostile during the war had been re-opened. They led me first to
Holland, Switzerland, and Denmark. The spring of 1923 saw a journey to
Spain. In the following year I was guest of honour of the newly established
PEN Club in London; two years later I accepted an invitation of the French
branch of the Carnegie Foundation, and I visited Warsaw in 1927.

Meanwhile, in the autumn of 1924, after many prolonged delays the two
volumes of *Der Zauberberg* were published. The interest of the public, as revealed by the hundred printings the book ran into within a few years, proved
that I had chosen the most favourable moment to come to the fore with
this composition of ideas epically conceived. The problems of the novel did
not essentially appeal to the masses, but they were of consuming interest to
the educated, and the distress of the times had increased the receptivity of
the public to a degree that favoured my product, which so wilfully played
fast and loose with the form of the novel.

Soon after the completion of the *Betrachtungen* I added to my longer narratives a prose idyll, the animal story *Herr und Hund* (1919) [*Bashan and I*]
Der Zauberberg was followed by a bourgeois novella from the period of revolution and inflation, *Unordnung und frühes Leid* (1926) [*Disorder and Early
Sorrow*]; *Mario und der Zauberer* [*Mario and the Magician*], written in 1929,
is for the time being my last attempt at compositions of this size. It was
written during my work on a new novel which in subject matter and intention is far different from all earlier works, for it leaves behind the bourgeois
individual sphere and enters into that of the past and myth. The Biblical story
for which the title *Joseph und seine Brüder* is planned, and of which individual
sections have been made known through public readings and publication
in journals, seems about half completed. A study trip connected with it led
me to Egypt and Palestine in February-March-April, 1930.

Ever since his early days the author of this biographical sketch has been
encouraged in his endeavours by the kind interest of his fellow men as well
as by official honours. An example is the conferment of an honorary doctor's
degree by the University of Bonn in 1919; and, to satisfy the German delight in title, the Senate of Lübeck, my home town, added the title of professor on the occasion of a city anniversary. I am one of the first members,
nominated by the state itself, of the new literary division of the Prussian
Academy of Arts; my fiftieth birthday was accompanied by expressions of
public affection that I can remember only with emotion, and the summit
of all these distinctions has been the award of the Nobel Prize in Literature
by the Swedish Academy last year. But I may say that no turmoil of success

as ever dimmed the clear apprehension of the relativity of my deserts or ven for a moment dulled the edge of my self-criticism. The value and gnificance of my work for posterity may safely be left to the future; for ie they are nothing but the personal traces of a life led consciously, that is, onscientiously.

Biographical note on Thomas Mann

'homas Mann (1875–1955) moved to Switzerland in 1933 shortly after the Iazis had come to power and begun a campaign of abuse against him. He vas formally expatriated in 1936. In 1937 the University of Bonn deprived im of his honorary doctorate (restored in 1946), which aroused Mann to famous and moving reply in which he epitomized the situation of the Ierman writer in exile. Mann, who had anticipated and warned against the ise of fascism during the Weimar Republic (e.g., in *Mario and the Magician*), ontinued to combat it in many pamphlets and talks throughout the period f the Nazi regime and the Second World War. He became an American itizen in 1940 and, from 1941 to 1953, lived in Santa Monica, California. After the war he frequently revisited Europe: in 1949 he received the Goethe 'rizes of Weimar (East Germany) and Frankfurt (West Germany), but when ie finally returned to Europe he settled near Zürich, where he died in 1955.

Among the chief works of Mann's later years are the novels *Lotte in Weimar* 1939) [*The Beloved Returns*], in which the fictional account of a meeting f the lovers of *Werther* grown old provides the framework for a psycho- ogically and technically ingenious portrait of the old Goethe; *Joseph und seine Brüder* (1933–43) [*Joseph and his Brothers*], a version of the Old Testament tory which interweaves myth and psychology; and *Dr. Faustus* (1947), the tory of an artist who chooses to pay with self-destruction for the powers f genius, a fate that echoes the last days of the Third Reich; the collections f essays *Leiden und Grösse der Meister* (1935) [*Suffering and Greatness of the Masters*]; and the essay on Schiller, *Versuch über Schiller* (1955). A complete dition of his works in twelve volumes was published in Berlin (1956) and n Frankfurt (1960).

Literature 1930

SINCLAIR LEWIS

«for his vigorous and graphic art of description and his ability to create, with wit and humour, new types of characters»

Presentation

by Erik Axel Karlfeldt, Permanent Secretary of the Swedish Academy

This year's winner of the Nobel Prize in Literature is a native of a part of America which for a long time has had Swedish contacts. He was born at Sauk Centre, a place of about two or three thousand inhabitants in the great cornland of Minnesota. He describes the place in his novel *Main Street* (1920), though there it is called Gopher Prairie.

It is the great prairie, an undulating land with lakes and oak groves, which has produced that little town and many others exactly like it. The pioneers have need of places to sell their grain, shops to purchase their supplies, banks for their mortgage loans, doctors for their bodies, and clergymen for their souls. There is cooperation between the country and the town, but at the same time there is conflict. Does the town exist for the sake of the country, or the country for the town?

The prairie makes its power felt. During the winters, long and cold as ours, terrific storms dump their snow in the wide streets, between low and shabby houses. The summer scorches with an intense heat and the town smells, because it lacks both sewers and street cleaning. Yet the town naturally feels its superiority; it is the flower of the prairie. It has the economic threads in its hands, and it is the focus of civilization – a concentrated, proud America amidst these earth-bound thralls of foreign origin, Germans and Scandinavians.

Thus the town lives happily in its self-confidence and its belief in true democracy, which does not exclude a proper stratification of the people, its faith in a sound business morality, and the blessings of being motorized; for there are many Fords in Main Street.

To this town comes a young woman filled with rebellious emotions. She wants to reform the town, inside and out, but fails completely, almost going under in the attempt.

As a description of life in a small town, *Main Street* is certainly one of the best ever written. To be sure, the town is first and foremost American, but it could, as a spiritual milieu, be situated just as well in Europe. Like Mr. Lewis, many of us have suffered from its ugliness and bigotry. The

strong satire has aroused local protests, but one need not be keensighted t
see the tolerant strain in Lewis's sketch of his native town and its people.

Behind the puffed-up complacency of Gopher Prairie, however, lurk
jealousy. At the edge of the plain stand cities like St. Paul and Minneapoli
already little metropolitan centres with their skyscraper windows gleamin
in the sunlight or the evening's electricity. Gopher Prairie wants to be lik
them and finds the time ripe for a campaign of progress, based on the risin
war price of wheat.

A stump orator is imported, a real rabble-rouser of the peppiest kind, an
with blatant eloquence he demonstrates that nothing will be easier than fc
Gopher Prairie to take the lead and reach the 200,000 class.

Mr. Babbitt – George Follansbee Babbitt – is the happy citizen of such
city (*Babbitt*, 1922). It is called Zenith, but probably it cannot be found o
the map under that name. This city with its enlarged horizons hereafter be
comes the starting point for Mr. Lewis's critical raids into the territoric
of Americanism. The city is a hundred times larger than Gopher Prairie anc
therefore, a hundred times richer in one hundred per cent Americanism an
one hundred times as satisfied with itself, and the enchantment of its optimisr
and progressive spirit is embodied in George F. Babbitt.

As a matter of fact, Babbitt probably approaches the ideal of an America
popular hero of the middle class. The relativity of business morals as we
as private rules of conduct is for him an accepted article of faith, and withou
hesitation he considers it God's purpose that man should work, increase h
income, and enjoy modern improvements. He feels that he obeys these com
mandments and therefore lives in complete harmony with himself and sc
ciety.

His profession, real estate, is the highest in existence, and his house nea
the city, with its trees and lawn, is standard, inside and out. The make c
his car corresponds to his position, and in it he whizzes through the street
proud as a young hero amidst the perils of the traffic. His family life als
corresponds to the bourgeois average. His wife has become used to h
masculine grumblings at home, and the children are impertinent, but tha
is what one expects.

He enjoys excellent health, is well-fed and thriving, alert and good-naturec
His daily lunches at the club are feasts of instructive business conversatio
and stimulating anecdotes; he is sociable and winning. Babbitt is furthe
more a man with the gift of speech. He has learned all the national slogar
and whirls them about with his flowing tongue in his popular talks befor

lubs and mass meetings. Not even for the most elevated spirituality does
he lack sympathy. He basks in the company of the noted poet, Cholmondeley
Frink, who concentrates his genius on the composition of striking, rhymed
advertisements for various firms and thereby earns a good annual income.

Thus Babbitt lives the life of the irreproachable citizen conscious of his
respectability. But the jealousy of the gods broods over a mortal whose
happiness grows too great. A soul such as Babbitt's is, of course, incapable
of growth; it is a ready-made article from the start. Then Babbitt discovers
that he has tendencies toward vice which he has neglected – although not
wholly, one ought to add. As he approaches fifty, he hastens to make up
for the neglect. He enters into an irregular relationship and joins a frivolous
gang of youths, in which he plays the role of a generous sugar daddy. But
his deeds find him out. His lunches at the club become more and more painful
through the silence and aloofness of his friends. They hint that he is spoiling
his chance of future membership in the committee of progress. Here it is
naturally New York and Chicago that loom before him. He succeeds in re-
covering his better self, and it is edifying to see him kneel in his pastor's
study, where he receives absolution. And then Babbitt can once more devote
himself to the Sunday school and other socially useful activities. His story
ends as it began.

That it is institutions as representatives of false ideas, and not individuals,
that Mr. Lewis wants to attack with his satire, he has himself indicated. It
is then a triumph for his art, a triumph almost unique in literature, that he
has been able to make this Babbitt, who fatalistically lives within the borders
of an earth-bound but at the same time pompous utilitarianism, an almost
lovable individual.

Babbitt is naive, and a believer who speaks up for his faith. At bottom
there is nothing wrong with the man, and he is so festively refreshing that
he almost serves as a recommendation for American snap and vitality. There
are bounders and Philistines in all countries, and one can only wish that half
of them were half as amusing as Babbitt.

To the splendour of the figure, as well as to other speaking characters in
the book, Mr. Lewis has added his unparalleled gift of words. Listen, for
example, to the conversation of a few commercial travellers, sitting together
in a compartment of the New York express. An unsuspected halo falls over
the profession of selling. «To them, the Romantic Hero was no longer the
knight, the wandering poet, the cowpuncher, the aviator, nor the brave
young district attorney, but the great sales manager, who had an Analysis

of Merchandizing Problems on his glass-topped desk, whose title of nobility was ‹Go-getter›, and who devoted himself and all his young samurai to the cosmic purpose of Selling – not of selling anything in particular, for or to anybody in particular, but pure Selling.»

Arrowsmith (1925) is a work of a more serious nature. Lewis has there attempted to represent the medical profession and science in all its manifestations. As is well known, American research in the natural sciences, physics, chemistry, and medicine ranks with the best of our age, and it has several times been recognized as such from this very platform. Tremendous resources have been placed at its command. Richly endowed institutions work unceasingly on its development.

That even here some speculative persons want to take advantage of their opportunities may be regarded as inevitable. Private industries are on the alert for scientific discoveries and want to profit from them before they have been tested and finally established. The bacteriologist, for instance, searches with infinite care for vaccines to cure widespread diseases, and the manufacturing chemist wants to snatch them prematurely from his hand for mass production.

Under the guidance of a gifted and conscientious teacher, Martin Arrowsmith develops into one of the idealists of science. The tragedy of his life as a research worker is that, after making an important discovery, he delays its announcement for constantly renewed tests until he is anticipated by a Frenchman in the Pasteur Institute.

The book contains a rich gallery of different medical types. We have the hum of the medical schools with their quarrelling and intriguing professors. Then there is the unpretentious country doctor, recalled from *Main Street*, who regards it as an honour to merge with his clientele and become their support and solace. Then we have the shrewd organizer of public health and general welfare, who works himself into popular favour and political power. Next we have the large institutes with their apparently royally independent investigators, under a management which to a certain extent must take into consideration the commercial interests of the donors and drive the staff to forced work for the honour of the institutes.

Above these types rises Arrowsmith's teacher, the exiled German Jew, Gottlieb, who is drawn with a warmth and admiration that seem to suggest a living model. He is an incorruptibly honest servant of science, but at the same time a resentful anarchist and a stand-offish misanthrope, who doubts whether the humanity whose benefactor he is amounts to as much as the animals he kills with his experiments. Further we meet the Swedish doctor, Gustaf Sondelius, a radiant Titan, who with singing and courage pursues pests in their lairs throughout the world, exterminates poisonous rats and burns infected villages, drinks and preaches his gospel that hygiene is destined to kill the medical art.

Alongside all of this runs the personal history of Martin Arrowsmith. Lewis is much too clever to make his characters without blemish, and Martin suffers from faults which at times seem obstructive to his development, both as a man and as a scientist. As a restless and irresolute young man he gets his best help from a little woman he encountered at a hospital where she was an insignificant nurse. When he begins to drift about the country as an unsuccessful medical student, he looks her up in a little village in the Far West, and there she becomes his wife. She is a devoted and simple soul, who demands nothing and who patiently waits in her solitude when, bewitched by the siren of science, her husband loses himself in the labyrinths of his work.

Later she accompanies him and Sondelius to the plague-infected island where Arrowsmith wants to test his serum. Her death in the abandoned hut, while her husband listens distractedly to another and more earthy siren than that of science, seems like a poetically crowning final act to a life of primitive self-sacrificing femininity.

The book is full of admirable learning, certified by experts as being accurate. Though a master of light-winged words, Lewis is never superficial when it comes to the foundations of his art. His study of details is always as careful and thorough as that of such a scientist as Arrowsmith or Gottlieb. In this work he has built a monument to the profession of his own father, that of the physician, which certainly is not represented by a charlatan or a faker.

His big novel *Elmer Gantry* (1927) is like a surgical operation on one of the most delicate parts of the social body. Presumably it would not pay to search anywhere in the world for the old Puritanical virtues, but possibly one might find in some of the oldest corners of America a remnant of the sect which regarded it as a sin to remarry, once it had pleased God to make one a widower or widow, and wicked to lend money at interest. But otherwise America has no doubt had to moderate its religious rigidity. To what extent a pulpiteer like Elmer Gantry is common over there, we cannot here have the slightest idea. Neither his slapdash style of preaching with his cocky pugilistic manners («Hello, Mr. Devil») nor his successful collecting of money and men inside the gates of the church can hide the sad fact that he is an unusually foul fish. Mr. Lewis has been neither willing nor able to give him any attractive traits. But as description the book is a feat of strength, genuine and powerful, and its full-flavoured, sombre satire has a devastating effect. It is unnecessary to point out that hypocrisy thrives a little everywhere and that any one who attacks it at such a close range places himself before a hydra with many dangerous heads.

Sinclair Lewis's latest work is called *Dodsworth* (1929). In his books we have previously caught glimpses of the family as one of the most artistocratic in Zenith–a circle where no Babbitt ever gains admission. «Most aristocratic» probably often means in America «richest», but Sam Dodsworth is both aristocratic and rich. Even after 300 years he notices the English blood in his veins and wants to know the land of his ancestors. He is an American, but not a jingo. With him travels his wife, Fran. She is already over forty, while he is fifty. She is a cool beauty, «virginal as the winter wind», though she has grown children. In the European atmosphere she blossoms as a brilliant flower of luxury, revelling in vanity, pleasure, and selfishness. She goes so far that the quiet man who loves her has to leave her to her fate.

Once alone he meditates on the problem «Europe-America», and as a real business man he wants to clear up his accounts with both. He thinks of many things, honestly and without prejudice. One of his observations is that the very soil of Europe has some of the old-time quiet, which is scorned by America, the land of restless record-hunters. But America is the land of youth and daring experiments. And when he returns there, we understand that the heart of Sinclair Lewis follows him.

Yes, Sinclair Lewis is an American. He writes the new language–American –as one of the representatives of 120,000,000 souls. He asks us to consider that this nation is not yet finished or melted down; that it is still in the turbulent years of adolescence.

The new great American literature has started with national self-criticism. It is a sign of health. Sinclair Lewis has the blessed gift of wielding his land-clearing implement not only with a firm hand but with a smile on his lips and youth in his heart. He has the manners of a new settler, who takes new land into cultivation. He is a pioneer.

Mr. Sinclair Lewis–I have spoken of you to this assembly in a language which you do not understand. I might have abused the occasion to speak ill of you. I have not done it. I have spoken of you as one of the strong, young chieftains of the great new American literature. Besides, you have a ecial recommendation to Swedish hearts. You were born among our ountrymen in America, and you have mentioned them in friendly terms your renowned books. We are glad to see you here today and glad that ur nation has a laurel of its own to bestow on you. And now I ask you descend with me and receive it from the hand of our King.

t the banquet, Tor Hedberg, Member of the Swedish Academy, addressed e laureate: «Finally, Mr. Lewis, in your person we greet that [American] ew building on its own American ground. It has been said that the Nobel rize in Literature has found its way across the Atlantic far too late. If so, has not been due to any indifference on the part of the Swedish Academy, or to any lack of knowledge, but rather to an «embarras de richesse». It as further been said that the award of a prize to your work, in which the ollies of mankind–not excluding those that are perhaps special to America have been scourged, is an expression of some kind of European or Swedish nimosity against America. I dare to assert that this is a complete mistake. is with living humour that you aim the blows of your scourge, and where here is humour, there is a heart too. It is not only the keen and lively in- llect, the masterly design of human shapes and characters but also the warm, pen, gaily-beating heart that we have appreciated in you.» Sinclair Lewis xpressed his gratitude and declared that he felt closely related to the Swedish eople because of his many acquaintances among the Swedish families of Minnesota. He said that the Nobel Prize had a great significance for him, at it had in fact created a new standard which implied an obligation to nprove on what he had done so far. Furthermore, he considered it a high onour to have been awarded the Nobel Prize along with the renowned holars who received the distinction. He said that, personally, he had the rofoundest respect for the integrity of the scientist, and thought that a man f letters, himself included, should strive for the same integrity.

SINCLAIR LEWIS

The American Fear of Literature

Nobel Lecture, December 12, 1930

Were I to express my feeling of honor and pleasure in having been awarded the Nobel Prize in Literature, I should be fulsome and perhaps tedious, and I present my gratitude with a plain «Thank you».

I wish, in this address, to consider certain trends, certain dangers, and certain high and exciting promises in present-day American literature. To discuss this with complete and unguarded frankness–and I should not insult you by being otherwise than completely honest, however indiscreet–it will be necessary for me to be a little impolite regarding certain institutions and persons of my own greatly beloved land.

But I beg of you to believe that I am in no case gratifying a grudge. Fortune has dealt with me rather too well. I have known little struggle, not much poverty, many generosities. Now and then I have, for my books or myself, been somewhat warmly denounced–there was one good pastor in California who upon reading my *Elmer Gantry* desired to lead a mob and lynch me, while another holy man in the state of Maine wondered if there was no respectable and righteous way of putting me in jail. And, much harder to endure than any raging condemnation, a certain number of old acquaintance among journalists, what in the galloping American slang we call the «I Knew Him When Club», have scribbled that since they know me personally, therefore I must be a rather low sort of fellow and certainly no writer. But if I have now and then received such cheering brickbats, still I, who have heaved a good many bricks myself, would be fatuous not to expect a fair number in return.

No, I have for myself no conceivable complaint to make, and yet for American literature in general, and its standing in a country where industrialism and finance and science flourish and the only arts that are vital and respected are architecture and the film, I have a considerable complaint.

I can illustrate by an incident which chances to concern the Swedish Academy and myself and which happened a few days ago, just before I took the ship at New York for Sweden. There is in America a learned and most amiable old gentleman who has been a pastor, a university professor, and a diplomat. He is a member of the American Academy of Arts and Letters and no few universities have honored him with degrees. As a writer he is chiefly known for his pleasant little essays on the joy of fishing. I do not suppose that professional fishermen, whose lives depend on the run of cod or herring, find it altogether an amusing occupation, but from these essays I learned, as a boy, that there is something very important and spiritual about catching fish, if you have no need of doing so.

This scholar stated, and publicly, that in awarding the Nobel Prize to a person who has scoffed at American institutions as much as I have, the Nobel Committee and the Swedish Academy had insulted America. I don't know whether, as an ex-diplomat, he intends to have an international incident made of it, and perhaps demand of the American Government that they land Marines in Stockholm to protect American literary rights, but I hope not.

I should have supposed that to a man so learned as to have been made a Doctor of Divinity, a Doctor of Letters, and I do not know how many other imposing magnificences, the matter would have seemed different; I should have supposed that he would have reasoned, «Although personally I dislike this man's books, nevertheless the Swedish Academy has in choosing him honored America by assuming that the Americans are no longer a puerile backwoods clan, so inferior that they are afraid of criticism, but instead a nation come of age and able to consider calmly and maturely any dissection of their land, however scoffing.»

I should even have supposed that so international a scholar would have believed that Scandinavia, accustomed to the works of Strindberg, Ibsen, and Pontoppidan, would not have been peculiarly shocked by a writer whose most anarchistic assertion has been that America, with all her wealth and power, has not yet produced a civilization good enough to satisfy the deepest wants of human creatures.

I believe that Strindberg rarely sang the «Star-Spangled Banner» or addressed Rotary Clubs, yet Sweden seems to have survived him.

I have at such length discussed this criticism of the learned fisherman not because it has any conceivable importance in itself, but because it does illustrate the fact that in America most of us–not readers alone but even writers –are still afraid of any literature which is not a glorification of everything American, a glorification of our faults as well as our virtues. To be not only a best-seller in America but to be really beloved, a novelist must assert that all American men are tall, handsome, rich, honest, and powerful at golf; that all country towns are filled with neighbors who do nothing from day to day save go about being kind to one another; that although American girls may be wild, they change always into perfect wives and mothers; and that, geographically, America is composed solely of New York, which is inhabited entirely by millionaires; of the West, which keeps unchanged all the boisterous heroism of 1870; and of the South, where everyone lives on a plantation perpetually glossy with moonlight and scented with magnolias.

It is not today vastly more true than it was twenty years ago that such novelists of ours as you have read in Sweden, novelists like Dreiser and Willa Cather, are authentically popular and influential in America. As it was revealed by the venerable fishing Academician whom I have quoted, we still most revere the writers for the popular magazines who in a hearty and edifying chorus chant that the America of a hundred and twenty million population is still as simple, as pastoral, as it was when it had but forty million; that in an industrial plant with ten thousand employees, the relationship between the worker and the manager is still as neighborly and uncomplex as in a factory of 1840, with five employees; that the relationships between father and son, between husband and wife, are precisely the same in an apartment in a thirty-story palace today, with three motor cars awaiting the family below and five books on the library shelves and a divorce imminent in the family next week, as were those relationships in a rose-veiled five-room cottage in 1880; that, in fine, America has gone through the revolutionary change from rustic colony to world empire without having in the least altered the bucolic and Puritanic simplicity of Uncle Sam.

I am, actually, extremely grateful to the fishing Academician for having somewhat condemned me. For since he is a leading member of the American Academy of Arts and Letters, he has released me, has given me the right to speak as frankly of that Academy as he has spoken of me. And in any honest study of American intellectualism today, that curious institution must be considered.

Before I consider the Academy, however, let me sketch a fantasy which has pleased me the last few days in the unavoidable idleness of a rough trip on the Atlantic. I am sure that you know, by now, that the award to me of the Nobel Prize has by no means been altogether popular in America. Doubtless the experience is not new to you. I fancy that when you gave the award even to Thomas Mann, whose *Zauberberg* seems to me to contain the whole of intellectual Europe, even when you gave it to Kipling, whose social significance is so profound that it has been rather authoritatively said that he created the British Empire, even when you gave it to Bernard Shaw,

ere were countrymen to those authors who complained because you did
t choose another.

And I imagined what would have been said had you chosen some American
ther than myself. Suppose you had taken Theodore Dreiser.

Now to me, as to many other American writers, Dreiser more than any
ther man, marching alone, usually unappreciated, often hated, has cleared
e trail from Victorian and Howellsian timidity and gentility in American
ction to honesty and boldness and passion of life. Without his pioneering,
doubt if any of us could, unless we liked to be sent to jail, seek to express
fe and beauty and terror.

My great colleague Sherwood Anderson has proclaimed this leadership
f Dreiser. I am delighted to join him. Dreiser's great first novel, *Sister Carrie*,
which he dared to publish thirty long years ago and which I read twenty-
ve years ago, came to housebound and airless America like a great free
Western wind, and to our stuffy domesticity gave us the first fresh air since
Mark Twain and Whitman.

Yet had you given the Prize to Mr. Dreiser, you would have heard groans
rom America; you would have heard that his style–I am not exactly sure
what this mystic quality «style» may be, but I find the word so often in
he writings of minor critics that I suppose it must exist–you would have
eard that his style is cumbersome, that his choice of words is insensitive,
hat his books are interminable. And certainly respectable scholars would
omplain that in Mr. Dreiser's world, men and women are often sinful and
ragic and despairing, instead of being forever sunny and full of song and
irtue, as befits authentic Americans.

And had you chosen Mr. Eugene O'Neill, who has done nothing much
n American drama save to transform it utterly, in ten or twelve years, from
false world of neat and competent trickery to a world of splendor and fear
nd greatness, you would have been reminded that he has done something
ar worse than scoffing–he has seen life as not to be neatly arranged in the
tudy of a scholar but as a terrifying, magnificent, and often quite horrible
hing akin to the tornado, the earthquake, the devastating fire.

And had you given Mr. James Branch Cabell the Prize, you would have
een told that he is too fantastically malicious. So would you have been told
hat Miss Willa Cather, for all the homely virtue of her novels concerning
he peasants of Nebraska, has in her novel, *The Lost Lady*, been so untrue
o America's patent and perpetual and possibly tedious virtuousness as to
icture an abandoned woman who remains, nevertheless, uncannily charm-

ing even to the virtuous, in a story without any moral; that Mr. Henr
Mencken is the worst of all scoffers; that Mr. Sherwood Anderson viciousl
errs in considering sex as important a force in life as fishing; that Mr. Upto
Sinclair, being a Socialist, sins against the perfectness of American capitalisti
mass production; that Mr. Joseph Hergesheimer is un-American in regardin
graciousness of manner and beauty of surface as of some importance in th
endurance of daily life; and that Mr. Ernest Hemingway is not only to
young but, far worse, uses language which should be unknown to gentlemen
that he acknowledges drunkenness as one of man's eternal ways to happiness
and asserts that a soldier may find love more significant than the heart
slaughter of men in battle.

Yes, they are wicked, these colleagues of mine; you would have done al
most as evilly to have chosen them as to have chosen me; and as a chauvinisti
American–only, mind you, as an American of 1930 and not of 1880–I re
joice that they are my countrymen and countrywomen, and that I may speal
of them with pride even in the Europe of Thomas Mann, H. G. Wells
Galsworthy, Knut Hamsun, Arnold Bennett, Feuchtwanger, Selma Lager
löf, Sigrid Undset, Verner von Heidenstam, D'Annunzio, Romain Rolland

It is my fate in this paper to swing constantly from optimism to pessimisn
and back, but so is it the fate of anyone who writes or speaks of anything
in America–the most contradictory, the most depressing, the most stirring
of any land in the world today.

Thus, having with no muted pride called the roll of what seem to me to
be great men and women in American literary life today, and having indeed
omitted a dozen other names of which I should like to boast were there time
I must turn again and assert that in our contemporary American literature
indeed in all American arts save architecture and the film, we–yes, we who
have such pregnant and vigorous standards in commerce and science–have
no standards, no healing communication, no heroes to be followed nor vil
lains to be condemned, no certain ways to be pursued, and no dangerou
paths to be avoided.

The American novelist or poet or dramatist or sculptor or painter mus
work alone, in confusion, unassisted save by his own integrity.

That, of course, has always been the lot of the artist. The vagabond and
criminal François Villon had certainly no smug and comfortable refuge in
which elegant ladies would hold his hand and comfort his starveling sou
and more starved body. He, veritably a great man, destined to outlive in
history all the dukes and puissant cardinals whose robes he was esteemed

unworthy to touch, had for his lot the gutter and the hardened crust.

Such poverty is not for the artist in America. They pay us, indeed, only too well; that writer is a failure who cannot have his butler and motor and his villa at Palm Beach, where he is permitted to mingle almost in equality with the barons of banking. But he is oppressed ever by something worse than poverty—by the feeling that what he creates does not matter, that he is expected by his readers to be only a decorator or a clown, or that he is good-naturedly accepted as a scoffer whose bark probably is worse than his bite and who probably is a good fellow at heart, who in any case certainly does not count in a land that produces eighty-story buildings, motors by the million, and wheat by the billions of bushels. And he has no institution, no group, to which he can turn for inspiration, whose criticism he can accept and whose praise will be precious to him.

What institutions have we?

The American Academy of Arts and Letters does contain, along with several excellent painters and architects and statesmen, such a really distinguished university president as Nicholas Murray Butler, so admirable and courageous a scholar as Wilbur Cross, and several first-rate writers: the poets Edwin Arlington Robinson and Robert Frost, the free-minded publicist James Truslow Adams, and the novelists Edith Wharton, Hamlin Garland, Owen Wister, Brand Whitlock, and Booth Tarkington.

But it does not include Theodore Dreiser, Henry Mencken, our most vivid critic, George Jean Nathan, who, though still young, is certainly the dean of our dramatic critics, Eugene O'Neill, incomparably our best dramatist, the really original and vital poets, Edna St. Vincent Millay and Carl Sandburg, Robinson Jeffers and Vachel Lindsay and Edgar Lee Masters, whose *Spoon River Anthology* was so utterly different from any other poetry ever published, so fresh, so authoritative, so free from any gropings and timidities that it came like a revelation and created a new school of native American poetry. It does not include the novelists and short-story writers, Willa Cather, Joseph Hergesheimer, Sherwood Anderson, Ring Lardner, Ernest Hemingway, Louis Bromfield, Wilbur Daniel Steele, Fannie Hurst, Mary Austin, James Branch Cabell, Edna Ferber, nor Upton Sinclair, of whom you must say, whether you admire or detest his aggressive socialism, that he is internationally better known than any other American artist whosoever, be he novelist, poet, painter, sculptor, musician, architect.

I should not expect any Academy to be so fortunate as to contain all these writers, but one which fails to contain any of them, which thus cuts itself off from so much of what is living and vigorous and original in American letters, can have no relationship whatever to our life and aspirations. It does not represent the literary America of today—it represents only Henry Wadsworth Longfellow.

It might be answered that, after all, the Academy is limited to fifty members; that, naturally, it cannot include every one of merit. But the fact is that while most of our few giants are excluded, the Academy does have room to include three extraordinarily bad poets, two very melodramatic and insignificant playwrights, two gentlemen who are known only because they are university presidents, a man who was thirty years ago known as a rather clever, humorous draughtsman, and several gentlemen of whom—I sadly confess my ignorance—I have never heard.

Let me again emphasize the fact—for it is a fact—that I am not attacking the American Academy. It is a hospitable and generous and decidedly dignified institution. And it is not altogether the Academy's fault that it does not contain many of the men who have significance in our letters. Sometimes it is the fault of those writers themselves. I cannot imagine that grizzly bear Theodore Dreiser being comfortable at the serenely Athenian dinners of the Academy, and were they to invite Mencken, he would infuriate them with his boisterous jeering. No, I am not attacking—I am reluctantly considering the Academy because it is so perfect an example of the divorce in America of intellectual life from all authentic standards of importance and reality.

Our universities and colleges, or gymnasia, most of them, exhibit the same unfortunate divorce. I can think of four of them, Rollins College in Florida, Middlebury College in Vermont, the University of Michigan, and the University of Chicago—which has had on its roll so excellent a novelist as Robert Herrick, so courageous a critic as Robert Morss Lovett—which have shown an authentic interest in contemporary creative literature. Four of them. But universities and colleges and musical emporiums and schools for the teaching of theology and plumbing and signpainting are as thick in America as the motor traffic. Whenever you see a public building with Gothic fenestration on a sturdy backing of Indiana concrete, you may be certain that it is another university, with anywhere from two hundred to twenty thousand students equally ardent about avoiding the disadvantage of becoming learned and about gaining the social prestige contained in the possession of a B.A. degree.

Oh, socially our universities are close to the mass of our citizens, and so are they in the matter of athletics. A great college football game is passionately vitnessed by eighty thousand people, who have paid five dollars apiece and motored anywhere from ten to a thousand miles for the ecstasy of watching twenty-two men chase one another up and down a curiously marked field. During the football season, a capable player ranks very nearly with our greatest and most admired heroes–even with Henry Ford, President Hoover, and Colonel Lindbergh.

And in one branch of learning, the sciences, the lords of business who rule us are willing to do homage to the devotees of learning. However bleakly one of our trader aristocrats may frown upon poetry or the visions of a painter, he is graciously pleased to endure a Millikan, a Michelson, a Banting, a Theobald Smith.

But the paradox is that in the arts our universities are as cloistered, as far from reality and living creation, as socially and athletically and scientifically they are close to us. To a true-blue professor of literature in an American university, literature is not something that a plain human being, living to-day, painfully sits down to produce. No; it is something dead; it is something magically produced by superhuman beings who must, if they are to be regarded as artists at all, have died at least one hundred years before the diabolical invention of the typewriter. To any authentic don, there is something slightly repulsive in the thought that literature could be created by any ordinary human being, still to be seen walking the streets, wearing quite commonplace trousers and coat and looking not so unlike a chauffeur or a farmer. Our American professors like their literature clear and cold and pure and very dead.

I do not suppose that American universities are alone in this. I am aware that to the dons of Oxford and Cambridge, it would seem rather indecent to suggest that Wells and Bennett and Galsworthy and George Moore may, while they commit the impropriety of continuing to live, be compared to anyone so beautifully and safely dead as Samuel Johnson. I suppose that in the universities of Sweden and France and Germany there exist plenty of professors who prefer dissection to understanding. But in the new and vital and experimental land of America, one would expect the teachers of literature to be less monastic, more human, than in the traditional shadows of old Europe.

They are not.

There has recently appeared in America, out of the universities, an astonishing circus called «the New Humanism». Now of course «humanism» means so many things that it means nothing. It may infer anything from a belief that Greek and Latin are more inspiring than the dialect of contemporary peasants to a belief that any living peasant is more interesting than a dead Greek. But it is a delicate bit of justice that this nebulous word should have been chosen to label this nebulous cult.

Insofar as I have been able to comprehend them—for naturally in a world so exciting and promising as this today, a life brilliant with Zeppelins and Chinese revolutions and the Bolshevik industrialization of farming and ships and the Grand Canyon and young children and terrifying hunger and the lonely quest of scientists after God, no creative writer would have the time to follow all the chilly enthusiasms of the New Humanists—this newest of sects reasserts the dualism of man's nature. It would confine literature to the fight between man's soul and God, or man's soul and evil.

But, curiously, neither God nor the devil may wear modern dress, but must retain Grecian vestments. Oedipus is a tragic figure for the New Humanists; man, trying to maintain himself as the image of God under the menace of dynamos, in a world of high-pressure salesmanship, is not. And the poor comfort which they offer is that the object of life is to develop self-discipline – whether or not one ever accomplishes anything with this self-discipline. So the whole movement results in the not particularly novel doctrine that both art and life must be resigned and negative. It is a doctrine of the blackest reaction introduced into a stirringly revolutionary world.

Strangely enough, this doctrine of death, this escape from the complexities and danger of living into the secure blankness of the monastery, has become widely popular among professors in a land where one would have expected only boldness and intellectual adventure, and it has more than ever shut creative writers off from any benign influence which might conceivably have come from the universities.

But it has always been so. America has never had a Brandes, a Taine, a Goethe, a Croce.

With a wealth of creative talent in America, our criticism has most of it been a chill and insignificant activity pursued by jealous spinsters, ex-baseball-reporters, and acid professors. Our Erasmuses have been village schoolmistresses. How should there be any standards when there has been no one capable of setting them up?

The great Cambridge-Concord circle of the middle of the nineteenth century – Emerson, Longfellow, Lowell, Holmes, the Alcotts – were sentimental reflections of Europe, and they left no school, no influence. Whitman and Thoreau and Poe and, in some degree, Hawthorne, were outcasts.

en alone and despised, berated by the New Humanists of their generation.
was with the emergence of William Dean Howells that we first began
have something like a standard, and a very bad standard it was.

Mr. Howells was one of the gentlest, sweetest, and most honest of men,
ut he had the code of a pious old maid whose greatest delight was to have
a at the vicarage. He abhorred not only profanity and obscenity but all
f what H. G. Wells has called «the jolly coarsenesses of life». In his fantastic
ision of life, which he innocently conceived to be realistic, farmers and
amen and factory hands might exist, but the farmer must never be covered
ith muck, the seaman must never roll out bawdy chanteys, the factory
and must be thankful to his good kind employer, and all of them must
ng for the opportunity to visit Florence and smile gently at the quaintness
f the beggars.

So strongly did Howells feel this genteel, this New Humanistic philosophy
at he was able vastly to influence his contemporaries, down even to 1914
d the turmoil of the Great War.

He was actually able to tame Mark Twain, perhaps the greatest of our
riters, and to put that fiery old savage into an intellectual frock coat and
p hat. His influence is not altogether gone today. He is still worshipped
y Hamlin Garland, an author who should in every way have been greater
an Howells but who under Howells' influence was changed from a harsh
d magnificent realist into a genial and insignificant lecturer. Mr. Garland
, so far as we have one, the dean of American letters today, and as our
an, he is alarmed by all of the younger writers who are so lacking in taste
to suggest that men and women do not always love in accordance with
e prayer-book, and that common people sometimes use language which
ould be inappropriate at a women's literary club on Main Street. Yet this
me Hamlin Garland, as a young man, before he had gone to Boston and
come cultured and Howellsised, wrote two most valiant and revelatory
orks of realism, *Main-Traveled Roads* and *Rose of Dutcher's Coolie*.

I read them as a boy in a prairie village in Minnesota—just such an envi-
nment as was described in Mr. Garland's tales. They were vastly exciting
me. I had realized in reading Balzac and Dickens that it was possible to
scribe French and English common people as one actually saw them. But
had never occurred to me that one might without indecency write of the
ople of Sauk Centre, Minnesota, as one felt about them. Our fictional
adition, you see, was that all of us in Midwestern villages were altogether
ble and happy; that not one of us would exchange the neighborly bliss

of living on Main Street for the heathen gaudiness of New York or Paris or Stockholm. But in Mr. Garland's *Main-Traveled Roads* I discovered that there was one man who believed that Midwestern peasants were sometimes bewildered and hungry and vile–and heroic. And, given this vision, I was released; I could write of life as living life.

I am afraid that Mr. Garland would be not pleased but acutely annoyed to know that he made it possible for me to write of America as I see it, and not as Mr. William Dean Howells so sunnily saw it. And it is his tragedy, it is a completely revelatory American tragedy, that in our land of freedom men like Garland, who first blast the roads to freedom, become themselves the most bound.

But, all this time, while men like Howells were so effusively seeking to guide America into becoming a pale edition of an English cathedral town, there were surly and authentic fellows–Whitman and Melville, then Dreiser and James Huneker and Mencken–who insisted that our land had something more than tea-table gentility.

And so, without standards, we have survived. And for the strong young men, it has perhaps been well that we should have no standards. For, after seeming to be pessimistic about my own and much beloved land, I want to close this dirge with a very lively sound of optimism.

I have, for the future of American literature, every hope and every eager belief. We are coming out, I believe, of the stuffiness of safe, sane, and incredibly dull provincialism. There are young Americans today who are doing such passionate and authentic work that it makes me sick to see that I am a little too old to be one of them.

There is Ernest Hemingway, a bitter youth, educated by the most intense experience, disciplined by his own high standards, an authentic artist whose home is in the whole of life; there is Thomas Wolfe, a child of, I believe, thirty or younger, whose one and only novel, *Look Homeward, Angel,* worthy to be compared with the best in our literary production, a Gargantuan creature with great gusto of life; there is Thornton Wilder, who in an age of realism dreams the old and lovely dreams of the eternal romantics; there is John Dos Passos, with his hatred of the safe and sane standards of Babbitt and his splendor of revolution; there is Stephen Benét, who to American drabness has restored the epic poem with his glorious memory of old John Brown; there are Michael Gold, who reveals the new frontier of the Jewish East Side, and William Faulkner, who has freed the South from hoopskirts; and there are a dozen other young poets and fictioneers, most of them living ow in Paris, most of them a little insane in the tradition of James Joyce, who, however insane they may be, have refused to be genteel and traditional and dull.

I salute them, with a joy in being not yet too far removed from their determination to give to the America that has mountains and endless prairies, enormous cities and lost far cabins, billions of money and tons of faith, to an America that is as strange as Russia and as complex as China, a literature worthy of her vastness.

Autobiography

To recount my life for the Nobel Foundation, I would like to present it as possessing some romantic quality, some unique character, like Kipling's early adventures in India, or Bernard Shaw's leadership in the criticism of British arts and economics. But my life, aside from such youthful pranks as sailing on cattleships from America to England during university vacations, trying to find work in Panama during the building of the Canal, and serving for two months as janitor of Upton Sinclair's abortive co-operative colony, Helicon Hall, has been a rather humdrum chronicle of much reading, constant writing, undistinguished travel à la tripper, and several years of comfortable servitude as an editor.

I was born in a prairie village in that most Scandinavian part of America, Minnesota, the son of a country doctor, in 1885. Until I went East to Yale University I attended the ordinary public school, along with many Madsens, Olesons, Nelsons, Hedins, Larsons. Doubtless it was because of this that I made the hero of my second book, *The Trail of the Hawk*, a Norwegian, and Gustaf Sondelius, of *Arrowsmith*, a Swede – and to me, Dr. Sondelius is the favorite among all my characters.

Of Carl Ericson of *The Trail of the Hawk*, I wrote – back in 1914, when I was working all day as editor for the George H. Doran Publishing Company, and all evening trying to write novels – as follows:

«His carpenter father had come from Norway, by way of steerage and a farm in Wisconsin, changing his name (to Americanize it) from Ericsen... Carl was second-generation Norwegian; American-born, American in speech, American in appearance, save for his flaxen hair and china-blue eyes... When he was born the ‹typical Americans› of earlier stocks had moved to city palaces or were marooned on run-down farms. It was Carl Ericson, not a Trowbridge or a Stuyvesant or a Lee or a Grant, who was the ‹typical American› of his period. It was for him to carry on the American destiny of extending the Western horizon; his to restore the wintry Pilgrim virtues and the exuberant October, partridge-drumming days of Daniel Boone; then to add, in his own or another generation, new American aspirations for beauty.»

My university days at Yale were undistinguished save for contributions
to the *Yale Literary Magazine*. It may be interesting to say that these contributions were most of them reeking with a banal romanticism; that an author
who was later to try to present ordinary pavements trod by real boots should
through university days have written nearly always of Guinevere and Lan-
celot–of weary bitterns among sad Irish reeds–of story-book castles with
troubadours vastly indulging in wine, a commodity of which the author was
singularly ignorant. What the moral is, I do not know. Whether imaginary
castles at nineteen lead always to the sidewalks of Main Street at thirty-five,
and whether the process might be reversed, and whether either of them is
desirable, I leave to psychologists.

I drifted for two years after college as a journalist, as a newspaper reporter
in Iowa and in San Francisco, as–incredibly–a junior editor on a magazine
for teachers of the deaf, in Washington, D.C. The magazine was supported
by Alexander Graham Bell, inventor of the telephone. What I did not know
about teaching the deaf would have included the entire subject, but that did
not vastly matter, as my position was so insignificant that it included typing
hundreds of letters every week begging for funds for the magazine and, on
days when the Negro janitress did not appear, sweeping out the office.

Doubtless this shows the advantages of a university education, and it was
further shown when at the age of twenty-five I managed to get a position
in a New York publishing house at all of fifteen dollars a week. This was
my authentic value on the labor market, and I have always uncomfortably
suspected that it would never have been much higher had I not, accidentally,
possessed the gift of writing books which so acutely annoyed American
smugness that some thousands of my fellow citizens felt they must read these
scandalous documents, whether they liked them or not.

From that New York position till the time five years later when I was
selling enough short stories to the magazines to be able to live by free-lancing,
I had a series of typical white-collar, unromantic, office literary jobs with
two publishing houses, a magazine (*Adventure*), and a newspaper syndicate,
reading manuscripts, writing book advertising, writing catalogues, writing
uninspired book reviews–all the carpentry and plumbing of the city of letters.
Nor did my first five novels rouse the slightest whispers: *Our Mr. Wrenn*,
The Trail of the Hawk, *The Job*, *The Innocents*, and *Free Air* they were called,
published between 1914 and 1919, and all of them dead before the ink was
dry. I lacked sense enough to see that, after five failures, I was foolish to
continue writing.

Main Street, published late in 1920, was my first novel to rouse the em
battled peasantry and, as I have already hinted, it had really a success o
scandal. One of the most treasured American myths had been that all Ameri
can villages were peculiarly noble and happy, and here an American attacke
that myth. Scandalous. Some hundreds of thousands read the book with th
same masochistic pleasure that one has in sucking an aching tooth.

Since *Main Street*, the novels have been *Babbitt* (1922); *Arrowsmith* (1925)
Mantrap (1926); *Elmer Gantry* (1927); *The Man Who Knew Coolidge* (1928)
and *Dodsworth* (1929). The next novel, yet unnamed, will concern idealisn
in America through three generations, from 1818 till 1930 – an idealisn
which the outlanders who call Americans «dollar-chasers» do not understand
It will presumably be published in the autumn of 1932, and the author's chie
difficulty in composing it is that, after having received the Nobel Prize, h
longs to write better than he can.

I was married, in England, in 1928, to Dorothy Thompson, an America
who had been the Central European correspondent and *chef de bureau* of th
New York Evening Post. My first marriage, to Grace Hegger, in New York
in 1914, had been dissolved.

During these years of novelwriting since 1915, I have lived a quite unro
mantic and unstirring life. I have travelled much; on the surface it woul
seem that one who during these fifteen years had been in forty states of th
United States, in Canada, Mexico, England, Scotland, France, Italy, Sweden
Germany, Austria, Czechoslovakia, Jugoslavia, Greece, Switzerland, Spain
the West Indies, Venezuela, Colombia, Panama, Poland, and Russia mus
have been adventurous. That, however, would be a typical error of biog
raphy. The fact is that my foreign travelling has been a quite uninspire
recreation, a flight from reality. My real travelling has been sitting in Pull
man smoking cars, in a Minnesota village, on a Vermont farm, in a hote
in Kansas City or Savannah, listening to the normal daily drone of wha
are to me the most fascinating and exotic people in the world – the Averag
Citizens of the United States, with their friendliness to strangers and thei
rough teasing, their passion for material advancement and their shy idealism
their interest in all the world and their boastful provincialism – the intricat
complexities which an American novelist is privileged to portray.

And nowadays, at forty-six, with my first authentic home – a farm in th
pastoral state of Vermont – and a baby born in June 1930, I am settled dow
to what I hope to be the beginning of a novelist's career. I hope the awkwar
apprenticeship with all its errors is nearly done.

Biographical note on Sinclair Lewis

inclair Lewis (1885–1951) continued to be a prolific writer, but none of his
ıter writings equalled the success or stature of his chief works of the twenties.
ıfter his divorce from his second wife in 1942, Sinclair Lewis lived chiefly in
ıurope. His later novels include *Ann Vickers* (1933), *It Can't Happen Here*
1935), *The Prodigal Parents* (1938), *Gideon Planish* (1943), *Cass Timberlane*
1945), *Kingsblood Royal* (1947), *The God-Seeker* (1949), and *World So Wide*
1951). *From Main Street to Stockholm: Letters of Sinclair Lewis 1919–1930* was
ıublished in 1952, one year after his death in Rome.

Literature 1931

ERIK AXEL KARLFELDT

«the poetry of Erik Axel Karlfeldt»

Presentation

by Anders Österling, Member of the Nobel Committee of the Swedish Academy

f an interested foreigner were to ask one of Erik Axel Karlfeldt's countrymen what we admire most in this poet and on what qualities his national
greatness depends, it would at first seem easy to give an answer. People like
to talk of what they love. The Swede would say that we celebrate this poet
because he represents our character with a style and a genuineness that we
should like to be ours, and because he has sung with singular power and
exquisite charm of the tradition of our people, of all the precious features
which are the basis for our feeling for home and country in the shadow of
the pine-covered mountains.

But the Swede would soon check himself, realizing that such a general
explanation is insufficient, that in Karlfeldt there are many things, beloved
but difficult to define, which a proper appraisal must take into account but
which are inaccessible to the foreigner. Hence we can offer no ready-made
expression of our conviction of the high rank of Karlfeldt's poetry, for there
are elements of mysticism in it, powers and instincts that elude analysis.

We face a similar difficulty on this occasion when we are to briefly sketch
the life-work of the great lyrical poet, since it has now been made the object
of a great international award. It is the deliberate self-limitation of lyrical
poetry, and at the same time its fate, that its most profound qualities and
values are indissolubly connected with the character and rhythm of its original
language, with the meaning and weight of every single word. Karlfeldt's
individuality may be dimly felt in a translation, but only in Swedish can it
be fully comprehended. However, if one attempts to find independent comparative criteria, he is forced to admit that even the treasures of the so-called
great literatures have only rarely been enriched by such jewels as Karlfeldt
has created in a so-called minor language.

If we look back on Karlfeldt's notable career from its début in 1895 and
follow it through the works of three decades, steady though limited in size
by his austere standards, we see very clearly how this man used his talents
with a rare instinct for the fruitful, the solid, and the genuine. He began as
a minstrel and a singer of nature, conscious of his ability but still doubtful

of his calling. Was there any use for the dreams that thronged his breast
Could they have a meaning for a whole people? Early in his career, the poe
looked for a deputy, an alter ego, an independent figure suited to represen
his feelings, his sufferings, and his longing as well as his sarcasm. The famou
Fridolin was at first a creation of shyness, for the poet was reluctant to appea
in his own person and expose the private life of his soul. Fridolin soon be
came a classic, and he has his place in the rout of Northern Bacchus, a rusti
cousin of the characters of Bellman, with a firmer gait, but with flower
on his hat from the harvest festival at Pungmakarebo. Karlfeldt's home be
came more and more an artistic microcosm in which the universe was mir
rored in the same manner as Biblical scenes are mirrored in the baroqu
fantasies of the frescoes in the farmhouses of Dalekarlia. With his sense o
humour, which was often reverence in disguise, he kept his being unstained
and he preserved the magic ring of harmony. But his seemingly peacefu
development must have contained many struggles and tensions, just enougl
to create the necessary pressure for the creative spring. Poetry was for Karl
feldt a continuous test of the strength and substance of his being. Thus he
gave a powerful finale to his poetry in *Hösthorn* (1927) [The Horn of Au
tumn], his epilogue played on a winter organ, whose pipes reach from eartl
to heaven but at the same time sound a childhood echo of the small whit
churches in Dalarna.

The unity of his work is a rarity in our time. If one asks about Karlfeldt'
main problem, one word may serve as an answer: self-discipline. His orig
inality grew on the soil of a pagan and luxuriant wilderness, and he woul
not have been drawn so often to witch motifs and the pitchy brew of Urie
if he had not felt the presence of demons. The muffled tumult of nature unde
the moon of pagan festivals is one of the visions that he evokes. The contras
between the heavy intoxication of the blood and the pure celestial yearning
of the soul recurs constantly in his poetry. Yet the different elements neve
destroy each other. He tames them as does an artist by remaining faithfu
to himself and by giving a personal touch even to the smallest detail.

In Karlfeldt we find scarcely a single expression of poetic self-conscious
ness. The increasing response to his work would have made such an expres
sion superfluous even if his solid peasant blood had not been a protectio
against aesthetic arrogance. We find everywhere proof of the integrity o
professional honour that is revealed in beautiful and permanent work. In a
age in which handmade things have become rare, there is a new and almos
moral value in the masterly, chiselled, and resonant language of his verse

Karlfeldt's poetry possesses precisely this stamp of miraculous perfection. Which of us does not remember such stanzas ringing like bells or vibrating like strings, but above all sung with that peculiar and resounding voice that differs from all others? Perhaps we should remember in this context the beautiful song about the old turner, the village craftsman, who played the fiddle for the people on the banks of the Opplimen and made spinning wheels for them...

In all great poetry there is an interrelation between tradition and experiment, and the principles of renewal and conservation are contained in such poetry. The national tradition survives in Karlfeldt because it is renewed personally and has the character of a conquest dearly bought. We may rejoice that this poet, whose inspiration is drawn predominantly from a past that is disappearing or has disappeared, is thoroughly unconventional in his means of expression and shows daring innovations, whereas busy modernists often content themselves with following the latest trends and fads. Nor can there be any doubt that, despite his provincial subject matter, the singer of Dalarna is one of the contemporary poets who have most boldly tried the wings of imagination and experimented with the possibilities of poetic form.

Thus the decision to honour the poetry of Erik Axel Karlfeldt with this year's Nobel Prize is intended as an expression of justice by international standards. Death has stepped between the laureate and his reward; under the circumstances the Prize will be given to his family. He has left us, but his work remains. The tragic world of chance is outshone by the imperishable summer realm of poetry. Before our eyes we see the tomb in the dusk of winter. At the same time we hear the great victorious harmonies sung by the happiness of the creative genius; we feel the scents from the Northern pleasure garden that his poetry created for the comfort and joy of all receptive hearts.

At the banquet, Professor C. W. Oseen spoke about the deceased laureate, "Is there nothing that is only beneficial, to humanity as well as to the individual? Perhaps there is! What the poems of Erik Axel Karlfeldt have meant to the Swedish people, you, honoured guests, cannot know, but for us it remains unforgettable. For thirty-five years they have accompanied the ups and downs of our lives. That nothing may emerge from Karlfeldt's work, his world of beauty, for the benefit of humanity and the individual, I cannot

believe, I will not believe. And yet–how far are we from the intentions o
Alfred Nobel even here? Out of the prize meant to help a needy artist w
have made a wreath, a wreath to adorn the coffin of our most beloved poet

If today's award does not strictly follow Nobel's intentions, does tha
mean that the result of this procedure will be less than what Nobel intended
I say not! What we have created is not less but more! This festive ceremony
is a tribute to genius. It may not have much in common with Alfred Nobel'
dreams but it is akin to his work. He was a genius himself. His work ha
served humanity, to build and to destroy. It has served and destroyed life
The festive occasion we are celebrating is dedicated to genius with its goo
and evil faces, with this double significance, because we do not know wha
humanity needs most and what furthers its prospering most: ‹good› o
‹evil›. We dedicate this ceremony to genius, brother of madness, to whom
we owe everything that makes our lives worthwhile.»

Biography

Erik Axel Karlfeldt (1864–1931) was born in Karlbo in the province of Dalekarlia. The name Karlfeldt, which he assumed in 1889, was derived from the name of his father's farm; his parents were Erik Janson and Anna tina Jansdotter, both of whom came from old mining families. Karlfeldt attended schools at his birthplace and at Västerås, where he graduated in 1885. He studied at the University of Uppsala and received his degree in 1898. Between 1893 and 1896, he taught at the private grammar school at Djursholm and at the school for adult education at Molkom. For a short time he worked for a Stockholm paper.

After completing his studies, he held a position at the Royal Library in Stockholm for five years. In 1903 he was appointed librarian of the Agricultural Academy. Meanwhile he had found recognition as a poet, and in 1904 was elected to the Swedish Academy. In 1905 he became a member of the Nobel Institute of the Academy and in 1907 of the Nobel Committee. In 1912 he was appointed permanent secretary of the Academy and henceforth devoted all his time to this position (although he did remain a member of the Nobel Committee) and to his poetry. In 1917 he received an honorary doctorate from the University of Uppsala.

Individual poems of his had appeared even during his school days; his first collection *Vildmarks-och kärleksvisor* [Songs of the Wilderness and of Love] was printed in the autumn of 1895. It was followed by *Fridolins visor* (1898) [Fridolin's Song], *Fridolins lustgård* (1901) [Fridolin's Pleasure Garden], *Flora och Pomona* (1906) [Flora and Pomona], *Flora och Bellona* (1918) [Flora and Bellona], and *Hösthorn* (1927) [The Horn of Autumn]. Selections of his poetry, translated into English by Charles Wharton Stork under the title *Arcadia Borealis*, were published in 1938.

Karlfeldt wrote a short life of the Swedish poet Lucidor (1909) and a necrologue for Carl Fredrik Dahlgren in the proceedings of the Swedish Academy. A collection of his speeches appeared in print shortly after his death in 1931.

Literature 1932

JOHN GALSWORTHY

«for his distinguished art of narration, which takes its highest form in
The Forsyte Saga»

Presentation

by Anders Österling, Member of the Nobel Committee of the Swedish Academy

When we survey John Galsworthy's authorship, it seems to develop unusually smoothly, pushed on by a conscientious and indefatigable creative impulse. Yet he is not one of those who have turned to the literary career rapidly and without resistance. Born, as the English put it, with a silver spoon in his mouth, that is, economically independent, he studied at Harrow and Oxford, chose the law without practising it, and travelled all over the world. When, at the age of twenty-eight, he began writing for the first time, the immediate reason was the exhortation of a woman friend, and it was to Galsworthy a mere recreation, evidently not without the inherent prejudices of the gentleman, against the vocation of writing. His first two collections of tales were published under the pen name of John Sinjohn, and the editions were soon withdrawn by the self-critical beginner. Not until he was thirty-seven did he begin his real authorship by publishing the novel *The Island Pharisees* (1904), and two years later appeared *The Man of Property*, the origin of his fame and at the same time of his monumental chief work, *The Forsyte Saga*.

In Galsworthy's satire against the Island Pharisees, the fundamental feature that was to mark all his subsequent works was already apparent. The book deals with an English gentleman's having stayed abroad long enough to forget his conventional sphere of thoughts and feelings; he criticizes the national surroundings severely, and in doing so he is assisted by a Belgian vagabond, who casually makes his acquaintance in an English railway compartment and who becomes his fate. At that time Galsworthy was himself a cosmopolite returned home, prepared to fight against the old capitalistic aristocratic society with about the same program as Bernard Shaw, although the Englishman, contrary to the Irishman who fought with intellectual arms, above all aimed at capturing feeling and imagination. The pharisaical egoism of England's ruling classes, the subject of Galsworthy's debut, remained his program for the future, only specialized in his particular works. He never tired of fighting against all that seemed narrow and harsh in the national character, and the persistence of his attacks on social evil indicates his strong impressions and deeply wounded feeling of justice.

With the Forsyte type he now aimed at the upper middle class, the rich businessmen, a group not yet having reached real gentility, but striving with its sympathies and instincts toward the well-known ideal of the gentleman of rigid, imperturbable, and imposing correctness. These people are particularly on their guard against dangerous feelings, a fact which, however does not exclude accidental lapses, when passion intrudes upon their life, and liberty claims its rights in a world of property instincts. Beauty, here represented by Irene, does not like to live with *The Man of Property*; in his bitter indignation at this, Soames Forsyte becomes almost a tragic figure. It seems uncertain if in the beginning Galsworthy thought of a sequel to that first Forsyte novel, which is a masterpiece of an energetic, firm, and independent account of human nature. At any rate it was not until fifteen years later that he again took up his Forsytes, and at this time the effects of the World War had radically changed the perspective. But now this work expanded; *In Chancery* (1920) and *To Let* (1921) and two short story interludes were added, and thus *The Forsyte Saga* proper was completed. Not finished with the younger members of the family, Galsworthy wrote *A Modern Comedy*, a new trilogy whose structure is exactly like that of its predecessor and consists of the three novels, *The White Monkey* (1924), *The Silver Spoon* (1926), and *Swan Song* (1928), united by two short story interludes. These two trilogies together form an unusual literary accomplishment. The novelist has carried the history of his time through three generations, and his success in mastering so excellently his enormously difficult material, both in its scope and in its depth, remains an extremely memorable feat in English literature – doubly remarkable, if we consider that it was performed in a field in which the European continent had already produced some of its best works.

In the foreground of this chronicle is everyday reality, as experienced by the Forsytes, all personal fortunes, conflicts, and tragicomedies. But in the background is visible the dark fabric of historical events. Every reader is sure to remember the chapter describing how Soames with his second wife witnesses the funeral of Queen Victoria in grey weather at the Hyde Park fence, and the rapid survey of the age from her accession to the throne: «Morals had changed, manners had changed, men had become monkeys twice removed, God had become Mammon – Mammon so respectable as to deceive himself.» In the Forsyte novels we observe the transformation and the dissolution of the Victorian age up to our days. In the first trilogy comes to life the period that in England effected the fusion of nobility and plutocracy with the accompanying change of the notion of a «gentleman», a kind of

Indian summer of wealth before the days of the storm. The second trilogy, no longer called «saga» but «comedy», describes the profound crisis of the new England whose task is to change the ruins of the past and the improvised barracks of wartime into its future home. The gallery of types is admirably complete. Robust businessmen, spoiled society ladies, aunts touching in an old-fashioned way, rebellious young girls, gentlemen of the clubs, politicians, artists, children, and even dogs – these last-mentioned especially favoured by Galsworthy – emerge in the London panorama in a concrete form, alive before our eyes and ears.

The situations recur as a curious documentation of the oscillation and the undulation in a family of given hereditary dispositions. The individual portraits are distinguished, and the law of social life is at work.

It is also instructive, however, to observe in these novels how Galsworthy's view gradually changes. The radical critic of culture rises by degrees to a greater objectivity in his appreciation and to a more liberal view of the purely human. An often cited example of this is his treatment of Soames, this standard national type, at first satirized, but then described with a respect that, reluctantly growing, finally changes into a genuine sympathy. Galsworthy has seized upon this sympathy; his characterization of Soames's personality thoroughly worked out becomes the most memorable feature of the Forsyte saga and the comedy of the descendants. One easily remembers one of those masterly final episodes of *Swan Song*, in which Old Soames, having driven to his ancestors' village on the west coast, finds with the help of an old census map the place where the Forsytes' farm had been situated, where only a single stone marks the site. Something like the ghost of a path leads him down into a valley of grass and furze. He breathes in the fresh, rough sea air which goes a little to his head; he puts on his overcoat and sits musing, his back against the stone. Had his ancestors built the house themselves at this lonely place, had they been the first to settle down here? he wonders. Their England rises before him, an England «of pack horses and very little smoke, of peat and wood fires, and wives who never left you, because they couldn't probably». He sits there a long time, absorbed in his feeling for the birthplace.

«And something moved in him, as if the salty independence of that lonely spot were still in his bones. Old Jolyon and his own father and the rest of his uncles – no wonder they'd been independent, with this air and loneliness in their blood; and crabbed with the pickling of it – unable to give up, to let go, to die. For a moment he seemed to understand even himself.»

To Galsworthy Soames thus becomes one of the last representatives of static old England. There was no humbug in him, we are told; he had his trying ways, but he was genuine. The sober prosaic respectability is in this manner duly honoured in Galsworthy's realism, and this has been pointed out as the essential factor in his judgment of human nature. As time passed, and the weary, cynical laxity grew more and more visibly modern, the chronicler found that several traits which under other circumstances had been little appreciated, perhaps really constituted the secret of the British power of resistance. On the whole, Galsworthy's later novels are permeated with a patriotic feeling of self-defence that appears also in his descriptions of the home and studies of nature. Even these last-mentioned are rendered with a more tender and more anxious poetry, with the feeling of protecting something precious yet already shadowed by certain loss. It may be old chambers where people have established themselves as if to remain there forever. Or it may be an English garden park, where the September sun is shining beautifully on bronze-coloured beech leaves and centenary hedges of yew.

Time does not permit me to dwell in the same detail upon other of Galsworthy's works, often quite comparable in quality to the Forsyte series, which surpasses them by virtue of its epic dimensions. It is above all in *The Country House* (1907), in *Fraternity* (1901), and in *The Dark Flower* (1913) that his mature essential character is to be sought. In the novel of the manor he created perhaps his most exquisite female portrait, Mrs. Pendyce, the type of the perfect, unaffected lady with all the modest tragedy which surrounds a truly noble nature, condemned to be restrained if not destroyed by the fetters of tradition. In *Fraternity* he represented, with a discreet mixture of pity and irony, the unfulfilled martyr of social conscience, the aesthete who is tortured by the shadows of the proletarian masses in London, but is not able to take the decisive step and carry out his altruistic impulse of action. There we also meet the old original Mr. Stone, the utopian dreamer with his eternal monologues beneath the night sky, indeed one of Galsworthy's most memorable types. Nor do we forget *The Dark Flower*, which may be called a psychological sonata, played with a masterly hand and based on the variations of passion and resignation in the ages of man. Even in the form of the short story Galsworthy has often been able to evoke an emotional response through contrasts of shadow and light which work rather graphically. He can do this in only a few pages which become animated by his personal style, for example, when he tells about such a simple case as that of the German shoemaker in «Quality», the story of the hopeless struggle of good craftsmanship against low-price industry.

By appealing to education and the sense of justice, his narrative art has always gently influenced contemporary notions of life and habits of thought. The same is true of his dramatic works, which were often direct contributions to social discussion and led to definite reforms at least in one area, the administration of public prisons in England. His dramas show an unusual richness of ideas combined with great ingenuity and technical skill in the working out of scenic effect. When certain inclinations are found, they are always just and humane. In *The Forest* (1924), for example, he brands the inconsiderate spirit of greed that, for crass purposes, exploits the heroism of the British world-conquering mind. *The Show* (1925) represents the defencelessness of the individual against the press in a family tragedy where brutal newspaper curiosity functions like a deaf and unchecked machine, removing the possibility of any one being held responsible for the resultant evil.

Loyalties depicts a matter of honour in which loyalty is tested and impartially examined in the different circles where it is at work, that is, the family, the corporation, the profession, and the nation. The force of these and other plays is in their logical structure and their concentrated action; sometimes they also possess an atmosphere of poetic feeling that is far from trivial. I am thinking especially of *A Pigeon* (1912) and *A Bit o' Love* (1915) which, however, did not meet with such brilliant success on the stage. Although on the whole Galsworthy's plays cannot be rated artistically with his novels, they confirm quite as plainly how strongly he sticks to his early ideal of liberty, that which in Shelley put on the wings and flames of dawn. Even in his rather cool dramatic works we meet a steady enemy of all oppression, spiritual as well as material, a sensitive man who with all his heart reacts against lack of consideration and never gives way in his demand for fair play.

In technique Turgenev is one of his first teachers. As in the charming Russian narrator, we find in Galsworthy a definite musical charm catching and keeping the hidden feelings. His intuition is so infallible that he can content himself with a slight allusion and a broken hint. But then there is Galsworthy's irony, such a singular instrument that even the tone separates him from any other writer. There are many different kinds of irony. One principal kind is negative and can be compared to the hoar-frost of the windows in a house where there is no fire, where the hearth has grown cold long ago. But there is also an irony friendly to life, springing from warmth, interest, and humanity; such is Galsworthy's. His is an irony that, in the presence of tragicomic evil, seems to question why it must be so, why it is necessary, and whether there is nothing to remedy it. Sometimes Galsworthy

makes nature herself take part in that ironic play about human beings, t
underline the bitterness or sweetness of the incidents with the help of wind
clouds, fragrances, and bird cries. Assisted by this irony he successfully ap
peals to the psychological imagination, always the best ally of understandin
and sympathy.

Galsworthy once formulated his artistic motto in words such as harmony
proportion, balance. They mark his natural turn of mind, a spiritual idea
now often suspect, perhaps because it is so difficult to reach. We soon discove
that this poet who so severely and persistently attacked the typical gentlema
of self-sufficiency, himself indisputably succeeded in filling the old notio
with new life, so that it preserved its contact with both the immediatel
human and the unrestricted aesthetic instinct. In the artist Galsworthy flouris
exactly those qualities of temper that in English are comprehended in th
word: *gentleness*. These qualities are expressed in his works, and in this wa
they have become a cultural contribution to our own times.

As Mr. Galsworthy has unfortunately been prevented by illness from bein
here today, as he had wished, to receive personally the Nobel Prize in Litera
ture for 1932, it will now be delivered to the representative of Great Britai
here present, Minister Clark Kerr.

Your Excellency – May I ask you to receive from His Majesty's hands th
Nobel Prize in Literature, awarded to your famous countryman.

At the banquet, Gunnar Holmgren, Rector of the Caroline Institute, mad
these remarks: «Finally, we are today paying homage to John Galsworthy
If this our homage is marked by a feeling of very special warmth, it is largel
because his noble personality and his exquisite artistic gifts, as displayed i
his numerous literary works, have long been famous and highly appreciate
all over the world. But the reason is no less to be found in that spirit c
idealism, that warm sympathy and true humanity that radiate from all h
writings and render him especially worthy to receive a gift from Alfre
Nobel's Foundation. We regret very deeply that unfortunate circumstance
have prevented John Galsworthy from being present here today. We shoul
have been happy indeed to have had the privilege at the same time of hor
ouring in his person the incarnation of that high-minded and idealist
England which we all love and admire. I beg to request His Excellency th
British Minister kindly to convey to him our sincere greetings and heartie
congratulations.»

Biography

John Galsworthy (1867–1933) was educated at Harrow and studied law at New College, Oxford. He travelled widely and at the age of twenty-eight began to write, at first for his own amusement. His first stories were published under the pseudonym John Sinjohn and later were withdrawn. He considered *The Island Pharisees* (1904) his first important work. As a novelist Galsworthy is chiefly known for his *roman fleuve, The Forsyte Saga*. The first novel of this vast work appeared in 1906. *The Man of Property* was a harsh criticism of the upper middle classes, Galsworthy's own background. Galsworthy did not immediately continue it; fifteen years and with them the First World War intervened until he resumed work on the history of the Forsytes with *In Chancery* (1920) and *To Let* (1921). Meanwhile he had written a considerable number of novels, short stories, and plays. *The Forsyte Saga* was continued by the three volumes of *A Modern Comedy, The White Monkey* (1924), *The Silver Spoon* (1926), *Swan Song* (1928), and its two interludes *A Silent Wooing* and *Passersby* (1927). To these should be added *On Forsyte Change* (1930), a collection of short stories. With growing age Galsworthy came more and more to identify himself with the world of his novels, which at first he had judged very harshly. This development is nowhere more evident than in the author's changing attitude toward Soames Forsyte, the «man of property», who dominates the first part of the work.

Galsworthy was a dramatist of considerable technical skill. His plays often took up specific social grievances such as the double standard of justice as applied to the upper and lower classes in *The Silver Box* (1906) and the confrontation of capital and labour in *Strife* (1909). *Justice* (1910), his most famous play, led to a prison reform in England. Galsworthy's reaction to the First World War found its expression in *The Mob* (1914), in which the voice of a statesman is drowned in the madness of the war-hungry masses; and in the enmity of the two families of *The Skin Game* (1920).

Literature 1933

IVAN ALEKSEEVICH BUNIN

«for the strict artistry with which he has carried on the classical Russian traditions in prose writing»

Presentation

by Per Hallström, Permanent Secretary of the Swedish Academy

Ivan Bunin's literary career has been clear and uncomplicated. He came from a family of country squires and grew up in the literary tradition of the times in which that social class dominated Russian culture, created a literature occupying a place of honour in contemporary Europe, and led to fatal political movements. «The lords of the scrupulous consciences» is what the following generation ironically called these men who, full of indignation and pity, set themselves up against the humiliation of the serfs. They deserved a better name, for they would soon have to pay with their own prosperity for the upheaval that they were going to cause.

Only the debris of the family possessions remained about the young Bunin; it was in the world of poetry that he could feel a strong rapport with the past generations. He lived in a world of illusions without any energy, rather than of national sentiment and hope for the future. Nonetheless he did not escape the influence of the reform movement; as a student, he was deeply struck by the appeal of Tolstoy's proclaiming fraternity with the humble and poor. Thus he learned like others to live by the toil of his hands, and for his part he chose the craft of cooper in the home of a co-religionist who greatly loved discussion. (He might well have tried a less difficult craft–the staves come apart easily, and it takes much skill to make a vessel that will hold its content.)

For a guide in more spiritual doctrines he had a man who fought with wavering energy against the temptations of the flesh in a very literal sense, and here vegetarianism entered his doctrine. During a voyage with him– to Tolstoy's home to be presented to the master–Bunin was able to observe his victories and defeats. He was victorious over several refreshment stands in railroad stations but finally the temptation of the meat pâtés was too strong. Having finished chewing, he found ingenious excuses for his particular fall: «I know, however, that it is not the pâté that holds me in its power but I who hold it. I am not its slave; I eat when I want to; when I don't want to, I don't eat.» It goes without saying that the young student did not want to stay long in this company.

Tolstoy himself did not attach great importance to Bunin's religious zeal. «You wish to live a simple and industrious life? That is good, but don' be priggish about it. One can be an excellent man in all kinds of lives.» And of the profession of poet he said, «Oh well, write if you have a great fancy for it, but remember well that it can never be the goal of your life.» This warning was lost on Bunin; he was already a poet with all his being.

He quickly attracted attention for verses that followed austere classical models; their subject was often descriptions of melancholic beauty of past life in the old manors. At the same time he developed in prose poems his power to render nature with all the fullness and richness of his impressions, having exercised his faculties with an extraordinary subtlety to reproduce them faithfully. Thus he continued the art of the great realists while his contemporaries devoted themselves to the adventures of literary programs, symbolism, neo-naturalism, Adamism, futurism, and other names of such passing phenomena. He remained an isolated man in an extremely agitated era.

When Bunin was forty, his novel *Derévnya* (1910) [*The Village*] made him famous and indeed notorious, for the book provoked a violent discussion. He attacked the essential point of the Russian faith in the future, the Slavophiles' dream of the virtuous and able peasant, through whom the nation must someday cover the world with its shadow. Bunin replied to this thesis with an objective description of the real nature of the peasants' virtues. The result was one of the most sombre and cruel works even in Russian literature, where such works are by no means rare.

The author gives no historical explanation of the decadence of the *muzhikí* except for the brief information that the grandfather of the two principal characters in the novel was deliberately tracked to death by his master's greyhounds. This deed expresses well, in fact, the imprint borne by the spirit of the suppressed. But Bunin shows them just as they are without hesitating before any horror, and it was easy for him to prove the truthfulness of his severe judgment. Violence of the most cruel kind had recently swept the province in the wake of the first revolution–a foreshadowing of a later one.

For lack of another name, the book is called a novel in the translations, but it really bears little resemblance to that genre. It consists of a series of immensely tumultuous episodes from lower life; truth of detail has meant everything to the author. The critic questioned not so much the details but their disinterested selection–the foreigner cannot judge the validity of the criticism. Now the book has had a strong revival because of events since then, and it remains a classic work, the model of a solid, concentrated, and sure art, in the eyes of the Russian *émigrés* as well as of those in the homeland.

The descriptions of villages were continued in many shorter essays, sometimes devoted to the religious element which, in the eyes of the enthusiastic national generation, made the *muzhikí* the people of promise. In the writer's pitiless analysis the redemptive piety of the world is reduced to anarchic instincts and to the taste for self-humiliation, essential traits of the Russian spirit according to him. He was indeed far from his youthful Tolstoyian faith. But he had retained one thing from it: his love of the Russian land. He has hardly ever painted his marvellous countryside with such great art as in some of these novellas. It is as if he had done it to preserve himself, to be able to breathe freely once more after all he had seen of the ugly and the false.

In a quite different spirit *Sukhodól* (1911–12), the short novel of a manor, was written as a counterpart to *Derévnya*. The book is not a portrayal of the present times, but of the heyday of the landed proprietors, as remembered by an old servant in the house where Bunin grew up. The author is not an optimist in this book, either; these masters have little vital force, they are as unworthy of being responsible for their own destinies and those of their subordinates as the severest accuser could have desired. In effect one finds here in large measure the materials for that defence of the people which Bunin silently passed over in *Derévnya*.

But nonetheless the picture appears now in a totally different light; it is filled with poetry. This is due in part to the kind of reconciliation that the past possesses, having paid its debt by death; but also to the sweet vision of the servant who gives charm to the confused and changing world in which, however, her youth was ruined. But the chief source of poetry is the author's imaginative power, his faculty for giving this book, with an intense concentration, the richness of life. *Sukhodól* is a literary work of *very* high order.

During the years which remained before the World War, Bunin made long trips through the Mediterranean countries and to the Far East. They provided him with the subjects of a series of exotic novellas, sometimes inspired by the world of Hindu ideas, with its peace in the abnegation of life, but more often by the strongly accentuated contrast between the dreaming Orient and the harsh and avid materialism of the West. When the war came, these studies in the spirit of the modern globe-trotters with the imprint created by the world tragedy were to result in the novella that came to be his most famous work: *Gospodín iz San Francisco* (1916) [*The Gentleman from San Francisco*].

As often elsewhere, Bunin here simplifies the subject extremely by restrict-
ing himself to developing the principal idea with types rather than complex
characters. Here he seems to have a special reason for this method: it is as
if the author were afraid to come too close to his figures because they awaken
his indignation and his hate. The American multi-millionaire, who after a
life of ceaseless thirst for money, sets out as an old man into the world to
refresh the dry consciousness of his power, his blindness of soul, and his
avidity for senile pleasure, interests the author only in so far as he can show
in what a pitiable manner he succumbs, like a bursting bubble. It is as if
a judgment of the pitiless world were pronounced against his character. In
place of a portrait of this pitifully insignificant man, the novella gives by its
singularly resolute art a portrait of destiny, the enemy of this man, without
any mysticism but only with strictly objective description of the game of
the forces of nature with human vanity. The mystical feeling, however, is
awakened in the reader and becomes stronger and greater through the perfect command of language and tone. *Gospodín iz San Francisco* was immediately accepted as a literary masterpiece; but it was also something else:
the portent of an increasing world twilight; the condemnation of the essential
guilt in the tragedy; the distortion of human culture which pushed the world
to the same fate.

The consequences of the war expelled the author from his country, so
dear to him despite everything, and it seemed a duty to remain silent under
the severe pressure of what he had suffered. But his lost country lived again
doubly dear in his memory, and regret gave him more pity for men. Still,
he sometimes, with stronger reason, painted his particular enemy, the *muzhík*,
with a sombre clear-sightedness of all his vices and faults; but sometimes
he looked forward. Under all repellent things, he saw something of indestructible humanity, which he represented not with moral stress but as a
force of nature, full of the immense possibilities of life. «A tree of God»,
one of them calls himself, «I see thus that God provides it; where the wind
goes, there I follow.» In this manner he has taken leave of them for the
present.

From the inexhaustible treasures of his memories of the Russian nature,
Bunin was later able to draw anew the joy and the desire to create. He gave
colour and brilliance to new Russian destinies, conceived in the same austerity
as in the era when he lived among them. In *Mítina lyubóv* (1924–25) [*Mitya's
Love*], he analyzed young feelings with all the mastery of a psychology in
which sense impressions and states of mind, marvellously rendered, are

articularly essential. The book was very successful in his country, although
signalled the return to literary traditions which, with many other things,
ad seemed condemned to death. In what has been published of *Zhizn Arsén-
va* (Part I, *Istóki dnéy*, 1930 [*The Well of Days*]), partially an autobiography,
e has reproduced Russian life in a manner broader than ever before. His
ld superiority as the incomparable painter of the vast and rich beauty of
he Russian land remains fully confirmed here.

In the literary history of his country, the place of Ivan Bunin has been
learly defined and his importance recognized for a long time and almost
vithout divergence of opinions. He has followed the great tradition of the
rilliant era of the nineteenth century in stressing the line of development
vhich can be continued. He perfected concentration and richness of expres-
ion – of a description of real life based on an almost unique precision of ob-
ervation. With the most rigorous art he has well resisted all temptations
o forget things for the charm of words; although by nature a lyric poet,
e has never embellished what he has seen but has rendered it with the most
xact fidelity. To his simple language he has added a charm which, according
o the testimonies of his compatriots, has made of it a precious drink that
ne can often sense even in the translations. This ability is his eminent and
ecret talent, and it gives the imprint of the masterpiece to his literary work.

Mr. Bunin – I have tried to present a picture of your work and of that
ustere art which characterizes it, a picture doubtlessly quite incomplete be-
ause of the little time at my disposal for a task so demanding. Please receive
ow, sir, from the hands of His Majesty the King, those marks of distinction
vhich the Swedish Academy is conferring on you, together with its heartfelt
ongratulations.

Acceptance

On November ninth, very far from here in a poor country house in an ol
Provençal town, I received the telephone call that informed me of the choic
of the Swedish Academy. I would not be honest if I told you, as one doe
in such cases, that it was the profoundest emotional moment of my life. A
great philosopher has said that even the most vehement feelings of joy hardl
count in comparison with those which provoke sorrow. I do not wish t
strike a note of sadness at this dinner, which I shall forever remember, bu
let me say nonetheless that in the course of the past fifteen years my sorrow
have far exceeded my joys. And not all of those sorrows have been persona
–far from it. But I can certainly say that in my entire literary life no othe
event has given me so much legitimate satisfaction as that little technica
miracle, the telephone call from Stockholm to Grasse. The prize establishe
by your great countryman, Alfred Nobel, is still the highest reward that ca
crown the work of a writer. Ambitious like most men and all writers, I wa
extremely proud to receive that reward at the hands of the most competen
and impartial of juries, and be assured, gentlemen of the Academy, I wa
also extremely grateful. But I should have proved a paltry egotist if on tha
ninth of November I had thought only of myself. Overwhelmed by th
congratulations and telegrams that began to flood me, I thought in the solitud
and silence of night about the profound meaning in the choice of the Swedis
Academy. For the first time since the founding of the Nobel Prize you hav
awarded it to an exile. Who am I in truth? An exile enjoying the hospitalit
of France, to whom I likewise owe an eternal debt of gratitude. But, gentle
men of the Academy, let me say that irrespective of my person and my wor
your choice in itself is a gesture of great beauty. It is necessary that ther
should be centres of absolute independence in the world. No doubt, all dif
ferences of opinion, of philosophical and religious creeds, are represente
around this table. But we are united by one truth, the freedom of though
and conscience; to this freedom we owe civilization. For us writers, especially
freedom is a dogma and an axiom. Your choice, gentlemen of the Academy
has proved once more that in Sweden the love of liberty is truly a national cult

Finally, a few words to end this short speech: my admiration for your
royal family, your country, your people, your literature, does not date from
his day alone. Love of letters and learning has been a tradition with the
royal house of Sweden as with your entire noble nation. Founded by an
illustrious soldier, the Swedish dynasty is one of the most glorious in the
world. May His Majesty the King, the chivalrous King of a chivalrous people, permit a stranger, a free writer honoured by the Swedish Academy, to
express to him these sentiments of profound respect and deep emotion.

The acceptance speech of the laureate was preceded by the following remarks by Professor Wilhelm Nordenson of the Caroline Institute: «Not only
he efforts to explore the subtleties of atoms and chromosomes have been
rewarded today; also brilliant efforts to describe the subtleties of the human
soul have been crowned with the golden laurel of the Nobel Prize. You have,
Mr. Bunin, thoroughly explored the soul of vanished Russia, and in doing
so, you have most meritoriously continued the glorious traditions of the great
Russian literature. You have given us the most valuable picture of Russian
society as it once was, and well do we understand the feelings with which
you must have seen the destruction of the society with which you were so
intimately connected. May our feelings of sympathy be of some comfort
to you in the melancholy of exile.»

Autobiography

I come from an old and noble house that has given to Russia a good man illustrious persons in politics as well as in the arts, among whom two poet of the early nineteenth century stand out in particular: Anna Búnina an Vasíly Zhukóvsky, one of the great names in Russian literature, the son o Athanase Bunin and the Turk Salma.

All my ancestors had close ties with the soil and the people: they wer country gentlemen. My parents were no exception. They owned estates i Central Russia, in those fertile steppes in which the ancient Muscovite czar had settled colonists from all over the country for their protection agains Tartar invasions from the South. That is why in that region there develope the richest of all Russian dialects, and almost all of our great writers from Turgenev to Leo Tolstoy have come from there.

I was born in Vorónezh in 1870; my childhood and youth were spen almost entirely in the country on my father's estates. During my adolescenc the death of my little sister caused a violent religious crisis, but it left n permanent scars on my soul. I had a passion for painting, which, I think shows in my writings. I wrote both poetry and prose fairly early and m works were also published from an early date.

Ever since I began to publish, my books have been both in prose an poetry, original writings as well as translations (from the English). If on divides my work by genre, one would find volumes of original poetry, tw volumes of translations, and ten volumes of prose.

My works were soon recognized by the critics. They were subsequentl honoured on several occasions, receiving in particular the Pushkin Prize, th highest prize awarded by the Russian Academy of Sciences. In 1909 tha Academy elected me one of its twelve honorary members, a position tha corresponds to the immortals of the French Academy. Among their numbe was Leo Tolstoy.

Nonetheless, there were several reasons why I was not widely known fo a considerable time. I kept aloof from politics and in my writings did no touch upon questions concerning it. I did not belong to any literary school

was neither decadent, nor symbolist, romantic, or naturalist. Moreover, I
frequented few literary circles. I lived chiefly in the country; I travelled much
in Russia as well as abroad; I visited Italy, Sicily, Turkey, the Balkans,
Greece, Syria, Palestine, Egypt, Algeria, Tunisia, and the tropics. According
to the words of Saadi I tried to «look at the world and leave upon it the
imprint of my soul». I was interested in problems of philosophy, religion,
morals, and history.

In 1910 I published my novel *Derévnya* [*The Village*]. It was the first of
a series of works to give a picture of the Russian without make-up: his
character and his soul, his original complexity, his foundations at once luminous and obscure, but almost always essentially tragic. These «ruthless»
works caused passionate discussions among our Russian critics and intellectuals
who, owing to numerous circumstances peculiar to Russian society and–in
these latter days–to sheer ignorance or political advantage, have constantly
idealized the people. In short, these works made me notorious; this success
has been confirmed by more recent works.

I left Moscow because of the Bolshevik regime in May, 1918; until Feb-
ruary, 1920, when I finally emigrated abroad, I lived in the south of Russia.
Since then I have lived in France, dividing my time between Paris and the
Maritime Alps.

Biographical note on Ivan Bunin

In addition to *Derévnya*, Bunin (1870–1953) wrote such novels as *Sukhodól*
(1911–12) and *Mítina lyubóv* (1924–25) [*Mitya's Love*], the short story *Gospodín iz San Francisco* (1916) [*The Gentleman from San Francisco*], and the autobiographical novel in two volumes, *Zhizn Arsénieva* (Part I, *Istóki dnéy* [1930],
translated as *The Well of Days*; Part II, *Lika* [1939]). He is the author of several
volumes of short stories mixed with poetry, and, in 1950, he published the
autobiography *Vospominániya* [*Memories and Portraits*]. Bunin died in France
in 1953. There are two editions of his collected works–one in twelve volumes
(Berlin, 1934–36) and the other in six volumes (Moscow, 1956)–as well as
collections of his stories (Moscow, 1961) and of his poetry (Leningrad, 1961).

Literature 1934

LUIGI PIRANDELLO

«for his bold and ingenious revival of dramatic and scenic art»

Presentation

by Per Hallström, Permanent Secretary of the Swedish Academy

The work of Luigi Pirandello is extensive. As an author of novellas he certainly is without equal in output, even in the primary country of this literary genre. Boccaccio's *Decameron* contains one hundred novellas; Pirandello's *Novelle per un anno* (1922–37) has one for each day of the year. They offer much variation in subject matter as well as in character: descriptions of life either purely realistic or philosophically profound or paradoxical, as often marked by humour as by satire. There are also creations of a jaunty poetic imagination in which the demands of reality give way to an ideal and creative truth.

The common feature of all these novellas is the effortless improvisation that gives them spontaneity, *élan*, and life. But since the limited scope of the novella demands a particularly strict composition, we also find the result of improvisation. In his hurried treatment of the subject Pirandello may soon lose control, without any concern for the overall impression. Although his novellas reveal much originality, they are hardly representative of the accomplished master; this is readily apparent when one notes the many motifs which were later employed in his dramatic work.

Nor do his novels mark the zenith of his literary achievement. Although his early novels were imbued with the same ideas with which he made his profoundly original contribution to the modern theatre, he reserved the definitive shaping of these ideas for the theatre.

In the short survey that is possible here, we can mention only one of these novels in which a distinctive feature of his concept of our times, his disgust and fear of materialism which mechanizes life, appears most strongly. The novel is *Si gira* (1916) [*Shoot!*], titled after a technical term of the cinema, «Shoot one». The expression warns the actors when the shooting of a scene begins. The narrator is the one who «shoots», that is, the cameraman of a large film industry. He finds a special meaning in his work. For him, life with all its good and evil is reduced to the material of images mechanically produced for a thoughtless pastime; it has no other purpose. The photographic apparatus becomes a demon which swallows everything and unrolls it on the film reel, thus giving it an outward appearance of reality, an appearance which is, in essence, spiritual death and emptiness. Our modern existence revolves and runs with the same lifeless speed, completely mechanized as if it were destroyed and annihilated. The author's attitude is expressed with extreme intensity. The mere plot is devastating enough.

That is the background of Pirandello's dramas, limited as they most often are to purely psychological problems. The bitterness of our present era must have had much influence on the plays' pessimistic philosophy even if this philosophy is based on the author's nature.

Maschere Nude (1918–21), the title he gave to his collection of plays, is difficult to translate because of its complexity. Literally this expressions means «naked masks», but «masks» usually indicates a bare surface. In this case however, the word is applied to the disguise which hides one from other and from one's self and which signifies to Pirandello the form of the self, a surface with an unfathomable being behind it. «Veiled» masks, analyzed and dissolved with penetrating clarity: this is the portrayal of human being in his dramas–men are unmasked. That is the meaning of the phrase.

The most remarkable feature of Pirandello's art is his almost magical power to turn psychological analysis into good theatre. Usually the theatre requires human stereotypes; here the spirit is like a shadow, obscurity behind obscurity, and one cannot decide what is more or less central inside. Finally one racks his brains, for there is no centre. Everything is relative, nothing can be grasped completely, and yet the plays can sometimes seize, captivate and charm even the great international public. This result is wholly paradoxical. As the author himself explained, it depends on the fact that his works «arise out of images taken from life which have passed through a filter of ideas and which hold me completely captive». It is the image which is fundamental, not, as many have believed, the abstract idea disguised afterwards by an image.

It has been said that Pirandello has but a «single» idea, the illusory nature of the personality, of the «I». The charge is easy to prove. The author is indeed obsessed with that idea. However, even if the idea is expanded to include the relativity of everything man believes he sees and understands, this charge is unfair.

Pirandello's dramatic art did not at first break with general literary tendencies. He treated social and ethical problems, the conflict between parenthood and the social structure with its inflexible notions of honour and decency, and the difficulties that human goodness finds in protecting itself against the same adversaries. All this was presented in morally as well as

ogically complicated situations and ended either in victory or defeat. These
roblems had their natural counterpart in the analysis of the «I» of the cha-
acters who were as relative as the idea against which they were fighting.

In several of his plays it is the idea others have of a personality and the
ffect they experience from it which becomes the principal subject. Others
now us only as we know them, imperfectly; and yet we make definitive
udgments. It is under the atmospheric pressure of these judgments that the
onsciousness of one's self can be changed. In *Tutto per bene* (1920) [*All For
The Best*] this psychological process is carried to its conclusion. In *Vestire gli
nudi* (1923) [*To Clothe the Naked*] the motif is turned upside down and as-
umes a moving tragic character. A lost life, an «I», no longer finding any-
ning in itself, desires death but, turning entirely to the outside, has a last
athetic wish to have a proper shroud in the beautifying idea which others
ave of its former being. In this gripping play even lying appears by its an-
uish as a kind of innocence.

But the author does not stop here; several of his plays deal with the lie
a the world of relativity and examine with a penetrating logic how more
r less criminal this lie is. In *La vita che ti diedi* (1924) [*The Life I Gave You*] the
ght to unreality receives beautiful and great expression. A woman, having
ost her only son, no longer has anything which holds her to life; yet the
ery violence of the blow reawakens in her a strength which dispels death,
s light dispels darkness. All has become shadows; she feels that not only
erself but all existence is «such stuff as dreams are made of». In her heart
ne guards both the memory and the dream, and now they are able to surpass
ll other things. The son to whom she gave life, who always filled her soul,
lls it still. There no void is possible; the son cannot be removed. He remains
a her presence, a form she cannot grasp; she feels him there as much as she
able to feel anything. Thus the relativity of truth has taken the shape of
simple and sublime mystery.

The same relativity appears as an enigma in *Così è (se vi pare)* (1918) [*Right
'ou Are (If You Think You Are)*]. The play is called a parable, which means
nat its singular story makes no pretensions to reality. It is a bold and ingenious
abrication which imparts wisdom. The circumstances of a family, recently
ettled in a provincial city, become intolerable to the other inhabitants of
ne town. Of the three members of the family, the husband, the wife, and
ne mother-in-law, either the husband or the mother-in-law, each otherwise
easonable, must be viewed as seized with absurd ideas about the identity
f the wife. The last speaker always has the final say on the issue, but a com-

parison of the conflicting statements leaves it in doubt. The questionings an
the confrontation of the two characters are described with great dramati
art and with a knowledge of the most subtle maladies of the soul. The wif
should be able to resolve the puzzle, but when she appears she is veiled lik
the goddess of knowledge and speaks mysteriously; to each of the intereste
parties she represents what she must be in order for that person to preserv
his image of her. In reality she is the symbol of the truth which no one ca
grasp in its entirety.

The play is also a brilliant satire on man's curiosity and false wisdom; i
it Pirandello presents a catalogue of types and reveals a penetrating self
conceit, either partially or completely ridiculous, in those attempting to dis
cover truth. The whole remains a masterpiece in its own right.

The central problem in the author's dramatic work, however, is the analysi
of the «I»–its dissolution in contrary elements, the negation of its unity a
illusory, and the symbolical description of the *Maschere nude*. Thanks to th
inexhaustible productivity of his mind, Pirandello attacks the problem fron
different sides, some of which have already been mentioned.

By sounding the depths of madness, he makes important discoveries. I
the tragedy of *Enrico IV* (1922) [*Henry IV*], for example, the strongest im
pression comes from the struggle of the personality for its identity in th
eternally flowing torrent of time. In *Il giuoco delle parti* (1919) [*The Rules c
the Game*] Pirandello creates a drama of pure abstractions: he uses the arti
ficial notions of duty to which members of society can be subjected by th
force of tradition with resolute logic for an action completely contrary t
expectation. As by a stroke of a magic wand, the game of abstractions fill
the scene with an extremely captivating life.

Sei Personaggi in cerca d'autore (1921) [*Six Characters in Search of an Author*
is a game similar to that described earlier and at the same time its very op
posite; it is both profoundly serious and full of ideas. Here unrestraine
creative imagination rather than abstraction dominates. It is the true dram
of poetic creation; it is also the settling of accounts between the theatre an
truth, between appearance and reality. Moreover, it is the half-despairin
message of art to the soul of a ravaged age, of fragmentary scenes bot
fulminating and explosive. This flood of violent feeling and superior intel
lectuality, rich in poetry, is truly the inspiration of genius. The world-wid
success of the play, which proves that it has to some extent been understoo
is as extraordinary as the piece itself. There is neither the necessity nor th
time to recall its magically startling details.

The sceptical psychology on which Pirandello has based his remarkable production is purely negative. If it were adopted by the general public with the same naiveté with which new and bold ideas are generally received, it would indeed entail more than one risk. But there is no danger that this will happen. It applies itself to purely intellectual realms and the general public scarcely follows it there. If by chance someone might be persuaded that his «I» is a fiction, he would soon be convinced that in practice this «I» does possess a certain degree of reality. Just as it is impossible to prove the freedom of the will, which is however constantly proved by experience, so the «I» manifestly finds means to make itself remembered. These means are gross or subtle. The most subtle of them perhaps consists in the faculty of thought itself; among others, the thought which wants to annihilate the «I».

But the analytical work of this great writer retains its value, especially if compared to several other things to which we have been treated in our time. Psychological analysis has given us complexes, which have spread immense pleasure and joy. They have even been worshipped as fetishes by apparently pious minds. Barbarous fetishes! To a person with some visual imagination, they resemble seaweed entangled in the water. Small fish often hover before this seaweed meditating until, their heads clear at last, they sink into it and disappear. Pirandello's scepticism protects us from such adventures; furthermore, he can help us. He warns us not to touch the delicate tissue of the human soul in a coarsely dogmatic and blind manner.

As a moralist, Pirandello is neither paradoxical nor destructive. Good remains good, and evil, evil. A nobly old-fashioned humanity dominates his ideas about the world of men. His bitter pessimism has not stifled his idealism; his penetrating analytical reason has not cut the roots of life. Happiness does not occupy a large place in the world of his imagination, but what gives dignity to life still finds enough air to breathe in it.

Dear Dr. Pirandello – Mine was the difficult task of presenting a concise synopsis of your profound literary work. Although such a brief sketch is hardly adequate, I have carried out my charge with pleasure.

May I now ask you to receive from His Majesty the Nobel Prize in Literature, of which the Swedish Academy has deemed you worthy.

Acceptance

I take deep satisfaction in expressing my respectful gratitude to Your Majesties
for having graciously honoured this banquet with your presence. May I be
permitted to add the expression of my deep gratitude for the kind welcome
I have been given as well as for this evening's reception, which is a worthy
epilogue to the solemn gathering earlier today at which I had the incomparable honour of receiving the Nobel Prize in Literature for 1934 from the
august hands of His Majesty the King.

I also wish to express my profound respect and sincere gratitude to the eminent Royal Swedish Academy for its distinguished judgment, which crowns
my long literary career.

For the success of my literary endeavours, I had to go to the school of
life. That school, although useless to certain brilliant minds, is the only thing
that will help a mind of my kind: attentive, concentrated, patient, truly
childlike at first, a docile pupil, if not of teachers, at least of life, a pupil who
would never abandon his complete faith and confidence in the things he
learned. This faith resides in the simplicity of my basic nature. I felt the need
to believe in the appearance of life without the slightest reserve or doubt.

The constant attention and deep sincerity with which I learned and pondered this lesson revealed humility, a love and respect for life that were indispensable for the assimilation of bitter disillusions, painful experiences,
frightful wounds, and all the mistakes of innocence that give depth and value
to our experiences. This education of the mind, accomplished at great cost,
allowed me to grow and, at the same time, to remain myself.

As my true talents developed, they left me completely incapable of life
as becomes a true artist, capable only of thoughts and feelings; of thought
because I felt, and of feelings because I thought. In fact, under the illusion
of creating myself, I created only what I felt and was able to believe.

I feel immense gratitude, joy, and pride at the thought that this creation
has been considered worthy of the distinguished award you have bestowed
on me.

I would gladly believe that this Prize was given not so much to the vir-

uosity of a writer, which is always negligible, but to the human sincerity of
ny work.

rior to the acceptance, Professor Göran Liljestrand of the Caroline Institute
emarked: «Society is a higher unit of life than the individual; it has a greater
complexity and involves adjustments of different kinds. The conflicts arising
rom the necessity of such adaptations have been the subject of Mr. Pirandello's work. At present the problems concerned call for investigations along
other lines than those followed by medicine and the other sciences. Mr.
Pirandello, at once philosopher, poet, and dramatist, has been able to under-
tand and describe different phases of human mentality. He has studied its
changes in disease and their subtle relations to the normal mind. He has
penetrated deeply into the obscure borderland between reality and dream.
We honour him as one of the great masters of dramatic art.»

Biography

Luigi Pirandello (1867–1936) was born in Girgenti, Sicily. He studied phi lology at Rome and at Bonn and wrote a dissertation on the dialect of hi native town (1891). From 1897 to 1922 he was professor of aesthetics an stylistics at the *Real Istituto di Magistere Femminile* at Rome. Pirandello's wor is impressive by its sheer volume. He wrote a great number of novellas whic were collected under the title *Novelle per un anno* (15 vols., 1922–37). O his six novels the best known are *Il fu Mattia Pascal* (1904) [*The Late Matti Pascal*], *I vecchi e i giovani* (1913) [*The Old and the Young*], *Si gira* (1916 [*Shoot!*], and *Uno, nessuno e centomila* (1926) [*One, None, and a Hundred thousand*].

But Pirandello's greatest achievement is in his plays. He wrote a larg number of dramas which were published, between 1918 and 1935, unde the collective title of *Maschere nude* [*Naked Masks*]. The title is programmatic Pirandello is always preoccupied with the problem of identity. The self exist to him only in relation to others; it consists of changing facets that hide an in scrutable abyss. In a play like *Cosí è (se vi pare)* (1918) [*Right You Are (If Yo Think You Are)*], two people hold contradictory notions about the identity o a third person. The protagonist in *Vestire gli ignudi* (1923) [*To Clothe the Naked* tries to establish her individuality by assuming various identities, which ar successively stripped from her; she gradually realizes her true position in th social order and in the end dies «naked», without a social mask, in both he own and her friends' eyes. Similarly in *Enrico IV* (1922) [*Henry IV*] a ma supposedly mad imagines that he is a medieval emperor, and his imaginatio and reality are strangely confused. The conflict between illusion and realit is central in *La vita che ti diedi* (1924) [*The Life I Gave You*] in which Anna' long-lost son returns home and contradicts her mental conception of him However, his death resolves Anna's conflict; she clings to illusion rather tha to reality. The analysis and dissolution of a unified self are carried to an extrem in *Sei personaggi in cerca d'autore* (1921) [*Six Characters in Search of An Author* where the stage itself, the symbol of appearance versus reality, becomes th setting of the play.

The attitudes expressed in *L'Umorismo* [*Humour*], an early essay (1908), re fundamental to all of Pirandello's plays. His characters attempt to fulfil heir self-seeking roles and are defeated by life itself which, always changing, nables them to see their perversity. This is Pirandello's humour, an irony vhich arises from the contradictions inherent in life.

Literature 1935

Prize not awarded

Literature 1936

EUGENE GLADSTONE O'NEILL

«for the power, honesty, and deep-felt emotions of his dramatic works, which embody an original concept of tragedy»

Presentation

by Per Hallström, Permanent Secretary of the Swedish Academy

Eugene O'Neill's dramatic production has been of a sombre character from the very first, and for him life as a whole quite early came to signify tragedy.

This has been attributed to the bitter experiences of his youth, more especially to what he underwent as a sailor. The legendary nimbus that gathers around celebrities in his case took the form of heroic events created out of his background. With his contempt for publicity, O'Neill straightway put a stop to all such attempts; there was no glamour to be derived from his drab hardships and toils. We may indeed conclude that the stern experiences were not uncongenial to his spirit, tending as they did to afford release of certain chaotic forces within him.

His pessimism was presumably on the one hand an innate trait of his being, on the other an offshoot of the literary current of the age, though possibly it is rather to be interpreted as the reaction of a profound personality to the American optimism of old tradition. Whatever the source of his pessimism may have been, however, the line of his development was marked out, and O'Neill became by degrees the uniquely and fiercely tragic dramatist that the world has come to know. The conception of life that he presents is not a product of elaborate thinking, but it has the genuine stamp of something lived through. It is based upon an exceedingly intense, one might say heart-rent, realization of the austerity of life, side by side with a kind of rapture at the beauty of human destinies shaped in the struggle against odds.

A primitive sense of tragedy, as we see, lacking moral backing and achieving no inner victory–merely the bricks and mortar for the temple of tragedy in the grand and ancient style. By his very primitiveness, however, this modern tragedian has reached the well-spring of this form of creative art, a naive and simple belief in fate. At certain stages it has contributed a stream of pulsating life-blood to his work.

That was, however, at a later period. In his earliest dramas O'Neill was a strict and somewhat arid realist; those works we may here pass by. Of more moment were a series of one-act plays, based upon material assembled during his years at sea. They brought to the theatre something novel, and hence he attracted attention.

Those plays were not, however, dramatically notable; properly speaking, merely short stories couched in dialogue-form; true works of art, however, of their type, and heart-stirring in their simple, rugged delineation. In one of them, *The Moon of the Caribbees* (1918), he attains poetic heights, partly by the tenderness in depicting the indigence of a sailor's life with its naive illusions of joy, and partly by the artistic background of the play: dirge-like Negro songs coming from a white coral shore beneath metallically glittering palms and the great moon of the Caribbean Sea. Altogether it is a mystical weave of melancholy, primitive savagery, yearning, lunar effulgence, and oppressive desolateness.

The drama *Anna Christie* (1921) achieves its most striking effect through the description of sailors' life ashore in and about waterfront saloons. The first act is O'Neill's masterpiece in the domain of strict realism, each character being depicted with supreme sureness and mastery. The content is the raising of a fallen Swedish girl to respectable human status by the strong and wholesome influences of the sea; for once pessimism is left out of the picture, the play having what is termed a happy ending.

With his drama *The Hairy Ape* (1922), also concerned with sailors' lives, O'Neill launches into that expressionism which sets its stamp upon his «idea-dramas». The aim of expressionism in literature and the plastic arts is difficult to determine; nor need we discuss it, since for practical purposes a brief description suffices. It endeavours to produce its effects by a sort of mathematical method; it may be said to extract the square root of the complex phenomena of reality, and build with those abstractions a new world on an enormously magnified scale. The procedure is an irksome one and can hardly be said to achieve mathematical exactitude; for a long time, however, it met with great success throughout the world.

The Hairy Ape seeks to present on a monumental scale the rebellious slave of steam power, intoxicated with his force and with superman ideas. Outwardly he is a relapse to primitive man, and he presents himself as a kind of beast, suffering from yearning for genius. The play depicts his tragical discomfiture and ruin on being brought up against cruel society.

Subsequently O'Neill devoted himself for a number of years to a boldly expressionistic treatment of ideas and social questions. The resulting plays have little connection with real life; the poet and dreamer isolates himself, becoming absorbed in feverishly pursued speculation and phantasy.

The Emperor Jones (1920), as an artistic creation, stands rather by itself; through it the playwright first secured any considerable celebrity. The theme embraces the mental breakdown of a Negro despot who rules over a Negro-populated island in the West Indies. The despot perishes on the flight from his glory, hunted in the dead of night by the troll-drums of his pursuers and by recollections of the past shaping themselves as paralyzing visions. These memories stretch back beyond his own life to the dark continent of Africa. Here lies concealed the theory of the individual's unconscious inner life being the carrier of the successive stages in the evolution of the race. As to the rightness of the theory we need form no opinion; the play takes so strong a hold upon our nerves and senses that our attention is entirely absorbed.

The «dramas of ideas» proper are too numerous and too diversified to be included in a brief survey. Their themes derive from contemporary life or from sagas and legends; all are metamorphosed by the author's fancy. They play on emotional chords all tightly strung, give amazing decorative effects, and manifest a never-failing dramatic energy. Practically speaking, everything in human life in the nature of struggle or combat has here been used as a subject for creative treatment, solutions being sought for and tried out of the spiritual or mental riddles presented. One favourite theme is the cleavage of personality that arises when an individual's true character is driven in upon itself by pressure from the world without, having to yield place to a make-believe character, its own live traits being hidden behind a mask. The dramatist's musings are apt to delve so deep that what he evolves has an urge, like deep-sea fauna, to burst asunder on being brought into the light of day. The results he achieves, however, are never without poetry; there is an abundant flow of passionate, pregnant words. The action, too, yields evidence in every case of the never-slumbering energy that is one of O'Neill's greatest gifts.

Underneath O'Neill's fantastic love of experimenting, however, is a hint of a yearning to attain the monumental simplicity characteristic of ancient drama. In his *Desire Under the Elms* (1924) he made an attempt in that direction, drawing his motif from the New England farming community, hardened in the progress of generations into a type of Puritanism that had gradually come to forfeit its idealistic inspiration. The course embarked upon was to be followed with more success in the «Electra» trilogy.

In between appeared *A Play; Strange Interlude* (1928), which won high praise and became renowned. It is rightly termed «A Play», for with its broad and loose-knit method of presentation it cannot be regarded as a trag-

dy; it would rather seem most aptly defined as a psychological novel in
scenes. To its subtitle, «Strange Interlude», a direct clue is given in the course
of the play: «Life, the present, is the strange interlude between the past and
that is to come.» The author tries to make his idea clear, as far as possible,
by resorting to a peculiar device: on the one hand, the characters speak and
reply as the action of the play demands; on the other, they reveal their real
natures and their recollections in the form of monologues, inaudible to the
other characters upon the stage. Once again, the element of masking!

Regarded as a psychological novel, up to the point at which it becomes
so improbable for any psychology, the work is very notable for its wealth
of analytical and above all intuitive acumen, and for the profound insight
it displays into the inner workings of the human spirit. The training bore
fruit in the real tragedy that followed, the author's grandest work: *Mourning
Becomes Electra* (1931). Both in the story it unfolds and in the destiny-charged
atmosphere enshrouding it, this play keeps close to the tradition of the ancient
drama, though in both respects it is adjusted to modern life and to modern
lines of thought. The scene of this tragedy of the modern-time house of
Atreus is laid in the period of the great Civil War, America's *Iliad*. That
choice lends the drama the clear perspective of the past and yet provides it
with a background of intellectual life and thought sufficiently close to the
present day. The most remarkable feature in the drama is the way in which
the element of fate has been further developed. It is based upon up-to-date
hypotheses, primarily upon the natural-scientific determinism of the doctrine
of heredity, and also upon the Freudian omniscience concerning the unconscious, the nightmare dream of perverse family emotions.

These hypotheses are not, as we know, established beyond dispute, but
the all-important point regarding this drama is that its author has embraced
and applied them with unflinching consistency, constructing upon their
foundation a chain of events as inescapable as if they had been proclaimed
by the Sphinx of Thebes herself. Thereby he has achieved a masterly example
of constructive ability and elaborate motivation of plot, and one that is surely
without a counterpart in the whole range of latter-day drama. This applies
specially to the first two parts of the trilogy.

Two dramas, wholly different and of a new type for O'Neill, followed.
They constitute a characteristic illustration of the way he has of never resting
content with a result achieved, no matter what success it may have met with.
They also gave evidence of his courage, for in them he launched a challenge
to a considerable section of those whose favourable opinions he had won,

and even to the dictators of those opinions. Though it may not at the present time be dangerous to defy natural human feelings and conceptions, it is not by any means free from risk to prick the sensitive conscience of critics. In *Ah, Wilderness* (1933) the esteemed writer of tragedies astonished his admirers by presenting them with an idyllic middle-class comedy and carried his audiences with him. In its depiction of the spiritual life of young people the play contains a good deal of poetry, while its gayer scenes display unaffected humour and comedy; it is, moreover, throughout simple and human in its appeal.

In *Days Without End* (1934) the dramatist tackled the problem of religion, one that he had until then touched upon only superficially, without identifying himself with it, and merely from the natural scientist's combative standpoint. In this play he showed that he had an eye for the irrational, felt the need of absolute values, and was alive to the danger of spiritual impoverishment in the empty space that will be all that is left over the hard and solid world of rationalism. The form the work took was that of a modern miracle play, and perhaps, as with his tragedies of fate, the temptation to experiment was of great importance in its origination. Strictly observing the conventions of the drama form chosen, he adopted medieval naiveté in his presentation of the struggle of good against evil, introducing, however, novel and bold features of stage technique. The principal character he cleaves into two parts, white and black, not only inwardly but also corporeally, each half leading its own independent bodily life – a species of Siamese twins contradicting each other. The result is a variation upon earlier experiments. Notwithstanding the risk attendant upon that venture, the drama is sustained by the author's rare mastery of scenic treatment, while in the spokesman of religion, a Catholic priest, O'Neill has created one of his most lifelike characters. Whether that circumstance may be interpreted as indicating a decisive change in his outlook upon life remains to be seen in the future.

O'Neill's dramatic production has been extraordinarily comprehensive in scope, versatile in character, and abundantly fruitful in new departures; and still its originator is at a stage of vigorous development. Yet in essential matters, he himself has always been the same in the exuberant and unrestrainably lively play of his imagination, in his never-wearying delight in giving shape to the ideas, whether emanating from within or without, that have jostled one another in the depths of his contemplative nature, and, perhaps first and foremost, in his possession of a proudly and ruggedly independent character.

In choosing Eugene O'Neill as the recipient of the 1936 Nobel Prize in Literature, the Swedish Academy can express its appreciation of his peculiar and rare literary gifts and also express their homage to his personality in these words: the Prize has been awarded to him for dramatic works of vital energy, sincerity, and intensity of feeling, stamped with an original conception of tragedy.

Acceptance

by James E. Brown, Jr., American Chargé d'Affaires

It is an extraordinary privilege that has come to me to take before this gathering of eminent persons the place of my fellow-countryman, Mr. Eugene O'Neill, recipient of the Nobel Prize in Literature, who unfortunately is unable to be present here today.

It is an extraordinary privilege because the significance and true worth of the Nobel Prizes are fully recognized in all advanced parts of the world. The Prizes are justly held in honor and esteem, for it is well known that they are awarded without prejudice of any kind by the several committees whose members generously devote much time and thought to the task in their charge.

In addition to being a stimulus to endeavour and a high recognition of achievement, the Prizes are valuable in another respect. Owing to the complete absence of partiality in the awarding of them, they induce people of all countries to think in terms of the world and mankind, heedless of classifications or boundaries of any character. The good influence of such conspicuous recognition of a particular achievement thus spreads far beyond its special purpose.

Mr. O'Neill has been prevented from being here today principally because the state of his health, damaged by overwork, has forced him to follow his doctor's orders to live absolutely quietly for several months. It is his hope and I follow his own words in a letter to me, that all those connected with the festival will accept in good faith his statement of the impossibility of his attending, and not put it down to arbitrary temperament, or anything of the sort.

In view of his inability to attend, he promptly sent a speech to be read on his behalf on this occasion. Mr. O'Neill in a letter to me said regarding his speech, «It is no mere artful gesture to please a Swedish audience. It is a plain statement of fact and my exact feeling, and I am glad of this opportunity to get it said and on record.» It affords me great pleasure to read now the speech addressed to this gathering by Mr. Eugene O'Neill.

«First, I wish to express again to you my deep regret that circumstances

ave made it impossible for me to visit Sweden in time for the festival, and
o be present at this banquet to tell you in person of my grateful appreciation.

It is difficult to put into anything like adequate words the profound grat-
ude I feel for the greatest honor that my work could ever hope to attain,
he award of the Nobel Prize. This highest of distinctions is all the more
grateful to me because I feel so deeply that it is not only my work which
s being honored, but the work of all my colleagues in America—that this
Nobel Prize is a symbol of the recognition by Europe of the coming-of-age
f the American theatre. For my plays are merely, through luck of time and
circumstance, the most widely-known examples of the work done by Amer-
can playwrights in the years since the World War—work that has finally
made modern American drama in its finest aspects an achievement of which
Americans can be justly proud, worthy at last to claim kinship with the mod-
rn drama of Europe, from which our original inspiration so surely derives.

This thought of original inspiration brings me to what is, for me, the
greatest happiness this occasion affords, and that is the opportunity it gives
me to acknowledge, with gratitude and pride, to you and to the people of
Sweden, the debt my work owes to that greatest genius of all modern dramatists, your August Strindberg.

It was reading his plays when I first started to write back in the winter of
913—14 that, above all else, first gave me the vision of what modern drama
ould be, and first inspired me with the urge to write for the theatre myself.
f there is anything of lasting worth in my work, it is due to that original
mpulse from him, which has continued as my inspiration down all the
ears since then—to the ambition I received then to follow in the footsteps of
is genius as worthily as my talent might permit, and with the same integrity
f purpose.

Of course, it will be no news to you in Sweden that my work owes much
o the influence of Strindberg. That influence runs clearly through more than
a few of my plays and is plain for everyone to see. Neither will it be news
or anyone who has ever known me, for I have always stressed it myself.
have never been one of those who are so timidly uncertain of their own
contribution that they feel they cannot afford to admit ever having been
influenced, lest they be discovered as lacking all originality.

No, I am only too proud of my debt to Strindberg, only too happy to
have this opportunity of proclaiming it to his people. For me, he remains,
as Nietzsche remains in his sphere, the Master, still to this day more modern
than any of us, still our leader. And it is my pride to imagine that perhaps

his spirit, musing over this year's Nobel award for literature, may smile with a little satisfaction, and find the follower not too unworthy of his Master.

Prior to the acceptance, Robert Fries, Director of the Bergius Foundation, remarked: «It is difficult to explain the vital processes in the living organism, it is difficult to interpret the inmost essence of matter, but it is perhaps most difficult to sound the human mind and to understand the soul in its shifting phases. With passionate intensity and impulsive genius Eugene O'Neill has done this in his dramas, and one cannot but be captivated by the masterly way in which he deals with the great problems of life.»

Autobiography

Born October 16th, 1888, in New York City. Son of James O'Neill, the popular romantic actor. First seven years of my life spent mostly in hotels and railroad trains, my mother accompanying my father on his tours of the United States, although she never was an actress, disliked the theatre, and held aloof from its people.

From the age of seven to thirteen attended Catholic schools. Then four years at a non-sectarian preparatory school, followed by one year (1906–1907) at Princeton University.

After expulsion from Princeton I led a restless, wandering life for several years, working at various occupations. Was secretary of a small mail order house in New York for a while, then went on a gold prospecting expedition in the wilds of Spanish Honduras. Found no gold but contracted malarial fever. Returned to the United States and worked for a time as assistant manager of a theatrical company on tour. After this, a period in which I went to sea, and also worked in Buenos Aires for the Westinghouse Electrical Co., Swift Packing Co., and Singer Sewing Machine Co. Never held a job long. Was either fired quickly or left quickly. Finished my experience as a sailor as able-bodied seaman on the American Line of transatlantic liners. After this, was an actor in vaudeville for a short time, and reporter on a small town newspaper. At the end of 1912 my health broke down and I spent six months in a tuberculosis sanatorium.

Began to write plays in the Fall of 1913. Wrote the one-act *Bound East for Cardiff* in the Spring of 1914. This is the only one of the plays written in this period which has any merit.

In the Fall of 1914, I entered Harvard University to attend the course in dramatic technique given by Professor George Baker. I left after one year and did not complete the course.

The Fall of 1916 marked the first production of a play of mine in New York—*Bound East for Cardiff*, which was on the opening bill of the Provincetown Players. In the next few years this theatre put on nearly all of my short plays, but it was not until 1920 that a long play *Beyond the Horizon* was

produced in New York. It was given on Broadway by a commercial manage
ment–but, at first, only as a special matinee attraction with four afternoo
performances a week. However, some of the critics praised the play and i
was soon given a theatre for a regular run, and later on in the year wa
awarded the Pulitzer Prize. I received this prize again in 1922 for *Anna Christi*
and for the third time in 1928 for *Strange Interlude*.

The following is a list of all my published and produced plays which ar
worth mentioning, with the year in which they were written:

Bound East for Cardiff (1914), *Before Breakfast* (1916), *The Long Voyage Hom*
(1917), *In the Zone* (1917), *The Moon of the Caribbees* (1917), *Ile* (1917), *Th*
Rope (1918), *Beyond the Horizon* (1918), *The Dreamy Kid* (1918), *Where th*
Cross is Made (1918), *The Straw* (1919), *Gold* (1920), *Anna Christie* (1920)
The Emperor Jones (1920), *Diff'rent* (1920), *The First Man* (1921), *The Fountai*
(1921–22), *The Hairy Ape* (1921), *Welded* (1922), *All God's Chillun Got Wing*
(1923), *Desire Under the Elms* (1924), *Marco Millions* (1923–25), *The Grea*
God Brown (1925), *Lazarus Laughed* (1926), *Strange Interlude* (1926–27), *Dy*
namo (1928), *Mourning Becomes Electra* (1929–31), *Ah, Wilderness* (1932), *Day*
Without End (1932–33).

Biographical note on Eugene O'Neill

After an active career of writing and supervising the New York production
of his own works, O'Neill (1888–1953) published only two new plays be
tween 1934 and the time of his death. In *The Iceman Cometh* (1946), he ex
posed a «prophet's» battle against the last pipedreams of a group of derelicts a
another pipedream and managed to infuse into the «Lower Depths» atmo
sphere a sense of the tragic. *A Moon for the Misbegotten* (1952) contains a strong
autobiographical content, which it shares with *Long Day's Journey into Nigh*
(posth. 1956), one of O'Neill's most important works. The latter play, writ
ten, according to O'Neill, «in tears and blood...with deep pity and under
standing and forgiveness for *all* the four haunted Tyrones», had its premier
at the Royal Dramatic Theatre in Stockholm. Sweden grew into an O'Neil
centre with the first productions of the one-act play *Hughie* (posth. 1959) a
well as *A Touch of the Poet* (posth. 1958) and an adapted version of *Mor*
Stately Mansions (posth. 1962)–both plays being parts of an unfinished cycl
in which O'Neill returned to his earlier attempts at making psychologica
analysis dramatically effective.

Literature 1937

ROGER MARTIN DU GARD

*for the artistic vigour and truthfulness with which he has pictured human con-
trasts as well as some fundamental aspects of contemporary life in the series of
novels entitled* Les Thibault»

Presentation

by Per Hallström, Permanent Secretary of the Swedish Academy

The recipient of the Nobel Prize in Literature for 1937, Roger Martin d Gard, has dedicated most of his activity to a single work, a long series of nov els with the collective title, *Les Thibault* (1922–40). It is a vast work both in th number of its volumes and in its scope. It represents modern French life b means of a whole gallery of characters and an analysis of the intellectual cur rents and the problems that occupied France during the ten years precedin the First World War, a gallery as full and an analysis as complete as the subjec of the novel permitted. The work has therefore taken a form especially char acteristic of our era, called the «roman fleuve» in the country of its origin

The term designates a narrative method that is relatively little concerne with composition and advances like a river across vast countries, reflectin everything that is found on its way. The essence of such a novel, in large a well as small matters, consists in the exactitude of this reflection rather thar in the harmonious balance of its parts; it has no shape. The river lingers at wil and only rarely does the undercurrent disturb the smooth flow of its surfac

Our age can hardly be called calm; on the contrary, the speed of th machines accelerates the rhythm of life to the point of agitation. It is strang therefore, that in such an age the most popular literary form, the novel, shoul have developed in a totally opposite direction, and by so doing have becom only the more popular. Still, if the novel offered us the satisfying world o fantasy, one could explain this phenomenon in psychological terms as a sor of poetic compensation for the frustrations of daily life. But it is precisel the heart-rending anguish of reality that the novel takes such time to soun and to emphasize.

Nevertheless, the novel is there, with its boundless substance, and th reader finds a certain solace in the heightened awareness which he acquire from the inevitable element of tragedy inherent in all life. With a kind o heroism, it swallows reality in large draughts and encourages us to bear eve great sufferings with joy. The reader's aesthetic demands will be satisfied i isolated sections of the work which are more condensed and therefore bette suited to call forth his feelings. *Les Thibault* does not lack such sections.

The essential characters of the novel are three members of the same family: the father and two sons. The father remains in the background; his passive role, one of weight and massiveness, is presented by a special technique. The two sons and the countless secondary characters of the work are presented in a dramatic manner. Unprepared by anything in the story, we see them before us, acting and speaking in the present; and we are given a detailed and complete description of the setting. The reader must be quick to grasp what he sees and hears, for the capricious and irregular rhythm of life beats everywhere. He is helped in his task by the writer's most perfected tool: the analysis of his heroes' thoughts, expressed beyond words, an insight into the darkness which engenders conscious actions. Martin du Gard goes even further; he shows how thoughts, feelings, and the will can be transformed before becoming words and acts. Sometimes exterior considerations–habit, vanity, or even a simple gaucherie–alter expressions and personality. This examination, at once subtle and bold, of the dynamic processes of the soul obviously constitutes Martin du Gard's most original and most remarkable contribution to the art of characterizing human beings. From the aesthetic point of view, this is not always an advantage, for the analysis may appear cumbersome when its results do not seem necessary to the story.

This introspective method is used even for the father's character, but it is less complicated in his case. His personality is already clear-cut and complete at the beginning of the novel, for he belongs to the past. Events of the present no longer affect him.

He is a member of the upper middle class, conscious of his status and his duties, a faithful servant of the Church and a generous benefactor of society, full of prudent advice. He really belongs to a generation before his own, to the France of the July Monarchy; that is why he is to come into more than one conflict with the next generation, in particular with his sons. But this conflict rarely reaches the verbal level, for the old man is too convinced of his proper worth to engage in discussions. Hence the perennial theme of the opposition of youth to age is not specially treated here.

The representative of age appears above all in an attitude of introspection and immutability; he relies heavily and complacently on all that he thinks wise and just. No word can influence him. In the isolation of his life, one might see the whole tragedy of age if he were not himself so completely unaware of the possibility of such a tragedy.

He is characterized rather by comic traits; profounder sentiments are expressed only at the time of his death, in the face of his human destiny. This expression is not direct but results from a strictly objective, concrete de scription of the long martyrdom of his agony. It is a moving description despite its minute detail. Up to now he had been considered only from without, with the exception of some rare instances when he had revealed what, even in him, was hidden behind the façade he presented to the world.

The difference between him and his oldest son receives little emphasis. Antoine Thibault is a doctor. Entirely absorbed by his profession, his father's moral and ethical points of view are entirely alien to him. Morality is replaced in him by an intense and conscientious devotion to research and to the exercise of his profession. Master of himself, prudent, tactful, he has not the least desire for opposition; he has not even time to think of it. In the novel one witnesses his rapid evolution within prescribed limits. He is a man ambitious for the future. At first he is occasionally a little fatuous, but he soon commands respect by his work.

Antoine becomes a sympathetic representative of the intellectuals of his day, full of ideas, without prejudices in his conceptions, but as a determinist convinced of the inability of the individual to change whatever the general course of events may be. He is not a revolutionary.

Quite different is his brother Jacques, who is several years younger. The latter is too close to the writer's heart to suffer any criticism. He is the hero of the work, and the exterior world is examined and judged according to his ideals. His father's responsibility for his evolution is considerable, but actually Jacques, by his whole nature, is destined to be a revolutionary. When the story begins, he is a schoolboy of fourteen in a college run by priests. Although he dislikes and neglects his studies, he commands respect by his intelligence. The catastrophe occurs when he discovers a friend among his schoolmates, and their affection, at this dangerous period of adolescence, takes an exalted and seemingly erotic form. Their feelings are betrayed by their letters, misinterpreted (as, indeed, they are bound to be) by the priests who intervene with disciplinary measures. The strict surveillance and the very intrusion into his emotional private life are an unbearable offense to Jacques. Furthermore, he has to await his father's rage, stirred up by this scandal. His revolt is expressed in action. He carries along his friend in his escape far from all yokes, those he endured and those he feared in a hostile and harsh world. He feels that his whole being, in the grip of romantic poetry and of more dangerous tendencies, is irreconcilable with the real world. Seeking happiness and freedom, the two boys leave for Africa, but their visionary project is destroyed in Marseilles by the efforts of the police who had been alerted.

On his return, his father, in an excess of pedagogic zeal, makes a psychological mistake; he condemns his son to solitary confinement in a reformatory
founded by himself. The oppression of this confinement causes Jacques' indomitable personality to emerge even stronger and fiercer. The account of
this development is the most moving episode in the work.

After he has been released owing to his brother's influence, Jacques is
permitted to pursue his studies, his only consolation. He does brilliantly and
is easily accepted by the École Normale, the supreme goal of all ambitious
and talented students and the open door to all top literary or scientific careers.
But Jacques cannot be attracted by an official career that for him is only a
void and an illusion; he soon sets out for adventure and reality. Once more
the boy escapes to Africa, but this time he succeeds and he remains absent
from the narrative for a long time.

He is seen again when Antoine discovers his residence – in Switzerland
among the revolutionaries – and brings him back to their father's deathbed.
He arrives too late for a reconciliation, even if one considered a reconciliation
between these two diametrically opposed concepts of life possible. The old
man does not recognize him, but Jacques feels a deep sorrow, for he is not
one of those people who, obsessed with mankind's future happiness, begin
by stifling every trace of humanity in themselves.

Such is the outline of Jacques' inner life as far as it is known. For the rest
he remains rather elusive, as before, but we notice the author's great appreciation of his faculties and of his character.

We get to know him fully when the novel approaches its conclusion and
at the same time its height of epic grandeur – in the summer of 1914 just before the world catastrophe. Jacques is in Geneva, having left Paris soon after
his father's death in order to escape the necessity of inheriting a fortune in
a society which he scorns. He belongs to a group of socialist and communist
reformers whose immediate mission is to halt the threat of war by the revolt
of the masses. The description of these agitators is one of the least successful
passages in the book; the overall impression, whether intended or not, is that
these men are not worthy of their mission.

But Jacques' stature increases in everyone's eyes when he leaves Geneva
and returns to Paris to accomplish his mission. His development is moral
rather than intellectual; his actions have no great results, but he saves his soul.
The description of the last days of July in Paris, with Jacques wavering between hope and despair in this surcharged atmosphere, is a veritable *tour de
force* in Martin du Gard's novelistic achievement. The history of this period re-

vives, reawakens, as far as the masses' role is concerned. But, as almost always, the role is not decisive. The masses are impotent, blind, and in this case even less familiar than usual with the game of politics that causes such tragedies. The author himself seems not to be particularly initiated, but he is tolerant and human, and his description, as far as it goes, is truthful.

Against the background of this bewildering anxiety there occurs a brief but highly illuminating episode of a completely different character. Jacques meets again a young girl with whom he had almost fallen in love several years before, but from whom he had run away as he had run away from everything else. This time the true spark is kindled between them. This fatal love story is one of the most significant episodes in the novel; it is profoundly felt and rendered in all its pure beauty precisely because it is restricted to the dimensions that the breathless flight of days imposes on the story. It lasts only a short time, but that is enough to give it a tragic and simple beauty.

When all the political illusions vanish for Jacques at the declaration of war, he recreates for himself a new illusion, born of his despair and of his will to sacrifice. Right at the front lines he tries to ward off the catastrophe by appealing from an airplane to the two opposing armies, seeking to inspire in them a common revolt and a desire to overthrow the powers which hold them captive. Without hesitating he leaves Paris and the woman he loves.

The adventure is stamped with the same schoolboy romanticism and lack of reality as was his first flight out of the world, but Jacques nonetheless carries out his plan with his customary energy. His call for revolution is printed in Switzerland, the airplane and pilot are ready, the expedition begins. It will not last long, for he has hardly flown over the battlefield when the plane crashes and catches fire with its whole load, men and bundles of paper. Jacques himself falls, a heap of bruised and burned flesh, among the retreating French troops. All his perception is restricted to a vague sensation of the bitterness of defeat and to unbearable and infinite physical torments, which are finally relieved by the bullet of a compatriot tired of dragging along this ill-fated person whom he holds to be a spy anyhow.

It is difficult to imagine a bitterer dénouement to a tragedy or a crueller irony in a defeat. But Martin du Gard did not direct his irony toward his hero. Perhaps he wanted to show the brutality and the cruelty of world events as opposed to idealistic tendencies. His bitterness is certainly justified here, but the long detailed description of the whole episode becomes almost intolerable in its scrupulous exactitude.

Jacques Thibault, as we finally get to know him, lives in our memory as a heroic figure. Without the least grandiloquent attitude or word, this up-right, silent, and reserved man receives at last the seal of grandeur: grandeur of will and courage. Whenever the novel centres on him, the writer's un-tiring work achieves persuasive eloquence. After his pointed and sceptical analysis of the human soul, which almost consumes its object with its often extreme exactness in detail, through the most minute realism possible, Martin du Gard finally pays homage to the idealism of the human spirit.

Acceptance

The presence of so many illustrious persons assembled under the patronage of His Highness, the Crown Prince, heightens the emotions that I feel at finding myself here and hearing the words of praise that have just been addressed to me. I feel rather like an owl, suddenly roused from its nest and exposed to the daylight, whose eyes, used to the dark, are blinded by dazzling brightness.

I am proud of the exceptional mark of esteem the Swedish Academy has bestowed on me, but I cannot conceal my surprise from you. Ever since I felt your favour lie upon and almost overwhelm me, I have asked myself how to interpret it.

My first thought was of my country. I am happy that in making a *French* author its choice for this year, the distinguished Swedish Academy has thought fit to glorify our French literature in particular. On the other hand, I know some great poets among my compatriots, noble and powerful minds, whom your votes might have chosen with much better reason. Why then am I today in this place of honour?

The demon of vanity, never completely silenced, at first whispered to me some flattering presumptions. I even went so far as to ask myself whether by granting this distinction to the «man without dogma» that I profess to be, the Academy did not wish to emphasize that in this century, when everyone «believes» and «asserts», it is perhaps useful that there should be some who «hesitate», «put in doubt», and «question»—independent minds that escape the fascination of partisan ideologies and whose constant care is to develop their individual consciences in order to maintain a spirit of «inquiry» as objective, liberal, and fair-minded as is humanly possible.

I should also like to think that this sudden honour acknowledges certain principles dear to me. «Principles» is a big word to be used by a man who says that he is always ready to revise his opinions. I must, however, admit that in the practice of my art I have imposed upon myself certain guidelines to which I have tried to be faithful.

I was still very young when I encountered, in a novel by the English writer

Thomas Hardy, this reflection on one of his characters: «The true value of life seemed to him to be not so much its beauty, as its tragic quality.» It spoke to an intuition deep within me, closely allied to my literary vocation. Ever since that time I have thought that the prime purpose of the novel is to give voice to the tragic element in life. Today I would add: the tragic element in the life of an individual, the tragedy of a «destiny in the course of being fulfilled».

At this point I cannot refrain from referring to the immortal example of Tolstoy, whose books have had a determining influence on my development. The born novelist recognizes himself by his passion to penetrate ever more deeply into the knowledge of man and to lay bare in each of his characters that individual element of his life which makes each being unique. It seems to me that any chance of survival which a novelist's work may have rests solely on the quantity and the quality of the individual lives that he has been able to create in his books. But that is not all. The novelist must also have a sense of life in general; his work must reveal a personal vision of the universe. Here again Tolstoy is the great master. Each of his creatures is more or less secretly haunted by a metaphysical obsession, and each of the human experiences that he has recorded implies, beyond an inquiry into man, an anxious question about the meaning of life. I admit that I take pleasure in the thought that, in crowning my work as a novelist, the members of the Swedish Academy wished to pay indirect homage to my devotion to that unapproachable model and to my efforts to profit from the instruction of his genius.

I should like to conclude with a more sombre hypothesis, although I am embarrassed to disturb this festive mood by arousing those painful thoughts that haunt all of us. However, perhaps the Swedish Academy did not hesitate to express a special purpose by drawing the attention of the intellectual world to the author of *L'Été 1914* [*Summer 1914*].

That is the title of my last book. It is not for me to judge its value. But at least I know what I set out to do: in the course of these three volumes I tried to revivify the anguished atmosphere of Europe on the eve of the mobilizations of 1914. I tried to show the weakness of the governments of that day, their hesitations, indiscretions, and unavowed desires; I tried above all to give an impression of the stupefaction of the peaceful masses before the approach of that cataclysm whose victims they were going to be, that cataclysm which was to leave nine million men dead and ten million men crippled.

When I see that one of the highest literary juries in the world supports these books with the prestige of its incontestable authority, I ask myself whether the reason may not be that these books through their wide circulation have appeared to defend certain values that are again being threatened and to fight against the evil contagion of the forces of war.

For I am a son of the West, where the noise of arms does not let our minds rest. Since we have come together today on the tenth of December, the anniversary of the death of Alfred Nobel (that man of action, «no mere shadow», who in the last years of his life seems indeed to have put his supreme hope in the brotherhood of nations), permit me to confess how good it would be to think that my work – the work that has just been honoured in his name – might serve not only the cause of letters, but even the cause of peace. In these months of anxiety in which we are living, when blood is already being shed in two extreme parts of the globe, when practically everywhere in an atmosphere polluted by misery and fanaticism passions are seething around pointed guns, when too many signs are again heralding the return of that languid defeatism, that general consent which alone makes wars possible: at this exceptionally grave moment through which humanity is passing, I wish, without vanity, but with a gnawing disquietude in my heart, that my books about «Summer 1914» may be read and discussed, and that they may remind all – the old who have forgotten as well as the young who either do not know or do not care – of the sad lesson of the past.

Prior to the acceptance, Professor A. E. Lindh of the University of Uppsala spoke: «It is with great pleasure and gratification that we find among our distinguished guests this evening Roger Martin du Gard, crowned today with the golden laurel of the Nobel Prize. We thank you most heartily for what you have given us through the medium of your literary work, and particularly for your great masterpiece, *Les Thibault*, which has come into being as a result of an intense study of reality, and of a profound knowledge of human dissimilitudes. In your psychological work survives that classical French realism which dauntlessly portrays life in all its naked truths, and which demands of its practitioners an incorruptible conscience and a great sense of justice. We admire the way in which you have permitted the family chronicles in *Les Thibault* to develop into a tragic and complete picture of Europe such as it appeared before those calamitous years of the World War. In acknowledging your powerful accomplishments we add our respect for the earnest pathos which runs through your literary works.»

Biography

Roger Martin du Gard (1881–1958) was born in Neuilly-sur-Seine, attended two of the finest Paris lycées and, in 1906, was graduated from the École des Chartes with a thesis on an archaeological subject and with the degree of archivist-paleographer. To this training in history and scholarship he attributes his scrupulous realism and attention to minute detail.

Martin du Gard's first success was the novel *Jean Barois*, published by his former school friend Gaston Gallimard in 1913. It anticipates some of the thematic material of *Les Thibault*. Largely in dialogue form, *Jean Barois* is the story of a life deeply divided by two world views, that of the Catholic Church and that of a freethinking, unflinching, humanistic philosophy of facing and mastering reality. In 1920 he published the peasant farce *Le Testament du Père Leleu*. He became attached to the circle of the *Nouvelle Revue Française* and was close to Gide, Copeau, and J. Schlumberger.

After the years of the First World War, which Martin du Gard spent almost entirely in the front lines, he devoted most of his time to the writing of the «roman-fleuve», *Les Thibault*, which culminates in the three volumes of *L'Été 1914* [*Summer 1914*]. The twelve individual volumes of the series of novels appeared between 1922 and 1940.

Les Thibault is a monumental picture of the world before the outbreak of the First World War. Its rambling plot traces the history of Jacques Thibault, the rebel son of an upper middle-class family, against the background of the more staid destinies of his relatives. The work gives a detailed account of the hero's despair at the outbreak of fighting and the failure of his insane attempt to stop it. Various minor works, written for distraction or relaxation, include the drama *Un Taciturne* (1932) [*The Silent One*], the short novel *Confidence africaine* (1931) [*African Secret*], and a collection of village sketches, *Vieille France* (1933) [*The Postman*]. His *Notes sur André Gide 1913–1951* [*Recollections of André Gide*] appeared in 1951. The complete works of Martin du Gard were published in two volumes in 1955.

Literature 1938

PEARL S. BUCK

(pen name of Pearl Walsh, *née* Sydenstricker)

«for her rich and truly epic descriptions of peasant life in China and for he
biographical masterpieces»

Presentation

by Per Hallström, Permanent Secretary of the Swedish Academy

Pearl Buck once told how she had found her mission as interpreter to the West of the nature and being of China. She did not turn to it as a literary speciality at all; it came to her naturally.

«It is people that have always afforded me my greatest pleasure and interest», she said, «and as I live among the Chinese, it has been the Chinese people. When I am asked what sort of people they are, I cannot answer. They are not this or that, they are just people. I can no more define them than I can define my own relatives and kinsmen. I am too near to them and I have lived too intimately with them for that.»

She has been among the people of China in all their vicissitudes, in good years and in famine years, in the bloody tumults of revolutions and in the delirium of Utopias. She has associated with the educated classes and with primordially primitive peasants, who had hardly seen a Western face before they saw hers. Often she has been in deadly peril, a stranger who never thought of herself as a stranger; on the whole, her outlook retained its profound and warm humanity. With pure objectivity she has breathed life into her knowledge and given us the peasant epic which has made her world-famous, *The Good Earth* (1931).

As her hero she took a man who led the same existence as his forefathers had during countless centuries, and who possessed the same primitive soul. His virtues spring from one single root: affinity with the earth, which yields its crops in return for a man's labours.

Wang Lung is created from the same stuff as the yellow-brown earth in the fields, and with a kind of pious joy he bestows upon it every ounce of his energy. The two belong to each other in origin, and they will become one again with the death he will meet with tranquility. His work is also a duty done, and thus his conscience is at rest. Since dishonesty avails nothing in his pursuits, he has become honest. This is the sum total of his moral conceptions, and equally few are his religious ones, which are almost entirely comprehended in the cult of ancestor-worship.

He knows that man's life is a gleam of light between two darknesses; from the one behind him runs the chain of forefathers from father to son, and the chain must not be broken by him, if he is not to lose his dim hope of survival in a surmised, unknown region. For then would expire a spark of the life-fire of the race, which each individual man has to care for.

And thus the story begins with Wang Lung's marriage and his dreams of sons in the house. Of his wife, O'Lan, he does not dream, for–as is proper and fitting–he has never seen her. She is a slave at the great house in the neighbouring town and cheap to buy, since she is said to be ugly. For that reason she has probably been left alone by the young sons of the house, and to this the bridegroom attaches great value.

Their life together is happy, for the wife proves to be an excellent help-mate, and the children soon make their appearance. She satisfies all the demands laid upon her, and she has no claims of her own. Behind her mute eyes is hidden a mute soul. She is all submission, but wise and prompt in action; a wife also in her paucity of words, springing from a philosophy of life learned in a hard school.

Success attends the two. They are able to set aside a little money, and Wang Lung's great passion, next to parenthood, his longing for more ground to cultivate, may now venture forth from subconsciousness. He is able to buy more fields, and everything promises happiness and increase.

Then comes a blow from the hand of fate; a drought descends upon the district. The good earth is changed into yellow, whirling dust. By selling land they could avert starvation, but that would be to bolt and lock the door to the future. Neither of them wishes to do that, so they set forth in company with the growing army of beggars to a city in the south, to live on the crumbs from the rich man's table.

O'Lan had made the journey once before in her childhood, when the end of it was that she was sold to save her parents and brothers.

Thanks to her experience, they accommodate themselves to the new life. Wang Lung toils as a beast of burden and the others beg with an acquired aptitude. Autumn and winter pass. With the spring, their yearning for their own land and its tilling becomes unendurable, but they have no money for the journey.

Then again fate intervenes–as natural a fate in China as drought and plague and flood. War, which is ever present somewhere in that great country, and the ways of which are as inscrutable as those of the powers of the air, stalks across the city and makes chaos of law and order. The poor plunder the homes of the rich.

Wang Lung goes with the mob without any definite motives, for his peasant soul revolts at deeds of violence, but by pure chance a handful of gold coins is almost forced into his hand. Now he can go home and begin the spring work on his rain-soaked soil. More than that, he can buy new fields; he is rich and happy.

He becomes still richer, though ultimately not happier, through the plunder acquired by O'Lan. From her days of slavery she knows something about hiding places in palaces, and she discovers a handful of precious stones. She takes them nearly as unpremeditatedly as a magpie steals glittering things, and hides them as instinctively. When her husband discovers them in her bosom, his whole world is transformed. He buys farm after farm. He becomes the leading man in the district, no longer peasant but lord, and his character changes colour. Simplicity and harmony with the earth vanish. In their place comes, slowly but surely, a curse for the desertion.

Wang Lung no longer has any real peace in his lordly leisure, with a young concubine in the house and O'Lan pushed into a dark corner, to die there when she has worn herself out.

The sons are not attractive figures. The eldest devotes himself to an empty life of indulgence, the second is swallowed up by greed for gold as a merchant and usurer. The youngest becomes one of the «war lords» who drain the unhappy country. Around them the Middle Empire is torn asunder in the tumult of new creation, which has become so agonizing in our days.

The trilogy does not carry us so far, however; it concludes with a sort of reconciliation between the third generation and the good earth. One of Wang Lung's grandsons, a man educated in the West, returns to the family estate and applies the knowledge he has acquired to the improvement of the conditions of work and life among the peasants.

The rest of the family live without roots in that conflict between old and new which Pearl Buck has described in other works—mostly in the tone of tragedy.

Of the many problems in this novel, the most serious and sombre one is the position of the Chinese woman. From the very beginning it is on this point that the writer's pathos emerges most strongly, and amid the calm of the epic work it constantly makes itself felt. An early episode in the work gives the most poignant expression of what a Chinese woman has been worth since time immemorial. It is given with impressive emphasis, and also with a touch of humour which is naturally rare in this book. In a moment of happiness, with his little first-born son dressed in fine clothes on his arm, and seeing the future bright before him, Wang Lung is on the point of breaking into boastful words but restrains himself in sudden terror. There, under the open sky, he had almost challenged the invisible spirits and drawn their evil glances upon himself. He tries to avert the menace by hiding his son under his coat and saying in a loud voice, «What a pity that our child is a girl, which no one wants, and is pitted with smallpox into the bargain! Let us pray that it may die!» And O'Lan joins in the comedy and acquiesces –probably without thinking at all.

In reality the spirits need not waste their glances on a girl child. Its lot is hard enough in any case. It is Pearl Buck's female characters which make the strongest impression. There is O'Lan with her scanty words, which carry all the more weight. Her whole life is portrayed in equally scanty but telling lines.

Quite a different figure is the chief character in the novel *The Mother* (1934). She is not referred to by any other designation, as if to indicate that her whole destiny is expressed in that word. She is, however, vividly individualized, a brave, energetic, strong character, of a more modern type than O'Lan's, perhaps, and without her slave temperament. The husband soon deserts his home, but she keeps it together for her children. The whole story ends in sorrow, but not in defeat. The mother cannot be crushed, not even when her younger son is beheaded as a revolutionary, and she has to seek a stranger's grave to weep by, for he has none. Just then a grandson is born, and she again has someone to love and sacrifice herself for.

The mother is the most finished of Pearl Buck's Chinese female figures, and the book is one of her best. But in character descriptions and the story-teller's art she is at her best in the two biographies of her parents, *The Exile* (1936) and *Fighting Angel* (1936). These should be called classics in the fullest sense of the word; they will endure, for they are full of life. In this respect the models from which the portraits are drawn are of great significance.

One seldom feels any great sense of gratitude for the company proffered in contemporary novels, and it is gladly forgotten. The characters have no great wealth of qualities, and the writer puts forth all his powers to lessen them, often by a persistent analysis with foregone results.

Here, however, one encounters two consummate characters, living un-selfish lives of action, free from brooding and vacillation. They are profoundly unlike each other, and the fact that they are thrown together in a common struggle in a hard and strange world often leads to great tragedy–but not to defeat: they stand erect even to the very last. There is a spirit of heroism in both stories.

The mother, Carie, is richly gifted, brave and warm, of a genuine nature, harmonious amid ever-straining forces. She is tested to the utmost in sorrows and dangers; she loses many children because of the harshness of the conditions of life, and at times a terrible death threatens her in those troubled times. It is almost as hard for her to witness the never-ending suffering around her. She does what she can to mitigate it, and that is not a little, but no power is sufficient for such a task.

Even inwardly she passes through a hard and unceasing struggle. In her calling, and with her nature, she needs more than the conviction of faith. It is not enough for her that she has dedicated herself to God; she must also feel that the sacrifice has been accepted. But the sign of this, for which she begs and prays, never comes. She is compelled to persist in an untiring endeavour to find God and to content herself with trying to be good without divine help.

However, she preserves her spiritual health, her love for the life which has shown her so much that is terrible, and her eye for the beauty the world has to offer; she even retains her happiness and her humour. She resembles a fresh fountain springing from the heart of life.

The daughter tells her story with rare and lively perspicuity. The biography is precise in regard to the course of events, but creative imagination plays its part in the various episodes and in the description of the inner life of the character. Nothing is falsified, for this imagination is intuitive and true.

The language has vivid spontaneity; it is clear and suffused with a tender and soulful humour. There is, however, a flaw in the story. The daughter's devotion to her mother makes it impossible for her to do justice to her father. In his family life his limitations were obvious, limitations sharp and at times painful. As a preacher and soldier of Christ he was without blemish, in many respects even a great character; but he ought to have lived his life alone, free of the familial duties he hardly found time to notice, duties which in any case weighed lightly with him against his all-absorbing calling. Thus he was of little help to his wife, and in her biography he could not be fully understood.

This was accomplished, however, in another book, whose title is the key to his life and being: *Fighting Angel*. Andrew did not possess his wife's richly composite nature; his was narrow but deep, and as bright as a gleaming sword. He devoted every thought to his goal of opening the way to salvation for the heathens. Everything was insignificant compared to that. What Carie prayed for in vain, communion with God, he possessed wholly and unshakeably in the firm conceptions of his Biblical faith. With this faith he walked like a conqueror, further than any other in the immense heather country, he endured all hardships without noticing them, and he encountered threats and dangers in the same manner. For the poor, blind, strange brown people he felt tenderness and love. Among them his stern nature broke into blossom. When he had won their souls to a confession of faith, he did not doubt the genuineness of the confession; with the naiveté of a child, he accepted it as good. The door to God, always denied them before, had been opened to them, and to weigh them and judge them was now in the hands of Him who knows best. They had been given their possibility of salvation, and for Andrew it was urgent to give this possibility to all he could reach in that immense country, where thousands were dying every hour. His enthusiasm burned, and his work had something of genius in its magnitude and depth.

He strained his forces to the utmost in never-ending action, and the repose he allowed himself was the mystic's abandonment to the infinite amid ardent prayers. The whole of his life was a flame which rose straight and high, in spite of all storms; it could not be judged by ordinary conceptions. The daughter, whose portrait conceals none of his repellent features, maintained pure reverence before the nobility of the whole. One is profoundly thankful for both these perfectly executed pictures—each in its way so rare.

By awarding this year's Prize to Pearl Buck for the notable works which pave the way to a human sympathy passing over widely separated racial boundaries and for the studies of human ideals which are a great and living art of portraiture, the Swedish Academy feels that it acts in harmony and accord with the aim of Alfred Nobel's dreams for the future.

Mrs. Walsh, I have attempted a short survey of your work, indeed hardly necessary here, where the audience is so well acquainted with your remarkable books.

I hope, though, that I have been able to give some idea of their trend, toward opening a faraway and foreign world to deeper human insight and sympathy within our Western sphere—a grand and difficult task, requiring all your idealism and greatheartedness to fulfil as you have done.

May I now ask you to receive from the hands of His Majesty the King the Nobel Prize in Literature, conferred upon you by the Swedish Academy.

Acceptance

t is not possible for me to express all that I feel of appreciation for what as been said and given to me. I accept, for myself, with the conviction of aving received far beyond what I have been able to give in my books. I an only hope that the many books which I have yet to write will be in ome measure a worthier acknowledgment than I can make tonight. And, ndeed, I can accept only in the same spirit in which I think this gift was riginally given—that it is a prize not so much for what has been done, as or the future. Whatever I write in the future must, I think, be always benefited nd strengthened when I remember this day.

I accept, too, for my country, the United States of America. We are a eople still young and we know that we have not yet come to the fullest f our powers. This award, given to an American, strengthens not only one, ut the whole body of American writers, who are encouraged and heartened y such generous recognition. And I should like to say, too, that in my ountry it is important that this award has been given to a woman. You who have already so recognized your own Selma Lagerlöf, and have long ecognized women in other fields, cannot perhaps wholly understand what t means in many countries that it is a woman who stands here at this moment. But I speak not only for writers and for women, but for all Americans, for we all share in this.

I should not be truly myself if I did not, in my own wholly unofficial way, peak also of the people of China, whose life has for so many years been ny life also, whose life, indeed, must always be a part of my life. The minds f my own country and of China, my foster country, are alike in many ways, ut above all, alike in our common love of freedom. And today more than ver, this is true, now when China's whole being is engaged in the greatest f all struggles, the struggle for freedom. I have never admired China more han I do now, when I see her uniting as she has never before, against the nemy who threatens her freedom. With this determination for freedom, which is in so profound a sense the essential quality in her nature, I know hat she is *unconquerable*. Freedom—it is today more than ever the most precious human possession. We –Sweden and the United States–we have it still My country is young–but it greets you with a peculiar fellowship, you whose earth is ancient and free.

Prior to the acceptance, Bertil Lindblad, Director of the Stockholm Observatory at Saltsjöbaden, made the following remarks: «Mrs. Pearl Buck you have in your literary works, which are of the highest artistic quality advanced the understanding and the appreciation in the Western world of a great and important part of mankind, the people of China. You have taught us by your works to see the individuals in that great mass of people. You have shown us the rise and fall of families, and the land as the foundation upon which families are built. In this you have taught us to see those qualities of thought and feeling which bind us all together as human beings on this earth, and you have given us Westerners something of China's soul. When by the development of technical inventions the peoples of the earth are drawn closer to each other, the surface of the earth shrinks, so that East and West are no longer separated by almost insurmountable voids of distance, and when on the other hand, partly as a natural effect of this phenomenon, the differences of national character and ambitions clash to form dangerous discontinuities, it is of the greatest importance that the peoples of the earth learn to understand each other as individuals across distances and frontiers. When works of literature succeed in this respect they are certainly in a very direct way idealistic in the sense in which this word was meant by Alfred Nobel.»

PEARL S. BUCK

The Chinese Novel

Nobel Lecture, December 12, 1938

When I came to consider what I should say today it seemed that it would
be wrong not to speak of China. And this is none the less true because I am
an American by birth and by ancestry and though I live now in my own
country and shall live there, since there I belong. But it is the Chinese and
not the American novel which has shaped my own efforts in writing.
My earliest knowledge of story, of how to tell and write stories, came
to me in China. It would be ingratitude on my part not to recognize this
today. And yet it would be presumptuous to speak before you on the
subject of the Chinese novel for a reason wholly personal. There is another
reason why I feel that I may properly do so. It is that I believe the Chinese novel has an illumination for the Western novel and for the Western
novelist.

When I say Chinese novel, I mean the indigenous Chinese novel, and not
that hybrid product, the novels of modern Chinese writers who have been
too strongly under foreign influence while they were yet ignorant of the
riches of their own country.

The novel in China was never an art and was never so considered, nor
did any Chinese novelist think of himself as an artist. The Chinese novel,
its history, its scope, its place in the life of the people, so vital a place, must
be viewed in the strong light of this one fact. It is a fact no doubt strange
to you, a company of modern Western scholars who today so generously
recognize the novel.

But in China art and the novel have always been widely separated. There,
literature as an art was the exclusive property of the scholars, an art they
made and made for each other according to their own rules, and they found
no place in it for the novel. And they held a powerful place, those Chinese
scholars. Philosophy and religion and letters and literature, by arbitrary classical rules, they possessed them all, for they alone possessed the means of
learning, since they alone knew how to read and write. They were powerful
enough to be feared even by emperors, so that emperors devised a way of
keeping them enslaved by their own learning, and made the official examina-

tions the only means to political advancement, those incredibly difficul
examinations which ate up a man's whole life and thought in preparing fo
them, and kept him too busy with memorizing and copying the dead an
classical past to see the present and its wrongs. In that past the scholars foun
their rules of art. But the novel was not there, and they did not see it bein
created before their eyes, for the people created the novel, and what livin
people were doing did not interest those who thought of literature as a
art. If scholars ignored the people, however, the people, in turn, laughed a
the scholars. They made innumerable jokes about them, of which this is
fair sample: One day a company of wild beasts met on a hillside for a hunt
They bargained with each other to go out and hunt all day and meet agai
at the end of the day to share what they had killed. At the end of the day
only the tiger returned with nothing. When he was asked how this happene
he replied very disconsolately, «At dawn I met a schoolboy, but he was,
feared, too callow for your tastes. I met no more until noon, when I foun
a priest. But I let him go, knowing him to be full of nothing but wind
The day went on and I grew desperate, for I passed no one. Then as dar
came on I found a scholar. But I knew there was no use in bringing hin
back since he would be so dry and hard that he would break our teeth i
we tried them on him.»

The scholar as a class has long been a figure of fun for the Chinese people
He is frequently to be found in their novels, and always he is the same, a
indeed he is in life, for a long study of the same dead classics and their forma
composition has really made all Chinese scholars look alike, as well as thin
alike. We have no class to parallel him in the West—individuals, perhaps, only
But in China he was a class. Here he is, composite, as the people see him
a small shrunken figure with a bulging forehead, a pursed mouth, a nose a
once snub and pointed, small inconspicuous eyes behind spectacles, a high
pedantic voice, always announcing rules that do not matter to anyone bu
himself, a boundless self-conceit, a complete scorn not only of the commo
people but of all other scholars, a figure in long shabby robes, moving wit
a swaying haughty walk, when he moved at all. He was not to be seen excep
at literary gatherings, for most of the time he spent reading dead literatur
and trying to write more like it. He hated anything fresh or original, fo
he could not catalogue it into any of the styles he knew. If he could no
catalogue it, he was sure it was not great, and he was confident that only
he was right. If he said, «Here is art», he was convinced it was not to b
found anywhere else, for what he did not recognize did not exist. And a

e could never catalogue the novel into what he called literature, so for him
, did not exist as literature.

Yao Hai, one of the greatest of Chinese literary critics, in 1776 enumerated
he kinds of writing which comprise the whole of literature. They are essays,
overnment commentaries, biographies, epitaphs, epigrams, poetry, funeral
ulogies, and histories. No novels, you perceive, although by that date the
Chinese novel had already reached its glorious height, after centuries of development among the common Chinese people. Nor does that vast compilation
f Chinese literature, *Ssŭ Ku Chuen Shu*, made in 1772 by the order of the
great Emperor Ch'ien Lung, contain the novel in the encyclopedia of its
terature proper.

No, happily for the Chinese novel, it was not considered by the scholars
s literature. Happily, too, for the novelist! Man and book, they were free
rom the criticisms of those scholars and their requirements of art, their
echniques of expression and their talk of literary significances and all that
liscussion of what is and is not art, as if art were an absolute and not the
hanging thing it is, fluctuating even within decades! The Chinese novel was
ree. It grew as it liked out of its own soil, the common people, nurtured
oy that heartiest of sunshine, popular approval, and untouched by the cold
nd frosty winds of the scholar's art. Emily Dickinson, an American poet,
once wrote, «Nature is a haunted house, but art is a house that tries to be
naunted.» «Nature», she said,

> Is what we see,
> Nature is what we know
> But have no art to say—
> So impatient our wisdom is,
> To her simplicity.

No, if the Chinese scholars ever knew of the growth of the novel, it was
only to ignore it the more ostentatiously. Sometimes, unfortunately, they
found themselves driven to take notice, because youthful emperors found
novels pleasant to read. Then these poor scholars were hard put to it. But
hey discovered the phrase «social significance», and they wrote long literary
reatises to prove that a novel was not a novel but a document of social
ignificance. Social significance is a term recently discovered by the most
modern of literary young men and women in the United States, but the
old scholars of China knew it a thousand years ago, when they, too, demanded

that the novel should have social significance, if it were to be recognized
as an art.

But for the most part the old Chinese scholar reasoned thus about the novel

> *Literature is art.*
> *All art has social significance.*
> *This book has no social significance.*
> *Therefore it is not literature.*

And so the novel in China was not literature.

In such a school was I trained. I grew up believing that the novel had
nothing to do with pure literature. So I was taught by scholars. The art of
literature, so I was taught, is something devised by men of learning. Out
of the brains of scholars came rules to control the rush of genius, that wild
fountain which has its source in deepest life. Genius, great or less, is the spring
and art is the sculptured shape, classical or modern, into which the water
must be forced, if scholars and critics were to be served. But the people of
China did not so serve. The waters of the genius of story gushed out as they
would, however the natural rocks allowed and the trees persuaded, and only
common people came and drank and found rest and pleasure.

For the novel in China was the peculiar product of the common people
And it was solely their property. The very language of the novel was their
own language, and not the classical Wen-li, which was the language of literature and the scholars. Wen-li bore somewhat the same resemblance to
the language of the people as the ancient English of Chaucer does to the
English of today, although ironically enough, at one time Wen-li, too, was
a vernacular. But the scholars never kept pace with the living, changing
speech of the people. They clung to an old vernacular until they had made
it classic, while the running language of the people went on and left them
far behind. Chinese novels, then, are in the «Pei Hua», or simple talk, of
the people, and this in itself was offensive to the old scholars because it resulted in a style so full of easy flow and readability that it had no technique
of expression in it, the scholars said.

I should pause to make an exception of certain scholars who came to China
from India, bearing as their gift a new religion, Buddhism. In the West
Puritanism was for a long time the enemy of the novel. But in the Orient
the Buddhists were wiser. When they came into China, they found literature
already remote from the people and dying under the formalism of that pe-

riod known in history as the Six Dynasties. The professional men of literature were even then absorbed not so much in what they had to say as in pairing into couplets the characters of their essays and their poems, and already they scorned all writing which did not conform to their own rules. Into this confined literary atmosphere came the Buddhist translators with their great treasures of the freed spirit. Some of them were Indian, but some were Chinese. They said frankly that their aim was not to conform to the ideas of style of the literary men, but to make clear and simple to common people what they had to teach. They put their religious teachings into the common language, the language which the novel used, and because the people loved story, they took story and made it a means of teaching. The preface of *Fah Shu Ching*, one of the most famous of Buddhist books, says, «When giving the words of gods, these words should be given forth simply.» This might be taken as the sole literary creed of the Chinese novelist, to whom, indeed, gods were men and men were gods.

For the Chinese novel was written primarily to amuse the common people. And when I say amuse I do not mean only to make them laugh, though laughter is also one of the aims of the Chinese novel. I mean amusement in the sense of absorbing and occupying the whole attention of the mind. I mean enlightening that mind by pictures of life and what that life means. I mean encouraging the spirit not by rule-of-thumb talk about art, but by stories about the people in every age, and thus presenting to people simply themselves. Even the Buddhists who came to tell about gods found that people understood gods better if they saw them working through ordinary folk like themselves.

But the real reason why the Chinese novel was written in the vernacular was because the common people could not read and write and the novel had to be written so that when it was read aloud it could be understood by persons who could communicate only through spoken words. In a village of two hundred souls perhaps only one man could read. And on holidays or in the evening when the work was done he read aloud to the people from some story. The rise of the Chinese novel began in just this simple fashion. After a while people took up a collection of pennies in somebody's cap or in a farm wife's bowl because the reader needed tea to wet his throat, or perhaps to pay him for time he would otherwise have spent at his silk loom or his rush weaving. If the collections grew big enough he gave up some of his regular work and became a professional storyteller. And the stories he read were the beginnings of novels. There were not many such stories

written down, not nearly enough to last year in and year out for people
who had by nature, as the Chinese have, a strong love for dramatic story.
So the storyteller began to increase his stock. He searched the dry annals of
the history which the scholars had written, and with his fertile imagination,
enriched by long acquaintance with common people, he clothed long-dead
figures with new flesh and made them live again; he found stories of court
life and intrigue and names of imperial favorites who had brought dynasties
to ruin; he found, as he traveled from village to village, strange tales from
his own times which he wrote down when he heard them. People told him
of experiences they had had and he wrote these down, too, for other people.
And he embellished them, but not with literary turns and phrases, for the
people cared nothing for these. No, he kept his audiences always in mind
and he found that the style which they loved best was one which flowed
easily along, clearly and simply, in the short words which they themselves
used every day, with no other technique than occasional bits of description,
only enough to give vividness to a place or a person, and never enough to
delay the story. Nothing must delay the story. Story was what they wanted.

And when I say story, I do not mean mere pointless activity, not crude
action alone. The Chinese are too mature for that. They have always demanded of their novel character above all else. *Shui Hu Chuan* they have
considered one of their three greatest novels, not primarily because it is full
of the flash and fire of action, but because it portrays so distinctly one hundred
and eight characters that each is to be seen separate from the others. Often
I have heard it said of that novel in tones of delight, «When anyone of the
hundred and eight begins to speak, we do not need to be told his name. By
the way the words come from his mouth we know who he is.» Vividness
of character portrayal, then, is the first quality which the Chinese people
have demanded of their novels, and after it, that such portrayal shall be by
the character's own action and words rather than by the author's explanation.

Curiously enough, while the novel was beginning thus humbly in teahouses, in villages and lowly city streets out of stories told to the common
people by a common and unlearned man among them, in imperial palaces
it was beginning, too, and in much the same unlearned fashion. It was an
old custom of emperors, particularly if the dynasty were a foreign one, to
employ persons called «imperial ears», whose only duty was to come and
go among the people in the streets of cities and villages and to sit among them
in teahouses, disguised in common clothes and listen to what was talked
about there. The original purpose of this was, of course, to hear of any dis-

ontent among the emperor's subjects, and more especially to find out if
discontents were rising to the shape of those rebellions which preceded the
all of every dynasty.

But emperors were very human and they were not often learned scholars.
More often, indeed, they were only spoiled and willful men. The «imperial
ars» had opportunity to hear all sorts of strange and interesting stories,
nd they found that their royal masters were more frequently interested in
these stories than they were in politics. So when they came back to make
their reports, they flattered the emperor and sought to gain favor by telling
him what he liked to hear, shut up as he was in the Forbidden City, away
from life. They told him the strange and interesting things which common people did, who were free, and after a while they took to writing
down what they heard in order to save memory. And I do not doubt that
f messengers between the emperor and the people carried stories in one
direction, they carried them in the other, too, and to the people they told
tories about the emperor and what he said and did, and how he quarreled
with the empress who bore him no sons, and how she intrigued with the
chief eunuch to poison the favorite concubine, all of which delighted the
Chinese because it proved to them, the most democratic of peoples, that their
emperor was after all only a common fellow like themselves and that he,
too, had his troubles, though he was the Son of Heaven. Thus there began
another important source for the novel that was to develop with such form
and force, though still always denied its right to exist by the professional
man of letters.

From such humble and scattered beginnings, then, came the Chinese novel,
written always in the vernacular, and dealing with all which interested the
people, with legend and with myth, with love and intrigue, with brigands
and wars, with everything, indeed, which went to make up the life of the
people, high and low.

Nor was the novel in China shaped, as it was in the West, by a few great
persons. In China the novel has always been more important than the nov-
list. There has been no Chinese Defoe, no Chinese Fielding or Smollett,
no Austin or Brontë or Dickens or Thackeray, or Meredith or Hardy, any
more than Balzac or Flaubert. But there were and are novels as great as the
novels in any other country in the world, as great as any could have written,
had he been born in China. Who then wrote these novels of China?

That is what the modern literary men of China now, centuries too late,
are trying to discover. Within the last twenty-five years literary critics,

trained in the universities of the West, have begun to discover their ow
neglected novels. But the novelists who wrote them they cannot discove
Did one man write *Shui Hu Chuan*, or did it grow to its present shape, adde
to, rearranged, deepened and developed by many minds and many a hand
in different centuries? Who can now tell? They are dead. They lived in thei
day and wrote what in their day they saw and heard, but of themselves the
have told nothing. The author of *The Dream of the Red Chamber* in a far late
century says in the preface to his book, «It is not necessary to know the time
of Han and T'ang–it is necessary to tell only of my own times.»

They told of their own times and they lived in a blessed obscurity. The
read no reviews of their novels, no treatises as to whether or not what the
did was well done according to the rules of scholarship. It did not occu
to them that they must reach the high thin air which scholars breathed no
did they consider the stuff of which greatness is made, according to th
scholars. They wrote as it pleased them to write and as they were abl
Sometimes they wrote unwittingly well and sometimes unwittingly the
wrote not so well. They died in the same happy obscurity and now the
are lost in it and not all the scholars of China, gathered too late to do then
honor, can raise them up again. They are long past the possibility of literar
post-mortems. But what they did remains after them because it is the com
mon people of China who keep alive the great novels, illiterate people wh
have passed the novel, not so often from hand to hand as from mouth t
mouth.

In the preface to one of the later editions of *Shui Hu Chuan*, Shih Nai Ar
an author who had much to do with the making of that novel, writes, «Wha
I speak of I wish people to understand easily. Whether the reader is goo
or evil, learned or unlearned, anyone can read this book. Whether or no
the book is well done is not important enough to cause anyone to worry
–Alas, I am born to die. How can I know what those who come after m
who read my book will think of it? I cannot even know what I mysel
born into another incarnation, will think of it. I do not know if I mysel
then can even read. Why therefore should I care?»

Strangely enough, there were certain scholars who envied the freedon
of obscurity, and who, burdened with certain private sorrows which the
dared not tell anyone, or who perhaps wanting only a holiday from th
weariness of the sort of art they had themselves created, wrote novels, too
under assumed and humble names. And when they did so they put asid
pedantry and wrote as simply and naturally as any common novelist. Fo

he novelist believed that he should not be conscious of techniques. He should
write as his material demanded. If a novelist became known for a particular
style or technique, to that extent he ceased to be a good novelist and became
literary technician.

A good novelist, or so I have been taught in China, should be above all
else *tse ran*, that is, natural, unaffected, and so flexible and variable as to be
wholly at the command of the material that flows through him. His whole
duty is only to sort life as it flows through him, and in the vast fragmentariness
of time and space and event to discover essential and inherent order and
rhythm and shape. We should never be able, merely by reading pages, to
know who wrote them, for when the style of a novelist becomes fixed, that
style becomes his prison. The Chinese novelists varied their writing to accompany like music their chosen themes.

These Chinese novels are not perfect according to Western standards. They
are not always planned from beginning to end, nor are they compact, any
more than life is planned or compact. They are often too long, too full of
incident, too crowded with character, a medley of fact and fiction as to
material, and a medley of romance and realism as to method, so that an impossible event of magic or dream may be described with such exact semblance
of detail that one is compelled to belief against all reason. The earliest novels
are full of folklore, for the people of those times thought and dreamed in
the ways of folklore. But no one can understand the mind of China today
who has not read these novels, for the novels have shaped the present mind,
too, and the folklore persists in spite of all that Chinese diplomats and Western-
trained scholars would have us believe to the contrary. The essential mind
of China is still that mind of which George Russell wrote when he said of
the Irish mind, so strangely akin to the Chinese, « that mind which in its
folk imagination believes anything. It creates ships of gold with masts of
silver and white cities by the sea and rewards and faeries, and when that vast
folk mind turns to politics it is ready to believe anything.»

Out of this folk mind, turned into stories and crowded with thousands
of years of life, grew, literally, the Chinese novel. For these novels changed
as they grew. If, as I have said, there are no single names attached beyond
question to the great novels of China, it is because no one hand wrote them.
From beginning as a mere tale, a story grew through succeeding versions,
into a structure built by many hands. I might mention as an example the
well-known story, *The White Snake*, or *Pei Shê Chuan*, first written in the
T'ang dynasty by an unknown author. It was then a tale of the simple

supernatural whose hero was a great white snake. In the next version in the following century, the snake has become a vampire woman who is an evil force. But the third version contains a more gentle and human touch. The vampire becomes a faithful wife who aids her husband and gives him a son. The story thus adds not only new character but new quality, and ends not as the supernatural tale it began but as a novel of human beings.

So in early periods of Chinese history, many books must be called not so much novels as source books for novels, the sort of books into which Shakespeare, had they been open to him, might have dipped with both hands to bring up pebbles to make into jewels. Many of these books have been lost, since they were not considered valuable. But not all – early stories of Han, written so vigorously that to this day it is said they run like galloping horses, and tales of the troubled dynasties following – not all were lost. Some have persisted. In the Ming dynasty, in one way or another, many of them were represented in the great collection known as *T'ai P'ing Kuan Shi*, wherein are tales of superstition and religion, of mercy and goodness and reward for evil and well doing, tales of dreams and miracles, of dragons and gods and goddesses and priests, of tigers and foxes and transmigration and resurrection from the dead. Most of these early stories had to do with supernatural events of gods born of virgins, of men walking as gods, as the Buddhist influence grew strong. There are miracles and allegories, such as the pens of poor scholars bursting into flower, dreams leading men and women into strange and fantastic lands of Gulliver, or the magic wand that floated an altar made of iron. But stories mirrored each age. The stories of Han were vigorous and dealt often with the affairs of the nation, and centered on some great man or hero. Humor was strong in this golden age, a racy, earthy, lusty humor, such as was to be found, for instance, in a book of tales entitled *Siao Ling*, presumed to have been collected, if not partly written, by Han Tang Suan. And then the scenes changed, as that golden age faded, though it was never to be forgotten, so that to this day the Chinese like to call themselves sons of Han. With the succeeding weak and corrupt centuries, the very way the stories were written became honeyed and weak, and their subjects slight, or as the Chinese say, «In the days of the Six Dynasties, they wrote of small things, of a woman, a waterfall, or a bird.»

If the Han dynasty was golden, then the T'ang dynasty was silver, and silver were the love stories for which it was famous. It was an age of love, when a thousand stories clustered about the beautiful Yang Kuei Fei and her scarcely less beautiful predecessor in the emperor's favor, Mei Fei. These ove stories of T'ang come very near sometimes to fulfilling in their unity and complexity the standards of the Western novel. There are rising action and crisis and dénouement, implicit if not expressed. The Chinese say, «We must read the stories of T'ang, because though they deal with small matters, yet they are written in so moving a manner that the tears come.»

It is not surprising that most of these love stories deal not with love that ends in marriage or is contained in marriage, but with love outside the marriage relationship. Indeed, it is significant that when marriage is the theme the story nearly always ends in tragedy. Two famous stories, *Pei Li Shi* and *Chiao Fang Chi*, deal entirely with extramarital love, and are written apparently to show the superiority of the courtesans, who could read and write and sing and were clever and beautiful besides, beyond the ordinary wife who was, as the Chinese say even today, «a yellow-faced woman», and usually literate.

So strong did this tendency become that officialdom grew alarmed at the popularity of such stories among the common people, and they were denounced as revolutionary and dangerous because it was thought they attacked that foundation of Chinese civilization, the family system. A reactionary tendency was not lacking, such as is to be seen in *Hui Chen Chi*, one of the earlier forms of a famous later work, the story of the young scholar who loved the beautiful Ying Ying and who renounced her, saying prudently as he went away, «All extraordinary women are dangerous. They destroy themselves and others. They have ruined even emperors. I am not an emperor and I had better give her up»—which he did, to the admiration of all wise men. And to him the modest Ying Ying replied, «If you possess me and leave me, it is your right. I do not reproach you.» But five hundred years later the sentimentality of the Chinese popular heart comes forth and sets the thwarted romance right again. In this last version of the story the author makes Chang and Ying Ying husband and wife and says in closing, «This is in the hope that all the lovers of the world may be united in happy marriage.» And as time goes in China, five hundred years is not long to wait for a happy ending.

This story, by the way, is one of China's most famous. It was repeated in the Sung dynasty in a poetic form by Chao Teh Liang, under the title *The Reluctant Butterfly*, and again in the Yuan dynasty by Tung Chai-yuen as a drama to be sung, entitled *Suh Hsi Hsiang*. In the Ming dynasty, with two versions intervening, it appears as Li Reh Hua's *Nan Hsi Hsiang Chi*, written in the southern metrical form called «ts'e», and so to the last and most famous *Hsi Hsiang Chi*. Even children in China know the name of Chang Sen.

If I seem to emphasize the romances of the T'ang period, it is because romance between man and woman is the chief gift of T'ang to the novel, and not because there were no other stories. There were many novels of a humorous and satirical nature and one curious type of story which concerned itself with cockfighting, an important pastime of that age and particularly in favor at court. One of the best of these tales is *Tung Chen Lao Fu Chuan*, by Ch'en Hung, which tells how Chia Chang, a famous cockfighter, became so famous that he was loved by emperor and people alike.

But time and the stream pass on. The novel form really begins to be clear in the Sung dynasty, and in the Yuan dynasty it flowers into that height which was never again surpassed and only equalled, indeed, by the single novel *Hung Lou Meng*, or *The Dream of the Red Chamber*, in the Ts'ing dynasty. It is as though for centuries the novel had been developing unnoticed and from deep roots among the people, spreading into trunk and branch and twig and leaf to burst into this flowering in the Yuan dynasty, when the young Mongols brought into the old country they had conquered their vigorous, hungry, untutored minds and demanded to be fed. Such minds could not be fed with the husks of the old classical literature, and they turned therefore the more eagerly to the drama and the novel, and in this new life, in the sunshine of imperial favor, though still not with literary favor, there came two of China's three great novels, *Shui Hu Chuan* and *San Kuo* – *Hung Lou Meng* being the third.

I wish I could convey to you what these three novels mean and have meant to the Chinese people. But I can think of nothing comparable to them in Western literature. We have not in the history of our novel so clear a moment to which we can point and say, «There the novel is at its height.» These three are the vindication of that literature of the common people, the Chinese novel. They stand as completed monuments of that popular literature, if not of letters. They, too, were ignored by men of letters and banned by censor and damned in succeeding dynasties as dangerous, revolutionary, decadent. But they lived on, because people read them and told them as stories and sang them as songs and ballads and acted them as dramas, until at last grudgingly even the scholars were compelled to notice them and to begin to say they were not novels at all but allegories, and if they were allegories perhaps then they could be looked upon as literature after all, though the people paid no heed to such theories and never read the long treatises which scholars wrote to prove them. They rejoiced in the novels they had made as novels and for no purpose except for joy in story and in story through which they could express themselves.

And indeed the people had made them. *Shui Hu Chuan*, though the modern versions carry the name of Shi Nai An as author, was written by no one man. Out of a handful of tales centering in the Sung dynasty about a band of robbers there grew this great, structured novel. Its beginnings were in history. The original lair which the robbers held still exists in Shantung, or did until very recent times. Those times of the thirteenth century of our Western era were, in China, sadly distorted. The dynasty under the emperor Huei Chung was falling into decadence and disorder. The rich grew richer and the poor poorer and when none other came forth to set this right, these righteous robbers came forth.

I cannot here tell you fully of the long growth of this novel, nor of its changes at many hands. Shih Nai An, it is said, found it in rude form in an old book shop and took it home and rewrote it. After him the story was still told and re-told. Five or six versions of it today have importance, one with a hundred chapters entitled *Chung I Shui Hu*, one of a hundred and twenty-seven chapters, and one of a hundred chapters. The original version attributed to Shih Nai An, had a hundred and twenty chapters, but the one most used today has only seventy. This is the version arranged in the Ming dynasty by the famous Ching Shen T'an, who said that it was idle to forbid his son to read the book and therefore presented the lad with a copy revised by himself, knowing that no boy could ever refrain from reading it. There is also a version written under official command, when officials found that nothing could keep the people from reading *Shui Hu*. This official version is entitled *Tung K'ou Chi*, or, *Laying Waste the Robbers*, and it tells of the final defeat of the robbers by the state army and their destruction. But the common people of China are nothing if not independent. They have never adopted the official version, and their own form of the novel still stands. It is a struggle they know all too well, the struggle of everyday people against a corrupt officialdom.

I might add that *Shui Hu Chuan* is in partial translation in French under the title *Les Chevaliers Chinois*, and the seventy-chapter version is in complete English translation by myself under the title *All Men Are Brothers*. The original title, *Shui Hu Chuan*, in English is meaningless, denoting merely the watery margins of the famous marshy lake which was the robbers' lair. To Chinese the words invoke instant century-old memory, but not to us.

This novel has survived everything and in this new day in China has taken on an added significance. The Chinese Communists have printed their own edition of it with a preface by a famous Communist and have issued it anew as the first Communist literature of China. The proof of the novel's greatness is in this timelessness. It is as true today as it was dynasties ago. The people of China still march across its pages, priests and courtesans, merchants and scholars, women good and bad, old and young, and even naughty little boys. The only figure lacking is that of the modern scholar trained in the West, holding his Ph.D. diploma in his hand. But be sure that if he had been alive in China when the final hand laid down the brush upon the pages of that book, he, too, would have been there in all the pathos and humor of his new learning, so often useless and inadequate and laid like a patch too small upon an old robe.

The Chinese say «The young should not read *Shui Hu* and the old should not read *San Kuo*.» This is because the young might be charmed into being robbers and the old might be led into deeds too vigorous for their years. For if *Shui Hu Chuan* is the great social document of Chinese life, *San Kuo* is the document of wars and statesmanship, and in its turn *Hung Lou Meng* is the document of family life and human love.

The history of the *San Kuo* or *Three Kingdoms* shows the same architectural structure and the same doubtful authorship as *Shui Hu*. The story begins with three friends swearing eternal brotherhood in the Han dynasty and ends ninety-seven years later in the succeeding period of the Six Dynasties. It is a novel rewritten in its final form by a man named Lo Kuan Chung, thought to be a pupil of Shih Nai An, and one who perhaps even shared with Shih Nai An in the writing, too, of *Shui Hu Chuan*. But this is a Chinese Bacon-and-Shakespeare controversy which has no end.

Lo Kuan Chung was born in the late Yuan dynasty and lived on into the Ming. He wrote many dramas, but he is more famous for his novels, of which *San Kuo* is easily the best. The version of this novel now most commonly used in China is the one revised in the time of K'ang Hsi by Mao Chen Kan, who revised as well as criticised the book. He changed, added and omitted material, as for example when he added the story of Suan Fu Ren, the wife of one of the chief characters. He altered even the style. If *Shui Hu Chuan* has importance today as a novel of the people in their struggle for liberty, *San Kuo* has importance because it gives in such detail the science and art of war as the Chinese conceive it, so differently, too, from our own. The guerillas, who are today China's most effective fighting units against

Japan, are peasants who know *San Kuo* by heart, if not from their own reading, at least from hours spent in the idleness of winter days or long summer evenings when they sat listening to the storytellers describe how the warriors of the Three Kingdoms fought their battles. It is these ancient tactics of war which the guerillas trust today. What a warrior must be and how he must attack and retreat, how retreat when the enemy advances, how advance when the enemy retreats – all this had its source in this novel, so well known to every common man and boy of China.

Hung Lou Meng, or *The Dream of the Red Chamber*, the latest and most modern of these three greatest of Chinese novels, was written originally as an autobiographical novel by Ts'ao Hsüeh Ching, an official highly in favor during the Manchu regime and indeed considered by the Manchus as one of themselves. There were then eight military groups among the Manchus, and Ts'ao Hsüeh Ching belonged to them all. He never finished his novel, and the last forty chapters were added by another man, probably named Kao O. The thesis that Ts'ao Hsüeh Ching was telling the story of his own life has been in modern times elaborated by Hu Shih, and in earlier times by Yuan Mei. Be this as it may, the original title of the book was *Shih T'ou Chi*, and it came out of Peking about 1765 of the Western era, and in five or six years, an incredibly short time in China, it was famous everywhere. Printing was still expensive when it appeared, and the book became known by the method that is called in China, «You-lend-me-a-book-and-I-lend-you-a-book».

The story is simple in its theme but complex in implication, in character study and in its portrayal of human emotions. It is almost a pathological study, this story of a great house, once wealthy and high in imperial favor, so that indeed one of its members was an imperial concubine. But the great days are over when the book begins. The family is already declining. Its wealth is being dissipated and the last and only son, Chia Pao Yü, is being corrupted by the decadent influences within his own home, although the fact that he was a youth of exceptional quality at birth is established by the symbolism of a piece of jade found in his mouth. The preface begins, «Heaven was once broken and when it was mended, a bit was left unused, and this became the famous jade of Chia Pao Yü.» Thus does the interest in the supernatural persist in the Chinese people; it persists even today as a part of Chinese life.

This novel seized hold of the people primarily because it portrayed the problems of their own family system, the absolute power of women in the home, the too great power of the matriarchy, the grandmother, the mother, and even the bondmaids, so often young and beautiful and fatally dependent, who became too frequently the playthings of the sons of the house and ruined them and were ruined by them. Women reigned supreme in the Chinese house, and because they were wholly confined in its walls and often illiterate, they ruled to the hurt of all. They kept men children, and protected them from hardship and effort when they should not have been so protected. Such a one was Chia Pao Yü, and we follow him to his tragic end in *Hung Lou Meng*.

I cannot tell you to what lengths of allegory scholars went to explain away this novel when they found that again even the emperor was reading it and that its influence was so great everywhere among the people. I do not doubt that they were probably reading it themselves in secret. A great many popular jokes in China have to do with scholars reading novels privately and publicly pretending never to have heard of them. At any rate, scholars wrote treatises to prove that *Hung Lou Meng* was not a novel but a political allegory depicting the decline of China under the foreign rule of the Manchus, the word Red in the title signifying Manchu, and Ling Tai Yü, the young girl who dies, although she was the one destined to marry Pao Yü, signifying China, and Pao Ts'ai, her successful rival, who secures the jade in her place, standing for the foreigner, and so forth. The very name Chia signified, they said, falseness. But this was a farfetched explanation of what was written as a novel and stands as a novel and as such a powerful delineation, in the characteristic Chinese mixture of realism and romance, of a proud and powerful family in decline. Crowded with men and women of the several generations accustomed to living under one roof in China, it stands alone as an intimate description of that life.

In so emphasizing these three novels, I have merely done what the Chinese themselves do. When you say «novel», the average Chinese replies, «*Shui Hu, San Kuo, Hung Lou Meng*.» Yet this is not to say that there are not hundreds of other novels, for there are. I must mention *Hsi Yü Chi*, or *Record of Travels in the West*, almost as popular as these three. I might mention *Feng Shen Chuan*, the story of a deified warrior, the author unknown but said to be a writer in the time of Ming. I must mention *Ru Ling Wai Shi*, a satire upon the evils of the Ts'ing dynasty, particularly of the scholars, full of a double-edged though not malicious dialogue, rich with incident, pathetic and humorous. The fun here is made of the scholars who can do nothing practical, who are lost in the world of useful everyday things, who are so bound by conven-

ion that nothing original can come from them. The book, though long,
has no central character. Each figure is linked to the next by the thread of
incident, person and incident passing on together until, as Lu Hsün, the
famous modern Chinese writer, has said, «they are like scraps of brilliant silk
and satin sewed together».

And there is *Yea Shou Pei Yin*, or *An Old Hermit Talks in the Sun*, written
by a famous man disappointed in official preferment, Shia of Kiang-yin, and
here is that strangest of books, *Ching Hua Yuen*, a fantasy of women, whose
ruler was an empress, whose scholars were all women. It is designed to show
that the wisdom of women is equal to that of men, although I must acknowledge that the book ends with a war between men and women in which the
men are triumphant and the empress is supplanted by an emperor.

But I can mention only a small fraction of the hundreds of novels which
delight the common people of China. And if those people knew of what
I was speaking to you today, they would after all say «tell of the great three,
and let us stand or fall by *Shui Hu Chuan* and *San Kuo* and *Hung Lou Meng*».
In these three novels are the lives which the Chinese people lead and have
long led, here are the songs they sing and the things at which they laugh
and the things which they love to do. Into these novels they have put the
generations of their being and to refresh that being they return to these novels
again and again, and out of them they have made new songs and plays and
other novels. Some of them have come to be almost as famous as the great
originals, as for example *Ching P'ing Mei*, that classic of romantic physical
love, taken from a single incident in *Shui Hu Chuan*.

But the important thing for me today is not the listing of novels. The
aspect which I wish to stress is that all this profound and indeed sublime
development of the imagination of a great democratic people was never in
its own time and country called literature. The very name for story was
«hsiao shuo», denoting something slight and valueless, and even a novel was
only a «ts'ang p'ien hsiao shuo», or a longer something which was still slight
and useless. No, the people of China forged their own literature apart from
letters. And today this is what lives, to be part of what is to come, and all
the formal literature, which was called art, is dead. The plots of these novels
are often incomplete, the love interest is often not brought to solution,
heroines are often not beautiful and heroes often are not brave. Nor has the
story always an end; sometimes it merely stops, in the way life does, in the
middle of it when death is not expected.

In this tradition of the novel have I been born and reared as a writer. My ambition, therefore, has not been trained toward the beauty of letters or the grace of art. It is, I believe, a sound teaching and, as I have said, illuminating for the novels of the West.

For here is the essence of the attitude of Chinese novelists—perhaps the result of the contempt in which they were held by those who considered themselves the priests of art. I put it thus in my own words, for none of them has done so.

The instinct which creates *the arts* is not the same as that which produces art. The creative instinct is, in its final analysis and in its simplest terms, an enormous extra vitality, a super-energy, born inexplicably in an individual, a vitality great beyond all the needs of his own living—an energy which no single life can consume. This energy consumes itself then in creating more life, in the form of music, painting, writing, or whatever is its most natural medium of expression. Nor can the individual keep himself from this process, because only by its full function is he relieved of the burden of this extra and peculiar energy—an energy at once physical and mental, so that all his senses are more alert and more profound than another man's, and all his brain more sensitive and quickened to that which his senses reveal to him in such abundance that actuality overflows into imagination. It is a process proceeding from within. It is the heightened activity of every cell of his being, which sweeps not only himself, but all human life about him, or in him, in his dreams, into the circle of its activity.

From the product of this activity, art is deducted—but not by him. The process which creates is not the process which deduces the shapes of art. The defining of art, therefore, is a secondary and not a primary process. And when one born for the primary process of creation, as the novelist is, concerns himself with the secondary process, his activity becomes meaningless. When he begins to make shapes and styles and techniques and new schools, then he is like a ship stranded upon a reef whose propeller, whirl wildly as it will, cannot drive the ship onward. Not until the ship is in its element again can it regain its course.

And for the novelist the only element is human life as he finds it in himself or outside himself. The sole test of his work is whether or not his energy is producing more of that life. Are his creatures alive? That is the only question. And who can tell him? Who but those living human beings, the people? Those people are not absorbed in what art is or how it is made—are not, indeed, absorbed in anything very lofty, however good it is. No, they are absorbed only in themselves, in their own hungers and despairs and joys and above all, perhaps, in their own dreams. These are the ones who can really judge the work of the novelist, for they judge by that single test of reality. And the standard of the test is not to be made by the device of art, but by the simple comparison of the reality of what they read, to their own reality.

I have been taught, therefore, that though the novelist may see art as cool and perfect shapes, he may only admire them as he admires marble statues standing aloof in a quiet and remote gallery; for his place is not with them. His place is in the street. He is happiest there. The street is noisy and the men and women are not perfect in the technique of their expression as the statues are. They are ugly and imperfect, incomplete even as human beings, and where they come from and where they go cannot be known. But they are people and therefore infinitely to be preferred to those who stand upon the pedestals of art.

And like the Chinese novelist, I have been taught to want to write for these people. If they are reading their magazines by the million, then I want my stories there rather than in magazines read only by a few. For story belongs to the people. They are sounder judges of it than anyone else, for their senses are unspoiled and their emotions are free. No, a novelist must not think of pure literature as his goal. He must not even know this field too well, because people, who are his material, are not there. He is a storyteller in a village tent, and by his stories he entices people into his tent. He need not raise his voice when a scholar passes. But he must beat all his drums when a band of poor pilgrims pass on their way up the mountain in search of gods. To them he must cry, «I, too, tell of gods!» And to farmers he must talk of their land, and to old men he must speak of peace, and to old women he must tell of their children, and to young men and women he must speak of each other. He must be satisfied if the common people hear him gladly. At least, so I have been taught in China.

Biography

Pearl Buck (1892–) was born in Hillsboro, West Virginia. She grew up in China, where her parents were missionaries, but was educated at Randolph-Macon College. After her graduation she returned to China and lived there until 1934 with the exception of a year spent at Cornell University, where she took an M.A. in 1926. Pearl Buck began to write in the twenties; her first novel, *East Wind, West Wind*, appeared in 1930. It was followed by *The Good Earth* (1931), *Sons* (1932), and *A House Divided* (1935), together forming a trilogy on the saga of the family of Wang. *The Good Earth* stood on the American list of «best sellers» for a long time and earned her several awards, among them the Pulitzer Prize and the William Dean Howells Medal. She also published *The First Wife and Other Stories* (1933), *All Men are Brothers* (a translation of the Chinese novel *Shui Hu Chuan*) (1933), *The Mother* (1934), and *This Proud Heart* (1938). The biographies of her mother and father, *The Exile* and *Fighting Angel*, were published in 1936 and later brought out together under the title of *The Spirit and the Flesh* (1944). *The Time Is Now*, a fictionalized account of the author's emotional experiences, although written much earlier, did not appear in print until 1967.

Pearl Buck's works after 1938 are too many to mention. Her novels have continued to deal with the confrontation of East and West, her interest spreading to such countries as India and Korea. Her novelist's interest in the interplay of East and West has also led to some activity in political journalism.

Pearl Buck has been active in many welfare organizations; in particular she set up an agency for the adoption of Asian-American children (Welcome House, Inc.) and has taken an active interest in retarded children (*The Child Who Never Grew*, 1950).

Literature 1939

FRANS EEMIL SILLANPÄÄ

«for his deep comprehension and exquisite art in painting the nature of his country and the life of its peasants in their mutual relations»

Critical Essay

by Per Hallström, Permanent Secretary of the Swedish Academy

Frans Eemil Sillanpää took the motifs for his novels and novellas, which are almost exclusively about his native land (a small region of Finnish peasants), from the scanty, limited circumstances in which he grew up. From the very beginning of his work, he aspired to represent the reality of what he had seen around him, in the most truthful and complete fashion, in the most minute detail, without avoiding the common or even the ugly that might strike his eyes. His work consists of purely naturalistic description, with a large amount of psychoanalytical interpretation, of the actions and feelings of his figures.

He satisfied aesthetic demands by his singular stylistic qualities. His style is artistically formed, terse and simple, facile and lucid, personal and highly expressive. Even in translation one can glimpse the mastery which his compatriots have recognized in him, mastery in a language of rather limited literary background. His stylistic qualities are most fascinating in his descriptions of nature, for there the artist's joy truly finds its broadest domain. In the human destinies he described, there was no great room for joy. The pictures are most often in very sombre colours, but his artistic power never fails.

The novel which gave rise to his reputation was perhaps his *tour de force* as an intrepid and bitter painter of life. It dates from the disastrous year 1918 and was written under the pressure of the events which the author had witnessed in the civil war between the Nationalists and the Communists. Sillanpää left it to others to describe the heroic corollary of the civil war, the liberation from Russian domination, for he mistrusted grand postures. Devoting himself to social struggles, he applied himself solely to his self-appointed task of explaining the reasons and aggravations that had led to the catastrophe. He had lived for a long time with these ideas, and he was never to abandon them, wherever they led him.

He named his book *Hurskas kurjuus* (1919) [*Meek Heritage*] in memory of the extremely poor conditions in which a large part of the Finnish people lived, the class in which he grew up and to which he felt closest. These peasants armed insufficient parcels of land which belonged to the landowners whose half-servants they were, without the protection of a mutual contract. Their fate depended entirely on the good will of their little despots. He called their heritage meek because it was accepted with apathetic resignation tinged with religion, like an ineluctable destiny.

The principal personage Sillanpää chose for his novel, Jussi Toivola, can hardly be called his hero. With his predilection for all that is very simple, all that pertains to the dullness of daily life, with his aversion to all that is purely aesthetic and his rectitude in describing characters, he made him an extremely primitive and weak person. Jussi was from the very beginning only a vulgar instrument, the laughing-stock of his community, scorned and ill-treated by all. It is questionable whether, in some other social condition, he might have been able to become something truly different. In addition there was his marriage with a woman quite as benighted as he. She began by duping him, making him accept another man's child. In her housework she was as incapable as he was in his trade. There was never any intelligence or foresight on their small farm, which they had obtained on very bad terms. They had many children, and, with them, greater and greater worries and needs.

Jussi was attracted by the revolutionary peasant movement which, merging with other rebellions against the social order, led at the end to anarchy and error. A certain development of his personality followed from it–the only progress that life had to offer him.

He began to reflect on his capacities and, as much as he was able to do so, took an active part in this movement. In the meetings in which there was a matter for all to speak about, Jussi also spoke and discovered that he could do it and that his words were heard. He derived a joy from it that he had never found before and he felt like a man. With his native naiveté and without knowing where the current would carry him, he followed the flood with ardour and played his small part. He carried arms he never used but of which he was very proud. He could thus serve as a sentinel around the houses of the landowners. One day, one of them was killed without his participating in the murder. Soon after the country was reconquered by the Nationalists in the fight against the Communists and the Russians, Jussi was one of those condemned to death for murder.

The description of the death of this blind victim of this era's events is the crucial episode of the novel. It is the expression of a painful tragedy, as much as this term can be applied to so forlorn and drifting a destiny, with details of a grotesque comedy, making a whole, however, of a very moving unity

One of the earlier parts of this book–the story of Jussi Toivola's half grown daughter, the daughter who, to his inexpressible joy, had the honou of being promoted to servant in a fashionable home–was taken out by th author to become a short novel in itself, *Hiltu ja Ragnar* (1923) [Hiltu an Ragnar]. It was written with even greater bitterness, if that is possible.

This child of nature, whose ignorance and innocence were prodigious, wa seduced by the son of the house. When the consequences began to appea she did not understand them and believed herself the victim of an illnes She was driven to suicide by the despair and terror that she felt before a existence which must be her fate. This innocent figure was in a way mad poetic by the author's sober and profound sense of pity.

This poetry became truly poignant in a later novel, treating a feminin destiny of the same kind, *Nuorena nukkunut* (1931) [*The Maid Silja*], tha work of Sillanpää's which was admired most. Silja, like Hiltu, came fror a family inevitably condemned to ruin, but she grew up in less severe povert and, actually, without ugliness. She is presented in a quite different manne Not deformed by the unhappy destiny of her kindred, she had preserve her personality, imbued with instinctive purity and delicacy. This child ha sprung up like a flower in the transient magnificence of full summer, wit all the beauty and frailty of the season, in perpetual light, on the shore c the dazzling blue lakes. She appeared as the symbol of that short and ravish ing summer, without seeming strange to the poor peasants' world in whic she worked to earn her bread.

Silja's story is quite simple but very significant. After the ruin of her hom she goes into domestic service, but none of the brutality and ugliness of he new surroundings can tarnish her inner feelings. She goes through the wor without being touched by it.

She can at last live her love story, but it is almost as short and as etherea as that of a butterfly. The student who had been her unworthy lover ha abandoned her almost immediately, buts he kept the most delightful mem ories of the affair and bore her loneliness without the least complaint.

In the war year of 1918 she proved her determination and courage i danger. She performed a fine act but she scarcely noticed it, silent and discre as she always was. When her congenital tuberculosis began to make its effec felt, she felt no terror. Grateful for the one unforgettable hour that life ha given her, she now awaited the end with a sweet and silent dignity. T prevent transmitting her disease to others, she took her few possessions an

1ade herself a tranquil asylum in the wash-house, protected on the land of
er masters. From that time on she no longer had any cares.

There she was more alone than ever, with nothing to look forward to
xcept the end which she knew was near, but she felt happy and free. She
repared herself to meet the great adventure by dreaming of all that she had
ound of beauty, all so simple in itself but resplendent in the light of the love
1e had really lived. Sometimes she floated in her dreams in the eternal hap-
iness of the beyond.

In this episode, the bitter realist took pleasure in finding the beauty of
uman nature and, freed from all psychoanalytic doctrine, he remained quite
imply the poet and was able to create pure poetry with a flash of grandeur.

Outside of that, only in his description of the countryside did Sillanpää's
rtistic mastery flourish so richly, and then only when he chose motifs as
imple as possible while avoiding all that could give immediate delight to
1e eye, without letting himself be seduced by the colours of a traditional
eauty. With the delicacy of a painter, he wished quite simply to render
1e beauty of what the ordinary observer would have overlooked.

In his last important novel, *Ihmiset suviyössä* (1934) [*People in the Summer
Night*], he dropped these restrictions and allowed the nature of his homeland
o lend all it could. There are large vistas of sweet, fresh verdure, with lakes
1eandering and glistening with azure brilliance and, above all, the magic
f the light of days and nights caught in all its shifting moments. Space gives
epth and expanse to his pictures.

Human life in this setting has diverse destinies, some menacing and sombre,
thers in perfect harmony with the happiness which, devoid of cares, is
roper to this summer season. One finds here a view of life not influenced
y a purely literary taste – a striving for free, rich, and complete beauty.
verything is in tune with the infinite and the calm of space.

The pattern of the human figures does not always reach great profundity,
ut in their quickness and their lightness they are in harmony with the flight
f the clouds and the play of lights at dusk or at the dawn of a new day.
1 the subtle art of this stylist, the verbal pictures take on sonority and their
1usic is that of a violin made of rays and colours.

Considered from the purely artistic point of view, this book is perhaps
tronger than any of those preceding, even if *Silja*, in its final episode, has
more profoundly human poetry and is thus more moving.

Presentation

by Per Hallström, Permanent Secretary of the Swedish Academy, at its regular meeting on December 14, 1939

The diploma of a Nobel Prize has just been given to you and you have hear the reasons which led the Swedish Academy to accord this distinctio to your literary work. These reasons are very briefly stated on this parch ment, but you have been deprived of the many homages which woul have been paid you at the ceremony of the distribution of the Nob Prizes.

These homages you will find equally in our company, in the simplicit characteristic of our gatherings, but with the same warmth as that whic you would have received in the festival room on the day of the ceremony None of us knows your Finnish language; we have been able to appreciat your works only in the translations, but no doubt exists about your master as a writer. This mastery is so great that it appears clearly even in a foreig attire. Simple, brief, objective, without the least affectation, your languag flows with the clarity of a spring and reflects what your artist's eye has seized You have chosen your motifs with the greatest delicacy and, one could a most say, with a sort of timidity before what is immediately beautiful. Yo wish to create beauty from what exists in everyday nature, and the mann in which you can do it often remains your secret. It is not at the writer desk that one sees you work but before the easel of the watercolourist, an over your shoulder, one often accustoms one's eye to see in a new mar ner. Sometimes, when painting spaces and clouds in the light of a summe day, you forget the fear that you have of a too favourable motif and yo then employ the musical art with the hand of a master. This characterist trait, your fondness for the simple and the typical, you show also in yor description of man. This description takes pleasure in rendering the everyda life of the peasants, strongly attached to the earth from which it draws i strength. When it is a question of deeds, you show an equal mastery, an the effect is produced only with the simplest means.

Concerning your most celebrated work, you have said some words whic no one else could have found: «Everything that touches Silja is generall of a magnificent insignificance.» No artist can go farther in the desire to r main respectfully faithful to the reality of things. Thus you have represented your people, without the least finery.

At the present moment, even the name of your country is significant everywhere. As simple as you see them, your people find themselves a prey to fateful powers, heroically great in their indomitable courage, faithful to their duty to the very end, to the death which they confront without trembling. In our thanks for what you have given, our thoughts go still further; they go, with all our admiration and the emotion which grips us, to your people, to your nation.

Autobiography

Frans Eemil Sillanpää was born on the 16th of September, 1888, at Ylä-Satakunta in the Hämeenkyrö Parish of Finland on a desolate croft of the same name. The cottage had been built by his parents, his father Frans Henrik Henriksson, who had moved there some ten years before from Kauvatsa in the Kumo Valley, and his mother, Loviisa Vilhelmiina Iisaksdotter, whose family had lived in the Hämeenkyrö Parish from times immemorial.

Sillanpää's parents had experienced all the trials and tribulations common to generations of settlers in those parts of Finland. Frosts had killed their seeds, farm animals had perished, and the farmer's children, too, had died until only Frans Eemil, the youngest of the offspring, was left.

There was only a mobile school for the farm children, and it was purely by accident – young Sillanpää's life was to abound in accidents – that the crofter's son, who was regarded as a bright lad, came to attend a regular school where he displayed a real aptitude for learning. Some idealists decided that nothing less than a secondary school at Tampere would do and, after giving the matter some thought, old Sillanpää consented to send his son away. For five years, Sillanpää's parents pinched and scraped to keep their son in school, after which he supported himself for another three years and, in 1908, matriculated with good marks. This was a time in Finland when a promising young man could study almost indefinitely on borrowed money, and young Sillanpää was not slow to avail himself of this miscarriage of educational zeal. He plunged into learning and his studies were as chaotic as they were long drawn-out. He did, however, choose biology as his basic subject and worked hard in the laboratory, cutting up things, studying them under the microscope, and drawing what he saw until, one fine day, he woke up to find that five years had gone by; his examination day was still far off and the kind old gentlemen who had been lending him money were not prepared to do so any longer. He scraped together enough cash to return to his home, where he found his father and mother poorer than ever. He lived in their hut and shared their meals, which could hardly excite a gourmet's palate.

His student days were over, his amorous escapades a thing of the past, out at least it was easy enough for him to start from nothing. Sillanpää acquired at a nearby village shop some stationary of the type favoured by village lads for private correspondence and wrote a short story, which he sent to the editor of a large city paper without much hope of seeing it published. To use an expression popular in those days, the story must have been written with his heart's blood because, after a very short time, it appeared on the front page of the aforesaid paper and its author received a very handsome letter from the editor's secretary, as well as his fee, which was more than welcome. The story had been published under a pen name but the literary world of Helsinki soon discovered the identity of the author and the erstwhile eternal scholar found himself, to his amazement, receiving letters of extravagant praise. After several more of his stories had been published in the same paper, something very unusual happened. He was approached by a well-known publisher who asked to be borne in mind should Sillanpää's literary output stretch to a whole book. The publisher went so far as to offer him a reasonable advance to enable him to work in peace.

Yet another wonder–one of a series–occurred at that time. At an unimportant village dance, Sillanpää met a shy seventeen-year-old girl who, insisting that she could not dance, sat far at the back of the dance hall. In spite of her resistance, Sillanpää dragged her out onto the dance floor to discover that she could dance after all, which she proceeded to do with the utmost seriousness and concentration. This was the beginning of a twenty-five-year saga, during which Sigrid Maria (for such was the name of the seventeen-year-old girl) bore Sillanpää eight children, one of whom died. Mrs. Sillanpää died on an April morning in 1939. In early November, the widower who, six months earlier, had been in deep mourning, was standing before the mayor of Helsinki being asked if he would take Anna Armia von Hertzen to be his wedded wife, to love her, and so on. To this, Sillanpää replied with obvious eagerness, nor was Anna Armia's «yes» a timid whisper. Some days before a telegram had come from the Secretary of the Swedish Academy telling Sillanpää that he had been awarded the Nobel Prize in Literature. A new point had been reached in the long series of wonderful events with which Sillanpää's life has been punctuated. As for the changes which may have occurred in it since that memorable event, they are, historically speaking, too recent to be worth recording. May his autobiography, therefore, end with this red-letter day.

It should perhaps be added that, in 1936, the University of Helsinki conferred on Sillanpää an honorary doctorate.

Books published by Sillanpää, of which *The Maid Silja* in particular ha
been translated into nearly every civilized language from Icelandic to Hebrew
are *Elämä ja aurinko* (1916) [Life and Sun]; *Ihmislapsia elämän saatossa* (1917
[Children of Man in Life's Procession]; *Hurskas kurjuus* (1919) [*Meek Heri
tage*]; *Rakas isänmaani* (1919) [Beloved Fatherland]; *Hiltu ja Ragnar* (1923
[Hiltu and Ragnar]; *Enkelten suojatit* (1923) [Wards of the Angels]; *Omistan
ja omilleni* (1924) [About my Own and to my Own]; *Maan tasalta* (1924
[From the Earth's Level]; *Töllinmäki* (1925) [Shanty Hill]; *Rippi* (1928
[Confession]; *Kiitos hetkistä, Herra...* (1930) [Thanks for the Moments
Lord...]; *Nuorena nukkunut* (1931) [*The Maid Silja*]; *Miehen tie* (1932) [*A
Man's Way*]; *Virranpohjalta* (1933) [From the Bottom of the Stream]; *Ihmi
set suviyössä* (1934) [*People in the Summer Night*]; *Viidestoista* (1936) [Th
Fifteenth].

Biographical note on Frans Eemil Sillanpää

After 1939, Sillanpää (1880–1964) wrote the novels *Elokuu* (1944) [August
and *Ihmiselon ihanuus ja kurjuus* (1945) [The Loveliness and Wretchedness o
Human Life]. An account of his life, *Poika eli elämäänsä* [The Boy Lived Hi
Life], based mainly on the Finnish radio broadcasts of his memoirs, was pub
lished in 1953. A collection of his political and social essays and his trave
accounts came out in 1956 under the title *Päivä korkeimmillaan* [Day at it
Highest].

Sillanpää's family name was Koskinen and was later changed to Sillanpää
His collected works were published in twelve volumes between 1932 an
1948.

Literature 1940-1943

Prizes not awarded

Literature 1944

JOHANNES VILHELM JENSEN

«for the rare strength and fertility of his poetic imagination, with which is combined an intellectual curiosity of wide scope and a bold, freshly creative style»

Broadcast Lecture

by Per Hallström, Chairman of the Nobel Committee of the Swedish Academy

Among Johannes V. Jensen's prose works *Den lange rejse* (1908–22) [*The Long Journey*] stands foremost in popular estimation. The theme of this immense epic is man's development from the soulless and inarticulate herd-life – when more than any other creature he was a prey to the forces of nature – to a state of primitive and gradually progressive civilization. The six long stories are full of adventures actuated, Jensen thinks, by obscure but profound nostalgia for the tropical world that was man's first home.

The first saga takes place somewhere in the primeval forests of Europe near a huge volcano. Fire glows on its summit and sometimes burning lava pours down the slopes, destroying everything in its path. For countless ages, primitive man has worshipped the fire-god in dumb terror. But at last comes the first great moment in the history of mankind: the emergence from the herd of a man with a mind and a will, a Prometheus.

Fearlessly confronting the unknown, he solves the riddle of fire and brings it down on a torch to serve man. With it he lights campfires to keep off wild beasts. But he does much more. Observing the movements of the stars he infers the notion of time, the first abstract idea won from the darkness of chaos. He also takes the first step toward civilized intercourse between individuals, discovering tenderness in sexual relations, the inaugural burgeoning of what we know as love. In the end he dies a prophet's death at the hands of the obtuse masses, but he bequeathes a rich legacy to posterity.

Thus ends the first saga. The next, with a second prehistoric patriarch, begins after another measureless lapse of time. The world has changed now, the volcano is extinct, the climate cooling. There is a general migration to the south. But one man sets off in the opposite direction to grapple with hardship. He is a sort of Cain, a slayer avoided by his fellow men, whom he holds in such contempt that he does not even condescend to take their god, fire, with him to the icy lands of the North. Defying the cold, he grows hardy and strong. With a woman who has somehow found her way up there he becomes the father of the Nordic race which is so dear to Jensen, who follows its destiny.

He rediscovers fire, not simply borrowing it as before but by a stroke of genius striking it out of two minerals. And thus he founds a new civilization.

The theme is repeated in a third saga with another genius who invents means of locomotion: wagons and boats driven by oar or sail. The men of the North, ready now to listen to the old call to the summer lands, begin the long journey proper.

The later sagas describing the journey take us down to historical times: we see the Cimbrians marching on Rome and the Vikings' raids. But the story does not end until Columbus realizes that dream of a tropical paradise which is the leading idea of the book.

Jensen's imaginative resources are rich and inexhaustible, his power of vivid presentation unfailing.

The whole book is like a series of huge decorative paintings in which characterization is less important than the range of composition and the incomparable skill of the brush strokes.

Characters of much greater psychological interest will be found in Jensen's tales from life in his native Himmerland, *Himmerlandshistorier* (1898–1910). Its inhabitants, descendants of the Cimbrians, have kept much of their ancestors' primitive savage energy, forced as they are to struggle hard for meagre reward in a country of heath and sand. They are men of action, rugged, swayed by strong passions. On intimate terms with tragedy, they bear it staunchly. They have their own mordant humour, too, and Jensen renders the tragic and the comic in the most congenial way. The art of these peasant tales is so consummate that they already rank as Danish classics.

The master hand is even more apparent in a later Himmerland story of very different flavour, a short novel called *Jørgine* (1926). This book shows us another facet of Jensen's remarkably versatile talent. It is a simple, quiet story: a deceived peasant girl saves herself from disaster and shame by an unromantic marriage and becomes a dutiful, hard-working wife and self-sacrificing mother. *Jørgine* is an excellent piece of work, deep in feeling, penetrating in its knowledge of life, wonderfully fresh and alert, and written with that virtuosity of style which is always at Jensen's command. Since *Jørgine* he has more than once turned his attention to similar placid lives, creating from them minor works of classic art.

For many years Jensen has collected very heterogeneous pieces of writing in volumes entitled *Myter* (1907–45) [Myths]. The whole series of these is so well known that the word «myth» has acquired in Danish the additional sense of a new literary genre. That sense is not easy to define. Sometimes it means that Jensen has left the everyday world to explore that realm of fantasy which is the domain he masters. This can happen even when he is telling his own experiences in the first person. Just as often he tells in a «myth» events and experiences which must be taken as factual, or he expounds, with utmost sincerity, his ideas and theories. His presentation then is of unique graphic clarity and verisimilitude.

Sometimes natural phenomena are described with such profound intuition and imaginative insight that the word «myth» can be understood in its ordinary sense. The common factor in all these diverse works is indeed only their brilliant and direct style. This same style in Jensen's innumerable studies and manifestoes in popular science allows us to classify them as belles-lettres.

The exigencies of space prevent me from mentioning more than one of these works here. I choose *Vor oprindelse* (1941) [Our Origin] since it constitutes a sort of parallel and complement to the sagas in *Den lange rejse*. The book opens at the point in time when man himself, ceasing to be merely passive, begins to influence the forces of evolution.

In the introduction Jensen says important things about the blessings of work – a subject on which he is undoubtedly an authority, for he has been an indefatigable worker all his life.

This becomes evident in more ways than one in *Vor oprindelse*. He has re-enacted every one of the advances made by man in that long history he so brilliantly relates – from the mastery of fire and the making of the first weapons to the slowly perfected mastery of the crafts. It is a most impressive book, one of his best.

The Danes think as highly of his verse as of his prose. As a poet his major characteristic is an ever-deepening devotion to his native soil, expressed in quite varying tones. Sometimes he uses a revived old alliterative measure; sometimes modern «free verse» – but with the great improvement that rhythm is retained and syntax respected. Some of his poems are in regular verse, their pure melodies recalling the golden age of Danish poetry. In them Jensen rises to the zenith of his powers and reveals yet another aspect, new and surprising, of his art and his personality.

Primarily he directed all his love to the machine age. He seemed spellbound by the astonishing and ever more rapid march of science. The faster the pace, the greater his enchantment. Such an outlook has no use for old values. It flies high over the nations, has no thought for them. Its Utopia needs no flowering meadows to walk in, no infinite space for dreams.

Fortunately, Johannes V. Jensen's richly creative mind has taken frequent holidays from the marvels of the future to dwell instead on those inherited aesthetic and emotional values which are fundamental to the spirit of man.

On December 10, 1944, a luncheon was held under the auspices of the American-Scandinavian Foundation at the Waldorf-Astoria Hotel in New York to take the place of the customary ceremonies in Stockholm. Mr. Jensen was not present at the gathering. The lecture was broadcast in Stockholm on the same date.

Mr. Jensen participated in the official ceremonies of the Nobel Foundation in Stockholm in 1945. On that occasion, he received his diploma and the gold medal.

Presentation

by Anders Österling, Permanent Secretary of the Swedish Academy

'oday Johannes V. Jensen will receive in person the Nobel Prize in Literature
or 1944, and we are happy to salute the great Danish writer who since the
eginning of the century has been in the front rank, always active, for a long
me controversial, but universally admired for his vitality. This child of the
ry and windy moors of Jutland has, almost out of spite, astonished his con-
mporaries by a remarkably prolific production. He could well be consider-
d one of the most fertile Scandinavian writers. He has constructed a vast and
nposing literary *œuvre*, comprising the most diverse genres: epic and lyric,
naginative and realistic works, as well as historical and philosophical essays,
ot to mention his scientific excursions in all directions.

This bold iconoclast and stylistic innovator has increasingly become a pa-
riarchal classic, and in his heart he feels close to the poetry of the golden age
nd hopes that one day he will be counted among the life-giving tutelary
pirits of his nation.

Johannes V. Jensen has been such a passionate student of biological and
hilosophical evolution that he should be amazed at the singular course of
is own development. A conquering instinct forms the basis of his being. He
vas a native of Himmerland, a relatively dry region in western Jutland, and
is impressions of men and things were engraved indelibly on his conscious-
ess. Later he was to remember those resources that were hidden beneath the
ensations of childhood, the ancient treasure of family memories. His father,
he veterinarian of Farsö, came from that area, and through his paternal
randfather, the old weaver of Guldager, Jensen is directly descended from
easants. Characteristically enough, his first book dealt with the province of
is origin. His incomparable *Himmerlandshistorier* offer an original portrait
allery of primitive and half-savage creatures who are still subject to ancient
ears. The promised land of his childhood, powerful and alive with the past,
found again in his mature poetry.

The first books of Johannes V. Jensen reveal him as a young man from the
rovinces; a student of opposition, living in Copenhagen; an arduous and
gitated youth, fighting passionately against intellectual banality and narrow-

mindedness. This native of Jutland, self-conscious, difficult to approach, but sensitive, was soon to find his country too narrow. Stifled by the familiar climate of the Danish isles, he threw himself into exotic romanticism with the cool passion of a gambler. His travels across foreign continents for the first time opened to him the space needed by his restless, unchained imagination. During that period of his life he sang the praise of technology and mechanization. Just as his compatriot H. C. Andersen was perhaps the first to describe the charms of railway travel, Johannes V. Jensen was the prophet of the marvels of our age, of skyscrapers, motor cars, and cinemas, which he never tired of praising in his American novels, *Madame D'Ora* (1904) and *Hjulet* (1905) [The Wheel]. But soon he entered into a new stage of his development; at the risk of simplifying matters we might say that, having satisfied his passion for distant travel, he began to look in time for what he had pursued in space. The same man who had sung the modern life, with its rapid pace and noisy machines, has become the spectator of ancient epochs and has devoted himself to the study of the long, slow periods during which man first sought adventure.

Thus we come to perhaps his most important creation, the six volumes combined under the title *Den lange rejse*, which leads us from the ice age to Christopher Columbus. The central theme or one of the central themes of this work is the universal mission of the Scandinavian people, from the great migrations and the Norman invasion to the discovery of America. Jensen considers Christopher Columbus a descendant of the Lombards, in short Nordic man, if not a Jutlander like himself. In this monumental series appears a legendary figure, Nornagestr. He is not at all the same person who appears at the court of King Olaf Tryggvason to tell his stories and die there. According to the Icelandic saga he was three hundred years old; but Jensen makes him even older and turns him into a kind of Ahasverus, ubiquitous, always behind his time, a stranger among the new generations, but nevertheless younger than they because he lived at a time when existence itself was young and mankind closer to its origins. The writer has followed tradition only as far as it was useful to him. Three prophetesses came to Nornagestr's mother to see the child and one of them predicted that he would die as soon as the candle could no longer burn. Gro, the mother, immediately extinguished the candle and gave it to the child as an amulet. In the work of Johannes V. Jensen, Nornagestr sometimes lights it in foreign lands and whenever he does so a deep abyss of time opens before him. When he comes to again, seized by the love of life, he is transported to his country, the fresh and green Zealand

All legends exist because reason alone cannot clarify experience. What then Nornagestr, who plays such an important role in the epic of the Danish master? Perhaps it is the spirit of the Nordic people rising from the night like phantom or like an atavistic creature. One suspects that this unique globe-trotter with his harp is closely related to the author himself, who has given him many ideas about life and death, and about the close relation between the present and eternity – the precious fruits of experiences gathered from the lands and seas of the globe.

For Johannes V. Jensen, who grew up on a Jutland moor where the horizon often indented by a line of tumuli, it was natural to divide his interests between facts and myths and to seek his way between the shadows of the past and the realities of the present. His example reveals to us both the attraction of the primitive for a sensitive man and the necessity of transforming brute force into tenderness. He has attained the summit of his art by means of these violent contrasts. A fresh, salty breeze blows through his work, which unfolds with vivid language, powerful expression, and singular energy. Precisely in the poets most deeply rooted in their country do we find this poetic genius for words. Jensen is the voice of Jutland and of Denmark. With his talents he deserves the title of the most eminent narrator of the victorious struggle of the Nordic people against nature, and of the continuity of the Nordic spirit throughout the ages.

Mr. Jensen – If you have listened to what I have just said you will certainly think that the few moments I had were much too short to accomplish the long voyage through your work, and that I have neglected important aspects of it. It is fortunate for us as well as for you that a proper presentation is hardly necessary at all in your case. You are a well-known member of our great family and as such you are now asked to receive from the hands of our King the distinction which the Swedish Academy has awarded you.

At the banquet, Professor A. H. T. Theorell, Director of the Department of Biochemistry at the Nobel Institute of Medicine, called Mr. Jensen «the splendid representative of the proud literary tradition of our dear sister country, Denmark».

Acceptance

I thank the venerable Swedish Academy and the Swedish nation for the honour they have bestowed upon me in awarding me the Nobel Prize in Literature. Present in all our thoughts today is the founder, Alfred Nobel whose generosity has done so much good for science, literature, and peace throughout the world. This great Swedish scientist and humanist linked the name of Sweden with a broad vision that stretches far beyond the frontier of one nation and serves to bring all nations closer to one another.

When one thinks of great Swedish minds of international fame, our thoughts turn to Alfred Nobel's forerunner, that great genius of natural science, Linné, who gave animals their proper names and, long before any one had ever dreamt of evolution, classified monkeys, apes, and man under the name of primates. Passion for nature, for all that stirred and breathed was the driving force in Linné's genius. Whenever one reads of the determi nation of the species, or opens a book on natural science and history, in what ever language, one inevitably comes across the name of Linné. There is some thing of the freshness of mind, of the lightness of spirit in Linné which for centuries has been linked in people's minds with the mountains of Sweden and Swedish joy in nature.

I cannot talk of Linné without being reminded of Charles Darwin, re membering him not only as a man of science who has drawn a line between two epochs, but also as the most lovable, the kindest of human beings, the best of fathers; his distinguished name is now carried by the third and fourth generation of his descendants. To him, evolution was not only the subject of a life's study but the very essence of life, proof of the inexhaustible richness and wonder of nature, revealed each day and taken to heart.

Were one to determine the degree of maturity of each nation according to its capacity for reasoning and comprehension, England would come out on top for her sense of realism, and the man who put forward these basically English ideas in a simple, unaffected manner was Charles Darwin.

Linné's designation of species was the foundation which subsequently en abled Darwin to form his conclusions on their origin. This Anglo-Swedish

nse of reality, derived from our common Nordic background, has establish-
d for all time the place of mankind in nature.

I should like to mention on this occasion another name in Danish literature
vhich is linked with Swedish tradition, that of Adam Oehlenschläger. You
vill remember that when he met Sweden's national poet, Esaias Tegnér, at
und in 1829, he was hailed by him as the great poet and simple man that he
vas. A hundred years later, in 1929, it was my lot to receive in the same town
degree from the University of Lund. I am not Oehlenschläger's successor,
ut I do count myself among his followers and admirers.

It is with a feeling of Scandinavian fellowship that I now wish to thank the
reat and free Swedish nation which once crowned my countryman Adam
Oehlenschläger with laurels, and has on two occasions judged my literary
fforts worthy of distinction.

Autobiography

I was born on the 20th of January, 1873, in a village in North Jutland, the second son of the district veterinary surgeon, H. Jensen, a descendant on both sides of farmers and craftsmen. In 1893, at the age of twenty, I graduated from the Cathedral School of Viborg, and subsequently studied medicine for three years at the University of Copenhagen. I earned my living by my pen until it became necessary for me to choose between further studies and literature. The grounding in natural sciences which I obtained in the course of my medical studies, including preliminary examinations in botany, zoology, physics and chemistry, was to become decisive in determining the trend of my literary work.

My literary career began near the turn of the century with the publication of *Himmerlandshistorier* (1898–1910) [Himmerland Stories], comprising a series of tales set in that part of Denmark where I was born. This was followed in the years up to 1944 by «legends» and «myths», representing literary forms have particularly liked, and of which nine volumes have appeared (*Myter* 1907–45 [Myths]). I have also written poetry, a few plays, and many essays chiefly on anthropology and the philosophy of evolution.

For many years I was engaged in journalism, writing articles and chronicles for the daily press without ever joining the staff of any newspaper. Nor have I ever belonged to any political party. After extensive journeys to the East, to Malaya and China, and several visits to the United States, I inspired a change in the Danish literature and press by introducing English and American vigour, which was to replace the then dominant trend of decadent Gallicism. The essence of my literary work is to be found in my collection of poems, which may be regarded as a reaction against the fastidious style of the day bearing Baudelaire's poisonous hall-mark. My poems represented a return to simple style and sound subject matter (*Digte, 1904–41, 1943* [Poems])

A probing analysis of the problems of evolution forms the basis of my prose. During half a century of literary work, I have endeavoured to introduce the philosophy of evolution into the sphere of literature, and to inspire my readers to think in evolutionary terms. I was prompted to do this because of the misinterpretation and distortion of Darwinism at the end of the 19th century. The concept of the *Übermensch* had disastrous consequences in that it led to two world wars, and was destroyed only with the collapse of Germany in 1945. In the course of opposing this fallacious doctrine, I have arrived at a new interpretation of the theory of evolution and its moral implications.

Biographical note on Johannes V. Jensen

Johannes V. Jensen (1873–1950) developed his theories of evolution in a cycle of six novels, *Den lange rejse* (1908–22) [*The Long Journey*], which was published in a two-volume edition in 1938.

Literature 1945

GABRIELA MISTRAL

(pen name of Lucila Godoy y Alcayaga)

«for her lyric poetry which, inspired by powerful emotions, has made her name a symbol of the idealistic aspirations of the entire Latin American world»

Presentation

by Hjalmar Gullberg, Member of the Swedish Academy

One day a mother's tears caused a whole language, disdained at that time in good society, to rediscover its nobility and gain glory through the power of its poetry. It is said that when [Frédéric] Mistral, the first of the two poets bearing the name of the Mediterranean wind, had written his first verses in French as a young student, his mother began to shed inexhaustible tears. An ignorant country woman from Languedoc, she did not understand this distinguished language. Mistral then wrote *Mirèio*, recounting the love of the pretty little peasant for the poor artisan, an epic that exudes the perfume of the flowering land and ends in cruel death. Thus the old language of the troubadours became again the language of poetry. The Nobel Prize of 1904 drew the world's attention to this event. Ten years later the poet of *Mirèio* died.

In that same year, 1914, the year in which the First World War broke out, a new Mistral appeared at the other end of the world. At the Floral Games of Santiago de Chile, Gabriela Mistral obtained the prize with some poems dedicated to a dead man.

Her story is so well known to the people of South America that, passed on from country to country, it has become almost a legend. And now that she has at last come to us, over the crests of the Cordilleran Andes and across the immensities of the Atlantic, we may retell it once again.

In a small village in the Elquis valley, several decades ago, was born a future schoolteacher named Lucila Godoy y Alcayaga. Godoy was her father's name, Alcayaga her mother's; both were of Basque origin. Her father, who had been a schoolteacher, improvised verses with ease. His talent seems to have been mixed with the anxiety and the instability common to poets. He left his family when his daughter, for whom he had made a small garden, was still a child. Her beautiful mother, who was to live a long time, has said that sometimes she discovered her lonely little daughter engaged in intimate conversations with the birds and the flowers of the garden. According to one version of the legend, she was expelled from school. Apparently she was considered too stupid for teaching hours to be wasted on her. Yet she taught herself by her own methods, educating herself to the extent that she became a teacher in the small village school of Cantera. There her destiny was fulfilled at the age of twenty, when a passionate love arose between her and a railroad employee.

We know little of their story. We know only that he betrayed her. One day in November, 1909, he fatally shot himself in the head. The young girl was seized with boundless despair. Like Job, she lifted her cry to the Heaven that had allowed this. From the lost valley in the barren, scorched mountains of Chile a voice arose, and far around men heard it. A banal tragedy of every day life lost its private character and entered into universal literature. Lucila Godoy y Alcayaga became Gabriela Mistral. The little provincial school teacher, the young colleague of Selma Lagerlöf of Maarbacka, was to become the spiritual queen of Latin America.

When the poems written in memory of the dead man had made known the name of the new poet, the sombre and passionate poems of Gabriela Mistral began to spread over all South America. It was not until 1922, however, that she had her large collection of poems, *Desolación* (Despair), printed in New York. A mother's tears burst forth in the middle of the book, in the fifteenth poem, tears shed for the son of the dead man, a son who would never be born...

Gabriela Mistral transferred her natural love to the children she taught. For them she wrote the collections of simple songs and rounds, collected in Madrid in 1924 under the title *Ternura* (Tenderness). In her honour, four thousand Mexican children at one time sang these rounds. Gabriela Mistral became the poet of motherhood by adoption.

In 1938 her third large collection, *Tala* (a title which can be translated as «ravage» but which is also the name of a children's game), appeared in Buenos Aires for the benefit of the infant victims of the Spanish Civil War. Contrasting with the pathos of *Desolación*, *Tala* expresses the cosmic calm which envelopes the South American land whose fragrance comes all the way to us. We are again in the garden of her childhood; I listen again to the intimate dialogues with nature and common things. There is a curious mixture of sacred hymn and naive song for children; the poems on bread and wine, salt, corn, and water – water that can be offered to thirsty men – celebrate the primordial foods of human life!...

From her maternal hand this poet gives us a drink which tastes of the earth and which appease the thirst of the heart. It is drawn from the spring which ran for Sappho on a Greek island and for Gabriela Mistral in the valley of Elquis, the spring of poetry that will never dry up.

Madame Gabriela Mistral–You have indeed made a long voyage to be received by so short a speech. In the space of a few minutes I have described to the compatriots of Selma Lagerlöf your remarkable pilgrimage from the chair of a schoolmistress to the throne of poetry. In rendering homage to the rich Latin American literature, we address ourselves today quite specially to its queen, the poet of *Desolación*, who has become the great singer of sorrow and of motherhood.

I ask you now to receive from the hands of His Majesty the King the Nobel Prize in Literature, which the Swedish Academy has awarded you.

Acceptance

Today Sweden turns toward a distant Latin American country to honour it in the person of one of the many exponents of its culture. It would have pleased the cosmopolitan spirit of Alfred Nobel to extend the scope of his protectorate of civilization by including within its radius the southern hemisphere of the American continent. As a daughter of Chilean democracy, I am moved to have before me a representative of the Swedish democratic tradition, a tradition whose originality consists in perpetually renewing itself within the framework of the most valuable creations of society. The admirable work of freeing a tradition from deadwood while conserving intact the core of the old virtues, the acceptance of the present and the anticipation of the future, these are what we call Sweden, and these achievements are an honour to Europe and an inspiring example for the American continent.

The daughter of a new people, I salute the spiritual pioneers of Sweden, by whom I have been helped more than once. I recall its men of science who have enriched its national body and mind. I remember the legion of professors and teachers who show the foreigner unquestionably exemplary schools, and I look with trusting love to those other members of the Swedish people: farmers, craftsmen, and workers.

At this moment, by an undeserved stroke of fortune, I am the direct voice of the poets of my race and the indirect voice for the noble Spanish and Portuguese tongues. Both rejoice to have been invited to this festival of Nordic life with its tradition of centuries of folklore and poetry.

May God preserve this exemplary nation, its heritage and its creations, its efforts to conserve the imponderables of the past and to cross the present with the confidence of maritime people who overcome every challenge.

My homeland, represented here today by our learned Minister Gajardo, respects and loves Sweden, and it has sent me here to accept the special honour you have awarded to it. Chile will treasure your generosity among her purest memories.

rior to the acceptance, Professor A. H. T. Theorell of the Department of
iochemistry, Nobel Institute of Medicine, addressed the Chilean poet: «To
ou, Gabriela Mistral, I wish to convey our admiring homage. From a dis-
int continent, where the summer sun now shines, you have ventured the
ong journey to Gösta Berling's land, when the darkness of winter broods at
s deepest. A worthier voice than mine has praised your poetry earlier today.
May I nevertheless be permitted to say that we all share in the gladness that
he Nobel Prize has this time been awarded to a poetess who combines
nagnificent art with the deepest and noblest aims.»

Biography

Gabriela Mistral (1889–1957), pseudonym for Lucila Godoy y Alcayaga was born in Vicuña, Chile. The daughter of a dilettante poet, she began to write poetry as a village schoolteacher after a passionate romance with a railway employee who committed suicide. She taught elementary and secondary school for many years until her poetry made her famous. She played an important role in the educational systems of Mexico and Chile, was active in cultural committees of the League of Nations, and was Chilean consul in Naples, Madrid, and Lisbon. She held honorary degrees from the Universities of Florence and Guatemala and was an honorary member of various cultural societies in Chile as well as in the United States, Spain, and Cuba. She taught Spanish literature in the United States at Columbia University, Middlebury College, Vassar College, and at the University of Puerto Rico.

The love poems in memory of the dead, *Sonetos de la muerte* (1914), made her known throughout Latin America, but her first great collection of poems, *Desolación* [Despair], was not published until 1922. In 1924 appeared *Ternura* [Tenderness], a volume of poetry dominated by the theme of childhood; the same theme, linked with that of maternity, plays a significant role in *Tala*, poems published in 1938. Her complete poetry was published in 1958.

Literature 1946

HERMANN HESSE

«for his inspired writings which, while growing in boldness and penetration, exemplify the classical humanitarian ideals and high qualities of style»

Presentation

by Anders Österling, Permanent Secretary of the Swedish Academy

This year's Nobel Prize in literature has been awarded to a writer of German origin who has had wide critical acclaim and who has created his work regardless of public favour. The sixty-nine-year-old Hermann Hesse can look back on a considerable achievement consisting of novels, short stories, and poems, partly available in Swedish translation.

He escaped from political pressure earlier than other German writers and, during the First World War, settled in Switzerland where he acquired citizenship in 1923. It should not be overlooked, however, that his extraction as well as his personal connections had always justified Hesse in considering himself as much Swiss as German. His asylum in a country that was neutral during the war allowed him to continue his important literary work in relative quiet, and at present Hesse, together with Mann, is the best representative of the German cultural heritage in contemporary literature.

With Hesse, more than with most writers, one has to know his personal background to understand the rather surprising components that make up his personality. He comes from a strictly pietist Swabian family. His father was a well-known church historian, his mother the daughter of a missionary. She was of French descent and was educated in India. It was taken for granted that Hermann would become a minister, and he was sent to the seminary at the cloister of Maulbronn. He ran away, became an apprentice to a watchmaker, and later worked in bookshops in Tübingen and Basle.

The youthful rebellion against the inherited piety that nonetheless always remained in the depth of his being, was repeated in a painful inner crisis, when in 1914 as a mature man and an acknowledged master of regional literature he went new ways which were far removed from his previous idyllic paths. There are, briefly, two factors that caused this profound change in Hesse's writings.

The first was, of course, the World War. When at its beginning he wanted to speak some words of peace and contemplation to his agitated colleagues and in his pamphlet used Beethoven's motto, «O Freunde, nicht diese Töne», he aroused a storm of protest. He was savagely attacked by the German press and was apparently deeply shocked by this experience. He took it as evidence that the entire civilization of Europe in which he had so long believed was sick and decaying. Redemption had to come from beyond the accepted norms, perhaps from the light of the East, perhaps from the core hidden in anarchic theories of the resolution of good and evil in a higher unity. Sick and doubt-ridden, he sought a cure in the psychoanalysis of Freud, eagerly preached and practised at that time, which left lasting traces in Hesse's increasingly bold books of this period.

This personal crisis found its magnificent expression in the fantastical novel *Der Steppenwolf* (1927) [*Steppenwolf*], an inspired account of the split in human nature, the tension between desire and reason in an individual who is outside the social and moral notions of everyday life. In this bizarre fable of a man without a home, hunted like a wolf, plagued by neuroses, Hesse created an incomparable and explosive book, dangerous and fateful perhaps, but at the same time liberating by its mixture of sardonic humour and poetry in the treatment of the theme. Despite the prominence of modern problems Hesse even here preserves a continuity with the best German traditions; the writer whom this extremely suggestive story recalls most is E. T. A. Hoffmann, the master of the *Elixiere des Teufels*.

Hesse's maternal grandfather was the famous Indologist Gundert. Thus even in his childhood the writer felt drawn to Indian wisdom. When as a mature man he travelled to the country of his desire he did not, indeed, solve the riddle of life; but the influence of Buddhism soon entered his thought, an influence by no means restricted to *Siddhartha* (1922), the beautiful story of a young Brahman's search for the meaning of life on earth.

Hesse's work combines so many influences from Buddha and St. Francis to Nietzsche and Dostoevsky that one might suspect that he is primarily an eclectic experimenter with different philosophies. But this opinion would be quite wrong. His sincerity and his seriousness are the foundations of his work and remain in control even in his treatment of the most extravagant subjects.

In his most accomplished novellas we are confronted both directly and indirectly with his personality. His style, always admirable, is as perfect in rebellion and demonic ecstasy as in calm philosophical speculation. The story of the desperate embezzler Klein, who flees to Italy to seek there his last chance, and the marvellously calm description of his late brother Hans in the *Gedenkblätter* (1937) [Reminiscences] are masterly examples from different fields of his creativity.

In Hesse's more recent work the vast novel *Das Glasperlenspiel* (1943)

[*Magister Ludi*] occupies a special position. It is a fantasy about a mysterious intellectual order, on the same heroic and ascetic level as that of the Jesuits, based on the exercise of meditation as a kind of therapy. The novel has an imperious structure in which the concept of the game and its role in civilization has surprising parallels with the ingenious study *Homo ludens* by the Dutch scholar Huizinga. Hesse's attitude is ambiguous. In a period of collapse it is a precious task to preserve the cultural tradition. But civilization cannot be permanently kept alive by turning it into a cult for the few. If it is possible to reduce the variety of knowledge to an abstract system of formulas, we have on the one hand proof that civilization rests on an organic system; on the other, this high knowledge cannot be considered permanent. It is as fragile and destructible as the glass pearls themselves, and the child that finds the glittering pearls in the rubble no longer knows their meaning. A philosophical novel of this kind easily runs the risk of being called recondite, but Hesse defended his with a few gentle lines in the motto of the book, «...then in certain cases and for irresponsible men it may be that non-existent things can be described more easily and with less responsibility in words than the existent, and therefore the reverse applies for pious and scholarly historians; for nothing destroys description so much as words, and yet there is nothing more necessary than to place before the eyes of men certain things the existence of which is neither provable nor probable, but which, for this very reason, pious and scholarly men treat to a certain extent as existent in order that they may be led a step further toward their being and their becoming.»

If Hesse's reputation as a prose writer varies, there has never been any doubt about his stature as a poet. Since the death of Rilke and George he has been the foremost German poet of our time. He combines exquisite purity of style with moving emotional warmth, and his musical form is unsurpassed in our time. He continues the tradition of Goethe, Eichendorf, and Mörike and renews its poetic magic by a colour peculiar to himself. His collection of poems, *Trost der Nacht* (1929) [The Solace of Night], mirrors with unusual clarity not only his inner drama, his healthy and sick hours, and his intense self-examination, but also his devotion to life, his pleasure in painting, and his worship of nature. A later collection, *Neue Gedichte* (1937) [New Poems], is full of autumnal wisdom and melancholy experience, and its hows a heightened sensibility in image, mood, and melody.

In a summary introduction it is impossible to do justice to the many changing qualities which make this writer particularly attractive to us and which have justly given him a faithful following. He is a problematic and a con-

ssional poet with the wealth of the South German mind, which he express-
in a very individual mixture of freedom and piety. If one overlooked the
assionate tendency to protest, the ever-burning fire that makes the dreamer
fighter as soon as the matters at stake are sacred to him, one might call him
romantic poet. In one passage Hesse says that one must never be content with
ality, that one should neither adore nor worship it, for this low, always dis-
ppointing, and desolate reality cannot be changed except by denying it
rough proving our superior strength.

Hesse's award is more than the confirmation of his fame. It honours a poetic
chievement which presents throughout the image of a good man in his
ruggle, following his calling with rare faithfulness, who in a tragic epoch
cceeded in bearing the arms of true humanism.

Unfortunately, reasons of health have prevented the poet from making
he journey to Stockholm. In his stead the envoy of the Swiss Federal Repub-
c will accept the Prize.

Your Excellency, I ask you now to receive from the hands of His Majesty
he King the Prize awarded by the Swedish Academy to your countryman,
Hermann Hesse.

Acceptance

by Henry Vallotton, Swiss Minister

We deeply regret that illness keeps Hermann Hesse in Switzerland. But his thoughts are with us, and his gratitude speaks through this message which he asked me to read to you: «In sending cordial and respectful greetings to your festive gathering, I should like above all to express my regrets at not being able to be your guest in person, to greet and to thank you. My health has always been delicate, and I have been left a permanent invalid by the afflic tions of the years since 1933 that have destroyed my life's work and have again and again burdened me with heavy duties. But my mind has not been broken, and I feel akin to you and to the idea that inspired the Nobel Founda tion, the idea that the mind is international and supra-national, that it ought to serve not war and annihilation, but peace and reconciliation.

My ideal, however, is not the blurring of national characteristics, such as would lead to an intellectually uniform humanity. On the contrary, may diversity in all shapes and colours live long on this dear earth of ours. What a wonderful thing is the existence of many races, many peoples, many lan guages, and many varieties of attitude and outlook! If I feel hatred and irre concilable enmity toward wars, conquests, and annexations, I do so for many reasons, but also because so many organically grown, highly individual, and richly differentiated achievements of human civilization have fallen victim to these dark powers. I hate the *grands simplificateurs*, and I love the sense of quality, of inimitable craftsmanship and uniqueness. As your grateful guest and colleague I therefore extend my greetings to Sweden, your country, to her language and civilization, her rich and proud history, and her persever ance in maintaining and shaping her individual nature. I have never been to Sweden, but for decades many a good and kind thing has come to me from your country since that first present which I received from it: it is now forty years ago and it was a Swedish book, a copy of the first edition of *Christ Legends* with a personal dedication by Selma Lagerlöf. In the course of years there has been many a valuable exchange with your country until you have now surprised me with the final great present. Let me express to you my profound gratitude.»

Prior to the acceptance, Sigurd Curman, President of the Royal Academy of Sciences, made the following remarks: «Hermann Hesse has carried on his battle against these microbes of the soul in the field of literature. He has endeavoured, in his stylistically exquisite poems and stories, to show us the way to rise out of this slough. He shouts to all of us the motto of young Joseph Knecht in *Das Glasperlenspiel*: ‹Transzendieren!› Advance, mount higher, conquer yourself! For to be human is to suffer an incurable duality, to be drawn toward both good and evil. And we can achieve harmony and peace only when we have killed the selfishness within us. This is Hesse's message to the people of a ravaged age, resounding with screams of self-vindication from East and West. It is principally as a profound philosopher and bold critic of the contemporary period in his stories that Hesse deserves the Nobel Prize.»

Autobiography

I was born in Calw in the Black Forest on July 2, 1877. My father, a Baltic German, came from Estonia; my mother was the daughter of a Swabian and a French Swiss. My father's father was a doctor, my mother's father a missionary and Indologist. My father, too, had been a missionary in India for a short while, and my mother had spent several years of her youth in India and had done missionary work there.

My childhood in Calw was interrupted by several years of living in Basle (1880–86). My family had been composed of different nationalities; to this was now added the experience of growing up among two different peoples, in two countries with their different dialects.

I spent most of my school years in boarding schools in Wuerttemberg and some time in the theological seminary of the monastery at Maulbronn. I was a good learner, good at Latin though only fair at Greek, but I was not a very manageable boy, and it was only with difficulty that I fitted into the framework of a pietist education that aimed at subduing and breaking the individual personality. From the age of twelve I wanted to be a poet, and since there was no normal or official road, I had a hard time deciding what to do after leaving school. I left the seminary and grammar school, became an apprentice to a mechanic, and at the age of nineteen I worked in book and antique shops in Tübingen and Basle. Late in 1899 a tiny volume of my poems appeared in print, followed by other small publications that remained equally unnoticed until in 1904 the novel *Peter Camenzind*, written in Basle and set in Switzerland, had a quick success. I gave up selling books, married a woman from Basle, the mother of my sons, and moved to the country. At that time a rural life, far from the cities and civilization, was my aim. Since then I have always lived in the country, first, until 1912, in Gaienhofen on Lake Constance, later near Bern, and finally in Montagnola near Lugano, where I am still living.

Soon after I settled in Switzerland in 1912, the First World War broke out and each year brought me more and more into conflict with German nationalism; ever since my first shy protests against mass suggestion and violence I have been exposed to continuous attacks and floods of abusive letters from

Germany. The hatred of the official Germany, culminating under Hitler, was compensated for by the following I won among the young generation that thought in international and pacifist terms, by the friendship of Romain Rolland, which lasted until his death, as well as by the sympathy of men who thought like me even in countries as remote as India and Japan. In Germany I have been acknowledged again since the fall of Hitler, but my works, partly suppressed by the Nazis and partly destroyed by the war, have not yet been republished there.

In 1923, I resigned German and acquired Swiss citizenship. After the dissolution of my first marriage I lived alone for many years, then I married again. Faithful friends have put a house in Montagnola at my disposal.

Until 1914 I loved to travel; I often went to Italy and once spent a few months in India. Since then I have almost entirely abandoned travelling, and have not been outside of Switzerland for over ten years.

I survived the years of the Hitler regime and the Second World War through the eleven years of work that I spent on the *Glasperlenspiel* (1943) [*Magister Ludi*], a novel in two volumes. Since the completion of that long book, an eye disease and increasing sicknesses of old age have prevented me from engaging in larger projects.

Of the Western philosophers, I have been influenced most by Plato, Spinoza, Schopenhauer, and Nietzsche as well as the historian Jacob Burckhardt. But they did not influence me as much as Indian and, later, Chinese philosophy. I have always been on familiar and friendly terms with the fine arts, but my relationship to music has been more intimate and fruitful. It is found in most of my writings. My most characteristic books in my view are the poems collected edition, Zürich, 1942), the stories *Knulp* (1915), *Demian* (1919), *Siddhartha* (1922), *Der Steppenwolf* (1927) [*Steppenwolf*], *Narziss und Goldmund* 1930), *Die Morgenlandfahrt* (1932) [*The Journey to the East*], and *Das Glasperlenspiel* (1943) [*Magister Ludi*]. The volume *Gedenkblätter* (1937, enlarged ed. 1962) [Reminiscences] contains a good many autobiographical things. My essays on political topics have recently been published in Zürich under the title *Krieg und Frieden* (1946) [*War and Peace*].

I ask you, gentlemen, to be contented with this very sketchy outline; the state of my health does not permit me to be more comprehensive.

Biographical note on Hermann Hesse

Hermann Hesse (1877–1962) received the Goethe Prize of Frankfurt in 1946 and the Peace Prize of the German Booksellers in 1955. A complete edition of his works in six volumes appeared in 1952; a seventh volume (1957) contains essays and miscellaneous writings. *Beschwörungen* (1955) [Evocations], a volume of late prose, and his correspondence with Romain Rolland (1954) were published separately.

Literature 1947

ANDRÉ GIDE

«for his comprehensive and artistically significant writings, in which human problems and conditions have been presented with a fearless love of truth and keen psychological insight»

Presentation

by Anders Österling, Permanent Secretary of the Swedish Academy

On the first page of the remarkable journal kept by André Gide for half a century, the author, then twenty years old, finds himself on the sixth floor of a building in the Latin Quarter, looking for a meeting place for «The Symbolists», the group of youths to which he belonged. From the window he looked at the Seine and Notre Dame during the sunset of an autumn day and felt like the hero of a Balzac novel, a Rastignac ready to conquer the city lying at his feet: «And now, we two!» However, Gide's ambition was to find long and twisting paths ahead; nor was it to be contented with easy victories.

The seventy-eight-year-old writer who this day is being honoured with the award of the Nobel Prize has always been a controversial figure. From the beginning of his career he put himself in the first rank of the sowers of spiritual anxiety, but this does not keep him today from being counted almost everywhere among the first literary names of France, or from enjoying an influence that has persisted unabatedly through several generations. His first works appeared in the 1890's; his last one dates from the spring of 1947. A very important period in the spiritual history of Europe is outlined in his work, constituting a kind of dramatic foundation to his long life. One may ask why the importance of this work has only so recently been appreciated at its true value: the reason is that André Gide belongs unquestionably to that class of writers whose real evaluation requires a long perspective and a space adequate for the three stages of the dialectic process. More than any of his contemporaries, Gide has been a man of contrasts, a veritable Proteus of perpetually changing attitudes, working tirelessly at opposite poles in order to strike flashing sparks. This is why his work gives the appearance of an uninterrupted dialogue in which faith constantly struggles against doubt, asceticism against the love of life, discipline against the need for freedom. Even his external life has been mobile and changing, and his famous voyages to the Congo in 1927 and to Soviet Russia in 1935 –to cite only those–are proof enough that he did not want to be ranked among the peaceful stay-at-homes of literature.

Gide comes from a Protestant family whose social position permitted him to follow his vocation freely and to devote greater attention than most others can afford to the cultivation of his personality and to his inner development. He described this family milieu in his famous autobiography whose title *Si le grain ne meurt* (1924) [*If It Die...*] is taken from St. John's words about the grain of wheat that must die before its fruition. Although he has strongly reacted against his Puritan education, he has nonetheless all his life dwelled on the fundamental problems of morality and religion, and at times he has defined with rare purity the message of Christian love, particularly in his short novel, *La Porte étroite* (1909) [*Strait Is the Gate*], which deserves to be compared with the tragedies of Racine.

On the other hand, one finds in André Gide still stronger manifestations of that famous «immoralism»–a conception which his adversaries have often misinterpreted. In reality it designates the free act, the «gratuitous» act, the liberation from all repressions of conscience, something analagous to what the American recluse Thoreau expressed, «The worst thing is being the slave dealer of one's soul.» One should always keep in mind that Gide found some difficulty in presenting as virtue that which is composed of the absence of generally recognized virtues. *Les Nourritures terrestres* (1897) [*Fruits of the Earth*] was a youthful attempt from which he later turned away, and the diverse delights he enthusiastically sings of evoke for us those beautiful fruits of southern lands which do not bear keeping. The exhortation which he addresses to his disciple and reader, «And now, throw away my book. Leave me!», has been followed first of all by himself in his later works. But what leaves the strongest impression, in *Nourritures* as elsewhere, is the intense poetry of separation, of return, captured by him in so masterly a fashion in the flute-song of his prose. One rediscovers it often, for example in this brief journal entry, written later, near a mosque at Brusa on one May morning: «Ah! begin anew and on again afresh! Feel with rapture this exquisite tenderness of the cells in which emotion filters like milk... Bush of the dense gardens, rose of purity, indolent rose in the shade of plane trees, can it be that thou hast not known my youth? Before? Is it a memory I dwell in? Is it indeed I who am seated in this little corner of the mosque, I who breathe and I who love thee? or do I only dream of loving thee?... If I were indeed real, would this swallow have stolen so close to me?»

Behind the strange and incessant shift in perspective that Gide's work offers to us, in the novels as well as in the essays, in the travel diaries, or in the analyses of contemporary events, we always find the same supple intelligence, the same incorruptible psychology, expressed in a language which, by thet

most sober means, attains a wholly classic limpidity and the most delicate
variety. Without going into the details of the work, let us mention in this
connection the celebrated *Les Faux Monnayeurs* (1926) [*The Counterfeiters*],
with its bold and penetrating analysis of a group of young French people.
Through the novelty of its technique, this novel has inspired a whole new
orientation in the contemporary art of the narrative. Next to it, put the volume of memoirs already mentioned, in which the author intended to recount his life truthfully without adding anything that could be to his advantage or hiding what would be unpleasant. Rousseau had had the same intention, with this difference, that Rousseau exhibits his faults in the conviction
that all men being as evil as he, none will dare to judge or condemn him.
Gide, however, quite simply refuses to admit to his fellows the right to pass
any judgment on him; he calls on a higher tribunal, a vaster perspective, in
which he will present himself before the sovereign eye of God. The significance of these memoirs thus is indicated in the mysterious Biblical quotation
of the «grain of wheat» which here represents the personality: as long as the
latter is sentient, deliberate, and egocentric, it dwells alone and without ger-
minating power; it is only at the price of its death and its transmutation that
it will acquire life and be able to bear fruit. «I do not think,» Gide writes, «that
there is a way of looking at the moral and religious question or of acting in
the face of it that I have not known and made my own at some moment in
my life. In truth, I have wished to reconcile them all, the most diverse points
of view, by excluding nothing and by being ready to entrust to Christ the
solution of the contest between Dionysus and Apollo.»

Such a statement throws light on the intellectual versatility for which Gide
is often blamed and misunderstood, but which has never led him to betray
himself. His philosophy has a tendency toward regeneration at any price and
does not fail to evoke the miraculous phoenix which out of its nest of flames
hurls itself to a new flight.

In circumstances like those of today, in which, filled with admiring gratitude, we linger before the rich motifs and the essential themes of this work,
it is natural that we pass over the critical reservations which the author himself seems to enjoy provoking. For even in his ripe age, Gide has never argued
in favor of a full and complete acceptance of his experiences and his conclusions. What he wishes above all is to stir up and present the problems. Even
in the future, his influence will doubtless be noted less in a total acceptance
than in a lively controversy about his work. And in this lies the foundation
of his true greatness.

His work contains pages which provoke like a defiance through the almost unequalled audacity of the confession. He wishes to combat the Pharisees, but it is difficult, in the struggle, to avoid shocking certain rather delicate norms of human character. One must always remember that this manner of acting is a form of the impassioned love of truth which, since Montaigne and Rousseau, has been an axiom of French literature. Through all the phases of his evolution, Gide has appeared as a true defender of literary integrity, founded on the personality's right and duty to present all its problems resolutely and honestly. From this point of view, his long and varied activity, stimulated in so many ways, unquestionably represents an idealistic value.

Since Mr. André Gide, who has declared with great gratitude his acceptance of the distinction offered him, has unfortunately been prevented from coming here by reasons of health, his Prize will now be handed to His Excellency the French Ambassador.

Acceptance

read by Gabriel Puaux, French Ambassador

«It would no doubt be of little purpose to dwell on my regrets at not being able to be present on this solemn occasion nor to have my own voice bear witness to my gratitude, compelled as I am to forgo a trip that promised to be both pleasant and instructive.

I have, as you know, always declined honours, at least those which as a Frenchman I could expect from France. I confess, gentlemen, that it is with a sense of giddiness that I suddenly receive from you the highest honour to which a writer can aspire. For many years I thought that I was crying in the wilderness, later that I was speaking only to a very small number, but you have proved to me today that I was right to believe in the virtue of the small number and that sooner or later it would prevail.

It seems to me, gentlemen, that your votes were cast not so much for my work as for the independent spirit that animates it, that spirit which in our time faces attacks from all possible quarters. That you have recognized it in me, that you have felt the need to approve and support it, fills me with confidence and an intimate satisfaction. I cannot help thinking, however, that only recently another man in France represented this spirit even better than I do. I am thinking of Paul Valéry, for whom my admiration has steadily grown during a friendship of half a century and whose death alone prevents you from electing him in my place. I have often said with what friendly deference I have constantly and without weakness bowed to his genius, before which I have always felt ‹human, only too human›. May his memory be present at this ceremony, which in my eyes takes on all the more brilliance as the darkness deepens. You invite the free spirit to triumph and through this signal award, given without regard for frontiers or the momentary dissensions of factions, you offer to this spirit the unexpected chance of extraordinary radiance.»

rior to the acceptance, Arne Tiselius, Deputy Chairman of the Nobel oundation, made the following comment: «Unfortunately, Mr. André Gide, ue to ill health, has had to give up his original intention to attend the cere-nonies. We regret this, indeed, and would like to extend our reverence and ur sympathy to the venerable master of French literature whose genius has ɔ profoundly influenced our time.»

Biography

André Gide (1869–1951) came from a family of Huguenots and recent con
verts to Catholicism. As a child he was often ill and his education at the École
Alsacienne was interrupted by long stays in the South, where he was instruc
ted by private tutors. His *Les Cahiers d'André Walter* (1891) [*The Notebooks o
André Walter*] opened the door to the symbolist literary circles of the day, bu
the decisive event of these years was a journey to Algeria, where a severe ill
ness brought him to the verge of death and precipitated his revolt against hi
puritanical background. Henceforth his work lived on the never resolve
tensions between a strict artistic discipline, a puritanical moralism, and th
desire for unlimited sensual indulgence and abandonment to life. *Les Nour
ritures terrestres* (1897)[*Fruits of the Earth*], the drama *Saül* (1903), and later *L
Retour de l'enfant prodigue* (1907) [*The Return of the Prodigal*], are the chie
documents of his revolt.

A result of Gide's revolt was the unprecedented freedom with which he
wrote about sexual matters in *Corydon* (privately published 1911, publi
version 1924), his autobiography *Si le grain ne meurt* (1924) [*If It Die…*], an
Gide's lifelong diary *Journal 1889 à 1939* (1939), *Journal 1939 à 1942* (1948
and *Journal 1942 à 1949* (1950).

Gide divided his narrative works into *soties* such as *Les Caves du Vatica
(1914) [*Lafcadio's Adventures*] and classically restrained *récits*, for example, *L
Porte étroite* (1909) [*Strait is the Gate*] and *La Symphonie pastorale* (1919). Th
only work which he considered a novel was the structurally complex an
experimental *Les Faux Monnayeurs* (1926) [*The Counterfeiters*].

Until the twenties Gide was known chiefly in avant-garde and esoteri
literary circles (he was one of the founders of *La Nouvelle Revue Française*
but in his later years he became a highly influential, although always con
troversial figure. He travelled widely. His trip to the Congo led to a scathin
report on economic abuses by French firms and resulted in reforms. If in th
thirties Gide put off one part of the public by his sympathies with commu
nism, his disillusioned report of his journey to Russia, *Le Retour de L'U.R.S.*
(1936), scandalized another. Gide's interests went far beyond the confines o

rench literature. He translated Shakespeare, Whitman, Conrad, and Rilke.
He was an influential literary critic (*Prétextes*, 1903; *Nouveaux Prétextes*, 1911)
and was especially attracted to problematic writers like Dostoevsky, about
whom he wrote a book (1923).

Among Gide's last work was *Thésée* (1946), like the earlier *Oedipe* (1931)
the reworking of an old myth. Gide's collected works have been published
in fifteen volumes (1933–39).

Literature 1948

THOMAS STEARNS ELIOT

«for his outstanding, pioneer contribution to present-day poetry»

Presentation

by Anders Österling, Permanent Secretary of the Swedish Academy

In the impressive succession of Nobel Prize winners in Literature, T. S. Eliot marks a departure from the type of writer that has most frequently gained that distinction. The majority have been representatives of a literature which seeks its natural contacts in the public consciousness, and which, to attain this goal, avails itself of the media lying more or less ready at hand. This year's Prize winner has chosen to take another path. His career is remarkable in that, from an extremely exclusive and consciously isolated position, he has gradually come to exercise a very far-reaching influence. At the outset he appeared to address himself to but a small circle of initiates, but this circle slowly widened, without his appearing to will it himself. Thus in Eliot's verse and prose there was quite a special accent, which compelled attention just in our own time, a capacity to cut into the consciousness of our generation with the sharpness of a diamond.

In one of his essays Eliot himself has advanced, as a purely objective and quite uncategorical assumption, that poets in our present civilization have to be difficult to approach. «Our civilization», he says, «comprehends great variety and complexity, and this variety and complexity, playing upon a refined sensibility, must produce various and complex results. The poet must become more and more comprehensive, more allusive, more indirect, in order to force, to dislocate if necessary, language into his meaning.»

Against the background of such a pronouncement, we may test his results and learn to understand the importance of his contribution. The effort is worth-while. Eliot first gained his reputation as the result of his magnificent experiment in poetry, *The Waste Land*, which appeared in 1922 and then seemed bewildering in several ways, due to its complicated symbolic language, its mosaic-like technique, and its apparatus of erudite allusion. It may be recalled that this work appeared in the same year as another pioneer work, which had a still more sensational effect on modern literature, the much discussed *Ulysses*, from the hand of an Irishman, James Joyce. The parallel is by no means fortuitous, for these products of the nineteen-twenties are closely akin to one another, in both spirit and mode of composition.

The Waste Land–a title whose terrifying import no one can help feeling when the difficult and masterly word-pattern has finally yielded up its secrets. The melancholy and sombre rhapsody aims at describing the aridity and impotence of modern civilization, in a series of sometimes realistic and sometime mythological episodes, whose perspectives impinge on each other with an indescribable total effect. The cycle of poems consists of 436 lines, but actually it contains more than a packed novel of as many pages. *The Waste Land* now lies a quarter of a century back in time, but unfortunately it has proved that its catastrophic visions still have undiminished actuality in the shadow of the atomic age.

Since then Eliot has passed on to a series of poetic creations of the same brilliant concentration, in pursuance of the agonized, salvation-seeking main theme. The *horror vacui* of modern man in a secularized world, without order, meaning, or beauty, here stands out with poignant sincerity. In his latest work, *Four Quartets* (1943), Eliot has arrived at a meditative music of words with almost liturgical refrains and fine, exact expressions of his spiritual experiences. The transcendental superstructure rises ever clearer in his world picture. At the same time a manifest striving after a positive, guiding message emerges in his dramatic art, especially in the mighty historical play about Thomas of Canterbury, *Murder in the Cathedral* (1935), but also in *The Family Reunion* (1939), which is a bold attempt to combine such different conceptions as the Christian dogma of original sin and the classical Greek myths of fate, in an entirely modern environment, with the scene laid in a country house in northern England.

The purely poetical part of Eliot's work is not quantitatively great, but as it now stands out against the horizon, it rises from the ocean like a rocky peak and indisputably forms a landmark, sometimes assuming the mystic contours of a cathedral. It is poetry impressed with the stamp of strict responsibility and extraordinary self-discipline, remote from all emotional clichés, concentrated entirely on essential things, stark, granitic, and unadorned, but from time to time illuminated by a sudden ray from the timeless space of miracles and revelations.

Insight into Eliot must always present certain problems to be overcome, obstacles which are at the same time stimulating. It may appear to be contradictory to say that this radical pioneer of form, the initiator of a whole revolution in style within present-day poetry, is at the same time a coldly reasoning, logically subtle theorist, who never wearies of defending historical perspectives and the necessity of fixed norms for our existence. As early as he 1940's, he had become a convinced supporter of the Anglican Church n religion and of classicism in literature. In view of this philosophy of life, which implies a consistent return to ideals standardized by age, it might seem hat his modernistic practice would clash with his traditional theory. But his is hardly the case. Rather, in his capacity as an author, he has uninterrupedly and with varying success worked to bridge this chasm, the existence of which he must be fully and perhaps painfully conscious. His earliest poetry, o convulsively disintegrated, so studiously aggressive in its whole technical form, can finally also be apprehended as a negative expression of a mentality which aims at higher and purer realities and must first free itself of abhorrence and cynicism. In other words, his revolt is that of the Christian poet. It should also be observed in this connection that, on the whole, Eliot is careful not to magnify the power of poetry in relation to that of religion. In one place, where he wishes to point out what poetry can really accomplish for our inner life, he does so with great caution and reserve: «It may make us from time o time a little more aware of the deeper, unnamed feelings which form the substratum of our being, to which we rarely penetrate; for our lives are mostly a constant evasion of ourselves.»

Thus, if it can be said with some justification that Eliot's philosophical position is based on nothing but tradition, it ought nevertheless to be borne in mind that he constantly points out how generally that word has been misused in today's debates. The word «tradition» itself implies movement, something which cannot be static, something which is constantly handed on and assimilated. In the poetic tradition, too, this living principle prevails. The existing monuments of literature form an idealistic order, but this is slightly modified every time a new work is added to the series. Proportions and values are unceasingly changing. Just as the old directs the new, this in its turn directs he old, and the poet who realizes this must also realize the scope of his difficulties and his responsibility.

Externally, too, the now sixty-year-old Eliot has also returned to Europe, the ancient and storm-tossed, but still venerable, home of cultural traditions. Born an American, he comes from one of the Puritan families who emigrated from England at the end of the seventeenth century. His years of study as a young man at the Sorbonne, at Marburg, and at Oxford, clearly revealed to him that at bottom he felt akin to the historical milieu of the Old World, and since 1927 Mr. Eliot has been a British subject.

It is not possible in this presentation to indicate more than the most immediate fascinating features in the complicated multiplicity of Eliot's characteristics as a writer. The predominating one is the high, philosophically schooled intelligence, which has succeeded in enlisting in its service both imagination and learning, both sensitivity and the analysis of ideas. His capacity for stimulating a reconsideration of pressing questions within intellectual and aesthetic opinion is also extraordinary, and however much the appraisement may vary, it can never be denied that in his period he has been an eminent poser of questions, with a masterly gift for finding the apt wording, both in the language of poetry and in the defence of ideas in essay form.

Nor is it due only to chance that he has written one of the finest studies of Dante's work and personality. In his bitter moral pathos, in his metaphysical line of thought, and in his burning longing for a world order inspired by religion, a *civitas dei*, Eliot has indeed certain points of contact with the great Florentine poet. It redounds to his honour that, amidst the varied conditions of his milieu, he can be justly characterized as one of Dante's latest-born successors. In his message we hear solemn echoes from other times, but that message does not by any means therefore become less real when it is given to our own time and to us who are now living.

Mr. Eliot – According to the diploma, the award is made chiefly in appreciation of your remarkable achievements as a pioneer within modern poetry. I have here tried to give a brief survey of this very important work of yours which is admired by many ardent readers in this country.

Exactly twenty-five years ago, there stood where you are now standing another famous poet who wrote in the English tongue, William Butler Yeats. The honour now passes to you as being a leader and a champion of a new period in the long history of the world's poetry.

With the felicitations of the Swedish Academy, I now ask you to receive your Prize from the hands of His Royal Highness the Crown Prince.

Acceptance

When I began to think of what I should say to you this evening, I wished only to express very simply my appreciation of the high honour which the Swedish Academy has thought fit to confer upon me. But to do this adequately proved no simple task: my business is with words, yet the words were beyond my command. Merely to indicate that I was aware of having received the highest international honour that can be bestowed upon a man of letters, would be only to say what everyone knows already. To profess my own unworthiness would be to cast doubt upon the wisdom of the Academy; to praise the Academy might suggest that I, as a literary critic, approved the recognition given to myself as a poet. May I therefore ask that it be taken for granted, that I experienced, on learning of this award to myself, all the normal emotions of exaltation and vanity that any human being might be expected to feel at such a moment, with enjoyment of the flattery, and exasperation at the inconvenience, of being turned overnight into a public figure? Were the Nobel Award similar in kind to any other award, and merely higher in degree, I might still try to find words of appreciation: but since it is different in kind from any other, the expression of one's feelings calls for resources which language cannot supply.

I must therefore try to express myself in an indirect way, by putting before you my own interpretation of the significance of the Nobel Prize in Literature. If this were simply the recognition of merit, or of the fact that an author's reputation has passed the boundaries of his own country and his own language, we could say that hardly any one of us at any time is, more than others, worthy of being so distinguished. But I find in the Nobel Award something more and something different from such recognition. It seems to me more the election of an individual, chosen from time to time from one nation or another, and selected by something like an act of grace, to fill a peculiar role and to become a peculiar symbol. A ceremony takes place, by which a man is suddenly endowed with some function which he did not fill before. So the question is not whether he was worthy to be so singled out, but whether he can perform the function which you have assigned to him:

the function of serving as a representative, so far as any man can be, of some-thing of far greater importance than the value of what he himself has written.

Poetry is usually considered the most local of all the arts. Painting, sculp-ture, architecture, music, can be enjoyed by all who see or hear. But language, especially the language of poetry, is a different matter. Poetry, it might seem, separates peoples instead of uniting them.

But on the other hand we must remember, that while language constitutes a barrier, poetry itself gives us a reason for trying to overcome the barrier. To enjoy poetry belonging to another language, is to enjoy an understanding of the people to whom that language belongs, an understanding we can get in no other way. We may think also of the history of poetry in Europe, and of the great influence that the poetry of one language can exert on another; we must remember the immense debt of every considerable poet to poets of other languages than his own; we may reflect that the poetry of every coun-try and every language would decline and perish, were it not nourished by poetry in foreign tongues. When a poet speaks to his own people, the voices of all the poets of other languages who have influenced him are speaking also. And at the same time he himself is speaking to younger poets of other lan-guages, and these poets will convey something of *his* vision of life and some-thing of the spirit of *his* people, to their own. Partly through his influence on other poets, partly through translation, which must be also a kind of re-creation of his poems by other poets, partly through readers of his language who are not themselves poets, the poet can contribute toward understanding between peoples.

In the work of every poet there will certainly be much that can only appeal to those who inhabit the same region, or speak the same language, as the poet. But nevertheless there is a meaning to the phrase «the poetry of Europe», and even to the word «poetry» the world over. I think that in poetry people of different countries and different languages – though it be apparently only through a small minority in any one country – acquire an understanding of each other which, however partial, is still essential. And I take the award of the Nobel Prize in Literature, when it is given to a poet, to be primarily an assertion of the supra-national value of poetry. To make that affirmation, it is necessary from time to time to designate a poet: and I stand before you not on my own merits, but as a symbol, for a time, of the significance of poetry.

Prior to the acceptance, Gustaf Hellström of the Swedish Academy made these remarks: «Humility is also the characteristic which you, Mr. Eliot, have come to regard as man's virtue. ‹The only wisdom we can hope to acquire is the wisdom of humility.› At first it did not appear that this would be the final result of your visions and your acuity of thought. Born in the Middle West, where the pioneer mentality was still alive, brought up in Boston, the stronghold of Puritan tradition, you came to Europe in your youth and were there confronted with the pre-war type of civilization in the Old World: the Europe of Edward VII, Kaiser Wilhelm, the Third Republic, and *The Merry Widow*. This contact was a shock to you, the expression of which you brought to perfection in *The Waste Land*, in which the confusion and vulgarity of the civilization became the object of your scathing criticism. But beneath that criticism there lay profound and painful disillusionment, and out of this disillusionment there grew forth a feeling of sympathy, and out of that sympathy was born a growing urge to rescue from the ruins of the confusion the fragments from which order and stability might be restored. The position you have long held in modern literature provokes a comparison with that occupied by Sigmund Freud, a quarter of a century earlier, within the field of psychic medicine. If a comparison might be permitted, the novelty of the therapy which he introduced with psychoanalysis would match the revolutionary form in which you have clothed your message. But the path of comparison could be followed still further. For Freud the most profound cause of the confusion lay in the *Unbehagen in der Kultur* of modern man. In his opinion there must be sought a collective and individual balance, which should constantly take into account man's primitive instincts. You, Mr. Eliot, are of the opposite opinion. For you the salvation of man lies in the preservation of the cultural tradition, which, in our more mature years, lives with greater vigour within us than does primitiveness, and which we must preserve if chaos is to be avoided. Tradition is not a dead load which we drag along with us, and which in our youthful desire for freedom we seek to throw off. It is the soil in which the seeds of coming harvests are to be sown, and from which future harvests will be garnered. As a poet you have, Mr. Eliot, for decades, exercised a greater influence on your contemporaries and younger fellow writers than perhaps anyone else of our time.»

Biography

Thomas Stearns Eliot (1888–1965) was born in St. Louis, Missouri, of an old New England family. He was educated at Harvard and did graduate work in philosophy at the Sorbonne, Harvard, and Merton College, Oxford. He settled in England, where he was for a time a schoolmaster and a bank clerk, and eventually literary editor for the publishing house Faber & Faber, of which he later became a director. He founded and, during the seventeen years of its publication (1922–1939), edited the exclusive and influential literary journal *Criterion*. In 1927, Eliot became a British citizen and about the same time entered the Anglican Church.

Eliot has been one of the most daring innovators of twentieth-century poetry. Never compromising either with the public or indeed with language itself, he has followed his belief that poetry should aim at a representation of the complexities of modern civilization in language and that such representation necessarily leads to difficult poetry. Despite this difficulty his influence on modern poetic diction has been immense. Eliot's poetry from *Prufrock* (1917) to the *Four Quartets* (1943) reflects the development of a Christian writer: the early work, especially *The Waste Land* (1922), is essentially negative, the expression of that horror from which the search for a higher world arises. In *Ash Wednesday* (1930) and the *Four Quartets* this higher world becomes more visible; nonetheless Eliot has always taken care not to become a «religious poet» and often belittled the power of poetry as a religious force. However, his dramas *Murder in the Cathedral* (1935) and *The Family Reunion* (1939) are more openly Christian apologies. In his essays, especially the later ones, Eliot advocates a traditionalism in religion, society, and literature that seems at odds with his pioneer activity as a poet. But although the Eliot of *Notes towards the Definition of Culture* (1948) is an older man than the poet of *The Waste Land*, it should not be forgotten that for Eliot tradition is a living organism comprising past and present in constant mutual interaction. Eliot's plays *Murder in the Cathedral* (1935), *The Family Reunion* (1939), *The Cocktail Party* (1949), *The Confidential Clerk* (1954), and *The Elder Statesman* (1959) were published in one volume in 1962; *Collected Poems 1909–62* appeared in 1963.

Literature 1949

WILLIAM FAULKNER

(Prize awarded in 1950)

«for his powerful and artistically unique contribution to the modern American novel»

Presentation

by Gustaf Hellström, Member of the Swedish Academy

William Faulkner is essentially a regional writer, and as such reminds Swedish readers now and then of two of our own most important novelists, Selma Lagerlöf and Hjalmar Bergman. Faulkner's Värmland is the northern part of the state of Mississippi and his Vadköping is called Jefferson. The parallelism between him and our two fellow countrymen could be extended and deepened, but time does not allow such excursions now. The difference–the great difference–between him and them is that Faulkner's setting is so much darker and more bloody than that against which Lagerlöf's cavaliers and Bergman's bizarre figures lived. Faulkner is the great epic writer of the southern states with all their background: a glorious past built upon cheap Negro slave labour; a civil war and a defeat which destroyed the economic basis necessary for the then existing social structure; a long drawn-out and painful interim of resentment; and, finally, an industrial and commercial future whose mechanization and standardization of life are strange and hostile to the Southerner and to which he has only gradually been able and willing to adapt himself. Faulkner's novels are a continous and ever-deepening description of this painful process, which he knows intimately and feels intensely, coming as he does from a family which was forced to swallow the bitter fruits of defeat right down to their worm-eaten cores: impoverishment, decay, degeneration in its many varied forms. He has been called a reactionary. But even if this term is to some extent justified, it is balanced by the feeling of guilt which becomes clearer and clearer in the dark fabric at which he labours so untiringly. The price of the gentlemanly environment, the chivalry, the courage, and the often extreme individualism was inhumanity. Briefly, Faulkner's dilemma might be expressed thus: he mourns for and, as a writer, exaggerates a way of life which he himself, with his sense of justice and humanity, would never be able to stomach. It is this that makes his regionalism universal. Four bloody years of war brought about the changes in the social structure which it has taken the peoples of Europe, except the Russians, a century and a half to undergo.

It is against a background of war and violence that the fifty-two-year-old writer sets his more important novels. His grandfather held a high command during the Civil War. He himself grew up in the atmosphere created by warlike feats and by the bitterness and the poverty resulting from the never admitted defeat. When he was twenty he entered the Canadian Royal Air Force, crashed twice, and returned home, not as a military hero but as a physically and psychically war-damaged youth with dubious prospects, who for some years faced a precarious existence. He had joined the war because, as his *alter ego* expressed it in one of his early novels, «one doesn't want to waste a war». But out of the youth who once had been thirsting for sensation and battle, there gradually developed a man whose loathing of violence is expressed more and more passionately and might well be summed up by the fifth Commandment: Thou shalt not kill. On the other hand, there are things which man must always show himself unwilling to bear: «Some things», says one of his latest characters, «you must always be unable to bear. Injustice and outrage and dishonor and shame. Not for kudos and not for cash—Just refuse to bear them.» One might ask how these two maxims can be reconciled or how Faulkner himself envisages a reconciliation between them in times of international lawlessness. It is a question which he leaves open.

The fact is that, as a writer, Faulkner is no more interested in solving problems than he is tempted to indulge in sociological comments on the sudden changes in the economic position of the southern states. The defeat and the consequences of defeat are merely the soil out of which his epics grow. He is not fascinated by men as a community but by man in the community, the individual as a final unity in himself, curiously unmoved by external conditions. The tragedies of these individuals have nothing in common with Greek tragedy: they are led to their inexorable end by passions caused by inheritance, traditions, and environment, passions which are expressed either in a sudden outburst or in a slow liberation from perhaps generations-old restrictions. With almost every new work Faulkner penetrates deeper into the human psyche, into man's greatness and powers of self-sacrifice, lust for power, cupidity, spiritual poverty, narrow-mindedness, burlesque obstinacy, anguish, terror, and degenerate aberrations. As a probing psychologist he is the unrivalled master among all living British and American novelists. Neither do any of his colleagues possess his fantastic imaginative powers and his ability to create characters. His subhuman and superhuman figures, tragic or comic in a macabre way, emerge from his mind with a reality that few existing people—even those nearest to us—can give us, and they move in a milieu whose odours of subtropical plants, ladies' perfumes, Negro sweat, and the smell of horses and mules penetrate immediately even into a Scandinavian warm and cosy den. As a painter of landscapes he has the hunter's intimate knowledge of his own hunting-ground, the topographer's accuracy, and the impressionist's sensitivity. Moreover–side by side with Joyce and perhaps even more so–Faulkner is the great experimentalist among twentieth-century novelists. Scarcely two of his novels are similar technically. It seems as if by this continuous renewal he wanted to achieve the increased breadth which his limited world, both in geography and in subject matter, cannot give him. The same desire to experiment is shown in his mastery, unrivalled among modern British and American novelists, of the richness of the English language, a richness derived from its different linguistic elements and the periodic changes in style–from the spirit of the Elizabethans down to the scanty but expressive vocabulary of the Negroes of the southern states. Nor has anyone since Meredith–except perhaps Joyce–succeeded in framing sentences as infinite and powerful as Atlantic rollers. At the same time, few writers of his own age can rival him in giving a chain of events in a series of short sentences, each of which is like a blow of a hammer, driving the nail into the plank up to the head and securing it immovably. His perfect command over the resources of the language can–and often does–lead him to pile up words and associations which try the reader's patience in an exciting complicated story. But this profusion has nothing to do with literary flamboyance. Nor does it merely bear witness to the abounding agility of his imagination; in all their richness, every new attribute, every new association is intended to dig deeper into the reality which his imaginative power conjures up.

Faulkner has often been described as a determinist. He himself, however, has never claimed to adhere to any special philosophy of life. Briefly, his view of life may perhaps be summed up in his own words: that the whole thing (perhaps?) signifies nothing. If this were not the case, He or They who set up the whole fabric would have arranged things differently. And yet it must mean something, because man continues to struggle and must continue to struggle until, one day, it is all over. But Faulkner has one belief, or rather one hope: that every man sooner or later receives the punishment he deserves, and that self-sacrifice not only brings with it personal happiness but also adds to the sum total of the good deeds of mankind. It is a hope, the latter part of which reminds us of the firm conviction expressed by the Swedish poet Viktor Rydberg in the recitative of the Cantata presented at the Jubilee Degree Conferment at Uppsala in 1877.

Mr. Faulkner – The name of the southern state in which you were born and reared has long been well known to us Swedes, thanks to two of the closest and dearest friends of your boyhood, Tom Sawyer and Huckleberry Finn. Mark Twain put the Mississippi River on the literary map. Fifty years later you began a series of novels with which you created out of the state of Mississippi one of the landmarks of twentieth-century world literature; novels which with their ever-varying form, their ever-deeper and more intense psychological insight, and their monumental characters – both good and evil – occupy a unique place in modern American and British fiction.

Mr. Faulkner – It is now my privilige to ask you to receive from the hands of His Majesty the King the Nobel Prize in Literature, which the Swedish Academy has awarded you.

At the banquet, Robin Fåhraeus, Member of the Royal Academy of Sciences, addressed the American author: « Mr. William Faulkner – We heard with great pleasure that you were coming to our country to receive your Prize in person. We are indeed happy to greet you as an eminent artist, as a detached analyst of the human heart, as a great author who in a brilliant manner has enlarged man's knowledge of himself.»

Acceptance*

I feel that this award was not made to me as a man, but to my work – a life'
work in the agony and sweat of the human spirit, not for glory and least of
all for profit, but to create out of the materials of the human spirit something
which did not exist before. So this award is only mine in trust. It will not be
difficult to find a dedication for the money part of it commensurate with the
purpose and significance of its origin. But I would like to do the same with
the acclaim too, by using this moment as a pinnacle from which I might be
listened to by the young men and women already dedicated to the same
anguish and travail, among whom is already that one who will some day
stand here where I am standing.

Our tragedy today is a general and universal physical fear so long sustained
by now that we can even bear it. There are no longer problems of the spirit.
There is only the question: When will I be blown up? Because of this, the
young man or woman writing today has forgotten the problems of the human heart in conflict with itself which alone can make good writing because
only that is worth writing about, worth the agony and the sweat.

He must learn them again. He must teach himself that the basest of all
things is to be afraid; and, teaching himself that, forget it forever, leaving no
room in his workshop for anything but the old verities and truths of the
heart, the old universal truths lacking which any story is ephemeral and
doomed – love and honor and pity and pride and compassion and sacrifice.
Until he does so, he labors under a curse. He writes not of love but of lust, of
defeats in which nobody loses anything of value, of victories without hope
and, worst of all, without pity or compassion. His griefs grieve on no universal bones, leaving no scars. He writes not of the heart but of the glands.

Until he relearns these things, he will write as though he stood among and
watched the end of man. I decline to accept the end of man. It is easy enough

* The acceptance speech was apparently revised by the author for publication in *Th
Faulkner Reader*. These minor changes, all of which improve the address stylistically
have been incorporated here.

say that man is immortal simply because he will endure: that when the
st dingdong of doom has clanged and faded from the last worthless rock
anging tideless in the last red and dying evening, that even then there will
ill be one more sound: that of his puny inexhaustible voice, still talking. I
fuse to accept this. I believe that man will not merely endure: he will
revail. He is immortal, not because he alone among creatures has an inex-
austible voice, but because he has a soul, a spirit capable of compassion and
crifice and endurance. The poet's, the writer's, duty is to write about these
ings. It is his privilege to help man endure by lifting his heart, by reminding
im of the courage and honor and hope and pride and compassion and pity
d sacrifice which have been the glory of his past. The poet's voice need not
erely be the record of man, it can be one of the props, the pillars to help
im endure and prevail.

Biography

William Faulkner (1897–1962), who came from an old southern family grew up in Oxford, Mississippi. He joined the Canadian, and later the British, Royal Air Force during the First World War, studied for a while at the University of Mississippi, and temporarily worked for a New York bookstore and a New Orleans newspaper. Except for some trips to Europe and Asia, and a few brief stays in Hollywood as a scriptwriter, he worked on his novels and short stories on a farm in Oxford.

In an attempt to create a saga of his own, Faulkner has invented a host of characters typical of the historical growth and subsequent decadence of the South. The human drama in Faulkner's novels is then built on the model of the actual, historical drama extending over almost a century and a half. Each story and each novel contributes to the construction of a whole, which is the imaginary Yoknapatawpha County and its inhabitants. Their theme is the decay of the old South, as represented by the Sartoris and Compson families, and the emergence of ruthless and brash newcomers, the Snopeses. Theme and technique–the distortion of time through the use of the inner monologue–are fused particularly successfully in *The Sound and the Fury* (1929), the downfall of the Compson family seen through the minds of several characters. The novel *Sanctuary* (1931) is about the degeneration of Temple Drake, a young girl from a distinguished southern family. Its sequel, *Requiem For A Nun* (1951), written partly as a drama, centered on the courtroom trial of a Negro woman who had once been a party to Temple Drake's debauchery. In *Light in August* (1932), prejudice is shown to be most destructive when it is internalized, as in Joe Christmas, who believes, though there is no proof of it, that one of his parents was a Negro. The theme of racial prejudice is brought up again in *Absalom, Absalom!* (1936), in which a young man is rejected by his father and brother because of his mixed blood. Faulkner's most outspoken moral evaluation of the relationship and the problems between Negroes and whites is to be found in *Intruder In the Dust* (1948).

In 1940, Faulkner published the first volume of the Snopes trilogy, *The Hamlet*, to be followed by two volumes, *The Town* (1957) and *The Mansion*

1959), all of them tracing the rise of the insidious Snopes family to positions of power and wealth in the community. *The Reivers*, his last—and most humorous—work, with a great many similarities to Mark Twain's *Huckleberry Finn*, appeared in 1962, the year of Faulkner's death.

Literature 1950

Earl BERTRAND ARTHUR WILLIAM RUSSELL

«*in recognition of his varied and significant writings, in which he champion humanitarian ideals and freedom of thought*»

Presentation

by Anders Österling, Permanent Secretary of the Swedish Academy

he great work on Western philosophy which Bertrand Russell brought out
1946, that is, at the age of seventy-four, contains numerous characteristic
eflections giving us an idea of how he himself might like us to regard his
ong and arduous life. In one place, speaking of the pre-Socratic philosophers,
e says, «In studying a philosopher, the right attitude is neither reverence
or contempt, but first a kind of hypothetical sympathy, until it is possible to
now what it feels like to believe in his theories, and only then a revival of
he critical attitude, which should resemble, as far as possible, the state of
mind of a person abandoning opinions which he has hitherto held.»

And in another place in the same work he writes, «It is not good either to
orget the questions that philosophy asks, or to persuade ourselves that we
ave found indubitable answers to them. To teach how to live without cer-
ainty, and yet without being paralyzed by hesitation, is perhaps the chief
hing that philosophy, in our age, can still do for those who study it.»

With his superior intellect, Russell has, throughout half a century, been at
he centre of public debate, watchful and always ready for battle, as active as
ver to this very day, having behind him a life of writing of most imposing
cope. His works in the sciences concerned with human knowledge and
mathematical logic are epoch-making and have been compared to Newton's
undamental results in mechanics. Yet it is not these achievements in special
ranches of science that the Nobel Prize is primarily meant to recognize. What
important, from our point of view, is that Russell has so extensively ad-
ressed his books to a public of laymen, and, in doing so, has been so eminent-
y successful in keeping alive the interest in general philosophy.

His whole life's work is a stimulating defence of the reality of common
ense. As a philosopher he pursues the line from the classical English em-
iricism, from Locke and Hume. His attitude toward the idealistic dogmas
a most independent one and quite frequently one of opposition. The great
hilosophical systems evolved on the Continent he regards, so to speak, from
he chilly, windswept, and distinctive perspective of the English Channel.
With his keen and sound good sense, his clear style, and his wit in the midst

of seriousness, he has in his work evinced those characteristics which are found among only the elite of authors. Time does not permit even the briefest survey of his works in this area, which are fascinating also from a purely literary point of view. It may suffice to mention such books as the *History of Western Philosophy* (1946), *Human Knowledge* (1948), *Sceptical Essays* (1948), and the sketch «My Mental Development» (in *The Philosophy of Bertrand Russell*, 1951); but to these should be added a great number of equally important books on practically all the problems which the present development of society involves.

Russell's views and opinions have been influenced by varied factors and cannot easily be summarized. His famous family typifies the Whig tradition in English politics. His grandfather was the Victorian statesman, John Russell. Familiar from an early age with the ideas of Liberalism, he was soon confronted by the problems of rising socialism and since then he has, as an independent critic, weighed the advantages and disadvantages of this form of society. He has consistently and earnestly warned us of the dangers of the new bureaucracy. He has defended the right of the individual against collectivism, and he views industrial civilization as a growing threat to humanity's chances of simple happiness and joy in living. After his visit to the Soviet Union in 1920 he strongly and resolutely opposed himself to Communism. On the other hand, during a subsequent journey in China, he was very much attracted by the calm and peaceable frame of mind of China's cultivated classes and recommended it as an example to a West ravaged by wild aggression.

Much in Russell's writings excites protest. Unlike many other philosophers, he regards this as one of the natural and urgent tasks of an author. Of course, his rationalism does not solve all troublesome problems and cannot be used as a panacea, even if the philosopher willingly writes out the prescription. Unfortunately, there are–and obviously always will be–obscure forces which evade intellectual analysis and refuse to submit to control. Thus even if Russell's work has, from a purely practical point of view, met with but little success in an age which has seen two world wars – even if it may look as if, in the main, his ideas have been bitterly repudiated – we must nevertheless admire the unwavering valour of this rebellious teller of the truth and the sort of dry, fiery strength and gay buoyancy with which he presents his convictions, which are never dictated by opportunism but are often directly unpopular. To read the philosopher Russell often gives very much the same pleasure as to listen to the outspoken hero in a Shaw comedy when in loud and cheerful tones he throws out his bold retorts and keen arguments.

In conclusion, Russell's philosophy may be said in the best sense to fulfil just those desires and intentions that Alfred Nobel had in mind when he instituted his Prizes. There are quite striking similarities between their outlooks on life. Both of them are at the same time sceptics and utopians, both take a gloomy view of the contemporary world, yet both hold fast to a belief in the possibility of achieving logical standards for human behaviour. The Swedish Academy believes that it acts in the spirit of Nobel's intention when, on the occasion of the fiftieth anniversary of the Foundation, it wishes to honour Bertrand Russell as one of our time's brilliant spokesmen of rationality and humanity, as a fearless champion of free speech and free thought in the West.

My lord – Exactly two hundred years ago Jean Jacques Rousseau was awarded the prize offered by the Academy of Dijon for his famous answer to the question of «whether the arts and sciences have contributed to improve morals». Rousseau answered «No», and this answer–which may not have been a very serious one–in any case had most serious consequences. The Academy of Dijon had no revolutionary aims. This is true also of the Swedish Academy, which has now chosen to reward you for your philosophical works just because they are undoubtedly of service to moral civilization and, in addition, most eminently answer to the spirit of Nobel's intentions. We honour you as a brilliant champion of humanity and free thought, and it is a pleasure for us to see you here on the occasion of the fiftieth anniversary of the Nobel Foundation. With these words I request you to receive from the hands of His Majesty the King the Nobel Prize in Literature for 1950.

At the banquet, Robin Fåhraeus, Member of the Royal Academy of Sciences, made the following comment: «Dear Professor Bertrand Russell–We salute you as one of the greatest and most influential thinkers of our age, endowed with just those four characteristics which on another occasion you have regarded to be the criteria of prominent fellow men; namely, vitality, courage, receptivity, and intelligence.»

BERTRAND RUSSELL

What Desires Are Politically Important?

Nobel Lecture, December 11, 1950

I have chosen this subject for my lecture tonight because I think that most
current discussions of politics and political theory take insufficient account of
psychology. Economic facts, population statistics, constitutional organization, and so on, are set forth minutely. There is no difficulty in finding out
how many South Koreans and how many North Koreans there were when
the Korean War began. If you will look into the right books you will be able
to ascertain what was their average income per head, and what were the sizes
of their respective armies. But if you want to know what sort of person a
Korean is, and whether there is any appreciable difference between a North
Korean and a South Korean; if you wish to know what they respectively
want out of life, what are their discontents, what their hopes and what their
fears; in a word, what it is that, as they say, «makes them tick», you will look
through the reference books in vain. And so you cannot tell whether the
South Koreans are enthusiastic about UNO, or would prefer union with
their cousins in the North. Nor can you guess whether they are willing to
forgo land reform for the privilege of voting for some politician they have
never heard of. It is neglect of such questions by the eminent men who sit in
remote capitals, that so frequently causes disappointment. If politics is to become scientific, and if the event is not to be constantly surprising, it is imperative that our political thinking should penetrate more deeply into the springs
of human action. What is the influence of hunger upon slogans? How does
their effectiveness fluctuate with the number of calories in your diet? If one
man offers you democracy and another offers you a bag of grain, at what
stage of starvation will you prefer the grain to the vote? Such questions are
far too little considered. However, let us, for the present, forget the Koreans
and consider the human race.

All human activity is prompted by desire. There is a wholly fallacious
theory advanced by some earnest moralists to the effect that it is possible to
resist desire in the interests of duty and moral principle. I say this is fallacious,
not because no man ever acts from a sense of duty, but because duty has no
hold on him unless he desires to be dutiful. If you wish to know what men

will do, you must know not only, or principally, their material circumstances, but rather the whole system of their desires with their relative strengths.

There are some desires which, though very powerful, have not, as a rule, any great political importance. Most men at some period of their lives desire to marry, but as a rule they can satisfy this desire without having to take any political action. There are, of course, exceptions; the rape of the Sabine women is a case in point. And the development of northern Australia is seriously impeded by the fact that the vigorous young men who ought to do the work dislike being wholly deprived of female society. But such cases are unusual, and in general the interest that men and women take in each other has little influence upon politics.

The desires that are politically important may be divided into a primary and a secondary group. In the primary group come the necessities of life: food and shelter and clothing. When these things become very scarce, there is no limit to the efforts that men will make, or to the violence that they will display, in the hope of securing them. It is said by students of the earliest history that, on four separate occasions, drought in Arabia caused the population of that country to overflow into surrounding regions, with immense effects, political, cultural, and religious. The last of these four occasions was the rise of Islam. The gradual spread of Germanic tribes from southern Russia to England, and thence to San Francisco, had similar motives. Undoubtedly the desire for food has been, and still is, one of the main causes of great political events.

But man differs from other animals in one very important respect, and that is that he has some desires which are, so to speak, infinite, which can never be fully gratified, and which would keep him restless even in Paradise. The boa constrictor, when he has had an adequate meal, goes to sleep, and does not wake until he needs another meal. Human beings, for the most part, are not like this. When the Arabs, who had been used to living sparingly on a few dates, acquired the riches of the Eastern Roman Empire, and dwelt in palaces of almost unbelievable luxury, they did not, on that account, become inactive. Hunger could no longer be a motive, for Greek slaves supplied them with exquisite viands at the slightest nod. But other desires kept them active: four in particular, which we can label acquisitiveness, rivalry, vanity, and love of power.

Acquisitiveness–the wish to possess as much as possible of goods, or the title to goods–is a motive which, I suppose, has its origin in a combination of fear with the desire for necessaries. I once befriended two little girls from

Estonia, who had narrowly escaped death from starvation in a famine. They lived in my family, and of course had plenty to eat. But they spent all their leisure visiting neighbouring farms and stealing potatoes, which they hoarded. Rockefeller, who in his infancy had experienced great poverty, spent his adult life in a similar manner. Similarly the Arab chieftains on their silken Byzantine divans could not forget the desert, and hoarded riches far beyond any possible physical need. But whatever may be the psychoanalysis of acquisitiveness, no one can deny that it is one of the great motives–especially among the more powerful, for, as I said before, it is one of the infinite motives. However much you may acquire, you will always wish to acquire more; satiety is a dream which will always elude you.

But acquisitiveness, although it is the mainspring of the capitalist system, is by no means the most powerful of the motives that survive the conquest of hunger. Rivalry is a much stronger motive. Over and over again in Mohammedan history, dynasties have come to grief because the sons of a sultan by different mothers could not agree, and in the resulting civil war universal ruin resulted. The same sort of thing happens in modern Europe. When the British Government very unwisely allowed the Kaiser to be present at a naval review at Spithead, the thought which arose in his mind was not the one which we had intended. What he thought was, «I must have a Navy as good as Grandmamma's.» And from this thought have sprung all our subsequent troubles. The world would be a happier place than it is if acquisitiveness were always stronger than rivalry. But in fact, a great many men will cheerfully face impoverishment if they can thereby secure complete ruin for their rivals. Hence the present level of taxation.

Vanity is a motive of immense potency. Anyone who has much to do with children knows how they are constantly performing some antic, and saying «Look at me». «Look at me» is one of the most fundamental desires of the human heart. It can take innumerable forms, from buffoonery to the pursuit of posthumous fame. There was a Renaissance Italian princeling who was asked by the priest on his deathbed if he had anything to repent of. «Yes», he said, «there is one thing. On one occasion I had a visit from the Emperor and the Pope simultaneously. I took them to the top of my tower to see the view, and I neglected the opportunity to throw them both down, which would have given me immortal fame.» History does not relate whether the priest gave him absolution. One of the troubles about vanity is that it grows with what it feeds on. The more you are talked about, the more you will wish to be talked about. The condemned murderer who is allowed to see the account of his trial in the press is indignant if he finds a newspaper which has reported it inadequately. And the more he finds about himself in other newspapers, the more indignant he will be with the one whose reports are meagre. Politicians and literary men are in the same case. And the more famous they become, the more difficult the press-cutting agency finds it to satisfy them. It is scarcely possible to exaggerate the influence of vanity throughout the range of human life, from the child of three to the potentate at whose frown the world trembles. Mankind have even committed the impiety of attributing similar desires to the Deity, whom they imagine avid for continual praise.

But great as is the influence of the motives we have been considering, there is one which outweighs them all. I mean the love of power. Love of power is closely akin to vanity, but it is not by any means the same thing. What vanity needs for its satisfaction is glory, and it is easy to have glory without power. The people who enjoy the greatest glory in the United States are film stars, but they can be put in their place by the Committee for Un-American Activities, which enjoys no glory whatever. In England, the King has more glory than the Prime Minister, but the Prime Minister has more power than the King. Many people prefer glory to power, but on the whole these people have less effect upon the course of events than those who prefer power to glory. When Blücher, in 1814, saw Napoleon's palaces, he said, «Wasn't he a fool to have all this and to go running after Moscow.» Napoleon, who certainly was not destitute of vanity, preferred power when he had to choose. To Blücher, this choice seemed foolish. Power, like vanity, is insatiable. Nothing short of omnipotence could satisfy it completely. And as it is especially the vice of energetic men, the causal efficacy of love of power is out of all proportion to its frequency. It is, indeed, by far the strongest motive in the lives of important men.

Love of power is greatly increased by the experience of power, and this applies to petty power as well as to that of potentates. In the happy days before 1914, when well-to-do ladies could acquire a host of servants, their pleasure in exercising power over the domestics steadily increased with age. Similarly, in any autocratic regime, the holders of power become increasingly tyrannical with experience of the delights that power can afford. Since power over human beings is shown in making them do what they would rather not do, the man who is actuated by love of power is more apt to inflict pain than to permit pleasure. If you ask your boss for leave of absence from the office on some legitimate occasion, his love of power will derive more satisfaction from a refusal than from a consent. If you require a building permit, the petty official concerned will obviously get more pleasure from saying «No» than from saying «Yes». It is this sort of thing which makes the love of power such a dangerous motive.

But it has other sides which are more desirable. The pursuit of knowledge is, I think, mainly actuated by love of power. And so are all advances in scientific technique. In politics, also, a reformer may have just as strong a love of power as a despot. It would be a complete mistake to decry love of power altogether as a motive. Whether you will be led by this motive to actions which are useful, or to actions which are pernicious, depends upon the social system, and upon your capacities. If your capacities are theoretical or technical, you will contribute to knowledge or technique, and, as a rule, your activity will be useful. If you are a politician you may be actuated by love of power, but as a rule this motive will join itself on to the desire to see some state of affairs realized which, for some reason, you prefer to the status quo. A great general may, like Alcibiades, be quite indifferent as to which side he fights on, but most generals have preferred to fight for their own country, and have, therefore, had other motives besides love of power. The politician may change sides so frequently as to find himself always in the majority, but most politicians have a preference for one party to the other, and subordinate their love of power to this preference. Love of power as nearly pure as possible is to be seen in various different types of men. One type is the soldier of fortune, of whom Napoleon is the supreme example. Napoleon had, I think, no ideological preference for France over Corsica, but if he had become Emperor of Corsica he would not have been so great a man as he became by pretending to be a Frenchman. Such men, however, are not quite pure examples, since they also derive immense satisfaction from vanity. The purest type is that of the *eminence grise* – the power behind the throne that never appears in public, and merely hugs itself with the secret thought: «How little these puppets know who is pulling the strings.» Baron Holstein, who controlled the foreign policy of the German Empire from 1890 to 1906, illustrates this type to perfection. He lived in a slum; he never appeared in society; he avoided meeting the Emperor, except on one single occasion when the Emperor's importunity could not be resisted; he refused all invitations to Court functions, on the ground that he possessed no court dress. He had acquired secrets which enabled him to blackmail the Chancellor and many of the Kaiser's intimates. He used the power of blackmail, not to acquire wealth, or fame, or any other obvious advantage, but merely to compel the adoption of the foreign policy he preferred. In the East, similar characters were not very uncommon among eunuchs.

I come now to other motives which, though in a sense less fundamental than those we have been considering, are still of considerable importance. The first of these is love of excitement. Human beings show their superiority to the brutes by their capacity for boredom, though I have sometimes thought, in examining the apes at the zoo, that they, perhaps, have the rudiments of this tiresome emotion. However that may be, experience shows that escape from boredom is one of the really powerful desires of almost all human beings. When white men first effect contact with some unspoilt race of savages, they offer them all kinds of benefits, from the light of the gospel to pumpkin pie. These, however, much as we may regret it, most savages receive with indifference. What they really value among the gifts that we bring to them is intoxicating liquor which enables them, for the first time in their lives, to have the illusion for a few brief moments that it is better to be alive than dead. Red Indians, while they were still unaffected by white men, would smoke their pipes, not calmly as we do, but orgiastically, inhaling so deeply that they sank into a faint. And when excitement by means of nicotine failed, a patriotic orator would stir them up to attack a neighbouring tribe, which would give them all the enjoyment that we (according to our temperament) derive from a horse race or a General Election. The pleasure of gambling consists almost entirely in excitement. Monsieur Huc describes Chinese traders at the Great Wall in winter, gambling until they have lost all their cash, then proceeding to lose all their merchandise, and at last gambling away their clothes and going out naked to die of cold. With civilized men, as with primitive Red Indian tribes, it is, I think, chiefly love of excitement which makes the populace applaud when war breaks out; the emotion is exactly the same as at a football match, although the results are sometimes somewhat more serious.

It is not altogether easy to decide what is the root cause of the love of excitement. I incline to think that our mental make-up is adapted to the stage when men lived by hunting. When a man spent a long day with very primitive weapons in stalking a deer with the hope of dinner, and when, at the end of the day, he dragged the carcass triumphantly to his cave, he sank down in contented weariness, while his wife dressed and cooked the meat. He was sleepy, and his bones ached, and the smell of cooking filled every nook and cranny of his consciousness. At last, after eating, he sank into deep sleep. In such a life there was neither time nor energy for boredom. But when he took to agriculture, and made his wife do all the heavy work in the fields, he had time to reflect upon the vanity of human life, to invent mythologies and systems of philosophy, and to dream of the life hereafter in which he would perpetually hunt the wild boar of Valhalla. Our mental make-up is suited to a life of very severe physical labor. I used, when I was younger, to take my holidays walking. I would cover twenty-five miles a day, and when the evening came I had no need of anything to keep me from boredom, since the delight of sitting amply sufficed. But modern life cannot be conducted on these physically strenuous principles. A great deal of work is sedentary, and most manual work exercises only a few specialized muscles. When crowds assemble in Trafalgar Square to cheer to the echo an announcement that the government has decided to have them killed, they would not do so if they had all walked twenty-five miles that day. This cure for bellicosity is, however, impracticable, and if the human race is to survive – a thing which is, perhaps, undesirable – other means must be found for securing an innocent outlet for the unused physical energy that produces love of excitement. This is a matter which has been too little considered, both by moralists and by social reformers. The social reformers are of the opinion that they have more serious things to consider. The moralists, on the other hand, are immensely impressed with the seriousness of all the permitted outlets of the love of excitement; the seriousness, however, in their minds, is that of Sin. Dance halls, cinemas, this age of jazz, are all, if we may believe our ears, gateways to Hell, and we should be better employed sitting at home contemplating our sins. I find myself unable to be in entire agreement with the grave men who utter these warnings. The devil has many forms, some designed to deceive the young, some designed to deceive the old and serious. If it is the devil that tempts the young to enjoy themselves, is it not, perhaps, the same personage that persuades the old to condemn their enjoyment? And is not condemnation perhaps merely a form of excitement appropriate to old age? And is it not, perhaps, a drug which – like opium – has to be taken in continually stronger doses to produce the desired effect? Is it not to be feared that, beginning with the wickedness of the cinema, we should be led step by step to condemn the opposite political party, dagoes, wops, Asiatics, and, in short, everybody except the fellow members of our club? And it is from just such condemnations, when widespread, that wars proceed. I have never heard of a war that proceeded from dance halls.

What is serious about excitement is that so many of its forms are destructive. It is destructive in those who cannot resist excess in alcohol or gambling

It is destructive when it takes the form of mob violence. And above all it is destructive when it leads to war. It is so deep a need that it will find harmful outlets of this kind unless innocent outlets are at hand. There are such innocent outlets at present in sport, and in politics so long as it is kept within constitutional bounds. But these are not sufficient, especially as the kind of politics that is most exciting is also the kind that does most harm. Civilized life has grown altogether too tame, and, if it is to be stable, it must provide harmless outlets for the impulses which our remote ancestors satisfied in hunting. In Australia, where people are few and rabbits are many, I watched a whole populace satisfying the primitive impulse in the primitive manner by the skillful slaughter of many thousands of rabbits. But in London or New York some other means must be found to gratify primitive impulse. I think every big town should contain artificial waterfalls that people could descend in very fragile canoes, and they should contain bathing pools full of mechanical sharks. Any person found advocating a preventive war should be condemned to two hours a day with these ingenious monsters. More seriously, pains should be taken to provide constructive outlets for the love of excitement. Nothing in the world is more exciting than a moment of sudden discovery or invention, and many more people are capable of experiencing such moments than is sometimes thought.

Interwoven with many other political motives are two closely related passions to which human beings are regrettably prone: I mean fear and hate. It is normal to hate what we fear, and it happens frequently, though not always, that we fear what we hate. I think it may be taken as the rule among primitive men, that they both fear and hate whatever is unfamiliar. They have their own herd, originally a very small one. And within one herd, all are friends, unless there is some special ground of enmity. Other herds are potential or actual enemies; a single member of one of them who strays by accident will be killed. An alien herd as a whole will be avoided or fought according to circumstances. It is this primitive mechanism which still controls our instinctive reaction to foreign nations. The completely untravelled person will view all foreigners as the savage regards a member of another herd. But the man who has travelled, or who has studied international politics, will have discovered that, if his herd is to prosper, it must, to some degree, become amalgamated with other herds. If you are English and someone says to you, «The French are your brothers», your first instinctive feeling will be, «Nonsense. They shrug their shoulders, and talk French. And I am even told that they eat frogs.» If he explains to you that we may have to fight the Russians, that, if so, it will be desirable to defend the line of the Rhine, and that, if the line of the Rhine is to be defended, the help of the French is essential, you will begin to see what he means when he says that the French are your brothers. But if some fellow-traveller were to go on to say that the Russians also are your brothers, he would be unable to persuade you, unless he could show that we are in danger from the Martians. We love those who hate our enemies, and if we had no enemies there would be very few people whom we should love.

All this, however, is only true so long as we are concerned solely with attitudes towards other human beings. You might regard the soil as your enemy because it yields reluctantly a niggardly subsistence. You might regard Mother Nature in general as your enemy, and envisage human life as a struggle to get the better of Mother Nature. If men viewed life in this way, co-operation of the whole human race would become easy. And men could easily be brought to view life in this way if schools, newspapers, and politicians devoted themselves to this end. But schools are out to teach patriotism; newspapers are out to stir up excitement; and politicians are out to get re-elected. None of the three, therefore, can do anything towards saving the human race from reciprocal suicide.

There are two ways of coping with fear: one is to diminish the external danger, and the other is to cultivate Stoic endurance. The latter can be reinforced, except where immediate action is necessary, by turning our thoughts away from the cause of fear. The conquest of fear is of very great importance. Fear is in itself degrading; it easily becomes an obsession; it produces hate of that which is feared, and it leads headlong to excesses of cruelty. Nothing has so beneficent an effect on human beings as security. If an international system could be established which would remove the fear of war, the improvement in everyday mentality of everyday people would be enormous and very rapid. Fear, at present, overshadows the world. The atom bomb and the bacterial bomb, wielded by the wicked communist or the wicked capitalist as the case may be, make Washington and the Kremlin tremble, and drive men further along the road toward the abyss. If matters are to improve, the first and essential step is to find a way of diminishing fear. The world at present is obsessed by the conflict of rival ideologies, and one of the apparent causes of conflict is the desire for the victory of our own ideology and the defeat of the other. I do not think that the fundamental motive here has much to do with ideologies. I think the ideologies are merely a way of grouping people, and that the passions involved are merely those which always arise between rival groups. There are, of course, various reasons for hating communists. First and foremost, we believe that they wish to take away our property. But so do burglars, and although we disapprove of burglars our attitude towards them is very different indeed from our attitude towards communists–chiefly because they do not inspire the same degree of fear. Secondly, we hate the communists because they are irreligious. But the Chinese have been irreligious since the eleventh century, and we only began to hate them when they turned out Chiang Kai-shek. Thirdly, we hate the communists because they do not believe in democracy, but we consider this no reason for hating Franco. Fourthly, we hate them because they do not allow liberty; this we feel so strongly that we have decided to imitate them. It is obvious that none of these is the real ground for our hatred. We hate them because we fear them and they threaten us. If the Russians still adhered to the Greek Orthodox religion, if they had instituted parliamentary government, and if they had a completely free press which daily vituperated us, then–provided they still had armed forces as powerful as they have now–we should still hate them if they gave us ground for thinking them hostile. There is, of course, the *odium theologicum*, and it can be a cause of enmity. But I think that this is an offshoot of herd feeling: the man who has a different theology feels strange, and whatever is strange must be dangerous. Ideologies, in fact, are one of the methods by which herds are created, and the psychology is much the same however the herd may have been generated.

You may have been feeling that I have allowed only for bad motives, or, at best, such as are ethically neutral. I am afraid they are, as a rule, more powerful than more altruistic motives, but I do not deny that altruistic motives exist, and may, on occasion, be effective. The agitation against slavery in England in the early nineteenth century was indubitably altruistic, and was thoroughly effective. Its altruism was proved by the fact that in 1833 British taxpayers paid many millions in compensation to Jamaican landowners for the liberation of their slaves, and also by the fact that at the Congress of Vienna the British Government was prepared to make important concessions with a view to inducing other nations to abandon the slave trade. This is an instance from the past, but present-day America has afforded instances equally remarkable. I will not, however, go into these, as I do not wish to become embarked in current controversies.

I do not think it can be questioned that sympathy is a genuine motive, and that some people at some times are made somewhat uncomfortable by the sufferings of some other people. It is sympathy that has produced the many humanitarian advances of the last hundred years. We are shocked when we hear stories of the ill-treatment of lunatics, and there are now quite a number of asylums in which they are not ill-treated. Prisoners in Western countries are not supposed to be tortured, and when they are, there is an outcry if the facts are discovered. We do not approve of treating orphans as they are treated in *Oliver Twist*. Protestant countries disapprove of cruelty to animals. In all these ways sympathy has been politically effective. If the fear of war were removed, its effectiveness would become much greater. Perhaps the best hope for the future of mankind is that ways will be found of increasing the scope and intensity of sympathy.

The time has come to sum up our discussion. Politics is concerned with herds rather than with individuals, and the passions which are important in politics are, therefore, those in which the various members of a given herd can feel alike. The broad instinctive mechanism upon which political edifices have to be built is one of co-operation within the herd and hostility towards other herds. The co-operation within the herd is never perfect. There are members who do not conform, who are, in the etymological sense, «egregious», that is to say, outside the flock. These members are those who have fallen below, or risen above, the ordinary level. They are: idiots, criminals, prophets, and discoverers. A wise herd will learn to tolerate the eccentricity of those who rise above the average, and to treat with a minimum of ferocity those who fall below it.

As regards relations to other herds, modern technique has produced a conflict between self-interest and instinct. In old days, when two tribes went to war, one of them exterminated the other, and annexed its territory. From the point of view of the victor, the whole operation was thoroughly satisfactory. The killing was not at all expensive, and the excitement was agreeable. It is not to be wondered at that, in such circumstances, war persisted. Unfortunately, we still have the emotions appropriate to such primitive warfare, while the actual operations of war have changed completely. Killing an enemy in a modern war is a very expensive operation. If you consider how many Germans were killed in the late war, and how much the victors are paying in income tax, you can, by a sum in long division, discover the cost of a dead German, and you will find it considerable. In the East, it is true, the enemies of the Germans have secured the ancient advantages of turning out the defeated population and occupying their lands. The Western victors, however, have secured no such advantages. It is obvious that modern war is not good business from a financial point of view. Although we won both the world vars, we should now be much richer if they had not occurred. If men were ctuated by self-interest, which they are not – except in the case of a few aints – the whole human race would co-operate. There would be no more vars, no more armies, no more navies, no more atom bombs. There would ot be armies of propagandists employed in poisoning the minds of Nation A gainst Nation B, and reciprocally of Nation B against Nation A. There vould not be armies of officials at frontiers to prevent the entry of foreign ooks and foreign ideas, however excellent in themselves. There would not e customs barriers to ensure the existence of many small enterprises where ne big enterprise would be more economic. All this would happen very quickly if men desired their own happiness as ardently as they desired the nisery of their neighbours. But, you will tell me, what is the use of these itopian dreams? Moralists will see to it that we do not become wholly selfish, nd until we do the millenium will be impossible.

I do not wish to seem to end upon a note of cynicism. I do not deny that here are better things than selfishness, and that some people achieve these hings. I maintain, however, on the one hand, that there are few occasions ipon which large bodies of men, such as politics is concerned with, can rise bove selfishness, while, on the other hand, there are a very great many cir- cumstances in which populations will fall below selfishness, if selfishness is in- erpreted as enlightened self-interest.

And among those occasions on which people fall below self-interest are most of the occasions on which they are convinced that they are acting from dealistic motives. Much that passes as idealism is disguised hatred or disguised love of power. When you see large masses of men swayed by what appear to be noble motives, it is as well to look below the surface and ask yourself what it is that makes these motives effective. It is partly because it is so easy to be taken in by a façade of nobility that a psychological inquiry, such as I have been attempting, is worth making. I would say, in conclusion, that if what I have said is right, the main thing needed to make the world happy is intel- ligence. And this, after all, is an optimistic conclusion, because intelligence is a thing that can be fostered by known methods of education.

Biography

Bertrand Russell (1872–) was born in Trelleck, Wales. His parents died when he was three years old. He was educated privately and went to Trinity College, Cambridge, where he was a brilliant student of mathematics and philosophy. In 1900, Russell became acquainted with the work of the Italian mathematician Peano, which inspired him to write *The Principles of Mathematics* (1903), expanded in collaboration with Alfred North Whitehead into three volumes of *Principia Mathematica* (1910–13). The research, which Russell did during this period together with Whitehead and which is preserved in many books and essays, establishes him as one of the founding fathers of modern analytical philosophy. Throughout his life Russell has also been an extremely outspoken and aggressive moralist in the rationalist tradition of Locke and Hume. His many essays, often in the form of short reflections or observations on moral or psychological topics, are written in a terse, vivid, and provocative style. His greatest literary achievement has been his *History of Western Philosophy* (1946).

Russell's external career has been chequered. The descendant of one of the great families of the Whig aristocracy, he has always delighted in standing up for his radical convictions with wilful stubbornness. In 1916, he was deprived of his lectureship at Trinity College, Cambridge, after his pacifist activities had brought him into conflict with the government, but in 1946 he was re-elected a Fellow. In 1918, he even went to prison for six months, where he wrote his *Introduction to Mathematical Philosophy* (1919). In 1920, Russell travelled in Russia and, subsequently, taught philosophy at Peking for a year. He went to the United States in 1938 and taught there for several years at various universities. Lord Russell has been a Fellow of the Royal Society since 1908; he succeeded to the earldom in 1931 and, in 1949, received the Order of Merit.

In recent years Lord Russell has been active in political organizations such as the Campaign for Nuclear Disarmament and other groups with similar aims. The first two volumes of his autobiography, covering the years from 1872 to 1944, appeared in 1967 and 1968, respectively.

Literature 1951

PÄR FABIAN LAGERKVIST

«for the artistic vigour and true independence of mind with which he endeavours in his poetry to find answers to the eternal questions confronting mankind»

Presentation

by Anders Österling, Permanent Secretary of the Swedish Academy

In a youthful manifesto of 1913 entitled *Ordkonst och bildkonst* [Verbal Art and Pictorial Art], Pär Lagerkvist, whose name was then unknown, had the audacity to find fault with the decadence of the literature of his time which according to him, did not answer the requirements of art. His essay contains declarations which in their far too categorial form border on truism, but which in the light of his later work take on another, more profound meaning. Thus the young writer declared, «The writer's mission is to explain his time from an artist's point of view and to express the thought and feeling of this time for us and generations to come.» Today we can affirm that Lagerkvist himself, as far as one can follow him in his ascent toward maturity and greatness, amply accomplished this goal.

Today we call attention to this Swedish writer, not to present him in a general fashion – which would indeed seem superfluous – but to render to his work and to his person the homage due to them. Our attention is drawn above all to the impassioned, unfaltering sincerity, the ardent, unwearying patience, that have been the living forces behind his work. By these purely spiritual qualities, Pär Lagerkvist should answer fairly well, at least as a type of creative mind, to what Nobel said in the Sibylline terms of his will: «in an idealistic sense». Undeniably he belongs to that group of writers who, boldly and directly, have dedicated themselves to the vital questions of humanity and who have tirelessly returned to the fundamental problems of our existence, with all that is overwhelming and sorrowful. The era in which he lived, whose materials determined his vocation, was menaced by rising clouds and by the eruptions of catastrophes. It is on this sombre and chaotic scene that he began to fight; it is in this country without sun that he discovered the flame of his inspiration.

Lagerkvist, with a precocious instinct of the imagination, apprehended the approaching disaster so far in advance that he was the prophet of anguish in Nordic literature; but he is also one of the most vigilant guardians of the spirit's sacred fire which threatens to be extinguished in the storm. A number of those listening to me surely recall the short story in Lagerkvist's *Onda Sagor*

1924) [Evil Tales], in which one sees the child of ten, on a luminous spring day, walking with his father along the railroad track; they hear together the songs of the birds in the forest, and then, on their way back, in the dusk, they are suddenly surprised by the unknown noise which cleaves the air. «I had an obscure foreboding of what that meant; it was the anguish which was going to come, all the unknown, which Father did not know, and from which he could not protect me. Here is what this world will be, what this life will be for me, not like Father's life in which everything was reassuring and well established. It was not a real world, not a real life. It was only something ablaze which rushed into the depths of obscurity, obscurity without end.» This childhood memory now appears to us as a symbol of the theme that dominates Pär Lagerkvist's work; at the same time, one might say that it proves to us that his subsequent works are authentic and logically necessary.

It is impossible, with the short time at our disposal today, to examine all these works in turn. The important thing is that, while Pär Lagerkvist makes use of different genres, dramatic or lyric, epic or satiric, his way of grasping reality remains fundamentally the same. It does not matter in his case if the results are not always on a level with the intentions, for each work plays the role of a stone in an edifice he intends to build; each is a part of his mission, a mission that always bears on the same subject: the misery and grandeur of what is human, the slavery to which earthly life condemns us, and the heroic struggle of the spirit for its liberation. This is the theme in all the works we choose to recall at this time: *Gäst hos verkligheten* (1925) [*Guest of Reality*]; *Hjärtats sånger* (1926) [Songs from the Heart]; *Han som fick leva om sitt liv* 1928) [He Who Lived His Life Over Again]; *Dvärgen* (1944) [*The Dwarf*]; *Barabbas* (1950). It is needless to cite others to give an idea of the scope of Lagerkvist's inspirations and the power of his genius.

One of the foreign experts who, on the fiftieth anniversary of the Nobel Foundation, criticized the historic series of Nobel Prize laureates, gave as criteria two conditions which seemed equally indispensable to him: on the one hand the artistic value of the finished work, on the other its international reputation. Insofar as this last condition is concerned, it can immediately be objected that those who write in a language that is not widespread will find themselves at a great disadvantage. In any case, it is extremely rare that a Nordic writer could make a reputation with the international public, and, therefore, a fair judgment on this kind of candidate is an especially delicate matter. However, Nobel's will explicitly prescribes that the Prizes should be awarded «without any consideration of nationality, so that they should be

awarded to the worthiest, be he Scandinavian or not.» That should also signi-
fy that if a writer seems worthy of the Nobel Prize, the fact that he is Swedish,
for example, should not in the end hinder him from obtaining it. As for Pär
Lagerkvist, we must consider another factor, which pleases us very much:
his last work has attracted much sympathy and esteem outside our frontiers.
This was further proved by the insistent recommendations with which
Lagerkvist's candidacy has been sustained by a majority of foreign advisers.
He does not owe his Prize to the Academy circle itself. That the moving interpretations of the inner conflicts of Barabbas have found such repercussions
even in foreign languages clearly shows the profoundly inspired character of
this work, which is all the more remarkable as the style of it is original and in
a sense untranslatable. Indeed, in this language at once harsh and sensitive,
Lagerkvist's compatriots often hear the echo of Småland folklore reechoing
under the starry vault of Biblical legend. This reminds us once more that
regional individuality can sometimes be transformed into something universal and accessible to all.

On each page of Pär Lagerkvist's work are words and ideas which, in their
profound and fearful tenderness, carry at the very heart of their purity a message of terror. Their origin is in a simple, rustic life, laborious and frugal of
words. But these words, these thoughts, handled by a master, have been
placed at the service of other designs and have been given a greater purpose,
that of raising to the level of art an interpretation of the time, the world, and
man's eternal condition. That is why in the statement of the reasons for
awarding the Nobel Prize to Pär Lagerkvist, it seems legitimate to us to affirm that this national literary production has risen to the European level.

Dr. Lagerkvist—We who have followed you from close by know how re-
pugnant it is to you to be placed in the limelight. But since that seems inevitable at this moment, I beg you only to believe in the sincerity of our congratulations at the moment when you receive this award which, according to
us, you have deserved more than any other at the present time. I have been
obliged to sing your praises in front of you. But if the occasion were less
solemn, I would be tempted to tell you quite simply, in the old Swedish manner: may it bring you happiness.

And now, it remains for me to ask you to receive from the hands of our
King the Nobel Prize in Literature for 1951.

Acceptance

I wish to express my warm thanks to the Swedish Academy for awarding me the Nobel Prize in Literature. This is so great an honour that one may be excused for asking oneself – have I really deserved it? Speaking for myself, I dare not even pose the question! Having taken no part in making this decision, however, I can enjoy it with a free conscience. The responsibility rests with my esteemed colleagues and for this, too, I am truly thankful!

We have heard great speeches today and will presently hear more. I shall therefore refrain from making one but will ask you instead to bear with me while I read you a passage from a book of mine that has never been published. I was wondering what I should say on this solemn occasion, when something rather strange happened; I unearthed an old manuscript dating back to 1922, twenty-nine years ago. As I read it, I came upon a passage which more or less expressed what I would have said in my speech, except that it did so in the form of a story, which is much better suited to my taste. It is about the enigma of our life which makes human destiny at once so great and so hard.

I wrote it nearly thirty years ago. I was staying at the time in a little place in the Pyrenees on the shores of the Mediterranean, a very lovely part of the world. I will now read you the first part of it as well as I can.

The Myth of Mankind

Once upon a time there was a world, and a man and a woman came to it on a fine morning, not to dwell there for any length of time, but just for a brief visit. They knew many other worlds, and this one seemed to them shabbier and poorer than those others. True, it was beautiful enough with its trees and mountains, its forests and copses, the skies above with ever-changing clouds and the wind which came softly at dusk and stirred everything so mysteriously. But, for all that, it was still a poor world compared to those they possessed far, far away. Thus they decided to remain here for only a short while, for they loved each other and it seemed as though nowhere else was their love so wonderful as in just this world. Here, love was not something one took for granted and that permeated everyone and everything, but was like a visitor from whom wondrous things were expected. Everything that had been clear and natural in their life became mysterious, sinister, and veiled. They were strangers abandoned to unknown powers. The love that united them was a marvel–it was perishable; it could fade away and die. So for a while they wished to remain in this new world they had found for themselves.

It was not always daylight here. After the light of day, dusk would fall upon all things, wiping out, obliterating them. The man and woman lay together in the darkness listening to the wind as it whispered in the trees. They drew closer to each other, asking: why are we here at all?

Then the man built a house for himself and the woman, a house of stones and moss, for were they not to move on shortly? The woman spread sweet-scented grass on the earthen floor and awaited him home at dusk. They loved each other more than ever and went about their daily chores.

One day, when the man was out in the fields, he felt a great longing come upon him for her whom he loved above all things. He bent down and kissed the earth she had lain upon. The woman began to love the trees and the clouds because her man walked under them when he came home to her, and she loved twilight too, for it was then that he returned to her. It was a strange new world, quite unlike those other worlds they owned far, far away.

And so the woman gave birth to a son. The oak trees outside the house sang to him, he looked about him with startled eyes and fell asleep lulled by the sound of the wind in the trees. But the man came home at night carrying gory carcasses of slain animals; he was weary and in need of rest. Lying in the darkness, the man and woman talked blissfully of how they would soon be moving on.

What a strange world this was; summer followed by autumn and frosty winter, winter followed by lovely spring. One could see time pass as one season released another; nothing ever stayed for long. The woman bore another son and, after a few years, yet another. The children grew up and went about their business; they ran and played and discovered new things every day. They had the whole of this wonderful world to play with and all that was in it. Nothing was too serious to be turned into a toy. The hands of the man became calloused with hard work in the fields and in the forest. The woman's features became drawn and her steps less sprightly than before, but her voice was as soft and melodious as ever. One evening, as she sat down tired after a busy day, with the children gathered round her, she said to them,

«Now we shall soon be moving from here. We will be going to the other worlds where our home is.» The children looked amazed. «What are you saying, Mother? Are there any other worlds than this?» The mother's eyes met the husband's and pain pierced their hearts. Softly, she replied, «Of course there are other worlds», and she began to tell them of the worlds so unlike the one in which they were living, where everything was so much more spacious and wonderful, where there was no darkness, no singing trees, no struggle of any sort. The children sat huddled around her, listening to her story. Now and then, they would look up at their father as if asking, «Is this true, what Mother is telling us?» He only nodded and sat there deep in his own thoughts. The youngest son sat very close to his mother's feet; his face was pale, his eyes shone with a strange light. The eldest boy, who was twelve, sat further away and stared out. Finally, he rose and went out into the darkness.

The mother went on with her story and the children listened avidly. She seemed to behold some far-off country with eyes that stared unseeing; from time to time she paused as though she could see no more, remember no more. After a while, though, she would resume her story in a voice that grew fainter and fainter. The fire was flickering in the sooty fireplace; it shone upon their faces and cast a glow over the warm room. The father held his hand over his eyes. And so they sat without stirring until midnight. Then the door opened; a gust of cold air invaded the room and the eldest son appeared. He was holding in his hand a large black bird with blood gushing from its breast. This was the first bird he had killed on his own. He threw it down by the fire where it reeked of warm blood. Then, still without uttering a word, he went into a dark corner of the room at the back and lay down to sleep.

All was quiet now; the mother had finished her story. They gazed bewildered at each other, as if waking from a dream, and stared at the bird as it lay there dead, the red blood seeping from its breast, staining the floor about it. All arose silently and went to bed.

After that night, little was said for a time; each one went his own way. It was summer, bumblebees were buzzing in the lush meadows, the copses had been washed a bright green colour by the soft rains of spring, and the air was crystal clear. One day, at noon, the smallest child came up to his mother as he was sitting outside the house. He was very pale and quiet and asked her to tell him about the other world. The mother looked at him in amazement. «Darling,» she said, «I cannot speak of it now. Look, the sun is shining! Why aren't you out playing with your brothers?» He went quietly away and cried, but no one knew.

He never asked her again but only grew paler and paler, his eyes burning with a strange light. One morning, he could not get up at all, but just lay there. Day after day, he lay still, hardly saying a word, gazing into space with his strange eyes. They asked him where the pain was and promised that he would soon be out again in the sun and see all the fine new flowers that had come up. He did not reply, but only lay there not even seeming to see them. His mother watched over him and cried and asked him if she should tell him of all the wonderful things she knew, but he only smiled at her.

One night, he closed his eyes and died. They all gathered round him, his mother folded his small hands over his breast and, when the dusk fell, they sat huddled together in the darkening room and talked about him in whispers. He had left this world, they said, and gone to another world, a better and happier one, but they said it with heavy hearts and sighed. Finally, they all walked away frightened and confused, leaving him lying there, cold and forsaken.

In the morning, they buried him in the earth. The meadows were scented, the sun was shining softly, and there was gentle warmth everywhere. The mother said, «He is no longer here.» A rose tree near his grave burst into blossom.

And so the years came and went. The mother often sat by the grave in the afternoons, staring over the mountains that shut everything out. The father paused by the grave whenever he passed it on his way, but the children would not go near it, for it was like no other place on earth.

The two boys grew up into tall strapping lads, but the man and the woman began to shrink and fade away. Their hair turned grey, their shoulders stooped, and yet a kind of peace and dignity came upon them. The father still tried to go out hunting with his sons, but it was they who coped with the animals when they were wild and dangerous. The mother, aging, sat outside the house and groped about with her hands when she heard them returning home. Her eyes were so tired now that they could only see at noon when the sun was at its highest in the sky. At other times, all was darkness about her and she used to ask why that was so. One autumn day, she went inside and lay down, listening to the wind as to a memory of long long ago. The man sat by her side and, together, they talked about things as if they were alone in the world once more. She had grown very frail but an inner light illuminated her features. One night, she said to them in her failing voice, «Now I want to leave this world where I have spent my life and go to my home.» And so she went away. They buried her in the earth and there she lay.

Then it was winter once more and very cold. The old man no longer went out, but sat by the fire. The sons came home with carcasses and cut them up. The old man turned the meat on the spit and watched the fire turn a brighter red where the meat was roasting on it. When the spring came, he went out and looked at the trees and fields in all their greenery. He paused by each one and gave it a nod of recognition. Everything here was familiar to him. He stopped by the flowers he had picked for her he loved the first morning they had come here. He stopped by his hunting weapons, now covered with blood, for one of his sons had taken them. Then he walked back into the house and lay down and said to his sons as they stood by his deathbed, «Now I must depart from this world where I have lived all my life and leave it. Our home is not here.» He held their hands in his until he died. They buried him in the earth as he had bid them do, for it was there he wished to lie.

Now both the old people were gone and the sons felt a wonderful relief. There was a sense of liberation as though a cord tying them to something which was no part of them had been severed. Early next morning, they arose and went out into the open, savouring the smell of young trees and of the rain which had fallen that night. Side by side they walked together, the two tall youngsters, and the earth was proud to bear them. Life was beginning for them and they were ready to take possession of this world.

Prior to the acceptance, Einar Löfstedt, Member of the Swedish Academy and the Royal Academy of Sciences, made the following comments: «Is there a secret link between science and poetry? Perhaps there is. An English writer has said: ‹Poetry is the impassioned expression which is in the countenance of all science.› Whether these words apply to every science is open to question, but they do voice a very deep truth. Great poetry, as well as great science, is a form of obsession. They both want to lift man out of himself and to seek the answer to his eternal questions. With a visionary's strength and an ever deeper earnestness, you, Pär Lagerkvist, have sought to throw light on the problems of humanity in our time. Long before most, you have given expression to the *Anguish* occasioned by the threatening mechanization and barrenness of modern civilization. You have seen the human mind as a car, black and empty, roaring along in the dark through unknown towns to an unknown goal. But by degrees you have also heard the delicate flute of tenderness playing in the night, and you have seen *The Eternal Smile* in the life of humble folk when it is lived in love and trust. And in *Barabbas*, your recent great work, you have shown us man–torpid, uncertain, guilt-laden, like most of us–half unconsciously following the Unknown One who died to save mankind.

We offer you our thanks and congratulations and are happy to have been able to bestow on you, on the repeated recommendation from other countries, the honour of the Nobel Prize.»

Biography

'är Lagerkvist (1891–), the son of peasants, was born in the south of weden. He decided early that he was going to be a writer and, after a year t the University of Uppsala, he left for Paris (1913), where he came under he influence of expressionism, especially in painting. His impressions result-d in the programmatic *Ordkonst och bildkonst* (1913) [Verbal Art and Pictorial Art]. Until 1930 Lagerkvist lived chiefly in France and Italy, and even after is permanent return to Sweden he frequently travelled on the Continent and 1 the Mediterranean.

Lagerkvist has given an account of his early years in the autobiographical olumes *Gäst hos verkligheten* (1925) [*Guest of Reality*] and *Det besegrade livet* 1927) [The Conquered Life]. His poetry moves from the anxiety and de-pair of the war years, as in *Ångest* (1916) [*Anguish*], to the celebration of love s a «universal conciliatory power», as in *Hjärtats sånger* (1926) [Songs from he Heart].

As a playwright, Lagerkvist has been extremely versatile. While *Den svåra tunden* (1918) [*The Difficult Hour I, II, III*] shows the influence of the later trindberg, plays like *Himlens Hemlighet* (1919)[*The Secret of Heaven*] echo 'agore and the mystery play; *Han som fick leva om sitt liv* (1928) [He Who ived His Life Over Again], on the other hand, is realistic. His work during he thirties was determined by his violent opposition to totalitarianism: *ödeln* (1933) [*The Hangman*], *Mannen utan själ* (1936) [The Man without a oul], and *Seger i mörker* (1939) [Victory in the Darkness].

Lagerkvist increasingly has dealt with the problem of man's relation to od, particularly in his three important novels, *Dvärgen* (1944) [*The Dwarf*], *arabbas* (1950), and *Sibyllan* (1956) [*The Sibyl*]. *Barabbas*, the story of a believer without faith», was his first truly international success.

In 1940, Lagerkvist was elected to the Swedish Academy.

Literature 1952

FRANÇOIS MAURIAC

«for the deep spiritual insight and the artistic intensity with which he has in hi
novels penetrated the drama of human life»

Presentation

by Anders Österling, Permanent Secretary of the Swedish Academy

The student of François Mauriac's works will be struck from the very first by the insistence with which Mauriac devotes himself to describing a precise milieu, a corner of land one can point to on a map of France. The action of his novels nearly always unfolds in the Gironde, the Bordeaux region, that old vine-growing country where chateaux and small farms have taken possession of the earth, or in the Landes, the country of pine trees and sheep pastures where the song of the cicadas vibrates in the lonely spaces, and where the Atlantic sounds its far-off thunder. This is Mauriac's native country. He considers it his calling to describe this singular region and its people, especially those who own the land; and it can be said that his personal style partakes of the restrained energy which twists the branches of the grape vines and of the pitiless clarity of the light which falls from a torrid sky. In that sense, this writer, who is read the world over, is undeniably and markedly a man of the province, but his provincialism does not exclude the great human problems of universal scope. If one wants to dig deep one must first and always have a ground to thrust one's pick into.

Mauriac had a more than usually restricted childhood; he grew up in the shelter of a milieu in which the maternal influence made itself strongly felt, an influence which did not cease to act on his adolescent sensitivity. There is reason to believe that he had painful surprises later when he made contact with the outside world. Guided until then by pious advice, he had not suspected that evil dominated reality to such an extent as it appears in all the monotony and indifference of everyday life. Catholic by birth, brought up in a Catholic atmosphere which became his spiritual country, he has, in short, never had to decide for or against the Church. But he has on several occasions re-examined and publicly specified his Christian position, above all in order to question whether the demands a realist's position made on the writer could be reconciled with the commandments and prohibitions of the Church. Apart from these inevitable and insoluble antinomies, Mauriac, as a writer, uses the novel to expound a particular aspect of human life in which Catholic thought and sensitivity are at the same time backgroud and keystone. Hence,

his non-Catholic readers may to a certain extent feel that they are looking a
a world foreign to them; but to understand Mauriac, one must remember the
one fact without which no account of him can be complete: he does not belong to the group of writers who are converts. He himself is conscious of the
force that gives him those roots which permit him to cite a great and steri
tradition when he probes souls overwhelmed by the weight of their fault
and scrutinizes their secret intentions.

Mauriac has been assured a central position in modern literature for so long
and so unquestionably that the denominational barriers have almost lost al
importance. Whereas many writers of his generation who had a fleeting glory
are almost forgotten today, his profile stands out more and more distinctly
with the years. In his case it is not a question of fame achieved at the price o:
compromise, for his sombre and austere vision of the world is scarcely made
to please his contemporaries. He has always aimed high. With all the power
and all the consistency of which he is capable, he has tried to continue in hi
realistic novels the tradition of such great French moralists as Pascal, La
Bruyère, and Bossuet. To this let us add that he represents a tendency toward
religious inspiration which, particularly in France, has always been an extremely important element of spiritual formation. If I may in this context say
a few words about Mauriac as a distinguished journalist, we must not forget
in the interest of European thought, his work in that field, his commentaries
on daily events, the entire side of his literary activity which deserves public
esteem.

But if he is today the laureate of the Nobel Prize in Literature, it is obviously above all because of his admirable novels. Suffice it to name a few
masterpieces such as *Le Désert de l'amour* (1925) [*The Desert of Love*], *Thérès*
Desqueyroux (1927) [*Thérèse*], and its sequel *La Fin de la nuit* (1935) [*The
End of the Night*], *La Pharisienne* (1941) [*A Woman of the Pharisees*], and *L*
Noeud de vipères (1932) [*The Knot of Vipers*], without intending to say how
far the artistic qualities of these works place them in a class apart; for everywhere, in the whole series of Mauriac's novels, are found unforgettable scenes
dialogues, and situations, so mysteriously and so cruelly revealing. The repe-
tition of the same themes could create a certain monotony, but his acute analyses and sure touch awaken the same admiration with each new encounter
Mauriac remains unequalled in conciseness and expressive force of language
his prose can in a few suggestive lines shed light on the most complex and
difficult things. His most remarkable works are characterized by a purity of
logic and classic economy of expression that recall the tragedies of Racine.

The voiceless anxiety of youth, the abysses of evil and the perpetual menace of their presence, the deceitful temptations of the flesh, the ascendancy of avarice in the life of material goods, the havoc of self-satisfaction and pharisaism—these are the motifs that constantly reappear under Mauriac's pen. Small wonder that in his wielding of such a palette, he has been accused of blackening his subjects without cause, of writing as a misanthrope. But the response he gives is that, on the contrary, a writer who bases his whole concept of the world on grace and sees man's supreme recourse in God's love has the feeling of working in a spirit of hope and confidence. We have no right to doubt the sincerity of this declaration, but it is evident that in practice sin attracts him more than innocence. He detests what is edifying, and while he never grows tired of portraying the soul that persists in evil and is on its way to damnation, he generally prefers to bring down the curtain at the moment when the consciousness of its misery is about to push the soul toward repentance and salvation. This writer limits himself to the role of witness to the negative phase of this evolution, leaving all the positive side to the priest, who does not have to write a novel.

Mauriac himself once said that everyone is free to seek satisfaction in a literature that beautifies life and permits us to escape from reality, but the predilection which most people have for this kind of literature should not make us unjust toward the writers whose vocation is to know man. It is not we who hate life. Those alone hate life who, not being able to bear the sight of it, falsify it. The true lovers of life love it as it is. They have stripped it of its masks, one by one, and have given their hearts to this monster at last laid bare. In one of his controversies with André Gide, he returned to the cardinal point of his thought in affirming that the most complete sincerity is the form of honour which is linked to the writer's craft. Most often Tartuffe is made to appear under the ecclesiastical costume, but Mauriac assures us that this personage is found much more frequently in the midst of those supporting the theory of materialistic progress. It is easy to deride the principles of morality, but Mauriac objects to such derision; as he has stated quite simply, «Each of us knows he could become less evil than he is.»

This simple phrase is perhaps the key that opens the secret of good in the chapters of Mauriac's work, the secret of their sombre ardour and their subtle disharmony. His plunges into the midst of man's weaknesses and vices are more than the effect of a mania pushed to virtuosity. Even when he analyzes reality without pity, Mauriac preserves a last certainty, that there is a charity which passes understanding. He does not lay claim to the absolute; he knows that it does not exist with virtue in the pure state, and he views without indulgence those who call themselves pious. Faithful to the truth which he has made his, he strives to describe his characters in such a way that, seeing themselves as they are, they would be stricken with repentance and the desire to become, if not better, at least a little less evil. His novels can be compared to narrow but deep wells at the bottom of which a mysterious water is seen glistening in the darkness.

Dear Sir and colleague–In the few moments at my disposal I could speak about your work only in a sketchy manner. I know how much it deserves admiration; I also know how difficult it is to do it justice, to make general statements without ignoring the specific characteristics of your work. The Swedish Academy has awarded you this year's Nobel Prize in Literature «for the deep spiritual insight and the artistic intensity with which you have in your novels penetrated the drama of human life».

There remains for me to extend to you the most heartfelt congratulations of the Swedish Academy, this younger sister of your venerable Académie Française, and to ask you to receive the Prize from the hands of His Majesty the King.

Acceptance

he last subject to be touched upon by the man of letters whom you are
onouring, I think, is himself and his work. But how could I turn my thoughts
way from that work and that man, from those poor stories and that simple
rench writer, who by the grace of the Swedish Academy finds himself all of
sudden burdened and almost overwhelmed by such an excess of honour?
No, I do not think that it is vanity which makes me review the long road that
as led me from an obscure childhood to the place I occupy tonight in your
nidst.

When I began to describe it, I never imagined that this little world of the
past which survives in my books, this corner of provincial France hardly
nown by the French themselves where I spent my school holidays, could
apture the interest of foreign readers. We always believe in our uniqueness;
we forget that the books which enchanted us, the novels of George Eliot or
Dickens, of Tolstoy or Dostoevsky, or of Selma Lagerlöf, described countries
ery different from ours, human beings of another race and another religion.
ut nonetheless we loved them only because we recognized ourselves in them.
The whole of mankind is revealed in the peasant of our birthplace, every
ountryside of the world in the horizon seen through the eyes of our child-
ood. The novelist's gift consists precisely in his ability to reveal the univer-
lity of this narrow world into which we are born, where we have learned to
ove and to suffer. To many of my readers in France and abroad my world
as appeared sombre. Shall I say that this has always surprised me? Mortals,
ecause they are mortal, fear the very name of death; and those who have
ever loved or been loved, or have been abandoned and betrayed or have
ainly pursued a being inaccessible to them without as much as a look for the
reature that pursued them and which they did not love—all these are aston-
hed and scandalized when a work of fiction describes the loneliness in the
ery heart of love. «Tell us pleasant things», said the Jews to the prophet
saiah. «Deceive us by agreeable falsehoods.»

Yes, the reader demands that we deceive him by agreeable falsehoods.
Nonetheless, those works that have survived in the memory of mankind are

those that have embraced the human drama in its entirety and have not shied away from the evidence of the incurable solitude in which each of us must face his destiny until death, that final solitude, because finally we must die alone.

This is the world of a novelist without hope. This is the world into which we are led by your great Strindberg. This would have been my world were it not for that immense hope by which I have been possessed pratically since I awoke to conscious life. It pierces with a ray of light the darkness that I have described. My colour is black and I am judged by that black rather than by the light that penetrates it and secretly burns there. Whenever a woman in France tries to poison her husband or to strangle her lover, people tell me «Here is a subject for you.» They think that I keep some sort of museum of horrors, that I specialize in monsters. And yet, my characters differ in an essential point from almost any others that live in the novels of our time: they feel that they have a soul. In this post-Nietzschean Europe where the echo of Zarathustra's cry «God is dead» is still heard and has not yet exhausted its terrifying consequences, my characters do not perhaps all believe that God is alive, but all of them have a conscience which knows that part of their being recognizes evil and could not commit it. They know evil. They all feel dimly that they are the creatures of their deeds and have echoes in other destinies.

For my heroes, wretched as they may be, life is the experience of infinite motion, of an indefinite transcendence of themselves. A humanity which does not doubt that life has a direction and a goal cannot be a humanity in despair. The despair of modern man is born out of the absurdity of the world; his despair as well as his submission to surrogate myths: the absurd delivers man to the inhuman. When Nietzsche announced the death of God, he also announced the times we have lived through and those we shall still have to live through, in which man, emptied of his soul and hence deprived of a personal destiny, becomes a beast of burden more maltreated than a mere animal by the Nazis and by all those who today use Nazi methods. A horse, a mule, a cow has a market value, but from the human animal, procured without cost thanks to a well-organized and systematic purge, one gains nothing but profit until it perishes. No writer who keeps in the centre of his work the human creature made in the image of the Father, redeemed by the Son, and illuminated by the Spirit, can in my opinion be considered a master of despair, be his picture ever so sombre.

For his picture does remain sombre, since for him the nature of man is wounded, if not corrupted. It goes without saying that human history as told by a Christian novelist cannot be based on the idyll because he must not shy away from the mystery of evil.

But to be obsessed by evil is also to be obsessed by purity and childhood. It makes me sad that the too hasty critics and readers have not realized the place which the child occupies in my stories. A child dreams at the heart of all my books; they contain the loves of children, first kisses and first solitude, all the things that I have cherished in the music of Mozart. The serpents in my books have been noticed, but not the doves that have made their nests in more than one chapter; for in my books childhood is the lost paradise, and it introduces the mystery of evil.

The mystery of evil–there are no two ways of approaching it. We must either deny evil or we must accept it as it appears both within ourselves and without–in our individual lives, that of our passions, as well as in the history written with the blood of men by power-hungry empires. I have always believed that there is a close correspondence between individual and collective crimes, and, journalist that I am, I do nothing but decipher from day to day in the horror of political history the visible consequences of that invisible history which takes place in the obscurity of the heart. We pay dearly for the evidence that evil is evil, we who live under a sky where the smoke of crematories is still drifting. We have seen them devour under our own eyes millions of innocents, even children. And history continues in the same manner. The system of concentration camps has struck deep roots in old countries where Christ has been loved, adored, and served for centuries. We are watching with horror how that part of the world in which man is still enjoying his human rights, where the human mind remains free, is shrinking under our eyes like the «peau de chagrin» of Balzac's novel.

Do not for a moment imagine that as a believer I pretend not to see the objections raised to belief by the presence of evil on earth. For a Christian, evil remains the most anguishing of mysteries. The man who amidst the crimes of history perseveres in his faith will stumble over the permanent scandal: the apparent uselessness of the Redemption. The well-reasoned explanations of the theologians regarding the presence of evil have never convinced me, reasonable as they may be, and precisely because they are reasonable. The answer that eludes us presupposes an order not of reason but of charity. It is an answer that is fully found in the affirmation of St. John: God is Love. Nothing is impossible to the living love, not even drawing everything to itself; and that, too, is written.

Forgive me for raising a problem that for generations has caused many commentaries, disputes, heresies, persecutions, and martyrdoms. But it is after all a novelist who is talking to you, and one whom you have preferred to all others; thus you must attach some value to what has been his inspiration. He bears witness that what he has written about in the light of his faith and hope has not contradicted the experience of those of his readers who share neither his hope nor his faith. To take another example, we see that the agnostic admirers of Graham Greene are not put off by his Christian vision. Chesterton has said that whenever something extraordinary happens in Christianity ultimately something extraordinary corresponds to it in reality. If we ponder this thought, we shall perhaps discover the reason for the mysterious accord between works of Catholic inspiration, like those of my friend Graham Greene, and the vast dechristianized public that devours his books and loves his films.

Yes, a vast dechristianized public! According to André Malraux, «the revolution today plays the role that belonged formerly to the eternal life.» But what if the myth were, precisely, the revolution? And if the eternal life were the only reality?

Whatever the answer, we shall agree on one point: that dechristianized humanity remains a crucified humanity. What worldly power will ever destroy the correlation of the cross with human suffering? Even your Strindberg, who descended into the extreme depths of the abyss from which the psalmist uttered his cry, even Strindberg himself wished that a single word be engraved upon his tomb, the word that by itself would suffice to shake and force the gates of eternity: «o crux ave spes unica». After so much suffering even he is resting in the protection of that hope, in the shadow of that love. And it is in his name that your laureate asks you to forgive these all too personal words which perhaps have struck too grave a note. But could he do better, in exchange for the honours with which you have overwhelmed him, than to open to you not only his heart, but his soul? And because he has told you through his characters the secret of his torment, he should also introduce you tonight to the secret of his peace.

Prior to the acceptance, Harald Cramér, Member of the Royal Academy of Sciences, addressed the French writer: «Mr. Mauriac – In your work you have penetrated into the hearts of men, and you have shown them as you saw them: human, all too human. You did not hesitate to use the saddest and most sombre colours, if truth required it. Still, as one of your characters says, ‹ One can reach the supernatural through the base› –and if you have painted sad pictures of human life, you have also shown the rays of faith and divine grace which illuminate the darkness. Rest assured of our sincere and profound admiration.»

Biography

François Mauriac (1885) was born in Bordeaux. His father, a banker, died when he was eighteen months old, leaving his mother with five children, of which he was the youngest. François grew up in a closely sheltered world, first under the protection of his mother, later in a school run by the Marianites. He studied literature at Bordeaux and Paris but soon became an independent writer. *Les Mains jointes* [Clasped Hands], a collection of poems that appeared in 1909, aroused some interest, but it was not until the publication of *Le Baiser aux lepreux* (1922) [*A Kiss for the Leper*] that Mauriac became famous. In 1933, he was elected to the Académie Française. During the Second World War he lived in occupied territory, at his estate in Malagar and in Paris, and published *Le Cahier noir* [The Black Notebook] under the pseudonym Forez. After the war de Gaulle made Mauriac a Grand Officer of the Legion of Honour. Apart from his many novels, Mauriac has published several plays which have been produced by the Comédie Française. He is also a distinguished journalist and has been an editorial writer for *Figaro*.

The «religious» novels of Mauriac have been a puzzle to many critics, for they abound in evidences of the «dark side of life», and their religious content is not directly apparent. For instance, *Le Désert de l'amour* (1925) [*The Desert of Love*] portrays the triangle of a woman and her would-be lovers, father and son, whose «unused» passion, an illusion of escape, turns into the desert in whose isolation the characters live their frustrated lives. Other outstanding novels are *Thérèse Desqueyroux* (1927) [*Thérèse*], *Le Noeud de vipères* (1932) [*The Knot of Vipers*], *La Fin de la nuit* (1935) [The End of the Night], and *La Pharisienne* (1941) [*A Woman of the Pharisees*]. His most recent work has been a study of Charles de Gaulle (1964). Mauriac's complete works were published in twelve volumes between 1950 and 1956.

Literature 1953

Sir WINSTON LEONARD SPENCER CHURCHILL

«for his mastery of historical and biographical description as well as for brilliant oratory in defending exalted human values»

Presentation

by S. Siwertz, Member of the Swedish Academy

Very seldom have great statesmen and warriors also been great writers. One thinks of Julius Caesar, Marcus Aurelius, and even Napoleon, whose letters to Josephine during the first Italian campaign certainly have passion and splendour. But the man who can most readily be compared with Sir Winston Churchill is Disraeli, who also was a versatile author. It can be said of Disraeli as Churchill says of Rosebery, that «he flourished in an age of great men and small events». He was never subjected to any really dreadful ordeals. His writing was partly a political springboard, partly an emotional safety valve. Through a series of romantic and self-revealing novels, at times rather difficult to read, he avenged himself for the humiliation and setbacks that he, the Jewish stranger in an England ruled by aristocrats, suffered despite his fantastic career. He was not a great writer but a great actor, who played his leading part dazzlingly. He could very well repeat Augustus' words of farewell: «Applaud, my friends, the comedy is over!»

Churchill's John Bull profile stands out effectively against the elder statesman's chalk-white, exotic mask with the black lock of hair on the forehead. The conservative Disraeli revered the English way of life and tradition which Churchill, radical in many respects, has in his blood, including steadfastness in the midst of the storm and the resolute impetus which marks both word and deed. He wears no mask, shows no sign of cleavage, has no complex, enigmatic nature. The analytical *morbidezza*, without which the modern generation finds it hard to imagine an author, is foreign to him. He is a man for whom reality's block has not fallen apart. There, simply, lies the world with its roads and goals under the sun, the stars, and the banners. His prose is just as conscious of the goal and the glory as a runner in the stadium. His every word is half a deed. He is heart and soul a late Victorian who has been buffeted by the gale, or rather one who chose of his own accord to breast the storm.

Churchill's political and literary achievements are of such magnitude that one is tempted to resort to portray him as a Caesar who also has the gift of Cicero's pen. Never before has one of history's leading figures been so close to us by virtue of such an outstanding combination. In his great work about his ancestor, Marlborough, Churchill writes, «Words are easy and many, while great deeds are difficult and rare.» Yes, but great, living, and persuasive words are also difficult and rare. And Churchill has shown that they too can take on the character of great deeds.

It is the exciting and colourful side of Churchill's writing which perhaps first strikes the reader. Besides much else, *My Early Life* (1930) is also one of the world's most entertaining adventure stories. Even a very youthful mind can follow with the keenest pleasure the hero's spirited start in life as a problem child in school, as a polo-playing lieutenant in the cavalry (he was considered too dense for the infantry), and as a war correspondent in Cuba, in the Indian border districts, in the Sudan, and in South Africa during the Boer War. Rapid movement, undaunted judgments, and a lively perception distinguish him even here. As a word-painter the young Churchill has not only verve but visual acuteness. Later he took up painting as a hobby, and in *Thoughts and Adventures* (1932) discourses charmingly on the joy it has given him. He loves brilliant colours and feels sorry for the poor brown ones. Nevertheless, Churchill paints better with words. His battle scenes have a matchless colouring. Danger is man's oldest mistress and in the heat of action the young officer was fired to an almost visionary clear-sightedness. On a visit to Omdurman many years ago I discovered how the final struggle in the crushing of the Mahdi's rebellion, as it is depicted in *The River War* (1899), was branded on my memory. I could see in front of me the dervish hordes brandishing their spears and guns, the ochre-yellow sand ramparts shot to pieces, the Anglo-Egyptian troops' methodical advance, and the cavalry charge which nearly cost Churchill his life.

Even old battles which must be dug out of dusty archives are described by Churchill with awesome clarity. Trevelyan masterfully depicts Marlborough's campaigns, but in illusory power it is doubtful that Churchill's historic battle scenes can be surpassed. Take, for instance, the Battle of Blenheim. One follows in fascination the moves of the bloody chess game, one sees the cannon balls plough their furrows through the compact squares, one is carried away by the thundering charge and fierce hand-to-hand fighting of the cavalry; and after putting the book down one can waken in the night in a cold sweat, imagining he is right in the front rank of English redcoats who, without wavering, stand among the piles of dead and wounded loading their rifles and firing their flashing salvoes.

But Churchill became far more than a soldier and a delineator of war.

Even in the strict but brilliant school of the parliamentary gamble for power he was, perhaps from the outset, something of a problem child. The young Hotspur learned, however, to bridle his impetuosity, and he quickly developed into an eminent political orator with the same gift of repartee as Lloyd George. His sallies, often severe, excluded neither warmth nor chivalry. In his alternation between Toryism and radicalism, he followed in the footsteps of his father, Lord Randolph Churchill. He has also portrayed the latter's short, uneasy, tragically interrupted political and personal life in a work which has an undisputed place of honour in England's profuse biographical literature.

Even the First World War, despite all setbacks, meant a vast expansion for Churchill as both politician and writer. In his historical works the personal and the factual elements have been intimately blended. He knows what he is talking about. In gauging the dynamics of events, his profound experience is unmistakable. He is the man who has himself been through the fire, taken risks, and withstood extreme pressure. This gives his words a vibrating power. Occasionally, perhaps, the personal side gets the upper hand. Balfour called *The World Crisis* (1923–29) «Winston's brilliant autobiography, disguised as world history.» With all due respect to archives and documents, there is something special about history written by a man who has himself helped to make it.

In his great book on the Duke of Marlborough (1933–38), whose life's work is so similar to Churchill's own, he makes an intrepid attack on his ancestor's detractors. I do not know what professional historians say of his polemic against Macaulay, but these diatribes against the great general's persistent haters and revilers are certainly diverting and temperamental.

The Marlborough book is not only a series of vivid battle scenes and a skillful defence of the statesman and warrior. It is also a penetrating study of an enigmatic and unique personality; it shows that Churchill, in addition to all else, is capable of real character-drawing. He returns again and again to the confusing mixture in Marlborough of methodical niggardliness and dazzling virtuosity: «His private fortune was amassed», he says, «upon the same principles as marked the staff-work of his campaigns, and was a part of the same design. It was only in love or on the battlefield that he took all risks. In these supreme exaltations he was swept from his system and rule of living, and blazed resplendent with the heroic virtues. In his marriage and in his victories the worldly prudence, the calculation, the reinsurance, which regulated his ordinary life and sustained his strategy, fell from him like a too heavily embroidered cloak, and the genius within sprang forth in sure and triumphant command.» In his military enthusiasm Churchill forgets for a moment that Marlborough's famous and dearly loved Sarah was by no means one to let herself be ordered about. But it is a wonderful passage.

Churchill regretted that he had never been able to study at Oxford. He had to devote his leisure hours to educating himself. But there are certainly no educational gaps noticeable in his mature prose. Take, for example, *Great Contemporaries* (1937), one of his most charming books. He is said to have moulded his style on Gibbon, Burke, and Macaulay, but here he is supremely himself. What a deft touch and at the same time what a fund of human knowledge, generosity, and gay malice are in this portrait gallery!

Churchill's reaction to Bernard Shaw is very amusing, a piquant meeting between two of England's greatest literary personalities. Churchill cannot resist poking fun at Shaw's blithely irresponsible talk and flippancy, which contrasted with the latter's fundamental gravity. Half amused, half appalled, he winces at the way in which the incorrigibly clowning genius was forever tripping himself up and turning somersaults between the most extreme antitheses. It is the contrast between the writer, who must at all costs create surprises, and the statesman, whose task it is to meet and master them.

It is not easy to sum up briefly the greatness of Churchill's style. He says of his old friend, the Liberal statesman, John Morley, «Though in conversation he paraded and manœuvred nimbly and elegantly around his own convictions, offering his salutations and the gay compliments of old-time war to the other side, [he] always returned to his fortified camp to sleep.» As a stylist Churchill himself, despite his mettlesome chivalry, is not prone to such amiable arabesques. He does not beat about the bush, but is a man of plain speaking. His fervour is realistic, his striking - power is tempered only by broad-mindedness and humour. He knows that a good story tells itself. He scorns unnecessary frills and his metaphors are rare but expressive.

Behind Churchill the writer is Churchill the orator – hence the resilience and pungency of his phrases. We often characterize ourselves unconsciously through the praise we give others. Churchill, for instance, says of another of his friends, Lord Birkenhead, «As he warmed to his subject, there grew that glow of conviction and appeal, instinctive and priceless, which constitutes true eloquence.» The words might with greater justification have been said of Churchill himself.

The famous desert warrior, Lawrence of Arabia, the author of *The Seven Pillars of Wisdom*, is another who has both made and written history. Of him

Churchill says, «Just as an aeroplane only flies by its speed and pressure against the air, so he flew best and easiest in the hurricane.» It is again striking how Churchill here too speaks of the same genius that carried his own words through the storm of events.

Churchill's mature oratory is swift, unerring in its aim, and moving in its grandeur. There is the power which forges the links of history. Napoleon's proclamations were often effective in their lapidary style. But Churchill's eloquence in the fateful hours of freedom and human dignity was heart-stirring in quite another way. With his great speeches he has, perhaps, himself erected his most enduring monument.

Lady Churchill – The Swedish Academy expresses its joy at your presence and asks you to convey to Sir Winston a greeting of deep respect. A literary prize is intended to cast lustre over the author, but here it is the author who gives lustre to the prize. I ask you now to accept, on behalf of your husband, the 1953 Nobel Prize in Literature from the hands of His Majesty the King.

Acceptance

read by Lady Churchill

«The Nobel Prize in Literature is an honour for me alike unique and unexpected and I grieve that my duties have not allowed me to receive it myself here in Stockholm from the hands of His Majesty your beloved and justly respected Sovereign. I am grateful that I am allowed to confide this task to my wife.

The roll on which my name has been inscribed represents much that is outstanding in the world's literature of the twentieth century. The judgment of the Swedish Academy is accepted as impartial, authoritative, and sincere throughout the civilized world. I am proud but also, I must admit, awestruck at your decision to include me. I do hope you are right. I feel we are both running a considerable risk and that I do not deserve it. But I shall have no misgivings if you have none.

Since Alfred Nobel died in 1896 we have entered an age of storm and tragedy. The power of man has grown in every sphere except over himself. Never in the field of action have events seemed so harshly to dwarf personalities. Rarely in history have brutal facts so dominated thought or has such a widespread, individual virtue found so dim a collective focus. The fearful question confronts us; have our problems got beyond our control? Undoubtedly we are passing through a phase where this may be so. Well may we humble ourselves, and seek for guidance and mercy.

We in Europe and the Western world, who have planned for health and social security, who have marvelled at the triumphs of medicine and science, and who have aimed at justice and freedom for all, have nevertheless been witnesses of famine, misery, cruelty, and destruction before which pale the deeds of Attila and Genghis Khan. And we who, first in the League of Nations, and now in the United Nations, have attempted to give an abiding foundation to the peace of which men have dreamed so long, have lived to see a world marred by cleavages and threatened by discords even graver and more violent than those which convulsed Europe after the fall of the Roman Empire.

It is upon this dark background that we can appreciate the majesty and hope which inspired the conception of Alfred Nobel. He has left behind him a bright and enduring beam of culture, of purpose, and of inspiration to a generation which stands in sore need. This world-famous institution points a true path for us to follow. Let us therefore confront the clatter and rigidity we see around us with tolerance, variety, and calm.

The world looks with admiration and indeed with comfort to Scandinavia, where three countries, without sacrificing their sovereignty, live united in their thought, in their economic practice, and in their healthy way of life. From such fountains new and brighter opportunities may come to all mankind. These are, I believe, the sentiments which may animate those whom the Nobel Foundation elects to honour, in the sure knowledge that they will thus be respecting the ideals and wishes of its illustrious founder.»

Prior to the acceptance, G. Liljestrand, Member of the Royal Academy of Sciences, made the following remarks: «In the past, several prime ministers and ministers of foreign affairs and even two Presidents of the United States have been awarded the Nobel Peace Prize. Now, for the first time, a great statesman has received the Prize in Literature. But Sir Winston Churchill is a recognized master of the English language, that wonderful and flexible instrument of human thought. His monumental biographies are already classics, and his works on contemporary history are an outflow of deep and intimate first-hand knowledge, of lucidity of style as well as of humour and generosity. But to Sir Winston the English language has also provided an important tool, with the aid of which part of his job has been finished. His words, accompanied by corresponding deeds, have inspired hope and confidence in millions from all parts of the world during times of darkness. With a slight alteration we might use his own words: Never in the field of human conflict was so much owed by so many to one man. We would like to ask Lady Churchill to convey to her husband our respectful and sincere admiration and reverence for what he has given us in his writings and his speeches.»

Biography

The Right Honourable Sir Winston Leonard Spencer Churchill (1874–1965), the son of Lord Randolph Churchill and an American mother, was educated at Harrow and Sandhurst. After a brief but eventful career in the army, he became a Conservative Member of Parliament in 1900. He held many high posts in Liberal and Conservative governments during the first three decades of the century. At the outbreak of the Second World War, he was appointed First Lord of the Admiralty–a post which he had earlier held from 1911 to 1915. In May, 1940, he became Prime Minister and Minister of Defence and remained in office until 1945. He took over the premiership again in the Conservative victory of 1951 and resigned in 1955. However, he remained a Member of Parliament until the general election of 1964, when he did not seek re-election. Queen Elizabeth II conferred on Churchill the dignity of Knighthood and invested him with the insignia of the Order of the Garter in 1953. Among the other countless honours and decorations he received, special mention should be made of the honorary citizenship of the United States which President Kennedy conferred on him in 1963.

Churchill's literary career began with campaign reports: *The Story of the Malakand Field Force* (1898) and *The River War* (1899), an account of the campaign in the Sudan and the Battle of Omdurman. In 1900, he published his only novel, *Savrola*, and, six years later, his first major work, the biography of his father, *Lord Randolph Churchill*. His other famous biography, the life of his great ancestor, the Duke of Marlborough, was published in four volumes between 1933 and 1938. Churchill's history of the First World War appeared in four volumes under the title of *The World Crisis* (1923–29); his memoirs of the Second World War ran to six volumes (1948–1953/54). After his retirement from office, Churchill wrote a *History of the English-speaking Peoples* (4 vols., 1956–58). His magnificent oratory survives in a dozen volumes of speeches, among them *The Unrelenting Struggle* (1942), *The Dawn of Liberation* (1945), and *Victory* (1946).

Churchill, a gifted amateur painter, wrote *Painting as a Pastime* (1948). An autobiographical account of his youth, *My Early Life*, appeared in 1930.

Literature 1954

ERNEST MILLER HEMINGWAY

«for his powerful mastery of the art of storytelling, most recently displayed in The Old Man and the Sea, *and for his influence on contemporary style»*

Presentation

by Anders Österling, Permanent Secretary of the Swedish Academy

In our modern age, American authors have set their stamp more and more strongly on the general physiognomy of literature. Our generation in particular has, during the last few decades, seen a reorientation of literary interest which implies not only a temporary change in the market but, indeed, a shifting of the mental horizon, with far-reaching consequences. All these swiftly rising new authors from the United States, whose names we now recognize as stimulating signals, had one thing in common: they took full advantage of the Americanism to which they were born. And the European public greeted them with enthusiasm; it was the general wish that Americans should write as Americans, thereby making their own contribution to the contest in the international arena.

One of these pioneers is the author who is now the focus of attention. It is hardly an exaggeration to say that Ernest Hemingway, more than any of his American colleagues, makes us feel we are confronted by a still young nation which seeks and finds its exact form of expression. A dramatic tempo and sharp curves have also characterized Hemingway's own existence, in many ways so unlike that of the average literary man. With him, this vital energy goes its own way, independent of the pessimism and the disillusionment so typical of the age. Hemingway evolved his style in the hard school of journalistic reporting. In the editorial office of the Kansas City newspaper where he served his apprenticeship, there was a kind of pressman's catechism, the first dictum of which was: «Use short sentences. Use short paragraphs.» Hemingway's purely technical training clearly led to an artistic self-discipline of uncommon strength. Rhetoric, he has said, is merely the blue sparks from the dynamo. His master in older American literature was Mark Twain in *Huckleberry Finn*, with its rhythmical stream of direct and unconventional narrative prose.

The young journalist from Illinois was flung headlong into the First World War when he volunteered to serve as an ambulance driver in Italy, where he received his baptism of fire at the Piave front and was severely wounded by shell splinters. The nineteen-year-old's first violent experience of war is an essential factor in Hemingway's biography. Not that he was daunted by it; on the contrary, he found that it was a priceless asset for a writer to see war at first hand–like Tolstoy at Sevastopol–and to be able to depict it truthfully. Several years were to elapse, however, before he could bring himself to give an artistically complete account of his painfully confused impressions from the Piave front in 1918: the result was the novel *A Farewell to Arms* in 1929, with which he really made his name, even if two very talented books with a European post-war setting, *In Our Time* (1942) and *The Sun Also Rises* (1926), had already given proof of his individuality as a storyteller. In the following years, his instinctive predilection for harrowing scenes of action and grim spectacle drew him to Africa with its big-game hunting and to Spain with its bullfighting. When the latter country was transformed into a theatre of war, he found inspiration there for his second significant novel, *For Whom the Bell Tolls* (1940), in which an American champion of liberty fights for «man's dignity»–a book in which the writer's personal feelings seem more deeply involved than anywhere else.

When mentioning these principal elements in his production, one should not forget that his narrative skill often attains its highest point when cast in a smaller mould, in the laconic, drastically pruned short story, which, with a unique combination of simplicity and precision, nails its theme into our consciousness so that every blow tells. Such a masterpiece, more than any other, is *The Old Man and the Sea* (1952), the unforgettable story of an old Cuban fisherman's duel with a huge swordfish in the Atlantic. Within the frame of a sporting tale, a moving perspective of man's destiny is opened up; the story is a tribute to the fighting spirit, which does not give in even if the material gain is nil, a tribute to the moral victory in the midst of defeat. The drama is enacted before our eyes, hour by hour, allowing the robust details to accumulate and take on momentous significance. «But man is not made for defeat», the book says. «A man can be destroyed but not defeated.»

It may be true that Hemingway's earlier writings display brutal, cynical, and callous sides which may be considered at variance with the Nobel Prize's requirement for a work of an ideal tendency. But on the other hand, he also possesses a heroic pathos which forms the basic element in his awareness of life, a manly love of danger and adventure with a natural admiration for every individual who fights the good fight in a world of reality overshadowed by violence and death. In any event, this is the positive side of his cult of manliness, which otherwise is apt to become demonstrative, thereby defeating its own ends. It should be remembered, however, that courage is Hemingway's central theme—the bearing of one who is put to the test and who steels himself to meet the cold cruelty of existence, without, by so doing, repudiating the great and generous moments.

On the other hand, Hemingway is not one of those authors who write to illustrate theses and principles of one kind or another. A descriptive writer must be objective and not try to play God the Father—this he learned while still in the editorial office in Kansas City. That is why he can conceive of war as a tragic fate having a decisive effect on the whole of his generation; but he views it with a calm realism, void of illusion, which disdains all emotional comment, a disciplined objectivity, stronger because it is hard-won.

Hemingway's significance as one of this epoch's great moulders of style is apparent in both American and European narrative art over the past twenty-five years, chiefly in the vivid dialogue and the verbal thrust and parry, in which he has set a standard as easy to imitate as it is difficult to attain. With masterly skill he reproduces all the nuances of the spoken word, as well as those pauses in which thought stands still and the nervous mechanism is thrown out of gear. It may sometimes sound like small talk, but it is not trivial when one gets to know his method. He prefers to leave the work of psychological reflection to his readers, and this freedom is of great benefit to him in spontaneous observation.

When one surveys Hemingway's production, definite scenes flare up in the memory—Lieutenant Henry's flight in the rain and mud after the panic at Caporetto, the desperate blowing up of the bridge in the Spanish mountains when Jordan sacrifices his life, or the old fisherman's solitary fight with the sharks in the nocturnal glow of lights from Havana.

Moreover, one may trace a distinctive linking thread—let us say a symbolic warp reaching back a hundred years in the loom of time—between Hemingway's latest work, *The Old Man and The Sea*, and one of the classic creations of American literature, Herman Melville's novel *Moby Dick*, the white whale who is pursued in blind rage by his enemy, the monomaniac sea captain. Neither Melville nor Hemingway wanted to create an allegory; the salt ocean depths with all their monsters are sufficiently rewarding as a poetic element. But with different means, those of romanticism and of realism, they both attain the same theme—a man's capacity of endurance and, if need be, of at least daring the impossible. «A man can be destroyed but not defeated.»

This year's Nobel Prize in Literature has therefore been awarded to one of the great authors of our time, one of those who, honestly and undauntedly, reproduces genuine features in the hard countenance of the age. Hemingway, now fifty-six years old, is the fifth American author so far to be honoured in this way. As the Prize winner himself is unfortunately unable to be present for reasons of health, the Prize will now be handed to the United States Ambassador.

Acceptance

read by John C. Cabot, United States Ambassador

«Having no facility for speech-making and no command of oratory nor any domination of rhetoric, I wish to thank the administrators of the generosity of Alfred Nobel for this Prize.

No writer who knows the great writers who did not receive the Prize can accept it other than with humility. There is no need to list these writers. Everyone here may make his own list according to his knowledge and his conscience.

It would be impossible for me to ask the Ambassador of my country to read a speech in which a writer said all of the things which are in his heart. Things may not be immediately discernible in what a man writes, and in this sometimes he is fortunate; but eventually they are quite clear and by these and the degree of alchemy that he possesses he will endure or be forgotten.

Writing, at its best, is a lonely life. Organizations for writers palliate the writer's loneliness but I doubt if they improve his writing. He grows in public stature as he sheds his loneliness and often his work deteriorates. For he does his work alone and if he is a good enough writer he must face eternity, or the lack of it, each day.

For a true writer each book should be a new beginning where he tries again for something that is beyond attainment. He should always try for something that has never been done or that others have tried and failed. Then sometimes, with great luck, he will succeed.

How simple the writing of literature would be if it were only necessary to write in another way what has been well written. It is because we have had such great writers in the past that a writer is driven far out past where he can go, out to where no one can help him.

I have spoken too long for a writer. A writer should write what he has to say and not speak it. Again I thank you.»

Prior to the acceptance, H. S. Nyberg, Member of the Swedish Academy, made the following comment: «Another deep regret is that the winner of this year's Nobel Prize in Literature, Mr. Ernest Hemingway, on account of ill health has to be absent from our celebration. We wish to express our admiration for the eagle eye with which he has observed, and for the accuracy with which he has interpreted the human existence of our turbulent times; also for the admirable restraint with which he has described their naked struggle. The human problems which he has treated are relevant to all of us, living as we do in the confused conditions of modern life; and few authors have exercised such a wide influence on contemporary literature in all countries. It is our sincere hope that he will soon recover health and strength in pursuit of his life-work.»

Biography

Ernest Hemingway (1898–1961), born in Oak Park, Illinois, started his career as a writer in a newspaper office in Kansas City at the age of seventeen. Before the United States entered the First World War, he joined a volunteer ambulance unit in the Italian army. Serving at the front, he was wounded, was decorated by the Italian Government, and spent considerable time in hospitals. After his return to the United States, he became a reporter for Canadian and American newspapers and was soon sent back to Europe to cover such events as the Greek Revolution.

During the twenties, Hemingway became a member of the group of expatriate Americans in Paris, which he described in his first important work, *The Sun Also Rises* (1926). Equally successful was *A Farewell to Arms* (1929), the study of an American ambulance officer's disillusionment in the war and his role as a deserter. Hemingway used his experiences as a reporter during the civil war in Spain as the background for his most ambitious novel, *For Whom the Bell Tolls* (1940). Among his later works, the most outstanding is the short novel, *The Old Man and the Sea* (1952), the story of an old fisherman's journey, his long and lonely struggle with a fish and the sea, and his victory in defeat.

Hemingway–himself a great sportsman–liked to portray soldiers, hunters, bullfighters–tough, at times primitive people whose courage and honesty are set against the brutal ways of modern society, and who in this confrontation lose hope and faith. His straightforward prose, his spare dialogue, and his predilection for understatement are particularly effective in his short stories, some of which are collected in *Men Without Women* (1927) and *The Fifth Column and the First Forty-Nine Stories* (1938). Hemingway died in Idaho in 1961.

Literature 1955

HALLDÓR KILJAN LAXNESS

«for his vivid epic power, which has renewed the great narrative art of Iceland»

Presentation

by E. Wessén, Member of the Swedish Academy

Iceland is the cradle of narrative art here in the North. This is ultimately due to the peculiar nature and development of the Icelandic community. In Iceland there were no conditions for the rise of the class society elsewhere so characteristic of the Middle Ages, with its sharp contrast between Church and people, between the learned and the peasants. There books were not, as in other lands, the privilege of a few priests versed in Latin. Even in the Middle Ages literacy was far more widespread among the common people in Iceland than in other parts of Europe. This fact created the basic conditions for the writing down in the native tongue of the old vernacular poetry which, in the rest of northern Europe, our country included, was despised and forgotten.

So it came about that the poor little nation on its remote island created world literature, producing prose tales which the other European countries were unable to match for hundreds of years. *Snorre* and the sagas will always stand out as peaks in the art of historical narrative, as models of style in their perspicuity, clarity, and vigour. The Icelandic saga, very largely anonymous, is the product of a whole nation's literary talent and independent creative power.

In Iceland the saga has always been held in great honour. To the Icelanders themselves it has given consolation and strength during dark centuries of poverty and hardship. To this very day Iceland stands out as the literary nation of the North *par excellence*, in relation to its population and its resources.

Enormous power is necessary to renew in our time a narrative art which has such traditions. In the book which Halldór Laxness has written about the peasant poet Olafur Ljósvíkíngur, he especially touches on the problems and the mission of poetry, making one of the characters say: «That poem is good which reaches the heart of the people. There is no other criterion.» But in order to reach the people's heart, literary skill alone, however great, is not enough; the ability to depict events and exploits is not enough. If literature is to be a «light of the world», it must strive to give a true picture of human life and conditions. That goal runs like a continuous thread through most of what

Halldór Laxness has written. And as he has an extraordinarily fine sense of the concrete things of human life and at the same time an inexhaustible gift of storytelling, he has come to rank as his people's greatest writer of the present age.

One of the most remarkable testimonies of the conflicts in modern cultural life–not only in Iceland but in the whole of the West–is Laxness's early work, *Vefarinn mikli frá Kasmir* (1927) [The Great Weaver from Kashmir]. Despite a certain youthful immaturity, it carries weight as a contemporary document and as a personal confession. The main character is a young Icelander, a writer with an artistic temperament, who, during a roving life in Europe, experiences to the full the chaotic perplexity following the First World War. Like Hans Alienus at one time, he tries to get his bearings and to find a firm footing in life–but what a difference in situation! Far more than a generation in time separates them. On the one hand, peace, unshakable faith in progress, dreams of beauty; on the other, a shattered, bleeding world, moral laxity, anguish, and impotence. Steinn Elliði finally throws himself into the arms of the Catholic Church. Since Strindberg, few books in the literature of northern Europe have bared inner conflicts with such uncompromising candour and shown how the individual comes to terms with the forces of the age.

Halldór Laxness did not attain artistic balance until, toward the end of the twenties, he returned to Iceland and found his calling as bard of the Icelandic people. All his important books have Icelandic themes.

He is an excellent painter of Icelandic scenery and settings. Yet this is not what he has conceived as his chief mission. «Compassion is the source of the highest poetry. Compassion with Ásta Sóllilja on earth», he says in one of his best books. Art must be supported by sympathy and love for humanity; otherwise it is worth very little. And a social passion underlies everything Halldór Laxness has written. His personal championship of contemporary social and political questions is always very strong, sometimes so strong that it threatens to hamper the artistic side of his work. His safeguard then is the astringent humour which enables him to see even people he dislikes in a redeeming light, and which also permits him to gaze far down into the labyrinths of the human soul.

Individual people and their destinies always move us most deeply in Halldór Laxness's novels. Against the dark background of poverty, strikes, and strife in the little Icelandic fishing village, the shining, girlish figure of Salka Valka stands out, resolute, capable, and pure of heart.

Even more affecting, perhaps, is the story of Bjartur, the man with the indomitable will for freedom and independence, Geijer's yeoman farmer in an Icelandic setting and, with monumental, epic proportions, the settler, the *landnámsman* of Iceland's thousand-year-old history. Bjartur remains the same in sickness and misfortune, in poverty and starvation, in raging snowstorms and face to face with the frightening monsters of the moors, and pathetic to the last in his helplessness and his touching love for his foster daughter, Ásta Sóllilja.

The story of the peasant poet Olafur Ljósvíkíngur, *Ljós heimsins* (1937–40) [The Light of the World], is possibly his greatest work. It is based on the contrast between a miserable environment and the heaven-born dreams of one who is a friend and servant of beauty.

In *Islandsklukkan* (1943–46) [The Bell of Iceland], Laxness for the first time sets the scene in a bygone age. And he indeed succeeds in giving the atmosphere of the period both of Iceland and of Denmark. Stylistically, it is a masterpiece. But even here it is chiefly individuals and their destinies that one remembers: the wretched tatterdemalion Jón Hreggviðsson; «the fair maid» Snaefriður Eydalín; and above all, the learned collector of manuscripts, Arnas Arnaeus, in whom Iceland lives more robustly than in anyone else.

Halldór Laxness has guided literary development back to common and traditional ground. That is his great achievement. He has a vivid and personal style, easy and natural, and one gets a strong impression of how well and how flexibly it serves his ends.

One more thing must be emphasized if Laxness's position is to be properly understood. There was a time when the Icelandic authors chose another Scandinavian language for their art, not merely for economic reasons, but because they despaired of the Icelandic language as an instrument for artistic creation. Halldór Laxness has, in the field of prose, renewed the Icelandic language as an artistic means of expression for a modern content, and by his example he has given the Icelandic writers courage to use their native tongue. Broadly speaking, therein lies his greatest significance, and this is what has given him a strong and very respected position in his own land.

Acceptance

I was travelling in the south of Sweden a few weeks ago, when I heard the rumour that the choice of the Swedish Academy might possibly fall on me. Alone in my hotel room that night, I naturally began to ask myself what it would mean to a poor wanderer, a writer from one of the most remote islands in the world, to be suddenly singled out by an institution famous for its promotion of culture, and brought here to the platform by its command.

It is not so strange perhaps that my thoughts turned then – as they still do, not least at this solemn moment – to all my friends and relations, to those who had been the companions of my youth and are dead now and buried in oblivion. Even in their lifetime, they were known to few, and today they are remembered by fewer still. All the same they have formed and influenced me and, to this day, their effect on me is greater than that of any of the world's great masters or pioneers could possibly have been. I am thinking of all those wonderful men and women, the people among whom I grew up. My father and mother, but above all, my grandmother, who taught me hundreds of lines of old Icelandic poetry before I ever learned the alphabet.

In my hotel room that night, I thought – as I still do – of the moral principles she instilled in me: never to harm a living creature; throughout my life, to place the poor, the humble, the meek of this world above all others; never to forget those who were slighted or neglected or who had suffered injustice, because it was they who, above all others, deserved our love and respect, in Iceland or anywhere in the world. I spent my entire childhood in an environment in which the mighty of the earth had no place outside story books and dreams. Love of, and respect for, the humble routine of everyday life and its creatures was the only moral commandment which carried conviction when I was a child.

I recall my friends whose names the world never knew but who, in my youth, and long into my adult life, guided my literary work. Though no writers themselves, they nevertheless possessed infallible literary judgment and were able, better than most of the masters, to open my eyes to what was essential in literature. Many of those gifted men are no longer with us, but they are so vivid in my mind and in my thoughts that, many a time, I would have been hard put to distinguish between which was the expression of my own self and which the voice of my friends within me.

I am thinking, too, of that community of one hundred and fifty thousand men and women who form the book-loving nation that we Icelanders are. From the very first, my countrymen have followed my literary career, now criticizing, now praising my work, but hardly ever letting a single word be buried in indifference. Like a sensitive instrument that records every sound, they have reacted with pleasure or displeasure to every word I have written. It is a great good fortune for an author to be born into a nation so steeped in centuries of poetry and literary tradition.

My thoughts fly to the old Icelandic storytellers who created our classics, whose personalities were so bound up with the masses that their names, unlike their lives' work, have not been preserved for posterity. They live in their immortal creations and are as much a part of Iceland as her landscape. For century upon dark century those nameless men and women sat in their mud huts writing books without so much as asking themselves what their wages would be, what prize or recognition would be theirs. There was no fire in their miserable dwellings at which to warm their stiff fingers as they sat up late at night over their stories. Yet they succeeded in creating not only a literary language which is among the most beautiful and subtlest there is, but a separate literary genre. While their hearts remained warm, they held on to their pens.

As I was sitting in my hotel room in Skåne, I asked myself: what can fame and success give to an author? A measure of material well-being brought about by money? Certainly. But if an Icelandic poet should forget his origin as a man of the people, if he should ever lose his sense of belonging with the humble of the earth, whom my old grandmother taught me to revere, and his duty toward them, then what is the good of fame and prosperity to him?

Your Majesties, ladies and gentlemen—It is a great event in my life that the Swedish Academy should have chosen to link my name with the nameless masters of sagas. The reasons the Academy has given for singling me out in so spectacular a manner will serve as an encouragement to me for the rest of my days, but they will also bring joy to those whose support has been responsible for all that my work may have of value. The distinction you have conferred on me fills me with pride and joy. I thank the Swedish Academy for all this with gratitude and respect. Though it was I who today received the Prize from Your Majesty's hands, nevertheless I feel that it has also been bestowed on my many mentors, the fathers of Iceland's literary tradition.

Prior to the acceptance, H. Bergstrand, former Rector of the Caroline Institute, addressed Mr. Laxness: «We know that Alfred Nobel regarded life with the eyes of a poet, and that his gaze was fixed on a far-off dreamland. Accordingly, literature should have an idealistic tendency. This is something else than the admission of the lad who later called himself Halldór Kiljan Laxness when he listened to the sayings of the pipe-player. He said that the player's talk hid no deeper meaning than an ordinary landscape or a finely painted picture, and they therefore had the same self-evident charm. ‹From the day I learned to read›, he continued, ‹I have been irritated by stories with a moral, a hidden pointer, in the guise of adventure. I immediately stopped reading or listening as soon as I thought I understood that the purpose of the story was to force on me some kind of wisdom which someone else considered noteworthy, a virtue that someone else found admirable, instead of telling me a story. For a story is still the best thing that one can tell.›

I am convinced that the Swedish Academy was of the same opinion when it awarded the Nobel Prize in Literature to a modern incarnation of an Icelandic teller of sagas. And no one can deny that his tales move the mind, a prerequisite that Horace demanded for the works of a poet, in the words ‹et quocunque volent animum auditoris agunto›.»

Biography

Halldór Kiljan Laxness (1902–   ) was born in Reykjavik, the capital of Iceland, but spent his youth in the country. From the age of seventeen on, he travelled and lived abroad, chiefly on the European continent. He was influenced by expressionism and other modern currents in Germany and France. In the mid-twenties he was converted to Catholicism; his spiritual experiences are reflected in several books of an autobiographical nature, chiefly *Undir Helgahnúk* (1924) [Under the Holy Mountain]. In 1927, he published ed his first important novel, *Vefarinn mikli frá Kasmir* (The Great Weaver from Kashmir). Laxness' religious period did not last long; during a visit to America he became attracted to socialism. *Althýdubókin* (1929) [The Book of the People] is evidence of a change toward a socialist outlook. In 1930, Laxness settled in Iceland.

Laxness' main achievement consists of three novel cycles written during the thirties, dealing with the people of Iceland. *Pú vínvidur hreini* (1931) and *Fuglinn í fjörunni* (1932) [both translated as *Salka Valka*] tell the story of a poor fisher girl; *Sjalfstaettfolk* (1934–35) [*Independent People*] treats the fortunes of small farmers, whereas the tetralogy *Ljós heimsins* (1937–40) [The Light of the World] has as its hero an Icelandic folk poet. Laxness' later works are frequently historical and influenced by the saga tradition: *Islandsklukkan* (1943–46) [The Bell of Iceland], *Gerpla* (1952) [*The Happy Warriors*] and *Paradisarheimat* (1960) [*Paradise Reclaimed*]. Laxness is also the author of the topical and sharply polemical *Atómstödin* (1948) [*The Atom Station*].

Literature 1956

JUAN RAMÓN JIMÉNEZ

«for his lyrical poetry, which in the Spanish language constitutes an example of high spirit and artistic purity»

Presentation

by Hjalmar Gullberg, Member of the Swedish Academy

A long life consecrated to poetry and to beauty has been honoured this year with the Nobel Prize in Literature. He is an old gardener, this Juan Ramón, who has dedicated half a century to the creation of a new rose, a white mystical rose, which will bear his name.

Jardines lejanos (1904) [Distant Gardens] is one of his books from the beginning of the century. In the southern parts of Andalusia, far off the route from Jerez to Seville well known to Swedish tourists, the poet was born in 1881. But his poetry is not a strong and intoxicating wine, and his work not a grandiose mosque turned into a cathedral. It makes you think, rather, of one of those gardens circled by high, whitewashed walls which you see marking a landscape. He who stops a moment and goes in with his camera runs the risk of being deceived. There is nothing singular or picturesque here, only the usual things: fruit trees and the air which vibrates on passing through them, the pond that reflects the sun and the moon, a bird singing. No small minaret has been transformed into an ivory tower in this fertile garden planted in the soil of Arab culture. But the visitor who lingers will notice that the passivity within the walls is deceiving, that the isolation is only of the circumstantial and transitory, of what pretends to be present. He will not fail to observe that the rose has a radiance which demands sharper senses and a new sensibility. There is a beauty which is more than the play and delight of the senses; in front of the visitor the silent gardener suddenly appears like a strict director of souls. At the entrance of the Juanramonian garden the tourist ought to observe the same rules as on entering a mosque: wash his hands and rinse his mouth in the fountain for ablutions, take off his shoes, etc.

The year in which Ramón Jiménez began to publish his melodious verses was in the history of Spain a year for an examination of conscience. On December 10, 1898, in Paris, was signed the treaty with the United States by which Spain lost Cuba, Puerto Rico, and the Philippines, as well as what remained of its navy and its prestige. By a stroke of the pen the remnants of a whole colonial empire were eliminated. In Madrid a group of writers took up the pen to reconquer, in their fashion, the world within the boundaries of Spain.

Some of them ultimately attained their goals. The Machado brothers, Valle-Inclán, and Unamuno were among them. The «modernists», as they called themselves, had in turn grouped themselves around their leader, the Nicaraguan Rubén Darío, visiting in Spain. It was Darío also who, at the beginning of the century, sponsored the first book of verses of the new poet, Juan Ramón Jiménez, a book which bore the scarcely martial title, *Almas de violeta* (1900) [Souls of Violet].

He was not an audacious creator who would present himself on stage in full light. His song arrived, timid and intimate, from a penumbral background and spoke of the moon and of melancholy with echoes of Schumann and Chopin. He wept with Heine and with his countryman inspired by Heine, Gustavo Adolfo Bécquer, the exquisite poet to whom some shortsighted admirers gave the name, «golden-haired Nordic King». In the manner of Verlaine he murmured his *Arias tristes* (1903) [Sad Arias] in a half-voice. When, little by little but with sure step, he had freed himself from the gentle, captivating arms of French symbolism, the characteristic features of music and intimacy would remain forever impressed on him.

Music and painting–we can note that, in Seville, the young student also studied to be a painter. Just as we speak of the blue and rose periods of Picasso, who was born in the same year, as the historians of literature have called attention to the predominance of different colours in the work of Ramón Jiménez. To the first period belong all the poems in yellow and green – the famous green poem of his disciple Garcia Lorca has its origin here. Later, white predominates, and the nakedness of white characterizes the brilliant, decisive epoch which includes what has been called the second poetic style of Juan Ramón. Here we witness the long period of plenitude of a poet of light. Far off are the melancholy mood-pictures, far off also the anecdotal themes. The poems treat only of poetry and love, and of the landscape and the sea which are identified with poetry and love. A formal asceticism carried to perfection, rejecting every exterior embellishment of the verse, will be the road that will lead to the simplicity that is the supreme form of art, the poetry that the poet calls naked.

This «second style of Juan Ramón» reaches its full development in *Diario de un poeta recién casado* [Diary of a Newly-Wed Poet] in 1917. In this year the newly-wed poet made his first trip to America and his diary is full of an infinite feeling for the sea, full of oceanic poetry. His books *Eternidades* (1918) [Eternities] and *Piedra y cielo* (1919) [Stone and Sky] mark new stages toward the longed-for identification of the «I» with the world; poetry and thought have the purpose of finding «the exact name for things». Gradually the poems become more concise, naked, transparent; they are, in fact, maxims and aphorisms of the mystical poetics of Juan Ramón.

In his constant zeal to surpass previous achievements, Ramón Jiménez has made a clean slate of his earliest production and has radically modified old poems, gathering those meriting his approval into extensive anthologies. After his volumes *Belleza* [Beauty] and *Poesía* [Poetry] in 1923, in his zeal to experiment with new forms, he abandoned the publication of his works in book form and often published without title or author's name, in the form of sheets or leaflets scattered by the wind. In 1936 the civil war interrupted the projected edition of his works in twenty-one volumes. *Animal de fondo* (1949) [Animal of Depth], the last book from his period of exile, is, if read by itself, a sample of a work in progress. Today, therefore, it is still premature to discuss this phase which in literary history will perhaps carry the title «the last style of Juan Ramón».

Far away, in what was the colony of Puerto Rico, he is afflicted today by an immense sorrow. It will not be possible for us to see his thin face with its profound eyes and to ask ourselves if it has been taken directly from a painting by El Greco. We find a less solemn self-portrait in the delightful book, *Platero y yo* (1914) [*Platero and I*]. There, dressed in mourning, the poet passes with his Nazarene beard, riding his little donkey while the gypsy children shout at the top of their voices: The madman! The madman! The madman! ... And in truth it is not always easy to distinguish a madman from a poet. But for like spirits the madness of this man has been eminent wisdom. Rafael Alberti, Jorge Guillén, Pedro Salinas, and others who have written their names in the recent history of Spanish poetry have been his disciples; Federico García Lorca is one of them, and so are the Latin American poets, with Gabriela Mistral at their head. I cite the statement of a Swedish journalist on being informed of the Nobel Prize in Literature for this year: «Juan Ramón Jiménez is a born poet, one of those who are born one day with the same simplicity with which the sun's rays shine, one who purely and simply has been born and has given of himself, unconscious of his natural talents. We do not know when such a poet is born. We know only that one day we find him, we see him, we hear him, just as one day we see a plant flower. We call this a miracle.»

In the annals of the Nobel Prize, Spanish literature has been one of the distant gardens. Very rarely have we cast a glance inside. This year's laureate is the last survivor of the famous «generation of 1898». For a generation of poets on both sides of the ocean which separates and at the same time unites the Hispanic countries, he has been a master – the master, in effect. When the Swedish Academy renders homage to Juan Ramón Jiménez, it renders homage also to an entire epoch in the glorious Spanish literature.

Acceptance

by Jaime Benitez, Rector of the University of Puerto Rico

Juan Ramón Jiménez has given me the following message to convey to you:

«I accept with gratitude the undeserved honour which this illustrious Swedish Academy has seen fit to bestow upon me. Besieged by sorrow and sickness, I must remain in Puerto Rico, unable to participate directly in the solemnities. And so that you may have the living testimony of my own intimate feelings gathered in day-by-day association of friendship firmly established in this land of Puerto Rico, I have asked Rector Jaime Benitez of its University, where I am a member of the faculty, to be my personal representative before you in all ceremonies connected with the Nobel Prize awards of 1956.»

I have found such affection for Juan Ramón Jiménez and such understanding for his works that I trust you will excuse me if I single out for special thanks one among you so wise and penetrating that I am certain all others will be glad to be recognized in him. I refer to your own great poet Hjalmar Gullberg, whose presentation this afternoon we shall always remember and whose rendition of Juan Ramón Jiménez' poetry has brought to the Scandinavian people the clear purity of our Andalusian master.

Juan Ramón Jiménez has asked me also to say this: «My wife Zenobia is the true winner of this Prize. Her companionship, her help, her inspiration made, for forty years, my work possible. Today, without her, I am desolate and helpless.»

I have heard from the trembling lips of Juan Ramón Jiménez some of the most touching expressions of despair. For Juan Ramón is such a poet that his every word reflects his own internal kingdom. We fervently hope that someday his sorrow will be expressed in writing and that the memory of Zenobia will provide renewed and everlasting inspiration to that great master of Hispanic letters, Juan Ramón Jiménez, whom you have honoured so signally today.

Prior to the acceptance, R. Granit, Member of the Royal Academy of Sciences, made the following remarks about the Spanish poet: «Juan Ramón has been called a poet for poets, but the layman can approach him if willing first to partake passively of the sheer visual beauty of his landscape, lovely Andalusia, its birds, its flowers, pomegranates, and oranges. Once inside his world, by leisurely reading and rereading, one gradually awakens to a new ‹living insight› into it, refreshed by the depth and richness of a rare poetical imagination. While doing so I recalled a conversation between the painter Degas and the poet Mallarmé, as related by Paul Valéry. Degas, struggling with a sonnet, complained of the difficulties, and finally exclaimed: ‹And yet I do not lack ideas…› Mallarmé with great mildness replied: ‹But Degas, one does not create poetry with ideas. One does it with words.› If ever there has been inspired use of words, it is in Juan Ramón Jiménez' poetry, and in this sense he is a poet for poets. This is probably also the reason why, within the whole Spanish-speaking world, he is regarded as the teacher and master.

The literary awards may involve decisions more difficult than the scientific ones. Yet we should be grateful to the founder for having included a literary Prize in his will. It adds dignity to the other awards and to the act itself; it emphasizes the human and cultural element which the two worlds of creative imagination have in common; and perhaps, in the end, it expresses deeper insight than scientists ever can achieve.»

Biography

Juan Ramón Jiménez (1881–1958) belonged to the group of writers who in the wake of Spain's loss of her colonies to the United States (1898) staged a literary revival. The leader of this group of *modernistas*, as they called themselves, Rubén Darío, helped Juan Ramón to publish *Almas de violeta* (1900) [Souls of Violet], his first volume of poetry. The years between 1905 to 1912 Ramón Jiménez spent at his birthplace, Moguer, where he wrote *Elejías puras* (1908) [Pure Elegies], *La soledad sonora* (1911) [Sonorous Solitude], and *Poemas májicos y dolietes* (1911) [Magic Poems of Sorrow]. His early poetry was influenced by German Romanticism and French Symbolism. It is strongly visual and dominated by the colours yellow and green. His later style, decisive, formally ascetic, and dominated by white, emerges in the poetic prose of his delicate *Platero y yo* (1914) [*Platero and I*] and is fully developed in *Diario de un poeta recién casado* (1917) [Diary of a Newly-Wed Poet], written during a trip to the United States, as well as in *Eternidades* (1918) [Eternities], *Piedra y cielo* (1919) [Stone and Sky], *Poesía* (1923) [Poetry], and *Belleza* (1923) [Beauty]. In the twenties, Ramón Jiménez became the acknowledged master of the new generation of poets. He was active as a critic as well as an editor of literary journals. In 1930 he retired to Seville to devote himself to the revision of his earlier work. Six years later, as the result of the Spanish Civil War, he left Spain for Puerto Rico and Cuba. He remained in Cuba for three years and, in 1939, went to the United States, which became his residence until 1951, when he moved definitely to Puerto Rico. During these years Juan Ramón taught at various universities and published *Españoles de tres mundos* (1942) [Spaniards of Three Worlds], a book of prose portraits, and several collections of poems, among them *Voces de mi copla* (1945) [Voices of My Song] and *Animal de fondo* [Animal of Depth]. The latter book, perhaps his best, clearly reveals the religious preoccupations that filled the last years of the poet's life. Selections from most of his works were published in English translation in *Selected Writings of Juan Ramón Jiménez* and *Three Hundred Poems, 1903–1953*. Ramón Jiménez died in Puerto Rico in 1958.

Literature 1957

ALBERT CAMUS

«for his important literary production, which with clearsighted earnestness illuminates the problems of the human conscience in our times»

Presentation

by Anders Österling, Permanent Secretary of the Swedish Academy

French literature is no longer linked geographically to the frontiers of France in Europe. In many respects it reminds one of a garden plant, noble and irreplaceable, which when cultivated outside its territory still retains its distinctive character, although tradition and variation alternately influence it. The Nobel laureate for this year, Albert Camus, is an example of this evolution. Born in a small town in eastern Algeria, he has returned to this North African milieu to find the source of all the determining influences that have marked his childhood and youth. Even today the man Camus is aware of this great French overseas territory, and the writer in him is often pleased to recall this fact.

From a quasi-proletarian origin, Camus found it necessary to get ahead in life on his own; a poverty-stricken student, he worked at all sorts of jobs to meet his needs. It was an arduous schooling, but one which in the diversity of its teaching was certainly not useless to the realist he was to become. In the course of his years of study, which he spent at the University of Algiers, he belonged to a circle of intellectuals who later came to play an important role in the North African Resistance. His first books were published by a local publishing house in Algiers, but at the age of twenty-five he reached France as a journalist and soon came to make his reputation in the metropolis as a writer of the first rank, prematurely tempered by the harsh, feverish atmosphere of the war years.

Even in his first writings Camus reveals a spiritual attitude that was born of the sharp contradictions within him between the awareness of earthly life and the gripping consciousness of the reality of death. This is more than the typical Mediterranean fatalism whose origin is the certainty that the sunny splendour of the world is only a fugitive moment bound to be blotted out by the shades. Camus represents also the philosophical movement called Existentialism, which characterizes man's situation in the universe by denying it all personal significance, seeing in it only absurdity. The term «absurd» occurs often in Camus' writings, so that one may call it a leitmotif in his work, developed in all its logical moral consequences on the levels of freedom, responsibility, and the anguish that derives from it.

The Greek myth of Sisyphus, who eternally rolls his rock to the mountain top from which it perpetually rolls down again, becomes in one of Camus' essays a laconic symbol of human life. But Sisyphus, as Camus interprets him, is happy in the depth of his soul, for the attempt alone satisfies him. For Camus, the essential thing is no longer to know whether life is worth living but *how* one must live it, with the share of sufferings it entails.

This short presentation does not permit me to dwell longer on Camus' always fascinating intellectual development. It is more worthwhile to refer to the works in which, using an art with complete classical purity of style and intense concentration, he has embodied these problems in such fashion that characters and action make his ideas live before us, without commentary by the author. This is what makes *L'Étranger* (1942) [*The Stranger*] famous. The main character, an employee of a government department, kills an Arab following a chain of absurd events; then, indifferent to his fate, he hears himself condemned to death. At the last moment, however, he pulls himself together and emerges from a passivity bordering on torpor. In *La Peste* (1947) [*The Plague*], a symbolic novel of greater scope, the main characters are Doctor Rieux and his assistant, who heroically combat the plague that has descended on a North African town. In its calm and exact objectivity, this convincingly realistic narrative reflects experiences of life during the Resistance, and Camus extols the revolt which the conquering evil arouses in the heart of the intensely resigned and disillusioned man.

Quite recently Camus has given us the very remarkable story-monologue, *La Chute* (1956) [*The Fall*], a work exhibiting the same mastery of the art of storytelling. A French lawyer, who examines his conscience in a sailors' bar in Amsterdam, draws his own portrait, a mirror in which his contemporaries can equally recognize themselves. In these pages one can see Tartuffe shake hands with the Misanthrope in the name of that science of the human heart in which classical France excelled. The mordant irony, employed by an aggressive author obsessed with truth, becomes a weapon against universal hypocrisy. One may wonder, of course, where Camus is heading by his insistence on a Kierkegaardian sense of guilt whose bottomless abyss is omnipresent, for one always has the feeling that the author has reached a turning point in his development.

Personally Camus has moved far beyond nihilism. His serious, austere meditations on the duty of restoring without respite that which has been ravaged, and of making justice possible in an unjust world, rather make him a humanist who has not forgotten the worship of Greek proportion and beauty as they were once revealed to him in the dazzling summer light on the Mediterranean shore at Tipasa.

Active and highly creative, Camus is in the centre of interest in the literary world, even outside of France. Inspired by an authentic moral engagement, he devotes himself with all his being to the great fundamental questions of life, and certainly this aspiration corresponds to the idealistic end for which the Nobel Prize was established. Behind his incessant affirmation of the absurdity of the human condition is no sterile negativism. This view of things is supplemented in him by a powerful imperative, a «nevertheless», an appeal to the will which incites to revolt against absurdity and which, for that reason, creates a value.

Acceptance

In receiving the distinction with which your free Academy has so generously honoured me, my gratitude has been profound, particularly when I consider the extent to which this recompense has surpassed my personal merits. Every man, and for stronger reasons, every artist, wants to be recognized. So do I. But I have not been able to learn of your decision without comparing its repercussions to what I really am. A man almost young, rich only in his doubts and with his work still in progress, accustomed to living in the solitude of work or in the retreats of friendship: how would he not feel a kind of panic at hearing the decree that transports him all of a sudden, alone and reduced to himself, to the centre of a glaring light? And with what feelings could he accept this honour at a time when other writers in Europe, among them the very greatest, are condemned to silence, and even at a time when the country of his birth is going through unending misery?

I felt that shock and inner turmoil. In order to regain peace I have had, in short, to come to terms with a too generous fortune. And since I cannot live up to it by merely resting on my achievement, I have found nothing to support me but what has supported me through all my life, even in the most contrary circumstances: the idea that I have of my art and of the role of the writer. Let me only tell you, in a spirit of gratitude and friendship, as simply as I can, what this idea is.

For myself, I cannot live without my art. But I have never placed it above everything. If, on the other hand, I need it, it is because it cannot be separated from my fellow men, and it allows me to live, such as I am, on one level with them. It is a means of stirring the greatest number of people by offering them a privileged picture of common joys and sufferings. It obliges the artist not to keep himself apart; it subjects him to the most humble and the most universal truth. And often he who has chosen the fate of the artist because he felt himself to be different soon realizes that he can maintain neither his art nor his difference unless he admits that he is like the others. The artist forges himself to the others, midway between the beauty he cannot do without and the community he cannot tear himself away from. That is why true artists scorn nothing: they are obliged to understand rather than to judge. And if they have to take sides in this world, they can perhaps side only with that society in which, according to Nietzsche's great words, not the judge but the creator will rule, whether he be a worker or an intellectual.

By the same token, the writer's role is not free from difficult duties. By definition he cannot put himself today in the service of those who make history; he is at the service of those who suffer it. Otherwise, he will be alone and deprived of his art. Not all the armies of tyranny with their millions of men will free him from his isolation, even and particularly if he falls into step with them. But the silence of an unknown prisoner, abandoned to humiliations at the other end of the world, is enough to draw the writer out of his exile, at least whenever, in the midst of the privileges of freedom, he manages not to forget that silence, and to transmit it in order to make it resound by means of his art.

None of us is great enough for such a task. But in all circumstances of life, in obscurity or temporary fame, cast in the irons of tyranny or for a time free to express himself, the writer can win the heart of a living community that will justify him, on the one condition that he will accept to the limit of his abilities the two tasks that constitute the greatness of his craft: the service of truth and the service of liberty. Because his task is to unite the greatest possible number of people, his art must not compromise with lies and servitude which, wherever they rule, breed solitude. Whatever our personal weaknesses may be, the nobility of our craft will always be rooted in two commitments, difficult to maintain: the refusal to lie about what one knows and the resistance to oppression.

For more than twenty years of an insane history, hopelessly lost like all the men of my generation in the convulsions of time, I have been supported by one thing: by the hidden feeling that to write today was an honour because this activity was a commitment—and a commitment not only to write. Specifically, in view of my powers and my state of being, it was a commitment to bear, together with all those who were living through the same history, the misery and the hope we shared. These men, who were born at the beginning of the First World War, who were twenty when Hitler came to power and the first revolutionary trials were beginning, who were then confronted as a completion of their education with the Spanish Civil War, the Second World War, the world of concentration camps, a Europe of torture and prisons—these men must today rear their sons and create their works in a world threatened by nuclear destruction. Nobody, I think, can ask them to be optimists. And I even think that we should understand – without ceasing to fight it – the error of those who in an excess of despair have asserted their right to dishonour and have rushed into the nihilism of the era. But the fact remains that most of us, in my country and in Europe, have refused this nihilism and have engaged upon a quest for legitimacy. They have had to forge for themselves an art of living in times of catastrophe in order to be born a second time and to fight openly against the instinct of death at work in our history.

Each generation doubtless feels called upon to reform the world. Mine knows that it will not reform it, but its task is perhaps even greater. It consists in preventing the world from destroying itself. Heir to a corrupt history, in which are mingled fallen revolutions, technology gone mad, dead gods, and worn-out ideologies, where mediocre powers can destroy all yet no longer know how to convince, where intelligence has debased itself to become the servant of hatred and oppression, this generation starting from its own negations has had to re-establish, both within and without, a little of that which constitutes the dignity of life and death. In a world threatened by disintegration, in which our grand inquisitors run the risk of establishing forever the kingdom of death, it knows that it should, in an insane race against the clock, restore among the nations a peace that is not servitude, reconcile anew labour and culture, and remake with all men the Ark of the Covenant. It is not certain that this generation will ever be able to accomplish this immense task, but already it is rising everywhere in the world to the double challenge of truth and liberty and, if necessary, knows how to die for it without hate. Wherever it is found, it deserves to be saluted and encouraged, particularly where it is sacrificing itself. In any event, certain of your complete approval, it is to this generation that I should like to pass on the honour that you have just given me.

At the same time, after having outlined the nobility of the writer's craft, I should have put him in his proper place. He has no other claims but those which he shares with his comrades in arms: vulnerable but obstinate, unjust but impassioned for justice, doing his work without shame or pride in view of everybody, not ceasing to be divided between sorrow and beauty, and devoted finally to drawing from his double existence the creations that he obstinately tries to erect in the destructive movement of history. Who after all this can expect from him complete solutions and high morals? Truth is mysterious, elusive, always to be conquered. Liberty is dangerous, as hard to live with as it is elating. We must march toward these two goals, painfully but resolutely, certain in advance of our failings on so long a road. What writer would from now on in good conscience dare set himself up as a preacher of virture? For myself, I must state once more that I am not of this kind. I have never been able to renounce the light, the pleasure of being, and the freedom in which I grew up. But although this nostalgia explains many of my errors and my faults, it has doubtless helped me toward a better understanding of my craft. It is helping me still to support unquestioningly all those silent men who sustain the life made for them in the world only through memory of the return of brief and free happiness.

Thus reduced to what I really am, to my limits and debts as well as to my difficult creed, I feel freer, in concluding, to comment upon the extent and the generosity of the honour you have just bestowed upon me, freer also to tell you that I would receive it as an homage rendered to all those who, sharing in the same fight, have not received any privilege, but have on the contrary known misery and persecution. It remains for me to thank you from the bottom of my heart and to make before you publicly, as a personal sign of my gratitude, the same and ancient promise of faithfulness which every true artist repeats to himself in silence every day.

Prior to the acceptance, B. Karlgren, Member of the Royal Academy of Sciences, addressed the French writer: «Mr. Camus – As a student of history and literature, I address you first. I do not have the ambition and the boldness to pronounce judgment on the character or importance of your work - critics more competent than I have already thrown sufficient light on it. But let me assure you that we take profound satisfaction in the fact that we are witnessing the ninth awarding of a Nobel Prize in Literature to a Frenchman. Particularly in our time, with its tendency to direct intellectual attention, admiration, and imitation toward those nations who have – by virtue of their enormous material resources – become protagonists, there remains, nevertheless, in Sweden and elsewhere, a sufficiently large elite that does not forget, but is always conscious of the fact that in Western culture the French spirit has for centuries played a preponderant and leading role and continues to do so. In your writings we find manifested to a high degree the clarity and the lucidity, the penetration and the subtlety, the inimitable art inherent in your literary language, all of which we admire and warmly love. We salute you as a true representative of that wonderful French spirit.»

Biography

Albert Camus (1913–60) was a representative of non-metropolitan French literature. His origin in Algeria and his experiences there in the thirties were dominating influences in his thought and work. Of semi-proletarian parents, early attached to intellectual circles of strongly revolutionary tendencies, with a deep interest in philosophy (only chance prevented him from pursuing a university career in that field), he came to France at the age of twenty-five. The man and the times met: Camus joined the resistance movement during the occupation and after the liberation was a columnist for the newspaper *Combat*. But his journalistic activities had been chiefly a response to the demands of the time; in 1947 Camus retired from political journalism and besides writing his fiction and essays was very active in the theatre as producer and playwright (e.g., *Caligula*, 1944). He also adapted plays by Calderón, Lope de Vega, Dino Buzzati, and Faulkner's *Requiem for a Nun*. His love for the theatre may be traced back to his membership in *L'Équipe*, an Algerian theatre group, whose «collective creation» *Révolte dans les Asturies* (1934) was banned for political reasons.

The essay *Le Mythe de Sisyphe* (1942) [*The Myth of Sisyphus*] expounds Camus' notion of the absurd and of its acceptance with «the total absence of hope, which has nothing to do with despair, a continual refusal, which must not be confused with renouncement – and a conscious dissatisfaction.» Meursault, central character of *L'Étranger* (1942) [*The Stranger*], illustrates much of this essay: man as the nauseated victim of the absurd orthodoxy of habit, later – when the young killer faces execution – tempted by despair, hope, and salvation. Dr. Rieux of *La Peste* (1947) [*The Plague*], who tirelessly attends the plague-stricken citizens of Oran, enacts the revolt against a world of the absurd and of injustice and confirms Camus' words: «We refuse to despair of mankind. Without having the unreasonable ambition to save men, we still want to serve them.» Other well-known works of Camus are *La Chute* (1956) [*The Fall*] and *L'Exile et le royaume* (1957) [*Exile and the Kingdom*]. His austere search for moral order found its aesthetic correlative in the classicism of his art. He was a stylist of great purity and intense concentration and rationality.

Literature 1958

BORIS LEONIDOVICH PASTERNAK

«for his important achievement both in contemporary lyrical poetry and in the field of the great Russian epic tradition»

Announcement

by Anders Österling, Permanent Secretary of the Swedish Academy

This year's Nobel Prize in Literature has been awarded by the Swedish Academy to the Soviet Russian writer Boris Pasternak for his notable achievement in both contemporary poetry and the field of the great Russian narrative tradition.

As is well known, Pasternak has sent word that he does not wish to accept the distinction. This refusal, of course, in no way alters the validity of the award. There remains only for the Academy, however, to announce with regret that the presentation of the Prize cannot take place.

On October 25, 1958, two days after the official communication from the Swedish Academy that Boris Pasternak had been selected as the Nobel Prize winner in literature, the Russian writer sent the following telegram to the Swedish Academy: «Immensely thankful, touched, proud, astonished, abashed.» This telegram was followed, on October 29, by another one with this content: «Considering the meaning this award has been given in the society to which I belong, I must reject this undeserved prize which has been presented to me. Please do not receive my voluntary rejection with displeasure.»

Biography

Boris Leonidovich Pasternak (1890–1960), born in Moscow, was the son of talented artists: his father a painter and illustrator of Tolstoy's works, his mother a well-known concert pianist. Pasternak's education began in a German Gymnasium in Moscow and was continued at the University of Moscow. Under the influence of the composer Scriabin, Pasternak took up the study of musical composition for six years from 1904 to 1910. By 1912 he had renounced music as his calling in life and went to the University of Marburg, Germany, to study philosophy. After four months there and a trip to Italy, he returned to Russia and decided to dedicate himself to literature.

Pasternak's first books of verse went unnoticed. With *Sestra moya zhizn* (1922) [*My Sister Life*] and *Temy i variatsii* (1923) [*Themes and Variations*], the latter marked by an extreme, though sober style, Pasternak first gained a place as a leading poet among his Russian contemporaries. In 1924 he published *Vysokaya bolezn* [Sublime Malady], which portrayed the 1905 revolt as he saw it, and *Detstvo Lyuvers* [*The Childhood of Luvers*], a lyrical and psychological depiction of a young girl on the threshold of womanhood. A collection of four short stories was published the following year under the title *Vozdushnye puti* [*Aerial Ways*]. In 1927 Pasternak again returned to the revolution of 1905 as a subject for two long works: *Leytenant Shmidt*, a poem expressing threnodic sorrow for the fate of Lieutenant Schmidt, the leader of the mutiny at Sevastopol, and *Devyatsot pyaty god* [*The Year 1905*], a powerful but diffuse poem which concentrates on the events related to the revolution of 1905. Pasternak's reticent autobiography, *Okhrannaya gramota* [*Safe Conduct*], appeared in 1931 and was followed the next year by a collection of lyrics, *Vtoroye rozhdenie* (1932) [*Second Birth*]. In 1935 he published translations of some Georgian poets and subsequently translated the major dramas of Shakespeare, several of the works of Goethe, Schiller, Kleist, and Ben Jonson, and poems by Petöfi, Verlaine, Swinburne, Shelley, and others. *Na rannikh poyezdakh* [*In Early Trains*], a collection of poems written since 1936, was published in 1943 and enlarged and reissued in 1945 as *Zemnye prostory* [*Wide Spaces of the Earth*]. In 1957 *Doktor Zhivago*, Pasternak's only novel–except for the earlier «novel in verse», *Spektorsky* (1926)–first appeared in an Italian translation and has been acclaimed by some critics as a successful attempt at combining lyrical-descriptive and epic-dramatic styles. An autobiographical sketch, *Biograficbes-ky ocherk* [*An Essay in Autobiography*], was published in 1959, first in Italian and subsequently in English. Pasternak lived in Peredelkino, near Moscow, until his death in 1960.

Literature 1959

SALVATORE QUASIMODO

«for his lyrical poetry, which with classical fire expresses the tragic experience of life in our own times»

Presentation

by Anders Österling, Permanent Secretary of the Swedish Academy

Salvatore Quasimodo, the Italian poet who has been awarded this year's Nobel Prize in Literature, is a Sicilian by birth. He was born near Syracuse, to be more exact, in the little town of Modica some distance from the coast. It is not difficult to imagine that a region so rich in memories of the past must have been of the utmost importance for his future calling. The relics of the ancient Greek temples on the island, the theatres near the Ionian Sea, Arethusa's fountain, so famed in legend, the gigantic ruins at Girgenti and Slinunte – what a playground for a child's imagination! Here in days gone by the heroes of Greek poetry were guests at the court of King Hieron, here the voices of Pindar and Aeschylus linger like an echo through the ages.

Even if, as far as material matters are concerned, Quasimodo was reared in comparative poverty, the milieu in which he spent his youth was nevertheless something to be grateful for. Admittedly, many restless years of travel were to pass before he became conscious of his talent and began to find his way in the classical heritage that was his. In due course, however, his studies were to show their influence in his great contribution as a translator of the literature of classical antiquity which now forms the homogeneous background of his own work as one of the foremost poets in the Italian language. There can hardly be any doubt that his strict classical education acted as a stimulus, not to servile imitation, but to energetic self-discipline in the use of language and the achievement of artistic style. Although regarded as one of the principal innovators in modern poetry, Quasimodo is, nevertheless, bound to the classical tradition and occupies this place with all the natural confidence of a true heir.

Quasimodo made his debut as early as 1930 but it was not until the forties and fifties that he established his position as one of Italy's most outstanding poets, and by this time his reputation had become international. He belongs to the same generation as Silone, Moravia, and Vittorini, that is, the generation of left-wing authors who were able to prove their worth only after the fall of Fascism. Quasimodo is like these writers in that for him, too, the fate of present-day Italy is a reality in which he is deeply involved. His literary production is not very large. In actual fact it consists of five books of poetry, which reveal his development to complete individuality and originality. I quote the characteristic titles of the volumes: *Ed è subito sera* [And Suddenly It's Evening] published in 1942, *Giorno dopo giorno* [Day after Day] in 1946, *La vita non è sogno* [Life Is Not a Dream] in 1949, *Il falso e vero verde* [The False and the True Green] in 1956, and finally *La terra impareggiabile* [The Incomparable Earth] in 1958. Together they form one homogeneous work in which not a single line is unimportant.

Quasimodo has sung of the Sicily of his childhood and his youth with a love that, since he went to live in the north of Italy, has gained an ever-increasing depth and perspective – the windswept island scenery with its Greek temple columns, its desolate grandeur, its poverty–stricken villages, its dusty roads winding through olive groves, its strident music of pounding surf and shepherds' horns. Nonetheless, he cannot be called a provincial poet. The area from which he draws his themes gradually increases, while at the same time his human pathos breaks through the strict poetic form which first fettered him. Above all, the bitter experiences of the war provided the impulse for this change and made him an interpreter of the moral life of his fellow countrymen in their daily experience of nameless tragedies and constant confrontation with death. In this later period he has created a number of poems that are so monumental that one would like to believe that they will be accepted as a lasting contribution to the world's great poetry. Naturally, Quasimodo is far from being the only Italian poet to be deeply affected in this way by the martyrdom of his country and its people, but the Sicilian poet's dark and passionate earnestness rings with a special and individual note when he ends one of his lyrics with the cry:

> *However much everything else is distorted*
> *The dead can never be sold.*
> *Italy is my country, o stranger,*
> *It is of its people I sing, and of the sound*
> *Of secret lamentation that comes from its sea,*
> *I sing of its mothers' chaste grief, of all its life.*

Quasimodo is of the bold opinion that poetry does not exist for its own sake but has an irrefutable mission in the world, through its creative power to re-create man himself. To him, the road to freedom is the same as the conquest of isolation, and his own progress points in the same direction. In this way his work has become a living voice and his poetry an artistic expression of the consciousness of the Italian people, as far as this is possible for poetry with an otherwise so concise and individual structure. In his poems, Biblical turns of phrase are to be found side by side with allusions to classical mythology, that mythology which is an ever-present source of inspiration for a Sicilian. Christian compassion is the basic quality of his poetry, which in moments of greatest inspiration attains universality.

Dear Sir – The following statement pronounced by the Swedish Academy is the reason for which you have been awarded the Nobel Prize: «For his lyric poetry, which with classical fire expresses the tragic experience of life in our own times.»

Your poetry has come to us as an authentic and vivid message of that Italy which has had faithful friends and admirers in our nation for centuries. With our most cordial congratulations I ask you to receive the Nobel Prize in Literature from His Majesty the King.

Acceptance

I have always thought of Sweden as a country adopted by the men who received the Nobel Prize, that unique and brilliant distinction in contemporary civilization. No other nation, in fact, has succeeded in proposing, much less realizing, a similar prize. Although it originates in a country of a few million men, the Nobel Prize is a model of universality, charged with an active and spiritual significance.

The Prize, an award not easily attainable, arouses the passions of men of every political faction in every nation—a sign of its omnipresence and of that gulf which the writer, or poet, or philosopher finds opening before him. Culture, however, has always repulsed the recurrent threat of barbarism, even when the latter was heavily armed and seething with confused ideologies. Here around me are the representatives of one of the most ancient Northern civilizations, which in the course of its rugged history has found itself fighting next to those who have determined the extent of human liberties. It is a civilization which has produced humanist kings and queens, great poets and writers. These poets, both past and contemporary, are known in Italy today, even if only for the volatile side of their restless temperaments and their brooding spirits. From an allegorical presence, inspired by the fabled memories of the Vikings, these difficult and musical names have come to be honoured by us. They speak more forcefully to us than do the poets of other civilizations that are decaying or already buried in the dust of a Renaissance rhetoric. My purpose is neither to eulogize nor subtly to congratulate myself, but rather to criticize the intellectual condition of Europe, when I affirm that Sweden and her people through their choices have consistently challenged and influenced the culture of the world. I have already said that the poet and writer help change the world. This may seem presumptuous or merely a relative truth, but, in order to justify tumult or acquiescence, one need only think of the reactions that poets provoke, both in their own societies and elsewhere. You know that poetry reveals itself in solitude, and that from this solitude it moves out in every direction; from the monologue it reaches society without becoming either sociological or political. Poetry, even lyrical poetry, is always «speech». The listener may be the physical or metaphysical interior of the poet, or a man, or a thousand men. Narcissistic feeling, on the other hand, turns inward upon itself like a circle; and by means of alliteration and of evocative sounds it echoes the myths of other men in forgotten epochs of history.

Today we can talk of a neo-humanism on earth in an absolute sense–a neo-humanism without equal for man. And if the poet finds himself at the centre of this temporary physical structure, which was made in part by his spirit and intelligence, is he still a dangerous being? The question is not rhetorical but an ellipsis of the truth. The world today seems allied with the side opposed to poetry. And for the world, the poet's very presence is an obstacle to be overcome. He must be annihilated. The force of poetry, on the other hand, fans out in every direction in organized societies; and if literary games escape the sensibilities of men everywhere, a poetic activity that is inspired by humanism does not.

I have always thought that one of my poems was written for the men of the North, as well as for those of the Dark Continent or of the East. The universality of poetry is crucial to its form, its style, let us say (that is, the concentrated power of its language). But universality is also what was not there before and what one man contributes to the other men of his time. Such universality is not founded on abstract concepts or on a harmful morality–even worse when moralism is involved–but rather on a direct concreteness and on a unique spiritual condition.

My idea of beauty is embodied not only in harmony but also in dissonance, for even dissonance can attain the precision of a poetic form. Whether we think of painting or sculpture or music, the aesthetic, moral, and critical problems are the same; and likes and dislikes are similar. Greek beauty has been imperiled by contemporary man, who has destroyed form only to seek a new form for his imitation of life–an imitation, that is, which will reveal the very workings of nature. I speak of the poet, of this singular imperfection of nature, who builds his own real existence piece by piece out of the language of men. This language, however, is constructed from a sincerely reasoned syntax, not from a deceptive one. Every experience in life (whether lived or felt) initially involves an unexpected moral disintegration, a spiritual imbalance manifesting itself gradually, and a fear of prolonging a spiritual condition which has already collapsed under the weight of history. For the man of letters as for the transitory critic, the poet always keeps an inaccurate diary, always plays with a terrestrial theology. Indeed, it is certain that this critic will write that such poems are but ponderous restatements of an *ars nova*–restatements

of an art, of a new language which did not exist before these poems were written (thus the history of poetic form is overturned). Perhaps the latter is a way
of rendering solitude bearable and of naming the coldest objects that enclose
it. The poet's evil influence? Perhaps, because no one ever fills the silence of
those men who may read just one poem of a new poet, certainly not the fragile
critic, who fears that a sequence of fifteen or twenty verses may be true. The
investigation of the concept of purity is yet to be done in this century of divi-
sions which are, in appearance, political; a century in which the lot of the poet
is confused and hardly human. His latest rhapsodies are always viewed with
suspicion for their understanding of the heart.

I have spoken here not to propose a poetics nor to establish aesthetic standards but to salute a land for its sturdier men, who are very precious to our
civilization, and who come from the adopted country of which I spoke before.
I now find myself in this country.

I salute and profoundly thank your Majesties the King and Queen of Sweden, Your Royal Highnesses, and the Swedish Academy. Its eighteen members, wise and stern judges, have decided, in awarding the Nobel Prize to my
poetry, to honour Italy, which has been very rich during this first half century, up to the most recent generation, in works of literature, art, and thought
fundamental to our civilization.

Prior to the acceptance, E. Johnson, Member of the Swedish Academy, addressed the Italian poet: «You are, Mr. Salvatore Quasimodo, the winner of
this year's Prize in Literature. In you Italy has found a restorer of her modern
poetry. Your poetic work bears the mark of a country and basks in the light of
a culture both of which have for centuries given much to civilization. You
have entitled one of your poems ‹Uomo del mio tempo›. In it the tone and
the images evoke the often brutal reality in which we live. You yourself are a
man of our time, in the most profound sense of the word. Your work reflects
the trials, the miseries, and the hopes of our epoch. You understand the problems of our society, and your heart is compassionate toward the unfortunate,
the disinherited. Such is the fundamental quality of your poetry.»

The Poet and the Politician

Nobel Lecture, December 11, 1959

«The night is long that never finds the day.» These are Shakespeare's word[s] *Macbeth*, and they help us to define the poet's condition. At first, the rea[der] appears to the poet in his solitude as an image with the face and the gestu[re] of a childhood friend, perhaps of that more sensitive friend who is experien[ced] in solitary readings but a bit diffident in evaluating a presumed representati[on] or misrepresentation, of the world. This representation is attempted with rig[o] rous poetic measures extraneous to science and with words whose sounds [are] predetermined.

An exact poetic duplication of a man is for the poet a negation of the ear[th,] an impossibility of being, even though his greatest desire is to speak to ma[ny] men, to unite with them by means of harmonious verses about the truths [of] the mind or of things. Innocence is sometimes an acute quality which perm[its] the greatest representation of the sensible. And the innocence of the po[et's] friend, who requires, dialectically, that the first poetic rhythms have a logi[cal] form, will remain a fixed point of reference, a focus which will enable [the] poet to construct half of a parabola. The poet's other readers are the anci[ent] poets, who look upon the freshly written pages from an incorruptible distan[ce.] Their poetic forms are permanent, and it is difficult to create new forms wh[ich] can approach them.

The writer of stories or of novels settles on men and imitates them; [he] exhausts the possibilities of his characters. The poet is alone with infin[ite] objects in his own obscure sphere and does not know whether he should [be] indifferent or hopeful. Later that single face will multiply; those gestures w[ill] become approving or disapproving opinions. This happens at the publicati[on] of the first poems. As the poet has expected, the alarms now are sounded, f[or] –and it must be said again–the birth of a poet is always a threat to the existi[ng] cultural order, because he attempts to break through the circle of litera[ry] castes to reach the center.

He has a strange public now, with whom he begins to have silent a[nd] hostile rapport: critics, provincial professors, men of letters. In the po[et's] youth, the majority of these persons destroy his metaphysics, correct [his] images. They are abstract judges who revise «mistaken» poems according to an indifferent, poetic standard.

Poetry is also the physical self of the poet, and it is impossible to separate the poet from his poetry. However, I shall not indulge in autobiography by speaking of my own country, which, as everyone knows, has been filled in every century with Giovanni Della Casas, that is, with men of letters of metrical neatness and fully developed dexterity. These high priests of tradition have clairvoyance and imagination. Moreover, they are obsessed with allegories of the credible destruction of the world. They do not tolerate chronicles but only ideal figures and attitudes. For them the history of poetry is a gallery of ghosts. Even a polemic has some justification if one considers that my own first poetic experiments began during a dictatorship and mark the origin of the Hermetic movement.

From my first book, published in 1930, to the second and the third and the fourth (a translation of Greek lyrics published in 1940), I succeeded in seeing only a stratified public of humble or ambitious readers through the political haze and the academic aversion to harsh poetry that departed from the standard classical composition. The *Lirici Greci* (1940) [Greek Lyrics] entered fresh and new into the literary generation of the time; and they initiated a truer reading of the classics throughout Europe. I knew that young men quoted verses from my lyrics in their love letters; others were written on the walls of jails by political prisoners. What a time to be writing poetry! We wrote verses that condemned us, with no hope of pardon, to the most bitter solitude. Were such verses categories of the soul–great truths? Traditional European poetry, as yet unrestricted, was unaware of our presence: the Latin province, under the aegis of its Caesars, fostered bloodshed, not lessons in humanism.

My readers at that time were still men of letters; but there had to be other people waiting to read my poems. Students, white-collar workers, labourers? Had I sought only an abstract verisimilitude in my poetry? Or was I being overly presumptuous? On the contrary, I was an example of how solitude is broken. Solitude, Shakespeare's «long night», ill-borne by the politician–who wanted a poet such as Tyrtaeus during the African or Russian campaigns–became clearly poetic; taken to be a continuation of European decadence, it was rather the rough draft for neo-humanism. War, I have always said, forces men to change their standards, regardless of whether their country has won or lost. Poetics and philosophies disintegrate «when the trees fall and the walls collapse». At the point when continuity was interrupted by the first nuclear explosion, it would have been too easy to recover the formal sediment which linked us with an age of poetic decorum, of a preoccupation with poetic sounds.

After the turbulence of death, moral principles and even religious proofs are called into question. Men of letters who cling to the private successes of their petty aesthetics shut themselves off from poetry's restless presence. From the night, his solitude, the poet finds day and starts a diary that is lethal to the inert. The dark landscape yields a dialogue. The politician and the mediocre poets with their armour of symbols and mystic purities pretend to ignore the real poet. It is a story which repeats itself like the cock's crow; indeed, like the cock's third crow.

The poet is a nonconformist and does not penetrate the shell of the false literary civilization, which is full of defensive turrets as in the time of the Communes. He may seem to destroy his forms, while instead he actually continues them. He passes from lyric to epic poetry in order to speak about the world and the torment in the world through man, rationally and emotionally. The poet then becomes a danger. The politician judges cultural freedom with suspicion, and by means of conformist criticism tries to render the very concept of poetry immobile. He sees the creative act as being both extratemporal and ineffectual within society, as if the poet, instead of being a man, were a mere abstraction.

The poet is the sum total of the diverse «experiences» of the man of his times. His language is no longer that of the avant-garde, but is rather concrete in the classical sense. Eliot has pointed out that the language of Dante is «the perfection of a common language...nevertheless the ‹simple style› of which Dante is the greatest master, is a very difficult style». The poet's language must be given its proper emphasis. It is neither the language of the Parnassians, nor that of the linguistic revolutionaries, particularly in countries where contamination by dialects only produces additional doubts and literary hieroglyphs. Indeed, philologists will never revive a written language. This is a right which belongs exclusively to the poet. His language is difficult not because of philological reasons or spiritual obscurity, but because of its content. Poets can be translated; men of letters cannot, because they use intellectual skills to copy other poets' techniques and support Symbolism or Decadence for their very lack of content, for their derivative thought, for the truths on which they have been theoretically nourished when they are found to resemble Goethe or the great nineteenth-century French poets. A poet clings to his own tradition and avoids internationalism. Men of letters think of Europe or even of the whole world in the light of a poetics that isolates itself, as if poetry were an identical «object» all over the world. Then, with this understanding of poetics, formalistic men of letters may prefer certain kinds of content and violently reject others. But the problem on either side of the barricade is always content. Thus, the poet's word is beginning to strike forcefully upon the hearts of all men, while absolute men of letters think that they alone live in the real world. According to them, the poet is confined to the provinces with his mouth broken on his own syllabic trapeze. The politician takes advantage of the men of letters who do not assume a contemporary spiritual position, but rather one that has been outdated by at least two generations. Out of cultural unity he makes a game of sophisticated, turbulent decomposition wherein the religious forces can still press for the enslavement of man's intelligence.

Religious poetry, civic poetry, lyric or dramatic poetry are all categories of man's expression which are valid only if the endorsement of formal content is valid. It is a mistake to believe that a spiritual conquest, a particular emotional situation (a religious state) of the individual, can become «society» by extension. Pious abnegation, the renunciation of man by man, is nothing but a formula for death. The truly creative spirit always falls into the claws of wolves. The poet's spoken discourse often depends on a mystique, on the spiritual freedom that finds itself enslaved on earth. He terrifies his interlocutor (his shadow, an object to be disciplined) with images of physical decomposition, with complacent analyses of the horrid. The poet does not fear death, not because he believes in the fantasy of heroes, but because death constantly visits his thoughts and is thus an image of a serene dialogue. In opposition to this detachment, he finds an image of man which contains within itself man's dreams, man's illness, man's redemption from the misery of poverty–poverty which can no longer be for him a sign of the acceptance of life.

In order to assess the extent of the politician's power–and here religious power is also included–one need only recall the silence which lasted for a millennium in the fields of poetry and the arts after the close of the classical epoch, or recall the great paintings of the fifteenth century, a period in which the Church commissioned the work and dictated its content.

Formalistic criticism attempts to strike at the concept of art by focusing its attack on forms. It expresses reservations on the consistency of content in order to infringe upon artistic autonomy in an absolute sense. In fact, poetry will not accept the politician's «missionary» attempts, nor any other kind of critical interference, from whatever philosophy it may originate. The poet does not deviate from his moral or aesthetic path; hence his double solitude in the face of both the world and the literary militias.

But is there a contemporary aesthetics? And what philosophy offers truly significant suggestions? An existentialist or Marxist poetry has not yet appeared on the literary horizon; the philosophical dialogue or the chorus of new generations presupposes a crisis, even presupposes crises in man. The politician uses this confusion to give an air of illusory stability to fragmented poetry.

The antagonism between the poet and the politician has generally been evident in all cultures. Today the two blocs that govern the world are fashioning contradictory concepts of freedom, even though it is clear that for the politician there is but one sort of freedom, which leads in a single direction. It is difficult to break down this barrier which has stained the history of civilization with blood. There always exist as least two ways of regarding cultural freedom: the freedom found in those countries where a profound social revolution has occurred (the French Revolution, for example, or the October Revolution); and that found in other countries, which resist stubbornly before undergoing any change in their world view.

Can poet and politician cooperate? Perhaps they could in societies that are not yet fully developed, but never with complete freedom for both. In the contemporary world the politician may well take a variety of stands, but an accord between poet and politician will never be possible, because the one is concerned with the internal order of man, the other with the ordering of men. A quest for the internal order of man could, in a given epoch, coincide with the ordering and construction of a new society.

Religious power, which, as I have already said, frequently identifies itself with political power, has always been a protagonist of this bitter struggle, even when it seemingly was neutral. The reasons for which the poet, as moral barometer of his own people, becomes a danger to the politician are always those which Giovanni Villani cites in his *Croniche Fiorentine*. He says here that, for the benefit of his contemporaries, Dante «as a poet thoroughly enjoyed ranting and raving in his *Commedia* perhaps more than was proper; but possibly his exile was to blame».

Unlike Villani, Dante does not write chronicles. To the excellent «hermetic» poetry of the *dolce stil nuovo* Dante later adds, without ever betraying his own moral integrity, the violence of human and political invective, not dictated by his aversions, but by his internal standard of justice which is religious in the universal sense. The aesthetes have gingerly placed these verses, which burn in eternity, into the limbo of *non-poesia*. Verses like «Trivia ride tra le ninfe eterne» («Trivia smiles among the eternal nymphs») have always seemed poetically more sensible than the vituperation of the Pisans, or the liquid fires which, falling on the Florentines, burned Beatrice's charming city for centuries. The poetry of Dante has aroused suspicion just because of its greatness. And the false cult of his name, even today, is nothing but rhetoric, so small is the audience of his human *Commedia*. Every nation has poets who stand at the same level of civilization as Dante. Let us remember Schiller for the Germans. Shakespeare for the English, Molière and Corneille for the French, Cervantes for Spain, Dostoevsky for Russia; and as for the moderns, let us leave them for the moment in their hostile serenity at various places on this earth.

The attempts to define, unite, or separate the politician and the poet have at least served to measure historical quality in each of these two universal «types». If I wished to modify the two nouns with the attribute «man», I would increase its specific intensity in the poet and decrease it in the other type, thus making him a «political man», whereas by «politician» I mean the common denominator of an entire group of political numbers which are tied to each other by more or less equivalent ideologies.

Everybody knows the poet's function in the structure of an existing or a developing society. The importance of a Baudelaire, of a Mallarmé, of a Rimbaud, as architects of a «way» of life in France, is more evident today than it was to their contemporaries, who believed that the Symbolist poets were no more than a tortuous literary avant-garde who wrote in a language which had been violently forced into a provisional lyrical syntax. Does the politician recognize the poet's active role in society? It seems so, and–here I must repeat myself–the various forms of subservience or evasion adopted by men of culture in every age demonstrate this sufficiently.

Creative intelligence has always been considered a contagious disease. Hence the various reasons for patronage in the medieval courts–the chivalric or mildly heroic panegyrics, the interminable embellishments of the madrigals. Patronage in this form persisted to drag on to the threshold of our century, by which time the bourgeoisie was building its own state of freedom through reflex power of intelligence. Looking back, someone might observe that even Plato, as the architect of an ideal state, excluded poets from it because they were an element of disorder (or of order, one could say, considering the possibility of their unhinging a society established on anti-democratic foundations). Nevertheless, Plato's ostracism of the poet was only another form of political evasion.

Is the poet free today? According to the society that produces him, he is free

only if he remains the continuer of pseudo-existential enlightenment, the de
orator of placid human sentiments, or if he does not penetrate too profound
into the dialectic of his time, whether from political fear or simple inertia. F
example, Angelo Poliziano in the fifteenth century showed his artistic fre
dom in one of the *Stanze per la giostra di Giuliano de' Medici* [Stanzas Writt
for the Medici Joust], where he cautiously speaks of a confused nymph wl
goes to mass with secular ladies. But Leonardo da Vinci, a writer of a differe
kind, was not free. Here liberty assumes its true meaning; it is nothing but
permission granted by the political powers which allows the poet to enter l
society unarmed. Not even Ariosto and Tasso were free, nor the Abbot Parir
nor Alfieri, nor Foscolo: the rhetoric of these persecuted men places them
time among the propagators of the voice of man – a voice that seems to cry o
in the wilderness and instead corrodes society's untruths.

But is the politician free in his turn? No. In fact, the castes that besiege hii
determine a society's fate and act even upon the dictator. Around these tw
protagonists of history, both adversaries and neither of them free – and t
poets we mean all important writers of a given epoch – passions are stirred ar
conflict ensues. And there is peace only in time of war or revolution – revol
tion the bearer of order, and war the bearer of confusion.

The last war was a clash of systems, of politics, of civil orders, nation t
nation. Its violence twisted even the smallest liberties. A sense of life reappea
ed in the very resistance to the inimical but familiar invader, a resistance t
culture and by folk humanism which, in Vergil's words, «raised its head in tl
bitter fields» against the powerful.

In every country a cultural tradition remains detached from this militai
movement. This tradition is not merely provisional, although it is considere
as such by the conservative bankers who finance construction on civilization
«real estate». I insist upon saying not merely provisional, because the nuclei
of contemporary culture (including the philosophy of existence) is oriente
not toward the disasters of the soul and the spirit, but toward an attempt t
repair man's broken bones. Neither fear, nor absence, nor indifference, nc
impotence will ever allow the poet to communicate a non-metaphysical fa
to others.

The poet can say that man begins today; the politician can say, and indee
does say, that man has been and always may be caught in the trap of his mor
baseness, a baseness which is not congenital but rather implanted by a slo
secular infection.

This truth, concealed among the unattainable attitudes of political wisdon suggests as a first conclusion that the poet can speak only in periods of anarchy. The Resistance is a moral certainty, not a poetic one. The true poet never uses words in order to punish someone. His judgment belongs to a creative order; it is not formulated as a prophetic scripture.

Europeans know the importance of the Resistance; it has been the shining example of the modern conscience. The enemy of the Resistance, for all his shouting, is today only a shadow, without much strength. His voice is more impersonal than his proposals. The popular sensibility is not deceived about the condition of the poet or about that of his adversary. When the antagonism is increased, poetry replaces the subordinate thought of the politician who makes poetry into an idea that can be exploited or extinguished.

The Resistance is the perfect image of the conflict between the present and the past. The language of blood is not only a drama in the physical sense; it is the definitive expression of a continuous trial on man's moral «technology». Europe was born of the Resistance and of the admiration for the indeterminate figures who belong to that order which the war sought to establish. These figures have now been torn out by the roots. Death has an autonomous sleep, and any intervention to solicit this sleep either by logic or by skill of political intelligence is inhuman. Poetry's loyalty lies beyond any consideration of injustice or the intentions of death. The politician wants men to know how to die courageously; the poet wants men to live courageously.

While the poet is conscious of the politician's power, the politician notices the poet only when his voice reaches deep into the various social strata; that is, when lyrical or epic content is revealed as well as poetic form. At this moment, a subterranean struggle begins between the politician and the poet. In history the names of exiled poets are treated like human dice, while the politician claims to uphold culture but, in fact, tries only to reduce its power. His only purpose, as always, is to deprive man of three or four fundamental liberties, so that in his eternal cycle man continually retrieves what has been taken from him.

In our time the politician's defence against culture and thus against the poet operates both surreptitiously and openly in manifold ways. His easiest defence is the degradation of the concept of culture. Mechanical and scientific means, radio and television, help to break the unity of the arts, to favour a poetics that will not even disturb shadows. His most favoured poetics is always that which allies itself with the memory of Arcadia for the artistic disparagement of its own epoch. This is the meaning of Aeschylus' verse, «I maintain that the dead kill the living», which I used as the epigraph to my latest work, *La terra impareggiabile.* In this book man is compared to the earth. If it is a sin to speak of man's intelligence, we can also say that religious powers – and the adjective «lay» used to qualify intelligence is intended to indicate not an accidental quality but rather an intrinsic value – go beyond their bounds when they use their might to suppress the humble rather than to deal with the internal fire of the conscience.

The corruption of the concept of culture offered to the masses, who are led by it to believe that they are catching a glimpse of the paradise of knowledge, is not a modern political device; but the techniques used for this multiple dissipation of man's meditative interests are new and effective. Optimism has become a tangible item; it is nothing but a memory game. Myths and stories (anxiety about supernatural events, let us say) not only sink to the level of murder mysteries, but even undergo visible metamorphoses in the cinema or in the epic tales of criminals and pioneers. Any choice between the poet and the politician is precluded. Elegant urbanity, which sometimes pretends to be indifferent, ironically confines culture to the darker corners of its history, affirming that the scene of strife has been dramatized, that man and his suffering always have been and always will be in their habitual confines, yesterday as well as today and tomorrow. Surely. The poet knows that drama is still possible today – a provocative kind of drama. He knows that the adulators of culture are also its pyromaniacs. The *collage* composed of writers in any regime corrupts the literary groups in the center as easily as on the periphery. The former groups pretend to immortality with a tawdry calligraphy of the soul which they decorate with the colours of their impossible mental lives. In certain moments of history, culture secretly unites its forces against the politician. But it is a temporary unity which serves as a battering ram to beat down the doors of dictatorship. This force establishes itself under every dictatorship when it coincides with a search for man's fundamental liberties. When the dictator has been defeated, this unity disappears and factions again spring up. The poet is alone. Around him rises a wall of hate built with the stones thrown by literary mercenaries. The poet contemplates the world from the top of this wall, without ever descending either into the public places, like the wandering bards, or into the sophisticated circles, like the men of letters. From this very ivory tower, so dear to the corruptors of the romantic soul, he enters into the people's midst, not only into their emotional needs, but even into their jealous political thoughts.

This is not mere rhetoric. The story of the poet subjected to the silent siege is found in all countries and all chronicles of mankind. But the men of letters who are on the side of the politician do not represent the whole nation; they serve only – I say «serve» – to delay by a few moments the voice of the poet in the world. In time, according to Leonardo da Vinci, « every wrong is made right».

Biography

Salvatore Quasimodo (1901–1968) was born of Sicilian parents in Syracus. Desiring to become an engineer, he attended technical schools in Palermo an later enrolled at the Politecnico in Rome. In addition, he studied Latin an Greek at the University there. However, for economic reasons he was unab. to complete his studies. He obtained a position with the Italian government civil engineering corps and was sent to various parts of Italy. In 1930 he ha three poems published in the avant-garde review, *Solaria*, and later that san year appeared his first book of verse, *Acque e terre* [Waters and Lands]. Tw years later he published *Òboe sommerso* [Sunken Oboe], in which he prov a more mature poet. The «poetica della parola», the poetics of the wor which is for Quasimodo the fundamental and virtually limitless connotativ unit, pervades his first book. While this concept still serves as the basis fc *Òboe sommerso*, the main interest of this collection lies in the rhythmical a rangement of words around a lyrical nucleus. In both these and his later worl Sicily is the constant, ever-present factor.

Between 1930 and 1938, the year he left his government position, he mac the acquaintance of many prominent Italian authors and painters. In 1938 h became editor of the weekly magazine, *Tempo*, and three years later w appointed to the chair of Italian Literature at the Giuseppe Verdi Conserv tory in Milan.

During the 1930's Quasimodo was a leader of the «Hermetic» school c poetry; however, with the appearance of his translations *Lirici Greci* (194c [Greek Lyrics] it was obvious that his direction was no longer entirely alon the lines of that group. In *Nuove Poesie* (1942) [New Poems] Quasimod reveals both the influence of classical stylistics and a greater understanding c life in general. His subsequent translations, which range from the Greek an Latin poets (Sophocles, Aeschylus, Euripides, Ovid, Vergil, etc.) to Shak speare and Molière and twentieth-century writers (Neruda, e.e. cumming Aiken, etc.), reflect his full appreciation of the original works as well as h modern taste and sensibility.

During the Second World War Quasimodo experienced the need of th poet to feel one with the people and to declare himself as such in his poems. To him the role of the poet in society is a neccessarily active one; he should commit himself and his talents to contemporary struggles. Such views were first expressed in *Giorno dopo giorno* (1946) [Day after Day] and *La vita non è sogno* (1949) [Life Is Not a Dream].

Quasimodo's later works show this change from individualism toward sociality, and moreover affirm the positive characteristics of life even in a world where death is an omnipresent fear. In *La terra impareggiabile* (1958) [The Incomparable Earth] Quasimodo has eloquently attempted to fuse life and literature; he has developed a new language which coincides with man's new activities and ever-expanding investigations. Some of his poetry and two of his critical essays have appeared in English translation in *The Selected Writings of Salvatore Quasimodo* (1960); his *Selected Poems* were published in 1965.

The recipient of many literary prizes–in 1953, for instance, together with Dylan Thomas, he was awarded the Etna-Taormina International Prize in Poetry–, Quasimodo died in Naples on June 14, 1968.

Literature 1960

SAINT-JOHN PERSE

(pen name of Alexis Saint-Léger Léger)

«for the soaring flight and the evocative imagery of his poetry, which in a vision-
ry fashion reflects the conditions of our times»

Presentation

by Anders Österling, Permanent Secretary of the Swedish Academy

The Nobel Prize laureate in literature for this year bears a name of unusual sound, which he chose at first to protect himself from the curious. Saint-John Perse is the poet's name that was to be made internationally famous by a private man who in civil life is called Alexis Léger and as such was to acquire great prestige in another domain of public life. Thus his life is divided into two periods, one of which has ended whereas the other is continuing: Alexis Léger, the diplomat, has been transformed into Saint-John Perse, the poet.

Considered as a literary personage, he presents a biography remarkable in many respects. Born in 1887 in Guadeloupe, he belonged to a French family that came to settle there as early as the seventeenth century. He spent his childhood in this tropical Eden of the Antilles, all rustling with palms, but at the age of eleven he left for France with his family. He was educated at Pau and at Bordeaux, decided to take a degree in law, and in 1914 entered upon a diplomatic career. Sent first to Peking, he next found himself entrusted with increasingly important assignments. As Secretary General for the Ministry of Foreign Affairs for several years, with the rank of Councillor of State, he assumed major responsibilities during the political events that were the prelude to the Second World War.

After the defeat of France in 1940 he was abruptly suspended and went into exile, was considered a dangerous adversary by the Vichy regime, and was even deprived of his French citizenship. He found refuge in Washington, where he occupied a position as literary adviser to the Library of Congress. The French state was soon to reinstate him in his full rights, but the exile firmly refused to re-enter diplomacy. In recent years, however, he has repeatedly returned to France for private reasons.

Here is a career which opens vast vistas and which presupposes in the one who succeeds in it a breadth of perspective acquired under many conditions, combined with a spiritual tone of uncommon dynamic quality. This international versatility, the hallmark of the great traveller, constitutes moreover one of the themes often repeated in the poet's work. He owed his first success to the cycle of poems entitled «Pour fêter une enfance» (1910) [«To Celebrate

a Childhood»], whose dazzling imagery evokes in the golden dawn of child
hood memories the exotic paradise of Guadeloupe, its fabulous plants an
animals. From China he brought back an epic poem, Anabase (1924) [*Ana
basis*], which relates, in a form suggestive and hard as enamel, a mysteriou
warlike expedition into the Asian deserts. The same, uncompromisingl
dense form, in which verse and prose are united in a solemn flow blendin
Biblical verse with the rhythm of the Alexandrine, is found again in the col
lections of poems which followed: *Exil* (1942) [*Exile*] and *Vents* (1946
[*Winds*], both written in America. They constitute an imposing statement o
the uninterrupted cycle of degeneration and rejuvenation, while *Amers* (1957
[*Seamarks*] celebrates the sea, the eternal dispenser of power, the first cradle o
civilizations.

These works are, it is true, of marked singularity, complicated in form an
thought, but the master who created them is anything but exclusive, if on
means by that that he immures himself in a satisfied autonomy and is intereste
only in himself. Quite the contrary; his dominating quality is the wish t
express the human, seized in all its multiplicity, all its continuity; the wish t
describe man, forever the creator, struggling from century to century agains
the equally perpetual insubordination of the elements. He identifies himsel
with all the races who have lived on our stormy planet. «Our race is old,» h
said in a poem, «our face is nameless. And time knows much about all the me
that we may have been…the ocean of things besets us. Death is at the porthole
but our route is not there.»

In this exaltation of man's creative power, Saint-John Perse may sometime
recall the hymns of the German poet Hölderlin, who also was a magician o
speech, filled with the grandeur of the poetic vocation. It is very easy to trea
this sublime faith in the power of poetry as a paradox in order to belittle i
especially when it seems to assert itself with a force inversely proportional t
the need of arousing an immediate response to the thirst for human com
munion. On the other hand, Saint-John Perse is an eloquent example of th
isolation and estrangement which in our era are a vital condition for poeti
creation when its aim is high.

One can only admire the integrity of his poetic attitude, the lofty insistenc
with which he perseveres in the only mode of expression that allows him t
realize his intentions, an exclusive but always pertinent form. The inexhausti
ble luxuriance of the picturesque style of his rhapsodies is intellectuall
demanding and may weary the reader of whom the poet demands suc
efforts of concentration. He takes his metaphors from all disciplines, from a

eras, from all mythologies, from all regions; his cycles of poems call to mind those great sea shells from which a cosmic music seems to emanate. This expansive imagination is his strength. Exile, separation – evocations whose voiceless murmur gives his poetry its general tonality; and through the double theme of man's strength and helplessness a heroic appeal can be perceived, an appeal which is perhaps expressed more distinctly than before in the poet's latest work, *Chronique* (1960) [*Chronicle*], filled with a breath of grandeur, in which the poet recapitulates everything, at the end of the day, while making veiled allusions to the present state of the world. And he even makes a prophetic appeal to Europe to have it consider this fateful moment, this turning point in the course of history. The poem ends with these words: «Great age, here we are. Take measure of the heart of man.»

It is, then, correct to say that Saint-John Perse, behind an apparent abstruseness and symbols frequently difficult to grasp, brings a universal message to his contemporaries. One has every reason to add that in his own way he perpetuates a majestic tradition in French poetic art, especially the rhetorical tradition inherited from the classics. In short, this honour awarded to him only confirms the position he has acquired in letters as one of the great leaders in poetry.

Acceptance

I have accepted in behalf of poetry the honour which has been given to it here and which I am anxious to restore to it. Without you poetry would not often be held in esteem, for there appears to be an increasing dissociation between poetic activity and a society enslaved by materialism. The poet accepts this split, although he has not sought it. It would exist for the scientist as well, were it not for the practical uses of science. But it is the disinterested thought of both scientist and poet that is honoured here. In this place at least let them no longer be considered hostile brothers. For they are exploring the same abyss and it is only in their modes of investigation that they differ.

When one watches the drama of modern science discovering its rational limits in pure mathematics; when one sees in physics two great doctrines posit, the one a general theory of relativity, the other a quantum theory of uncertainty and indeterminism that would limit forever the exactitude even of physical measurements; when one has heard the greatest scientific innovator of this century, the initiator of a modern cosmology that reduces the vastest intellectual synthesis to the terms of an equation, invoke intuition to come to the aid of reason and proclaim that «the imagination is the true seed bed of science», going even so far as to claim for the scientist the benefit of a true artistic vision: is one not justified in considering the tool of poetry as legitimate as that of logic?

In truth, every creation of the mind is first of all «poetic» in the proper sense of the word; and inasmuch as there exists an equivalence between the modes of sensibility and intellect, it is the same function that is exercised initially in the enterprises of the poet and the scientist. Discursive thought or poetic ellipsis – which of these travels to, and returns from, more remote regions? And from that primal night in which two men born blind grope for their ways, the one equipped with the tools of science, the other helped only by the flashes of his imgi nation, which one returns sooner and more heavily laden with a brief phosphorescence? The answer does not matter. The mystery is common to both. And the great adventure of the poetic mind is in no way secondary to the dramatic advances of modern science. Astronomers have been bewildered by the theory of an expanding universe, but there is no less expansion in the moral infinite of the universe of man. As far as the frontiers of science are pushed back, over the extended arc of these frontiers one will hear the poet's hounds on the chase. For if poetry is not, as has been said, «absolute reality», it comes very close to it, for poetry has a strong longing for, and a deep perception of, reality, situated as it is at that extreme limit of cooperation where the real seems to assume shape in the poem. Through analogy and symbolism, through the remote illuminations of mediating imagery, through the interplay of their correspondences in a thousand chains of reactions and strange associations, and finally, through the grace of a language into which the very rhythm of Being has been translated, the poet invests himself with a surreality that cannot be that of science. Is there among men a more striking dialectic, one that engages them more completely? Since even the philosophers are deserting the threshold of metaphysics, it is the poets's task to retrieve metaphysics; thus poetry, not philosophy, reveals itself as the true «daughter of wonder», according to the words of that ancient philosopher to whom it was most suspect.

But more than a mode of perception, poetry is above all a way of life, of integral life. The poet existed among the cave men; he will exist among men of the atomic age, for he is an inherent part of man. Even religions have been born from the need for poetry, which is a spiritual need, and it is through the grace of poetry that the divine spark lives forever in the human flint. When mythologies vanish, the divine finds refuge and perhaps even continuation in poetry. As in the processions of antiquity the bearers of bread yielded their place to the bearers of torches, so now in the domain of social order and of the immediacies of human need it is the poetic imagination that is still illuminating the lofty passion of peoples in quest of light. Look at man walking proudly under the load of his eternal task; look at him moving along under his burden of humanity, when a new humanism opens before him, fraught with true universality and wholeness of soul. Faithful to its task, which is the exploration of the mystery of man, modern poetry is engaged in an enterprise the pursuit of which concerns the full integration of man. There is nothing Pythian in such poetry. Nor is it purely aesthetic. It is neither the art of the embalmer, nor that of the decorator. It does not breed cultured pearls, nor does it deal in semblances and emblems, and it would not be satisfied by any feast of music. Poetry allies itself with beauty–a supreme union–but never uses it as its ultimate goal or sole nourishment. Refusing to divorce art from life, love from perception, it is action, it is passion, it is power, and always the innovation which extend borders. Love is its hearth-fire, insurrection its law; its place is everywhere, in anticipation. It wants neither to deny nor to keep aloof; it expects no benefits from the advantages of its time. Attached to its own destiny and free from any ideology, it recognizes itself the equal of life, which is its own justification. And with one embrace, like a single great, living strophe, it clasps both past and future in the present, the human with the superhuman, planetary space with universal space. The obscurity for which it is reproached pertains not to its own nature, which is to illuminate, but to the night which it explores, the night of the soul and the mystery in which human existence is shrouded. Obscurity is banished from its expression and this expression is no less exacting than that of science.

Thus by his total adherence to that which is, the poet maintains for us a relationship with the permanence and unity of Being. And his lesson is one of optimism. For him the entire world of things is governed by a single law of harmony. Nothing can happen that by nature could exceed the measure of man. The worst upheavals of history are nothing but seasonal rhythms in a much vaster cycle of repetitions and renewals. And the Furies that cross the scene with lifted torches light only a fragment of the long historical process. Ripening civilizations do not die in the throes of one autumn: they merely change. Inertia is the only menace. The poet is the one who breaks through our habits. And in this way the poet finds himself tied to history despite himself. No aspect of the drama of his times is foreign to him. May he give all of us a clear taste of life in this great age. For this is a great and new time calling for a new self-appraisal. And, after all, to whom would we yield the honour of belonging to our age?

«Do not fear», says History, lifting one day her mask of violence, and with her hand making the conciliatory gesture of the Asiatic divinity at the climax of her dance of destruction, «Do not fear nor doubt, for doubt is sterile and fear servile. Listen instead to the rhytmic beat that my high innovating hand imposes on the great human theme in the constant process of creation. It is not true that life can renounce itself. There is nothing living which proceeds from nothingness or yearns for it. But neither does anything ever keep form or measure under the incessant flux of Being. The tragedy lies not in metamorphosis as such. The true drama of the age is in the widening gap between temporal and eternal man. Is man illuminated on one side going to grow dark on the other? And will his forced maturation in a community without communion be nothing but a false maturity?»

It is up to the true poet to bear witness among us to man's double vocation.

And that means holding up to his mind a mirror more sensitive to his spiritual possibilities. It means evoking in this our century a human condition more worthy of original man. It means, finally, bringing the collective soul into closer contact with the spiritual energy of the world. In the face of nuclear energy, will the poet's clay lamp suffice for his purpose? Yes, if man remembers the clay.

Thus it is enough for the poet to be the bad conscience of his age.

Prior to the acceptance, B. Lindblad, President of the Royal Academy of Sciences, made the following comment: «Mr. Saint-John Perse – With sublime intuition you know how to describe in brilliant metaphors the reaction of the soul of humanity to a world of inexhaustible richness. Your poetic opus covers past, present, and future with its wings; it reflects and illuminates all at once the genesis of our universe. You are one of the powerful defenders of the right of modern poetry to be recognized and accepted as a living force acting upon the emotional basis of the tumultuous world in which we live.»

Biography

Saint-John Perse (1887 –), pseudonym for Alexis Saint-Léger Léger, came from an old Bourguignon family which settled in the French Antilles in the seventeenth century and returned to France at the end of the nineteenth century. Perse studied law at Bordeaux and, after private studies in political science, went into the diplomatic service in 1914. There he had a brilliant career. He served first in the Peking embassy, and later in the Foreign Office where he held top positions under Aristide Briand and became its administrative head.

He left France for the United States in 1940 and was deprived of his citizenship and possessions by the Vichy regime. From 1941 to 1945, he was literary adviser to the Library of Congress. After the war he did not resume his diplomatic career and, in 1950, retired officially with the title of *Ambassadeur de France*. He has made the United States his permanent residence.

His literary work was published partly under his own name, but chiefly under the pseudonyms St. J. Perse and Saint-John Perse. After various poems that reflect the impressions of his childhood, he wrote *Anabase* (1924) [*Anabasis*] while in China. It is an epic poem which puzzled many critics and gave rise to the suggestion that it could be understood better by an Asian than by a Westerner. Much of his work was written after he settled in the United States: *Exil* (1942) [*Exile*], in which man and poet merge and imagery and diction are fully mastered; *Poème à l'Etrangère* (1943) [Poem to a Foreign Lady]; *Pluies* (1943) [*Rains*]; *Neiges* (1944) [*Snows*]; *Vents* (1946) [*Winds*], which are the winds of war and peace that blow within as well as outside of man; *Amers* (1957) [*Seamarks*], wherein the sea redounds as an image of the timelessness of man; and his abstract epic, *Chronique* (1960) [*Chronicle*].

Literature 1961

IVO ANDRIĆ

*«for the epic force with which he has traced themes and depicted human destinies
from his country's history»*

Presentation

by Anders Österling, Permanent Secretary of the Swedish Academy

The Nobel Prize in Literature has been awarded this year to the Yugoslav writer Ivo Andrić, who has been acknowledged in his own country as a novelist of unusual stature, and who in recent years has found an increasingly wide audience as more and more of his works have come to be translated. He was born in 1892 of a family of artisans that had settled in Bosnia, a province still under Austrian rule when he was a child.

As a young Serbian student he joined the national revolutionary movement, suffered persecution, and was imprisoned in 1914 when the war broke out. Nevertheless, he studied at several universities, finally obtaining his degree from Graz. For several years he served his country in the diplomatic service; at the outbreak of the Second World War he was the Yugoslav ambassador in Berlin. Only a few hours after his return to Belgrade, the city was bombed by German planes. Forced to retreat during the German occupation, Andrić nevertheless managed to survive and to write three remarkable novels. These are generally called the Bosnian trilogy, although they have nothing in common but their historical setting, which is symbolized by the Crescent and the Cross. The creation of this work, in the deafening roar of guns and in the shadow of a national catastrophe whose scope then seemed beyond calculation, is a singularly striking literary achievement. The publication of the trilogy did not take place until 1945.

The epic maturity of these chronicles in novel form, especially of his masterpiece *Na Drini ćuprija* (1945) [*The Bridge on the Drina*], was preceded by a phase during which Andrić, speaking in the first person of the lyric poet, sought to express the harsh pessimism of his young heart. It is significant that in the isolation of his years in prison he had found the greatest consolation in Kierkegaard. Later, in the asceticism of strict self-discipline, he discovered the way that could lead him back to what he called «the eternal unconscious and blessed patrimony», a discovery that also signified the introduction into his work of the objective epic form which he henceforth cultivated, making himself the interpreter of those ancestral experiences that make a people conscious of what it is.

Na Drini ćuprija is the heroic story of the famous bridge which the vizier Nehmed Pasha had built during the middle of the sixteenth century near the Bosnian city of Visegrad. Firmly placed on its eleven arches of light-coloured stone, richly ornamented, and raised in the middle by a superstructure, it proudly perpetuated the memory of an era throughout the following eventful centuries until it was blown up in the First World War. The vizier had wanted it to be a passage that would unite East and West in the centre of the Ottoman Empire. Armies and caravans would cross the Drina on this bridge, which for many generations symbolized permanence and continuity underneath the contingencies of history. This bridge became the scene for every important event in this strange corner of the world. Andrić's local chronicle is amplified by the powerful voice of the river, and it is, finally, a heroic and bloody act in world history that is played here.

In the following work, *Travnička hronika* (1945) [*Bosnian Story*], the action takes place at the time of the Napoleonic Wars. Here we witness the rivalry between the Austrian and French consuls in a desolated, old-fashioned city where a Turkish vizier has established his residence. We find ourselves in the midst of events which bring together tragic destinies. The discontent which stirs among the bazaars in the alleys of Travnik; the revolts of the Serbo-Croation peasants; the religious wars between Mohammedans, Christians, and Jews—all of this contributes to create the atmosphere that after a century of tension was going to be rent by the lightning at Sarajevo. Again, Andrić's power is revealed in the breadth of his vision and the masterly control of his complex subject matter.

The third volume, *Gospodjica* (1945) [*The Woman from Sarajevo*], is different; it is a purely psychological study of avarice in its pathological and demoniac aspect. It tells the story of a merchant's daughter who lives alone in Sarajevo. Her bankrupt father had told her on his death-bed to defend her interests ruthlessly, since wealth is the only means of escape from the cruelties of existence. Although the portrait is strikingly successful, Andrić here confines himself to a subject that does not permit him a full display of his great narrative gifts. They are revealed fully, however, in a minor work that should receive at least a brief mention: *Prokleta avilija* (1954) [*Devil's Yard*]. A story set in an Istanbul prison, it is as colourful in its pattern as an Oriental tale and yet realistic and convincing.

Generally speaking, Andrić combines modern psychological insight with the fatalism of the *Arabian Nights*. He feels a great tenderness for mankind, but he does not shrink from horror and violence, the most visible proof to him of the real presence of evil in the world. As a writer he possesses a whole network of original themes that belong only to him; he opens the chronicle of the world, so to speak, at an unknown page, and from the depth of the suffering souls of the Balkan slaves he appeals to our sensibility.

In one of his novellas, a young doctor recounting his experiences in the Bosnia of the 1920's says, «If you lie awake one whole night in Sarajevo you learn to distinguish the voices of the Sarajevian night. With its rich and firm strokes the clock of the Catholic cathedral marks the hour of two. A long minute elapses; then you hear, a little more feeble, but shrill, the voice of the Orthodox Church, which also sounds its two strokes. Then, a little more harsh and far away, there is the voice of the Beg Mosque clock; it sounds eleven strokes, eleven ghostly Turkish hours, counted after the strange division of time in those far-off regions. The Jews have no bell to toll their hours, and God alone knows what time it is for them, God alone knows the number indicated on the calendar of the Sephardims and the Ashkenazims. Thus, even in the deep of the night, when everybody sleeps, the world is divided; it is divided over the counting of the lost hours of a night that is coming to an end.»

Perhaps this suggestive nocturnal atmosphere also gives a key to the chief problems that have dominated Andrić's work. The study of history and philosophy has inevitably led him to ask what forces, in the blows and bitterness of antagonisms and conflicts, act to fashion a people and a nation. His own spiritual attitude is crucial in that respect. Considering these antagonisms with a deliberate and acquired serenity, he endeavours to see them all in the light of reason and with a profoundly human spirit. Herein lies, in the last analysis, the major theme of all his work; from the Balkans it brings to the entire world a Stoic message, as our generation has experienced it.

Dear Sir—It is written on your diploma that the Nobel Prize has been bestowed upon you «for the epic force with which you have traced themes and depicted human destinies from your country's history». It is with great satisfaction that the Swedish Academy honours in you a worthy representative of a linguistic area which, up to now, has not appeared on the list of laureates. Extending to you our most sincere congratulations, I ask you to receive from the hands of His Majesty the King the Prize awarded to you.

Acceptance

In carrying out the high duties entrusted to it, the Nobel Committee of the Swedish Academy has this year awarded the Nobel Prize in Literature, a signal mark of honour on the international scene, to a writer from a small country, as it is commonly called. In receiving this honour, I should like to make a few remarks about this country and to add a few considerations of a more general character about the storyteller's work to which you have graciously awarded your Prize.

My country is indeed a «small country between the worlds», as it has aptly been characterized by one of our writers, a country which, at break-neck speed and at the cost of great sacrifices and prodigious efforts, is trying in all fields, including the field of culture, to make up for those things of which it has been deprived by a singularly turbulent and hostile past. In choosing the recipient of this award you have cast a shining light upon the literary activity of that country, at the very moment when, thanks to a number of new names and original works, that country's literature is beginning to gain recognition through an honest endeavour to make its contribution to world literature. There is no doubt that your distinction of a writer of this country is an encouragement which calls for our gratitude; I am happy to have the opportunity to express this gratitude to you in this place and at this time, simply but sincerely.

It is a more difficult and more delicate task to tell you about the storyteller's work which you have honoured with your Prize. In fact, when it comes down to a writer and his work, can we expect him to be able to speak of that work, when in reality his creation is but a part of himself? Some among us would rather consider the authors of works of art either as mute and absent contemporaries or as famous writers of the past, and think that the work of art speaks with a clearer and purer voice if the living voice of the author does not interfere. This attitude is neither uncommon nor particularly new. Even in his day Montesquieu contended that authors are not good judges of their own works. I remember reading with understanding admiration Goethe's rule: «The artist's task is to create, not to talk»; and many years later I was moved to find the same thought brilliantly expressed by the greatly mourned Albert Camus.

Let me then, as seems fitting to me, concentrate in this brief statement on the story and the storyteller in general. In thousands of languages, in the most diverse climes, from century to century, beginning with the very old stories told around the hearth in the huts of our remote ancestors down to the works of modern storytellers which are appearing at this moment in the publishing houses of the great cities of the world, it is the story of the human condition that is being spun and that men never weary of telling to one another. The manner of telling and the form of the story vary according to periods and circumstances, but the taste for telling and retelling a story remains the same: the narrative flows endlessly and never runs dry. Thus, at times, one might almost believe that from the first dawn of consciousness throughout the ages, mankind has constantly been telling itself the same story, though with infinite variations, to the rhythm of its breath and pulse. And one might say that after the fashion of the legendary and eloquent Scheherazade, this story attempts to stave off the executioner, to suspend the ineluctable decree of the fate that threatens us, and to prolong the illusion of life and of time. Or should the storyteller by his work help man to know and to recognize himself? Perhaps it is his calling to speak in the name of all those who did not have the ability or who, crushed by life, did not have the power to express themselves. Or could it be that the storyteller tells his own story to himself, like the child who sings in the dark in order to assuage his own fear? Or finally, could the aim of these stories be to throw some light on the dark paths into which life hurls us at times and to tell us about this life, which we live blindly and unconsciously, something more than we can apprehend and comprehend in our weakness? And thus the words of a good storyteller often shed light on our acts and on our omissions, on what we should do and on what we should not have done. Hence one might wonder whether the true history of mankind is not to be found in these stories, oral or written, and whether we might not at least dimly catch the meaning of that history. And it matters little whether the story is set in the present or in the past.

Nevertheless, some will maintain that a story dealing with the past neglects, and to a certain degree turns its back on, the present. A writer of historical stories and novels could not in my opinion accept such a gratuitous judgment. He would rather be inclined to confess that he does not himself know very well when or how he moves from what is called the present into what we call the past, and that he crosses easily—as in a dream—the threshold of centuries. But in the end, do not past and present confront us with similar phenomena and with the same problems: to be a man, to have been born without knowing it or wanting it, to be thrown into the ocean of existence, to be obliged to swim, to exist; to have an identity; to resist the pressure and shocks from the outside and the unforeseen and unforeseeable acts–one's own and those of others–which so often exceed one's capacities? And what is more, to endure one's own thoughts about all this: in a word, to be human.

So it happens that beyond the imaginary demarcation line between past and present the writer still finds himself eye to eye with the human condition, which he is bound to observe and understand as best he can, with which he must identify, giving it the strength of his breath and the warmth of his blood, which he must attempt to turn into the living texture of the story that he intends to translate for his readers, in such a way that the result be as beautiful, as simple, and as persuasive as possible.

How can a writer arrive at this aim, by what ways, by what means? For some it is by giving free rein to their imagination, for others it is by studying with long and painstaking care the instructions that history and social evolution afford. Some will endeavour to assimilate the substance and meaning of past epochs, others will proceed with the capricious and playful nonchalance of the prolific French novelist who once said, «What is history but a peg to hang my novels on?» In a word, there are a thousand ways and means for the novelist to arrive at his work, but what alone matters and alone is decisive is the work itself.

The author of historical novels could put as an epigraph to his works, in order to explain everything to everyone, once and for all, the old saying: «Cogitavi dies antiquos et annos aeternos in mente habui» (I have pondered the days of yore and I have kept in mind the years of eternity). But with or without epigraph, his work, by its very existence, suggests the same idea.

Still, these are ultimately nothing but questions of technique, tastes, and methods, a fascinating intellectual pastime concerning a work or having vaguely to do with it. In the end it matters little whether the writer evokes the past, describes the present, or even plunges boldly into the future. The main thing is the spirit which informs his story, the message that his work conveys to mankind; and it is obvious that rules and regulations do not avail here. Each builds his story according to his own inward needs, according to the measure of his inclinations, innate or acquired, according to his conceptions and to the power of his means of expression. Each assumes the moral responsibility for his own story and each must be allowed to tell it freely. But, in conclusion, it is to be hoped that the story told by today's author to his contemporaries, irrespective of its form and content, should be neither tarnished by hate nor obscured by the noise of homicidal machines, but that it should be born out of love and inspired by the breadth of ideas of a free and serene human mind. For the storyteller and his work serve no purpose unless they serve, in one way or another, man and humanity. That is the essential point. And that is what I have attempted to bring out in these brief reflections inspired by the occasion and which, with your permission, I shall conclude as I began them, with the repeated expression of a profound and sincere gratitude.

Biography

Ivo Andrić (1892–) was born in the village of Dolac, near Travnik. After spending his youth in his native Bosnia, which was at the time part of the Austro-Hungarian Empire, he studied philosophy at the universities of Zagreb, Vienna, and Cracow. His studies were interrupted by the outbreak of the First World War, at the beginning of which he was jailed for his anti-Austrian activities. After receiving a doctorate in letters from the University of Graz in 1923, he entered the Yugoslav diplomatic service. The last diplomatic post he held was that of Yugoslav minister in Berlin. When Germany invaded Yugoslavia in 1939, Andrić returned to Belgrade and lived there in seclusion throughout the Second World War. He has continued to reside in the Yugoslav capital.

Andrić started his literary career as a poet. In 1914 he was one of the contributors to *Hrvatska mlada lirika* [Young Croatian Lyrics]. At the end of the war he published two books of lyrical prose–one of them entitled *Nemiri* (1919) [Anxieties]–which, written in the form of a diary, reflect Andrić's experiences of the war and his imprisonment. There followed a long period in which Andrić concentrated on the writing of short stories. His first novella, *Put Alije Djerzeleza* [*The Trip of Alija Djerzelez*], published in 1920, early manifests a dominant trait of his creative process. Andrić takes his material from the life of Bosnia, but through this local material he presents universal human problems. In the period between the two world wars Andrić published three books of short stories under the same title, *Pripovetke* (1924, 1931, 1936) [Stories].

During the Second World War, in the leisure imposed on him by the circumstances, Andrić wrote his three large works, all of which were published in 1945: *Na Drini ćuprija* [*The Bridge on the Drina*], *Travnička hronika* [*Bosnian Story*], and *Gospodjica* [*The Woman from Sarajevo*].

The first two of these works–both of them chronicles rather than novels in the strict sense – deal, like most of Andrić's work, with Bosnia and her history. The author describes the life of this region in which East and West have for centuries clashed with their interests and influences, a region whose population is composed of different nationalities and religions. Andrić is at his best when he limits himself to his native Bosnia and her people.

In *Gospodjica* and *Nove pripovetke* (1948) [New Stories] Andrić presented present-day people and problems. He dealt with the psychology of the wealthy, with the war and postwar periods, and with the formation of a new society. But in *Prokleta avilija* (1954) [*Devil's Yard*] Andrić returned to his favorite milieu and described the experiences of a Bosnian Franciscan, Fra Peter, who is put in an Istanbul jail, being wrongly accused of plotting against Ottoman rule. In 1960 Andrić published another collection of stories, *Lica* [Faces]. He has also written several essays, prominent among which is *Zapisi o Goji* (1961) [Notes on Goya].

Literature 1962

JOHN STEINBECK

«for his realistic as well as imaginative writings, distinguished by a sympathetic humour and a keen social perception»

Presentation

by Anders Österling, Permanent Secretary of the Swedish Academy

John Steinbeck, the author awarded this year's Nobel Prize in Literature, was born in the little town of Salinas, California, a few miles from the Pacific coast near the fertile Salinas Valley. This locality forms the background for many of his descriptions of the common man's everyday life. He was raised in moderate circumstances, yet he was on equal terms with the workers' families in this rather diversified area. While studying at Stanford University, he often had to earn his living by working on the ranches. He left Stanford without graduating and, in 1925, went to New York as a free-lance writer. After bitter years of struggling to exist, he returned to California, where he found a home in a lonely cottage by the sea. There he continued his writing.

Although he had already written several books by 1935, he achieved his first popular success in that year with *Tortilla Flat*. He offered his readers spicy and comic tales about a gang of *paisanos*, asocial individuals who, in their wild revels, are almost caricatures of King Arthur's Knights of the Round Table. It has been said that in the United States this book came as a welcome antidote to the gloom of the then prevailing depression. The laugh was now on Steinbeck's side.

But he had no mind to be an unoffending comforter and entertainer. The topics he chose were serious and denunciatory, as for example the bitter strikes on California's fruit and cotton plantations which he depicted in his novel *In Dubious Battle* (1936). The power of his literary style increased steadily during these years. The little masterpiece *Of Mice and Men* (1937), which is the story of Lennie, the imbecile giant who out of tenderness alone squeezes the life out of every living creature that comes into his hands, was followed by those incomparable short stories which he collected in the volume *The Long Valley* (1938). The way had now been paved for the great work that is principally associated with Steinbeck's name, the epic chronicle *The Grapes of Wrath* (1939). This is the story of the emigration to California which was forced upon a group of people from Oklahoma through unemployment and abuse of power. This tragic episode in the social history of the United States inspired in Steinbeck a poignant description of the experiences of one particular farmer and his family during their endless, heartbreaking journey to a new home.

In this brief presentation it is not possible to dwell at any length on individual works which Steinbeck later produced. If at times the critics have seemed to note certain signs of flagging powers, of repetitions that might point to a decrease in vitality, Steinbeck belied their fears most emphatically with *The Winter of Our Discontent* (1961), a novel published last year. Here he attained the same standard which he set in *The Grapes of Wrath*. Again he holds his position as an independent expounder of the truth with an unbiased instinct for what is genuinely American, be it good or bad.

In this recent novel, the central figure is the head of a family who has come down in the world. After serving in the war, he fails at whatever he tries until at last he is employed in the simple work of a grocery store clerk in the New England town of his forefathers. He is an honest man and he does not complain without due cause, although he is constantly exposed to temptation when he sees the means by which material success must be purchased. However, such means require both hard scrupulousness and moral obduracy, qualities he cannot muster without risking his personal integrity. Tellingly displayed in his sensitive conscience, irradiated like a prism, is a whole body of questions which bear on the nation's welfare problems. This is done without any theorizing, using concrete, or even trivial, everyday situations, which are nonetheless convincing when described with all of Steinbeck's vigorous and realistic verve. Even with his insistence on the factual, there are harmonic tones of daydreaming, fumbling speculations around the eternal theme of life and death.

Steinbeck's latest book is an account of his experiences during a three-month tour of forty American states (*Travels with Charley*, 1962). He travelled in a small truck equipped with a cabin where he slept and kept his stores. He travelled incognito, his only companion being a black poodle. We see here what a very experienced observer and *raisonneur* he is. In a series of admirable explorations into local colour, he rediscovers his country and its people. In its informal way this book is also a forceful criticism of society. The traveller in Rosinante—the name which he gave his truck—shows a slight tendency to praise the old at the expense of the new, even though it is quite obvious that he is on guard against the temptation. «I wonder why progress so often looks like destruction», he says in one place when he sees the bulldozers flattening out the verdant forest of Seattle to make room for the feverishly expanding residential areas and the skyscrapers. It is, in any case, a most topical reflection, valid also outside America.

Among the masters of modern American literature who have already been awarded this Prize–from Sinclair Lewis to Ernest Hemingway–Steinbeck more than holds his own, independent in position and achievement. There is in him a strain of grim humour which to some extent redeems his often cruel and crude motif. His sympathies always go out the oppressed, to the misfits and the distressed; he likes to contrast the simple joy of life with the brutal and cynical craving for money. But in him we find the American temperament also in his great feeling for nature, for the tilled soil, the wasteland, the mountains, and the ocean coasts, all an inexhaustible source of inspiration to Steinbeck in the midst of, and beyond, the world of human beings.

The Swedish Academy's reason for awarding the Prize to John Steinbeck reads, «For his realistic as well as imaginative writings, distinguished by a sympathetic humour and a keen social perception.»

Dear Mr. Steinbeck–You are not a stranger to the Swedish public any more than to that of your own country and of the whole world. With your most distinctive works you have become a teacher of good will and charity, a defender of human values, which can well be said to correspond to the proper idea of the Nobel Prize. In expressing the congratulations of the Swedish Academy, I now ask you to receive this year's Nobel Prize in Literature from the hands of His Majesty the King.

Acceptance

I thank the Swedish Academy for finding my work worthy of this highest honor.

In my heart there may be doubt that I deserve the Nobel award over other men of letters whom I hold in respect and reverence – but there is no question of my pleasure and pride in having it for myself.

It is customary for the recipient of this award to offer personal or scholarly comment on the nature and the direction of literature. At this particular time, however, I think it would be well to consider the high duties and the responsibilities of the makers of literature.

Such is the prestige of the Nobel award and of this place where I stand that I am impelled, not to squeak like a grateful and apologetic mouse, but to roar like a lion out of pride in my profession and in the great and good men who have practiced it through the ages.

Literature was not promulgated by a pale and emasculated critical priesthood singing their litanies in empty churches – nor is it a game for the cloistered elect, the tinhorn mendicants of low calorie despair.

Literature is as old as speech. It grew out of human need for it, and it has not changed except to become more needed.

The skalds, the bards, the writers are not separate and exclusive. From the beginning, their functions, their duties, their responsibilities have been decreed by our species.

Humanity has been passing through a gray and desolate time of confusion. My great predecessor, William Faulkner, speaking here, referred to it as a tragedy of universal fear so long sustained that there were no longer problems of the spirit, so that only the human heart in conflict with itself seemed worth writing about.

Faulkner, more than most men, was aware of human strength as well as of human weakness. He knew that the understanding and the resolution of fear are a large part of the writer's reason for being.

This is not new. The ancient commission of the writer has not changed. He is charged with exposing our many grievous faults and failures, with dredging up to the light our dark and dangerous dreams for the purpose of improvement.

Furthermore, the writer is delegated to declare and to celebrate man's proven capacity for greatness of heart and spirit – for gallantry in defeat – for courage, compassion and love. In the endless war against weakness and despair, these are the bright rally-flags of hope and of emulation.

I hold that a writer who does not passionately believe in the perfectibility of man, has no dedication nor any membership in literature.

The present universal fear has been the result of a forward surge in our knowledge and manipulation of certain dangerous factors in the physical world.

It is true that other phases of understanding have not yet caught up with this great step, but there is no reason to presume that they cannot or will not draw abreast. Indeed it is a part of the writer's responsibility to make sure that they do.

With humanity's long proud history of standing firm against natural enemies, sometimes in the face of almost certain defeat and extinction, we would be cowardly and stupid to leave the field on the eve of our greatest potential victory.

Understandably, I have been reading the life of Alfred Nobel – a solitary man, the books say, a thoughtful man. He perfected the release of explosive forces, capable of creative good or of destructive evil, but lacking choice, ungoverned by conscience or judgment.

Nobel saw some of the cruel and bloody misuses of his inventions. He may even have foreseen the end result of his probing – access to ultimate violence – to final destruction. Some say that he became cynical, but I do not believe this. I think he strove to invent a control, a safety valve. I think he found it finally only in the human mind and the human spirit. To me, his thinking is clearly indicated in the categories of these awards.

They are offered for increased and continuing knowledge of man and of his world – for understanding and communication, which are the functions of literature. And they are offered for demonstrations of the capacity for peace – the culmination of all the others.

Less than fifty years after his death, the door of nature was unlocked and we were offered the dreadful burden of choice.

We have usurped many of the powers we once ascribed to God.

Fearful and unprepared, we have assumed lordship over the life or death of the whole world – of all living things.

The danger and the glory and the choice rest finally in man. The test of his perfectibility is at hand.

Having taken Godlike power, we must seek in ourselves for the responsibility and the wisdom we once prayed some deity might have.

Man himself has become our greatest hazard and our only hope.

So that today, St. John the apostle may well be paraphrased: In the end is the Word, and the Word is Man–and the Word is with Men.

Prior to the acceptance, R. Sandler, Member of the Royal Academy of Sciences, commented, «Mr. John Steinbeck–In your writings, crowned with popular success in many countries, you have been a bold observer of human behaviour in both tragic and comic situations. This you have described to the reading public of the entire world with vigour and realism. Your *Travels with Charley* is not only a search for but also a revelation of America, as you yourself say: ‹This monster of a land, this mightiest of nations, this spawn of the future turns out to be the macrocosm of microcosm me.› Thanks to your instinct for what is genuinely American you stand out as a true representative of American life.»

Biography

John Steinbeck (1902–1968), born in Salinas, California, came from a family of moderate means. He worked his way through college at Stanford University but never graduated. In 1925 he went to New York, where he tried for a few years to establish himself as a free-lance writer, but he failed and returned to California. After publishing some novels and short stories, Steinbeck first became widely known with *Tortilla Flat* (1935), a series of humorous stories about Monterey *paisanos*.

Steinbeck's novels can all be classified as social novels dealing with the economic problems of rural labour, but there is also a streak of worship of the soil in his books, which does not always agree with his matter-of-fact sociological approach. After the rough and earthy humour of *Tortilla Flat*, he moved on to more serious fiction, often aggressive in its social criticism, to *In Dubious Battle* (1936), which deals with the strikes of the migratory fruit pickers on California plantations. This was followed by *Of Mice and Men* (1937), the story of the imbecile giant Lennie, and a series of admirable short stories collected in the volume *The Long Valley* (1938). In 1939 he published what is considered his best work, *The Grapes of Wrath*, the story of Oklahoma tenant farmers who, unable to earn a living from the land, moved to California where they became migratory workers.

Among his later works should be mentioned *East of Eden* (1952), *The Winter of Our Discontent* (1961), and *Travels with Charley* (1962), a travelogue in which Steinbeck wrote about his impressions during a three-month tour in a truck that led him through forty American states. He died in New York City in 1968.

Literature 1963

GIORGOS SEFERIS

(pen name of Giorgos Seferiades)

«for his eminent lyrical writing, inspired by a deep feeling for the Hellenic world of culture»

Presentation

by Anders Österling, Permanent Secretary of the Swedish Academy

This year's Nobel Prize in Literature has been awarded to the Greek poet Giorgos Seferis, who was born in 1900 at Smyrna, which he left at an early age to accompany his family to Athens. After the Greeks were driven out of Asia Minor and Seferis' home town had gone up in flames, homelessness–ever the fate of an oppressed and scattered people–was to play a decisive role during his adult years in more ways than one. Seferis studied in Paris, then entered the diplomatic service, went into exile with the Free Greek Government when Greece was occupied in 1941, and was moved about from country to country during the Second World War, when he served his country in Crete, in Cairo, in South Africa, in Turkey, and in the Middle East. After six years as ambassador in London, he retired last year and returned to Athens to devote himself entirely to his literary work.

Seferis' poetic production is not large, but because of the uniqueness of its thought and style and the beauty of its language, it has become a lasting symbol of all that is indestructible in the Hellenic affirmation of life. Now that Palamas and Sikelianos are dead, Seferis is today the representative Hellenic poet, carrying on the classical heritage; a leading national figure, he is also acclaimed abroad in so far as his poetry has been made available in translation. Here in Sweden his work was presented thirteen years ago by Hjalmar Gullberg, whose translations included the famous «The King of Asine», the theme of which has a connection with Sweden because of our archaeologists' successful excavations on this site. Using imagination as a tool, Seferis tries in this poem to penetrate the secret behind a name that is merely mentioned in a verse of the *Iliad*.

When reading Seferis we are forcibly reminded of a fact that is sometimes forgotten: geographically, Greece is not only a peninsula but also a world of water and foam, strewn with myriad islands, an ancient sea kingdom, the perilous and stormy home of the mariner. This Greece is the constant background of his poetry, in which it is conjured up as the vision of a grandeur both harsh and tender. Seferis does this with a language of rare subtlety, both rhythmical and metaphorical. It has rightly been said that he, better than anyone else, has interpreted the mystery of the stones, of the dead fragments of marble, and of the silent, smiling statues. In his evocative poems, figures from ancient Greek mythology appear together with recent events in the Mediterranean's bloody theatre of war. His poetry sometimes seems difficult to interpret, particularly because Seferis is reluctant to expose his inner self, preferring to hide behind a mask of anonymity. He often expresses his grief and bitterness through the medium of a central narrative figure, a kind of Odysseus with features borrowed from the old seamen in the lost Smyrna of the poet's youth. But in his hollow voice is dramatized much of Greece's historical fatality, its shipwrecks and its rescues, its disasters and its valour. Technically, Seferis has received vital impulses from T. S. Eliot, but underneath the tone is unmistakably his own, often carrying a broken echo of the music from an ancient Greek chorus.

Seferis once described himself, «I am a monotonous and obstinate man who for twenty years has not ceased to say the same things over and over again.» There is perhaps some truth in this description, but one must remember that the message he feels bound to convey is inseparable from the intellectual life of his generation as it finds itself confronted with ancient Greek civilization, a heritage that presents a formidable challenge to the impoverished heir. In one of his most significant poems Seferis describes a dream in which a marble head–too heavy for his arms, yet impossible to push aside–fell upon him at the moment of awakening. It is in this state of mind that he sings the praise of the dead, for only communication with the dead conversing on their asphodel meadows can bring to the living a hope of peace, confidence, and justice. In Seferis' interpretation the story of the Argonauts becomes a parable halfway between myth and history, a parable of oarsmen who must fail before they reach their goal.

But Seferis animates this background of melancholy resignation with the eloquent joy inspired in him by his country's mountainous islands with their whitewashed houses rising in terraces above an azure sea, a harmony of colours that we find again in the Greek flag. In concluding this brief presentation, I should like to add that the Prize has been awarded to Seferis «for his eminent lyrical writing, inspired by a deep feeling for the Hellenic world of culture».

Dear Sir–In honouring you, it has been a great privilege for the Swedish Academy to pay its tribute to the Greece of today, whose rich literature has had to wait perhaps too long for the Nobel laurels. Extending to you the congratulations of the Swedish Academy, I ask you to receive from the hands of His Majesty the King this year's Prize in Literature.

Acceptance

I feel at this moment that I am a living contradiction. The Swedish Academy has decided that my efforts in a language famous through the centuries but not widespread in its present form are worthy of this high distinction. It is paying homage to my language – and in return I express my gratitude in a foreign language. I hope you will accept the excuses I am making to myself.

I belong to a small country. A rocky promontory in the Mediterranean, it has nothing to distinguish it but the efforts of its people, the sea, and the light of the sun. It is a small country, but its tradition is immense and has been handed down through the centuries without interruption. The Greek language has never ceased to be spoken. It has undergone the changes that all living things experience, but there has never been a gap. This tradition is characterized by love of the human; justice is its norm. In the tightly organized classical tragedies the man who exceeds his measure is punished by the Erinyes. And this norm of justice holds even in the realm of nature.

«Helios will not overstep his measure;» says Heraclitus, «otherwise the Erinyes, the ministers of Justice, will find him out.» A modern scientist might profit by pondering this aphorism of the Ionian philosopher. I am moved by the realization that the sense of justice penetrated the Greek mind to such an extent that it became a law of the physical world. One of my masters exclaimed at the beginning of the last century, «We are lost because we have been unjust.» He was an unlettered man, who did not learn to write until the age of thirty-five. But in the Greece of our day the oral tradition goes back as far as the written tradition, and so does poetry. I find it significant that Sweden wishes to honour not only this poetry, but poetry in general, even when it originates in a small people. For I think that poetry is necessary to this modern world in which we are afflicted by fear and disquiet. Poetry has its roots in human breath – and what would we be if our breath were diminished? Poetry is an act of confidence – and who knows whether our unease is not due to a lack of confidence?

Last year, around this table, it was said that there is an enormous difference between the discoveries of modern science and those of literature, but little difference between modern and Greek dramas. Indeed, the behaviour of human beings does not seem to have changed. And I should add that today we need to listen to that human voice which we call poetry, that voice which is constantly in danger of being extinguished through lack of love, but is always reborn. Threatened, it has always found a refuge; denied, it has always instinctively taken root again in unexpected places. It recognizes no small nor large parts of the world; its place is in the hearts of men the world over. It has the charm of escaping from the vicious circle of custom. I owe gratitude to the Swedish Academy for being aware of these facts; for being aware that languages which are said to have restricted circulation should not become barriers which might stifle the beating of the human heart; and for being a true Areopagus, able «to judge with solemn truth life's ill-appointed lot», to quote Shelley, who, it is said, inspired Alfred Nobel, whose grandeur of heart redeems inevitable violence.

In our gradually shrinking world, everyone is in need of all the others. We must look for man wherever we can find him. When on his way to Thebes Oedipus encountered the Sphinx, his answer to its riddle was: «Man». That simple word destroyed the monster. We have many monsters to destroy. Let us think of the answer of Oedipus.

Prior to the acceptance, I. Svennilson of the Royal Academy of Sciences addressed the poet: «Giorgos Seferis-Nathan Söderblom, a friend of Alfred Nobel, later Sweden's Archbishop and one of the Nobel Peace Prize winners, developed on the basis of his scientific studies the idea that religion should be regarded as a continuous revelation of spiritual values by a long procession of prophets and saints. We know that the great classics are dear to the Greek people, and we greet you as an innovator within that living tradition.»

Some Notes on Modern Greek Tradition

Nobel Lecture, December 11, 1963

A poet who is especially dear to me, the Irishman W. B. Yeats, Nobel laureate of 1923, on his return from Stockholm wrote an account of his trip entitled «The Bounty of Sweden». I was reminded of it when the Swedish Academy honoured me so greatly by its choice. «The bounty of Sweden» is for us much older and extends much further. I do not think that any Greek, on learning of the homage you have paid to my country, could forget the good that Sweden has done in our country with altruism, patience, and such perfect humanity, whether it was done by your archaeologists in times of peace or by your Red Cross missions during the war. I pass over many other gestures of solidarity that we have seen more recently.

When your King, His Majesty Gustav Adolf VI, handed me the diploma of the Nobel Prize, I could not but remember with emotion the days when as Crown Prince he was determined to make his personal contribution to the excavations of the Acropolis of Asine. When I first met Axel Persson, that generous man who had devoted himself to the same excavation, I called him my godfather–godfather because Asine had given me a poem.

In the town of Missolonghi a granite monument has been dedicated to the Swedes who died for Greece in her struggle for independence. Our gratitude is even more durable than that granite.

One evening at the beginning of the last century, in a street on the island of Zante, Dionysios Solomos heard an old beggar at the door of a tavern reciting a popular ballad on the burning of the Holy Sepulchre at Jerusalem. Extending his hand, the beggar said:

> *The Holy Sepulchre of Christ, it did not burn;*
> *Where the holy light shines, no other fire can burn.*

Solomos, we are told, was seized with such enthusiasm that he entered the tavern and ordered free drinks for all those present. This anecdote is significant for me; I have always considered it as a symbol of the gift of poetry that our people are left in the hands of a prince of the spirit at the very moment when the resurrection of modern Greece begins.

This symbol represents a long development that has not yet been completed. It is my intention to speak to you of some men who have been important in the struggle for Greek expression ever since we started breathing the air of liberty. Forgive me if my account is sketchy, but I do not wish to tax your patience.

Our difficulties began with the Alexandrians who, dazzled by the Attic classics, began to teach what is correct and incorrect in writing, began, in other words, to teach purism. They did not consider that language is a living organism and that nothing can stop its growth. They were indeed very successful and brought forth generation after generation of purists, who have survived even to our day. They represent one of the two great currents in our language and our tradition that have never been interrupted.

The other current, long disregarded, is the vulgar, popular, or oral tradition. It is as old as the former and has its own written documents. I was moved when one day I happened to read a letter from a sailor to his father, preserved on a second-century papyrus. I was struck by the actuality and the presence of its language, and I grieved that for many centuries a wealth of sentiments had remained unexpressed, stifled forever by the vast shroud of purism and the niceties of the rhetorical style. The Gospels, too, as you know, were written in the popular language of their period. If one thinks of the Apostles, who wanted to be understood and appreciated by the common people, one can only view with anguish the human perversity that caused uproars in Athens at the beginning of the century on the occasion of a translation of the Gospels, and which even today would brand as unlawful the translation of the words of Christ.

But I am anticipating. The two currents ran parallel until the fall of the Greek Byzantine Empire. On the one hand, there were the scholars, refined by a thousand embellishments of the mind. On the other hand, there were the common people, who regarded them with respect but nevertheless continued in their own modes of expression. I do not think that during the Byzantine era there ever was a rapprochement between the two currents, that is, a phenomenon such as one observes in the frescoes and mosaics of the years preceding the end of the Empire under the Paleologues. At that time imperial art and the popular art of the provinces merged to produce a splendid renewal.

However, Constantinople underwent a long agony before she fell. When she was finally taken, a servitude, which was to last for several centuries, descended on the entire nation. Many then were the scholars who, «carrying the heavy urns filled with the ashes of their ancestors», as the poet says, came to the Occident to spread the seeds of what came to be called the Renaissance. But that Renaissance – I mean the word in its strict sense, as we use it to indicate the transition from the Middle Ages to the modern age, whether it was good or bad – that Renaissance was not known in Greece, with the exception of certain islands, notably Crete, which was then under Venetian rule. There, toward the sixteenth century, was developed a poetry and a verse drama in a language splendidly alive and perfectly sure of itself. Considering that at the same time important schools of painting were flourishing in Crete and that toward the middle of the century the great Cretan painter Domenicos Theotocopoulos, who came to be known as El Greco, was born and grew up on that island, the fall of Crete is an even more painful event than the fall of Constantinople.

Constantinople had, after all, received a fatal blow from the Crusaders in 1204. She was merely outliving herself. Crete, on the other hand, was full of vigour, and one can only brood with a curious mixture of grief and faith over the destiny of that Greek land whose people are always ready to rebuild what the squalls of history are to overthrow again. One is reminded of what the poet Kalvos wrote to General Lafayette: «God and our Despair».

At any rate, the revival in Crete began to decline in the middle of the seventeenth century. At that time many Cretans sought refuge in the Ionian Islands and in other parts of Greece. They brought with them their poems, which they knew by heart and which were immediately adopted in their new surroundings. These poems sometimes blended with the popular songs preserved by the Greeks of the mainland, together with their legends, for many generations. There is evidence that some of them may date back to pagan times; others emerged in the course of the centuries, such as the cycle of *Digenis Acritas*, a product of the Byzantine era. They make us realize that throughout the ages the same attitudes toward work, suffering, joy, love, and death persisted without change. But at the same time their expression is so fresh, so free and full of humanity, that they make us feel intuitively to what extent the spirit of Greece has always remained faithful to itself. I have so far avoided giving you examples. However much I am indebted to my translators – it is through them that you are able to know me – I have the painful feeling of a distortion beyond recovery when I translate my language into a language that is not mine. Forgive me if for the moment I cannot help making an exception. It is a very short poem about the death of a loved one:

*To protect you I placed three guards: the sun on
the mountain, the eagle on the plain, and the fresh
north wind on the ships. The sun has set;
the eagle has fallen asleep; and the ships have
carried away the fresh north wind. Charon saw
his chance and took you away.*

I have given you a pale reflection of the poem, which is radiant in Greek.

Here you have in very simplified terms the antecedents of modern Greece. It is the heritage which the old beggar in front of the tavern on Zante bequeathed to Dionysios Solomos one evening. That image comes to my mind whenever I think of him and of what he has given to us.

In the history of modern Greek poetry there is no lack of strange figures and cases. It would have been much more natural, for instance, if the poetry of a country of sailors, peasants, and soldiers had begun with rough and simple songs. But the opposite happened. It began with a man driven by the daemon of the absolute, who was born on the island of Zante. The level of culture on the Ionian Islands was at that time much superior to that on the mainland. Solomos had studied in Italy. He was a great European and very much aware of the problems faced by the poetry of his century. He could have made his career in Italy. He wrote poems in Italian, and he did not lack encouragement; but he preferred the narrow gate and decided to do his work in Greek. Solomos certainly knew the poems that the Cretan refugees had brought with them. He was a fervent partisan of the popular language and an enemy of purism. His views on the subject have been preserved in his *Dialogue between the Poet and the Pedant Scholar* (we should understand that word in the sense in which Rabelais uses the word Sorbonicole). I cite at random: «Is there anything in my mind», he exclaims, «but liberty and language?» Or again: «Submit to the language of the people, and if you are strong enough, conquer it.» He undertook this conquest and through this undertaking he became a great Greek. Solomos is without doubt the author of the «Hymn to Freedom», the first stanzas of which have became our national anthem, and of other poems that have been set to music and widely sung in the course of the last century. But it is not for this reason that his heritage is so valuable to us; it is because he charted as definitively as his age permitted him the course that Greek expression was to take. He loved the living language and worked all his life to raise it to the level of the poetry of which he dreamt. It was an effort beyond the powers of any single individual. Of his great poems–for instance «The Free

Besieged», inspired by the siege and sufferings of the town of Missolonghi—
only fragments remain to us, the dust from a diamond that the craftsman took
into his tomb. We have nothing but fragments and blank spaces to represent
the struggle of this great soul which was as tense as a bow-string that is about
to snap. Many generations of Greek writers have bent over those fragments
and those blank spaces. Solomos died in 1857. In 1927, *I Gynaika tis Zakynthos*
[*Woman of Zante*] was published for the first time and established him as a
great prose writer just as he had long been acknowledged as a great poet. It is a
magnificent work that makes a profound impact on our minds. In a significant
manner fate willed that seventy years after his death Solomos would reply
by means of this message to the inquietude of new generations. He has always
been a beginning.

I have made a pilgrimage to those regions haunted by the shadows of Ten-

Andreas Kalvos, a contemporary of Solomos, was one of the most isolated
figures in Greek literature. There is not even a portrait of him. A friend of the
Italian poet Ugo Foscolo, he soon was embroiled in a quarrel with him. He
was born on the island of Zante and lived for many years on Corfu. He does
not seem to have had any contact with Solomos. His entire work consists of a
slender volume of twenty odes published when he was barely thirty. In his
youth he travelled extensively in Italy, Switzerland, and England. He had a
lofty mind, imbued with the moral ideas of the end of the eighteenth century,
devoted to virtue, fiercely opposed to tyranny. His poetry is inspired by the
grandeur and sorrow of a martyred nation. It is moving to see how this man,
who lost his mother as a child, in the depth of his consciousness identifies the
love for his lost mother with that for his country. His language is irregular; his
rhymes idiosyncratic; he had a classical ideal in mind and despised what he
called «the monotony of the Cretan poems» that had given so much to Solomos. But his images are flashes of lightning and of such immediate power that
they seem to tear his poetry apart. After a solitary life on Corfu, devoted to
teaching, he left the Ionian Islands for good. He married a second time in
London and with his wife opened a boarding school for girls in a small provincial town in England. There he lived for fourteen years until his death,
without ever renewing contact with Greece.

I have made a pilgrimage to those regions haunted by the shadows of Tennyson. An old man who loved that part of the country told me that he had
once interviewed old women of eighty who had been pupils of Kalvos and
whose memories were full of respect for their old master. But again I was unable to free myself from the image of that faceless man, clad in black, striking
his lyre on an isolated promontory. His work fell into oblivion; doubtless his

voice did not conform to the taste for unreal and romantic rhetoric that swept Athens at that period. He was rediscovered about 1890 by Kostis Palamas. Greece had matured meanwhile, and it was the time when the young forces of modern Greece were beginning to burst forth. The struggle for a living language was widening. There were exaggerations, but that was only natural. The struggle, continuing for many years, went beyond literature and was characterized by the will to challenge every aspect of the present. It turned enthusiastically toward public education. One rejected ready-made forms and ideas. One certainly wanted to preserve the heritage of the ancients, but at the same time there was an interest in the common people; one wanted to illuminate the one by the other. One wondered about the identity of the Greek of today. Scholars and schoolmasters took part in this struggle. Important studies of Greek folklore appeared during this period, and there was a growing realization of the continuity of our tradition as well as of the need for a critical spirit.

Kostis Palamas played a great role in this movement. I was an adolescent when I first saw him; he was giving a lecture. He was a very short man, who impressed one by his deep eyes and by his voice, which was rich with a somewhat tremulous quality. His work was vast and influenced decades of Greek literary life. He expressed himself in all genres of poetry–lyric, epic, and satirical; at the same time he was our most important critic. He had an astonishing knowledge of foreign literatures, proving once again that Greece is a crossroads, and that since the time of Herodotus or Plato it has never been closed to foreign currents, especially in its best moments. Palamas inevitably had enemies, often among those who had profited from the road he had opened. I consider him a force of nature in comparison with which the critics look petty. When he appeared, it was as if a force of nature, held back and accumulated for over a thousand years of purism, had finally burst the dikes. When the waters are freed to flood a thirsty plain, one must not ask that they carry only flowers. Palamas was profoundly aware of all the components of our civilization, ancient, Byzantine, and modern. A world of unexpressed things thronged his soul. It was that world, his world, which he liberated. I would not maintain that his abundance never harmed him, but the people that assembled about his coffin in 1943 clearly felt something of what I have just told you when at the moment of final farewell they spontaneously sang our national anthem, the hymn to freedom, under the eyes of the occupation authorities.

One hundred and fifty-four poems constitute the known work of Constantine Cavafy, who is at the opposite pole from Palamas. He is that rare case among poets whose motivating force is not the word; the danger lies in the abundance of words. He was part of the Hellenic culture that flourished in Egypt and is disappearing today. Except for a few absences, he spent all his life in Alexandria, his native city. His art is characterized by rejections and by his sense of history. By history I do not mean the account of the past, but the history that lives in the present and sheds light on our present life, on its drama and its destiny. I compare Cavafy to that Proteus of the Alexandrian shore who, Homer says, changed his form incessantly. His tradition was not that of the popular art which Solomos and Palamas had followed; it was the scholarly tradition. Whereas they took their inspiration from a popular song or tale, he would have recourse to Plutarch or to an obscure chronicler or to the deeds of a Ptolemy or a Seleucid. His language is a mixture of what he learned from his family (a fine family from Constantinople) and what his ear picked up in the streets of Alexandria, for he was a city man. He loved countries and periods in which the frontiers are not well defined, in which personalities and beliefs are fluid. Many of his characters are partly pagan and partly Christian, or live in a mixed environment: «Syrians, Greeks, Armenians, Medes», as he has said. Once you have became familiar with his poetry, you begin to ask yourself if it is not a projection of our present life into the past, or perhaps if history has not decided all of a sudden to invade our present existence. His world is a preliminary world that comes back to life with the grace of a young body. His friend E. M. Forster told me that, when he read to him for the first time a translation of his poems, Cavafy exclaimed in surprise, «But you understand, my dear Forster, you understand.» He had so completely forgotten what it was like to be understood!

Time has passed since then, and Cavafy has been abundantly translated and commented upon. I am thinking at this moment of your true poet and generous Hellenist, the late Hjalmar Gullberg, who introduced Cavafy to Sweden. But Greece has several facets, and not all of them are obvious. I am thinking of the poet Anghelos Sikelianos. I knew him well, and it is easy to recall his magnificent voice as he recited his poetry. He had something of the splendour of a bard of a former age, but at the same time he was uncommonly familiar with our land and the peasants. Everybody loved him. He was called simply «Anghelos», as if he were one of them. He knew instinctively how to establish a relation between the words and the behaviour of a Parnassus shepherd or a village woman and the sacred world which he inhabited. He was possessed by a god, a force made up of Apollo, Dionysus, and Christ. A poem he wrote one Christmas night during the last war, «Dionysus in the Manger», begins «My sweet child, my Dionysus and my Christ. » And it is truly amazing to see how in Greece the old pagan religion has blended with orthodox Christianity. In Greece Dionysus, too, was a crucified god. Cavafy, who has so strongly felt and expressed the resurrection of man and the world, is nonetheless the same man who has written, «Death is the only way.» He understood that life and death are two faces of the same thing. I used to visit him whenever I passed through Greece. He suffered from a long illness, but the force that inspired him never left him to the end. One evening at his home, after his fainting spell had alarmed us, he told me, «I have seen the absolute black; it was unspeakably beautiful.»

Now, I should like to end this brief account with a man who has always been dear to me; he has supported me in difficult hours, when all hope seemed gone. He is an extreme case of contrasts, even in my country. He is not an intellectual. But the intellect thrown back upon itself sometimes needs freshness, like the dead who needed fresh blood before answering Ulysses. At the age of thirty-five he learned to read and write a little in order to record, so he said, what he had seen during the war of independence, in which he had taken a very active part. His name is Ioannis Makriyannis. I compare him to one of those old olive trees in our country which were shaped by the elements and which can, I believe, teach a man wisdom. He, too, was shaped by human elements, by many generations of human souls. He was born near the end of the eighteenth century on the Greek mainland near Delphi. He tells us how his poor mother, while she was gathering faggots, was seized by labour pains and gave birth to him in a forest. He was not a poet, but song was in him, as it has always been in the soul of the common people. When a foreigner, a Frenchman, visited him, he invited him for a meal; he tells us, «My guest wanted to hear some of our songs, so I invented some for him.» He had a singular talent for expression; his writing resembles a wall built stone by stone; all his words perform their function and have their roots; sometimes there is something Homeric in their movement. No other man has taught me more how to write prose. He disliked the false pretences of rhetoric. In a moment of anger he exclaimed, «You have appointed a new commander to the citadel of Corinth — a pedant. His name was Achilles, and in hearing the name you thought that it was the famous Achilles and that the name was going to fight. But a name never fights; what fights is valour, love of one's country, and virtue.» But at the same time one perceives his love for the ancient heritage, when he said to soldiers who were about to sell two statues to foreigners: «Even if they pay you ten thousand thalers, don't let the statues leave our soil. It is for them that we fought.» Considering that the war had left many scars on the body of this man, one may rightly conclude that these words carried some weight. Toward the end of his life his fate became tragic. His wounds caused him intolerable pain. He was persecuted, thrown into prison, tried, and condemned. In his despair he wrote letters to God. «And You don't hear us, You don't see us.» That was the end. Makriyannis died in the middle of the last century. His memoirs were deciphered and published in 1907. It took many more years for the young to realize his true stature.

I have spoken to you about these men because their shadows have followed me ever since I started on my journey to Sweden and because their efforts represent to my mind the efforts of a body shackled for centuries which, with its chains finally broken, regains life and gropes and searches for its natural activity. No doubt, my account has many limitations. I have distorted by oversimplifying. The limitation I particularly dislike is inherent in any personal matter. I have certainly omitted great names, for instance, Adamantios Korais and Alexandros Papadiamantis. But how to talk about all this without making a choice? Forgive my shortcomings. In any case, I have only indicated some landmarks, and that I have done as simply as possible. In addition to those men, and in the periods that separated them, there were of course many generations of dedicated workers who sacrificed their lives to advance the spirit a little more toward that many-faced expression which is the Greek expression. I also wanted to express my solidarity with my people, not only with the great masters of the mind, but with the unknown, the ignored, those who pored over a book with the same devotion with which one bends over an icon; with the children who had to walk for hours to get to schools far away from their villages «to learn the letters, the things of God», as their song has it. To echo once more my friend Makriyannis, one must not say «I», one must say «we», because no one does anything alone. I think it is good that it be so. I need that solidarity because, if I do not understand the men of our country with their virtues and vices, I feel that I could not understand the other men in the wide world.

I have not spoken to you of the ancients. I did not want to tire you. Perhaps I should add a few words. Since the fifteenth century, since the fall of Byzantium, they have increasingly become the heritage of mankind. They have been integrated into what we have come to call European civilization. We rejoice that so many nations contribute to bring them closer to our life. Still, there are certain things that have remained our inalienable possessions. When I read in Homer the simple words«φάος ἠελίοιο»–today I would say «φῶς του ἠλίου» (the sunlight)–I experience a familiarity that stems from a collective soul rather than from an intellectual effort. It is a tone, one might say, whose harmonies reach quite far; it feels very different from anything a translation can give. For we do, after all, speak the same language–a language changed, if you insist, by an evolution of several thousand years, but despite everything faithful to itself–and the feeling for a language derives from emotions as much as from knowledge. This language shows the imprints of deeds and attitudes repeated throughout the ages down to our own. These imprints sometimes have a surprising way of simplifying problems of interpretation that seem very difficult to others. I will not say that we are of the same blood, for I abhor racial theories, but we have always lived in the same country and have seen the same mountains slope into the sea. Perhaps I have used the word «tradition» without pointing out that it does not mean habit. On the contrary, tradition holds us by the ability to break habits, and thus proves its vitality.

Nor have I talked to you of my own generation, the generation on which fell the burden of a moral reorientation after the exodus of one and a half million people from Asia Minor and which witnessed a unique phenomenon in Greek history, the reflux to the Greek mainland, the concentration of our population, once dispersed in flourishing centres the world over.

And, finally, I have not spoken to you of the generation that came after us, whose childhood and adolescence were mangled during the years of the last war. It undoubtedly has new problems and other points of view: Greece is becoming more and more industrialized. Nations are moving more closely together. The world is changing. Its movements are speeding up. One might say that it is characteristic of the new generation to point out abysses, whether in the human soul or in the universe about us. The concept of duration has changed. It is a sorrowful and restless young generation. I understand its difficulties; they are, after all, not so different from ours. A great worker for our liberty, Righas Pheraios, has taught us: «Free thoughts are good thoughts.» But I should like our youth to think at the same time of the saying engraved on the lintel above the gate of your university at Uppsala: «Free thoughts are good; just thoughts are better.»

I have come to the end. I thank you for your patience. I am also grateful that «the bounty of Sweden» has permitted me in the end to feel as if I were «nobody»–understanding this word in the sense that Ulysses gave it when he replied to the Cyclops, Polyphemus: «οὖτις»–nobody, in that mysterious current which is Greece.

Biography

Giorgos Seferis (1900–) was born in Smyrna, Asia Minor. He attended school in Smyrna and finished his studies at the Gymnasium in Athens. When his family moved to Paris in 1918, Seferis studied law at the University of Paris and became interested in literature. He returned to Athens in 1925 and was admitted to the Royal Greek Ministry of Foreign Affairs in the following year. This was the beginning of a long and successful diplomatic career, during which he held posts in England (1931–1934) and Albania (1936–1938). During the Second World War, Seferis accompanied the Free Greek Government in exile to Crete, Egypt, South Africa, and Italy, and returned to liberated Athens in 1944. He continued to serve in the Ministry of Foreign Affairs and held diplomatic posts in Ankara (1948–1950) and London (1951–1953). He was appointed minister to Lebanon, Syria, Jordan, and Iraq (1953–1956), and was Royal Greek Ambassador to the United Kingdom from 1957 to 1961, the last post before his retirement in Athens. Seferis received many honours and prizes, among them honorary doctoral degrees from the universities of Cambridge (1960), Oxford (1964), Salonika (1964), and Princeton (1965).

His wide travels provide the backdrop and colour for much of Seferis' writing, which is filled with the themes of alienation, wandering, and death. Seferis' early poetry consists of *Strophe* (1931) [*Turning Point*], a group of rhymed lyrics strongly influenced by the Symbolists, and *E Sterna* (1932) [*The Cistern*], conveying an image of man's most deeply felt being which lies hidden from and ignored by the everyday world. His mature poetry, in which one senses an awareness of the presence of the past and particularly of Greece's great past as related to her present, begins with *Mythistorema* (1935) [*Mythistorema*], a series of twenty-four short poems which translate the Odyssean myths into modern idiom. In *Tetradio Gymnasmaton* (1940) [*Book of Exercises*], *Emerologio Katastromatos* (1940) [*Logbook I*], *Emerologio Katastromatos B* (1944) [*Logbook II*], *Kihle* (1947) [*Thrush*], and *Emerologio Katastromatos C* (1955) [*Logbook III*], Seferis is preoccupied with the themes he developed in *Mythistorema*, using Homer's *Odyssey* as his symbolic source; however, in

«The King of Asine» (in *Logbook I*), considered by many critics his finest poem, the source is a single reference in the *Iliad* to this all-but-forgotten king. The recent book of poetry, *Tria Krypha Poiemata* (1966) [*Three Secret Poems*], consists of twenty-eight short lyric pieces verging on the surrealistic.

In addition to poetry, Seferis has published a book of essays, *Dokimes* (1962) [*Essays*], translations of works by T.S.Eliot, and a collection of translations from American, English, and French poets entitled *Antigrafes* (1965) [*Copies*]. Seferis' collected poems (1924–1955) have appeared both in a Greek edition (Athens, 1965) and in an American one with translations *en face* (Princeton, 1967).

Literature 1964

JEAN-PAUL SARTRE

«for his work which, rich in ideas and filled with the spirit of freedom and the quest for truth, has exerted a far-reaching influence on our age»

Address

by Anders Österling, Member of the Swedish Academy

This year the Nobel Prize in Literature has been granted by the Swedish Academy to the French writer Jean-Paul Sartre «for his work which, rich in ideas and filled with the spirit of freedom and the quest for truth, has exerted a far-reaching influence on our age.»

It will be recalled that the laureate has made it known that he did not wish to accept the Prize. The fact that he has declined this distinction does not in the least modify the validity of the award. Under the circumstances, however, the Academy can only state that the presentation of the Prize cannot take place.

Refusal

In a public announcement, printed in *Le Figaro* of October 23, 1964, Mr. Sartre expressed his regret that his refusal of the Prize had given rise to scandal, and wished it to be known that, unaware of the irrevocability of the Swedish Academy's decisions, he had sought by letter to prevent their choice falling upon him. In this letter, he specified that his refusal was not meant to slight the Swedish Academy but was rather based on personal and objective reasons of his own.

As to personal reasons, Mr. Sartre pointed out that due to his conception of the writer's task he had always declined official honours and thus his present act was not unprecedented. He had similarly refused membership in the Legion of Honour and had not desired to enter the Collège de France, and he would refuse the Lenin Prize if it were offered to him. He stated that a writer's accepting such an honour would be to associate his personal commitments with the awarding institution, and that, above all, a writer should not allow himself to be turned into an institution.

Among his objective reasons, Mr. Sartre listed his belief that interchange between East and West must take place between men and between cultures without the intervention of institutions. Furthermore, since the conferment of past Prizes did not, in his opinion, represent equally writers of all ideologies and nations, he felt that his acceptance might be undesirably and unjustly interpreted.

Mr. Sartre closed his remarks with a message of affection for the Swedish public.

At the banquet, S. Friberg, Rector of the Caroline Institute, made the following remarks: «Mr. Sartre found himself unable to accept this year's Prize in Literature. There is always discussion about this Prize, which every one considers himself capable of judging, or which he does not understand and consequently criticizes. But I believe that Nobel would have had a great understanding of this year's choice. The betterment of the world is the dream of every generation, and this applies particularly to the true poet and scientist. This was Nobel's dream. This is one measure of the scientist's significance. And this is the source and strength of Sartre's inspiration. As an author and philosopher, Sartre has been a central figure in postwar literary and intellectual discussion – admired, debated, criticized. His explosive production, in its entirety, has the impress of a message; it has been sustained by a profoundly serious endeavour to improve the reader, the world at large. The philosophy, which his writings have served, has been hailed by youth as a liberation. Sartre's existentialism may be understood in the sense that the degree of happiness which an individual can hope to attain is governed by his willingness to take his stand in accordance with his ethos and to accept the consequences thereof; this is a more austere interpretation of a philosophy admirably expressed by Nobel's contemporary, Ralph Waldo Emerson: ‹Nothing is at last sacred but the integrity of your own mind.›

The quality of human life depends not only on external conditions but also on individual happiness. In our age of standardization and complex social systems, awareness of the meaning of life for the individual has perhaps not been lost, but it has certainly been dulled; and it is as urgent for us today as it was in Nobel's time to uphold the ideals which were his. »

Biography

Jean-Paul Sartre (1905–), born in Paris, studied at the École Normale Supérieure from 1924 to 1929 and became Professor of Philosophy at Le Havre in 1931. With the help of a stipend from the Institut Français he studied in Berlin (1932) the philosophies of Edmund Husserl and Martin Heidegger. After further teaching at Le Havre, and then in Laon, he taught at the Lycée Pasteur in Paris from 1937 to 1939. Since the end of the Second World War, Sartre has been living as an independent writer.

Sartre is one of those writers for whom a determined philosophical position is the centre of their artistic being. Although drawn from many sources, for example, Husserl's idea of a free, fully intentional consciousness and Heidegger's existentialism, the existentialism Sartre formulated and popularized is profoundly original. Its popularity and that of its author reached a climax in the forties, and Sartre's theoretical writings as well as his novels and plays constitute one of the main inspirational sources of modern literature. In his philosophical view atheism is taken for granted; the «loss of God» is not mourned. Man is condemned to freedom, a freedom from all authority, which he may seek to evade, distort, and deny but which he will have to face if he is to become a moral being. The meaning of man's life is not established before his existence. Once the terrible freedom is acknowledged, man has to make this meaning himself, has to commit himself to a role in this world, has to commit his freedom. And this attempt to make oneself is futile without the «solidarity» of others.

The conclusions a writer must draw from this position were set forth in «Qu'est-ce que la littérature?» (1948) [*What Is Literature?*]: literature is no longer an activity for itself, nor primarily descriptive of characters and situations, but is concerned with human freedom and its (and the author's) commitment. Literature is committed; artistic creation is a moral activity.

While the publication of his early, largely psychological studies, *L'Imagination* (1936), *Esquisse d'une théorie des émotions* (1939) [Outline of a Theory of the Emotions], and *L'Imaginaire: psychologie phénoménologique de l'imagination* (1940) [The Psychology of Imagination], remained relatively unnoticed,

Sartre's first novel, *La Nausée* (1938) [*Nausea*], and the collection of stories *Le Mur* (1938) [*Intimacy*] brought him immediate recognition and success. They dramatically express Sartre's early existentialist themes of alienation and commitment, and of salvation through art.

His central philosophical work, *L'Etre et le néant* (1943) [*Being and Nothingness*], is a massive structuralization of his concept of being, from which much of modern existentialism derives. The existentialist humanism which Sartre propagates in his popular essay *L'Existentialisme est un humanisme* (1946) [*Existentialism is a Humanism*] can be glimpsed in the series of novels, *Les Chemins de la Liberté* (1945–49) [*The Roads to Freedom*].

Sartre is perhaps best known as a playwright. In *Les Mouches* (1943) [*The Flies*], the young killer's committed freedom is pitted against the powerless Jupiter, while in *Huis Clos* (1947) [*No Exit*] hell emerges as the togetherness of people.

Sartre has engaged extensively in literary critisicm and has written studies on Baudelaire (1947) and Jean Genet (1952). A biography of his childhood, *Les Mots* [*The Words*], appeared in 1964.

Literature 1965

MIKHAIL ALEKSANDROVICH
SHOLOKHOV

«for the artistic power and integrity with which, in his epic of the Don, he has given expression to a historic phase in the life of the Russian people»

Presentation

by Anders Österling, Member of the Swedish Academy

This year's Nobel Prize in Literature, as you all know, has been awarded to the Russian writer Mikhail Sholokhov, born in 1905 and now in his sixty-first year. Sholokhov's childhood was spent in the country of the Don Cossacks; the strong ties that have always bound him to this district grew out of his sympathy for the highly individual temperament of its people and the wildness of its landscape. He saw his native province pass through the various phases of the Revolution and the Russian civil war. After trying his hand at manual work in Moscow, he soon began to concentrate on writing and produced a series of sketches describing the battles along the Don, a subject that was later to bring him fame. It is striking evidence of the precociousness of the war generation that Sholokhov was only twenty-one when he began the first parts of the great epic novel *Tikhi Don* (1928–1940) [*And Quiet Flows the Don*]. Its Russian title is simply «The Quiet Don», which acquires an undeniably ironic undertone in view of the extreme violence of the action in Sholokhov's masterpiece.

It took Sholokhov fourteen years to complete the highly exacting project, which covers the period including the First World War, the Revolution, and the civil war, having as its main theme the tragic Cossack revolt. The four parts of the epic appeared at relatively long intervals between 1928 and 1940, and were long viewed with some concern by Soviet critics, whose political affiliation made it difficult for them to accept wholeheartedly Sholokhov's quite natural commitment to his theme, the Cossacks' revolt against the new central authorities; nor could they easily accept his endeavour to explain and defend objectively the defiant spirit of independence that drove these people to resist every attempt at subjection.

In view of the controversial aspects of his theme, there can surely be no doubt that in undertaking the writing of this novel Sholokhov was taking a daring step, a step which at that point in his career also meant the settling of a conflict with his own conscience.

And Quiet Flows the Don is so well known to Swedish readers that an introduction may well seem superfluous. With magnificent realism the book portrays the unique character of the Cossack, the traditional mixture of cavalryman and farmer, whose instincts seem to conflict with one another but nevertheless are welded together to form a firmly coordinated whole. There is no glamorization. The coarse and savage streaks in the Cossack temperament are displayed openly; nothing is hidden or glossed over, but at the same time one is aware of an undercurrent of respect for all that is human. Although a convinced Communist, Sholokhov keeps ideological comment out of his book completely. We are compensated for the amount of blood shed in the battles he describes by the fullblooded vigour of his narrative.

The Cossack's son, Gregor, who changes allegiance from the Reds to the Whites and is forced against his will to continue the struggle to its hopeless conclusion, is both hero and victim. The conception of honour that he has inherited is put to the sternest of tests, and he is defeated by a necessity of history which here plays the same role as the classical Nemesis. But our sympathy goes out to him and to the two unforgettable women, Natalja, his wife, and Aksinia, his mistress, who both meet disaster for his sake. When he finally returns to his native village after digging Aksinia's grave in the steppe with his sabre, he is a grey-haired man who has lost everything in life but his young son.

Stretching away behind the whole gallery of figures, seen either in their personal relationships or playing their parts as military personnel, lies the mighty landscape of the Ukraine: the steppes in all the changing seasons, the villages with their sweet-smelling pastures and grazing horses, the grass billowing in the wind, the banks of the river, and the never-ending murmur of the river itself. Sholokhov never tires of describing the Russian steppes. Sometimes he interrupts the narrative right in the middle to burst out in exultation: «My beloved steppes under the low sky of the Don country! Ravines winding across the plain with their walls of red earth, a sea of waving feather-grass, marked only by the print of horses' hoofs leaving a trail like a myriad of birds' nests, and by the graves of the Tartars who in wise silence watch over the buried glory of the Cossacks... I bow low before you and as a son kiss your fresh earth, unspoiled steppe of the Don Cossacks, watered with blood.»

It may well be said that Sholokhov, breaking no new ground, is using a well-tried realistic technique, a technique that may seem naive in its simplicity if compared to many a later model in the art of novel-writing. But his subject surely could not have been presented in any other way, and the powerful, evenly sustained, epic flow of writing makes *And Quiet Flows the Don* a genuine *roman fleuve* in more than one sense.

Sholokhov's more recent work, for example, *Podnyataya tselina* (1932 and 1959) [*Virgin Soil Upturned*] – a novel describing compulsory collectivization and the introduction of *kolkhozy* – has a constant vitality and shows us Sholokhov's fondness for richly comic yet sympathetic characters. But of course, *And Quiet Flows the Don* would, by itself, thoroughly merit the present award, a distinction which has come rather late in the day, but happily not too late to add to the roll of Nobel Prize winners the name of one of the most outstanding writers of our time.

In support of its choice the Swedish Academy speaks of «the artistic power and integrity with which, in his epic of the Don, Sholokhov has given expression to a historic phase in the life of the Russian people».

Sir – This distinction is intended as a tribute of justice and gratitude to you for your important contribution to modern Russian literature, a contribution as well known in this country as it is all over the world. May I offer you the congratulations of the Swedish Academy, and at the same time ask you to receive from His Majesty the King this year's Nobel Prize in Literature.

Acceptance

On this solemn occasion I find it my pleasant duty to extend my thanks once more to the Swedish Academy, which has awarded me the Nobel Prize.

As I have already had occasion to testify in public, the feeling of satisfaction which this award arouses in me is not solely due to the international recognition of my professional merits and my individual characteristics as a writer. I am proud that this Prize has been awarded to a Russian, a Soviet writer. Here I represent a multitude of writers from my native land.

I have also previously expressed my satisfaction that, indirectly, this Prize is yet another recognition of the novel as a genre. I have not infrequently read and heard recent statements which have quite frankly astonished me, in which the novel has been declared an outdated form that does not correspond to present-day demands. Yet it is just the novel that makes possible the most complete comprehension of the world of reality, that permits the projection of one's attitude to this world, to its burning problems. One might say that the novel is the genre that most predisposes one to a profound insight into the tremendous life around us, instead of putting forward one's own tiny ego as the centre of the universe. This genre, by its very nature, affords the very widest scope for a realistic artist.

Many fashionable currents in art reject realism, which they assume has served its time. Without fear of being accused of conservatism, I wish to proclaim that I hold a contrary opinion and am a convinced supporter of realistic art. There is a lot of talk nowadays about literary avantgardism with reference to the most modern experiments, particularly in the field of form. In my opinion the true pioneers are those artists who make manifest in their works the new content, the determining characteristics of life in our time.

Both realism as a whole and the realistic novel are based upon artistic experiences presented by great masters in the past. During their development, however, they have acquired important new features that are fundamentally modern.

I am speaking of a realism that carries within itself the concept of life's regeneration, its reformation for the benefit of mankind. I refer, of course, to the realism we describe as socialist. Its peculiar quality is that it expresses a philosophy of life that accepts neither a turning away from the world nor a flight from reality, a philosophy that enables one to comprehend goals that are dear to the hearts of millions of people and that lights up their path in the struggle.

Mankind is not divided into a flock of individuals, people floating about in a vacuum, like cosmonauts who have penetrated beyond the pull of Earth's gravity. We live on Earth, we are subject to its laws and, as the Gospel puts it, sufficient unto the day is the evil thereof, its troubles and trials, its hopes for a better future. Vast sections of the world's population are inspired by the same desires, and live for common interests that bind them together far more than they separate them. These are the working people, who create everything with their hands and their brains. I am one of those authors who consider it their highest honour and their highest liberty to have a completely untrammelled chance of using their pens to serve the working people.

This is the ultimate foundation. From it are derived the conclusions as to how I, a Soviet writer, view the place of the artist in the world of today.

The era we live in is full of uncertainty. Yet there is not one nation on Earth that desires a war. There are, however, forces that hurl whole nations into the furnaces of war. Is it not inevitable that the ashes from the indescribable conflagration of the Second World War should move the writer's heart? Is not an honest writer bound to stand up against those who wish to condemn mankind to self-destruction?

What, then, is the vocation and what are the tasks of an artist who sees himself, not as an image of a god who is indifferent to the sufferings of mankind, enthroned far above the heat of battle, but as a son of his people, a tiny particle of humanity?

To be honest with the reader, to tell people the truth – which may sometimes be unpleasant but is always fearless. To strengthen men's hearts in their belief in the future, in the belief in their own ability to build this future. To be a champion of peace throughout the world and with his words breed such champions wherever those words penetrate. To unite people in their natural, noble striving toward progress.

Art possesses a great ability to influence people's intellects and brains. I believe that anyone has the right to call himself an artist, if he channels this ability into creating someting beautiful in the minds of men, if he benefits humanity.

My own people have not followed beaten tracks in their historical journey. Their journey has been that of the explorers, the pioneers for a new life. I have regarded and still regard it as my task as an author in all that I have written and in whatever I may come to write, to show my great respect for this nation of workers, this nation of builders, this nation of heroes, which has never attacked anyone but which knows how to put up an honourable defence of what it has created, of its freedom and dignity, of its right to build the future as it chooses.

I should like my books to assist people in becoming better, in becoming purer in their minds; I should like them to arouse love of one's fellow men, a desire to fight actively for the ideal of humanity and the progress of mankind. If I have managed to do this in some measure, then I am happy.

I thank all those of you here tonight, and all those who have sent me greetings and good wishes in connection with the Nobel Prize.

Prior to the acceptance, Karl Ragnar Gierow of the Swedish Academy addressed the Soviet novelist: «Mr. Sholokhov – You received news of the Nobel Prize when in the Ural Mountains for a couple of weeks' shooting, and, according to a Moscow newspaper, that same day you brought down two fine greylag geese at a long range with a single shot. But if you are celebrated tonight as the crack marksman amongst the Nobel laureates, it is because that coincidental hit has a certain relevance to your work.

An epic achievement like yours could be written on that enormous scale, with that breadth of view, with that wild and still majestic flow of events and figures, with that imposing execution of the theme – with all that, and be a masterpiece, never to be forgotten. Or the epic could be presented with that vivid sense of the dramatic situation, with that sharp eye for every detail of artistic value, with that passionate feeling for its characters – with all that, and be a work of art, always to be loved. The combination of both is the mark of the genius, of your genius. It is about as common as seeing two birds in flight aligned with one's gunsight. You brought the two down with one shot.

Your great epic of an old rule, desperately defending itself, and a new rule, as desperately fighting for every foot of blood-drenched earth, keeps posing from the outset the question: who – or what – rules? It also provides an answer. It says: the heart. The human heart, with all it holds of love and cruelty, hope and sorrow, pride and debasement. The human heart, which is the real battlefield of all victories and defeats that befall this earth of ours. Thus your art ranges beyond all frontiers, and we take it to our hearts with the deepest gratitude.»

Biography

Mikhail Aleksandrovich Sholokhov (1905–) was born in the land of the Cossacks, now known as the Kamenskaya region of the R.S.F.S.R. He attended several high schools until 1918. During the civil war he fought on the side of the revolutionaries, and in 1922 he moved to Moscow to become a journalist. There he published a number of short stories in newspapers. He made his literary debut in 1926 with a volume of stories, *Donskie rasskazy* (1926) [*Tales from the Don*], about the Cossacks of his native region, to which he had returned two years earlier.

In the same year, 1926, Sholokhov began writing *Tikhi Don* (1928–1940) [*And Quiet Flows the Don*], which matured slowly and took him fourteen years to complete. Reminiscent of Tolstoy in its vividly realistic scenes, its stark character descriptions and, above all, its vast panorama of the revolutionary period, Sholokhov's epic became the most-read work of Soviet fiction. Deeply interested in human destinies which are played against the background of the transformations and troubles in Russia, he unites in his work the artistic heritage of Tolstoy and Gogol with a new vision introduced into Russian literature by Maxim Gorky.

His other major work in the Don cycle, *Podnyataya tselina* (1932 and 1959) [*Virgin Soil Upturned*], deals in part with the collectivization of the Don area. There are a number of works such as the short story «Sudba cheloveka»(1957) [«The Fate of a Man»]–made into a popular Russian film–which treat the power and the resilience of human love under adversity. His collected works, *Sobranie sochineny*, were published in eight volumes between 1956 and 1960.

In 1932 Sholokhov joined the Communist Party and, on several occasions, has been a delegate to the Supreme Soviets. In 1939 he became a member of the Soviet Academy of Sciences and later vice president of the Association of Soviet Writers.

Literature 1966

SHMUEL YOSEF AGNON

« For his profoundly distinctive narrative art with motifs from the life of the Jewish people »

LEONIE NELLY SACHS

« for her outstanding lyrical and dramatic writings, which interpret Israel's destiny with touching strength »

Presentation

by Anders Österling, Member of the Swedish Academy

This year's Nobel Prize in Literature has been awarded to two outstanding Jewish authors–Shmuel Yosef Agnon and Nelly Sachs–each of whom represents Israel's message to our time. Agnon's home is in Jerusalem and Miss Sachs has been an immigrant in Sweden since 1940 and is now a Swedish subject. The purpose of combining these two Prize winners is to do justice to the individual achievements of each, and the sharing of the Prize has its special justification: to honour two writers who, although they write in different languages, are united in a spiritual kinship and complement each other in a superb effort to present the cultural heritage of the Jewish people through the written word. Their common source of inspiration has been for both of them a vital power.

I

Shmuel Agnon's reputation as the foremost writer in modern Hebrew literature has gradually penetrated linguistic barriers which in this case are particularly obstructive. His most important works are now available in Swedish under the title *I havets mitt* (In the Heart of the Seas). Agnon, now seventy-eight years old, began writing in Yiddish but soon changed to Hebrew, which, according to experts, he handles with absolute mastery, in a taut and sonorous prose style of extraordinary expressiveness. He was only twenty when he left his native town in East Galicia, where, as the scion of an old and respected family, he had been brought up in a scholarly tradition. He felt drawn to Palestine, where now, as an aged classical author, he can look back on the long struggle for national re-establishment, and where the so-called cultural Zionism possesses in him one of its finest creative champions.

Agnon's unique quality as a writer is apparent chiefly in the great cycle of novels set in his native town of Buczacz, once a flourishing centre of Jewish piety and rabbinical learning, now in ruins. Reality and legend stand side by side in his narrative art. *Hakhnasat Kalah* (1922) [*The Bridal Canopy*] is one of his most characteristic stories, in its ingenious and earthy humour a Jewish counterpart to *Don Quixote* and *Till Eulenspiegel*. But perhaps his greatest achievement is his novel *Oreach Nata Lalun* (1939) [*A Guest for the Night*], which tells of a visit to Buczacz, the war-ruined city of his childhood, and of the narrator's vain attempts to assemble the congregation for a service in the synagogue. Within the framework of a local chronicle we see a wonderful portrayal of destinies and figures, of experience and meditation. The lost key to the prayer house, which the traveller finds in his knapsack only after his return to Jerusalem, is for Agnon a symbolic hint that the old order can never be rebuilt in the Diaspora, but only under the protection of Zionism. Agnon is a realist, but there is always a mystical admixture which lends to even the greyest and most ordinary scenes a golden atmosphere of strange fairy-tale poetry, often reminiscent of Chagall's motifs from the world of the Old Testament. He stands out as a highly original writer, endowed with remarkable gifts of humour and wisdom and with a perspicacious play of thought combined with naive perception – in all, a consummate expression of the Jewish character.

II

Nelly Sachs, like so many other German-Jewish writers, suffered the fate of exile. Through Swedish intervention she was saved from persecution and the threat of deportation and was brought to this country. She has since then worked in peace as a refugee on Swedish soil, attaining the maturity and authority that are now confirmed by the Nobel Prize. In recent years she has been acclaimed in the German world as a writer of convincing worth and irresistible sincerity. With moving intensity of feeling she has given voice to the world-wide tragedy of the Jewish people, which she has expressed in lyrical laments of painful beauty and in dramatic legends. Her symbolic language boldly combines an inspired modern idiom with echoes of ancient Biblical poetry. Identifying herself totally with the faith and ritual mysticism of her people, Miss Sachs has created a world of imagery which does not shun the terrible truth of the extermination camps and the corpse factories, but which at the same time rises above all hatred of the persecutors, merely revealing a genuine sorrow at man's debasement. Her purely lyrical production is now collected under the title *Fahrt ins Staublose* (1961) [Journey to the Beyond], which comprises six interconnected works written during a twenty-year creative period of increasing concentration. There is also a series of dramatic poems, equally remarkable in their way, under the joint title *Zeichen im Sand* (1961) [Signs in the Sand], the themes of which might have been taken from the dark treasure house of Hassidic mysticism but which here have taken on new vigour and vital meaning. Let it suffice here to mention the mystery play *Eli* (1950) about an eight-year-old boy who is beaten to death by a German soldier in Poland when he blows on his shepherd's pipe to call on heaven's help when his parents are taken away. The visionary cobbler Michael manages to trace the culprit to the next village. The soldier has been seized by remorse and, at the encounter in the forest, he collapses without Michael's having to raise his hand against him. This ending denotes a divine justice which has nothing to do with earthly retribution.

Nelly Sachs' writing is today the most intense artistic expression of the reaction of the Jewish spirit to suffering, and thus it can indeed be said to fulfil the humane purpose underlying Alfred Nobel's will.

Doctor Agnon–According to the wording of the diploma, this year's Nobel Prize in Literature has been awarded to you for your «profoundly distinctive narrative art with motifs from the life of the Jewish people». We should be happy if you would consider this international distinction as a sign that your writing need not be isolated within the boundary of its language and that it has proved to have the power to reach out beyond all confining walls and to arouse mankind's sympathy, understanding, and respect. Through me the Swedish Academy conveys its sincere congratulations, and I now ask you to receive the Prize from the hands of His Majesty the King.

Miss Nelly Sachs –You have lived a long time in our country, first as an obscure stranger and then as an honoured guest. Today the Swedish Academy honours your «outstanding lyrical and dramatic writings, which interpret Israel's destiny with touching strength». On an occasion like this it is natural also to recall the invaluable interest you have shown in Swedish literature, a token of friendship which in turn has found a response in the desire of our Swedish writers to translate your work. Offering you the congratulations of the Swedish Academy, I ask you now to receive this year's Nobel Prize in Literature from the hands of His Majesty the King.

Acceptance

by Shmuel Yosef Agnon

Our sages of blessed memory have said that we must not enjoy any pleasure in this world without reciting a blessing. If we eat any food, or drink any beverage, we must recite a blessing over them before and after. If we breathe the scent of goodly grass, the fragrance of spices, the aroma of good fruits, we pronounce a blessing over the pleasure. The same applies to the pleasures of sight: when we see the sun in the Great Cycle of the Zodiac in the month of Nissan, or the trees first bursting into blossom in the spring, or any fine, sturdy, and beautiful trees, we pronounce a blessing. And the same applies to the pleasures of the ear. Through you, dear sirs, one of the blessings concerned with hearing has come my way.

It happened when the Swedish Chargé d'Affaires came and brought me the news that the Swedish Academy had bestowed the Nobel Prize upon me. Then I recited in full the blessing that is enjoined upon one that hears good tidings for himself or others: «Blessed be He, that is good and doeth good.» «Good», in that the good God put it into the hearts of the sages of the illustrious Academy to bestow that great and esteemed Prize upon an author who writes in the sacred tongue; «that doeth good», in that He favoured me by causing them to choose me. And now that I have come so far, I will recite one blessing more, as enjoined upon him who beholds a monarch: «Blessed art Thou, O Lord, our God, King of the Universe, Who hast given of Thy glory to a king of flesh and blood.» Over you, too, distinguished sages of the Academy, I say the prescribed blessing: «Blessed be He, that has given of His wisdom to flesh and blood.»

It is said in the Talmud (Tractate Sanhedrin 23a): «In Jerusalem, the men of discrimination did not sit down to dine in company until they knew who their companions were to be»; so I will now tell you who am I, whom you have agreed to have at your table.

As a result of the historic catastrophe in which Titus of Rome destroyed Jerusalem and Israel was exiled from its land, I was born in one of the cities of the Exile. But always I regarded myself as one who was born in Jerusalem. In a dream, in a vision of the night, I saw myself standing with my brother-Levites in the Holy Temple, singing with them the songs of David, King of Israel, melodies such as no ear has heard since the day our city was destroyed and its people went into exile. I suspect that the angels in charge of the Shrine of Music, fearful lest I sing in wakefulness what I had sung in dream, made me forget by day what I had sung at night; for if my brethren, the sons of my people, were to hear, they would be unable to bear their grief over the happiness they have lost. To console me for having prevented me from singing with my mouth, they enable me to compose songs in writing.

(Out of respect for the time, the rest of my words will be read in translation only.)

I belong to the Tribe of Levi; my forebears and I are of the minstrels that were in the Temple, and there is a tradition in my father's family that we are of the lineage of the Prophet Samuel, whose name I bear.

I was five years old when I wrote my first song. It was out of longing for my father that I wrote it. It happened that my father, of blessed memory, went away on business. I was overcome with longing for him and I made a song. After that I made many songs, but nothing has remained of them all. My father's house, where I left a roomful of writings, was burned down in the First World War and all I had left there was burned with it. The young artisans, tailors, and shoemakers, who used to sing my songs at their work, were killed in the First World War and of those who were not killed in the war, some were buried alive with their sisters in the pits they dug for themselves by order of the enemy, and most were burned in the crematories of Auschwitz with their sisters, who had adorned our town with their beauty and sung my songs with their sweet voices.

The fate of the singers who, like my songs, went up in flame was also the fate of the books which I later wrote. All of them went up in flame to Heaven in a fire which broke out one night at my home in Bad Homburg as I lay ill in a hospital. Among the books that were burned was a large novel of some seven hundred pages, the first part of which the publisher had announced he was about to bring out. Together with this novel, called *Eternal Life*, was burned everything I had written since the day I had gone into exile from the Land of Israel, including a book I had written with Martin Buber as well as four thousand Hebrew books, most of which had come down to me from my forebears and some of which I had bought with money set aside for my daily bread.

I said, «since the day I had gone from the Land of Israel», but I have not yet related that I had dwelt in the Land of Israel. Of this I will now speak.

At the age of nineteen and a half, I went to the Land of Israel to till its soil

and live by the labour of my hands. As I did not find work, I sought my liveli-
hood elsewhere. I was appointed Secretary of the Hovevei Zion (Lovers of
Zion) Society and Secretary of the Palestine Council—which was a kind of
parliament-in-the-making—and I was also the first Secretary of the voluntary
Jewish Magistrate's Court. Through these offices it was my privilege to get to
know almost every Jewish person, and those whom I did not come to know
through these offices I came to know through love and a desire to know my
brethren, the members of my people. It is almost certain that in those years
there was not a man, woman, or infant in the Land of Israel whom I did not
know.

After all my possessions had been burned, God gave me the wisdom to return to Jerusalem. I returned to Jerusalem, and it is by virtue of Jerusalem that
I have written all that God has put into my heart and into my pen. I have also
written a book about the Giving of the Torah, and a book on the Days of
Awe, and a book on the books of Israel that have been written since the day
the Torah was given to Israel.

Since my return to the Land of Israel, I have left it twice: once in connection
with the printing of my books by the late Zalman Schocken, and once I
travelled to Sweden and Norway. Their great poets had implanted love and
admiration for their countries in my heart, and I decided to go and see them.
Now I have come a third time, to receive your blessing, sages of the Academy.

During the time I have dwelt in Jerusalem, I have written long stories and
short ones. Some have been printed; most I still have in manuscript.

I have already told how my first songs came out of longing for my father.
The beginnings of my studies also came to me from my father, as well as from
the Rabbinical Judge of our town. But they were preceded by three tutors
under whom I studied, one after the other, from the time I was three and a half
till I turned eight and a half.

Who were my mentors in poetry and literature? That is a matter of opinion.
Some see in my books the influences of authors whose names, in my ignorance, I have not even heard, while others see the influences of poets whose
names I have heard but whose writings I have not read. And what is my opinion? From whom did I receive nurture? Not every man remembers the name
of the cow which supplied him with each drop of milk he has drunk. But in
order not to leave you totally in the dark, I will try to clarify from whom I
received whatever I have received.

First and foremost, there are the Sacred Scriptures, from which I learned
how to combine letters. Then there are the Mishna and the Talmud and the

Midrashim and Rashi's commentary on the Torah. After these come the *Poskim*—the later explicators of Talmudic Law—and our sacred poets and the medieval sages, led by our Master Rabbi Moses, son of Maimon, known as Maimonides, of blessed memory.

When I first began to combine letters other than Hebrew, I read every book in German that came my way, and from these I certainly received according to the nature of my soul. As time is short, I shall not compile a bibliography or mention any names. Why, then, did I list the Jewish books? Because it is they that gave me my foundations. And my heart tells me that they are responsible for my being honoured with the Nobel Prize.

There is another kind of influence, which I have received from every man, every woman, every child I have encountered along my way, both Jews and non-Jews. People's talk and the stories they tell have been engraved on my heart, and some of them have flown into my pen. It has been the same way with the spectacles of nature. The Dead Sea, which I used to see every morning at sunrise from the roof of my house, the Arnon Brook in which I used to bathe, the nights I used to spend with devout and pious men beside the Wailing Wall—nights which gave me eyes to see the land of the Holy One, Blessed be He—the Wall which He gave us, and the city in which He established His name.

Lest I slight any creature, I must also mention the domestic animals, the beasts and birds from whom I have learned. Job said long ago (35:11): «Who teacheth us more than the beasts of the earth, And maketh us wiser than the fowls of heaven?» Some of what I have learned from them I have written in my books, but I fear that I have not learned as much as I should have, for when I hear a dog bark, or a bird twitter, or a cock crow, I do not know whether they are thanking me for all I have told of them, or calling me to account.

Before I conclude my remarks, I will say one more thing. If I have praised myself too much, it is for your sake that I have done so, in order to reassure you for having cast your eyes on me. For myself, I am very small indeed in my own eyes. Never in all my life have I forgotten the Psalm (131:1) in which David said: «Lord, my heart is not haughty, nor mine eyes lofty; neither do I exercise myself in great matters, or in things too high for me.» If I am proud of anything, it is that I have been granted the privilege of living in the land which God promised our forefathers to give us, as it is written (Ezekiel 37:25): «And they shall dwell in the land that I have given unto Jacob my servant, wherein your fathers have dwelt; and they shall dwell therein, even they, and their children, and their children's children forever.»

Before concluding, I would say a brief prayer: He who giveth wisdom unto the wise and salvation unto kings, may He increase your wisdom beyond measure and exalt your sovereign. In his days and in ours may Judah be redeemed and Israel dwell in safety. May a redeemer come to Zion, may the earth be filled with knowledge and eternal joy for all who dwell therein, and may they enjoy much peace. May all this be God's will. Amen.

Acceptance

by Nelly Sachs

In the summer of 1939 a German girl friend of mine went to Sweden to visit Selma Lagerlöf, to ask her to secure a sanctuary for my mother and myself in that country. Since my youth I had been so fortunate as to exchange letters with Selma Lagerlöf; and it is out of her work that my love for her country grew. The painter-prince Eugen and the novelist helped to save me.

In the spring of 1940, after tortuous months, we arrived in Stockholm. The occupation of Denmark and Norway had already taken place. The great novelist was no more. We breathed the air of freedom without knowing the language or any person. Today, after twenty-six years, I think of what my father used to say on every tenth of December, back in my home town, Berlin: «Now they celebrate the Nobel ceremony in Stockholm.» Thanks to the choice of the Swedish Academy, I am now in the midst of that ceremony. To me a fairy tale seems to have become reality.

> *In der Flucht*
> *welch grosser Empfang*
> *unterwegs–*
>
> *Eingehüllt*
> *in der Winde Tuch*
> *Füsse im Gebet des Sandes*
> *der niemals Amen sagen kann*
> *denn er muss*
> *von der Flosse in den Flügel*
> *und weiter–*
>
> *Der kranke Schmetterling*
> *weiss bald wieder vom Meer–*
> *Dieser Stein*
> *mit der Inschrift der Fliege*
> *hat sich mir in die Hand gegeben–*

An Stelle von Heimat
halte ich die Verwandlungen der Welt–

(An English translation by Ruth and Matthew Mead appeared in Nelly Sachs' collection O *the Chimneys* [Farrar, Straus and Giroux, Inc., 1967].)

Prior to the two acceptances, Ingvar Andersson of the Swedish Academy made the following comments: «Shmuel Yosef Agnon, Nelly Sachs – This year's literary Prize goes to you both with equal honour for a literary production which records Israel's vicissitudes in our time and passes on its message to the peoples of the world.

Mr. Agnon – In your writing we meet once again the ancient unity between literature and science, as antiquity knew it. In one of your stories you say that some will no doubt read it as they read fairy tales, others will read it for edification. Your great chronicle of the Jewish people's spirit and life has therefore a manifold message. For the historian it is a precious source, for the philosopher an inspiration, for those who cannot live without literature it is a mine of never-failing riches. We honour in you a combination of tradition and prophecy, of saga and wisdom.

Miss Sachs – About twenty years ago, through the Swedish poet Hjalmar Gullberg, I first learned of your fate and your work. Since then you have lived with us in Sweden and I could talk to you in our own language. But it is through your mother tongue that your work reflects a historical drama in which you have participated. Your lyrical and dramatic writing now belongs to the great laments of literature, but the feeling of mourning which inspired you is free from hate and lends sublimity to the suffering of man. We honour you today as the bearer of a message of solace to all those who despair of the fate of man.

We honour you both this evening as the laurel-crowned heroes of intellectual creation and express our conviction that, in the words of Alfred Nobel, you ‹have conferred the greatest benefit on mankind›, and that you have given it clearsightedness, wisdom, uplift, and beauty. A famous speech at a Nobel banquet – that of William Faulkner, held in this same hall sixteen years ago – contained an idea which he developed with great intensity. It is suitable as a concluding quotation which points to the future: ‹I do not believe in the end of man.›»

Biography

Shmuel Yosef Agnon (1888–) was born in Buczacz, Eastern Galicia. Raised in a mixed cultural atmosphere, in which Yiddish was the language of the home, and Hebrew the language of the Bible and the Talmud which he studied formally until the age of nine, Agnon also acquired a knowledge of German literature from his mother and of the teachings of Maimonides and of the Hassidim from his father. In 1907 he left home and made his way to Palestine, where, except for an extended stay in Germany from 1913 to 1924, he has remained to this day.

At an early age, Agnon began writing the stories which form a chronicle of the decline of Jewry in Galicia. Included among these is his first major publication, *Hakhnasat Kalah* (1922) [*The Bridal Canopy*], which re-creates the golden age of Hassidism, and his apocalyptic novel, *Oreach Nata Lalun* (1939) [*A Guest for the Night*], which vividly depicts the ruin of Galicia after the First World War. Nearly all of his other writings are set in his adopted Palestine and deal with the replacement of the early Jewish settlement of that country by the more organized Zionist movement after the Second World War. The early pioneer immigrants are portrayed in his epic *Temol Shilshom* (1945) [*Only Yesterday*], considered his greatest work, and also in the nightmarish stories of *Sefer Hamaasim* (1932) [*The Book of Deeds*].

While these and other works, such as *Pat Shlema* (1933) [*A Whole Loaf*] and *Shevuat Emunim* (1943) [*Two Tales*], are enough to assure his stature as the greatest living Hebrew writer, Agnon has also occupied himself with commentaries on the Jewish High Festival, *Yamin Noraim* (1938) [*Days of Awe*], on the giving of the Torah, *Atem Reitem* (1959) [*Ye Have Seen*], and on the gathering of Hassidic lore, *Sifreihem Shel Tzadikim* (1960–1961) [*Books of the Tzadikim*].

Autobiography

Leonie Nelly Sachs, born in Berlin on December 10, 1891. As refugee arrived in Sweden with my mother on May 16, 1940. Since then living in Stockholm and active as writer and translator.

Biographical note

Nelly Sachs (1891–   ), daughter of a wealthy manufacturer, grew up in a fashionable area of Berlin. She studied music and dancing and at an early age began writing poetry. After her escape to Sweden in 1940, Miss Sachs took up the study of Swedish and devoted much of her time to the translation of such Swedish poets as Gunnar Ekelöf, Johannes Edfelt, and Karl Vennberg.

Nelly Sachs' career as a poet of note started only after her emigration, when she was nearly fifty years old. Her first volume of poetry, *In den Wohnungen des Todes* (1947) [In the Houses of Death], creates a cosmic frame for the suffering of her time, particularly that of the Jews. Although her poems are written in a keenly modern style, with an abundance of lucid metaphors, they also intone the prophetic language of the Old Testament. The collections *Sternverdunkelung* (1949) [Eclipse of Stars], *Und niemand weiss weiter* (1957) [And No One Knows Where to Go], and *Flucht und Verwandlung* (1959) [Flight and Metamorphosis] repeat, develop, and reinforce the cycle of suffering, persecution, exile, and death which characterizes the life of the Jewish people and becomes transformed, in Nelly Sachs' powerful metaphorical language, into the terms of man's bitter, but not hopeless, destiny. Of her poetic dramas, the miracle play *Eli* (1950), broadcast in West Germany as a radio play, has been widely acclaimed. Nelly Sachs has received awards in Sweden and Germany, among them the Prize of the Swedish Poets' Association (1958) and the «Friedenspreis des deutschen Buchhandels» (1965). In 1961 her collected poems were published under the title of *Fahrt ins Staublose* [Journey to the Beyond]; her verse dramas in *Zeichen im Sand* [Signs in the Sand]. *O the Chimneys*, English translations of some of her poetry and of her play *Eli*, appeared in 1967.

Literature 1967

MIGUEL ANGEL ASTURIAS

«for the vividness of his literary work, rooted in national traits and Indian traditions»

Presentation

by Anders Österling, Permanent Secretary of the Swedish Academy

This year the Nobel Prize in Literature has been awarded to the Guatemalan writer Miguel Angel Asturias, a prominent representative of the modern literature of Latin America, in which such interesting developments are now taking place. Born in 1899 in the capital of Guatemala, Asturias became imbued, even as a child, with the characteristically Guatemalan love of nature and of the mythical world. He devoted to this native heritage and to its libertarian spirit a fervour which was to dominate his whole literary production. After studying law and folklore, he lived in France during the twenties and for a time represented his country in the diplomatic service. He condemned himself to a long exile after the antidemocratic coup d'état of 1954, but returned when the legitimate regime took office again. He is presently the Guatemalan ambassador in Paris.

During the last few years, Asturias has gained international recognition, as his most important works came to be translated into various languages; today they can be read even in Swedish. His first work was a collection of Guatemalan legends, strange evocations of the Mayas' past, a treasure of images and symbols which has ever since been the inexhaustible source of his inspiration. But he did not get his real start as a writer until 1946, the year of the publication of the novel *El Señor Presidente* [*The President*]. This magnificent and tragic satire criticizes the prototype of the Latin-American dictator who appeared in several places at the beginning of the century and has since reappeared, his existence being fostered by the mechanism of tyranny which for the common man makes every day a hell on earth. The passionate vigour with which Asturias evokes the terror and distrust which poisoned the social atmosphere of the time makes his work a challenge and an invaluable aesthetic gesture. The narrative entitled *Hombres de maíz* [Men of Maize] appeared three years later. It might be considered as a folk tale whose chief inspiration is in the imagination but which nevertheless remains true to life. Its motifs are from the mythology of that tropical land where man must struggle simultaneously against a mysteriously beautiful but hostile nature and against unbearable social distortions, oppression, and tyranny. Such an accumulation of nightmares and totemic phantasms may overwhelm our sensibilities, but we cannot help being fascinated by a poetry so bizarre and terrifying.

With the trilogy of novels begun in 1950–*Viente fuerte* (1950) [*Strong Wind*], *El Papa verde* (1954) [The Green Pope], and *Los ojos de los enterrados* (1960) [The Eyes of the Buried]–a new topical concern appears in Asturias' epic work: the theme of the struggle against the domination of American trusts, epitomized by the United Fruit Company and its political and economic effects upon the contemporary history of the «Banana Republic». Here again we see the violent effervescence and the visionary vehemence which stem from the author's intense involvement in the situation of his country.

Asturias has completely freed himself from obsolete narrative techniques. Very early he came under the influence of the new tendencies appearing in European literature; his explosive style bears a close kinship to French surrealism. It must be noted, however, that he always takes his inspiration from real life. In his impressive cycle of poems entitled *Clarivigilia primaveral* [1965] (Bright and Awake in Spring), on which a Swedish critical study has just appeared, Asturias deals with the very genesis of the arts and of poetic creation, in a language which seems to have assumed the bright splendour of the magical quetzal's feathers and the glimmering of phosphorescent insects.

Latin America today can boast an active group of prominent writers, a multivoiced chorus in which individual contributions are not readily discernible. Asturias' work is nevertheless vast, bold, and outstanding enough to arouse interest outside of his own literary milieu, beyond a geographically limited area situated far away from us. One of the Indian legends Asturias alludes to evokes the belief that dead ancestors are forced to witness, with open eyes, the struggles and sufferings of their offspring. Only when justice is reestablished and the stolen soil restituted, will the dead finally be able to close their eyes and sleep peacefully in their tombs. It is a beautiful and poignant popular belief, and we can easily imagine that the militant poet has often felt upon him the gaze of his ancestors and has often heard the silent, symbolic appeal reaching to his heart.

Mr. Ambassador–You come from a distant country; but do not let this fact make you feel today that you are a stranger among us. Your work is known and appreciated in Sweden. We take pleasure in welcoming you as a messenger from Latin America, its people, its spirit, and its future. I congratulate you in the name of the Swedish Academy, which pays tribute to the «vividness of your literary work, rooted in national traits and Indian traditions». I now invite you to receive your Prize from His Majesty the King.

Acceptance

My voice on the threshold. My voice coming from afar. On the threshold of the Academy. It is difficult to become a member of a family. And it is easy. The stars know it. The families of luminous torches. To become a member of the Nobel family. To become an heir of Alfred Nobel. To blood ties, to civil relationship, a new consanguinity is added, a more subtle kinship, born of the spirit and the creative task. And this was perhaps the unspoken intention of the founder of this great family of Nobel Prize winners. To enlarge, through time, from generation to generation, the world of his own kin. As for me, I enter the Nobel family as the least worthy to be called among the many who could have been chosen.

I enter by the will of this Academy, whose doors open and close once a year in order to consecrate a writer, and also because of the use I made of the word in my poems and novels, the word which, more than beautiful, is responsible, a concern not foreign to that dreamer who with the passing of time would shock the world with his inventions—the discovery of the most destructive explosives then known—for helping man in his titanic chores of mining, digging tunnels, and constructing roads and canals.

I do not know if the comparison is too daring. But it is necessary. The use of destructive forces, the secret which Alfred Nobel extracted from nature, made possible in our America the most colossal enterprises. Among them, the Panama Canal. A magic of catastrophe which could be compared to the thrust of our novels, called upon to destroy unjust structures in order to make way for a new life. The secret mines of the people, buried under tons of misunderstanding, prejudices, and taboos, bring to light in our narrative—between fables and myths—with blows of protest, testimony, and denouncement, dikes of letters which, like sands, contain reality to let the dream flow free or, on the contrary, contain the dream to let reality escape.

Cataclysms which engendered a geography of madness, terrifying traumas, such as the Conquest: these cannot be the antecedents of a literature of cheap compromise; and, thus, our novels appear to Europeans as illogical or aberrant. They are not shocking for the sake of shock effects. It is just that what happened to us was shocking. Continents submerged in the sea, races castrated as they surged to independence, and the fragmentation of the New World. As the antecedents of a literature these are already tragic. And from there we have had to extract not the man of defeat, but the man of hope, that blind creature who wanders through our songs. We are peoples from worlds which have nothing like the orderly unfolding of European conflicts, always human in their dimensions. The dimensions of our conflicts in the past centuries have been catastrophic.

Scaffoldings. Ladders. New vocabularies. The primitive recitation of the texts. The rhapsodists. And later, once again, the broken trajectory. The new tongue. Long chains of words. Thought unchained. Until arriving, once again, after the bloodiest lexical battles, at one's own expressions. There are no rules. They are invented. And after much invention, the grammarians come with their language-trimming shears. American Spanish is fine with me, but without the roughness. Grammar becomes an obsession. The risk of anti-grammar. And that is where we are now. The search for dynamic words. Another magic. The poet and the writer of the active word. Life. Its variations. Nothing prefabricated. Everything in ebullition. Not to write literature. Not to substitute words for things. To look for word-things, word-beings. And the problems of man, in addition. Evasion is impossible. Man. His problems. A continent that speaks. And which was heard in this Academy. Do not ask us for genealogies, schools, treatises. We bring you the probabilities of a world. Verify them. They are singular. Singular is the movement, the dialogue, the novelistic intrigue. And most singular of all, throughout the ages there has been no interruption in the constant creation.

Prior to the acceptance, Hugo Theorell, Professor at the Caroline Institute, made the following remarks: «One of our most competent literary critics has pointed out that this year's Nobel Prize winner in Literature, Miguel Angel Asturias, in one of his most important books, *El Señor Presidente*, produces a strong effect by skilfully working with time and light–again our common ‹theme with variations›. Asturias paints in dark colours–against this background the rare light makes a so much stronger impression with his passionate, but artistically well balanced, protest against tyranny, injustice, slavery, and arbitrariness. He transforms glowing indignation into great literary art. This is indeed admirable.

May times come when conditions like those condemned by Mr. Asturias belong to history; when human beings live peacefully and happily together. This was indeed what Alfred Nobel hoped to promote by his Prizes.

Mr. Asturias – We sincerely admire your literary craftsmanship, and we hope that your work will contribute to ending the shameful social conditions that you have described with such impressive intensity. We congratulate you on your Nobel Prize, which you so very much deserve. »

Biography

Miguel Angel Asturias (1899–) was born in Guatemala and spent his childhood and adolescence in his native country. He studied for his baccalaureate at the state high school and later took a law degree at the University of San Carlos. His thesis on «The Social Problem of the Indian» was published in 1923.

After he finished his law studies, he founded with fellow students the Popular University of Guatemala, whose aim was to offer courses to those who could not afford to attend the national university. In 1923 he left for Europe, intending to study political economy in England. He spent a few months in London and then went to Paris, where he was to stay for ten years. At the Sorbonne he attended the lectures on the religions of the Mayas by Professor Georges Raynaud, whose disciple he became. Also, as correspondent for several important Latin American newspapers, he travelled in all the Western European countries, in the Middle East, in Greece, and in Egypt.

In 1928 Asturias returned for a short time to Guatemala, where he lectured at the Popular University. These lecture were collected in a volume entitled *La arquitectura de la vida nueva* (1928) [*Architecture of the New Life*]. He then went back to Paris, where he finished his *Leyendas de Guatemala* (1930) [*Legends of Guatemala*]. Published in Madrid, the book was translated into French by Francis de Miomandre, who sent his translation to Paul Valéry. The French poet was greatly impressed, and his letter to Miomandre was used as the preface to the 1931 edition published in the *Cahiers du Sud* series. The same year, *Leyendas de Guatemala* received the Silla Monsegur Prize, a reward for the best Spanish-American book published in France.

During his stay in Paris from 1923 to 1933, Asturias wrote his novel *El Señor Presidente* [*The President*], which slashed at the social evil and malignant corruption to which an insensitive dictator dooms his people. Because of its political implications Asturias was unable to bring the book with him when, in 1933, he returned to Guatemala, which at the time was ruled by the dictator Jorge Ubico. The original version was to remain unpublished for thirteen years. The fall of Ubico's regime in 1944 brought to the presidency Professor

Juan José Arévalo, who immediately appointed Asturias cultural attaché to the Guatemalan Embassy in Mexico, where the first edition of *El Señor Presidente* appeared in 1946.

In late 1947, Asturias went to Argentina as cultural attaché to the Guatemalan Embassy and, two years later, obtained a ministerial post. While in Buenos Aires, he published *Sien de alondra* (1949) [Temple of the Lark], an anthology of his poems written between 1918 and 1948. In 1948 he returned to Guatemala for a few months, during which time he wrote his novel *Viento fuerte* (1950) [*Strong Wind*], an indictment of the effect of North American imperialism on the economic realities of his country. That same year, the second edition of *El Señor Presidente* was published in Buenos Aires.

When the government of President Jacobo Arbenz Guzman fell in 1954, Asturias went into exile in Argentina, his wife's native country, where he remained until 1962. A year later, the Argentine publisher Losada brought out his novel *Mulata de tal* [*Mulata*]. This story, a surrealistic blend of Indian legends, tells of a peasant whose greed and lust consign him to a dark belief in material power from which, Asturias warns us, there is only one hope for salvation: universal love.

In 1966 Asturias was awarded the Lenin Peace Prize. In the same year, he was appointed the Guatemalan ambassador to France by President Julio Mendez Montenegro.

Index of Laureates

Name Index